KF   Patrick, John J.

DATE	BORROWER'S NAME	
APR - 8 1996		
FEB 1 4 1998		
NOV 3 0 1998		
FEB 2 0 1999		
MAR 1 1 2000		
NOV - 9 2002		
NOV 0 5 2005		
DEC - 7 2005		

The
Young Oxford Companion
to the

SUPREME
COURT
OF THE UNITED STATES

The
Young Oxford Companion
to the

SUPREME
COURT
OF THE UNITED STATES

John J. Patrick

Oxford University Press
New York

Oxford University Press

Oxford New York Toronto
Delhi Bombay Calcutta Madras Karachi
Kuala Lumpur Singapore Hong Kong Tokyo
Nairobi Dar es Salaam Cape Town
Melbourne Auckland Madrid

and associated companies in

Berlin Ibadan

Design: Sandy Kaufman
Layout: Valerie Sauers
Consultant: David J. Bodenhamer, Professor of History and Director,
POLIS Research Center, Indiana University–Purdue University at Indianapolis;
author, *Fair Trial: Rights of the Accused in American History*

Library of Congress Cataloging-in-Publication Data

Patrick, John J.
    The young Oxford companion to the Supreme Court of the United States /
John J. Patrick.
    Includes bibliographical references and index.
    ISBN 0-19-507877-2
    1. United States. Supreme Court—Encyclopedias, Juvenile. [1. United States. Supreme
Court—Encyclopedias.]
KF8742.A35P38 1994
347.73'26'03—dc20
[347.3073503]
93-6467
CIP

Printing (last digit): 9 8 7 6 5 4 3 2 1

Printed in the United States of America
on acid-free paper.

On the cover: *(top left) The bronze statue of Chief Justice John Marshall in the Supreme Court Building; (top right) Justice Thurgood Marshall; (bottom) the Supreme Court Building*

Frontispiece: Authority of Law, *one of two marble statues by James Earl Fraser that flank the front portico of the Supreme Court Building*

CONTENTS

PREFACE

Liberty, a desired end of constitutional government in the United States, is dependent upon law and justice. This truth is captured by two phrases carved on the marble exterior of the Supreme Court Building: over the east portico, "Justice the Guardian of Liberty," and over the west portico, "Equal Justice Under Law."

According to its framers, the U.S. Constitution was designed to "secure the Blessings of Liberty." The framers knew, however, that this lofty ideal could not be attained without workable instruments of government crafted for this end. The Supreme Court was intended to be a major means of securing the people's liberty.

The Supreme Court has the special duty of guarding the individual's rights to liberty through judicial review, its power to void government actions that violate the supreme law of the Constitution.

James Madison, the major architect of the Constitution, presciently observed that "independent tribunals of justice [headed by the Supreme Court] will consider themselves in a peculiar manner the guardians of those [constitutional] rights; they will be an impenetrable bulwark against every assumption of power in the legislative or executive; they will be naturally led to resist every encroachment upon rights expressly stipulated for in the Constitution."

During the 1830s, a perceptive French visitor to the United States, Alexis de Tocqueville, confirmed the enduring vision of the Constitution's framers about the critical importance of the Supreme Court to the vitality and destiny of their work. "Without [justices of the Supreme Court], the Constitution would be a dead letter," wrote Tocqueville in his classic 1835 commentary about the United States, *Democracy in America*. "Their power is enormous," Tocqueville wrote, "but it is the power of public opinion. [The justices] are all-powerful as long as the people respect the law; but they would be impotent against popular neglect or contempt of the law."

The Court has no power to guard the rights of the people through its rulings about the law unless particular people assume responsibility for bringing cases to the judiciary. Further, the Court's rulings, no matter how wise or just, may practically amount to nothing unless the people are vigilant about their enforcement.

The Supreme Court cannot serve the cause of the people's liberty without popular support. And to be effective, this support depends upon widespread public knowledge of the Court's work and a public commitment, based on reason, to the constitutional values for which it works.

The entries in this volume were written to further the spread of knowledge and understanding about law and its relationship to liberty. The articles introduce the reader to the origins and development of the Supreme Court. They discuss controversies and failures along with the achievements of the justices during different periods of U.S. history. The entries in this book will answer many of your questions about the Court. They are also likely to raise new questions, which can be investigated through use of the many suggestions for further reading.

As I worked on this book two young people, very dear to me, were constantly in my thoughts. And so I dedicate this work to them: my granddaughter, Rachel Patrick, and my niece, Laurel Ellet. I hope that this book will contribute to the education of their generation, the responsible citizens of the future.

HOW TO USE
THIS BOOK

The articles in this *Companion* are arranged alphabetically, so you can look up words, ideas, or names as you come across them in other readings. You can then use the SEE ALSO listings at the end of the article to read about related subjects. Sometimes you may find that the *Companion* deals with information under a different article name than what you looked up. The book will then refer you to the proper article. For example, if you look up Judicial Conference of the United States, you will find the notation "SEE Administration of Federal Courts." If you cannot find a separate article on a particular subject, look in the index, which will guide you to the relevant articles. All people are listed alphabetically by last name; for example, the entry for Sandra Day O'Connor is listed as O'Connor, Sandra Day, under O.

You can also use this *Companion* topically, by reading all the articles about a particular aspect of the Supreme Court. Below are several groupings of topics around common themes.

Biographies: There are articles on all the chief justices and associate justices of the Supreme Court, listed by surname. The biographical entries include personal data about each justice, including the place and dates of birth and death, education, previous government experience, and period of service on the Court. The articles emphasize participation in notable Court decisions and significant contributions to constitutional law.

Decisions of the Court: The book contains articles on 100 of the most historically significant cases decided by the Supreme Court. Each article on a case opens with standard information. The name of the case is followed by the official citation from *United States Reports* (for cases since 1875). For example, for *Abington School District* v. *Schempp* the citation is 374 U.S. 203 (1963). This means that the opinion in the case is published in volume 374 of *United States Reports,* beginning on page 203. The year the case was decided follows in parentheses.

Before 1875, official reports of Supreme Court cases were published under the names of the Court reporters. Thus, these names (full or abbreviated) appear in the citations of the Court's decisions before 1875. For example, the citation for *McCulloch* v. *Maryland* is 4 Wheat. 316 (1819). Wheat. is an abbreviation for Henry Wheaton, the Supreme Court Reporter from 1816 to 1827. Thus, this citation indicates that this case can be found in the 4th volume compiled by Wheaton, that it begins on page 316, and that it was decided in 1819.

Each case article in the *Companion* also provides the vote of the justices on the case; who wrote the majority opinion for the Court; who, if anyone, joined with a concurring opinion; and who, if anyone, dissented. Each article on a Supreme Court case also includes background information on the case; the issue or issues before the Court; the Court's opinion and legal reasoning in deciding the case; the dissenting opinions, if any, and reasons for them; and the significance of the case in constitutional law and history.

Core Concepts: Another category includes articles that define and discuss concepts central to the meaning of constitutionalism in the United States and decision making by the Court. There are articles, for example, on the Bill of Rights, Commerce power, Constitutional law, Due process of law, Federalism, Incorporation doctrine, Independent judiciary, Judicial activism and judicial restraint, Judicial review, Jurisdiction, Republicanism, Separation of powers, and Trial by jury.

Ideas and Issues: There are several essays on constitutional ideas and issues that have come before the Court. These essays show how decisions of the U.S. Supreme Court have affected the choices and opportunities of many people throughout American history. These essays include Abortion rights; Affirmative action; Capital punishment; Civil rights; Equality under the Constitution; Freedom of speech and press; Gun control and the right to bear arms; Juvenile justice; Liberty under the Constitution; Privacy, right to; Property rights; Religious issues under the Constitution; Rights of the accused; and Student rights under the Constitution.

Legal Terms and Phrases: The *Companion* contains definitions of many legal terms and phrases involved in the Court's work. For example, you can find definitions of basic technical terms, such as certiorari, writ of; habeas corpus, writ of; precedent; and seditious libel. There are also famous phrases associated with the Court, such as "separate but equal" (used in *Plessy* v. *Ferguson,* 1896) and Lemon Test (derived from *Lemon* v. *Kurtzman,* 1971).

Procedures, Practices, and Personnel: You can read about the procedures and practices by which the Supreme Court operates. Some examples of these entries are: Administration of federal courts, Conference, Decision days, Discuss list, Opinions, Oral argument, Rules of the Court, and Seniority.

Supreme Court Building: If you visit Washington, D.C., you may want to visit the Supreme Court Building. To learn more about this building, as well as the Court's previous homes, see the article on Buildings, Supreme Court, and Appendix 2, Visiting the Supreme Court Building.

Further Reading: If you want to know more about a specific topic, you can use the FURTHER READING entries at the end of many of the articles as well as the FURTHER READING guide at the end of the book, which lists more general sources.

Abington School District v. Schempp

☆ *374 U.S. 203 (1963)*
☆ *Vote: 8–1*
☆ *For the Court: Clark*
☆ *Concurring: Brennan, Douglas, and Goldberg*
☆ *Dissenting: Stewart*

A PENNSYLVANIA law required that each public school day must be started with the reading of at least 10 verses from the Bible, without comment. A student could be excused from this requirement by presenting to school authorities a written request from a parent or guardian. The Schempp family challenged the state law. They refused to request an exception for their child, a student at Abington High School, from the Bible-reading exercise. And they refused to allow their child to attend this exercise. The Schempps brought suit against the Abington School District to block enforcement of the Bible-reading statute.

The Issue Did the Pennsylvania law on Bible reading in public schools violate the 1st Amendment provision against laws "respecting an establishment of religion"?

Opinion of the Court The Court decided in favor of the Schempp family and struck down the state law on Bible reading in public schools. Writing for the Court, Justice Tom Clark concluded that the government may not promote religion in public schools. For the first time, the Court specified a test for determining whether a law violates the establishment clause of the 1st Amendment. Justice Clark wrote:

> The test may be stated as follows: What are the purposes and primary effect of the enactment? If either is the advancement or inhibition of religion then the enactment exceeds the scope of legislative power as circumscribed by the Constitution.... [T]o withstand the strictures of the Establishment Clause there must be a secular legislative purpose and a primary effect that neither advances nor inhibits religion.

According to the Court, the Pennsylvania law on daily Bible reading in public schools failed to pass this establishment clause test. The state law failed because it

Petitioners work to convince Congress to return Bible reading to public schools. The Abington *case had decided that such Bible reading was unconstitutional.*

advances religion. The Pennsylvania Bible-reading statute was therefore ruled unconstitutional.

Dissent Justice Potter Stewart claimed that the Court had incorrectly applied the 1st Amendment's establishment clause in this case. He emphasized that by striking down the state law, the Court was denying free exercise of religion to the majority of citizens. According to Justice Stewart, this Pennsylvania law was constitutional because it did not force students to participate in a religious exercise. Justice Stewart wrote:

> We err in the first place if we do not recognize, as a matter of history and as a matter of imperatives of our free society, that religion and government must necessarily interact in countless ways….
>
> [T]he central value embodied in the First Amendment…is the safeguarding of an individual's right to free exercise of his religion…. [T]here is involved in these cases a substantial free exercise claim on the part of those who affirmatively desire to have their children's school day open with the reading of passages from the Bible.

Significance This case clearly stated the Court's position that the government cannot foster or promote religious doctrine in public schools through state-legislated religious exercises. By reinforcing the *Engel* v. *Vitale* (1962) decision, the Court in this case seemed to settle the question of state-sponsored religious exercises in public schools. However, public opinion polls from the 1960s to the 1990s have shown that more than 60 percent of Americans disagree with the Court's decisions on the prohibition of prayer in public school–sanctioned programs. Vigorous debate about the separation of church and state continues.

SEE ALSO

Engel v. Vitale; Establishment clause; Religious issues under the Constitution

Abortion rights

ABORTION IS the termination of a pregnancy before the embryo or fetus is capable of survival outside the mother's womb. Should a woman have the right to decide whether or when to have an abortion?

In the United States, the state governments traditionally have regulated the performance of abortions. In 1960 every state government had a law making abortion a crime except when it was done to save the mother's life. By 1973, however, 14 states had passed laws permitting abortions under certain other conditions, such as when the pregnancy resulted from rape or incest, or when the baby, if born, would likely suffer from a severe defect. Alaska, Hawaii, and New York repealed most previous restrictions on the woman's right to an abortion.

In 1973 the U.S. Supreme Court made its landmark ruling on abortion rights in *Roe* v. *Wade*. The Court struck down a Texas law regulating abortion as an unconstitutional infringement of a woman's right to privacy, which had been established in *Griswold* v. *Connecticut* (1965). In *Griswold* the Court invalidated a Connecticut law prohibiting the use of birth control devices by ruling that it violated a person's constitutional right to a zone of privacy based on several provisions of the Bill of Rights and the due process clause of the 14th Amendment. In *Roe* the Court held that the "right of privacy [established in *Griswold*] is broad enough to encompass a woman's decision whether or not to terminate her pregnancy."

Writing for the Court, Justice Harry Blackmun stated that a woman's right to abortion could be limited, however, by "a compelling state interest" to protect her health and life. The Court decided that during the second trimester of a woman's pregnancy (months 4 to 6), the state might intervene to regulate abortion to protect the mother's health and that the state might regulate or prohibit abortion during the third trimester (months 7 to 9). During the first trimester (months 1 to 3) of a pregnancy, however, it seemed unlikely that there would be a reason to restrict abortion rights in order to protect the health and life of the mother.

Writing in dissent, Justice Byron White could not find in the Constitution the right to privacy upon which the *Roe* decision was based. Justice White helped to frame the controversy about abortion rights that has continued since the *Roe* decision. Many critics, like Justice White, have believed that questions about abortion rights should be resolved by state governments, not by the Court, as had been the long-standing practice in the American federal system of government.

Many critics of the *Roe* decision, however, have opposed it on religious or moral grounds. They reject abortion rights because, in their system of belief, abortion is a sin or morally wrong.

Activities to counter or overturn the *Roe* decision have persisted and have led to legal challenges in federal courts. But attempts to erect barriers to abortion rights have mostly failed, as have efforts to overturn *Roe.*

In *Harris* v. *McRae* (1980), however, the Court held that "although government may not place obstacles in the path of a woman's exercise of her freedom of choice [to have an abortion], it need not remove those not of its own creation. Indigency [being poor] falls in the latter category." As a result of this ruling, poor women who could not afford to pay for an abortion were no longer able to use federal Medicaid funds for one, except in cases of rape or incest or when the mother's life is threatened. Further, in *Ohio* v. *Akron Center*

Protesters march in 1988 to show their support for laws guaranteeing a woman's right to an abortion.

for Reproductive Health (1990), the Court upheld a state law that required minors (those below adult age) seeking an abortion either to notify one parent or get approval from a local court of law.

A major legal challenge to *Roe* emerged in *Webster* v. *Reproductive Health Services* (1989). This case concerned the constitutionality of a 1986 Missouri law that included several provisions for restricting a woman's right to an abortion. The Court upheld only two. One banned the use of public facilities or public employees to carry out an abortion. The other restriction pertained to the performance of an abortion on a woman carrying a fetus thought to be more than 20 weeks old. Before performing such an abortion, the physician must determine, through medical testing, whether the fetus is viable, or capable of living outside the mother's womb. If it is viable, the abortion may be prohibited.

The *Webster* decision thus modified the second-trimester rule in *Roe,* which held that all regulations on abortion rights must be related to protecting the health of the mother. The *Webster* decision, however, stopped short of overturning *Roe,* which antiabortion rights advocates had wanted.

SEE ALSO

Griswold v. Connecticut; Privacy, right to; Roe v. Wade; Webster v. Reproductive Health Services

FURTHER READING

Garrow, David J. *Liberty and Sexuality: The Right to Privacy and the Making of Roe v. Wade, 1923–1973.* New York: Macmillan, 1993.

Tribe, Laurence H. *Abortion: The Clash of Absolutes.* New York: Norton, 1990.

Abrams v. United States

☆ *250 U.S. 616 (1919)*
☆ *Vote: 7–2*
☆ *For the Court: Clarke*
☆ *Dissenting: Holmes and Brandeis*

JACOB ABRAMS was arrested in New York City on August 23, 1918. He and several friends had written, printed, and distributed copies of a leaflet that severely criticized President Woodrow Wilson and the U.S. government. The leaflet opposed President Wilson's decision to send a small U.S. military force to Russia during the civil war that followed the communist revolution of 1917. The communists, led by Vladimir Lenin, were fighting against anticommunist Russians and various foreign military forces to retain control of the government. Abrams's leaflet urged American workers to walk off their jobs in protest against President Wilson and the U.S. government and in support of the new communist government in Russia.

Abrams and his friends were arrested for violating the Espionage Act of 1917 and the Sedition Act of 1918. These laws made it a crime to write and publish disloyal or profane statements that were intended to interfere with production of goods necessary to the defense of the United States during wartime. The laws were passed to control antiwar activity after the United States entered World War I.

The Issue The specific question facing the Court pertained to the constitutionality of the Espionage Act and the Se-

dition Act. These federal laws were designed to limit freedom of expression in order to protect national security during wartime. However, the 1st Amendment says, "Congress shall make no law... abridging the freedom of speech, or of the press, or the right of the people peaceably to assemble, and to petition the Government for a redress of grievances." Did enforcement of the Espionage Act and the Sedition Act violate the 1st Amendment free speech and press rights of Jacob Abrams?

Opinion of the Court Justice John H. Clarke, writing for the Court, decided against Abrams's claims that his 1st Amendment rights were violated. Clarke based his decision on the "clear and present danger" and "bad tendency" tests stated by Justice Oliver Wendell Holmes in *Schenck* v. *United States* (1919). According to these two tests, which Holmes used interchangeably in *Schenck*, free speech and press could be limited if they were intended to cause an illegal action or if they threatened national security.

Justice Clarke wrote that "men must be held to have intended, and to be accountable for, the effects which their acts were likely to produce." Clarke argued that "the obvious effect" of the leaflet "would be to persuade persons...not to

Jacob Abrams (far right) and these other Russian immigrants dumped leaflets criticizing President Woodrow Wilson from the tops of New York City buildings.

work in ammunition factories, where their work would produce bullets, bayonets, cannons, and other munitions" needed by U.S. military forces in World War I.

Dissent Justice Oliver Wendell Holmes disagreed, for himself and Justice Louis Brandeis, with Justice Clarke's use of the "clear and present danger" test in this case. And he repudiated the "bad tendency" test. Justice Holmes maintained that the government had the right to protect itself against speech that immediately and directly threatens the security and safety of the country. He wrote that the 1st Amendment protected the expression of all opinions "unless they so imminently threaten immediate interference with the lawful and pressing purposes of the law that an immediate check is required to save the country." Justice Holmes denied that Abrams's actions and intentions represented a danger sufficient to justify limitation of his freedom of expression.

Justice Holmes concluded his dissent with a compelling theory of free speech in a constitutional democracy. Arguing for "free trade in ideas," Holmes said: "[T]he best test of truth is the power of the thought to get itself accepted in the competition of the market…. That at any rate is the theory of our Constitution. It is an experiment, as all life is an experiment."

Significance The Court's opinion in this case prevailed only in the short run. The dissent of Justice Holmes eventually had more influence on the Court and the American people. Holmes modified the "clear and present danger" test he had stated in *Schenck*, which had been used interchangeably with the "bad tendency" test. In *Abrams*, Holmes rejected the "bad tendency" test, which emphasized a person's intentions to encourage lawless behavior. Instead, Holmes stated in his *Abrams* dissent that a "clear and

present danger" exists only when speech can be immediately and directly connected to specific actions that cause illegal behavior threatening the safety or security of the United States. If an imminent danger could not be demonstrated, then speech could not be lawfully limited. The *Abrams* dissent has been called the best defense of free speech ever written by an American.

SEE ALSO

Freedom of speech and press; Schenck v. United States; Seditious libel

FURTHER READING

Polenberg, Richard. *Fighting Faiths: The Abrams Case, the Supreme Court, and Free Speech*. New York: Viking, 1987.

Administration of federal courts

THE SUPREME COURT is in charge of the administration of the federal judicial system. The chief justice and associate justices participate in the work of the Judicial Conference of the United States, the Administrative Office of the United States Courts, and the Federal Judicial Center.

Judicial Conference of the United States

The chief justice presides over the Judicial Conference of the United States, a board of trustees for the federal courts. Created by an act of Congress in 1922, the Judicial Conference has 27 members who represent the district or trial courts, the intermediate appellate courts, and the Supreme Court. By law, the mission of the Judicial Conference of the United States is to oversee the practices and procedures of the federal courts and to recommend changes to improve the functioning of the federal judicial system.

The conference meets twice a year at the Supreme Court Building in Washington, D.C.

Administrative Office of the United States Courts

Budgeting services and staff support for the Judicial Conference of the United States are provided by the Administrative Office of the U.S. Courts. The Administrative Office, created in 1939 by an act of Congress, operates under direction of the Judicial Conference to oversee and provide administrative services for the lower federal courts. More than 600 people work for the Administrative Office. The director, appointed by the Supreme Court, reports to the Judicial Conference of the United States.

Federal Judicial Center

In 1967 Congress enacted legislation to create the Federal Judicial Center, which carries out research and training programs to improve the operations of the federal courts. The chief justice presides over the seven-member board of the center, which meets four times each year and oversees the work of the center's staff of more than 100 people. Findings of the center's research projects are reported to the Judicial Conference of the United States.

Admiralty and maritime law

ARTICLE 3, SECTION 2, of the U.S. Constitution says, "The judicial Power shall extend…to all Cases of admiralty and maritime Jurisdiction." Admiralty or maritime law pertains to ships on the sea, including civil and criminal actions. In 1815 Justice Joseph Story, writing for the Court in *De Lovio* v. *Boit,* defined the scope of the Court's admiralty jurisdiction by stating that it extended to all transactions "which relate to the navigation, business, or commerce of the sea."

Advisory opinions

AN ADVISORY OPINION is a legal opinion given before a case is tried. Federal judges do not provide advisory opinions because Article 3 of the U.S. Constitution says their jurisdiction extends only to real cases and controversies "in Law and Equity, arising under this Constitution," and they therefore cannot issue statements about hypothetical cases.

A precedent against advisory opinions was established in 1793, when President George Washington asked Chief Justice John Jay and the Supreme Court to advise him about the federal government's obligations stemming from a 1778 treaty made by the Continental Congress with France. John Jay replied in a letter (August 8, 1793) that it was wrong, under the Constitution, for the Court to provide an advisory opinion to the President or anyone else. Jay's letter explained that the justices should not provide opinions on any matter unless it was brought to the Court through formal legal procedures as a real case.

The letter set a precedent against advisory opinions. It reinforced the principle of separation of powers and judicial independence from the executive branch. Thus, the President turns to the attorney general of the United States or to his own counsel, both of whom are officials of the executive branch, for legal advice.

SEE ALSO
Separation of powers

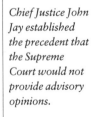

Chief Justice John Jay established the precedent that the Supreme Court would not provide advisory opinions.

Affirmative action

DURING THE 1950s and 1960s, the Supreme Court struck down laws that unfairly discriminated against individuals on the basis of race. Through its decisions in cases such as *Brown* v. *Board of Education* (1954) and *Heart of Atlanta Motel* v. *United States* (1964), the Court ruled that African Americans must have "equal protection of the laws," which the 14th Amendment says is a right available to all people in the United States. While lauding this major advance in civil rights for African Americans, many civil rights leaders said it was not sufficient to overcome the negative effects of more than two centuries of racial discrimination in the United States. So, during the 1970s and 1980s, leaders of civil rights organizations, such as the National Association for the Advancement of Colored People (NAACP) and the National Organization of Women (NOW), proposed programs designed to go beyond mere equality of opportunity to provide limited kinds of preferential treatment for victims of long-term racial or gender-based discrimination. These programs are called *affirmative action* because they involve plans designed, through specific actions, to bring about desired outcomes, such as increased job opportunities, job promotions, and admissions to colleges and universities.

Affirmative action plans, as conceived by civil rights leaders, have the following characteristics. First, they may be sponsored or instituted either by government agencies and public educational institutions or by private organizations, such as businesses, labor unions, vocational training schools, or private colleges.

Second, affirmative action plans take into account such personal factors as race, ethnicity, or gender when indi-

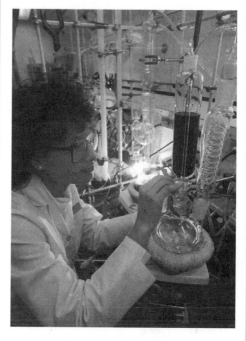

Dr. Yuhpyng Chen, a medical chemist, works in the lab at Pfizer Inc. Large corporations often design affirmative action programs to ensure that members of minority groups have access to job opportunities.

viduals are under consideration for employment in a job, promotion to a better job, or admission to a school or college. However, individuals must *not* receive education or employment benefits solely on the basis of such factors as race, ethnicity, or gender; rather, these personal factors will determine who receives or does not receive certain opportunities only when minority candidates are otherwise well qualified for the jobs, educational programs, and so forth that they seek to attain.

Third, affirmative action programs are based clearly on the educational or economic need of individuals resulting from unfair treatment in the past of racial, ethnic, or gender groups to which these people belong.

Fourth, affirmative action plans are supposed to be temporary remedies, not permanent programs.

Supporters of affirmative action plans have pointed out that most members of certain minority groups, such as African Americans, lag far behind most white Americans in income, educational attainment, job advancement, and general living standards. They claim that these differences are the result of long-term racial discrimination, rooted in the pre–Civil War institution of slavery. Further, they argue that affirmative action programs, whether required by the government or voluntarily undertaken by private employers and schools, are the best means to overcome the persistent negative consequences of past discrimination against minorities, especially African Americans.

Affirmative action programs have been widely established in education and economic institutions of the United States. These programs have raised a fundamental constitutional question. Does the 14th Amendment's guarantee of "equal protection of the laws" permit certain kinds of preferential treatment of certain categories of individuals, such as African Americans or women, in order to remedy the negative consequences of long-term discrimination against them?

The Supreme Court has upheld some affirmative action practices while striking down extreme versions of this concept. In *Regents of the University of California* v. *Bakke* (1978), for example, the Court ruled that a university could take into account race and ethnicity when making decisions about the admission of students. However, the Court ruled that an affirmative action plan based on rigid racial quotas to boost admission of minority students to a university was unconstitutional. In *United Steelworkers of America* v. *Weber* (1979), the Court permitted an employer's voluntarily imposed and temporary affirmative action program. That program would encourage unskilled black workers to obtain training that would lead to better, more skilled jobs, in which black Americans historically have been underrepresented. Once again, however, the Court rejected rigid, race-based quotas in hiring and job advancement.

In *United States* v. *Paradise* (1987)

the Court upheld a temporary and "narrowly tailored" quota system to bring about job promotion for black state troopers in Alabama. The state's affirmative action plan imposed a "one black for one white" promotion quota. This was justified, the Court said, by the "long and shameful record of delay and resistance" to employment opportunities for black Americans in the Alabama state police.

In 1987, in *Johnson* v. *Transportation Agency of Santa Clara County,* the Court endorsed a carefully crafted, temporary, and voluntary affirmative action plan to boost job promotion opportunities for women. The Court held it was permissible to take into account a woman's gender as a positive factor in promotion to a higher-ranking position because women had been systematically denied access to such positions in the past.

SEE ALSO

Brown v. Board of Education; Civil rights; Equality under the Constitution; Heart of Atlanta Motel v. United States; Johnson v. Transportation Agency of Santa Clara County; National Association for the Advancement of Colored People (NAACP); Regents of the University of California v. Bakke; United Steelworkers of America v. Weber

FURTHER READING

O'Neill, Robert M. *Discriminating against Discrimination.* Bloomington: Indiana University Press, 1975.
Rosenfeld, Michel. *Affirmative Action and Justice.* New Haven: Yale University Press, 1991.
Schwartz, Bernard. *Behind Bakke: Affirmative Action and the Supreme Court.* New York: New York University Press, 1988.

Amendments to the Constitution

THE AUTHORS of the U.S. Constitution realized that this document would

Women voting in New York City after the passage of the 19th Amendment, which guaranteed their right to vote nationwide.

have to be revised to meet new needs that would arise as times changed. George Washington expressed the inevitable need for, and value of, constitutional change in a letter to his nephew, Bushrod Washington (Nov. 10, 1787):

> The warmest friends and best supporters the Constitution has do not contend that it is free from imperfections.... I think the People (for it is with them to Judge) can...decide with as much propriety on the alterations and amendments which are necessary [as] ourselves. I do not think we are more inspired, have more wisdom, or possess more virtue than those who will come after us.

The amendment process

George Washington, who presided at the Constitutional Convention of 1787, recognized the importance of Article 5 of the Constitution, which specifies how formal changes, or amendments, may be made. Article 5 says:

> The Congress, whenever two thirds of both Houses shall deem it necessary, shall propose Amendments to this Constitution, or, on the Application of the Legislatures of two thirds of the several States, shall call a Convention for proposing Amendments, which, in either Case, shall be valid to all Intents and Purposes, as Part of this Constitution, when ratified by the Legislatures of three fourths of the several States, or by Conventions in three

fourths thereof, as the one or the other Mode of Ratification may be proposed by the Congress; Provided that no Amendment which may be made prior to the Year One thousand eight hundred and eight shall in any Manner affect the first and fourth Clauses in the Ninth Section of the first Article; and that no State, without its Consent, shall be deprived of its equal Suffrage in the Senate.

The usual procedure for making amendments is for two-thirds of the members of Congress to vote for the proposed amendments. Then the amendment is sent to the legislatures of the 50 states for approval. If three-fourths of the state legislatures ratify, or vote for, the proposal, it becomes an amendment to the U.S. Constitution. Of the 27 constitutional amendments, 26 of them have been made in this way. The 21st Amendment was approved by special conventions in three-fourths of the states, rather than by votes in state legislatures.

There is another method of proposing amendments to the Constitution— a method that has never been used. Congress, upon request of the states, can call for a special constitutional convention to write a proposed amendment. Article 5 states that Congress "shall call a convention for proposing amendments" whenever two-thirds of the states petition for one. This method of proposing amendments is known as an "Article 5 Convention."

The Bill of Rights

The Constitution was first amended in 1791. Amendments 1 through 10, known as the Bill of Rights, were ratified together by the end of 1791. This Bill of Rights limits the power of the federal government in order to protect the civil liberties and rights of individuals. These rights include the freedom of speech, protection against unwarranted searches and seizures, and provision of due process and other rights for people accused of criminal behavior.

Amendments 11 and 12

The 11th Amendment became part of the Constitution in 1795. It was proposed and ratified in response to an unpopular Supreme Court decision, *Chisholm* v. *Georgia* (1793). The Court decided that the citizens of one state can sue another state in a federal court without the consent of the state being sued. The 11th Amendment reversed the Court's decision by barring citizens of another state or a foreign country from suing a state in a federal court without the state's consent.

Amendment 12 was ratified in 1804 to correct a defect in the procedures for electing the President and Vice President. Article 2, Section 1, of the Constitution said that Presidential electors would vote for two people for President. The person who received the most votes would be the President, provided that he also received a majority of the votes cast. The person who came in second would be the Vice President. If no one received a majority of the electoral votes, then the House of Representatives had to elect the President from among the five candidates with the most votes.

This system broke down in the election of 1800, when Thomas Jefferson and Aaron Burr received an equal number of votes. It was generally understood that Jefferson was the candidate for President and Burr the candidate for Vice President. The Constitution, however, provided only that each elector vote for two people, without specifying which vote was for the Vice Presidential candidate. When Jefferson and Burr received the same number of votes, Burr tried to take advantage of the confusion to win the Presidency. Instead of stepping aside for his partner, Jefferson, he insisted that the contest be decided by the House of

Representatives, as provided by the Constitution. Jefferson was the winner in the House election, but it was clear that the Constitution had to be amended to prevent confusion of this kind from happening again. The 12th Amendment provided that electors would cast separate ballots for President and Vice President. If no one receives a majority of votes for President, the House of Representatives selects the President from the three candidates with the largest number of votes. Each state then has one vote, no matter how many representatives it has in the House. If no one receives a majority of the electoral votes for Vice President, then the Senate selects the Vice President from the two candidates with the most votes.

Civil War amendments

Amendments 13, 14, and 15 are known as the Civil War amendments. They were passed in the wake of the Union victory over the slaveholding states of the Confederacy. These three amendments were passed to protect the rights of former slaves.

The 13th Amendment, approved in 1865, prohibits slavery or involuntary servitude. The 14th Amendment, added to the Constitution in 1868, defined citizenship in such a way that state governments could not deny former slaves their rights and privileges as citizens. This amendment says that all people born in the United States are citizens, as are all individuals who are naturalized (foreign-born persons who become citizens through a legal process defined by Congress). According to Amendment 14, all citizens (natural-born and naturalized) have the same legal rights and privileges. This amendment forbids state governments from making and enforcing laws that would deprive any person of life, liberty, or property "without due process of law"; it also says that a state government may not deny to any person under its authority "the equal protection of the laws."

Amendment 15, adopted in 1870, barred the federal and state governments from denying any citizen the right to vote on the basis of race, color, or previous enslavement.

20th-century amendments

The 16th Amendment, passed in 1913, allows the federal government to collect taxes on income earned by citizens. In 1895, the Supreme Court had ruled that a federal income tax law passed in 1894 was unconstitutional. Representatives of the people in Congress and state legislatures overruled the Supreme Court through passage and ratification of this 16th Amendment.

The 17th Amendment was also passed in 1913. It provides for the election of two senators from each state by direct vote of the eligible voters of the state. Before passage of this amendment, two senators were selected by the legislature of each state.

The 18th Amendment, approved in 1919, prohibited the production, sale, or transportation of intoxicating liquors in the United States. The 21st Amendment was passed in 1933 to repeal the 18th Amendment.

Amendments 19, 23, 24, and 26 extended and protected the voting rights of certain groups of people. The 19th Amendment, ratified in 1920, guaranteed the voting rights of women. The 23rd Amendment, adopted in 1961, gave citizens residing in the District of Columbia the right to vote in Presidential elections. The 24th Amendment, ratified in 1964, prohibited state governments from requiring people to pay a tax to qualify to vote, thereby extending the right to vote to people who could not afford to pay a poll tax. The 26th Amendment, added to the Constitution in 1971, required that neither the federal nor state governments could deny to someone 18 years of age or older the right to vote on account of age.

The 20th Amendment, passed in 1933, provided that the term of office of the President and Vice President shall end at noon, January 20, of the year following the last Presidential election. The term of office of senators and representatives shall end at noon, January 3.

A supporter of the Equal Rights Amendment. The ERA failed to win ratification in 1982.

The 22nd Amendment was passed in 1951 to prevent a President from serving more than two four-year terms of office. It was passed in response to the four-time election of President Franklin D. Roosevelt. Previously, Presidents had followed a custom begun by George Washington and had retired from office after serving two terms. Many people feared that a President might gain too much power if permitted to hold office for too long. The Constitution was amended to avoid this risk.

The 25th Amendment, passed in 1967, specifies how vacancies are to be filled in the office of Vice President. The President nominates a Vice President to fill a vacancy, but this choice must be approved by a majority of the members of the Senate and House of Representatives. The 25th Amendment also specifies how the Vice President can assume the duties of the President if he is incapacitated. When the President recovers, he can take charge again, but if recovery is not likely to occur, the Vice President can be approved as the new President by a two-thirds vote of both houses of Congress. The 25th Amendment allows a President to resign from office and be replaced by the Vice President. The new President has the power to appoint a new Vice President, subject to approval by a majority of the members of both houses of Congress.

The 27th Amendment, passed in 1992, holds that if members of Congress vote a pay raise for themselves, their constituents must have the opportunity, before the pay raise takes effect, to vote out of office the members who voted for it. This amendment was originally proposed in 1789, along with the amendments that became parts of the Bill of Rights, but it was rejected. In the 18th century, six states ratified the amendment, and one more state ratified it in the 19th century. Thirty-three states approved it between 1978 and May 7, 1992, when Michigan became the final state needed to ratify it.

SEE ALSO
Bill of Rights

FURTHER READING
Bernstein, Richard B., with Jerome Agel. *Amending America: If We Love the Constitution So Much, Why Do We Keep Trying to Change It?* New York: Random House, 1993.
McComas, Maggie. "Amending the Constitution." *Constitution* 4, no. 2 (Spring–Summer 1992): 26–31.

American Bar Association Committee on Federal Judiciary

THE AMERICAN BAR ASSOCIATION (ABA) is the oldest and largest private organization of lawyers in the United States. In 1946 the ABA established a Standing Committee on Federal Judiciary to advise the government on the selection of Supreme Court justices and judges for federal district and appellate courts.

Sandra Day O'Connor is sworn in by Chief Justice Warren Burger. O'Connor was rated well qualified by the ABA committee.

The committee has 15 members, appointed by the ABA president. Members represent different regions of the country. There is at least one member from each of the geographical areas of the United States in which a circuit court of appeals is located.

The ABA committee's advisory ratings are an important part of the selection of Supreme Court justices. After the President of the United States nominates a person to be a Supreme Court justice, the ABA committee investigates the nominee's background and record of achievement. Then the Committee rates the nominee according to this scale: well qualified, not opposed, or not qualified. These ratings, although advisory, tend to have great influence on the Senate Judiciary Committee and on the Senate as a whole, which has the power to confirm or reject the President's nominations to the Court.

The ABA committee is also involved in the nomination of federal district and appellate court judges. It rates such nominees according to a slightly different scale: well qualified, qualified, qualified/not qualified (indicating a split vote), or not qualified. Its rating is sent to the Senate Judiciary Committee, which has the responsibility of recommending that the Senate approve or reject the nominee. The ABA committee also tries to publicize its ratings through the mass media.

SEE ALSO
Appointment of justices; Rejection of Supreme Court nominees

American Civil Liberties Union (ACLU)

FOUNDED IN 1920, the American Civil Liberties Union (ACLU) is a private organization, supported by dues-paying members, with the mission of defending the rights and liberties of individuals guaranteed by the U.S. Constitution. ACLU staff lawyers offer free legal services to individuals who claim that the government has violated their civil liberties. The ACLU defines civil liberties as those freedoms or rights that the government may not abridge or deny.

The ACLU claims nonpartisan support of the principle of civil liberties, and it has therefore defended the right to free speech of various individuals with conflicting political viewpoints because of its dedication to the idea of free speech for everyone. Moreover, ACLU lawyers have defended the free speech rights of people with whom they personally disagree, such as communists or Nazis, because they are dedicated to protecting the *principle* of free speech, not the *content* of any particular speech.

The ACLU has participated in numerous landmark cases before the U.S. Supreme Court that have greatly expanded the range and reach of the Bill of Rights during the 20th century. For example, in *Gitlow* v. *New York* (1925), a case involving 1st Amendment free speech issues, ACLU lawyers served as counsel for Benjamin Gitlow. The ACLU helped to influence the Court to recognize that the due process clause of the 14th Amendment could absorb or incorporate 1st Amendment freedoms. This case laid the foundations for the incorporation doctrine, which has led to the case-by-case application of most of the Bill of Rights to state laws. Lawyers for

the ACLU were involved in most of these cases. For example, *Stromberg* v. *California* (1931) involved the 1st Amendment right to freedom of speech; *Engel* v. *Vitale* (1962) dealt with the 1st Amendment prohibition against the establishment of a state religion; and *Miranda* v. *Arizona* (1966) upheld the 5th Amendment right to avoid self-incrimination. The ACLU also cooperated with the National Association for the Advancement of Colored People (NAACP) in landmark civil rights cases, such as *Brown* v. *Board of Education* (1954), which have used the "equal protection of the laws" clause of the 14th Amendment to end racial segregation and discrimination in public facilities and services.

The ACLU has more than 275,000 members. The national office in Washington, D.C., includes a legal staff, a public education department, and people working on several special projects on legal research and education. The ACLU also has a network of affiliates in all 50 states.

SEE ALSO

Civil rights; Gitlow v. New York; Incorporation doctrine; Miranda v. Arizona; Stromberg v. California

FURTHER READING

Lamson, Peggy. *Roger Baldwin: Founder of the American Civil Liberties Union.* Boston: Houghton Mifflin, 1976.
Walker, Samuel. *In Defense of American Liberties: A History of the ACLU.* New York: Oxford, 1990.

Roger Baldwin, founder of the American Civil Liberties Union.

Amicus curiae

AMICUS CURIAE is a Latin term meaning "friend of the court." An amicus curiae brief is a document regarding a case presented by someone who is not a direct party to the legal controversy. A friend of the court brief may be filed voluntarily, or it may be invited by the court. An amicus curiae brief is usually filed by individuals or groups with a special interest in the outcome of a case. However, no one who would benefit or be penalized directly, in a personal way, by the outcome of a case may file an amicus curiae brief.

In *Mapp* v. *Ohio* (1961), for example, the American Civil Liberties Union (ACLU) filed an amicus brief that argued for the exclusion from a criminal trial of evidence seized without a search warrant. Although this issue was not even mentioned by Mapp's own attorneys, the ACLU brief influenced the Supreme Court to apply the exclusionary rule against a state government for the first time.

SEE ALSO
Mapp v. Ohio

Appeal

AN APPEAL is the procedure by which a case is taken to a higher court for its review and possible reversal of the lower court's decision. The bases for an appeal are claims by the losing party that the lower court made an error or committed an injustice in reaching its decision. In most cases, the U.S. Supreme Court has discretion in deciding whether or not to accept the case for review. However, in some types of cases there is an automatic right of appeal to the U.S. Supreme Court. For example, decisions by the highest court of a state in cases involving federal constitutional issues are always open to appeal by the losing party to the U.S. Supreme Court. However, the Court may decide to let the decision of the lower court stand, without conducting a hearing into the case.

Cases reach the U.S. Supreme Court

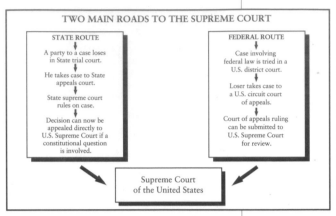

TWO MAIN ROADS TO THE SUPREME COURT

STATE ROUTE

A party to a case loses in State trial court.

He takes case to State appeals court.

State supreme court rules on case.

Decision can now be appealed directly to U.S. Supreme Court if a constitutional question is involved.

FEDERAL ROUTE

Case involving federal law is tried in a U.S. district court.

Loser takes case to a U.S. circuit court of appeals.

Court of appeals ruling can be submitted to U.S. Supreme Court for review.

Supreme Court of the United States

on appeal after either a lower federal court or a state court has made a decision on them. Decisions by the highest state court can be appealed directly to the U.S. Supreme Court if a constitutional question is involved. The losing party in a case generally has the right to appeal the case to a court of appellate jurisdiction. In the federal judicial system, the U.S. Supreme Court is the appellate court of last resort. It has the final decision, within the judicial system, on cases that come before it.

Courts of appellate jurisdiction give the losing party a new chance to win a case. This extra chance will be granted if there were errors of legal procedures, interpretation, or evidence in the lower court. Further, cases of great constitutional or national significance are likely to be accepted for determination by the highest appellate court, the U.S. Supreme Court.

SEE ALSO
Circuit Courts of Appeals; Courts of Appeals

Appellant

A PARTY who appeals a lower court decision to a higher court, such as the U.S. Supreme Court, is an appellant.

Appellate jurisdiction

SEE Jurisdiction

Appellee

THE PARTY to an appeal whose position in the case has been upheld by a lower court decision is the appellee. The appellant requires the appellee to respond in the higher court that accepts the case on appeal.

Appointment of justices

SUPREME COURT justices are appointed by the President, with the advice and consent of the Senate, according to Article 2, Section 2, of the Constitution. Although the President alone has the constitutional power to appoint a justice, he seeks advice from various important people and groups. In this way, the President tries to nominate someone for the Court who will have broad support or acceptance. Presidents tend to rely upon advice from the attorney general and the Department of Justice and the White House staff.

The American Bar Association Standing Committee on Federal Judiciary, established in 1946, is generally influential in the selection of justices. This committee rates Supreme Court nominees as well qualified, not opposed, or not qualified.

Many interest groups also express views about the selection of justices. For example, the National Association for the Advancement of Colored People (NAACP) tries to influence selection of justices who will protect and support civil rights for African Americans and other minority groups. Likewise, the National Organization of Women (NOW) pushes for selection of justices who are sympathetic to women's rights.

The Senate Judiciary Committee conducts hearings to investigate the qualifications and merits of a proposed Supreme Court justice. Witnesses are called before the committee to provide information and opinions about the nominee. And the nominee also appears before the committee to answer questions about his or her qualifications to be a justice. Today, these hearings are often broadcast live to large audiences and reported daily in the mass media.

The Senate Judiciary Committee concludes its hearings with a vote to recommend confirmation or rejection of the nomination by the full Senate. A nominee becomes a justice only after a favorable vote by a majority of the U.S. Senate.

There are no legal requirements for appointment to the U.S. Supreme Court. However, only lawyers have been selected for the Court. And it is unlikely that a nonlawyer could win approval to become a justice. Most justices have been judges on lower courts before becoming members of the Supreme Court. Since 1937, for example, 19 of the 32 justices had prior experience as either a state court judge or as a federal judge. Some of the greatest justices, however, did not serve previously as judges. For example, John Marshall, Joseph Story, Louis Brandeis, Harlan Fiske Stone, and Earl Warren have been rated as great achievers on the Court, but none of them had prior experience as a judge.

Presidents make a strong effort to select justices who will reflect favorably

This 1916 cartoon depicts "conservative" groups crying over the appointment of Louis Brandeis, who is shown walking away with a woman representing the Supreme Court.

In June 1986 President Ronald Reagan announces his new Supreme Court appointments—Antonin Scalia (far left) as associate justice and William Rehnquist (third from left) as chief justice. The retiring chief justice, Warren Burger, stands next to Rehnquist.

upon them and their administration. Legal scholars have noted the following personal characteristics that are expected of a nominee to the Supreme Court: substantial legal training and knowledge of law, personal integrity and high ethical standards, a strong sense of fair play, high intelligence, capacity for clear and cogent written and oral expression, and sound physical and mental health.

Presidents tend to nominate justices whose political and legal views appear to be compatible with their own. They usually do not seek agreement on specific cases or examples. Rather, they tend to want a nominee who shares their general views about constitutional interpretation and the process of making legal judgments.

SEE ALSO
American Bar Association Standing Committee on Federal Judiciary; Rejection of Supreme Court nominees; Senate Judiciary Committee

FURTHER READING
Abraham, Henry J. *Justices and Presidents: A Political History of Appointments to the Supreme Court.* New York: Oxford, 1992.

Assembly and petition, rights to

THE 1ST AMENDMENT to the U.S.

Constitution guarantees "the right of the people peaceably to assemble, and to petition the Government for a redress of grievances." The constitutional right of peaceful assembly means that people can gather in public to discuss their opinions about government or other concerns. This right to assemble also guarantees the right of association in groups, such as political parties, labor unions, and business organizations.

The right of petition means that individuals, acting alone or as part of a group, can freely send written criticisms or complaints to government officials. The right of petition also provides freedom to circulate documents for people to sign in order to demonstrate mass support for complaints against the government.

These fundamental freedoms of assembly and petition predate the U.S. Constitution, having their origins in the English legal heritage and the colonial governments of British North America. The English Bill of Rights of 1689 affirmed that "it is the right of the subjects to petition the King and all commitments and prosecutions for such petitioning are illegal." Forty-eight years earlier, in 1641, Section 12 of the Massachusetts Body of Liberties guaranteed freedom of speech and petition at public meetings, so that "Every man...shall have liberty to...present any necessary motion, complaint, petition, Bill or information."

From 1776 to 1783, the freedoms of assembly and petition were included in several of the original state constitutions, including the acclaimed Massachusetts Constitution of 1780, which greatly influenced the U.S. Constitution of 1787. By the 1780s, the twin freedoms of assembly and petition were recognized by Americans as rights of individuals that should be protected. Therefore, it would have been unusual if James Madison had not included them in his proposal to the first federal Congress, dated June 8, 1789, to add "the Great Rights of Mankind" to the Constitution.

In that address, Madison presciently said that "independent tribunals of justice will consider themselves in a peculiar manner the guardians of those rights; they will be an impenetrable bulwark against every assumption of power in the legislative or executive; they will be naturally led to resist every encroachment upon rights expressly stipulated for in the Constitution." Madison's prediction has proved correct, especially in this century, as the freedoms of assembly and petition, along with other fundamental constitutional rights of the people, have been protected by an independent federal judiciary using its power of judicial review.

First Amendment freedoms have been expanded through judicial interpretation throughout 200 years of American constitutional history, and today the rights of assembly and petition are protected against infringement by the states by the due process clause of the 14th Amendment. The Supreme Court affirmed these rights for the first time in *DeJonge* v. *Oregon* (1937) and *Hague* v. *Congress of Industrial Organizations* (1939). In *DeJonge,* the Court ruled that the Oregon state government could not make it a crime for a member of a radical group, such as the Communist party, merely to conduct and participate in a public meeting. Writing for the Court, Chief Justice Charles Evans Hughes declared, "The right of peaceable assembly is a right cognate to those of free speech and free press and is equally fundamental," and "peaceable assembly for lawful discussion cannot be made a crime."

In *Hague,* the Court struck down a Jersey City, New Jersey, ordinance requiring permits from a "director of public safety" in order to hold meetings in public places within the city or to distribute printed material in streets, parks, or other locations.

The freedoms of assembly and petition, like other constitutional rights, have limits. Justice Louis Brandeis wrote in 1927 (*Whitney* v. *California*), "Although the rights of free speech and assembly are fundamental, they are not in their nature absolute. Their exercise is subject to restriction, if the particular restriction proposed is required in order to protect the State from destruction or from serious injury, political, economic or moral." These limits must be justified, as Brandeis emphasized, by a compelling public interest. "Only an emergency can justify repression," said Brandeis. "Such must be the rule if authority is to be reconciled with freedom. Such, in my opinion, is the command of the Constitution. It is therefore always open to Americans to challenge a law abridging free speech [petition] and assembly by showing that there was no emergency justifying it."

Citizens of a constitutional democracy will forever be challenged to decide what constitutes an "emergency justifying" a particular limitation upon freedom of expression. They must respond, case by case, to this broad question: At what point, and under what circumstances, should majority rule be limited by the higher law of the Constitution in order to protect the fundamental free-

During the depression, World War I veterans marched in Washington to demand early payment of war bonuses. The Bill of Rights guarantees to all citizens the right to gather peaceably and voice their concerns.

doms and rights of individuals in the minority, such as their rights of peaceable assembly, petition, and speech? Justice Oliver Wendell Holmes reminded us about the occasional difficulty of answering this question, when he wrote, in *United States* v. *Schwimmer* (1929), "If there is any principle of the Constitution that more imperatively calls for attachment than any other, it is the principle of free thought—not free thought for those who agree with us but freedom for the thought that we hate."

An especially poignant example of Justice Holmes's "principle of free thought" was provided in *Collin* v. *Smith* (1978), a case decided by the U.S. Court of Appeals for the Seventh Circuit. In this decision, the federal appellate court decided to permit "followers of Nazism" flaunting the swastika to publicly and peaceably assemble to express their views in the village of Skokie, Illinois. In this decision, the court of appeals appeared to disregard the wishes of the majority in a community, as expressed by their representatives in government, who had passed ordinances prohibiting these American Nazis from publicly assembling to express their "hateful" political and social opinions. Judge Bernard Decker wrote:

> In this case, a small group of zealots, openly professing to be followers of Nazism, have succeeded in exacerbating the emotions of a large segment of the citizens of the Village of Skokie who are bitterly opposed to their views and revolted by the prospect of this public appearance.
>
> When feeling and tensions are at their highest peak, it is a temptation to reach for the exception to the rule announced by Mr. Justice Holmes,… freedom for the thought we hate.
>
> Freedom of thought carries with it the freedom to speak and to publicly assemble to express one's thoughts. … [I]t is better to allow those who

preach racial hate to expend their venom in rhetoric rather than to be panicked into embarking on a dangerous course of permitting the government to decide what its citizens must say and hear.

The U.S. Supreme Court refused to review the lower court decision in *Collin* v. *Smith*. Thus, Judge Decker's decision to overturn the Skokie ordinances was upheld.

This case presaged a heated controversy in the 1980s and 1990s about the limits of 1st Amendment freedoms of speech, press, assembly, and petition when these rights are used to assault the beliefs and sensitivities of vulnerable minorities, whether racial, ethnic, sexual, or religious. We are challenged today to decide critical questions about how to balance the 1st Amendment rights of various types of individuals, including some who are hateful, with our sense of the public good.

SEE ALSO
Whitney v. California

FURTHER READING
Friendly, Fred W., and Martha J. N. Elliott. "Protecting the Thought That We Hate. Freedom of Speech and the Right of Peaceable Assembly." In *The Constitution: That Delicate Balance*. New York: Random House, 1984.

Attainder, bill of

A BILL of attainder is a law that punishes a person without permitting him a trial or fair hearing in a court of law. It is punishment by legislation. Article 1, Section 9, of the U.S. Constitution forbids Congress to pass a bill of attainder, and Article 1, Section 10, prohibits any state government from enacting one. If the Constitution permitted bills of attainder, government officials could, by law, force the person *attained* or punished by legislative act to forfeit his liberty, property, or income. Using a bill of attainder, government officials could punish an individual who criticizes them or who belongs to an unpopular group. The U.S. Constitution protects the rights of individuals by denying to the government the power to pass a bill of attainder.

"Bad tendency" test

S E E Abrams v. United States; Freedom of speech and press

Bail

BAIL IS a pledge of money given by an accused person as security that he will appear in court for trial when requested. Bail enables the accused person to be out of jail during the period of time between the person's arrest and receipt of charges and the person's trial. Failure of the accused person to appear for trial may result in loss of the bail.

The 8th Amendment to the U.S. Constitution says, "Excessive bail shall not be required," thus assuring an accused person a fair opportunity to be free on bail. Permitting a person to be free on bail allows him to retain employment and income while awaiting trial. It also gives the defendant ample opportunity to prepare a defense to the charges. However, bail is usually denied to those accused of first-degree murder or other heinous crimes.

A bail bond office in Washington, D.C. Those who cannot afford to pay their own bail often turn to a bondsman, who puts up the bail money in return for a fee.

FURTHER READING

Buranelli, Vincent. *The Eighth Amendment.* Englewood Cliffs, N.J.: Silver Burdett Press, 1991.

Baker v. Carr

☆ *369 U.S. 186 (1962)*
☆ *Vote: 6–2*
☆ *For the Court: Brennan*
☆ *Concurring: Stewart and Clark*
☆ *Dissenting: Frankfurter and Harlan*
☆ *Not participating: Whittaker*

IN 1959, Charles Baker was mayor of Millington, Tennessee, a rapidly growing suburb of Memphis. He requested help from the state government in coping with the problems of urban growth. But he got no satisfaction because the urban areas of Tennessee were underrepresented in the state legislature. By contrast, the rural areas of the state were overrepresented. Approximately 11 percent of the population lived in rural areas of Tennessee, but more than 50 percent of the representatives in the state legislature were elected by the rural areas of the state. The outcome was neglect of the problems and the needs of urban people. The floor leader of the Tennessee House of Representatives said: "I believe in collecting the taxes where the money is—in the cities—and spending it where it's needed—in the country."

Charles Baker decided that the only way to solve the financial problems of Tennessee's cities was to force the government to reapportion the legislature—to draw the legislative districts equally according to population. In this way every citizen of the state, whether living in a rural or urban area, would be represented equally in the legislature—the principle of "one person, one vote." People's votes are equal when each member of the legislature represents about the same number of people. Charles Baker brought suit against Joseph Cordell Carr, the Tennessee secretary of state, to force reapportionment of the legislature. But the federal district court dismissed

STATE LEGISLATURES MUST REPRESENT POPULATION

Sanders in The Kansas City Star

"Great Scott! We've lost our vote!"

This cartoon satirizes the Baker v. Carr *decision as farm animals, representing rural voters, read about the reapportionment plan in the paper.*

the suit because the issue was political rather than legal. Thus, according to the trial court, the question should be resolved by the political (legislative and executive) branches of government, not the judicial branch (the courts).

The Issue Baker argued that urban voters in Tennessee were denied the equal protection of the laws guaranteed by the 14th Amendment. He requested that the state be ordered to equalize its legislative districts so that each person's vote was of equal weight. The Court, however, restricted its decision to questions of jurisdiction, standing, and justiciability. Did the court have the jurisdiction (authority) to make decisions about state legislative apportionment? Did Baker have standing (the right) to bring suit in a case of this kind? And was this issue appropriate for judicial decision or should it be left to the political branches of the government to decide?

Opinion of the Court Justice William Brennan, writing for the Court, ruled that the Court had jurisdiction in this case, Baker had standing to bring suit, and the issue was justiciable. He wrote that "the right [to equal districts in the Tennessee legislature] is within the reach of judicial protection under the Fourteenth Amendment."

Although the Court limited its decision to the questions of jurisdiction, standing, and justiciability, Justice Brennan clearly stated that failure to apportion legislative districts of a state equally was a violation of the equal protection clause of the 14th Amendment. He concluded that Baker was entitled to a trial, so the case was sent back to the federal district court.

Dissent Justice Felix Frankfurter and Justice John Marshall Harlan II strongly dissented. Frankfurter argued that the issue was essentially political, not judicial, and should be left to the legislative and executive branches to decide. Harlan argued that there was nothing in the U.S. Constitution that required state legislatures to be apportioned so as to equally represent each voter.

Significance This case was the first in a series that led to legislative reapportionment throughout the country. The culminating case was *Reynolds* v. *Sims* (1964), in which the Court decided that states were required to establish equally populated electoral districts for both houses of the state legislature. Within one year of the decision in *Baker* v. *Carr*, 36 states were involved in lawsuits about legislative reapportionment. Eventually, every state of the United States was required to redraw its legislative districts to provide equal representation for all voters of the state.

U.S. Attorney General Robert F. Kennedy called the *Baker* decision "a landmark in the development of representative government." And Chief Justice Earl Warren, near the end of his life, called this case the most important one decided during his 16 years as chief justice.

SEE ALSO
Reynolds v. Sims

FURTHER READING
Cortner, Richard C. *The Apportionment Cases.* Knoxville: University of Tennessee Press, 1970.

Baldwin, Henry

ASSOCIATE JUSTICE, 1830–44

☆ Born: Jan. 14, 1780, New Haven, Conn.
☆ Education: Yale College, LL.D., 1797; studied law under Alexander J. Dallas, Washington, D.C.
☆ Previous government service: U.S. representative from Pennsylvania, 1817–22
☆ Appointed by President Andrew Jackson Jan. 4, 1830; replaced Bushrod Washington, who died
☆ Supreme Court term: confirmed by the Senate Jan. 6, 1830, by a 41–2 vote; served until Apr. 21, 1844
☆ Died: Apr. 21, 1844, Philadelphia, Pa.

HENRY BALDWIN was a strong supporter of Andrew Jackson's 1828 Presidential campaign. In 1830, President Jackson rewarded Baldwin with an appointment to the Supreme Court. Justice Baldwin tended to support states' rights in cases involving conflict between federal power and state sovereignty. However, he argued against extreme positions in support of either state sovereignty or federal supremacy. He claimed to be searching for a middle-of-the-road position between the two extremes.

Justice Baldwin clashed with Chief Justice John Marshall and helped to destroy the unity of the Court. In 1831, for example, he dissented seven times from the majority opinions of the Court. This was a dramatic departure from the tradition of unanimity that Marshall had established.

Justice Baldwin became irritable and erratic as he aged, a striking change from the good humor of the early years of his career. Toward the end of his life, he was often angry and occasionally violent. He was deeply in debt by 1844, when he died of paralysis.

Barbour, Philip Pendleton

ASSOCIATE JUSTICE, 1836–41

☆ Born: May 25, 1783, Orange County, Va.
☆ Education: read law on his own; attended one term, College of William and Mary, 1801
☆ Previous government service: Virginia House of Delegates, 1812–14; U.S. representative from Virginia, 1814–25, 1827–30; Speaker of the House of Representatives, 1821–23; state judge, Virginia, 1825–27; president, Virginia Constitutional Convention, 1829–30; U.S. district judge, Court of Eastern Virginia, 1830–36
☆ Appointed by President Andrew Jackson Feb. 28, 1836; replaced Gabriel Duvall, who resigned
☆ Supreme Court term: confirmed by the Senate Mar. 15, 1836, by a 30–11 vote; served until Feb. 25, 1841
☆ Died: Feb. 25, 1841, Washington, D.C.

PHILIP PENDLETON BARBOUR belonged to a prominent family of Virginia landowners. He followed the family tradition to become a wealthy plantation owner and a leader in the state and federal governments. Barbour became an active supporter of Andrew Jackson's Democratic party and backed Jackson's successful campaign for the Presidency in 1828. Two years later, Jackson rewarded him with an appointment to the U.S. District Court for Eastern Virginia. In 1835, Jackson appointed Barbour to the U.S. Supreme Court.

During his brief period on the Court, Justice Barbour strongly supported states' rights and powers and strict limitations on the constitutional powers of the federal government. As a result, proponents of a strong federal government and those who believed in a loose interpretation of the Constitution

opposed Justice Barbour. Daniel Webster, for example, wrote in 1837, "His fear, or hatred, of the powers of this [federal] government is so great, his devotion to states' rights so absolute, that perhaps [a case] could hardly arise, in which he would be willing to exercise the power of declaring a state law void."

Bar of the Supreme Court

THE BAR of the Supreme Court consists of lawyers authorized by the Court to argue cases there. During the Supreme Court's first term in 1790, it established two main qualifications for these lawyers. First, the person must have a satisfactory professional and moral character and reputation. Second, the person must have met the standards to practice law before the highest court of one of the states or territories of the United States. The clerk of the Court's office examines all applications and notifies the lawyers whose applications are accepted.

Between 4,000 and 5,000 applicants are admitted each year to practice before the bar of the Court. After receiving notification of acceptance, the applicant is required to pay an admission fee of $100. Each applicant may then be officially admitted to the bar of the Supreme Court by taking an oath of admission either before a notary public or in the open Court. The oath asks the person to "solemnly swear that as an attorney and counselor of this Court, you will conduct yourself uprightly and according to law, and that you will support the Constitution of the United States. So help you God." The applicant replies, "I do."

This certificate authorizes Washington lawyer Pamela Stuart to argue cases before the Supreme Court.

Barron v. Baltimore

☆ 7 Pet. 243 (1833)
☆ Vote: 7–0
☆ For the Court: Marshall

JOHN BARRON owned docks and warehouses at the east side of the harbor of Baltimore, Maryland. Barron's wharf was a popular place for ships to tie up for off-loading cargoes into nearby warehouses. Barron and his partners made big profits by renting their wharf to ship owners.

Barron's prosperity was being ruined, however, by construction crews working for the city government of Baltimore. They were digging up land, building streets, and diverting streams. Rainfall caused dirt-laden runoff to flow into the Patapsco River, which deposited the debris under Barron's docks. As a result, the water level at Barron's wharf was lowered to the point of interfering with the safe entry of ships. Barron claimed his profitable business had been severely damaged, and he sued the city of Baltimore to compensate him for the financial losses it had caused.

The Issue Barron claimed that the city of Baltimore had violated his constitutional rights under the 5th Amendment, which says that "private property" shall not "be taken for public use without just compensation." Barron's claim raised this question: Could the 5th Amendment, or any other part of the federal Bill of Rights, be used to limit the powers of a state government? Or does the Bill of Rights restrain only the federal government?

Opinion of the Court Chief Justice John Marshall concluded that the first 10 amendments to the U.S. Constitution applied only to the federal government. This, he said, was the original intention of the framers of the first 10 amend-

Baltimore Harbor in 1830. John Barron claimed that the city was violating his constitutional right to property by allowing construction projects to interfere with the operation of his docks.

ments. Thus, the 5th Amendment could not be used by Barron to require Baltimore to pay him "just compensation" for taking his property. According to Marshall, the Supreme Court had no jurisdiction in the case, and so it was dismissed.

Significance This decision legally established the widely held view that the federal Bill of Rights was intended by its framers in 1789 to bind only the federal government. The constitutional issue of this case was settled until passage of the 14th Amendment in 1868, which was designed to limit the powers of state governments in order to protect the rights of individuals. However, the Supreme Court did not begin to use the 14th Amendment to incorporate, or apply, parts of the federal Bill of Rights to state governments until the second quarter of the 20th century, beginning with *Gitlow* v. *New York* (1925).

SEE ALSO

Incorporation doctrine

FURTHER READING

Friendly, Fred W., and Martha J. H. Elliott. "Barron's Wharf: The First Test of the Bill of Rights." In *The Constitution: That Delicate Balance*. New York: Random House, 1984.

Holmes, Burnham. *The Fifth Amendment*. Englewood Cliffs, N.J.: Silver Burdett Press, 1991.

Benton v. Maryland

☆ *395 U.S. 784 (1969)*
☆ *Vote: 7 2*
☆ *For the Court: Marshall*
☆ *Dissenting: Harlan and Stewart*

BENTON was charged by the state of Maryland with committing two crimes: larceny and burglary. The jury found Benton innocent of larceny and guilty of burglary. Benton appealed his conviction for burglary. This led to the reopening of the larceny charges. In the new trial, Benton was found guilty of both charges—larceny and burglary—and sent to prison.

The Issue The 5th Amendment to the Constitution provides protection against what is known as double jeopardy. It says that no person shall "be subject for the same offense to be twice put in jeopardy of life or limb." However, Benton had been tried twice by the state of Maryland for the same offense. Benton said that the state had violated his 5th Amendment right to protection against double jeopardy.

The state's attorneys pointed to the Court decision in *Palko* v. *Connecticut* (1937), which held that the 5th Amendment right to protection against double jeopardy was not applicable to the states because the due process clause of the 14th Amendment did not apply this right to the state courts. Therefore, this 5th Amendment right, they said, limited only federal government actions, not those of state governments. Was the 5th Amendment ban on double jeopardy applicable to state governments?

Opinion of the Court The Court ruled that the 5th Amendment protection against double jeopardy applied to the states. Justice Thurgood Marshall wrote that this 5th Amendment guarantee "represents a fundamental ideal." This right, wrote Marshall, is certainly among those rights that are central to the American concept of justice.

Significance The *Benton* decision overruled *Palko* by holding that the double jeopardy prohibition of the 5th Amendment is applicable to the states through the 14th Amendment. This case became part of the gradual process by which the Court, during the 20th century, has applied most parts of the federal Bill of Rights to the states, on a case-by-case basis.

SEE ALSO
Double jeopardy; Palko v. Connecticut

Bethel School District No. 403 v. Fraser

☆ *478 U.S. 675 (1986)*
☆ *Vote: 7–2*
☆ *For the Court: Burger*
☆ *Concurring: Blackmun and Brennan*
☆ *Dissenting: Marshall and Stevens*

MATTHEW FRASER, a 12th-grade student at Bethel High School in Pierce County, Washington, made a brief speech at a school assembly, in support of a friend's candidacy for the student government. The audience included ap-

proximately 600 students in grades 9 through 12.

Fraser's speech included no profane or "dirty" words. But it was filled with sexually suggestive comments and gestures. Fraser's performance caused an uproar among many students in the audience, who hooted, cheered, laughed uproariously, and mimicked the sexual activities implied by the suggestive language of the speech. Many other members of the audience, however, appeared to be shocked and upset.

School officials punished Fraser by suspending him from school for three days. Fraser's name was removed from a list of students eligible to speak at graduation exercises. He was charged with violating the school's disruptive conduct rule. According to this rule, "Conduct which materially and substantially interferes with the educational process is prohibited, including the use of obscene, profane language or gestures."

Fraser protested that his 1st Amendment right to freedom of speech had been violated. He sued school district officials.

The Issue Did the public school officials in this case violate a student's constitutional right to free speech by punishing him for violating the school's disruptive conduct rule? Do school officials have authority to impose limits on student speech of the kind specified in the disruptive conduct rule?

Opinion of the Court Writing for the Court, Chief Justice Warren E. Burger decided against Fraser's suit against the Bethel School District. He said, "The First Amendment does not prevent the school officials from determining that to permit a vulgar and lewd speech such as [Fraser's] would undermine the school's mission." Burger noted, "The undoubted freedom to advocate unpopular and controversial views in schools and classrooms must be balanced against the society's countervailing interest in teaching students the boundaries of socially appropriate behavior." The chief justice stressed that "the constitutional rights of students in public schools are not automatically coextensive with the rights of adults in other settings.... Nothing in the Constitution prohibits the states from insisting that certain modes of expression are inappropriate [in schools of the state] and subject to sanctions."

Dissent In a brief dissent, Justice Thurgood Marshall disagreed with the Court majority's conclusion that the student's remarks were disruptive of the school's educational mission. In a separate dissent, Justice John Paul Stevens said that the school district's disruptive conduct rule was too vague to be enforced fairly under the 1st Amendment's guarantee of free speech. He said, "I believe a strong presumption of free speech should apply whenever an issue of this kind is arguable."

Significance The Court's decision contributed to the concept that students in a public school do not necessarily have the same constitutional rights as adults outside of school. This point was also made in *New Jersey* v. *T.L.O.* (1985), which dealt with 4th Amendment protections against unlawful searches, and *Hazelwood School District* v. *Kuhlmeier* (1988), concerning free press rights. However, in *Tinker* v. *Des Moines Independent Community School District* (1969), Justice Abe Fortas, writing for the Court, said, "It can hardly be argued that either students or teachers shed their constitutional rights to freedom of speech or expression at the schoolhouse gate."

SEE ALSO

Freedom of speech and press; Hazelwood School District v. Kuhlmeier; New Jersey v. T.L.O.; Tinker v. Des Moines Independent Community School District

Betts v. Brady

☆ *316 U.S. 455 (1942)*
☆ *Vote: 6–3*
☆ *For the Court: Roberts*
☆ *Dissenting: Black, Douglas, and Murphy*

SMITH BETTS, a 43-year-old unemployed man, was indicted for robbing a store in Carroll County, Maryland. He pleaded not guilty, and because he could not afford to pay for a lawyer, he asked the trial court to appoint an attorney to defend him. The trial judge refused Betts's request because the courts in Maryland commonly appointed counsel only in special circumstances, such as cases involving mentally incompetent defendants or cases that involved the possibility of the death penalty. Smith Betts represented himself in court and was judged guilty. The judge sentenced him to eight years in the Maryland penitentiary.

While in jail, Betts filed habeas corpus petitions, which required the state either to justify holding him in jail or release him. He demanded to be released on the grounds that he was wrongfully convicted because his constitutional right to a lawyer had been denied. The courts refused his petitions. So Betts appealed his case to the U.S. Supreme Court.

The Issue Smith Betts argued that he had been deprived of the right to a lawyer guaranteed by the 6th Amendment, which says: "In all criminal prosecutions, the accused shall enjoy the right...to have the assistance of counsel for his defense." Furthermore, the 14th Amendment says that no state government "shall deprive any person of life, liberty, or property without due process of law."

Did the U.S. Constitution require the state of Maryland to provide a lawyer for a defendant too poor to pay for legal help? Could the right to "assistance of counsel" specified in the 6th Amendment be applied to a state government through the due process clause of the 14th Amendment?

Opinion of the Court The Court decided that "the Sixth Amendment of the Constitution applied only to trials in federal courts." The Court concluded that the Maryland legal system had given Smith Betts ample means to defend himself during his trial. In cases that did not involve capital punishment, a state did not have to provide a lawyer for a defendant too poor to pay for one.

Dissent Justice Hugo Black was joined in dissent by Justices William O. Douglas and Frank Murphy. Black argued that the due process clause of the 14th Amendment "incorporates" those rights spelled out in the federal Bill of Rights, which includes the 6th Amendment guarantee of the right "to have the assistance of counsel." Justice Black therefore concluded that the state of Maryland had denied Smith Betts one of his constitutional rights.

Justice Black wrote that no person should "be deprived of counsel merely because of his poverty. To do so, seems to me to defeat the promise of our democratic society to provide equal justice under the law."

Significance The Court's decision in *Betts* v. *Brady* prevailed until the 1960s. Justice Black's ringing dissent was not forgotten, however. The Court eventually overruled the *Betts* v. *Brady* decision in *Gideon* v. *Wainwright* (1963). And Justice Black, a dissenter in the *Betts* case, wrote the opinion for the Court in the *Gideon* case.

SEE ALSO

Gideon v. Wainwright; Incorporation doctrine; Rights of the accused

FURTHER READING

Force, Eden. *The Sixth Amendment*. Englewood Cliffs, N.J.: Silver Burdett Press, 1991.

Bill of Rights

THE BILL OF RIGHTS consists of Amendments 1 through 10 of the U.S. Constitution. This Bill of Rights sets limits on the power of government in order to protect liberties and rights of individuals from the government's abuse of its power.

Creation of the Bill of Rights

"[A] Bill of Rights is what the people are entitled to against every government on earth, general or particular [that is, federal or state], and what no just government should refuse, or rest on inference," wrote Thomas Jefferson to James Madison on December 20, 1787.

Jefferson was in Paris, serving as U.S. minister to France, when he received a copy of the Constitution drafted at the federal convention in Philadelphia during the summer of 1787 and found that it lacked a bill of rights. Jefferson generally approved of the new Constitution and reported in detail to Madison the many features of the proposed federal government that satisfied him. Then Jefferson declared in his December 20, 1787, letter to Madison that he did not like "the omission of a bill of rights providing clearly and without the aid of sophisms for freedom of religion, freedom of the press, protection against standing armies…and trial by jury in all matters of fact triable by the laws of the land."

A bill of rights consists of statements of civil liberties and rights that a government may not take away from the people who live under the government's authority. A bill of rights sets legal limits on the power of government to prevent public officials from denying liberties and rights to individuals, which they possess on the basis of their humanity.

Thomas Jefferson was concerned

The Bill of Rights was ratified in 1791 to ensure that the fundamental liberties and rights of individuals would not be violated by the federal government.

that the strong powers of government provided for by the U.S. Constitution could be used to destroy inherent civil liberties and rights of the people. He noted with pleasure that the Constitution of 1787 included means to limit the power of government, such as the separation of powers among three branches of government—legislative, executive, and judicial—to prevent any person or group from exercising power tyrannically. However, Jefferson strongly believed that additional guarantees of individual freedoms and rights were needed. He therefore demanded a bill of rights to protect certain liberties of the people, such as freedom to express ideas in public, from infringement by the government. Many Americans agreed with Jefferson, and they supported ratification of the Constitution only on the condition that a bill of rights would be added to it.

James Madison took up this cause at the first federal Congress in 1789. As a member of the Virginia delegation to the House of Representatives, Madison proposed several amendments to the Constitution to place certain liberties and rights of individuals beyond the reach of the government. The Congress approved 12 of these constitutional changes and sent them to the state governments for ratification. In 1791, 10 of these amendments were approved by the states and added to the Constitution. These 10 amendments are known as the Bill of Rights.

Contents of the Bill of Rights

Amendment 1 protects freedom of thought, belief, and expression. Amendment 1 says, for example, that the Congress of the United States is forbidden to pass any law "respecting an establishment of religion" or depriving individuals of certain fundamental civil liberties: religious freedom, the freedom of speech and the press, and the right of the people to gather together peacefully and petition the government to satisfy complaints they have against public policies and officials. The history of the 1st Amendment has involved the expansion of individual freedoms and the separation of church and state. For example, the 1st Amendment has been interpreted to mean that government may not establish an official religion, favor any or all religions, or stop individuals from practicing religion in their own way. Further, the right to assembly has been extended to include the right of association in organizations. Finally, the rights of free speech and press are generally understood to be very broad, if not absolute. There are, however, legal limits concerning the time, place, and manner of speech.

Amendment 2 protects the right of the state governments and the people to maintain militia or armed companies to guard against threats to their social order, safety, and security; and in connection with that state right the federal government may not take away the right of the people to have and use weapons.

Amendment 3 forbids the government, during times of peace, to house soldiers in a private dwelling without the consent of the owner. In a time of war the government may use private dwellings to quarter troops, if this is done lawfully.

Amendment 4 protects individuals against unreasonable and unwarranted searches and seizures of their property. It establishes conditions for the lawful issuing and use of search warrants—official documents authorizing a search—by government officials to protect the right of individuals to security "in their persons, houses, papers, and effects." There must be "probable cause" for issuing a warrant to authorize a search or arrest; and the place to be searched, the objects sought, and the person to be arrested must be precisely described.

Amendment 5 states certain legal and procedural rights of individuals. For example, the government may not act against an individual in the following ways:

• Hold an individual to answer for a serious crime unless the prosecution presents appropriate evidence to a grand jury that indicates the likely guilt of the individual.

• Try an individual more than once for the same offense.

• Force an individual to act as a witness against himself in a criminal case.

• Deprive an individual of life, liberty, or property without due process of law (fair and proper legal proceedings).

• Deprive an individual of his or her private property for public use without compensating the person fairly.

Amendment 6 guarantees individuals suspected or accused of a crime certain protections against the power of government. This amendment provides to individuals:

• The right to a speedy public trial before an unbiased jury picked from the community in which the crime was committed.

• The right to receive information about what the individual has been accused of and why the accusation has been made.

• The right to face, in court, witnesses offering testimony against the individual.

• The right to obtain favorable witnesses to testify for the defendant in court (that is, the right to subpoena witnesses).

• The right to help from a lawyer.

Amendment 7 provides for the right to a trial by jury in civil cases (common lawsuits or cases that do not involve a criminal action) where the value of the item(s) or the demanded settlement involved in the controversy exceeds $20.

Amendment 8 protects individuals from punishments that are too harsh, fines that are too high, and bail (the amount of money required to secure a person's liberty from legal custody) that is too high.

Amendment 9 says that the rights guaranteed in the Constitution are not the only rights that individuals may have. Individuals retain other rights, not mentioned in the Constitution, that the government may not take away.

Amendment 10 says that the state governments and the people of the United States retain any powers the Constitution does not specifically grant to the federal government or prohibit to the state governments, such as the power of the states to establish and manage public school systems.

Expanding the scope of the Bill of Rights

The framers of the first 10 amendments to the U.S. Constitution intended to limit only the powers of the national government, not those of the state governments. Amendment 1, for example, says that Congress may not take away the individual's rights to freedom of religion, speech, press, and so forth. This understanding of the Bill of Rights was supported by the Supreme Court's decision in *Barron* v. *Baltimore* (1833). Writing for a unanimous Court, Chief Justice John Marshall concluded that the Bill of Rights could be used to limit the power only of the federal government, not of the states.

However, the passage of the 14th Amendment in 1868 opened new possibilities. This amendment states that "no state...shall deprive any person of life, liberty, or property, without due process of law."

During the 20th century the Supreme Court has interpreted the due process clause of the 14th Amendment to require state and local governments to comply with most of the provisions of the Bill of Rights. Therefore, state and local governments are now prohibited from encroaching on most of the civil liberties and rights found in the U.S. Constitution. Under provisions of Amendment 14, the federal government has been empowered to act on behalf of individuals against state and local governments or people who would try to abridge other individuals' constitutional rights or liberties.

SEE ALSO

Amendments to the Constitution; Assembly and petition, rights to; Civil rights; Counsel, right to; Freedom of speech and press; Incorporation doctrine; Gun control and the right to bear arms; Liberty under the Constitution; Privacy, right to; Property rights; Religious issues under the Constitution; Rights of the accused; Searches and seizures; Self-incrimination, privilege against; Student rights under the Constitution

FURTHER READING

Bodenhamer, David J., and James W. Ely, Jr. *The Bill of Rights in Modern America after Two-Hundred Years.* Bloomington: Indiana University Press, 1993.

Hall, Kermit L., ed. *By and For the People: Constitutional Rights in American History.* Arlington Heights, Ill.: Harlan Davidson, 1991.

Levy, Leonard. "Why We Have a Bill of Rights." *Constitution* 3, no. 1 (Winter 1991): 6–13.

Meltzer, Milton. *The Bill of Rights: How We Got It and What It Means.* New York: Crowell, 1990.

Rakove, Jack. "Inspired Expedient: How James Madison Balanced Principle and Politics in Securing the Adoption of the Bill of Rights." *Constitution* 3, no. 1 (Winter 1991): 19–25.

A BILL OF RIGHTS CHRONOLOGY

June 8, 1789: James Madison, representative from Virginia, presented proposals about constitutional rights to the House of Representatives; he urged that these proposals be added to the Constitution.

September 25, 1789: More than two-thirds of both houses of Congress reacted favorably to most of Madison's proposals about individual rights, and they voted to approve 12 amendments to the Constitution. The amendments were proposed in response to the state ratifying conventions that had called for additional guarantees for civil liberties and rights in the Constitution.

October 2, 1789: President George Washington sent 12 proposed constitutional amendments to the states for their approval. According to Article 5 of the Constitution, three-fourths of the states had to ratify these proposed amendments before they could become part of the Constitution.

November 20, 1789: New Jersey became the first state to ratify 10 of the 12 Amendments, the Bill of Rights.

December 19, 1789: Maryland ratified the Bill of Rights.

December 22, 1789: North Carolina ratified the Bill of Rights.

January 19, 1790: South Carolina ratified the Bill of Rights.

January 25, 1790: New Hampshire ratified the Bill of Rights.

January 28, 1790: Delaware ratified the Bill of Rights.

February 27, 1790: New York ratified the Bill of Rights.

March 10, 1790: Pennsylvania ratified the Bill of Rights.

June 11, 1790: Rhode Island ratified the Bill of Rights.

November 3, 1791: Vermont ratified the Bill of Rights.

December 15, 1791: Virginia ratified the Bill of Rights; these 10 amendments became part of the Constitution of the United States of America.

Black, Hugo Lafayette

*ASSOCIATE JUSTICE,
1937–71*

☆ *Born: Feb. 27, 1886, Harlan, Ala.*
☆ *Education: Birmingham Medical
College, 1903–4; University of
Alabama, LL.B., 1906*
☆ *Previous government service: police
court judge, Birmingham, 1910–11;
solicitor, Jefferson County, Ala.,
1915–17; U.S. senator from
Alabama, 1927–37*
☆ *Appointed by President Franklin D.
Roosevelt Aug. 12, 1937; replaced
Willis Van Devanter, who retired*
☆ *Supreme Court term: confirmed by
the Senate Aug. 17, 1937, by a 63–16
vote; retired Sept. 17, 1971*
☆ *Died: Sept. 25, 1971, Bethesda, MD*

HUGO LAFAYETTE BLACK rose from
humble origins to become one of the
most highly regarded justices in the Supreme Court's history. He was the eighth
child of a farmer and storekeeper in rural
Clay County, Alabama. Through hard
work and determination, Hugo Black
overcame the hardships of his youth to
earn a law degree from the University of
Alabama and to begin a career as a lawyer and public official in his home state.

In 1926, Black won election to the
U.S. Senate, and he was reelected in
1932. During his second term, Senator
Black became a strong supporter of
President Franklin D. Roosevelt's New
Deal policies. Roosevelt responded in
1937 by making Black his first appoint-
ment to the U.S. Supreme Court.

Black's membership on the Court
became controversial when newspaper
reporters revealed that he had been a
member of the Ku Klux Klan from 1923
until 1926. The Ku Klux Klan had been
organized after the Civil War by white
supremacists who wanted to limit the
opportunities and rights of black people.
Justice Black repudiated his brief association with the racist Ku Klux Klan in a nationwide radio broadcast. "I did join the
Klan," said Black. "I later resigned. I
have never rejoined…. Before becoming
a Senator I dropped the Klan. I have had
nothing to do with it since that time."
From this controversial beginning on the
Court, Justice Black developed into one
of its leading members, often taking a
strong stand on behalf of the constitutional rights of individuals.

Justice Black favored a strict, literal
reading of the Constitution regarding the
government's power to infringe individual rights. For example, he wrote that
"the First Amendment does not speak
equivocally. It prohibits any law 'abridging the freedom of speech, or of the
press.' It must be taken as a command of
the broadest scope that explicit
language…will allow" (*Bridges* v. *California*, 1941). In line with this viewpoint,
Justice Black joined numerous decisions
and wrote several dissents, to advocate
virtually unlimited freedom of speech
and press. Near the end of his career,
however, he dissented from the majority
opinions in cases protecting picketing
and other nonverbal expression as examples of free speech (*Cox* v. *Louisiana*,
1965, and *Tinker* v. *Des Moines Independent Community School District*,
1969). In the *Tinker* case, for example,
Black dis-
sented from
the Court's
decision to
protect the
right of stu-
dents in a sec-
ondary school
to wear black
arm bands to
protest U.S.
government
policy in the
Vietnam War.
The Court de-

*A political car-
toon shows the
Ku Klux Klan, in
the form of a vul-
ture, hovering
over the White
House. Soon after
he joined the Su-
preme Court,
Hugo Black was
severely criticized
for his previous
membership in
the KKK.*

cided that by displaying the arm bands the students were expressing "symbolic speech."

Justice Black was a persistent leader of the Court's use of the federal Bill of Rights to limit the powers of state governments. He interpreted the due process clause of the 14th Amendment, which states, "No state shall…deprive any person of life, liberty, or property, without due process of law," to require state governments to comply with all provisions of the Bill of Rights. He stated this "total incorporation" position in his dissent in *Adamson* v. *California* (1947): "My study of the historical events that culminated in the Fourteenth Amendment… persuades me that one of the chief objects that the provisions of the Amendment's first section, separately, and as a whole, were intended to accomplish was to make the Bill of Rights applicable to the states."

The Court has not yet agreed with his "total incorporation" doctrine—the application of all provisions of the Bill of Rights to the states. Rather, the Court has continued to "incorporate" particular provisions of the Bill of Rights on a case-by-case basis. Through this process, most parts of the Bill of Rights have been incorporated under the due process clause of the 14th Amendment and applied to the states.

Although Justice Black's total incorporation doctrine has not prevailed, he greatly influenced the gradual application of more and more provisions of the Bill of Rights to the states. Thus, he greatly expanded the constitutional protection of individual rights available to the people of the United States.

Justice Black always carried a well-used copy of the Constitution in his pocket as a sign of his devotion to limited government and the rule of law. This faith in the Constitution lasted for the rest of his life. After 34 years of ser-

vice on the Court, he retired on September 17, 1971, because of ill health; he died eight days later.

SEE ALSO

Due process of law; Incorporation doctrine; Tinker v. Des Moines Independent Community School District

FURTHER READING

Ball, Howard, and Phillip J. Cooper. *Of Power and Right: Hugo Black, William O. Douglas, and America's Constitutional Revolution.* New York: Oxford University Press, 1992.
Dunne, Gerald T. *Hugo Black and the Judicial Revolution.* New York: Simon & Schuster, 1977.
Simon, James F. "The Antagonists: Hugo Black and Felix Frankfurter." *Constitution* 3, no. 1 (Winter 1991): 26–34.

Blackmun, Harry A.

ASSOCIATE JUSTICE, 1970–

☆ *Born: Nov. 12, 1908, Nashville, Ill.*
☆ *Education: Harvard College, A.B., 1929; Harvard Law School, LL.B., 1932*
☆ *Previous government service: clerk, Eighth Circuit Court of Appeals, 1932–33; judge, Eighth Circuit Court of Appeals, 1959–70*
☆ *Appointed by President Richard M. Nixon Apr. 14, 1970, to replace Abe Fortas, who resigned*
☆ *Supreme Court term: confirmed by the Senate May 12, 1970, by a 94–0 vote*

HARRY A. BLACKMUN spent most of his childhood in the Minneapolis–St. Paul area, where he began a lasting friendship with Warren E. Burger, a future chief justice of the United States. After graduation from Harvard Law School in 1932, Blackmun practiced law in Minnesota. In 1959 President Dwight Eisenhower appointed him to the Eighth Circuit Court of Appeals. In 1970 President Richard Nixon appointed him to the U.S. Supreme Court after the Senate had refused to confirm two preceding appointments (Clement F. Haynsworth of South Carolina and G. Harrold Carswell of Florida). The Senate confirmed Blackmun unanimously.

During his early years on the Court, Justice Blackmun tended to vote with his friend, Chief Justice Burger. Their opinions were so similar that news reporters named them "the Minnesota Twins." Later on, however, their views diverged and Blackmun often voted with Justices William Brennan and Thurgood Marshall, who were more liberal in decisions about civil liberties.

Justice Blackmun's most significant opinion was written for the majority in *Roe* v. *Wade* (1973). In this case, the Court defended the right of a pregnant woman to decide whether or not to have an abortion. Criminal penalties against doctors for performing abortions were declared unconstitutional. Justice Blackmun, writing for the Court, based his decision on the division of a pregnancy into three periods, called trimesters. He held that a state government could have no authority to prevent an abortion during the first trimester (the first three months of a pregnancy). During the second trimester, the state could regulate abortion only to protect the mother's well-being. During the third trimester, however, the state could legally prevent a woman from undergoing an abortion.

The *Roe* v. *Wade* decision was controversial. Since 1973, public response has been intense, whether for or against the Court's decision in this case. In the years following *Roe* v. *Wade,* Justice Blackmun has continued to defend the right of a pregnant woman to choose an abortion, in consultation with her doctor, during the first two trimesters of a pregnancy.

SEE ALSO

Privacy, right to; Roe v. Wade

FURTHER READING

Wasby, Stephen L. "Justice Harry A. Blackmun." In *The Burger Court: Political and Judicial Profiles,* edited by Charles M. Lamb and Stephen C. Halpern, 63–99. Urbana: University of Illinois Press, 1991.

Blair, John, Jr.

ASSOCIATE JUSTICE, 1789–95

☆ *Born: 1732, Williamsburg, Va.*
☆ *Education: College of William and Mary, B.A., 1754; studied law at Middle Temple, London, 1755–56*
☆ *Previous government service: Virginia House of Burgesses, 1766–70; clerk, Virginia Governor's Council, 1770–75; Virginia Constitutional Convention, 1776; Virginia Governor's Council, 1776; judge, Virginia General Court, 1777–78; chief justice, Virginia General Court, 1779; judge, first Virginia Court of Appeals, 1780–89; Constitutional Convention, 1787; judge, Virginia Supreme Court of Appeals, 1789*
☆ *Appointed by President George Washington Sept. 24, 1789, as one of the original members of the U.S. Supreme Court*
☆ *Supreme Court term: confirmed by the Senate Sept. 26, 1789, by a voice vote; resigned Oct. 25, 1795*
☆ *Died: Aug. 31, 1800, Williamsburg, Va.*

JOHN BLAIR, JR., was a member of a prominent Virginia family. He was an outstanding political leader of colonial Virginia and after 1776 continued his career of public service in the new state of Virginia. He participated in the Virginia Constitutional Convention of 1776 and the U.S. Constitutional Convention of 1787. He was one of three Virginians who signed the U.S. Constitution.

In recognition of his outstanding career as a political leader and Virginia state judge, George Washington appointed Blair to be one of the original six members of the U.S. Supreme Court. Blair's most important opinion was written in support of the Court's ruling in *Chisholm* v. *Georgia* (1793). In this decision, the Court ruled that Article 3, Section 2, of the U.S. Constitution gave a citizen of one state the right to sue another state in a federal court. This decision was overturned in 1795 by the 11th Amendment to the Constitution.

Justice Blair resigned from the Court on January 27, 1796. He retired to his home in Williamsburg, Virginia, where he died in 1800.

SEE ALSO

Chisholm v. Georgia

Blatchford, Samuel

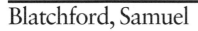

ASSOCIATE JUSTICE, 1882–93

☆ *Born: Mar. 9, 1820, New York, N.Y.*
☆ *Education: Columbia College, B.A., 1837*
☆ *Previous government service: judge, Southern District of New York, 1867–72; judge, Second Circuit Court of New York, 1872–82*
☆ *Appointed by President Chester Alan Arthur Mar. 13, 1882; replaced Ward Hunt, who retired*
☆ *Supreme Court term: confirmed by the Senate Mar. 27, 1882, by a voice vote; served until July 7, 1893*
☆ *Died: July 7, 1893, Newport, R.I.*

SAMUEL BLATCHFORD entered Columbia College at the age of 13 and graduated four years later at the top of his class. He spent the next four years preparing to become a lawyer by studying with and working for his father's friend New York governor William H. Seward. Samuel Blatchford became a lawyer in 1842 and practiced law first with his father and then with Seward's law firm. Later he established his own law firm.

After serving 15 years as a federal judge in New York (1867–82), Blatchford was appointed to the Supreme Court by President Chester Alan Arthur. Justice Blatchford served on the Supreme Court for 11 years, performing ably but without distinction. During the Court's memorial service for him in 1893, Attorney General Richard Olney said, "If he [Blatchford] was not brilliant, he was safe."

Bradley, Joseph P.

ASSOCIATE JUSTICE, 1870–92

☆ *Born: Mar. 14, 1813, Berne, N.Y.*
☆ *Education: Rutgers University, B.A., 1836*
☆ *Previous government service: none*
☆ *Appointed by President Ulysses S. Grant Feb. 7, 1870; replaced James Wayne, who died in 1867 and whose seat was unoccupied by act of Congress until 1870*
☆ *Supreme Court term: confirmed by the Senate Mar. 21, 1870, by a 46–9 vote; served until Jan. 22, 1892*
☆ *Died: Jan. 22, 1892, Washington, D.C.*

JOSEPH P. BRADLEY was a poor farm boy who became a very successful and wealthy man. He studied hard in school and attracted the attention of a local minister, who recommended him to Rutgers University. After graduating from Rutgers in 1836, Bradley studied law in the office of Arthur Gifford and became a lawyer in 1839. He worked hard and built a rewarding career as a lawyer.

In 1870, President Ulysses Grant appointed Joseph P. Bradley to the Supreme Court. During his 22 years of service on the Court, he was known for his careful research and detailed analysis of constitutional issues. He remained on the Court until the day of his death in 1892.

Brandeis, Louis Dembitz

ASSOCIATE JUSTICE, 1916–39

☆ *Born: Nov. 13, 1856, Louisville, Ky.*
☆ *Education: Harvard Law School, LL.B., 1877*
☆ *Previous government service: attorney, Massachusetts State Board of Trade, 1897–1911; counsel, Ballinger-Pinchot Investigation, 1910; chairman, arbitration board, New York garment workers' labor disputes, 1910–16*
☆ *Appointed by President Woodrow Wilson Jan. 28, 1916; replaced Joseph R. Lamar, who died*
☆ *Supreme Court term: confirmed by the Senate June 1, 1916, by a 47–22 vote; retired Feb. 13, 1939*
☆ *Died: Oct. 5, 1941, Washington, D.C.*

LOUIS DEMBITZ BRANDEIS was the first Jew to serve on the Supreme Court of the United States. His parents, Adolph and Fredericka Dembitz Brandeis, were immigrants from Bohemia who came to the United States in 1848.

The Brandeis family settled in Louisville, Kentucky, where Adolph Brandeis became a successful grain merchant who provided Louis with extraordinary opportunities for education and personal development. Louis completed two years of study at the highly regarded Annen-Realschule in Dresden, Germany. Brandeis returned to the United States to enter Harvard Law School, from which he graduated first in his class in 1877.

Soon after graduation, Brandeis began a law practice in Boston with his close friend and classmate Samuel Warren. By the turn of the century, Brandeis had become a nationally famous lawyer. News reporters called him the "people's attorney" because Brandeis often charged no fee for defending the rights of poor and disadvantaged people. He was also an active supporter of public reforms to bring about equal opportunities and fairness in the operations of businesses and government.

As the defense attorney in *Muller* v. *Oregon* (1908), Brandeis invented a new kind of legal argument, one based on sociological and economic evidence rather than legal precedent. Brandeis argued successfully for an Oregon law that limited the number of hours that women could work in laundries and other businesses. Brandeis's use of social science evidence to support legal reform of workplace conditions became a model for other lawyers, a type of document that they called "the Brandeis brief."

President Woodrow Wilson greatly respected Brandeis and often relied upon his advice. In 1916 Wilson appointed him to the U.S. Supreme Court to fill a vacancy created by the death of Justice Joseph R. Lamar. A vicious public controversy erupted over the nomination.

Many opponents disliked Brandeis because of his record as a political and social reformer. Others were against him because he was a Jew. One of his strongest supporters, Arthur Hill of Harvard Law School, explained the opposition to Brandeis's Supreme Court nomination: "Mr. Brandeis is an outsider, successful and a Jew."

The storm over President Wilson's appointment of Brandeis lasted for more than four months. This was the longest and most bitter battle over confirmation of an associate justice in the history of the Court. The closest example in recent times was the furor over the 1986 nomination of Robert Bork by President Ronald Reagan. Unlike the Bork nomination, however, the Brandeis appointment was eventually supported by the Senate Judiciary Committee, 10 votes to 8. Finally, the full Senate confirmed Brandeis by a vote of 47 to 22.

The new justice's troubles were not

over, however. One of his new colleagues, Justice James Clark McReynolds, refused to speak to Brandeis for more than three years. He would leave the conference table whenever Brandeis spoke, revealing his prejudice against the first Jew to serve on the Court.

Brandeis overcame this kind of hostility to become one of the greatest justices of all time. His most important opinions dealt with the constitutional rights of individuals. He sought to protect helpless individuals against oppression by uncaring government officials or an intolerant majority of the people. In *Olmstead* v. *United States* (1928), for example, Brandeis argued in a dissenting opinion for a general constitutional right to privacy. The Court had decided that wiretapping by federal government officials was not a violation of the 4th Amendment. Brandeis disagreed: "The makers of our Constitution...sought to protect Americans in their beliefs, their thoughts, their emotions and their sensations. They conferred, as against the Government, the right to be let alone—the most comprehensive of rights and the right most valued by civilized men."

Brandeis's dissent was vindicated in *Katz* v. *United States* (1967), when the Court overturned the *Olmstead* decision. In *Griswold* v. *Connecticut* (1965), the Court recognized a constitutional right to privacy for which Brandeis had argued many years before.

Brandeis was a leader in the movement to apply the federal Bill of Rights to the states through the due process clause of the 14th Amendment, a concept known as the incorporation doctrine. He first stated this idea in *Gilbert* v. *Minnesota* (1920). A few years later, the Court recognized this idea in *Gitlow* v. *New York* (1925). Since then, more and more parts of the Bill of Rights have been used to protect the liberties of individuals against state government violations.

Justice Brandeis was an especially vigorous defender of 1st Amendment freedoms. Through his Supreme Court opinions, he contributed mightily to the gradual expansion of these individual rights. He memorably expressed his commitment to 1st Amendment liberties in *Whitney* v. *California* (1927): "Those who won our independence believed that the final end of the State was to make men free to develop their faculties.... They believed liberty to be the secret of happiness."

Louis Brandeis served on the Court for 23 years, retiring in 1939 at the age of 82. A *New York Times* reporter noted: "The storm against him [when he was appointed to the Court] seems almost incredible now." Today, legal experts rate Louis Dembitz Brandeis one of the greatest justices in the history of the Supreme Court.

SEE ALSO

Incorporation doctrine; Muller v. Oregon; Olmstead v. United States; Privacy, right to

FURTHER READING

Baker, Leonard. *Brandeis and Frankfurter: A Dual Biography.* New York: New York University Press, 1984.
Paper, Lewis J. *Brandeis.* Englewood Cliffs, N.J.: Prentice-Hall, 1983.
Strum, Phillipa. *Louis D. Brandeis: Justice for the People.* Cambridge: Harvard University Press, 1984.

Brandeis brief

IN 1908 Louis D. Brandeis, as counsel for the state of Oregon in *Muller* v. *Oregon,* prepared a new kind of brief in support of an Oregon law that limited the number of hours that a woman could work each day in laundries and other industries. The brief included only two pages of discussion of the legal issues of the *Muller* case. The other 95 pages of this brief presented evidence about the

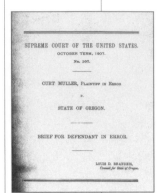

The first "Brandeis brief," which was submitted by Louis Brandeis in the case of Muller *v.* Oregon. *As counsel for the state of Oregon, Brandeis used sociological evidence to advocate that an Oregon law limiting working hours be upheld.*

harmful impact of long hours of strenuous labor on the "health, safety, and morals of women." The sociological evidence presented by Brandeis convinced the Court to support the Oregon law in order to protect public health and safety.

The success of the new kind of brief submitted by Brandeis in the *Muller* case influenced other lawyers to use sociological evidence, when appropriate, to make their arguments. This new kind of brief was named the Brandeis brief in honor of its creator, who later became a highly regarded justice of the U.S. Supreme Court.

SEE ALSO
Brief

Brandenburg v. Ohio

☆ *395 U.S. 444 (1969)*
☆ *Vote: Unanimous*
☆ *For the Court: Per curiam decision*

CLARENCE BRANDENBURG, a leader of the Ku Klux Klan, a white supremacist organization, was convicted of violating Ohio's Criminal Syndicalism Act. This state law outlawed speech that advocated violence as a means of achieving social or political reform. Brandenburg had urged violence against black people during a televised Ku Klux Klan rally.

The Issue The Ohio statute used to convict Brandenburg was identical to a California law upheld in *Whitney* v. *California* (1927). Brandenburg, however, claimed that his conviction violated his 1st Amendment free speech rights. What are the limits, if

any, to an individual's right to free speech?

Opinion of the Court The Court decided in favor of Brandenburg and struck down as unconstitutional the Ohio Criminal Syndicalism Act. This decision overturned *Whitney* v. *California*. The Court held that the constitutional guarantees of free speech do not permit a state to forbid people from speaking in favor of the use of force or other illegal actions unless it was likely to result in immediate violations of the law. The right to free speech can be limited only when the speech can be directly and immediately connected to specific actions that could result in lawless behavior.

Significance This decision greatly expanded the scope of political speech. The "clear and present danger" test set forth in *Schenck* v. *United States* (1919) and used in subsequent cases allowed restrictions on speech if it had a "bad tendency"—that is, if it appeared to encourage or cause illegal actions. However, the Brandenburg test allows virtually all political speech, unless it is demonstrably linked to immediate lawless behavior.

SEE ALSO
Freedom of speech and press; Schenck v. United States; Whitney v. California

The Ku Klux Klan, which promotes white supremacy, has the same right to free speech as other organizations.

Brennan, William J., Jr.
A S S O C I A T E   J U S T I C E , 1 9 5 6 – 9 0

☆ *Born: Apr. 25, 1906, Newark, N.J.*
☆ *Education: University of Pennsylvania, B.S., 1928; Harvard Law School, LL.B., 1931*
☆ *Previous government service: judge, New Jersey Superior Court, 1949–50; judge, New Jersey Appellate Division, 1950–52; associate judge, New Jersey Supreme Court, 1952–56*
☆ *Appointed by President Dwight D. Eisenhower as a recess appointment Oct. 16, 1956; replaced Sherman Minton, who resigned; nominated by Eisenhower Jan. 14, 1957*

☆ *Supreme Court term: confirmed by the Senate Mar. 19, 1957, by a voice vote; retired July 20, 1990*

WILLIAM J. BRENNAN was a leader on the Supreme Court during most of his 34 years of service. Chief Justice Earl Warren viewed Brennan as his closest associate and relied upon him for wise advice and strong partnership. After Warren's retirement in 1969, Brennan continued to influence his colleagues, although not as strongly or decisively as before.

William Brennan rose to national prominence through hard work, persistence, and continuous development of his sharp intellect. He was the second of eight children of Roman Catholic immigrants from Ireland. His working-class parents encouraged him to pursue higher education and to achieve excellence in his life. In response to his parents' encouragement, Brennan became a brilliant student at the University of Pennsylvania and Harvard Law School.

After leaving Harvard, Brennan practiced law in Newark, New Jersey, and served in the army during World War II. After the war, he returned to his law practice and became a judge in the state courts of New Jersey.

In 1956, Republican President Dwight Eisenhower appointed Brennan, a Democrat, to the Supreme Court. He immediately joined forces with Chief Justice Warren and wrote several of the Warren Court's landmark decisions between 1956 and 1969.

Brennan wrote the Court's opinion in *Baker* v. *Carr* (1962), which Warren called "the most important case that we decided in my time." In this case, the Court opened the way to a redrawing of voting districts that transferred political power from rural areas to urban ones throughout the United States. Before the *Baker* v. *Carr* decision, rural districts in many states had been unfairly favored over the urban districts to give them more representation in government than was deserved on the basis of population. *Baker* v. *Carr* led to a series of Court decisions (such as *Reynolds* v. *Sims* in 1964) that required state governments to eliminate or redraw voting districts that did not fairly represent various classes of voters.

Another of Brennan's landmark opinions came in *New York Times Co.* v. *Sullivan* (1964), which expanded freedom of the press by making it very difficult for a public official to recover damages for defamatory statements that are untrue. Justice Brennan argued that "debate on public issues should be uninhibited, robust, and wide open." He held that "wide open" freedom of expression is the purpose of the 1st Amendment, which would be undermined if critics of government officials had to conform to "any test of truth." He claimed that "erroneous statement is inevitable in free debate; and it must be protected if the freedoms of expression are to have the breathing space they need." Brennan concluded that all speech about public officials was protected by the Constitution unless it was expressed "with actual malice," that is, expressed "with knowledge that it was false or with reckless disregard of whether it was false or not." Thus, an "actual malice" standard was established as part of constitutional law.

Justice Brennan was a loose constructionist; that is, he gave the Constitution a broad interpretation to promote the rights and opportunities of individuals. He believed in a dynamic Constitution that should be adapted to changing circumstances by judicial interpretation. He wrote in the *South Texas Law Review* (1986) that "the genius of the Constitution rests not in any static meaning it might have had in a world that is dead and gone, but in the adaptability of its great principles to cope with current problems and current needs."

Critics charged that Brennan tried to overextend the powers of the judicial branch to involve federal judges in making policy decisions that belong only to the people's elected representatives in Congress. They accused him and his followers of wanting to make law through their judicial decisions instead of limiting themselves to making judgments in specific cases about the meaning of the Constitution and federal statutes. Critics also said that Brennan was wrong to disregard the intentions of those who wrote the Constitution and its amendments in his broad interpretations of this fundamental document.

Brennan retired in 1990 because of declining health. Both his supporters and his critics recognized Brennan's decisive influence on the development of the Constitution in the latter half of the 20th century.

SEE ALSO
Baker v. Carr; Judicial activism and judicial restraint; New York Times Co. v. Sullivan

FURTHER READING
Friedelbaum, Stanley H. "Justice William J. Brennan." In *The Burger Court: Political and Judicial Profiles*, edited by Charles M. Lamb and Stephen C. Halpern. Urbana: University of Illinois Press, 1991.

Brewer, David

*A S S O C I A T E   J U S T I C E ,
1 8 9 0 – 1 9 1 0*

☆ *Born: June 20, 1837, Smyrna, Turkey*
☆ *Education: Wesleyan University, 1852–53; Yale College, B.A., 1856; Albany Law School, LL.B., 1858*
☆ *Previous government service: commissioner, U.S. Circuit Court, Leavenworth, Kans., 1861–62; judge of probate and criminal courts, Leavenworth County, 1863–64; judge, First Judicial District of Kansas, 1865–*

69; *Leavenworth city attorney, 1869–70; justice, Kansas Supreme Court, 1870–84; judge, Eighth Federal Circuit Court, 1884–89*
☆ *Other government service: president, Venezuela–British Guiana Border Commission, 1895*
☆ *Appointed by President Benjamin Harrison Dec. 4, 1889; replaced Stanley Matthews, who died*
☆ *Supreme Court term: confirmed by the Senate Dec. 18, 1889, by a 53–11 vote; served until Mar. 28, 1910*
☆ *Died: Mar. 28, 1910, Washington, D.C.*

DAVID BREWER was the son of a Congregational missionary who lived in the Anatolian part of the Turkish Empire. The family returned to the United States while Brewer was an infant, and he was raised in Wethersfield, Connecticut.

After graduating from Albany Law School, Brewer went to Kansas, where he served on several state courts, including the Supreme Court of Kansas. During his nearly 21 years as an associate justice of the U.S. Supreme Court, Brewer tended to support decisions to limit government regulation of private businesses. He strongly believed in free enterprise, free markets, and private property rights as foundations of a free government. Brewer also spoke and wrote against acquisition of colonies by the United States after the victorious war against Spain in 1898.

Brief

A WRITTEN document known as a brief is prepared by the lawyers on each side of a case and submitted to a court. A brief presents the facts of a case and the counsel's legal argument. The term was first used in 1631.

In cases before the U.S. Supreme Court, the attorneys rely upon their written briefs to persuade the Court. Supreme Court rules require that a "brief must be compact, . . . concise, and free from burdensome, irrelevant, immaterial, and scandalous matter." Since 1980 there has been a 50-page limit on all briefs submitted to the Supreme Court.

SEE ALSO
Brandeis brief

Brown, Henry B.

ASSOCIATE JUSTICE, 1891–1906

☆ *Born: Mar. 2, 1836, South Lee, Mass.*
☆ *Education: Yale College, B.A., 1856; studied briefly at Yale Law School and Harvard Law School*
☆ *Previous government service: U.S. deputy marshal, 1861; assistant U.S. attorney, Detroit, Mich., 1863–68; circuit judge, Wayne County, Mich., 1868; federal judge, Eastern District of Michigan, 1875–90*
☆ *Appointed by President Benjamin Harrison Dec. 23, 1890; replaced Samuel Miller, who died*
☆ *Supreme Court term: confirmed by the Senate Dec. 29, 1890, by a voice vote; retired May 28, 1906*
☆ *Died: Sept. 4, 1913, New York, N.Y.*

HENRY B. BROWN became a lawyer in 1860 in Detroit, Michigan, after finishing his formal education at Yale. After a 15-year career as a federal district judge in Michigan, Brown joined the U.S. Supreme Court.

Justice Brown's strong support of property rights and free enterprise, and his tendency to resist strong government regulation of business, reflected the dominant opinions of his time. So did Brown's views about civil rights for black Americans, which were expressed in his opinion for the Court in *Plessy* v. *Ferguson* (1896). The Plessy decision supported a Louisiana state law that required black and white railroad passengers to sit in separate rail-

way cars. Justice Brown, writing for the Court, argued that this Louisiana law did not violate the "equal protection of the laws" clause of the 14th Amendment. Brown used a "separate but equal" doctrine to support the Court's decision. He stated that separate facilities could be required by law for blacks and whites as long as the facilities provided for one group were equal to the facilities provided for the other group. He wrote, "We consider the underlying fallacy of the plaintiff's argument to consist in the assumption that the enforced separation of the two races stamps the colored race with a badge of inferiority."

The Court's decision in the *Plessy* case led to widespread enactment of state laws to segregate blacks from whites, to keep them apart, in the use of public facilities, such as schools, rest rooms, parks, cemeteries, and so forth.

Justice Brown left the Court in 1906 because of failing eyesight. He was popular then, but is not well regarded today because of his opinion for the Court in the *Plessy* case. Most Americans today strongly reject the legal segregation of blacks and whites, which Justice Brown defended in the 1890s. However, Brown and his Supreme Court colleagues expressed the prevailing view of that era about black-white relationships.

SEE ALSO
Plessy v. Ferguson

Brown v. Board of Education

☆ *347 U.S. 483 (1954)*
☆ *Vote: 9–0*
☆ *For the Court: Warren*

THE 14TH AMENDMENT declares, "No state shall ... deny to any person

Thurgood Marshall (center) and two NAACP colleagues after he successfully argued the Brown v. Board of Education *case in favor of school desegregation.*

within its jurisdiction the equal protection of the laws." In 1896 the Supreme Court handed down a landmark decision on the meaning of this equal protection clause. In *Plessy* v. *Ferguson,* the Court ruled that the 14th Amendment allowed a state to segregate whites and blacks by providing "separate but equal" facilities for blacks.

For nearly 60 years this doctrine of "separate but equal" served as a constitutional justification for racial segregation in the United States. This doctrine sanctioned separating blacks and whites in schools, housing, transportation, and recreation.

Not all Americans accepted the view that the Constitution allowed racial discrimination. Those opposed to segregation agreed with Justice John Harlan, who dissented in *Plessy,* declaring, "Our Constitution is color-blind." In 1909 a group of black and white Americans formed the National Association for the Advancement of Colored People (NAACP) to fight segregation and racial injustice. In the 1930s and 1940s, NAACP legal counsel successfully argued a number of

Supreme Court cases in which the Court prohibited segregation in public universities, political primaries, and railroads. By 1950 many blacks and whites were ready to challenge the constitutionality of segregated elementary and high schools. In the early 1950s five separate cases—from South Carolina, Virginia, Delaware, Kansas, and Washington, D.C.—made their way through the court system. In each case the parents of black schoolchildren asked lower courts to strike down laws requiring segregated schools. The NAACP provided these parents with legal help. Eventually, the Supreme Court heard these cases together as *Brown* v. *Board of Education.* The case received its name when Mr. and Mrs. Oliver Brown sued the Topeka, Kansas, school board for denying their eight-year-old daughter, Linda, admission to a school only five blocks from their house. She had to leave her home at 7:40 every morning and travel 21 blocks in order to reach her assigned school by 9:00. The school board refused to let Linda attend the school in her own neighborhood solely because she was black and the school nearest to her home was for whites only.

The Issue Thurgood Marshall, later a Supreme Court justice, was director of the NAACP Legal Defense Fund. He provided legal counsel for the Browns and the other plaintiffs. Marshall presented evidence showing that separating black and white students discriminated against blacks, placing them at a severe disadvantage. He argued that segregated schools were not and could never be equal. Such schools, he said, violated the equal protection guarantee of the 14th Amendment.

John W. Davis, a distinguished attorney and a 1924 Presidential candidate, represented the defense. He argued that the authors of the 14th Amendment never intended that article to prevent segregation in the nation's schools. Further, he claimed, the courts did not possess the authority to order the states to desegregate their schools.

Those states with segregated schools claimed that the dual system provided "separate but equal" facilities for whites and blacks. In fact, virtually no black schools were equal to white schools. The South Carolina case, for example, began when the local school board, run by whites, refused to provide school buses for black children. The board also refused to pay for heating the black schools or to provide them with indoor plumbing—services and facilities provided to white students. In spite of these glaring inequities, the black plaintiffs did not argue that the school systems were separate but *unequal*. Rather, they focused on challenging the "separate but equal" doctrine itself. Did state-supported segregation in public schools, even when black and white schools had equal facilities, violate the equal protection clause of the 14th Amendment?

A 1958 cartoon reveals the continued conflict between the federal government and state governments in the wake of the Brown decision.

Opinion of the Court The Supreme Court unanimously struck down the "separate but equal" doctrine as an unconstitutional violation of the 14th Amendment. Chief Justice Earl Warren said that segregation clearly gave black children "a feeling of inferiority as to their status in the community that may affect their hearts and minds in a way unlikely to ever be undone." Even if segregated schools gave blacks access to equal physical facilities, Warren argued, they deprived students of equal educational opportunities.

Warren declared, "We conclude that in the field of public education the doctrine of 'separate but equal' has no place. Separate educational facilities are inherently unequal."

Significance The *Brown* decision overturned *Plessy* v. *Ferguson* (1896). The ruling in this case destroyed the constitutional foundations of all forms of state-supported segregation in the United States. It also prompted massive resistance to school integration in many states. That resistance, in turn, helped spur the growth of the civil rights movement. This movement encouraged the passage of the federal civil rights acts of 1957, 1960, 1964, 1965, and 1968, which increased black political and civil rights.

Resistance also slowed implementation of the *Brown* decision in schools and led to many additional court cases. For example, Prince Edward County, Virginia, closed all of its public schools—for whites as well as blacks—rather than integrate. The first additional case, *Brown* v. *Board of Education* (349 U.S. 294), known as *Brown II,* came in 1955.

Brown II came before the Court because, as Chief Justice Warren wrote, "[W]e requested further argument on the question of relief." The Court wanted to consider the issue of how to implement the ruling of *Brown I* to end segregation in public schools. In *Brown II* the Court set forth guidelines that placed the primary responsibility for doing so on local school officials. Federal district courts were to continue their jurisdiction and oversight of school desegregation cases. They could allow school districts to proceed carefully and gradually to complete school desegregation.

Although the Supreme Court ordered school districts to begin desegregation "with all deliberate speed," in reality just the opposite occurred. Fourteen years after *Brown,* less than 20 percent of black students in the South attended integrated schools. Faced with continued resistance, the Supreme Court ruled in 1968, in *Green* v. *County School Board of New Kent County, Virginia,* that segregation must end "at once." Eventually, lower federal court rulings and the work of the federal executive branch agencies began to change this pattern. By the 1980s most Americans fully accepted the Court's ruling in the *Brown* case as the correct decision. Today, it is hailed as one of the greatest and most important decisions in the history of the Supreme Court.

SEE ALSO

Civil rights; Equality under the Constitution; Marshall, Thurgood; Plessy v. Ferguson

FURTHER READING

Berman, Daniel M. *It Is So Ordered: The Supreme Court Rules on School Segregation.* New York: Norton, 1966.
Kluger, Richard. *Simple Justice.* New York: Knopf, 1976.

Buildings, Supreme Court

THE SUPREME COURT has had several homes since its first meeting, on February 1, 1790, in New York City.

The first federal government of the United States was located in New York from 1789 to 1790. The Supreme Court met, at first, on the second floor of the Royal Exchange Building at the intersection of Broad and Water streets.

In December 1790 the federal government moved to Philadelphia, where the Court occupied a room on the first floor of the State House, known today as Independence Hall. In August 1791, the Court moved to the newly built City Hall, located on the east side of State House Square, where it remained until 1801.

Early Years in Washington

At this time, the Court followed the rest of the federal government to its permanent headquarters, the new city of Washington, in the District of Columbia.

Buildings had been constructed especially for the President and the Congress in the new federal city, but there was no new building for the Supreme Court. So Congress permitted the justices to use a small room on the first floor of its still unfinished Capitol building. The Court stayed there until 1808, when it moved to another room in the Capitol that also housed the Library of Congress. But the Library was so crowded and inconvenient that the Court often met in a nearby tavern.

From February 1810 until August 1814, the Supreme Court met in a room specially created for it. This courtroom was located in the Capitol basement beneath the new chamber for the U.S. Senate. On the night of August 24, 1814, British troops invaded Washington, during the War of 1812, and burned the Capitol. The Supreme Court was therefore forced to meet in various temporary quarters until its former courtroom was repaired and ready for use in 1819. The Court remained in this location for 41 years. This room, known today as the Old Supreme Court Chamber, is open to visitors. It is furnished as it was when the Court met there long ago. This small courtroom has mahogany desks on a slightly raised platform, behind which the justices sat. There was also a very small room for the clerk of the Court.

A plaster relief entitled Justice *above the bench in the Old Supreme Court Chamber, in the U.S. Capitol.*

But there were neither offices nor a library for the justices. So, much of their work was done at home.

By 1860, two wings had been added to the Capitol to provide new, spacious chambers for the House of Representatives and the Senate. The Supreme Court moved from its cramped basement room to the old Senate chamber on the first floor of the Capitol. This large room, with anterooms for offices and storage, was by far the best home the Court had ever had. And the justices occupied the old Senate chamber for the next 75 years, until 1935.

The Supreme Court Building

The modern Supreme Court Building, opened in 1935, fulfilled the dream of Chief Justice William Howard Taft. He worked for several years to convince Congress to appropriate money to build a suitable, permanent home for the Court. The site chosen for the new Supreme Court Building was a full square block on First Street, across from the Capitol.

In 1928, Chief Justice Taft became chairman of the Supreme Court Building Commission, created by Congress. He picked Cass Gilbert to be the architect for the new Supreme Court Building and worked closely with him in overseeing development of the plans. The cornerstone was laid on October 13, 1932, but

The courtroom of the Supreme Court Building

Taft was not there to see it, having died on March 8, 1930. Gilbert died in 1934, but his son, Cass Gilbert, Jr., and John Rockart finished the project, under the supervision of David Lynn, Architect of the Capitol. The Court held its first session in its new home on October 7, 1935.

Gilbert, with Taft's approval, used the classical Greek style of architecture as his model. He selected marble to be the primary material for the building, which has four floors and a basement.

The basement contains a garage, laundry, carpentry shop, and police roll-call room. It also has offices and equipment storage rooms for the facilities manager and 32 maintenance workers.

The ground floor houses some of the administrative offices, including the Public Information Office, the clerk's office, the publications office, and police offices. It also has exhibit halls, a cafeteria, and a gift shop.

The first floor includes the courtroom, the chambers (offices) of the justices, the robing room, and conference rooms. The courtroom has seating for about 300 people. There is a raised bench along the east wall, where the justices sit to hear oral arguments on cases. The courtroom, at the center of the first floor, is surrounded by the justices' chambers. There is also a robing room, where justices go before sessions of the Court to put on their black judicial robes. Next to the robing room is the Justices' Conference Room, where cases are privately discussed and decided. Two other conference rooms (East and West Conference Rooms) are used for social events and meetings of Supreme Court staff members.

The second floor contains the dining room and library of the justices, the offices of the reporter of decisions and law clerks, and the legal office, which is occupied by the Court counsel and staff who do legal research for the justices.

The third floor is given to the large library. The fourth floor includes a gymnasium with a basketball court and exercise equipment, as well as storage space.

Both the exterior and interior of the Supreme Court Building are decorated with symbols of law and justice, liberty and order. On either side of the steps to the main (west) entrance to the building, for example, are two marble figures: the one at the left is a female symbolizing justice, the one at the right a male representing the authority of law. Also at the main entrance is a pediment with sculptures representing liberty, order, and authority, with an inscription below the panel of sculptures: "Equal Justice Under Law." Panels on the main door feature sculpted scenes in the history of law.

At the building's east side entrance, there is a pediment with a sculpted figure representing the benefits of law and the judicial resolution of conflicts. An inscription below this panel proclaims, "Justice, the Guardian of Liberty."

On the inside, along both sides of the Great Hall, are busts of former chief justices, profiles of great lawgivers in history, and other symbols of law and justice. The Great Hall leads to the Court chamber, or courtroom. Among the various sculpted symbols in this grand room, where the justices hear oral arguments, are figures and objects representing law, government, and the rights and liberty of the people, which the Court is committed to protect.

SEE ALSO
Appendix 2: Visiting the Supreme Court Building

Burger, Warren E.

CHIEF JUSTICE, 1969–86

☆ *Born: Sept. 17, 1907, St. Paul, Minn.*

☆ *Education: University of Minnesota, 1925–27; St. Paul College of Law, LL.B., 1931*
☆ *Previous government service: assistant U.S. attorney general, Civil Division, 1953–56; judge, U.S. Court of Appeals for the District of Columbia, 1956–69*
☆ *Appointed by President Richard Nixon May 29, 1969; replaced Chief Justice Earl Warren, who retired*
☆ *Supreme Court term: confirmed by the Senate June 9, 1969, by a 74–3 vote; retired Sept. 26, 1986*

WARREN E. BURGER worked hard to achieve an education. After high school, he worked at part-time jobs while going to college and law school in his home city of St. Paul, Minnesota. From 1931 to 1953, Burger practiced law and participated in Republican party politics in Minnesota. He attracted the attention of national Republican party leaders, and in 1953 President Dwight Eisenhower appointed Burger assistant attorney general of the United States.

In 1956, President Eisenhower named Burger to the U.S. Court of Appeals for the District of Columbia circuit. This position was a stepping-stone to the Supreme Court. In 1969, President Richard Nixon appointed Burger to be the 15th chief justice of the United States. He replaced Earl Warren, the strong leader of the Court during two decades of ground-breaking decisions that greatly expanded the legal opportunities and rights of minorities and individuals accused of crimes.

Chief Justice Burger tended to support the civil rights decisions of the Warren Court. However, in cases regarding the rights of criminal defendants, Burger tended to support the police and prosecutors. He believed that the Court under Earl Warren had moved too far in favor of supporting the rights of accused persons and criminals.

Burger's most important decision

was in the case of *United States* v. *Nixon* (1974), when the Court turned down President Nixon's claim of executive privilege as a reason for withholding tape recordings of private White House conversations from criminal investigators. The Court ordered the President to turn over the tapes, a ruling that established an important limitation on the powers of the President. This decision also affirmed the primacy of the Supreme Court in the interpretation of the Constitution.

Chief Justice Burger retired in 1986 to become chairman of the Commission on the Bicentennial of the United States Constitution. His greatest achievements as chief justice were his improvements in the ways in which the federal judicial system carries out its work. He reorganized many procedures for keeping records and for carrying out more efficiently the business of the federal courts. But Chief Justice Burger, unlike his predecessor, Earl Warren, did not exercise a decisive influence on the opinions of his associate justices.

SEE ALSO
Chief justice; United States v. Nixon

FURTHER READING
Lamb, Charles M. "Chief Justice Warren E. Burger." In *The Burger Court: Political and Judicial Profiles*, edited by Charles M. Lamb and Stephen C. Halpern. Urbana: University of Illinois Press, 1991.

☆ *Appointed by President Harry S. Truman Sept. 19, 1945; replaced Owen J. Roberts, who resigned*
☆ *Supreme Court term: confirmed by the Senate Sept. 19, 1945, by a voice vote; retired Oct. 13, 1958*
☆ *Died: Oct. 28, 1964, Washington, D.C.*

HAROLD BURTON, a Republican, was Democratic President Harry Truman's first appointment to the U.S. Supreme Court. He was the only Republican appointed to the Court between 1933 and 1953. Burton achieved an outstanding career in public life before joining the Court. He practiced law in Cleveland, where he had also been the mayor, and served one term in the U.S. Senate.

Justice Burton became a leading advocate of expanding the constitutional rights of African Americans. He spoke strongly against racial segregation and the "separate but equal" doctrine. He participated enthusiastically in the Court's decision in *Brown* v. *Board of Education* (1954) to end racial segregation in public schools. Burton resigned from the Court in 1958 because of illness; he died in 1964.

FURTHER READING
Berry, Mary F. *Stability, Security, and Continuity: Mr. Justice Burton and Decision-Making in the Supreme Court, 1945–1958*. Westport, Conn.: Greenwood, 1978.

Burton, Harold H.
ASSOCIATE JUSTICE, 1945–58

☆ *Born: June 22, 1888, Jamaica Plain, Mass.*
☆ *Education: Bowdoin College, B.A., 1909; Harvard Law School, LL.B., 1912*
☆ *Previous government service: Ohio House of Representatives, 1929; director of law, Cleveland, Ohio, 1929–32; mayor, Cleveland, 1935–40; U.S. senator from Ohio, 1941–45*

Butler, Pierce
ASSOCIATE JUSTICE, 1923–39

☆ *Born: Mar. 17, 1866, Pine Bend, Minn.*
☆ *Education: Carleton College, B.A., B.S., 1887*
☆ *Previous government service: assistant county attorney, Ramsey County, Minn., 1891–93; state's attorney, Ramsey County, 1893–97*

☆ Appointed by President Warren G. Harding Nov. 23, 1922; replaced William R. Day, who retired
☆ Supreme Court term: confirmed by the Senate Dec. 21, 1922, by a 61–8 vote; served until Nov. 16, 1939
☆ Died: Nov. 16, 1939, Washington, D.C.

PIERCE BUTLER was only the fourth Roman Catholic to be appointed to the Court. He was also a Democrat who was appointed by a Republican President, Warren G. Harding. Before joining the Court, he had practiced law and served as a prosecuting attorney in Minnesota.

Justice Butler tended to oppose government regulation of businesses. He was a strong opponent of government welfare programs and became a bitter foe of President Franklin D. Roosevelt's New Deal program of the 1930s. He voted against every New Deal policy that came before the Court. He also tended to oppose changes in racial segregation and the "separate but equal" doctrine.

FURTHER READING

Brown, Francis Joseph. *The Social and Economic Philosophy of Pierce Butler.* Washington, D.C.: Catholic University Press, 1945.

Byrnes, James F.

ASSOCIATE JUSTICE, 1941–42

☆ Born: May 2, 1879, Charleston, S.C.
☆ Education: studied law privately
☆ Previous government service: court reporter, Second Circuit of South Carolina, 1900–1908; solicitor, Second Circuit of South Carolina, 1908–10; U.S. representative from South Carolina, 1911–25; U.S. senator from South Carolina, 1931–41
☆ Appointed by President Franklin D. Roosevelt June 12, 1941; replaced James McReynolds, who retired

☆ Supreme Court term: confirmed by the Senate June 12, 1941, by a voice vote; resigned Oct. 3, 1942
☆ Subsequent government service: director of the Office of Economic Stabilization, 1942–43; director of the Office of War Mobilization and Reconversion, 1943–45; U.S. secretary of state, 1945–47; governor of South Carolina, 1951–55
☆ Died: Apr. 9, 1972, Columbia, S.C.

JAMES F. BYRNES was the son of Irish immigrants who settled in Charleston, South Carolina. His father died before the younger Byrnes was born. His mother raised the family alone, and James left school to help support himself and his family. He worked as a law clerk and then as a court reporter. These jobs led to an interest in the law, which he studied on his own. He passed the state bar exam in 1903 and began a career as solicitor, or district attorney, for South Carolina's Second Circuit.

In 1910, Byrnes became a Democratic party candidate for a seat in the House of Representatives. His victory launched a spectacular career in the federal government. He became a close friend of President Franklin D. Roosevelt and served in the U.S. Senate during Roosevelt's first two terms. The President rewarded Byrnes for his loyal support by appointing him to the Supreme Court in 1941.

Byrnes's service on the Court lasted less than 14 months. During this time he wrote only 16 opinions. He left the Court to serve President Roosevelt as director of the Office of Economic Stabilization (1942–43) and then as director of the Office of War Mobilization and Reconversion (1943–45). He was secretary of state from 1945 to 1947 under President Harry S. Truman. Byrnes was governor of South Carolina for one term, from 1951 to 1955.

Campbell, John A.

ASSOCIATE JUSTICE, 1853–61

☆ *Born: June 24, 1811, Washington, Ga.*
☆ *Education: University of Georgia, B.A., 1825; U.S. Military Academy, 1825–28*
☆ *Previous government service: Alabama House of Representatives, 1837, 1843*
☆ *Appointed by President Franklin Pierce Mar. 21, 1853; replaced Justice John McKinley, who died*
☆ *Supreme Court term: confirmed by the Senate Mar. 25, 1853, by a voice vote; resigned Apr. 30, 1861*
☆ *Died: Mar. 12, 1889, Baltimore, Md.*

JOHN A. CAMPBELL was a brilliant child who entered college at the age of 11 and graduated three years later. In 1828, he was admitted to the bar by a special act of the Georgia legislature and started his legal career in Alabama two years later. Campbell quickly became one of the best lawyers in Alabama.

Campbell joined the Supreme Court in 1853, during the political crisis that led to the Civil War. Important questions about human rights and property rights faced the Court. In response to these issues, Campbell supported states' rights and slavery. In *Scott* v. *Sandford* (1857), he joined Chief Justice Roger Taney to protect the property rights of slave owners, ruling that Congress could not prohibit slavery in U.S. territories.

When the Civil War started, Campbell left the Court and became assistant secretary of war for the Confederate States of America. After the war, he resumed his career as a lawyer and often represented clients in cases that went to the Supreme Court. For example, he represented the Butchers' Benevolent Association in oral argument in the *Slaughterhouse Cases* (1873).

Capital punishment

THE PENALTY of death for a person convicted of a serious crime, such as intentional murder, is called capital punishment. *Capital* is derived from the Latin word *capitalis,* which means "of the head." Throughout human history, beheading a person has been the most frequent form of killing someone as punishment for a serious crime. Current methods of carrying out capital punishment in the United States are electrocution, firing squad, hanging, poison gas, and lethal injection. The use of lethal injection has become the most common way of carrying out the death penalty in the United States; it is the method used in 17 states.

Capital punishment has been practiced in the United States since the founding of the republic. During the founding period, several crimes were punishable by death in the 13 states: murder, treason, piracy, arson, rape, robbery, burglary, sodomy, counterfeiting, horse theft, and slave rebellion. Today, in the 36 states that permit capital punishment, premeditated murder is virtually the only crime for which the punishment is death. Fourteen states and the District of Columbia have banned the death penalty. The United States government may impose the death penalty for certain federal crimes, such as treason.

In 1972 the U.S. Supreme Court ruled in *Furman* v. *Georgia* that the death penalty could not be imposed without legal guidelines that define precisely the crime and conditions for a sentence of death. A jury in Georgia had convicted William Furman, a black man, of murdering a white man and had sentenced him to death. Under Georgia law, the jury had complete power to decide

An electric chair used in Washington, D.C., before capital punishment was banned there.

The Passion of Sacco and Vanzetti, *by Ben Shahn. In 1927, Nicola Sacco and Bartolomeo Vanzetti were electrocuted after being convicted of a murder in Massachusetts. Their death was controversial because many believed they were found guilty primarily because they were foreigners and anarchists.*

whether a convicted murderer should receive the death penalty. The Legal Defense Fund of the National Association for the Advancement of Colored People (NAACP) filed an appeal on Furman's behalf. It argued that state laws that gave a jury free rein to impose capital punishment could be unfair. The NAACP lawyers pointed to evidence that blacks convicted of murdering whites were much more likely to be punished by death than whites convicted of murder.

A divided Court (5 to 4) agreed with the NAACP position and, for the first time, nullified a death penalty on the basis of the 8th Amendment, which forbids "cruel and unusual punishments." Justices William Brennan and Thurgood Marshall argued, in separate concurring opinions, that the death penalty is morally wrong and is always a violation of the "cruel and unusual punishments" clause of the 8th Amendment, as applied to the states through the due process clause of the 14th Amendment. Three other Justices—William O. Douglas, Potter Stewart, and Byron White—wrote separate concurring opinions in which they agreed only that the Georgia system for imposing capital punishment, at issue in this case, was unconstitutional because it led to random and unfair decisions about who should receive the death penalty.

After the *Furman* decision, there was a halt in the use of the death penalty by all 50 state governments. The Georgia government passed a new law regarding capital punishment to address the problems raised by the Court in *Furman*. It created a two-phase procedure for imposing the death penalty in murder cases: the trial phase and the sentencing phase.

In the trial phase, a jury would determine a defendant's guilt or innocence. If the defendant was found guilty, the state could request the death penalty. During phase two, there would be a second jury trial with the sole purpose of deciding whether to impose the death penalty. The Georgia law specified mandatory guidelines for determining whether to impose capital punishment. Thus, the law was designed to limit the jury's discretion and eliminate the kind of arbitrary application of the death penalty to which the Court objected in the *Furman* case.

The new Georgia law on capital punishment was tested in *Gregg* v. *Georgia* (1976), in which the Court decided that the death penalty for people convicted of first-degree murder is constitutional. The Court also upheld the Georgia law and praised it as a model for other states to follow. Many states have either adopted the Georgia law or created a similar one. The *Gregg* decision appears to have settled the capital punishment issue in favor of the death penalty, as long as it is imposed only in convictions for murder in the first degree and only according to certain clearly spelled out procedures and conditions.

Justices William Brennan and Thurgood Marshall were the two dissenters in the *Gregg* case. They continued to argue that capital punishment is always a violation of the 8th Amendment's "cruel and unusual punishments" clause. By contrast, the defenders of limited uses of capital punishment argue that the U.S. Constitution sanctions the death penalty. They point to the 5th and 14th Amendments, which restrain the government from taking away a person's "life, liberty, or property, without due process of law." These constitutional provisions imply that a person may, under certain conditions, be deprived of life, as long as due process of law is observed. A large majority of Americans have agreed, in public opinion polls, that the death penalty is an acceptable punishment for first-degree murder.

SEE ALSO

Cruel and unusual punishment

FURTHER READING

Bedau, Hugo Adam, ed. *The Death Penalty in America.* New York: Oxford, 1982.
Buranelli, Vincent. *The Eighth Amendment.* Englewood Cliffs, N.J.: Silver Burdett Press, 1991.
White, Welsh S. *The Death Penalty in the Nineties: An Examination of the Modern System of Capital Punishment.* Ann Arbor: University of Michigan Press, 1991.

Cardozo, Benjamin N.

ASSOCIATE JUSTICE, 1932–38

☆ *Born: May 24, 1870, New York, N.Y.*
☆ *Education: Columbia College, B.A., 1889; M.A., 1890; Columbia Law School, 1891*
☆ *Previous government service: justice, New York State Supreme Court, 1914; judge, New York State Court of Appeals, 1914–32, chief judge, New York State Court of Appeals, 1926–32*
☆ *Appointed by President Herbert Hoover Feb. 15, 1932; replaced Oliver Wendell Holmes, who retired*
☆ *Supreme Court term: confirmed by the Senate Feb. 24, 1932, by a voice vote; served until July 9, 1938*
☆ *Died: July 9, 1938, Port Chester, N.Y.*

BENJAMIN N. CARDOZO was only the second Jew to be appointed to the Supreme Court. He served on the Court with the first Jewish justice, Louis Brandeis.

Benjamin Cardozo was the youngest son of Albert and Rebecca Washington Cardozo, whose ancestors had settled in New York in the 1850s. He was a very bright child and entered Columbia University at age 15, graduating with honors four years later. In 1891, he began to practice law in New York City. Later, he served as a judge of the New York Supreme Court and the New York Court of Appeals.

As a New York State judge, Cardozo achieved a national reputation for his wise decisions and exemplary legal reasoning, which emphasized the effects of law on the lives of people. Cardozo opposed an overemphasis on precedent and tradition as constricting, too formal, and too likely to cause injustice by preventing constitutional changes to fit changing times.

Justice Cardozo served only six years on the U.S. Supreme Court. During this brief period, however, he established the doctrine of "selective incorporation" to guide the Court's use of the 14th Amendment to apply federal Bill of Rights provisions to the states. Cardozo stated this position in *Palko* v. *Connecticut* (1937). He wrote that to be "incorporated" under the due process clause of the 14th Amendment, a provision of the Bill of Rights must be "fundamental"; that is, it must be a right without which "neither liberty nor justice would exist," and the right "must be implicit in the concept of ordered liberty."

Cardozo recommended a case-by-case application of the 14th Amendment to use one or more parts of the Bill of Rights to limit the power of a state government and protect individual rights. This position was opposed by Justice Hugo Black, who wanted "total incorporation" of the Bill of Rights. Cardozo's position has prevailed, and the Court uses it today.

SEE ALSO

Incorporation doctrine; Palko v. Connecticut

FURTHER READING

Cardozo, Benjamin N. *The Nature of the Judicial Process.* New Haven: Yale University Press, 1921.
Posner, Richard A. *Cardozo: A Study in Reputation.* Chicago: University of Chicago Press, 1990.

New York police arrest bootleggers in 1921. In Carroll v. United States, *the Court decided that police can legally search a car without a warrant.*

Carroll v. United States

☆ *267 U.S. 132 (1925)*
☆ *Vote: 6–2*
☆ *For the Court: Taft*
☆ *Dissenting: McReynolds and Sutherland*

IN 1923, George Carroll and John Kiro were transporting alcoholic beverages in an automobile. Federal officers suspected they might be carrying liquor, stopped their car, and searched it. They found liquor and arrested Carroll and Kiro, who were charged with violating the Volstead Act (the federal law prohibiting the sale or transportation of alcoholic beverages). Carroll and Kiro were convicted, but they appealed because the federal officers had searched their automobile without a warrant.

The Issue Carroll claimed that the federal officers who searched his automobile had violated the 4th Amendment of the Constitution, which states, "The right of the people to be secure in their persons, houses, papers, and effects, against unreasonable searches and seizures, shall not be violated, and no Warrants shall issue, but upon probable cause, supported by Oath or affirmation, and particularly describing the place to be searched, and the persons or things to be seized." Carroll argued that the federal officers had no legal grounds for searching his car, so the evidence they found should have been excluded from his trial.

Opinion of the Court The Court decided against Carroll. The warrantless search of the car was constitutional, said Chief Justice William Howard Taft, because the vehicle could be driven away and the people in it could escape before a warrant could be obtained. Thus, an exception to the 4th Amendment warrant requirement could be made.

Dissent Justice George Sutherland joined Justice James McReynolds in dissent. McReynolds argued that no exceptions should be made in cases involving searches of cars to the 4th Amendment requirement of a warrant as protection against unreasonable searches and seizures. He concluded that Carroll had been wrongfully arrested.

Significance This case established a rule about searches of automobiles that has been upheld in subsequent cases such as *United States* v. *Ross* (1982). In *California* v. *Acevedo* (1991), the rule was strengthened by the Court's decision to eliminate a warrant requirement for searches and seizures of closed containers found in an automobile.

SEE ALSO
Searches and seizures; United States v. Ross

Catron, John

ASSOCIATE JUSTICE, 1837–65

☆ *Born: 1786, Pennsylvania*
☆ *Education: self-educated, studied law on his own*
☆ *Previous government service: judge, Tennessee Supreme Court of Errors and Appeals, 1824–31; chief justice of Tennessee, 1831–34*

☆ *Appointed by President Andrew Jackson Mar. 3, 1837, to fill a newly created seat on the Court*

☆ *Supreme Court term: confirmed by the Senate Mar. 8, 1837, by a 28–15 vote; served until May 30, 1865*

☆ *Died: May 30, 1865, Nashville, Tenn.*

JOHN CATRON was the son of German immigrants to Pennsylvania. The exact place of his birth is unknown, but the hardships of his childhood in Virginia and Kentucky, and his struggles to overcome them, have been recorded. Although Catron did not have an opportunity to go to school, he educated himself by reading at home.

Catron served under General Andrew Jackson in the War of 1812. His friendship with Jackson worked to his benefit after Jackson became President in 1828. Catron became a loyal Jacksonian Democrat, and the President rewarded him with an appointment to the U.S. Supreme Court in 1837. During his 28 years on the Court, Catron supported states' rights and slavery. But when the Civil War started, he remained loyal to the Union and remained at his job on the Supreme Court.

Certiorari, writ of

THE U.S. SUPREME COURT has the authority, given by Congress (according to Article 3, Section 2, of the Constitution), to issue a writ of certiorari, which is an order to a lower court to prepare the record of a case and submit it to the Supreme Court for review. The Latin term *certiorari* means "to be informed." A party to a case seeking review by the Supreme Court submits a petition to the Court for a writ of certiorari. If at least four justices vote in favor of it, "cert." is granted, and the case comes to the Court for its review and decision.

Each year approximately 5,000 petitions are sent to the Court seeking a writ of certiorari. Less than 5 percent are granted "cert." If the writ of certiorari is denied, the decision of the lower court is sustained. However, a denial of "cert." cannot be used as evidence of the Supreme Court's opinion on the issue in the case.

The rules of the Court provide general guidelines for accepting or rejecting appeals from lower courts. For example, the Court will likely accept a case for review if there appears to be an error in lower court proceedings, if the issue in the case involves an unsettled question of federal law, or if there are conflicting opinions on the case from the highest state court and a federal court of appeals.

According to Rule 10 of the *Rules of the Supreme Court of the United States,* "A review on writ of certiorari is not a matter of right, but of judicial discretion, and will be granted only when there are special and important reasons therefor." Making decisions about which cases to review, and which ones to reject, is among the most important judgments the Court makes. These decisions go a long way toward setting the agenda of the Court and determining who will and will not have access to it. Although there are other means by which a case comes before the U.S. Supreme Court, the writ of certiorari is the primary means for bringing a case to the Court for its review and disposition.

SEE ALSO

Jurisdiction

Chambers

THE OFFICES of Supreme Court justices are called chambers. Each justice has three connecting rooms on the main floor. One serves as the private office of the justice, and the other two are used by clerks and secretaries.

Charles River Bridge v. Warren Bridge

☆ *11 Pet. 420 (1837)*
☆ *Vote: 4–3*
☆ *For the Court: Taney*
☆ *Dissenting: McLean, Story, and Thompson*

IN 1828, the state government of Massachusetts granted a charter, or permit, for construction of a bridge across the Charles River to connect Boston with Cambridge. This new bridge, the Warren Bridge, was to span the river near an older bridge, the Charles River Bridge. The owners of the Charles River Bridge Company claimed that their charter, which they had obtained in 1785, gave them the right to prevent the construction of a new bridge. They claimed the new bridge would cause them to lose profits by attracting the patronage and the payments of those who had formerly used their bridge. The Charles River Bridge Company earned profits by charging a toll, or fee, to users of their bridge. The owners did not want competition from a new company that would also collect tolls from bridge users. Worse, the new Warren Bridge would become toll-free after six years.

The owners of the Charles River Bridge Company argued that in violating their charter, the new Warren Bridge Company charter violated the contract clause of the U.S. Constitution. They pointed to the Supreme Court's decision in *Dartmouth College* v. *Woodward* (1819), which seemed to support their

argument that the state should not violate the terms of a contract. They stated that the Court should not allow the Warren Bridge Company to compete with them.

The Issue Should a contract granted by a state government be interpreted so as to stop the state from granting another charter to build new public facilities that would meet important public needs? Would the granting of such a charter violate the contract clause of Article 1, Section 10, of the Constitution, which provides that no state shall pass a law "impairing the Obligation of Contracts"?

Opinion of the Court The court ruled against the Charles River Bridge Company. Chief Justice Roger Taney wrote the majority opinion, which emphasized that a state must interpret public charters so as to benefit public and community needs. Thus, the state of Massachusetts had the right, under the Constitution, to charter the building of a bridge that would compete with another bridge it had contracted for earlier.

Chief Justice Taney was not ignoring the contract clause of the Constitution. He believed in private property rights and the sanctity of contracts. However, he opposed any interpretation of a contract that infringed upon the rights or needs of the public. The contract granted to the Charles River Bridge Company did not say exactly that no other company could build a bridge nearby. Rather, the company interpreted the contract to give them exclusive rights. Taney and the majority of the Court, however, would not interpret the contract as giving exclusive rights to the older and established Charles River Bridge Company.

Dissent Justice Joseph Story argued for upholding the exclusive contract of the Charles River Bridge Company. He feared that the Court's decision in this case would undermine the faith of property owners in contracts as the means to protect their property rights.

Significance This decision opposed business monopolies (companies having exclusive control of the provision of goods or services) that hurt the public. It encouraged private businesses to compete freely with one another. The Court supported the right of state governments to decide, under the 10th Amendment, whether to grant charters to build new facilities such as highways, railroads, and bridges to serve the public.

SEE ALSO

Contract clause; Dartmouth College v. Woodward

FURTHER READING

Graff, Henry F. "The Charles River Bridge Case." In *Quarrels That Have Shaped the Constitution*, edited by John A. Garraty. New York: Harper & Row, 1987.

Chase, Salmon P.

CHIEF JUSTICE, 1864–73

☆ Born: Jan. 13, 1808, Cornish, N.H.
☆ Education: Dartmouth College, A.B., 1826
☆ Previous government service: U.S. senator from Ohio, 1849–55, 1861; governor of Ohio, 1856–60; U.S. secretary of the Treasury, 1861–64
☆ Appointed by President Abraham Lincoln Dec. 6, 1864; replaced Chief Justice Roger B. Taney, who died
☆ Supreme Court term: confirmed by the Senate Dec. 6, 1864, by a voice vote; served until May 7, 1873
☆ Died: May 7, 1873, New York, N.Y.

SALMON P. CHASE had a lifelong ambition to become President of the United States. He failed to realize his highest goal, but he did become the sixth Chief Justice of the United States.

After graduating from Dartmouth College in 1826, Chase studied law under U.S. Attorney General William Wirt and became a lawyer in Cincinnati. He achieved a national reputation as an opponent of slavery and a defender of escaped slaves who sought refuge in the free Northern states. His friends and foes called him the "attorney general for runaway Negroes."

In the 1850s, Chase became a leader in the new Republican party and its antislavery mission. After an unsuccessful bid to become the Republican party's Presidential candidate in 1860, he backed his party's choice, Abraham Lincoln. The new President appointed Chase to his cabinet as secretary of the Treasury. In 1864, Lincoln chose Chase to be Chief Justice of the United States, even though Chase had tried to take Lincoln's place as the Republican party Presidential candidate in the 1864 election.

As chief justice, Chase continued his concern for the rights of African Americans newly freed from slavery in 1865 by the 13th Amendment. Chief Justice Chase, however, also supported the constitutional rights of a Confederate sympathizer from Indiana in the landmark decision of *Ex parte Milligan* (1866). He joined in the unanimous decision that Lambdin Milligan, who lived in a non–war zone during the Civil War, had been unfairly and illegally tried in a military court, instead of a civilian court, for supposedly committing crimes against the federal government.

Chief Justice Chase presided with dignity and fairness over the 1868 impeachment trial of President Andrew

Johnson. And he wrote an enduring opinion for the Court in *Texas* v. *White* (1869) that endorsed the Republican party position that a state did not have a right to secede from the federal Union. Chase argued that Texas's Confederate government had been unlawful and that its acts, therefore, were null and void. Chase argued conclusively that the Constitution created "an indestructible union, composed of indestructible states" and that secession was illegal.

SEE ALSO

Chief Justice; Ex parte Milligan; Texas v. White

FURTHER READING

Blue, Frederick J. *Salmon P. Chase: A Life in Politics.* Kent, Ohio: Kent State University Press, 1987.

Chase, Samuel

ASSOCIATE JUSTICE, 1796–1811

☆ *Born: Apr. 17, 1741, Somerset County, Md.*
☆ *Education: tutored by father; studied law in an Annapolis, Md., law office*
☆ *Previous government service: Maryland General Assembly, 1764–84; Continental Congress, 1774–78, 1784–85; Maryland Convention and Council of Safety, 1775; judge, Baltimore Criminal Court, 1788–96; chief judge, General Court of Maryland, 1791–96*
☆ *Appointed by President George Washington Jan. 26, 1796; replaced John Blair, who resigned*
☆ *Supreme Court term: confirmed by the Senate Jan. 27, 1796, by a voice vote; served until June 19, 1811*
☆ *Died: June 19, 1811, Baltimore, Md.*

SAMUEL CHASE was a patriot in the American revolutionary war. He belonged to the Sons of Liberty and signed the Declaration of Independence.

Justice Chase wrote several impor-

tant opinions in early key decisions of the Supreme Court. In *Ware* v. *Hylton* (1796), for example, he helped to establish the supremacy of federal treaties over state laws that contradicted them. In *Hylton* v. *United States* (1796), Chase and the Supreme Court made a judgment about whether or not an act of Congress, the carriage tax of 1794, agreed with the Constitution. The Court supported the federal statute, which was its first judgment about the constitutionality of an act of the legislative branch of government. The Court, however, neither asserted or discussed the power of judicial review, which was established by Chief Justice John Marshall in *Marbury* v. *Madison* (1803).

Justice Chase was a harsh public critic of the Jeffersonian Republicans because he disagreed with their interpretations of the Constitution. When Thomas Jefferson became President in 1801, Chase sharpened his criticism of Jefferson and the Republican majority in Congress. In return, President Jefferson urged that Chase be removed from the Supreme Court. A majority of the House of Representatives voted to impeach Chase. As provided in the Constitution, the case went to the Senate for trial, where two-thirds of the Senators had to vote against Chase to remove him from office. Chase argued that he had done nothing wrong and that a federal judge should not be impeached and removed from office for criticizing the President. Chase was acquitted and remained on the Court until his death in 1811.

SEE ALSO

Hylton v. United States; Impeachment; Ware v. Hylton

FURTHER READING

Haw, James, et al. *Stormy Patriot: The Life of Samuel Chase.* Baltimore: Maryland Historical Society, 1980.

Checks and balances

S E E Separation of powers

Chief justice

THE CHIEF JUSTICE of the United States is the presiding officer of the Supreme Court and the head of the judicial branch of the federal government. The title chief justice is mentioned only once, however, in the U.S. Constitution: Article 1, Section 3, mandates that the chief justice serve as presiding officer of the Senate during an impeachment trial of a President. The office of chief justice is *not* mentioned in Article 3 of the Constitution, which deals with the judicial branch of the federal government.

The office of chief justice was established by the Judiciary Act of 1789. The position has truly been shaped by its occupants, who have established the roles and duties as they performed them. In addition, Congress contributed to development of this office through legislation.

Since 1789, the office of chief justice has developed into a complex and prestigious position. The person occupying this position must serve as Supreme

Court leader, judge, administrator, and national symbol of justice under the law.

The chief justice, like the eight associate justices of the Supreme Court, is appointed by the President of the United States "with the Advice and Consent of the Senate," as provided by Article 2, Section 2, of the Constitution. The chief justice, the eight associate justices, and the federal judges of the lower courts "shall hold their Offices during good Behaviour," according to Article 3, Section 1, of the Constitution, which provides lifetime job security for judges who want it. Further, Article 3, Section 1, says the pay of federal judges "shall not be diminished during their Continuance in Office." Thus, the Constitution provides for the independence of the chief justice, the eight associate justices, and other federal judges.

The chief justice has been called "first among equals" in his relationships with the eight associate justices. He has only one vote, as they do, in deciding cases. The chief justice and the eight associate justices are equal in their virtual lifetime tenure, in their protection against decreases in income, and in their independence as judicial decision makers on cases before the Court. The chief justice also must perform the work of a judge, along with his eight associates. Together, the chief and his associates review and make decisions on all petitions for certiorari (appeals from lower courts for a hearing before the Supreme Court); he must also examine, discuss, and decide, like his associates, all the cases that come to the Court. The chief shares with his associates the work of writing opinions for the Court.

Unlike his associates, however, the chief justice is the sole presiding officer of the Supreme Court. He presides at the conference during which the Court decides which cases to accept from the large number of appeals over which it

Chief Justice Earl Warren administers the oath of office to President Lyndon Johnson in 1965.

has discretionary power. He also presides over the public sessions, or hearings of cases, that come before the Court, and he chairs the private conference at which cases are discussed among the nine members of the Court and eventually decided by a vote of the justices. Finally, when the chief justice is in the majority, he has the authority to assign the task of writing the Court's opinion on the case either to himself or to one of the associate justices. Thus, the chief justice is able to influence directly or indirectly the style and substance of the Court's written opinion. When the chief justice is not part of the majority decision on a case, the most senior member of the majority assigns the writing of the Court's opinion.

In addition to his duties as presiding officer of the Supreme Court, the chief justice also serves as administrative head of the judicial branch of the federal government. He is chairman of the Judicial Conference of the United States. The conference includes 27 federal judges, who represent all the levels and regions of the federal judiciary. The conference meets twice a year to discuss common problems, to coordinate administrative policies, and to recommend to Congress measures for improving the operation of the federal courts. Administrative and budgetary functions for the conference are carried out by the Administrative Office of the United States Courts. The Administrative Office's director and deputy director are appointed by the Supreme Court and report to the chief justice. The chief justice is also the permanent chairman of the governing board of the Federal Judicial Center, which provides research and training services for the federal judiciary.

The chief justice has several extra-judicial responsibilities. He is manager of the Supreme Court Building. He serves as chancellor of the Smithsonian Institution, a complex of museums and

The chief justice's coat hook in the Old Supreme Court Chamber.

CHIEF JUSTICES

Justice	Tenure
John Jay	1789–1795
John Rutledge	1795
Oliver Ellsworth	1796–1800
John Marshall	1801–1835
Roger B. Taney	1836–1864
Salmon P. Chase	1864–1873
Morrison R. Waite	1874–1888
Melville W. Fuller	1888–1910
Edward D. White	1910–1921
William H. Taft	1921–1930
Charles E. Hughes	1930–1940
Harlan F. Stone	1941–1946
Frederick M. Vinson	1946–1952
Earl Warren	1953–1969
Warren E. Burger	1969-1986
William H. Rehnquist	1986–

research institutions operated by the federal government. And he is considered the head of the legal profession in the United States.

The chief justice is also the living symbol of the federal judiciary. In this role, the chief administers the oath of office to the President at every inauguration.

Since 1789, there have been 16 chief justices of the United States. The first chief justice was John Jay, appointed by President George Washington. President John Adams appointed the chief justice generally acclaimed as the greatest, John Marshall, who served from 1801 until his death in 1835. His tenure as chief justice was the longest. Other chief justices whom scholars and legal experts consider truly great are Roger B. Taney, Charles Evans Hughes, Harlan Fiske Stone, and Earl Warren. Five chief justices, nearly one-third of the total from 1789 to 1993, have performed well enough to receive such excellent ratings.

SEE ALSO
Administration of federal courts; Justices of
the Supreme Court

FURTHER READING
Morris, Jeffrey B. *First Among Equals: The
Office of the Chief Justice of the United
States.* Berkeley: University of California
Press, 1993.
Morris, Jeffrey B. "Hail to the Chief Justice."
Constitution 4, no. 2 (Spring–Summer
1992): 40–50.
Steamer, Robert J. *Chief Justice: Leadership
and the Supreme Court.* Columbia:
University of South Carolina Press, 1986.

Chisholm v. Georgia

☆ *2 Dall. 419 (1793)*
☆ *Vote: 4–1*
☆ *For the Court: seriatim opinions by
Jay, Cushing, Wilson, and Blair*
☆ *Dissenting: Iredell*

DURING THE American War of Independence, agents of the state government of Georgia purchased clothing, blankets, and other goods from Robert Farquhar, a merchant in Charleston, South Carolina. Farquhar died in 1784, and the executor of his estate was Alexander Chisholm. Acting for a minor (non-adult) heir of Farquhar, Chisholm sought payment from the Georgia state government for money that he claimed it owed Farquhar. Georgia officials refused to pay, however, because the state had already paid its agents for the goods. Chisholm was unable to collect the money owed his client from these agents. So he took his case to the newly established federal courts and sued the state of Georgia for the monetary value of the goods supplied by Farquhar.

The Issue The state of Georgia refused to send a representative to the Court. Georgia argued that the Court did not have jurisdiction in this case because a state government could not be sued by a citizen from another state.

When the Georgia government refused to pay a South Carolina merchant who had supplied army uniforms during the Revolution, the case went to the Supreme Court.

Opinion of the Court The Court ruled in favor of Chisholm. This decision was based on Article 3, Section 2, of the U.S. Constitution, which says, "The judicial Power shall extend to all Cases…between a State and Citizens of another State." Chief Justice John Jay wrote, "Any one state in the Union may sue another state in this court, that is, all the people of one state may sue all the people of another state. It is plain, then, that a state may be sued, and hence it plainly follows that suability and state sovereignty are not incompatible." In other words, a suit brought by citizens of one state against the government of another state does not diminish or threaten the authority or independent power of that state government.

Dissent Justice James Iredell argued that under common law no state could be sued unless it consented to the action. This state right was necessary in order for the state to retain its sovereignty (supreme power within its borders, free of external influences), said Iredell.

Significance This decision caused an uproar in Congress. A large majority in the House of Representatives (81–9) and the Senate (23–2) voted in favor of a proposed constitutional amendment that would effectively overturn the Supreme Court's decision in *Chisholm* v. *Georgia*. The state governments ratified this proposal, which became the 11th Amendment to the Constitution: "The Judicial power of the United States shall not be construed to extend to any suit in law or equity, commenced or prosecuted against one of the United States by citizens of another State, or by Citizens or Subjects of any Foreign State." This was the first time a Supreme Court decision was overturned by constitutional amendment.

What happened to Chisholm's financial claim against Georgia? It succeeded. Robert Farquhar's heir accepted securities (bonds) of the Georgia state government in full payment of his claim against the state. These bonds paid interest to the holder and could be exchanged for cash.

FURTHER READING

Orth, John V. *The Judicial Power of the United States: The Eleventh Amendment in American History.* New York: Oxford, 1987.

Circuit Courts of Appeals

THE JUDICIARY ACT of 1789 set up a system of lower federal courts, under the Supreme Court of the United States. At the bottom were federal district courts, one per state except for Massachusetts and Virginia, which had two apiece because of their greater population. Between the Supreme Court and the district courts were three circuit courts of appeal, one for each of three circuits, or districts, each of which included several states. In 1789 the Southern Circuit included South Carolina and Georgia (North Carolina was added in 1790 after it entered the Union). In 1789 the Eastern Circuit contained New York, Connecticut, Massachusetts, and New Hampshire (Rhode Island and Vermont were added when they joined the Union in 1790 and 1791, respectively). The Middle Circuit included Virginia, Maryland, Pennsylvania, Delaware, and New Jersey.

Until 1869 the circuit courts served both as trial courts and appellate courts; both federal district court judges and Supreme Court justices presided in these circuit courts. The judges and justices had to "ride circuit" in order to carry out their circuit court duties; that is, they had to travel from place to place, within the large area of the circuit, to hear cases and make decisions. In the early years of the United States, the judges and justices rode on horseback or in horse-drawn carriages.

Circuit riding was a great hardship, involving long hours of travel. The Supreme Court justices constantly complained to Congress, asking to be relieved of this heavy burden. In the Judiciary Act of 1869, Congress finally responded to their complaints. This law provided for the appointment of nine new circuit court judges, which relieved the Supreme Court justices of their ongoing circuit-riding duties. However, the law did require the justices to participate in circuit court duties once every two years.

The Judiciary Act of 1891 created, for the first time, the U.S. Circuit Courts of Appeals, one for each of nine regions, or circuits, to hear cases on appeal from the lower courts. The old circuit courts were retained, but their duties were merged with the federal district courts. So the federal judiciary consisted of two trial courts (circuit and district courts) and two appellate courts (the Supreme Court and the new Circuit Courts of Appeals). The act eliminated the circuit-riding duties of Supreme Court justices and assigned three judges to each of the nine new Circuit Courts of Appeals. This relieved the burden on the Supreme Court, which until then had carried out most of the federal appellate court work. In 1911 Congress acted to eliminate the old circuit courts because they merely duplicated the work of the district courts, which were retained as the trial courts of the federal judiciary. In 1948 the Circuit Courts of Appeals were given a new name, which they retain today, the Courts of Appeals.

SEE ALSO

Courts of Appeals

Citation

THE WAY in which opinions of the U.S. Supreme Court are identified, or cited, in legal literature is referred to as a citation. A Supreme Court case citation includes the following information, in this order: the names of the parties to the case, separated by "v.," for *versus* (Latin for "against"); the volume of *United States Reports* in which the case appears (for cases since 1875), or the volume of private reports, for pre-1875 cases; the beginning page number on which the report of the case appears; and the year the decision was made. For example, *Abrams* v. *United States,* 250 U.S. 616 (1919) means that the Supreme Court decision and opinion in this case will be found in Volume 250 of *United States Reports,* beginning on page 616. The case was decided in 1919.

United States Reports, published by the U.S. Government Printing Office, is one of several sources of Supreme Court opinions. Other sources are *Supreme Court Reporter,* published by West Publishing Company, and *United States Supreme Court Reports, Lawyers' Edition,* published by the Lawyers Cooperative Publishing Company.

Before 1875, official reports of Supreme Court cases were cited with the names of the Court reporters. These names (full or abbreviated) appear in the citations for those years. For example, in *Marbury* v. *Madison,* 1 Cr. 137 (1803), "Cr." is an abbreviation for William Cranch, the Supreme Court reporter from 1801 to 1815. The reporters of decisions from 1790 to 1875 were Alexander J. Dallas (1790–1800), William Cranch (1801–15), Henry Wheaton (1816–27), Richard Peters, Jr. (1828–42), Benjamin C. Howard (1843–60), Jeremiah S. Black (1861–62), and John W. Wallace (1863–75).

SEE ALSO
Reporter of decisions

Citizenship

THE 14TH AMENDMENT to the Constitution defines citizenship in the United States as follows: "All persons born or naturalized in the United States, and subject to the jurisdiction thereof, are citizens of the United States and of the state wherein they reside." Citizenship can be acquired by birth; anyone born in any of the 50 states, the District of Columbia, the Commonwealth of Puerto Rico, or the territories of Guam and the Virgin Islands, for example, is a natural-born citizen of the United States. Children born outside the country to at least one American parent are also U.S. citizens by birth. However, before they are 21 years old, they must become residents of the United States or declare their intention to become a U.S. citizen.

A second way to become a U.S. citizen, according to the 14th Amendment, is by naturalization. Article 1, Section 8, of the Constitution provides Congress the power "to establish a uniform law of naturalization." A person becomes a naturalized citizen by taking certain steps required by federal law. After five years of residence in the United States (three years if the person is married to an American citizen), a person may file a petition to become a citizen. Two

U.S. citizens must testify that the person has fulfilled the residence requirement, exhibits good moral behavior, and believes in the principles of the Constitution. Next, the person completes an examination to prove literacy in English

Immigrants become naturalized citizens in 1983 in Hawaii. The 14th Amendment guarantees the same protections to naturalized citizens as to the native-born.

and knowledge of U.S. history and government. Finally, the person pledges an oath of allegiance to the Constitution of the United States and signs a certificate of naturalization.

In *United States* v. *Wong Kim Ark* (1898), the Supreme Court ruled for the first time on a case arising under the 14th Amendment clause that defines citizenship. The Court decided that the race, ethnic identity, or place of birth of a person's parents could not be used to deny citizenship to a person born in the United States. The Court affirmed the fundamental importance of citizenship in *Trop* v. *Dulles* (1958) by refusing to take away a person's citizenship because he had deserted the army during wartime. Writing for the Court, Chief Justice Earl Warren held that such a loss of citizenship would be "cruel and unusual punishment," which is banned by the 8th Amendment.

Naturalized citizens have the same rights and duties as natural-born citizens, with one exception: they are not eligible to become President or Vice President of the United States (Article 2, Section 1, of the Constitution). According to the 14th Amendment, "No state shall make or enforce any law which shall abridge the privileges or immunities of citizens of the United States." Citizenship entitles a person to certain rights, such as the right to vote or to be a federal government official. (The Bill of Rights, however, applies to all individuals living in the United States, both citizens and noncitizens.) In return, all citizens have certain legal responsibilities, such as paying taxes, serving on a jury if called, serving in the country's armed forces if called, serving as a witness in court if summoned, and obeying the laws of the United States. (Noncitizens residing in the United States are also required to pay taxes and obey the law.) In exchange for the privileges and rights of citizenship, all citizens of

the United States have the obligation of loyalty and allegiance to their Constitution and their country.

SEE ALSO
United States v. Wong Kim Ark

FURTHER READING
Riesenberg, Peter. *Citizenship in the Western Tradition.* Chapel Hill: University of North Carolina Press, 1992.

Civil law

WITHIN THE legal system of the United States, civil law is a body of law pertaining to noncriminal private disputes among individuals, corporations, and governments. Thus, civil law is distinguished from criminal law, which deals with the enforcement of the laws against those accused of violating them. In a civil action, one private party takes legal action against another private party to seek relief in a court of law for an alleged wrong.

SEE ALSO
Criminal law

Civil rights

CIVIL RIGHTS and civil liberties often mean the same thing. The words are frequently used interchangeably to signify the protection of rights to liberty and equality under the Constitution, such as freedom of speech, protection against "unreasonable searches and seizures," and the right to due process of law. The term *civil rights,* however, is also used to refer to positive actions by the government to protect or extend the rights of people—to provide for individuals or

Byzantine emperor Justinian I consolidated Roman civil law into a collection that influenced legal systems of many countries in Europe and other parts of the world.

A taxicab with a sign that says "White Only" in Albany, Georgia, reveals that discrimination was part of everyday life in 1962.

groups opportunities that were previously denied to them. These kinds of civil rights guarantees usually are provided through statutes, such as the Civil Rights Act of 1964, which, for example, gives the federal government the power to prevent an employer from denying a job to someone because of the person's race, gender, religion, or ethnic origin.

Civil rights movements are organized efforts to obtain long-denied constitutional rights for individuals and groups such as African Americans, Hispanics, Native Americans, and women. These segments of the American population have not always enjoyed their full rights of citizenship under the U.S. Constitution.

The civil rights movement

The civil rights movement of African Americans, during most of the 20th century, has had a strong impact on the advancement of constitutional rights for all Americans, especially those who had been long-suffering victims of unjust discrimination and unfair treatment under the law. The early leader of this civil rights movement was the National Association for the Advancement of Colored People (NAACP), founded in 1909. After the formation in 1939 of its Legal Defense Fund (LDF), directed by Thurgood Marshall, the NAACP began to have a steady and significant effect on federal court rulings to obtain and expand the civil rights of African Americans with regard to voting and education. In *Smith* v. *Allwright* (1944) the Court ruled that a political party (the Democrats in this

case) could not exclude blacks from voting in a primary election to nominate party candidates for a subsequent general election. In *Sweatt* v. *Painter* (1950) the Court decided that a state may not deny admission of qualified blacks to a state law school on the grounds that a separate law school for blacks is available. The biggest breakthrough came with the legal victory, led by Thurgood Marshall and other NAACP attorneys, in *Brown* v. *Board of Education* (1954), which established that racial segregation in public schools is unconstitutional.

After the *Brown* decision, various African-American civil rights organizations, including the NAACP, launched political protest movements to influence enforcement of the *Brown* decision and to demand that the federal government pass laws to protect and promote civil rights for African Americans. Martin Luther King, Jr., and the Southern Christian Leadership Conference (SCLC), which he led, moved to the forefront.

Civil rights legislation

The political protest movement influenced enactment of two legislative milestones: the Civil Rights Act of 1964 and the Voting Rights Act of 1965. The 1964 Civil Rights Act forbids discrimination on the basis of race, color, religion, national origin, and, in employment, sex. The law provides protection from unfair discrimination in employment and in the use of public facilities. It also requires desegregation of public schools and facilities.

The Supreme Court has upheld as constitutional the major provisions of the Civil Rights Act of 1964. And the Court has interpreted this law broadly to expand the opportunities available to racial minorities often victimized by past discriminatory practices. In *Heart of Atlanta Motel* v. *United States* (1964), for example, the Court established beyond

President Lyndon Johnson (center) confers with Martin Luther King, Jr. (left) and other civil rights leaders in 1964. Later that year, Johnson signed the Civil Rights Act, which banned various kinds of discrimination based on race, ethnicity, gender, and religion.

challenge that no person can be excluded, because of race or color, from any facility that is open to the general public. Further, the Court has upheld programs of employers to emphasize recruitment of racial minorities that have suffered from the employer's racial discrimination in hiring in the past.

The 1965 Voting Rights Act outlawed discrimination by state governments against African Americans and other minority groups in voter registration and voting in state and federal elections. The Supreme Court upheld the law in *South Carolina* v. *Katzenbach* (1966), ruling that the law is a constitutional use of Congress's power to enforce the 15th Amendment ban on denying a citizen the right to vote because of the person's race or color. Congress renewed and reinforced this voting rights legislation in 1970, 1975, and 1982. The result has been a dramatic increase in the participation of African Americans in public elections as voters and candidates for government offices.

The African-American civil rights movement has become a model for other groups seeking to end legal discrimination against them, such as women, Hispanics, gays, the elderly, and the physically disabled. These groups, too, have tried to bring about favorable legislative acts and judicial decisions.

During the 1980s and 1990s, civil rights advocates have promoted affirmative action programs—the use of prefer-

ential treatment of racial, ethnic, or gender groups to provide access to education, employment, and other social benefits. The groups seeking and receiving these benefits are seen as having been victims of persistent and unfair discrimination. They look to affirmative action as a temporary means to overcome the harmful consequences of systematic discrimination in the past, which has unfairly denied opportunities to some people.

Congress passed the Civil Rights Act of 1991 to amend the Civil Rights Act of 1964. The purpose was to strengthen the scope of federal civil rights protections, which had been weakened by the Supreme Court's decision in *Ward's Cove Packing Company* v. *Atonio* (1989). In the *Ward's Cove* decision, the Court determined that those claiming discrimination by employers had to prove that a specific employment practice had been discriminatory. Even if the plaintiff were to provide the proof required, the employer could still claim that the discriminating practice was necessary to maintain his or her business.

The Civil Rights Act of 1991 overturned the *Ward's Cove* decision by eliminating, as illegal, an employer's claim of "business necessity" as a justification for intentional discrimination against an individual based on race, color, ethnic origin, and gender. Further, the Civil Rights Act of 1991 protects an employee against racial harassment after being hired. Finally, the 1991 law limits the opportunities to legally challenge employers' affirmative action programs.

SEE ALSO

Affirmative action; Brown v. Board of Education; Civil Rights Cases; Equality under the Constitution; Heart of Atlanta Motel v. United States; Johnson v. Transportation Agency of Santa Clara County; Liberty under the Constitution; National Association for the Advancement of Colored People (NAACP); Smith v. Allwright; Sweatt v. Painter

FURTHER READING

Branch, Taylor. *Parting the Waters: America in the King Years, 1954–63.* New York: Simon & Schuster, 1988.

Franklin, John Hope, and Alfred A. Moss, Jr. *From Slavery to Freedom.* New York: Knopf, 1988.

King, Martin Luther, Jr. *Stride Toward Freedom.* New York: Harper & Row, 1958.

King, Martin Luther, Jr. *Why We Can't Wait.* New York: Signet, 1964.

Konvitz, Milton R. *Century of Civil Rights.* New York: Columbia University Press, 1961.

Civil Rights Cases

☆ *109 U.S. 3 (1883)*
☆ *Vote: 8–1*
☆ *For the Court: Bradley*
☆ *Dissenting: Harlan*

The *Civil Rights Cases* were five cases that the Supreme Court decided together. In all five situations, the federal Civil Rights Act of 1875 had been enforced by the federal government against private facilities—a railroad company, theater owners, and innkeepers. In each case, a black American had been denied the same accommodations or services enjoyed by white Americans. The Civil Rights Act of 1875 forbade denial of access on the basis of race to theaters, hotels, railroad cars, and other privately owned facilities that served the public. The Civil Rights Act also forbade segregation of blacks and whites in their use of such privately owned facilities as hotels, theaters, and railroad cars. The defendants in these cases argued that the Civil Rights Act of 1875 was an unconstitutional regulation of their management of private property.

The Issue Congress passed the Civil Rights Act of 1875 to implement the "equal protection of the laws" clause of the 14th Amendment. This amendment restricted the power of a state *government* to violate the civil rights of people within its boundaries. But the primary intention of the framers of the 14th Amendment was to secure the rights of black people, which had been at risk. At issue was whether the 14th Amendment enabled Congress to forbid discrimination based on race by owners of *private* facilities used by the public.

Opinion of the Court
The Court ruled that the 14th Amendment banned the violation of individual rights only by state governments. According to Justice Joseph Bradley, the Civil Rights Act of 1875 was unconstitutional because it attempted to regulate the private conduct of individuals with regard to racial discrimination—an action that was beyond the scope of the 14th Amendment. According to Bradley, individuals faced with racial discrimination in their use of privately owned hotels, theaters, railroad cars, and so forth had to seek help from their state government. The federal government, according to the Court, had no constitutional authority to act in these cases.

Dissent Justice John Harlan stood against the Court in this case because its opinion rested "upon grounds entirely narrow and artificial." Harlan argued for a broad interpretation of the 13th and 14th Amendments as a suitable legal basis for the Civil Rights Act of 1875.

Harlan claimed that the federal government had the authority and the responsibility to protect individuals from racial discrimination in their access to privately owned facilities serving the public. He pointed out, for example, that roads and railroads were "established by the authority of these States" and theaters operated under state government licenses. Therefore, Harlan argued, the

This letter from the African M.E. Church praises Justice John Harlan for his dissent in the Civil Rights Cases. *Harlan argued that the 14th Amendment should protect African Americans from discrimination in public facilities even if those facilities are owned by private companies.*

state's association with these facilities justified federal action to provide all individuals, black and white, equal opportunity to use the facilities. Justice Harlan concluded:

> [T]here cannot be, in this republic, any class of human beings in practical subjection to another class, with power in the latter to dole out to the former just such privileges as they may choose to grant. The supreme law of the land has decreed that no authority shall be exercised in this country upon the basis of discrimination, in respect of civil rights, against freemen and citizens because of their race, color, or previous condition of servitude.

Significance Public opinion in the 1870s was solidly in support of the Court's ruling in the *Civil Rights Cases*. However, Harlan's dissent prevailed in the long run in federal legislation such as the Civil Rights Act of 1964 and in Supreme Court decisions such as *Heart of Atlanta Motel* v. *United States* (1964). It is Justice Harlan's dissent that is honored today, not Justice Bradley's opinion for the Court.

SEE ALSO

Heart of Atlanta Motel v. United States

FURTHER READING

Kull, Andrew. "The 14th Amendment That Wasn't." *Constitution* 5, no. 1 (Winter 1993): 68–75.
Westin, Alvin F. "The Case of the Prejudiced Doorkeeper: The Civil Rights Cases." In *Quarrels That Have Shaped the Constitution,* edited by John A. Garraty. New York: Harper & Row, 1987.

Clark, Tom

ASSOCIATE JUSTICE, 1949–67

☆ Born: Sept. 23, 1899, Dallas, Tex.
☆ Education: University of Texas, B.A., 1921; LL.B., 1922

☆ Previous government service: civil district attorney, Dallas County, Tex., 1927–32; special assistant, U.S. Department of Justice, 1937–43; assistant U.S. attorney general, 1943–45; U.S. attorney general, 1945–49
☆ Appointed by President Harry S. Truman Aug. 2, 1949; replaced Frank Murphy, who died
☆ Supreme Court term: confirmed by the Senate Aug. 18, 1949, by a 73–8 vote; retired June 12, 1967
☆ Died: June 13, 1977, New York, N.Y.

TOM CLARK worked in the U.S. Department of Justice and became friendly with Harry Truman, a senator from Missouri. In 1944, Clark supported Truman's bid to become the Democratic candidate for Vice President. When President Franklin D. Roosevelt died in 1945, Truman became President and he appointed Clark to be his attorney general. Four years later, Truman named Clark to the Supreme Court.

Both as attorney general and associate justice, Tom Clark supported government efforts to protect national security against Communist party activity in the United States. He also wrote opinions for the Court on landmark cases that protected individual rights. In *Mapp* v. *Ohio* (1961), for example, Clark declared that evidence seized illegally must be "excluded from" a state government's prosecution of a person accused of a crime. This "exclusionary rule" set forth by Clark in 1961 has endured as a guide to Court decisions.

Clark retired from the Supreme Court in 1967 when his son, Ramsay Clark, was appointed by President Lyndon Johnson to the job of U.S. attorney general, a position that Tom Clark had once filled. Tom Clark left the Court to avoid any possibility of conflict of interest in cases brought to the Court by his son.

He continued to serve the federal government, however, until his death in 1977. He was a founder and the first director of the Federal Judicial Center, which conducts research and training programs to improve operations of the federal courts. He also occasionally served as a judge on various circuits of the U.S. Court of Appeals.

SEE ALSO

Mapp v. Ohio

Clarke, John H.

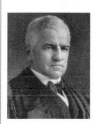

ASSOCIATE JUSTICE, 1916–22

☆ *Born: Sept. 18, 1857, New Lisbon, Ohio*

☆ *Education: Western Reserve University, B.A., 1877; M.A., 1880*

☆ *Previous government service: federal judge, U.S. District Court for the Northern District of Ohio, 1914–16*

☆ *Appointed by President Woodrow Wilson July 14, 1916; replaced Charles Evans Hughes, who resigned*

☆ *Supreme Court term: confirmed by the Senate July 24, 1916, by a voice vote; resigned Sept. 18, 1922*

☆ *Died: Mar. 22, 1945, San Diego, Calif.*

JOHN H. CLARKE served only six years on the Supreme Court. During this brief period, he often sided with Justice Louis Brandeis. His cooperation with Brandeis brought the hostility of Justice James McReynolds, who was persistently nasty to his two colleagues because he strongly disagreed with their legal ideas. McReynolds also seems to have disliked Brandeis because of a personal prejudice against Jews. McReynolds's ugly behavior was one of the reasons Clarke left the Court. McReynolds refused to sign the official letter expressing regret at Clarke's resignation.

Justice Clarke wrote the Court's opinion in *Abrams* v. *United States* (1919), in which he upheld limitations on free speech under the Espionage Act of 1918. In this opinion Clarke departed from his usual agreement with Brandeis, who joined Oliver Wendell Holmes in a strong dissent against the *Abrams* decision.

After leaving the Supreme Court, Clarke devoted the rest of his life to promoting the cause of world peace. He supported the work of the League of Nations and the creation of the United Nations in 1945.

SEE ALSO

Abrams v. United States

Class action

A LAWSUIT brought to court by one or more individuals on behalf of a category, or *class*, of people is called a *class action*. This type of lawsuit is used when there is a very large number of parties to a dispute who have common interests and stakes in the outcome. In a class action, the case is tried by one or a few parties who represent many others, and the judgment in the case is binding on all members of the class involved in the dispute. Many cases dealing with the civil rights of African Americans were class actions.

Clear and present danger test

SEE Abrams v. United States; Freedom of speech and press; Schenck v. United States

Clerk of the Court

DURING ITS first term, in 1790, the U.S. Supreme Court established the office of the clerk to be responsible for managing the Court's administrative work. The clerk manages the dockets (calendars, agendas, and schedules of events) of the Court, receives and records all documents filed on the various dockets and distributes these pages to the justices, notifies lower courts of all formal acts and decisions of the Supreme Court, and provides advice to lawyers who need information about the Court's rules and procedures. The clerk has a clerical and administrative staff of 25 people.

SEE ALSO
Staff of the Court, nonjudicial

Clerks of the justices

EACH SUPREME COURT justice may have a staff of four law clerks. Chief Justice William Rehnquist and Justice John Paul Stevens, however, chose to employ only three each. The justices have complete control over the hiring of these legal assistants. Most law clerks work at the job for only one year and use the prestigious position as a stepping stone to important jobs in law firms, on law school faculties, and in government service. Thirty-two former law clerks have become federal judges, and three have become Supreme Court justices: William H. Rehnquist, who clerked for Robert H. Jackson; John Paul Stevens, who clerked for Wiley B. Rutledge; and Byron White, who clerked for Fred M. Vinson.

The law clerks provide valuable re-

Sherry Colb, law clerk for Justice Harry Blackmun, working on upcoming Court cases.

search assistance for the justices. They also read, analyze, and write summaries of certiorari petitions, the requests to the Court for review of cases. The justices often depend upon their clerks' summaries and recommendations in deciding which cases to select for review.

Justice Horace Gray was the first member of the Court to employ a law clerk. In 1885 Gray hired a recent graduate of Harvard Law School, whom he paid with his own money. In 1922 Congress provided funds for the employment of one law clerk by each justice. In 1924 Congress established permanent law clerk positions at the Supreme Court.

Clifford, Nathan

ASSOCIATE JUSTICE, 1858–81

☆ Born: Aug. 18, 1803, Rumney, N.H.
☆ Education: studied law in the office of Josiah Quincy in Rumney
☆ Previous government service: Maine House of Representatives, 1830–34; attorney general of Maine, 1834–38; U.S. representative from Maine, 1839–43; U.S. attorney general, 1846–48; U.S. minister to Mexico, 1848–49
☆ Appointed by President James Buchanan Dec. 9, 1857; replaced Benjamin R. Curtis, who resigned
☆ Supreme Court term: confirmed by the Senate Jan. 12, 1858, by a 26–23 vote; served until July 25, 1881
☆ Died: July 25, 1881, Cornish, Maine

NATHAN CLIFFORD was a self-educated man who built a successful political career in Maine and in the federal government. He served as attorney general under President James Polk and was appointed by President James Buchanan to the U.S. Supreme Court. He was confirmed in a close vote because Republican senators believed he sympathized with the slave states that were threatening to secede from the Union.

Justice Clifford wrote no major opinions for the Court. He chaired the commission set up to settle the dispute over the Presidential election of 1876. There had been controversy about the correct vote totals and charges of voter fraud in three southern states. Clifford supported the case of Democrat Samuel Tilden but the commission decided in favor of Rutherford B. Hayes, the Republican.

Cohens v. Virginia

☆ *6 Wheat. 264 (1821)*
☆ *Vote: 6–0*
☆ *For the Court: Marshall*

TWO BROTHERS, Philip and Mendes Cohen, were charged with violating a Virginia law by selling lottery tickets within the state. They were tried, convicted, and fined by a local court in Norfolk, Virginia. The Cohens appealed the Virginia court decision to the U.S. Supreme Court under Section 25 of the Judiciary Act of 1789, which provides for review by the U.S. Supreme Court of decisions by state courts that involve issues of constitutional or federal law.

The Cohen brothers said that their lottery had been incorporated in Washington, D.C., according to terms of an act of Congress. Therefore they concluded that their lottery was conducted properly under federal law and could not be restricted by a state law.

The Issue Attorneys for the state of Virginia argued that according to the 11th Amendment to the Constitution, the U.S. Supreme Court could not have jurisdiction in this case. Furthermore, they held that there were no words in the U.S. Constitution that "set up the federal judiciary above the state judiciary." Therefore, they said, Section 25 of the Judiciary Act of 1789 could not be used to justify jurisdiction of the Supreme Court in this case. The issue was: Does the U.S. Supreme Court have jurisdiction in cases originating in state courts when these cases involve questions about federal law and the U.S. Constitution? Is the U.S. Supreme Court the final authority in such cases? Did the state of Virginia wrongfully convict the Cohens for violating a state law against lotteries?

Opinion of the Court Chief Justice John Marshall delivered the unanimous decision of the Court, which upheld the jurisdiction and authority of the U.S. Supreme Court to review decisions of state courts when they involve issues about federal law or the U.S. Constitution. He wrote eloquently in support of Section 25 of the Judiciary Act of 1789 and reaffirmed the Court's decision (written by Justice Joseph Story) in *Martin* v. *Hunter's Lessee* (1816).

Marshall also effectively dismissed Virginia's claim that the 11th Amendment precluded the Supreme Court from having jurisdiction in this case. Finally, after establishing the Court's authority and jurisdiction in this case, Marshall ruled against the Cohen brothers and upheld their conviction under Virginia state law.

Significance Chief Justice Marshall asserted the supremacy of the U.S. Constitution and federal law over state laws that conflicted with them. And he argued compellingly for the ultimate authority of the U.S. Supreme Court over state courts on *all* questions involving the U.S. Constitution and federal law. These views are no longer controversial, but in Marshall's time they were burning constitutional issues. The chief justice, however, framed and responded to these issues in a timeless fashion, and his decision undergirds our contemporary conceptions of federal-state relations.

SEE ALSO
Federalism; Judicial review; Jurisdiction; *Martin* v. *Hunter's Lessee*

Commerce power

ARTICLE 1, Section 8, of the U.S. Constitution gives Congress the power "to regulate Commerce with foreign Nations and among the several States, and with the Indian Tribes." Commerce refers to the production, selling, and transportation of goods. If these commercial activities affect more than one state, the federal government may use its "commerce power" to regulate them. Ever since the 1820s, the Supreme Court has tended to interpret broadly the meaning of Congress's power to regulate commerce.

The Supreme Court's first major decision to define the meaning of the commerce power involved a controversy over steamboats. In the early 1800s Robert Fulton developed the steamboat as a practical means of travel. Fulton's smoke-belching vessel started a chain of events that led to the case of *Gibbons* v. *Ogden* (1824).

The *Gibbons* case involved two key questions. First, did "commerce" include navigation, and did the commerce clause of the Constitution therefore give Congress the power to regulate navigation? Second, did Congress possess exclusive power to regulate interstate commerce or did it share that power with the states?

The *Gibbons* case interpreted the meaning of the term *commerce* to encompass not only "navigation" but also other forms of trade, movement, and business. However, the Court did not spell out exactly what these other forms were. For instance, did commerce include coal mining?

As a result, *Gibbons* v. *Ogden* did not immediately lead to extensive federal regulation of interstate commerce. Yet the decision did open the door for the vast expansion of national control over commerce that we have today. The

Workers at the H. J. Heinz Company wash and sort tomatoes. Since the 1820s, the courts have broadly interpreted Congress's power to regulate commercial activities.

Court's broad interpretation of the meaning of "commerce" ultimately enabled Congress to regulate manufacturing, child labor, farm production, wages and hours, labor unions, civil rights, and criminal conduct as well as buying and selling. Any activity affecting interstate commerce is now subject to national control. Moreover, the Court's broad interpretation of the commerce power has led to a steady growth of the federal government's power in its relationships with state governments.

Though the *Gibbons* ruling established a precedent, it was left to later courts to determine the scope of the commerce power on a case-by-case basis. The accompanying table lists some of the Court's major decisions on the commerce power made in the years since *Gibbons* v. *Ogden*. Through these decisions the Court has further defined Congress's power to regulate commerce in accordance with the commerce clause.

SEE ALSO

Federalism; Gibbons v. Ogden; Hammer v. Dagenhart; Heart of Atlanta Motel v. United States; National Labor Relations Board v. Jones & Laughlin Steel Corp.; United States v. Darby Lumber Co.

FURTHER READING

Corwin, Edward S. *The Commerce Power Versus States' Rights.* Princeton, N.J.: Princeton University Press, 1959.

DEVELOPMENT OF THE COMMERCE POWER

Kidd v. Pearson (1888) Manufacturing of goods, such as liquor, is not commerce. Congress cannot regulate such manufacturing as interstate commerce.

Champion v. Ames (1903) Congress may use its power to regulate commerce to outlaw the interstate sale and shipment of lottery tickets.

McCray v. United States (1904) Congress may regulate the sale of oleomargarine (a butter substitute) by placing a high tax on it. This decision, along with *Champion*, strengthened Congress's ability to use the commerce power as a regulatory power for the public good.

Swift and Co. v. United States (1905) The Court announces the "stream of commerce" doctrine. The meat-packing industry is part of a "stream of commerce" from the time an animal is purchased until it is processed and sold as meat. Congress could regulate at any point along that "stream." The "stream of commerce" doctrine became a basic legal concept in the expansion of the federal commerce power.

Adair v. United States (1908) Labor relations do not directly affect interstate commerce. Thus, Congress cannot use the commerce power to prohibit certain kinds of labor contracts.

Shreveport Rate Cases (1914) Court announces the "Shreveport doctrine." The federal government has power to regulate rail rates within states (intrastate) as well as between states (interstate). This sets the key precedent that whenever intrastate and interstate transactions (such as rail rates) become so related that regulation of one involves control of the other, Congress—not the states—has final authority.

Hammer v. Dagenhart (1918) Congress may not use the commerce power as a police power to regulate working conditions for child laborers or to prohibit the use of children in factories.

Bailey v. Drexel Furniture Co. (1922) Congress may not use its police power to place a high tax on the profits of companies employing child laborers. This decision, along with *Hammer* in 1918, greatly narrowed the federal police power. With these two decisions, the Court frustrated attempts by Congress to end child labor.

Railroad Retirement Board v. Alton Railroad (1935) The commerce clause does not give Congress the power to set up a pension system for railroad workers.

Carter v. Carter Coal Co. (1936) Mining is not commerce and does not affect commerce directly. Thus, Congress may not regulate labor relations in the coal mining industry.

National Labor Relations Board v. Jones & Laughlin Steel Corp. (1937) Congress may regulate labor relations in manufacturing to prevent possible interference with interstate commerce. With this decision, which overturned the *Adair* and *Carter* decisions, the Court gave up the narrow view of Congress's power to regulate commerce it had followed for many years. The Court based its decision on precedents set in the *Swift* and *Shreveport* cases.

Mulford v. Smith (1939) The commerce power gives Congress the authority to regulate market quotas for agricultural production. That is, Congress has the power to limit the amount of a product transported via interstate commerce.

United States v. Darby Lumber Co. (1941) Congress may use its commerce power to prohibit from interstate commerce goods made under substandard labor conditions. This decision overturns the *Hammer* decision.

Wickard v. Filburn (1942) Congress may regulate agricultural production affecting interstate commerce even if the produce is not meant for sale.

Heart of Atlanta Motel v. United States (1964) Congress may use its commerce power to prohibit public hotels and motels from discriminating against customers on the basis of race.

National League of Cities v. Usery (1976) Congress cannot use its commerce power to establish wage and hour standards for state and local government employees.

Garcia v. San Antonio Metropolitan Transit Authority (1985) Neither the 10th Amendment nor any other provision of the Constitution can be interpreted to limit the commerce power of Congress over the state governments. Thus, federal laws on minimum wages and overtime pay can be applied to workers of a transit system owned and operated by the city of San Antonio, Texas. This decision overruled *National League of Cities v. Usery*.

Common law

LAW MADE by judges through decisions in specific cases is known as the common law. These case-by-case decisions were used again and again in similar cases and thereby become customary, or common to all people living under the authority of the court of law. The common law used in the United States originated in England and was compiled in the 18th century by Sir William Blackstone in his *Commentaries on the Law of England.*

The English common law was taken by emigrants from the Old Country to the American colonies. After the American Revolution, English common law became the foundation of legal procedures in the United States of America. Today, the legal system in every American state, except Louisiana, is based on the Anglo-American common law. In Louisiana, once a French colony, certain French legal customs have been maintained. For instance, the word *parish,* derived from the French, is used instead of *county* to label administrative areas within the state.

Statutory law, the written law passed by a legislature, overrides the common law. Many statutes, however, are rooted in the common law tradition and are interpreted by judges according to this tradition.

There is no federal common law because the federal government functions on the basis of a written constitution, through which the people delegate power to the government. Federal judges, however, apply the common law to cases involving people from different states when there is no federal law that fits a particular case.

The U.S. Supreme Court's use of precedents in deciding cases is an ex-

The figure of William Blackstone appears in the north frieze in the courtroom of the Supreme Court building.

ample of the common law heritage. In its exercise of judicial review in particular cases, the Court sets precedents that apply to future cases. If a statute in a particular state is held unconstitutional, for example, this decision is applicable to similar statutes in all other states. The Supreme Court made this point strongly in *Cooper* v. *Aaron* (1958), in which the Court upheld the application of its decision in *Brown* v. *Board of Education* (1954), which concerned Kansas, to enforce an end to segregation of public schools in Arkansas.

SEE ALSO

Cooper v. Aaron; Precedent

FURTHER READING

Hogue, Arthur R. *Origins of the Common Law.* Indianapolis: Liberty Press, 1986.
Tribe, Lawrence H. *American Constitutional Law.* Mineola, N.Y.: Foundation Press, 1978.

Concurring opinion

JUSTICES OF the U.S. Supreme Court write concurring opinions on cases when they agree with the outcome of the majority opinion but disagree with the Court's reasons or explanations for the decision. In such a case a justice writes a separate concurring opinion, offering his or her own reasons about a decision with which he or she concurs, or agrees. On a few occasions, there have been so many concurring opinions in a case that there was no majority opinion of the Court. For example, in *Regents of the University of California* v. *Bakke* (1978), the Court decided the case by a

In a memo to the chief justice, Potter Stewart announces that he may write a concurring opinion, but he did not in this case.

vote of 5 to 4. However, eight of the justices wrote separate opinions, concurring in part and dissenting in part from the decision. As a result, there was no distinct opinion of the Court in this case. Rather, Justice Lewis Powell wrote an opinion announcing "the judgment of the Court," rather than an opinion for the majority of the Court. Cases decided without a clear-cut majority opinion written for the Court do not establish clear precedents.

SEE ALSO

Majority opinion; Opinions; Plurality opinion

The Conference Room in the Supreme Court Building. The justices meet here to discuss their cases in private sessions.

Conference

THE JUSTICES of the Supreme Court meet regularly in the Conference Room of the Supreme Court Building to discuss cases on which they have heard oral arguments. They also use the conference to screen and select petitions for review of new cases and to conduct other Court business. At least six justices must be present for a quorum, the minimum number required for the group to make a decision about a case.

In Wednesday afternoon conferences, the justices discuss cases argued orally before the Court on the previous Monday. The all-day conference on Friday is used to discuss cases argued orally the previous Tuesday and Wednesday.

Unlike the presentation of oral arguments in the Supreme Court chamber (courtroom), which is open to the public, the conference is always private and conducted in complete secrecy. Not even the justices' clerks or secretaries attend. No official records of the conferences are made, and no formal reports of the proceedings are issued. However, justices often make personal notes to help them recall main points or important details of a particular discussion.

Discussion of a case usually begins with the chief justice, who sets the context and reviews key facts and issues. The other justices present their views on the case in order of their seniority, beginning with the most senior. If a formal vote is taken on the case, the justices vote in the opposite order, beginning with the least senior. The chief justice is the last to vote. After everyone has voted, the chief justice announces the vote tally and goes on to the next case. Such a formal vote is often not taken, however, because the justices frequently reveal their votes in the preceding round of discussion.

A justice's views on a case sometimes change in the weeks following the conference, during which opinions are written and exchanged and informal discussions of the case continue. Before the final decision and the Court's opinion are announced, justices may modify the positions they expressed during the conference.

Confirmation process

SEE Appointment of justices; Rejection of Supreme Court nominees; Senate Judiciary Committee

Constitutional construction

ONE'S METHOD of interpreting the U.S. Constitution is called constitutional construction. Some interpreters of the Constitution favor a strict or narrow construction of the document. Strict constructionists interpret the Constitution according to their views of the framers' original intentions about the various parts of the document. Strict constructionists also tend to emphasize the literal meaning of the words of the Constitution.

Loose constructionists favor a broad interpretation of the ideas and words of the Constitution. They attempt to apply the purposes and the principles of the Constitution to meet changing circumstances and conditions. Loose constructionists point to the general welfare clause and the necessary and proper clause of Article 1, Section 8, of the Constitution, which grant Congress power "To...provide for the...general welfare of the United States" and "To make all Laws which shall be necessary and proper for carrying into Execution the foregoing Powers, and all other Powers vested by this Constitution in the Government of the United States or in any Department or Officer thereof."

Loose constructionists claim that the general welfare clause and the necessary and proper clause are the bases for broad or flexible interpretation of the Constitution to adjust its ideas to changing times. Loose constructionists also emphasize that they abide by the principles of the Constitution and respect precedents and historical developments.

A significant decision on the issue of strict versus broad construction was made in the landmark Supreme Court case of *McCulloch* v. *Maryland* (1819). The Court, under the leadership of Chief Justice John Marshall, argued strongly for loose construction and implied powers (powers not explicitly stated but considered logical extensions of Constitutional language). Since then, the loose constructionist position has prevailed most of the time. Occasionally, however, strict constructionists have exerted influence on the Court's decisions.

SEE ALSO
Marshall, John; McCulloch v. Maryland

Constitutional democracy

THE GOVERNMENT of the United States is called a constitutional democracy. It is a democracy because the government is based on the consent of the people. Further, the government operates according to the principle of majority rule. The people, for example, elect their representatives and senators in Congress by majority vote; and the members of Congress make laws according to majority rule.

The popular and democratic government of the United States, however, is limited by the higher law of the Constitution in order to secure, as the Declaration of Independence says, the "unalienable rights" of every person. These legal limitations on the people's government make the United States a constitutional democracy, not an unlimited democracy.

James Madison and other framers of the Constitution feared the new threat to liberty that could come from a tyrannical majority. In times past, the threat to lib-

In a speech delivered to Congress in August 1974, President Gerald Ford stressed that government in the United States is based on the rule of law.

erty came from the unrestrained powers of a king or an aristocracy. Madison, however, saw a new danger, which he expressed in a letter to Thomas Jefferson (Oct. 17, 1788):

> Wherever the real power in a Government lies, there is the danger of oppression. In our Governments, the real power lies in the majority of the Community, and the invasion of private rights is *chiefly* to be apprehended, not from acts of Government contrary to the sense of its constituents, but from acts in which the Government is the mere instrument of the major number [majority] of the constituents. This is a truth of great importance, but not yet sufficiently attended to.... Whenever there is an interest and power to do wrong, wrong will generally be done, and not less readily by [a majority of the people] than by a...prince.

Madison wanted government by majority rule of duly elected representatives of the people, but the majority's power must be limited by the higher law of a written constitution. If not, people that the majority disliked could lose basic freedoms and opportunities.

In *The Federalist* Nos. 10 and 51, James Madison argued for constitutional limits on power in government in order to protect the liberty and security of individuals. He opposed equally the absolut-

ism, or total power, of a monarch or military dictator (the tyranny of one), an aristocracy or oligarchy (tyranny of the few over the many), or a majority of the people (tyranny of the many over the few). In a republic or representative democracy (government by elected representatives of the people), the greatest threat to liberty would come from an unrestrained majority. This threat could be overcome by constructing constitutional limits on majority rule in order to protect minority rights.

A constitutional democracy, then, is government by majority rule with protection of minority rights. It is democratic because of its foundations of popular consent and majority rule. It is constitutional because the power of the majority to rule is limited by a supreme law.

In the constitutional democracy of the United States, the Supreme Court uses its power of judicial review to make decisions about issues in specific cases concerning limits on majority rule or on minority rights. In many landmark decisions, such as *West Virginia State Board of Education* v. *Barnette* (1943), the Court has limited the power of majority rule in order to protect the rights to liberty of individuals in the minority. Writing for the Court in the *Barnette* case, Justice Robert Jackson argued that a person's rights to liberty, such as the right to free exercise of religion, "are beyond the reach of majorities." They may not, he wrote, "be submitted to vote," and "they depend on the outcome of no elections."

In other landmark decisions, the Court has limited an individual's rights to liberty in order to maintain the democratic power of majority rule. For example, in *United States* v. *O'Brien* (1968), the Court upheld a federal law that made it a crime for anyone to destroy a draft card, the document that indicates that a person has registered with the government for possible induction into the armed forces. David O'Brien was denied the right to burn his draft card as a protest against the government. According to the Court, this violation of a federal law, enacted by majority rule of Congress, was not a permissible expression of freedom under the 1st Amendment.

SEE ALSO

Constitutionalism; Judicial review; Liberty under the Constitution; *United States* v. *O'Brien*; *West Virginia State Board of Education* v. *Barnette*

FURTHER READING

Agresto, John. *The Supreme Court and Constitutional Democracy.* Ithaca, N.Y.: Cornell University Press, 1984.

Berns, Walter. *Taking the Constitution Seriously.* Lanham, Md.: Madison Books, 1992.

Elster, Jon, and Rune Slagstad, eds. *Constitutionalism and Democracy.* New York: Cambridge, 1988.

Constitutionalism

LIMITED GOVERNMENT and the rule of law, as embodied in legal documents, institutions, and procedures, are the two essential elements of constitutionalism.

Limited government means that officials cannot act arbitrarily when they make and enforce public decisions. Public officials cannot simply do as they please. Rather, they are guided and limited by laws as they carry out the duties of their government offices. In the United States, the Constitution is the supreme law that guides and limits the exercise of power by government officials. Laws made in conformity with the Constitution also guide and limit the actions of government officials.

The rule of law means that neither government officials nor common citizens are allowed to break the law. Furthermore, people accused of crimes should be treated equally under the law and accorded due process, or fair and proper legal proceedings, in all official actions against them. Law governs the actions of everyone in the system—public officials and the citizenry, from highest to lowest ranks in both government and society. All laws and the actions based on those laws must conform to the highest law of the land, the Constitution.

In the United States, constitutionalism means there is a supreme law by which the people establish and limit the powers of their government. In 1787 representatives of the people of the United States drafted and ratified a Constitution, which stands above all laws made by any legislative body in the United States. Article 6 of the Constitution states this principle: "The Constitution, and the Laws of the United States which shall be made in Pursuance thereof...shall be the supreme Law of the Land." All laws, passed either by Congress or by state legislatures, must conform to the supreme law—the Constitution. As Alexander Hamilton explained in *The Federalist* No. 78: "No legislative act contrary to the Constitution, therefore, can be valid." On the contrary, a legislative or executive action that violates the Constitution can be declared unconstitutional, or unlawful, by the Supreme Court.

In the United States, the ultimate purpose of constitutionalism is stated in the Declaration of Independence: to secure the "unalienable rights" of all people through a government established by "consent of the governed." According to the Declaration, a good constitution limits the power of a government in order to secure the rights of every person, which belong equally to all human beings. If a government fails to secure these rights of individuals, then it is a bad gov-

James Madison wrote in The Federalist *that limits on the powers of government are necessary to protect the people from abuses.*

ernment and the people have the right to alter and replace it.

A continuing problem of constitutionalism, and of constitution makers, is how to establish a government with sufficient power to rule and maintain order yet with sufficient limitations on its power to prevent tyranny. The rights and liberties of individuals are supposed to be protected by law against abuses of power by government officials. However, if constitutional limits on government are too strict, the government will be too weak to carry out its duties effectively. A government that is too limited by law may not even be able to enforce the laws and maintain public order and security. By contrast, if the government is too strong, or unlimited in its use of power, then the liberties of individuals may be lost and tyranny might prevail. An effective constitutional government is neither too powerful nor too weak.

It is difficult to achieve a workable balance between power sufficient to govern effectively and limits on power sufficient to protect the people's liberties and rights. On the eve of the Civil War, Abraham Lincoln asked, "Must a government, of necessity, be too strong for the liberties of its own people, or too weak to maintain its own existence?" During the 1780s, James Madison and Alexander Hamilton argued in *The Federalist* that limited government under the Articles of Confederation (the document that formed the first government of the newly independent states) was too weak to maintain its own existence. The authors of *The Federalist* argued that limited government and the rule of law—principles of government reflected in the 1787 Constitution—would protect the people from abuses of power by would-be tyrants. They feared equally any unrestrained source of power. The power of an unlimited majority of the people, in their view, was just as dangerous to the

rights of individuals as the unlimited power of a king. They argued that the best government is both "energetic" (strong enough to act decisively and effectively in the public interest) and "limited by law" to protect individual rights.

The problem of constitutionalism—how to combine the contrary factors of power and restraint, order and liberty, in one constitution—was stated memorably by James Madison in *The Federalist* No. 51:

> But what is government itself but the greatest of all reflections of human nature? If men were angels, no government would be necessary. If angels were to govern men, neither external nor internal controls on government would be necessary. In framing a government which is to be administered by men over men, the great difficulty lies in this: you must first enable the government to control the governed; and in the next place oblige it to control itself. A dependence on the people is, no doubt, the primary control on the government; but experience has taught mankind the necessity of auxiliary precautions [limited government based on the supreme law of a written constitution].

Constitutionalism—limited government and the rule of law—is a means to the elusive end of securing the human rights of all people. This is the ultimate purpose of government under the U.S. Constitution.

SEE ALSO

Constitutional democracy; Constitutional law; Constitution, U.S.; Federalist, The; Judicial review; Liberty under the Constitution

FURTHER READING

Ketchum, Ralph. *Framed for Posterity: The Enduring Philosophy of the Constitution.* Lawrence: University Press of Kansas, 1993.
Lutz, Donald S. *The Origins of American Constitutionalism.* Baton Rouge: Louisiana State University Press, 1988.
Richards, David A. J. *Foundations of American Constitutionalism.* New York: Oxford, 1989.

Constitutional law

DECISIONS BY judges, who interpret and apply the Constitution to specific cases, create constitutional law. For example, judicial interpretation of the meaning of general phrases in the Constitution, such as "due process of law" or "unreasonable searches and seizures" or "interstate commerce," establishes constitutional law. In the United States, the Supreme Court plays a central role in developing constitutional law. In 1982, for instance, the Court decided in *United States* v. *Ross* that the 4th Amendment ban against "unreasonable searches and seizures" did not prevent police, under certain circumstances, from searching the contents of a car without a search warrant.

Constitutional law in the United States is the product of judicial interpretation of the U.S. Constitution in response to the constitutional issues in cases that come before the courts. Thus, the courts develop a body of case law. The decisions of the courts in these legal cases establish precedents, decisions that serve as models for future decisions. Thus, over time these precedents accumulate to become a body of constitutional law.

The development of American constitutional law is based on the power of the Supreme Court to consider whether particular federal and state laws and executive actions are consistent with the Constitution. If so, the laws or actions at issue are confirmed. If not, they are declared unconstitutional. Thus, the power of judicial review and the principle of constitutionalism are fundamental factors in the development of constitutional law by the judicial branch of government.

SEE ALSO
Constitutionalism; Judicial review; Precedent

FURTHER READING
Lieberman, Jethro K. *The Evolving Constitution: How the Supreme Court Has Ruled on Issues from Abortion to Zoning.* New York: Random House, 1993.

Constitution, U.S.

THE BASIC and supreme law of the land is the Constitution of the United States of America. It consists of 7 articles, which were drafted by the Constitutional Convention of 1787 in Philadelphia, and 27 amendments. More than 200 years old, this document is the oldest written constitution of a national state in use anywhere in the world today. (The oldest written constitution of any sort in use today is the Massachusetts state constitution of 1780.) Most of the national constitutions around the world have existed only since about 1970.

The U.S. Constitution, like other national constitutions, establishes a general framework for organizing and operating a government. It is not a detailed blueprint for governing on a day-to-day basis. The U.S. Constitution consists of only about 7,500 words. It does not attempt to consider the details of how to run the national government. Officials who run the government supply the de-

The Taft Court was one of the most distinguished in U.S. history. Seated: James McReynolds, Oliver Wendell Holmes, Chief Justice William Howard Taft, Willis Van Devanter, Louis D. Brandeis. Standing: Edward T. Stanford, George Sutherland, Pierce Butler, Harlan Fiske Stone.

tails that fit the general framework.

As the government's framework, the Constitution must be interpreted as specific problems arise. For example, the 4th Amendment to the Constitution protects people against "unreasonable searches and seizures" by police or other government officials. But what does "unreasonable searches and seizures" mean? The automobile did not exist in 1787, when the Constitution was written. Does the 4th Amendment allow the police to stop and search a car? In the case of *United States* v. *Ross* (1982), the Supreme Court decided that they could.

The Supreme Court is often called upon to answer such questions. Its decisions help to update the Constitution to reflect changing times and circumstances. Decisions by judges who interpret and apply the Constitution to specific cases help to add substance to the general framework of government established by the Constitution. These judicial decisions formulate *constitutional law*.

A constitution delegates powers to various types of public officials who run different parts of the government. For example, Article 1 of the Constitution grants the Congress certain lawmaking powers. Section 8 grants Congress such powers as regulation of commerce among the states, coining money and regulating its value, and raising and supporting the military forces.

The Constitution also specifies certain powers that the Congress may *not* exercise. According to Article 1, Section 9, Congress may not take money "from the treasury, but in consequence of appropriations made by law." Similarly, Amendment 1 limits the power of Congress: "Congress shall make no law...abridging the freedom of speech, or of the press."

Several other sections of the Constitution assign duties and powers to the public officials heading different branches of the government (Article 1,

The "Constitutional Centennial March" of 1887 celebrated the adoption of the U.S. Constitution.

Section 8, concerns the Congress; Article 2, Section 2, concerns the Presidency; and Article 3, Section 2, deals with the judiciary). For example, the President can dispatch military forces to put down civil disorder or rebellion or to enforce federal laws if necessary. The Constitution also places limits on the powers of officials such as the President, Supreme Court justices, and members of Congress.

Such limitations on the expressed powers granted to the government protect the liberties of the people. For example, although the U.S. Treasury Department collects taxes, an act of Congress must authorize any expenditure of that tax money. More generally, the first 10 amendments to the Constitution, known collectively as the Bill of Rights, protect the liberties of the people.

All government officials must follow the Constitution when carrying out their duties. For example, the Constitution (Article 6) says that "no religious test shall ever be required as a qualification to any office of public trust in the United States." Thus the President may not require any employees of the executive branch of government to attend church services in order to keep their jobs.

The U.S. Constitution grants powers in the name of the people, and the government draws its power from the consent of the governed. The document assumes that government officials will use their powers in the interests of the people. The preamble to the Constitution says, "We the People of the United States...do ordain and establish this Constitution for the United States of America."

Representatives of the people wrote and approved the Constitution of the United States. Granting certain powers to government in the name of the people gives legitimacy to the government because most of the people, viewing it as legal and proper, are likely to find it acceptable.

SEE ALSO

Amendments to the Constitution; Bill of Rights; Constitutional democracy; Constitutionalism; Constitutional law

FURTHER READING

Anastaplo, George. *The Constitution of 1787: A Commentary.* Baltimore: Johns Hopkins University Press, 1989.
Currie, David P. *The Constitution of the United States: A Primer for the People.* Chicago: University of Chicago Press, 1988.
Ritchie, Donald A. *The U.S. Constitution.* New York: Chelsea House, 1989.

Contempt power of the courts

THE JUDICIARY ACT of 1789 gives federal courts the power to punish an individual for contempt. A person is deemed in contempt of court when he disobeys a court's order or shows disrespect for its authority.

Contract clause

ARTICLE 1, Section 10, of the U.S. Constitution says, "No State shall…pass any…Law impairing the Obligation of Contracts." This contract clause prohibits any state government from passing a law that would interfere with contracts made by citizens, either by weakening the obligations assumed by parties to a contract or by making a contract difficult to enforce. The Supreme Court's decisions in *Fletcher* v. *Peck* (1810) and *Dartmouth College* v. *Woodward* (1819) were landmark decisions that used the contract clause to uphold the sanctity of contracts.

The contract clause applies to contracts between private individuals or contracts made by a state government.

However, if a contract endangers the health, safety, or welfare of the public, the state may regulate or void it. The state's authority to protect the public in this way is known as its police power. During the 20th century, the Court has often ruled in favor of state regulation or modification of contracts in the public interest.

SEE ALSO

Dartmouth College v. Woodward; Fletcher v. Peck

Cooper v. Aaron

☆ *358 U.S. 1 (1958)*
☆ *Vote: 9–0*
☆ *For the Court: Warren*
☆ *Concurring: Frankfurter*

In *Brown* v. *Board of Education* (1954), the Court ruled against racial segregation in public schools. However, school districts in most southern states were slow to carry out the *Brown* decision.

In the fall of 1957, the people of Little Rock, Arkansas, faced the first phase of the school board's very deliberate school desegregation plan. The day before desegregation was to begin, Governor Orval Faubus placed soldiers of the Arkansas National Guard at Central High School. The governor said they were there to keep order. But the federal district court ordered the National Guard removed because of a well-founded suspicion that Governor Faubus would use them to stop black students from entering the school.

The National Guard was withdrawn, and white protesters around the school rioted to prevent the black children from entering the high school. President Dwight Eisenhower sent in the 101st Airborne paratroopers to keep order and protect the nine black students at Central High School.

When a mob of white people gathered to protest the racial integration of Central High School in Little Rock, Arkansas, President Dwight Eisenhower sent federal troops to protect black students.

In February 1958 the federal district court gave the Little Rock school board permission for a two-year delay in carrying out school desegregation. In addition, the Arkansas legislature passed a law authorizing the governor to close all public schools required by the federal courts to desegregate. In this way, Governor Faubus and the state legislature directly challenged the supremacy of U.S. constitutional law—specifically, the *Brown* decision—with regard to the issue of school desegregation.

In response to the slow pace and threatened postponement of school desegregation in Little Rock, the National Association for the Advancement of Colored People (NAACP) filed suit in the federal district court. The suit was filed against William G. Cooper, president of the school board, on behalf of John Aaron and 32 other students.

The federal district and appellate courts had upheld the slow-paced desegregation plan. So the NAACP appealed to the U.S. Supreme Court. Chief Justice Earl Warren convened a special session of the Court in the summer of 1958 to hear this case.

The Issue The NAACP attorneys argued that the slow pace of school desegregation violated the Supreme Court's decision in *Brown* v. *Board of Education* (1954) and *Brown II* (1955) and the black students' rights to equal protection of the laws provided by the 14th Amendment. They pointed to the two-year postponement in implementation of desegregation permitted by the federal district court. Despite the importance of the NAACP's argument about the violation of constitutional rights, an even greater issue was enforcement of U.S. Supreme Court decisions. Could a state government enact and enforce legislation designed to prevent implementation of a Supreme Court decision?

Opinion of the Court The Court ruled against any delay by the Little Rock school board in carrying out its desegregation plan. And the Court strongly rejected the idea that a state government could ignore or actively oppose enforcement of U.S. Supreme Court decisions. Chief Justice Earl Warren wrote that the rights of black students could "neither be nullified openly and directly by state legislatures or state executive officials nor nullified indirectly by them by evasive schemes for segregation."

Significance The *Cooper* case was the Supreme Court's first opportunity to rule on the enforcement of its decision in *Brown* v. *Board of Education* (1954). Further, *Cooper* provided the Court a grand opportunity to assert the supremacy of constitutional law over the states. However, the immediate impact of the *Cooper* decision on school desegregation was slight. Not until the civil rights activities of the 1960s, and especially the passage of the Civil Rights Act of 1964, did school desegregation begin to occur extensively throughout the United States.

SEE ALSO

Brown v. Board of Education; Civil rights

FURTHER READING

Freyer, Tony. *The Little Rock Crisis: A Constitutional Interpretation.* Westport, Conn.: Greenwood Press, 1984.

Counsel, right to

THE 6TH AMENDMENT to the U.S. Constitution provides that "in all criminal prosecutions, the accused shall… have the assistance of counsel for his defence." This right of an accused person was not applied consistently to state governments until 1963, when the Court ruled in *Gideon* v. *Wainwright* that counsel must be provided for defendants in all state felony cases. If a defendant could not afford to pay for the services of counsel, then the state would be required to provide counsel for him. The guarantee of the right to counsel was extended to all state-level misdemeanor cases in *Argersinger* v. *Hamlin* (1972).

The *Gideon* case applied the right to counsel to the states through the due process clause of the 14th Amendment. This is an example of the Court's use of the incorporation doctrine to extend rights in the federal Bill of Rights to the state level.

SEE ALSO

Due process of law; Gideon v. Wainwright; Incorporation doctrine; Rights of the accused

Court-packing plan

ON FEBRUARY 5, 1937, President Franklin D. Roosevelt sent to Congress his Judicial Reorganization Bill. It called for adding one justice to the Supreme Court for every member over 70 years of age, up to a total of six additional justices.

The President claimed that he wanted to add new justices to increase the Court's efficiency in dealing with a heavy work load. His real motive, however, was to pack the Court with justices favorable to his New Deal political and economic reforms. The Supreme Court had struck down, as unconstitutional, such New Deal programs as the National Industrial Recovery Act, the Railroad Retirement Act, and the Agricultural Adjustment Act.

President Roosevelt's court-packing plan was controversial. Opponents claimed he was trying to destroy the independence of the judiciary to gain political advantage. Roosevelt, however, pushed hard for Congress to pass his bill, and it seemed that he had the votes needed to pass the Judicial Reorganization Bill.

In March 1937 the Court made two decisions favorable to President Roosevelt's New Deal policies in *West Coast Hotel Co.* v. *Parrish* and *National Labor Relations Board* v. *Jones & Laughlin Steel Corp.* Justice Owen Roberts, who had previously voted against New Deal programs, switched his position in these two critical cases. Newspaper writers called Justice Roberts's change in position the "switch in time that saved nine." The momentum for the President's court-packing plan declined in the wake of the two decisions. Further, anti–New Deal justice Willis Van Devanter announced his retirement, giving President Roosevelt the chance to nominate a justice favorable to his views. So the number of Supreme Court justices remained at nine, and the perceived political threat to judicial independence was ended.

Franklin Roosevelt shows off his plan for an expanded Supreme Court. FDR abandoned his controversial court-packing plan after the Court upheld important New Deal programs in 1937.

SEE ALSO
National Labor Relations Board v. Jones & Laughlin Steel Corp.; West Coast Hotel Co. v. Parrish

Court reporters

SEE Reporter of decisions

Courts of Appeals

THE U.S. COURTS OF APPEALS are the middle level of the federal judicial system. They stand between the federal district courts at the bottom and the Supreme Court of the United States at the top.

The Courts of Appeals have no original jurisdiction; they do not hear the first trial of a case. They hear only cases on appeal from the lower courts. In turn, cases may be appealed from the Court of Appeal to the highest court, the Supreme Court.

At present, the United States and its territories are divided into 12 circuits, or geographical areas in which a court of appeals is located. There are appellate circuits numbered 1 through 11 plus the Court of Appeals for the District of Columbia. In addition, the Federal Courts Improvement Act of 1982 created the U.S. Court of Appeals for the Federal Circuit, which takes cases on appeal from such specialized lower courts as the Court of Claims, the Court of Customs and Patent Appeals, and the Court of Veterans Appeals. There are more than 150 judges serving on the U.S. Courts of Appeals. The U.S. Court of Appeals for the Ninth Circuit (West Coast) has 28 judges, the largest number. The U.S. Court of Appeals for the First Circuit (the New England states) has only 6 judges, the least number. All appellate court judges are appointed by the President with the advice and consent of the Senate, as provided by Article 2, Section 3, of the Constitution.

The U.S. Courts of Appeals have appellate jurisdiction—they review the decisions of lower courts—over two main types of cases. The first type involves civil and criminal case appeals from the federal district courts, including the U.S. territorial courts (in U.S. territories such as Guam and Puerto Rico) and special courts such as the U.S. Tax Court. The second type involves appeals by individuals of decisions made by federal administrative agencies and independent regulatory commissions, such as the National Labor Relations Board. Most cases that come to the Courts of Appeals are of the first type.

SEE ALSO
Circuit Courts of Appeals; Federal judicial system

Criminal law

THE BODY of law that pertains to crimes against public authority—the federal or state governments, for example—is known as criminal law. These are the statutes that executive branch officials have the power to enforce. People who violate these laws may be apprehended by police and tried in a court of law. If convicted, they face the punishment prescribed by the trial court. If the convicted person feels that his constitutional rights have been violated, he may appeal the case to the Supreme Court.

SEE ALSO
Civil law; Rights of the accused

Cruel and unusual punishment

THE 8TH AMENDMENT to the Constitution prohibits the government from inflicting "cruel and unusual punishments." Individuals are protected from inhumane punishments, such as torture, burning at the stake, or crucifixion. Further, any punishment considered too severe in relation to the crime committed has been judged by the Court as "cruel and unusual punishment." In *Weems* v. *United States* (1910), for example, the Court overturned a sentence of 12 to 20 years in chains for a person convicted of giving false testimony. The Court judged this sentence to be cruel and unusual punishment because the penalty was out of proportion to the crime.

In 1972, in *Furman* v. *Georgia*, the Court decided that the death penalty was cruel and unusual punishment. In 1976, however, the Court held in *Gregg* v. *Georgia* that the death penalty is not necessarily an example of cruel and unusual punishment as long as systematic procedures are followed to eliminate arbitrary or racially discriminatory use of capital punishment.

Chief Justice Earl Warren aptly described the intent of the ban against cruel and unusual punishment in *Trop* v.

Dulles (1958): "The basic concept underlying the Eighth Amendment is nothing less than the dignity of man. While the State has the power to punish, the Amendment stands to assure that this power be exercised within the limits of civilized standards." Warren also discussed the relationship of the ban on cruel and unusual punishment to community standards: "The Court [has] recognized… that the words of the [Eighth] Amendment are not precise, and that their scope is not static. The Amendment draws its meaning from the evolving standards of decency that mark the progress of a maturing society."

SEE ALSO
Capital punishment; Furman v. Georgia

Curator, Office of the

SEE Staff of the Court, nonjudicial

Curtis, Benjamin R.

ASSOCIATE JUSTICE, 1851–57

☆ *Born: Nov. 4, 1809, Watertown, Mass.*
☆ *Education: Harvard College, A.B., 1829; Harvard Law School, LL.B., 1832*
☆ *Previous government service: Massachusetts state representative, 1849–51*
☆ *Appointed by President Millard Fillmore as a recess appointment Sept. 22, 1851; replaced Levi Woodbury, who died; nominated by Fillmore Dec. 11, 1851*
☆ *Supreme Court term: confirmed by the Senate Dec. 20, 1851, by a voice vote; resigned Sept. 30, 1857*
☆ *Died: Sept. 15, 1874, Newport, R.I.*

BENJAMIN R. CURTIS served only six years as an associate justice of the U.S. Supreme Court. But his dissent in the Dred Scott case is a lasting monument of

Various torture methods used in the Tower of London in the Middle Ages. The U.S. Constitution prohibits cruel and unusual punishments, such as torture, for crimes.

the struggle for equal rights by African Americans.

Dred Scott, a slave, brought suit against his master, claiming himself a free man because he had lived in areas that banned slavery. The Court decided against Scott and ruled that he had no right to bring a suit to the federal courts.

Justice Curtis disagreed with every major point of the majority opinion in *Scott* v. *Sandford* (1857). He argued that African Americans could be citizens of the United States, although the majority argued that slaves were merely property. If so, they had the right to bring suits to the federal courts. Curtis also held that the federal government had authority under the Constitution to regulate or prevent slavery in territories of the United States. By contrast, Chief Justice Roger Taney's argument for the Court was an attempt to protect slavery against federal government regulation and to deny all constitutional rights to African Americans.

Taney's ideas prevailed in the *Dred Scott* case, but Curtis won in the long run. The 14th Amendment, ratified in 1868, embodies Curtis's ideas about citizenship and constitutional rights. Today, Taney's opinion in the *Dred Scott* case is generally viewed as one of the worst decisions in the history of the Court.

Curtis left the Court a few months after the *Dred Scott* decision. This case caused serious conflict and hostility between Curtis and his associates on the Court. He decided he could no longer work comfortably and cooperatively with Chief Justice Taney and some other justices, and so he resigned.

Curtis returned to the practice of law and continued to attract national attention for his achievements. In 1868, for example, he successfully defended President Andrew Johnson in his impeachment trial. He also argued more than 50 cases before the U.S. Supreme Court.

SEE ALSO
Scott v. Sandford

FURTHER READING
Fehrenbacher, Don E. *The Dred Scott Case.* New York: Oxford, 1978.

Cushing, William

ASSOCIATE JUSTICE, 1790–1810

☆ *Born: Mar. 1, 1732, Scituate, Mass.*
☆ *Education: Harvard College, A.B., 1751, M.A., 1754; Yale University, M.A., 1753 studied law under Jeremiah Gridley, Boston*
☆ *Previous government service: judge, probate court for Lincoln, Mass. (now Maine), 1760–61; judge, Superior Court of Massachusetts Bay Province, 1772–77; chief justice, Superior Court of the Commonwealth of Massachusetts, 1777–89; Massachusetts Constitutional Convention, 1779; vice president, Massachusetts Ratifying Convention, 1788; delegate to the electoral college, 1788*
☆ *Appointed by President George Washington Sept. 24, 1789, to fill one of the original six seats on the U.S. Supreme Court*
☆ *Supreme Court term: confirmed by the Senate Sept. 26, 1789, by a voice vote; served until Sept. 13, 1810*
☆ *Died: Sept. 13, 1810, Scituate, Mass.*

WILLIAM CUSHING was an original member of the U.S. Supreme Court. He was the last judge in the United States to wear a full wig, a traditional adornment for British judges. Cushing did not stop wearing his wig until 1790.

Justice Cushing served 21 years on the Court, the longest term of President George Washington's original appointments, but wrote only 19 opinions. His most important opinion, *Ware* v. *Hylton* (1796), agreed with the Court's majority that a federal treaty cannot be violated by a state law.

SEE ALSO
Ware v. Hylton

Daniel, Peter V.

*ASSOCIATE JUSTICE,
1842–60*

☆ *Born: Apr. 24, 1784, Stafford County,
Va.*

☆ *Education: College of New Jersey
(Princeton), 1802–3; studied law with
Edmund Randolph in Richmond, Va.*

☆ *Previous government service: Virginia
House of Delegates, 1809–12; Virginia
Privy Council, 1812–35; lieutenant
governor of Virginia, 1818–35; U.S.
district judge, Eastern District of
Virginia, 1836–41*

☆ *Appointed by President Martin Van
Buren Feb. 26, 1841; replaced Philip
Barbour, who died*

☆ *Supreme Court term: confirmed by the
Senate Mar. 2, 1841, by a 22–5 vote;
served until May 31, 1860*

☆ *Died: May 31, 1860, Richmond, Va.*

PETER V. DANIEL was a loyal supporter of Andrew Jackson and the
Democratic party. After becoming President, Andrew Jackson rewarded Daniel
with an appointment to the federal judiciary in Virginia.

Daniel continued his support of the
Democrats and was appointed to the
U.S. Supreme Court by President Martin
Van Buren. Justice Daniel tended to support the rights and powers of state governments in cases regarding the exercise
of power in the federal system.

FURTHER READING

Frank, John P. *Justice Daniel Dissenting.*
Cambridge: Harvard University Press,
1964.

Dartmouth College v. Woodward

☆ *4 Wheat. 518 (1819)*
☆ *Vote: 5–1*
☆ *For the Court: Marshall*
☆ *Concurring: Story and Washington*
☆ *Dissenting: Duvall*

DARTMOUTH COLLEGE was established in 1769 by a charter from King
George III of England. After the formation of the United States, the agreement
with the king became an agreement with
the state of New Hampshire. In 1816
that state's legislature passed several
amendments to the college's charter. By
placing the school under the authority of
the state government, these amendments
had the effect of changing the private college into a state university.

Officials and friends of Dartmouth
College objected. They believed the state
legislature should not possess the authority to destroy the private nature of their
college.

The Issue Daniel Webster, arguing
for the Dartmouth College trustees,
maintained that the legislature had violated Article 1, Section 10, of the Constitution, which provides that "no State
shall…pass any…Law impairing the Obligation of Contracts." In an 1810 case
(*Fletcher* v. *Peck*), the Supreme Court
had ruled that a land grant is a contract.
Webster now argued that "a grant of
corporate powers and privileges is as
much a contract as a grant of land."

Is a charter a contract? Did the
Constitution's contract clause protect
private corporate charters, such as
Dartmouth's?

Opinion of the Court The Court
ruled in favor of Dartmouth College.
Chief Justice John Marshall's opinion
held that the charter of a private corporation was a contract. Thus, the Constitution forbade the state legislature from
changing that agreement. For the first
time, the Court extended the protection
of the Constitution's contract clause to a
corporate charter. Marshall intended
this ruling to be an important limitation
on the powers and rights of state governments within the federal Union.

In 1816, the New Hampshire legislature passed several amendments to the charter of Dartmouth College. Claiming that the state had violated its contract, the college took its case to the Supreme Court and won.

Dissent Justice Gabriel Duvall dissented in this case. However, he did not file an opinion.

Significance The decision increased the power of the federal government over the states. It reaffirmed that the U.S. Supreme Court could invalidate state laws when it found those laws unconstitutional. Further, the case reinforced the practice begun by *Fletcher* v. *Peck* of imposing restrictions upon state legislatures with regard to the regulation of corporations. The national government would not allow state legislatures to void or change existing charters because to do so would violate the contract clause of Article 1, Section 9, of the Constitution.

The *Dartmouth College* decision did not attract the attention of the press at the time. Yet it deserves recognition as one of the early Court's important decisions. Business corporations were just forming in a young nation, and the Court's decision gave these businesses security against unexpected legislative interference.

Such security was vital to those who might invest money in new industries and corporations. Investors could be sure that any rights granted a corporation by one state legislature could not be taken away by some future legislature. Such assurances encouraged investment in railroads and other new industries, which in turn stimulated the country's economic development. The *Dartmouth College* case did not, however, prevent states from regulating corporations. The decision merely held that a state government could not alter corporate charters it had already granted, unless the state reserved the right to do so when it initially granted the charter.

After the resolution of the *Dartmouth College* case, many state legislatures placed restrictions on companies they chartered. These new corporate charters often contained clauses allowing the state, under certain circumstances, to revoke the charters or to buy the companies. Nevertheless, the *Dartmouth College* decision encouraged investors by assuring them that the Supreme Court would regulate state grants and charters and that after the granting of a charter, the grantees could expect the courts to protect their rights.

SEE ALSO

Contract clause; Federalism; Fletcher v. Peck

FURTHER READING

Current, Richard N. "The Dartmouth College Case." In *Quarrels That Have Shaped the Constitution*, edited by John A. Garraty. New York: Harper & Row, 1987.

Data Systems Office

THE DATA SYSTEMS OFFICE maintains technological facilities and equipment, such as computers, printers, and photocopy machines, for the Court. The office electronically transmits (through computers) opinions of the Court to outside agencies. Court documents are processed (typed, printed, and copied) for the justices through the Data Systems Office. In addition, the office works with the Public Information Office to electronically transmit the bench copies of the Court's opinions to organizations outside the Court.

Davis, David

ASSOCIATE JUSTICE, 1862–77

☆ *Born: Mar. 9, 1815, Sassafras Neck, Md.*
☆ *Education: Kenyon College, B.A., 1832; Yale Law School, 1835*
☆ *Previous government service: Illinois House of Representatives, 1845–47; Illinois Constitutional Convention, 1847; Illinois State circuit court judge, 1848–62*
☆ *Appointed by President Abraham Lincoln as a recess appointment Oct. 17, 1862; replaced John A. Campbell, who resigned; nominated by Lincoln Dec. 1, 1862*
☆ *Supreme Court term: confirmed by the Senate Dec. 8, 1862, by a voice vote; resigned Mar. 4, 1877*
☆ *Died: June 26, 1886, Bloomington, Ill.*

DAVID DAVIS practiced law in Illinois, where he met Abraham Lincoln. Their friendship had a strong influence on Davis's career. He supported Lincoln's losing 1854 campaign for the U.S. Senate. Davis was Lincoln's campaign manager in 1860, when Lincoln won the Republican nomination for the Presidency and became the 16th President of the United States. In 1862, Lincoln appointed Davis to the Supreme Court.

Davis's outstanding contribution as an associate justice was his opinion for the Court in *Ex parte Milligan* (1866), a landmark decision. In the *Milligan* case, the Court decided that a military court in Indiana, created by order of the President, had illegally tried and convicted a man for the crime of aiding the Confederacy during the Civil War. Justice Davis argued that Indiana had not been a war zone and the civilian courts had remained open. Therefore, it was a denial of Milligan's constitutional rights to try him in a military court. Davis concluded that the Constitution could not be suspended in a national crisis, not even during a civil war, and that the Constitution

was "a law for rulers and people, equally in time of war and peace."

SEE ALSO
Ex parte Milligan

Day, William R.

ASSOCIATE JUSTICE, 1903–22

☆ *Born: Apr. 17, 1849, Ravenna, Ohio*
☆ *Education: University of Michigan, B.A., 1870; University of Michigan Law School, 1871–72*
☆ *Other government service: judge, Court of Common Pleas, Canton, Ohio, 1886–90; first assistant U.S. secretary of state, 1897–98; U.S. secretary of state, 1898; U.S. delegation, Paris Peace Conference, 1898–99; judge, U.S. Court of Appeals for the Sixth Circuit, 1899–1903; umpire, Mixed Claims Commission, 1922–23*
☆ *Appointed by President Theodore Roosevelt Feb. 19, 1903; replaced George Shiras, Jr., who resigned*
☆ *Supreme Court term: confirmed by the Senate Feb. 23, 1903, by a voice vote; resigned Nov. 13, 1922*
☆ *Died: July 9, 1923, Mackinac Island, Mich.*

WILLIAM R. DAY became a prominent lawyer and Republican party leader in Ohio. He developed a close friendship with William McKinley, who relied upon Day for support and advice. After McKinley became President, he appointed Day assistant secretary of state and later secretary of state. In 1899, McKinley further rewarded Day with an appointment to the U.S. Court of Appeals for the Sixth Circuit. McKinley's successor as President, Theodore Roosevelt, named Day to the Supreme Court.

During his 19 years on the Court, Justice Day tended to be an advocate for state powers and rights in the federal system. However, Day did support the power of the federal government to regulate businesses under the Sherman Anti-Trust Act.

FURTHER READING

McLean, Joseph E. *William Rufus Day: Supreme Court Justice from Ohio.* Baltimore: Johns Hopkins University Press, 1946.

Death penalty

SEE Capital punishment

Decision days

THE SUPREME COURT's decisions on cases are announced orally to the public in the Supreme Court chamber (courtroom). The justice who wrote the Court's opinion on the case announces the decision. Justices who wrote concurring or dissenting opinions may also state their position. The writers of the opinions may either briefly summarize their positions or simply state the result.

From 1857 until 1965 the Court followed a tradition of announcing decisions only on Mondays. But on April 15, 1965, the Court announced that it was ending the "Decision Monday" tradition. Now, in weeks when the Court hears oral arguments, opinions are announced on Tuesdays and Wednesdays. During other weeks, decisions are announced on Mondays.

Dennis v. United States

☆ *341 U.S. 494 (1951)*
☆ *Vote: 6–2*
☆ *For the Court: Vinson*
☆ *Concurring: Frankfurter and Jackson*
☆ *Dissenting: Black and Douglas*
☆ *Not participating: Clark*

IN 1940, Congress passed a law banning sedition. It was known as the Smith Act after its sponsor, Representative Howard Smith of Virginia. The Smith Act made it a crime "to knowingly and willfully advocate, abet, advise or teach the duty, necessity, desirability, or propriety of overthrowing or destroying any government in the United States by force or violence." Further, the Smith Act made it a crime for anyone to organize a group with the mission of violently overthrowing the U.S. government.

After World War II, the United States and the Soviet Union—allies during the war—became enemies locked in a cold war. Members of the Communist Party of the United States of America (CPUSA) were suspected of collaborating with the Communist party leaders of the Soviet Union. A central part of the communist ideology was the inevitability of violent revolution to advance the cause of communism throughout the world. Given this perceived threat, many American political leaders urged use of the Smith Act to crack down on American communists.

In 1949 the federal government arrested and convicted 11 members of the CPUSA, including Eugene Dennis, for violating the Smith Act. Dennis appealed on the grounds that the Smith Act was unconstitutional.

The Issue The 1st Amendment of the Constitution says, "Congress shall make no law…abridging the freedom of speech, or of the press." Eugene Dennis was convicted under the Smith Act, however, because of the political ideas he expressed. Did the Smith Act violate the 1st Amendment?

Opinion of the Court The Court voted to uphold the conviction of Dennis and 10 other members of the CPUSA. Chief Justice Fred M. Vinson announced

Eugene Dennis (second from left) and other members of the Communist party were arrested for advocating overthrow of the U.S. government. The Court upheld Dennis's conviction, ruling that free speech could be limited to protect national security.

the decision in this case. He argued that protecting the national security of the United States justified use of the Smith Act to limit the free speech of individuals advocating forcible overthrow of the national government.

Vinson wrote, "Overthrow of the government by force and violence…is certainly a substantial enough interest for the Government to limit speech. Indeed this is the ultimate value of any society, for if a society cannot protect its very structure from armed internal attack, it must follow that no subordinate value can be protected." According to Vinson's opinion, it was reasonable to limit free speech of communists to protect the security of the United States.

Dissent Justices Hugo Black and William O. Douglas believed the Smith Act was unconstitutional. Justice Black wrote:

> I cannot agree that the First Amendment permits us to sustain laws suppressing freedom of speech and press on the basis of Congress's or our own notions of mere "reasonableness." Such a doctrine waters down the First Amendment so that it amounts to little more than an admonition to Congress. The Amendment as so construed is not likely to protect any but those "safe"

or orthodox views which rarely need its protection….

Public opinion being what it now is, few will protest the conviction of these Communist petitioners. There is hope, however, that in calmer times when present pressures, passions and fears subside, this or some later Court will restore the First Amendment liberties to the high preferred place where they belong in a free society.

Significance In the short run, the *Dennis* judgment encouraged the U.S. Department of Justice to suppress free speech by Communist party members. In the long run, however, the Court did fulfill Justice Black's hope. In a similar case, *Yates* v. *United States* (1957), the Court refused to uphold the convictions of Communist party members for violating the Smith Act. From that point on, the Smith Act, though held to be constitutional, was no longer used to suppress political activities of communists or anyone else.

S E E   A L S O
Freedom of speech and press; Yates v. United States

Discuss list

THE JUSTICES make decisions at the Court's conference about which cases to hear. However, not all requests for hearings are discussed. The justices make decisions at the conference only on cases that appear on a discuss list, from which many requests have been eliminated. The chief justice is in charge of creating the discuss list. He includes cases that, in his judgment, merit discussion before a decision is made about whether the Court should review the cases.

The discuss list is circulated in advance of the conference to all the justices. Any justice who thinks a case has been wrongly omitted may add it to the list. Each appeal from lower courts for the Supreme Court to hear a case is reviewed by each justice. Only those cases on the discuss list, however, are discussed at the regular conference of the justices.

Only about 30 percent of all the cases sent to the Court for review make the discuss list. The other petitions for review are rejected without further consideration by the Court. The discuss list is a means for reducing the time-consuming work of the Court by greatly reducing the number of cases discussed at conferences.

Dissenting opinion

ONE OR more justices often disagree with the majority of the Court on how to decide a case. Justices who disagree with the majority are dissenters. They interpret the law, as it applies to a case, in a way that differs from the majority's interpretation. A dissenting opinion is different from the concurring opinion, which agrees with the Court's decision but provides an explanation that differs from the majority opinion.

A justice who disagrees with the verdict in a case usually writes a dissenting opinion, though there is no requirement that a dissent be accompanied by an opinion. However, most dissenting justices do write one to explain why they disagree with the majority decision. For example, in *Plessy* v. *Ferguson* (1896), the Court let stand a state law requiring trains to provide "separate but equal" facilities for black and white passengers. Justice John Marshall Harlan wrote a dissenting opinion in which he said that "the Constitution is color-blind, and neither knows nor tolerates classes among citizens."

A dissenting opinion is not an attempt to change the minds of the Court's majority because the Court has already reached a final decision before the dissenting opinion is written. Rather, the dissenter hopes to arouse public opinion against the majority opinion.

Ultimately, the dissenting judge hopes that the Court will reconsider the majority opinion and overrule it and that his opinion will someday become the basis for a majority opinion in a similar case. Chief Justice Charles Evans Hughes wrote: "A dissent in a court of last resort is an appeal to the brooding spirit of the law, to the intelligence of a future day, when a later decision may possibly correct the error into which the dissenting judge believes the court to have been betrayed."

For example, Justice Harlan's 1896 dissent in *Plessy* was vindicated by the majority opinion in *Brown* v. *Board of Education* (1954), in which the Court unanimously rejected the "separate but equal" doctrine and ruled that racially segregated public schools were inherently unequal. Similarly, Justice Hugo Black's dissenting opinion in *Betts* v. *Brady* (1942), in which he wrote that criminal defendants in state courts have the right to counsel, became the majority opinion in *Gideon* v. *Wainwright* (1963).

Over the course of history, however, dissenting opinions have rarely been incorporated into later decisions. Justice Oliver Wendell Holmes, who was known as the Great Dissenter, wrote 173 dissenting opinions during 30 years on the Supreme Court. Yet few of Holmes's dissenting opinions sparked reversals of court decisions.

The Supreme Court does not readily admit errors and overrule past decisions. The principle of *stare decisis* ("Let the decision stand") has a powerful influence on the Court. Justices usually accept precedents established in earlier Court decisions as guides in deciding later cases.

Oliver Wendell Holmes (left) and Louis D. Brandeis were known for their eloquent and frequent dissenting opinions.

SEE ALSO
Concurring opinion; Opinions; Precedent

FURTHER READING
Barth, Alan. *Prophets With Honor: Great Dissents and Great Dissenters on the Supreme Court.* New York: Random House, 1974.

Double jeopardy

THE 5TH AMENDMENT to the U.S. Constitution provides that no person shall "be subject for the same offence to be twice put in jeopardy of life or limb." This provision is known as the double jeopardy clause. It protects individuals against repeated prosecution by the government for a single alleged crime. In *Benton* v. *Maryland* (1969), the Court decided that the 5th Amendment's double jeopardy clause is incorporated by the due process clause of the 14th Amendment and thereby applicable to the states.

The double jeopardy clause protects an individual in three ways. First, it protects a person from being prosecuted a second time for the same offense after being declared innocent of this offense. Second, it protects a person from a second prosecution for the same crime after conviction for this offense. Third, in addition to prohibiting more than one prosecution, the double jeopardy clause protects an individual from being *punished* more than once for the same crime.

The great importance of the double jeopardy clause of the Constitution was emphasized by Justice Hugo L. Black in *Green* v. *United States* (1957): "The underlying idea…is that the State with all its resources and power should not be allowed to make repeated attempts to convict an individual for an alleged offense, thereby subjecting him to embarrassment, expense and ordeal and compel-

ling him to live in a continuing state of anxiety and insecurity; as well as enhancing the possibility that even though innocent he may be found guilty."

SEE ALSO
Benton v. Maryland

Douglas, William O.

ASSOCIATE JUSTICE, 1939–75

☆ *Born: Oct. 16, 1898, Maine, Minn.*
☆ *Education: Whitman College, B.A., 1920; Columbia Law School, LL.B., 1925*
☆ *Previous government service: Securities and Exchange Commission, 1936–39; chairman, 1937–39*
☆ *Appointed by President Franklin D. Roosevelt Mar. 20, 1939; replaced Louis D. Brandeis, who retired*
☆ *Supreme Court term: confirmed by the Senate Apr. 4, 1939, by a 62–4 vote; retired Nov. 12, 1975*
☆ *Died: Jan. 19, 1980, Washington, D.C.*

WILLIAM O. DOUGLAS served on the Supreme Court for 36 years, longer than any other justice. He wrote more opinions than any justice before or since. And he was honored, before his death, with a lasting monument: Congress designated a parkland in Washington as the William O. Douglas National Park to commemorate his concern for the environment.

Douglas overcame crushing poverty and a crippling illness in his childhood to earn the great achievements and honors of his adult life. His father died when Douglas was five years old, leaving his mother with three children and almost no money. Later, he struggled with polio, which seriously weakened his legs. He took long walks in the mountains near his home to build strength in his legs, and his contact with nature influenced him to become a lifelong advocate of environmental causes. His childhood experiences also led Douglas to have sympathy for the "underdog"—a person who copes with poverty, physical handicaps, or racial discrimination.

William Douglas was an outstanding student in school, which opened opportunities for him to become a teacher, lawyer, and government official. His achievements as a lawyer attracted the attention of President Franklin D. Roosevelt, who appointed him to the Securities and Exchange Commission. He became a strong supporter of Roosevelt's New Deal economic recovery programs, and the President appointed him to the Supreme Court in 1939, to fill the seat of Louis Brandeis, who had retired.

Justice Douglas sought to defend the constitutional rights of individuals and professed that the Bill of Rights was meant "to keep government off the backs of people." He joined Justice Hugo Black to extend the limits of free expression and to promote "incorporation" of the Bill of Rights into Section 1 of the 14th Amendment, so that these constitutional rights could be used to protect individuals against abuses by state and local governments. Further, Justice Douglas joined with the majority of the Court under Chief Justice Earl Warren to defend the rights of African Americans, as in *Brown* v. *Board of Education* (1954) and *Cooper* v. *Aaron* (1958).

Douglas's most notable opinion for the Court was *Griswold* v. *Connecticut* (1965), in which he argued for a constitutional right to privacy based on his interpretation of the 1st, 3rd, 4th, 5th, and 9th Amendments. Although this opinion has prevailed, it also has been controversial because a right to privacy is not written specifically into the Constitution.

Douglas was a frequent writer of dissenting opinions, usually in defense of the rights of unpopular persons. He dissented, for example, in *Dennis* v. *United States* (1951), to protest the Court's decision to uphold convictions of American Communist party members for stating and writing that the U.S. government should be overthrown and replaced by a communist form of government. Douglas believed that the 1st Amendment forbade all government limitations upon the content of speech, or what a person could say. According to Justice Douglas, the Constitution gives the government power only to regulate the conduct of the speaker, that is, actions that pose a serious threat to the safety or property of people.

Justice Douglas often spoke and wrote about his beliefs on many topics. Many of his public statements were controversial or in opposition to commonly held viewpoints. As a result, many people disliked Douglas. He faced three attempts to impeach him, the last and most serious occurring in 1970, five years before his retirement from the Court.

Justice Douglas suffered a stroke on Dec. 31, 1974, which partially paralyzed him. Nearly a year later, Douglas left the Court. He died some four years later, a hero to many for his unyielding advocacy of individual rights, especially the rights of persons disliked or neglected by a majority of the people.

SEE ALSO

Griswold v. Connecticut; Incorporation doctrine; Privacy, right to

FURTHER READING

Ball, Howard, and Phillip J. Cooper. *Of Power and Right: Hugo Black, William O. Douglas, and America's Constitutional Revolution.* New York: Oxford University Press, 1992.

Douglas, William O. *The Court Years, 1939–1975: The Autobiography of William O. Douglas.* New York: Vintage, 1981.

Simon, James F. *Independent Journey: The Life of William O. Douglas.* New York: Harper & Row, 1980.

Urofsky, Melvin I. "William O. Douglas, Common-Law Judge." *Constitution* 4, no. 3 (Fall 1992): 48–58.

Dred Scott case

SEE Scott v. Sandford

Due process of law

THE 5TH and 14th Amendments to the U.S. Constitution guarantee individuals the right of due process of law, which is often referred to simply as "due process." The 5th Amendment states, "No person shall be...deprived of life, liberty, or property, without due process of law." The 14th Amendment states, "No state shall...deprive any person of life, liberty, or property, without due process of law."

These two due process clauses provide that the government must act fairly, according to established legal procedures, with regard to a person's rights to life, liberty, and property. Due process means, for example, that an individual accused of a crime is guaranteed certain legal procedural rights, such as the right to know the charges against him, to confront his accusers in court, to have legal counsel, and to have a jury trial. These and other rights of the accused are specified in the 4th, 5th, 6th, and 8th Amendments to the Constitution.

Procedural due process

These rights of the accused are examples of *procedural due process*, and they are constitutional limits on the power of government designed to protect the rights and liberties of individuals.

Procedural due process—the idea that government must follow fair and generally accepted legal procedures in its actions against individuals—has been traced to the great English charter of liberty, the Magna Carta (1215). By signing this document, King John of England agreed to "obey the law of the land." This idea developed into the legal guarantee of procedural due process of law to protect people against arbitrary or lawless punishments or penalties imposed by the government.

Due process of law was included in an act of the English Parliament in 1354, which affirmed the Magna Carta and specified "that no man...shall be put out of Land or Tenement, nor taken, nor imprisoned, nor disinherited, nor put to death, without being brought to Answer by due Process of Law." This English concept of due process was brought to North America by English colonists and was included in their colonial charters and laws. The Massachusetts Body of Liberties (1641), for example, provided that an individual could not be deprived of life, liberty, and property except by "some express law of the country warranting the same, established by a General Court and sufficiently published." The first American statute to use the words "due process of law" was an act of the colonial government of Massachusetts in 1682.

The original state constitutions, drafted during the founding era of the United States (1776–83), included rights of procedural due process. They typically limited these rights to the traditional "law of the land" idea that stems from the Magna Carta. The Northwest Ordinance, enacted by the U.S. Congress in 1787 to regulate new territories north and west of the Ohio River, also guaranteed procedural due process rights by declaring, "[N]o man shall be deprived of his liberty or property but by the judgment of his peers, or the law of the land."

By 1789, when the federal Bill of Rights was drafted by the first Congress,

King John of England signs the Magna Carta, which established the concept of the rule of law.

the concept of due process was an established part of American constitutions and criminal law. Consequently, it was expected that the right of due process would be included in the Bill of Rights.

Substantive due process

During the 20th century, the Supreme Court has reinforced and extended individual rights. This has been done through the development of *substantive due process* and the nationwide application of the federal Bill of Rights through the due process clause of the 14th Amendment.

Substantive due process concerns specific behaviors of individuals that, according to the Court, are generally beyond the reach of government power, such as the free exercise of religion or participation in private organizations that petition the government about public problems and issues. The government may not regulate these actions, not even by the use of the fairest legal procedures, because to do so would violate the most fundamental rights of individuals in a constitutional government, such as rights to liberty, property, and equality under the law. If government officials want to regulate these kinds of usually protected actions, they must demonstrate that they cannot achieve a legitimate public purpose by any other means.

From the 1890s through the 1920s, the Court tended to use substantive due process to protect the property rights of business owners against state government regulations of working conditions, wages paid to employees, and hours of work. Since the 1930s, and especially since the 1960s, the Court has used substantive due process to protect the civil rights of individuals, especially racial minorities and women, against state government actions that threatened these fundamental rights. Thus, the Court has used substantive due process to invali-

date hundreds of state laws pertaining to a wide variety of social and economic concerns and civil rights, such as fair conditions of employment.

The Court has, however, permitted state governments to regulate minimum wages and the working hours of employees in private businesses. These state regulations have been upheld, as necessary for the public good, against claims by business owners that they violate private property rights of individuals. This was the Court's ruling in *West Coast Hotel Co.* v. *Parrish* (1937), an early example of the use of substantive due process to protect and extend the rights of employees.

In the 20th century, the Supreme Court has used the due process clause of the 14th Amendment, which limits the powers of state governments, to apply most of the rights guaranteed by the federal Bill of Rights to the states. This use of the due process clause to protect the individual rights specified in the Bill of Rights against infringement by state and local governments has been referred to as the incorporation doctrine. This process has occurred gradually, on a case-by-case basis.

The Court's use of the incorporation doctrine and substantive due process has been controversial. Critics charge that substantive due process is a distortion of the original meaning of due process, which involved only adherence to formal and fair procedures by government officials in actions against individuals. Further, critics say that substantive due process has been used by judges to interfere in matters that should be left to resolution by majority vote in Congress or state legislatures. Finally, critics claim that substantive due process and the incorporation doctrine have been used by the U.S. Supreme Court to wrongly suppress the authority and power of state governments.

Virtually no one challenges the general value of due process of law as a guarantee of procedural consistency and fairness. Justice Felix Frankfurter expressed a commonly held view about procedural due process in *Malinski* v. *New York* (1945): "The history of American freedom is, in no small measure, the history of procedure." And in *Shaughnessy* v. *United States* (1953), Justice Robert Jackson stressed that controversy about substantive due process does not change the most fundamental and general agreement about procedural fairness, which "is what it [due process] most uncompromisingly requires."

SEE ALSO

Bill of Rights; Incorporation doctrine; West Coast Hotel Co. v. Parrish

FURTHER READING

Graham, Fred. *The Due Process Revolution: The Warren Court's Impact on Criminal Law*. New York: Hayden, 1970.

Duncan v. Louisiana

☆ *391 U.S. 145 (1968)*
☆ *Vote: 7–2*
☆ *For the Court: White*
☆ *Concurring: Black, Douglas, and Fortas*
☆ *Dissenting: Harlan and Stewart*

GARY DUNCAN was convicted of a misdemeanor—battery—and sentenced to 60 days in jail and a fine of $150. The maximum penalty for this offense was two years in jail and a $300 fine. Duncan had requested a trial by jury. The request was denied because the Louisiana constitution did not require a jury trial in cases involving lesser felonies or misdemeanors. Duncan appealed on the grounds that his rights under the U.S. Constitution had been violated.

The Issue Duncan claimed a 6th Amendment right to a jury trial. However, the Court had not yet used the 14th Amendment to apply this part of the federal Bill of Rights to the states. Was it constitutional for the state of Louisiana to deny Duncan a trial by jury?

Opinion of the Court The Court decided to incorporate the 6th Amendment right to trial by jury under the due process clause of the 14th Amendment, which provides that no state may "deprive any person of life, liberty, or property, without due process of law." Thus, the state of Louisiana had to provide a jury trial in cases like this one. Duncan's conviction was reversed because his right to a jury trial had been unconstitutionally denied. The Court held, however, that prosecutions for certain very minor offenses may not require a jury trial. Since Duncan's case involved a possible maximum imprisonment of two years, the Court decided this case was too serious to be tried without a jury.

Significance This was the first time that the 6th Amendment right to trial by jury was applied to a state through the 14th Amendment. This case, therefore, was part of the gradual process by which the Court has applied most parts of the federal Bill of Rights to the states.

SEE ALSO

Incorporation doctrine; Trial by jury

Duvall, Gabriel

ASSOCIATE JUSTICE, 1811–35

☆ *Born: Dec. 6, 1752, Prince Georges County, Md.*
☆ *Education: studied law privately*
☆ *Previous government service: clerk, Maryland Convention, 1775–76; clerk, Maryland House of Delegates, 1777–87; Maryland State Council, 1782–85; Maryland House of Delegates, 1787–94; U.S. representative from Maryland, 1794–96; chief justice, General Court of Maryland,*

1796–1802; presidential elector, 1796, 1800; first comptroller of the U.S. Treasury, 1802–11
☆ *Appointed by President James Madison Nov. 15, 1811; replaced Samuel Chase, who died*
☆ *Supreme Court term: confirmed by the Senate Nov. 18, 1811, by a voice vote; resigned Jan. 14, 1835*
☆ *Died: Mar. 6, 1844, Prince Georges County, Md.*

GABRIEL DUVALL served on the Supreme Court for a little more than 23 years. Despite this long period of service, he had a very small impact on the work of the Court and neither wrote significant opinions nor developed ideas to guide the work of his successors.

Duvall's appointment to prominent positions in the federal government, including the Supreme Court, was his reward for many years of loyal service to the Republican party founded by Thomas Jefferson and James Madison. President Jefferson appointed Duvall to be comptroller of the U.S. Treasury in 1802. President Madison appointed Duvall to the Supreme Court in 1811.

During the final 10 years of his Supreme Court service, Duvall was chronically ill and gradually lost his hearing. The infirmities greatly interfered with his ability to do his job, and he was repeatedly asked by his colleagues to resign. Justice Duvall resisted this advice until satisfied that he would be replaced by someone of whom he approved. Duvall resigned in 1835 after President Andrew Jackson promised him that Roger B. Taney, a friend of Duvall's from Maryland, would be named to the Court. In 1835, President Jackson appointed Philip Barbour of Virginia to replace Duvall, and in 1836 he named Taney to replace John Marshall as chief justice.

Ellsworth, Oliver

CHIEF JUSTICE, 1796–1800

☆ *Born: Apr. 29, 1745, Windsor, Conn.*
☆ *Education: College of New Jersey (Princeton), B.A., 1766*
☆ *Other government service: Connecticut General Assembly, 1773–76; state's attorney, Hartford County, Conn., 1777–85; Continental Congress, 1776–83; Connecticut Council of Safety, 1779; Governor's Council, 1780–85, 1801–7; judge, Connecticut Supreme Court, 1785–89; Constitutional Convention, 1787; U.S. senator from Connecticut, 1789–96*
☆ *Appointed by President George Washington Mar. 3, 1796; replaced John Jay, who resigned*
☆ *Supreme Court term: confirmed by the Senate Mar. 4, 1796, by a 21–1 vote; resigned Dec. 15, 1800*
☆ *Died: Nov. 26, 1807, Windsor, Conn.*

OLIVER ELLSWORTH was one of the leading founders of the United States of America. He played a major role in writing and supporting ratification of the U.S. Constitution. Later, as a senator from Connecticut in the first U.S. Congress, Ellsworth drafted the Judiciary Act of 1789, which set up the federal judicial system in line with Article 3 of the Constitution.

In 1796 President George Washington named Ellsworth chief justice of the United States, a position he held for only three years. Ellsworth had very little influence on development of the Court during his brief term. In 1799, Ellsworth agreed to President John Adams's request that he travel to France to repair broken relationships between the United States and its former ally, with which the United States was fighting an undeclared naval war. Ellsworth helped to resolve the problems with France, but he became ill while overseas and resigned as chief justice before returning to the United States.

Eminent domain

THE GOVERNMENT's power to take land for public use is called eminent domain. According to the 5th Amendment, "No person shall…be deprived of life, liberty, or property, without due process of law; nor shall private property be taken for public use without just compensation."

SEE ALSO
Just compensation

Engel v. Vitale

☆ *370 U.S. 421 (1962)*
☆ *Vote: 7–1*
☆ *For the Court: Black*
☆ *Concurring: Douglas*
☆ *Dissenting: Stewart*
☆ *Not participating: White*

THE BOARD OF REGENTS of the state of New York has the authority to supervise the state's educational system. In 1961, this state education board composed a short prayer: "Almighty God, we acknowledge our dependence upon Thee, and we beg Thy blessings upon us, our parents, our teachers, and our Country." The Board of Regents recommended daily recitation in schools of this nondenominational prayer, on a voluntary basis.

Although the Regents prayer was only a recommendation, the New Hyde Park Board of Education required that this prayer be said aloud at the beginning of each school day by each class of students in the district and in the presence of a teacher. The parents of 10 students objected to this requirement as a violation of the principle of separation of church and state in the 1st Amendment to the Constitution. They took legal action to compel the local board of education to discontinue the use in public schools of an official prayer that was contrary to their beliefs and practices.

The Issue Did the New York Board of Regents and the New Hyde Park Board of Education violate the 1st Amendment ban on laws "respecting an establishment of religion"?

Opinion of the Court The Court decided to strike down the Regents prayer. Justice Hugo Black, writing for the majority, said that the primary concern in this case was the creation of the prayer and the subsequent distribution of it throughout the state by an official agency of the state government. These actions violated the establishment clause of the 1st Amendment, which was applicable to the state of New York through the due process clause of the 14th Amendment. Justice Black concluded, "Neither the fact that the prayer may be denominationally neutral nor the fact that its observance on the part of the students is voluntary [in school districts other than New Hyde Park] can serve to free it from the limitations of the Establishment Clause [which] is violated by the enactment of laws which establish an official religion whether those laws operate directly to coerce nonobserving individuals or not."

Dissent Justice Potter Stewart dis-

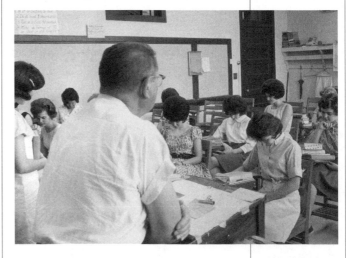

Prayer in public schools was a legal classroom activity before the Supreme Court ruled in Engel v. Vitale that such religious activity violated the separation of church and state.

sented on the grounds that the Regents prayer was nondenominational and voluntary. Justice Stewart wrote: "With all due respect, I think the Court has misapplied a great constitutional principle. I cannot see how an 'official religion' is established by letting those who want to say a prayer say it. On the contrary, I think that to deny the wish of these school children to join in reciting this prayer is to deny them the opportunity of sharing in the spiritual heritage of the Nation."

Significance This case, in combination with the decision in *Abington School District* v. *Schempp* (1963), established a strong position in favor of a strict separation of church and state. However, opponents have continued to challenge this view. In his dissent in *Wallace* v. *Jaffree* (1985), Justice William Rehnquist rejected the idea of strict separation of church and state. Rather, he argued, the establishment clause of the 1st Amendment was meant only to prevent the government from favoring one religion over another.

SEE ALSO

Abington School District v. Schempp; Establishment clause; Religious issues under the Constitution; Wallace v. Jaffree

Equality under the Constitution

THE UNITED STATES was born with a Declaration of Independence that proclaimed, as a self-evident truth, that, "all Men are created equal, that they are endowed by their Creator with certain unalienable Rights, that among these are Life, Liberty, and the Pursuit of Happiness—That to secure these Rights, Governments are instituted among Men."

According to the founders of the United States of America, all people are equal, by virtue of their humanity, in possession of certain rights (such as rights to liberty) that it is the responsibility of government to protect.

The founders were not claiming that all individuals are equal in their personal attributes, such as physical strength, intelligence, or artistic talent. They were not saying that a government is established to enforce equality or uniformity in the way people think, act, or live. Rather, the founders were committed to establishing a government that would guarantee equally to all individuals the rule of law and security for liberty under the law.

The word *equality,* however, did not appear in the Constitution of 1787 and the Bill of Rights of 1791. Further, the ideal of equal rights for all individuals under a government of laws was contradicted by the existence of slavery and the denial of rights to some people because of race or gender. Although the Constitution and Bill of Rights, as originally written, did not outlaw slavery and discrimination based on race or gender, one of the great early opponents of slavery and racial discrimination, Frederick Douglass, argued in a widely praised Fourth of July speech (1852) that "interpreted as it *ought* to be interpreted, the Constitution is a GLORIOUS LIBERTY DOCUMENT." According to Douglass—and many other opponents of slavery, racial discrimination, and gender discrimination—the Constitution of 1787 was neutral with regard to race and sex, thereby leaving the way open to equal protection under the law for women and racial minorities.

The American ideal of equal rights under law, however, was not explicitly included in the Constitution until after the Civil War, with passage of the three Reconstruction-era amendments. The

13th Amendment (1865) banned slavery. The 14th Amendment (1868) guaranteed equal rights of citizenship to all Americans, with the special intention of protecting the rights of former slaves. The 15th Amendment (1870) provided that voting rights of citizens "shall not be denied or abridged by the United States or by any State on account of race, color, or previous condition of servitude."

The 14th Amendment includes the word *equality* in Section 1, which prohibits a state government from denying "to any person within its jurisdiction the equal protection of the laws." This equal protection clause protects individuals from arbitrary discrimination by government officials. Federal courts have read the equal protection concept into their interpretation of the due process clause of the 5th Amendment, thereby applying the equal protection limitations to the federal government. Neither federal nor state governments may classify people in ways that violate their liberties or rights under the U.S. Constitution.

The equal protection clause does not require identical treatment in all circumstances. Discrimination is sometimes permitted. For example, laws denying people under 18 years old the right to vote or the right to marry without parental permission are considered reasonable classifications that do not violate the individual's constitutional rights and liberties because a relationship seems to exist between chronological age and the ability to perform in certain ways. However, a law prohibiting redheads from voting would be unreasonable and unconstitutional because no relationship exists between red hair and the ability to vote.

Racial equality and affirmative action

Despite the promise of the 14th Amendment, most black Americans did not enjoy equal protection of the laws until the second half of the 20th century. Indeed, the Supreme Court decision in *Plessy* v. *Ferguson* (1896) exemplified the denial of equality to black Americans in its sanction of "separate but equal" treatment of people based on race. Both before and after *Plessy,* racial segregation was a firmly established fact of American life, with the separate facilities for blacks hardly ever equal to those provided for white Americans.

If *Plessy* was a symbol of the unequal and unjust social conditions of racial segregation, it also contained a seed of social change toward legal equality. In the dissenting opinion, Justice John Marshall Harlan wrote, "Our Constitution is color-blind and neither knows nor tolerates classes among citizens. In respect of civil rights all citizens are equal before the law.... It is therefore to be regretted that this high tribunal…has reached the conclusion that it is competent for a state to regulate the enjoyment by citizens of their civil rights solely on the basis of race." Justice Harlan's argument for a color-blind Constitution became the rallying cry and goal of the National Association for the Advancement of Colored People (NAACP) and other participants in a civil rights movement committed to equal justice under the law.

The NAACP and its allies achieved several legal victories from the 1930s to the 1950s that advanced the cause of equal protection for the constitutional rights of black Americans. For example, *Smith* v. *Allwright* (1944) struck down barriers to participation by blacks in Democratic party primary elections. *Missouri ex rel. Gaines* v. *Canada* (1938) and *Sweatt* v. *Painter* (1950) provided access for black students to public law schools previously restricted to white students. The turning point, however, came in *Brown* v. *Board of Education* (1954), which overturned *Plessy* and outlawed state-sanctioned racial segregation in public schools. Several Court decisions after *Brown,* plus the federal Civil Rights Act of 1964, struck down racial segregation laws affecting all facets of American life and advanced the cause of equal security for the constitutional rights of all individuals, regard-

less of color or race. A key Court decision after *Brown* was *Cooper* v. *Aaron* (1958), which reaffirmed the court's decision in *Brown* against racial segregation in public schools. And *Heart of Atlanta Motel* v. *United States* (1964) buttressed the Civil Rights Act of 1964 in its prohibition of racial discrimination in privately owned accommodations open to the public, such as hotels and restaurants.

In 1967, in *Loving* v. *Virginia,* the Court struck down a state law prohibiting interracial marriages and held that all racial classifications are "inherently suspect classifications." Thus, any legal classification based on race would be subject to "strict scrutiny" by the Court. This means that the suspect classification would be judged unconstitutional unless the government could justify it with a compelling public interest, which is very difficult to do.

Since the 1970s the NAACP and other civil rights organizations have argued for both government-sponsored and private, voluntary affirmative action programs. Such programs are designed to give preferential treatment to racial minorities in order to provide greater access to jobs, competitive college and university programs, promotions to high-level professional and management positions, and government contracts. Advocates of affirmative action have argued that African Americans, for example, lag far behind whites in income, educational achievement, job advancement, and living standards. They claim that these differences are the consequence of many generations of racial discrimination and that affirmative action is the best way to overcome quickly the continuing negative effects of past discrimination.

Opponents of affirmative action view it as "reverse discrimination" based on race and, therefore, a violation of the idea that the Constitution is "color-blind."

The Court has upheld aspects of affirmative action while striking down extreme versions of this concept. In *Regents of the University of California* v. *Bakke* (1978), for example, the Court ruled that a university could take into account race and ethnicity when making decisions about the admission of students. However, the Court ruled that an affirmative action plan based on rigid racial quotas to boost admission of minority students to a university was unconstitutional. In *United Steelworkers of America* v. *Weber* (1979), the Court permitted an employer's voluntarily imposed and temporary affirmative action program. That program would encourage unskilled black workers to obtain training that would lead to better, more skilled jobs, in which black Americans historically have been underrepresented. Once again, however, the Court rejected rigid, race-based quotas in hiring and job advancement.

In *United States* v. *Paradise* (1987), the Court upheld a temporary and "narrowly tailored" quota system to bring about job promotion for black state troopers in Alabama. The state's affirmative action plan imposed a "one black-for-one-white" promotion quota. This was justified, the Court said, by the "long and shameful record of delay and resistance" to employment opportunities for black Americans in the Alabama state police force.

Gender-based issues of equality

Not until the 1970s did the Court extend to women the 14th Amendment's guarantee of "equal protection of the laws." One hundred years earlier, in *Bradwell* v. *Illinois* (1873), the Court had refused to use the equal protection clause to overturn a state government's ruling denying a woman a license to practice law. The denial was based strictly on the person's gender, but the Court ignored this flagrant violation of "equal protection of the laws." Writing for the Court, Justice Joseph P. Bradley justified the decision in *Bradwell* with a paternalistic explanation: "The natural and proper timidity and delicacy which belongs to the female sex evidently unfits it for many of the occupations of civil life [such as being a lawyer].... [T]he domestic sphere [is] that which properly belongs to the domain and functions of womanhood."

The Court's paternalism toward women reflected the general view of the public in the latter half of the 19th century. The late 19th-century Court also ruled that the 14th Amendment did not require state governments to permit women to vote (*Minor* v. *Happersett,* 1875) or to serve on juries (*Strauder* v. *West Virginia,* 1880). It took the 19th Amendment to the Constitution (1920) to overturn the Court's decision against women's voting rights. Not until 1975, in *Taylor* v. *Louisiana,* did the Court overturn *Strauder* and rule against state exclusion of women from jury duty.

Since the 1970s women have successfully challenged restrictions that appear to violate the 14th Amendment's equal protection clause. In *Reed* v. *Reed* (1971), for example, the Court used the 14th Amendment to nullify a state law that discriminated against women in serving as the administrators of the estates of the deceased.

In 1987, in *Johnson* v. *Transportation Agency of Santa Clara County,* the Court endorsed a carefully crafted, temporary, and voluntary affirmative action plan to boost job promotion opportunities for women. The Court held it was permissible to take into account a woman's gender as a positive factor in promotion to a higher-ranking position because women had been systematically denied access to such positions in the past.

Continuing controversy

Since the 1970s Americans have tended to agree about the constitutionality and justice of guaranteeing equality of civil rights and liberties to all individuals in the United States, regardless of race, ethnicity, or gender. Also since the 1970s, however, Americans have argued about the issue of affirmative action to remedy the effects of past discrimination against racial minorities and women.

Is any kind of affirmative action plan a violation of the equal protection clause? Or is affirmative action the best short-term and temporary means of reversing many generations of unjust discrimination?

The U.S. Congress endorsed limited uses of affirmative action to redress past injustices in the Civil Rights Act of 1991. Both the Court and citizens, however, are likely to continue to face controversies about affirmative action and equality under the Constitution.

SEE ALSO

Affirmative action; Brown v. Board of Education; Civil rights; Cooper v. Aaron; Heart of Atlanta Motel v. United States; Johnson v. Transportation Agency of Santa Clara County; Plessy v. Ferguson; Reed v. Reed; Regents of the University of California v. Bakke; Smith v. Allwright; Sweatt v. Painter; United Steelworkers of America v. Weber

FURTHER READING

Baer, Judith A. *Equality under the Constitution.* Ithaca: Cornell University Press, 1983.
Finkelman, Paul. "Race and the Constitution." In *By and for the People: Constitutional Rights in American History,* edited by Kermit L. Hall. Arlington Heights, Ill.: Harlan Davidson, 1991.
Jackson, Donald W. *Even the Children of Strangers: Equality under the U.S. Constitution.* Lawrence: University Press of Kansas, 1992.
Kull, Andrew. *The Color-Blind Constitution.* Cambridge: Harvard University Press, 1992.
Petrik, Paula. "Women and the Bill of Rights." In *By and for the People: Constitutional Rights in American History,* edited by Kermit L. Hall. Arlington Heights, Ill.: Harlan Davidson, 1991.
Pole, J. R. *The Pursuit of Equality in American History.* 2nd ed. Berkeley: University of California Press, 1993.
Van Burkleo, Sandra F. "No Rights But Human Rights." *Constitution* 2, no. 2 (Spring–Summer 1990): 4–19.

Equal protection of the laws

THE EQUAL protection clause of the 14th Amendment states, "No state shall...deny to any person within its jurisdiction the equal protection of the laws." The 14th Amendment, ratified in 1868, became part of the U.S. Constitution in the wake of the Civil War, with the direct purpose of protecting the legal rights of African Americans recently emancipated from slavery. The equal protection clause, however, has been applied by the courts to protect the rights of all individuals under the authority of the Constitution.

Until the 1940s, the equal protection clause was rarely used by the Supreme Court to overturn state laws as unconstitutional. Since the 1950s, however, the Court has used the equal protection clause to strike down, as unconstitutional, state laws supporting racial segregation in schools and other public facilities. For example, the Court's decision in *Brown* v. *Board of Education* (1954) was based on the equal protection clause. In *Reed* v. *Reed* (1971) the Court, for the first time, struck down a state law because it discriminated against women, in violation of the 14th Amendment's equal protection clause.

These demonstrators in 1969 claim that women face discrimination and fail to receive equal protection of the laws.

SEE ALSO

Equality under the Constitution

Establishment clause

THE 1ST AMENDMENT to the U.S. Constitution states, "Congress shall make no law respecting an establishment of religion." This establishment clause has been used by the Court to overturn, or declare unconstitutional, state laws involving the government in religious activities, such as prayers or religious programs in public schools. For example, the Court used the establishment clause to strike down state government laws in *Engel* v. *Vitale* (1962) and *Wallace* v. *Jaffree* (1985).

There is general agreement that the establishment clause prohibits an official religion endorsed by the government or preferential support by the government of some religions over others. There have been continuous arguments, however, about whether the establishment clause strictly prohibits all involvement by the government in support of religious activity as long as the involvement is conducted nonpreferentially.

SEE ALSO

Engel v. Vitale; Religious issues under the Constitution; Wallace v. Jaffree

Everson v. Board of Education of Ewing Township

☆ *330 U.S. 1 (1947)*
☆ *Vote: 5–4*
☆ *For the Court: Black*
☆ *Dissenting: Jackson, Frankfurter, Rutledge, and Burton*

IN 1941 the New Jersey legislature passed a law that said boards of educa-tion could pay the costs of bus transportation, to and from school, of students in public schools and Catholic parochial schools. Arch Everson, a resident of the school district governed by the Ewing Township Board of Education, claimed that this state law violated the 1st Amendment prohibition against the state establishment of religion. Everson claimed that it was unfair and illegal for the state government to use money from taxpayers, like himself, to pay for costs associated with private religious schools.

The Issue The 1st Amendment of the Constitution says, "Congress shall make no law respecting an establishment of religion." Furthermore, the 14th Amendment says, "No state shall…deprive any person of life, liberty, or property without due process of law." Everson argued that the 1st Amendment, which applies only to the U.S. Congress, could also be applied to state governments through the due process clause of the 14th Amendment.

The other constitutional issue was whether the New Jersey law challenged by Arch Everson actually involved the state government in religion in a way that violated the establishment clause of the 1st Amendment.

Opinion of the Court Justice Hugo Black, writing for the Court, argued that the 1st Amendment to the Constitution can be used to limit state governments through the due process clause of the 14th Amendment. On this issue, the Court agreed with Arch Everson. However, the Court disagreed with Everson with regard to the establishment clause and upheld the New Jersey law, which provided bus transportation for Catholic parochial school students at public expense. Justice Black claimed that this New Jersey law did not violate the establishment clause of the 1st Amendment.

Justice Black wrote the following rules to guide decisions about the establishment clause:

Governments are not allowed, under the Constitution, to support or prohibit the practice of religion. In the Everson *case, however, the Court decided that local governments could provide bus transportation for students in Catholic schools.*

Neither a state nor the Federal Government can set up a church. Neither can pass laws which aid one religion, aid all religions, or prefer one religion over another. Neither can force nor influence a person to go to or remain away from church against his will or force him to profess a belief or disbelief in any religion.... In the words of Jefferson, the clause against establishment of religion by law was intended to erect "a wall of separation between Church and State."

Justice Black concluded that the New Jersey statute at issue in this case did not violate the 1st Amendment because public payment for bus transportation of parochial school students had nothing to do with government promoting religion. Rather, this was only a program for moving children safely and easily to and from school, regardless of the religion or school of the children.

Dissent Justice Robert Jackson wrote that he agreed totally with the Court's rules for deciding what is an "establishment of religion." But he disagreed with the Court's conclusion that the *Everson* case did not fit these rules.

Justice Wiley Rutledge wrote a second dissenting opinion that also agreed with Black's rules and held that the New Jersey law *was* an example of an "establishment of religion." He concluded, "The [1st] Amendment's purpose…was to create a complete and permanent separation of the spheres of religious activity and civil authority by comprehensively forbidding every form of public aid or support for religion."

Significance The *Everson* case was the first to apply the establishment clause of the 1st Amendment to the states through the 14th Amendment. And it set standards to guide interpretation of the establishment clause that have been used to resolve later controversies, such as *Engel* v. *Vitale* (1962) and *Abington*

School District v. *Schempp* (1963).

S E E   A L S O

Abington School District v. Schempp (1963); Establishment clause; Engel v. Vitale; Religious issues under the Constitution

F U R T H E R   R E A D I N G

Miller, William Lee. *The First Liberty: Religion and the American Republic.* New York: Paragon House, 1985.

Exclusionary rule

EVIDENCE OBTAINED in violation of a person's constitutional rights cannot be used to prosecute the person. This restriction on the use of evidence obtained illegally is called the exclusionary rule, which was created in *Weeks* v. *United States* (1914). The Court applied the exclusionary rule to a state government for the first time in *Mapp* v. *Ohio* (1961).

The 4th Amendment to the Constitution protects individuals "against unreasonable searches and seizures" by government officials and provides that "no warrants [for searches and seizures] shall issue, but upon probable cause." If government officials seize evidence without a warrant, for example, it usually is excluded, or thrown out, from the legal proceedings against a person accused of a crime. However, in *United States* v. *Leon* (1984), the Court established a "good faith" exception to the exclusionary rule. This means that evidence seized on the basis of a mistakenly issued search warrant can still be used in a trial, if the warrant was issued on good faith—the belief that there were valid reasons for issuing it.

S E E   A L S O

Mapp v. Ohio; Searches and seizures; United States v. Leon; Weeks v. United States

President Richard Nixon meets with advisers in the Oval Office. Nixon tape recorded his conversations and later claimed he could withhold the tapes from the courts because of executive privilege.

Executive privilege

FROM TIME to time, Presidents of the United States have claimed the executive privilege of withholding information from Congress, the federal courts, or the general public. Executive privilege has been justified as necessary to protect national security against foreign enemies. President George Washington, for example, kept information on the Jay Treaty from the House of Representatives on behalf of the national interest.

In general, the U.S. Supreme Court has respected executive privilege. But the Court has insisted that executive privilege is not absolute and that the chief executive, under particular circumstances, may be required to disclose information in a judicial or congressional investigation.

In *United States* v. *Nixon* (1974), for instance, the Court ruled that President Richard Nixon was required, despite his claim of executive privilege, to give up to a special prosecutor tape recordings that were sought as evidence against Presidential assistants charged with criminal behavior. Writing for the court, Chief Justice Warren Burger upheld the general claim of executive privilege, while denying its use to President Nixon in this case.

SEE ALSO
United States v. Nixon

Ex parte

WHEN THE Latin phrase *ex parte* (meaning "from the part of") is used in the title of a court case, it means that the action was taken on behalf of the person named in the title of the case. It does not require the notification of or participation by an opposing party. For example, *Ex parte Milligan* (1866) was a legal action taken to the U.S. Supreme Court on behalf of Lambdin P. Milligan by his attorney. Milligan was in jail when the Supreme Court decided his case. He had been sentenced to death by a U.S. military court for treason against the United States during the Civil War. The Supreme Court ruled that the military court had no jurisdiction in this case, and Milligan was released.

Ex parte Milligan

☆ *4 Wall. 2 (1866)*
☆ *Vote: 9–0*
☆ *For the Court: Davis*

IN 1864, the general in command of the military district of Indiana arrested Lambdin P. Milligan. The Civil War still raged in other parts of the country. Federal agents alleged they had evidence of a conspiracy by Milligan and others to release and arm rebel prisoners so they could take part in a Confederate invasion of Indiana.

The army brought Milligan before a special military court instead of before the regular civil courts that were still operating in Indiana. The military court convicted Milligan of conspiracy and sentenced him to death.

Early in the Civil War, President Abraham Lincoln had placed some sections of the country under military rule and replaced civilian courts with military courts to try individuals accused of insurrection. Lincoln also suspended the writ of habeas corpus in such situations. A writ of habeas corpus orders an official who has a person in custody to bring the prisoner to court and explain why he is detaining the person. This basic civil liberty prevents arbitrary arrest and imprisonment.

Article 1, Section 9, of the Constitution says, "The privilege of the writ of habeas corpus shall not be suspended, unless when in cases of rebellion or invasion the public safety may require it." Lincoln believed that his order, later confirmed by Congress, was crucial to the preservation of the Union.

Milligan applied to a civilian court in Indiana for a writ of habeas corpus. He claimed his conviction was unconstitutional and asked for his right to a trial by jury in a civilian court.

The Issue The issue came before the Supreme Court in 1866, a year after the Civil War had ended with the defeat of the Confederacy. The appeal did not involve the question of Milligan's guilt or innocence. Rather, the Court dealt with the constitutional issue of whether the government in wartime could suspend citizens' constitutional rights under the 5th and 6th Amendments and set up military courts in areas that were free from invasion or rebellion and in which the civilian courts were still operating.

Opinion of the Court The Court ruled against the government on this question. It ruled that suspending the right of habeas corpus and trying civilians in military courts when civilian courts still operated violated the Constitution.

The Court declared that the civilian courts had been open in Indiana and that the state had been far removed from the battle zone. Thus, neither the President nor Congress could legally deny to an accused person a civilian trial by jury and due process of law as guaranteed by the 5th and 6th Amendments.

Significance The *Milligan* decision represented a great victory for American civil liberties in times of war or internal turmoil. The Court upheld the principle that civilian authorities should control the military even in times of great stress and emergency. Moreover, it reaffirmed that the right of citizens to due process of law remains absolute as long as civilian courts are operating.

SEE ALSO
Habeas corpus, writ of

FURTHER READING
Nevins, Allan. "The Case of the Copperhead Conspirator." In *Quarrels That Have Shaped the Constitution*, edited by John A. Garraty. New York: Harper & Row, 1987.

Ex post facto law

EX POST FACTO is a Latin term meaning "after the fact." Article 1, Section 9, of the Constitution prohibits the federal government from passing an ex post facto law, which is one that makes an action a crime even though it was not a crime when it was committed, or increases the penalty for a crime after it was committed, or changes the rules of evidence to make it easier to convict someone. Similarly, Article 1, Section 10, provides that no state shall pass an ex post facto law. The Constitution protects individuals by denying to the Congress or state legislatures the power to punish people by passing ex post facto laws.

Ex rel

THE TERM *ex rel* is an abbreviation of the Latin phrase *ex relative,* which means "on the relation of." When *ex rel* appears in the title of a case, it means that the legal proceeding was started by a government official in the name of the state or federal government but at the urging of a private individual with an interest in the issue of the case. For example, *Illinois ex rel. McCollum* v. *Board of Education* (1948) was a case brought by the state of Illinois against a local school board at the instigation of a private citizen, Ms. Vashti McCollum.

Federal district courts

THE U.S. DISTRICT COURTS have original jurisdiction in federal criminal cases and civil cases; that is, they are the first to hear these cases. They are the trial courts of the federal judicial system.

There are 94 federal district courts: 90 in the 50 states and the District of Columbia and 4 in the U.S. territories. Each state has at least one federal district court. Three large states—California, New York, and Texas—have four federal district courts each. Nine other states have three federal district courts apiece. In addition, there is a federal district court for each of the four U.S. territories: Guam, Puerto Rico, the Northern Mariana Islands, and the Virgin Islands.

Approximately 600 federal judges staff the district courts. They are appointed by the President and approved by the Senate, as specified in Article 2, Section 2, of the Constitution.

SEE ALSO
Federal judicial system

Federalism

FEDERALISM REFERS to the division of governmental powers between the national and state governments. The Founding Fathers created a federal sys-

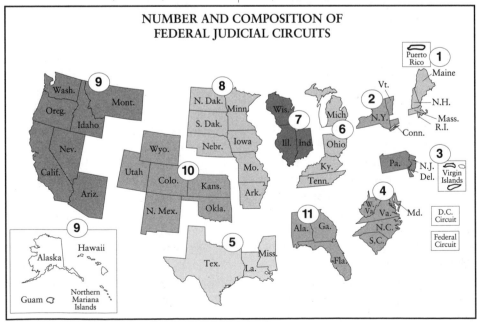

**NUMBER AND COMPOSITION OF
FEDERAL JUDICIAL CIRCUITS**

tem to overcome a tough political obstacle. They needed to convince independent states to join together to create a strong central government. Writing to George Washington before the Constitutional Convention, James Madison considered the dilemma. He said that establishing "one simple republic" that would do away with the states would be "unattainable." Instead, Madison wrote, "I have sought for a middle ground which may at once support a due supremacy of national authority, and not exclude [the states]." Federalism was the answer.

Under federalism, both state and national governments may directly govern through their own officials and laws. Both levels of government derive their legitimacy from the Constitution, which endows each with supreme power over certain areas of government. Both state and federal governments must agree to changes in the Constitution. Both exercise power separately and directly over the people living under their authority, subject to the limits specified in the U.S. Constitution, the supreme law of the country. The Constitution and acts of the national government that conform to it are superior to constitutions, laws, and actions of state and local governments.

In the American federal system, the national (federal) government has certain powers that are granted only to it by the Constitution. The 50 state governments also have powers that the national government is not supposed to exercise. For example, only the federal government may coin money or declare war. Only the state government may establish local governments and conduct elections within the state. Some powers are shared by both federal and state governments, such as the power to tax and borrow money. Some powers are denied to the federal and state governments, such as granting titles of nobility and passing bills of attainder.

The South Carolina State House in Columbia. The balance of power between state governments and the federal government has shifted over the years, as the Supreme Court has tended to grant more authority to the federal government.

In the American federal system, the powers of the national government are limited. However, within its field or range of powers, the national government is supreme. The states can neither ignore nor contradict federal laws and the Constitution. The core idea of American federalism is that two levels of government (national and state) exercise power separately and directly on the people at the same time. Under federalism, the state of Indiana has authority over its residents, but so does the federal government based in Washington, D.C. Indiana residents must obey the laws of their state government and their federal government.

Federalism is a central principle of the Constitution, but the balance of power between the state and national governments was not defined exactly at the Constitutional Convention of 1787. Since then, debates about the rights and powers of states in relation to the federal government have continued.

In *The Federalist* No. 45, James Madison gave his vision of how federalism would work:

> The powers delegated by the Constitution to the federal government are few and defined. Those which are to remain in state governments are numerous and indefinite. The former will be exercised principally on external objects, as war, peace, negotiation, and foreign

commerce.... The powers reserved to the several states will extend to all objects which, in the ordinary course of affairs, concern the lives, liberties, and properties of the people, and the internal order, improvement, and prosperity of the states.

However, the balance of power within the federal system—between the national government and state governments—has changed steadily since Madison's time. Through constitutional amendments, Supreme Court decisions, federal statutes, and executive actions, the powers of the national government have generally expanded to overshadow those of the states.

The development of national government power within the federal system was advanced initially by decisions of the U.S. Supreme Court under Chief Justice John Marshall. For example, the Court's decisions in *Fletcher* v. *Peck* (1810), *McCulloch* v. *Maryland* (1819), *Cohens* v. *Virginia* (1821), and *Gibbons* v. *Ogden* (1824) struck down state government actions that were judged in violation of federal law and the U.S. Constitution.

The Civil War (1861–65) established, once and for all, that in American federalism a state has no right to secede from the federal Union. In the wake of this war, the U.S. Supreme Court set forth the inviolable terms of federal Union in *Texas* v. *White* (1869): "The Constitution in all its provisions looks to an indestructible Union, composed of indestructible States."

During the 20th century, the Supreme Court has tended to make decisions that have diminished the power of state governments in their relationships with the national government. This trend was advanced strongly after 1937, in cases such as *West Coast Hotel Co.* v. *Parrish* (1937), when the Supreme Court began to uphold actions of the federal government to regulate economic activities in the states. During the 1950s and 1960s, the Supreme Court under Chief Justice Earl Warren upheld federal civil rights laws that restricted the actions of state governments to deprive racial minorities of individual rights. Further, in numerous landmark decisions the Court used the due process clause of the 14th Amendment to apply most of the federal Bill of Rights to state governments. These kinds of decisions have limited the powers of state governments in regard to the civil rights and liberties of individuals.

SEE ALSO

Incorporation doctrine; Texas v. White; West Coast Hotel Co. v. Parrish

FURTHER READING

Elazar, Daniel J. *American Federalism: A View from the States.* New York: Harper & Row, 1984.
Goldwin, Robert A., and William A. Schambra, eds. *How Federal Is the Constitution?* Washington, D.C.: American Enterprise Institute, 1987.
Kaye, Judith S. "Federalism's Other Tier." *Constitution* 3, no. 1 (Winter 1991): 48–55.

Federalist, The

THE FEDERALIST, a collection of 85 papers, or essays, was written to explain and support ratification of the Constitution of 1787. Seventy-seven essays were first printed in New York City newspapers between October 27, 1787, and April 2, 1788. The complete set of 85 essays was published in May 1788 by McLean and Company of New York City.

Alexander Hamilton, the major author of *The Federalist,* wrote 51 of the 85 papers (Nos. 1, 6–9, 11–13, 15–17, 21–36, 59–61, and 65–85). James Madison wrote 29 essays (Nos. 10, 14, 18–20, 37–58, and 62–63). Illness forced John Jay to withdraw from the project, and he wrote only five essays (Nos. 2–5 and 64).

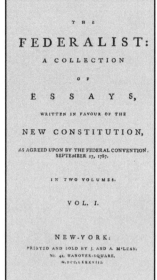

THE

FEDERALIST:

A COLLECTION

OF

E S S A Y S,

WRITTEN IN FAVOUR OF THE

NEW CONSTITUTION,

AS AGREED UPON BY THE FEDERAL CONVENTION,
SEPTEMBER 17, 1787.

IN TWO VOLUMES.

VOL. I.

NEW-YORK:

PRINTED AND SOLD BY J. AND A. M'LEAN,
No. 41, HANOVER-SQUARE,
M,DCC,LXXXVIII.

The Federalist *was first published in book form in 1788 after appearing as a series of essays in New York newspapers.*

Each paper was signed with the pseudonym Publius, after Publius Valerius Publicola, a great defender of the Roman Republic of ancient times.

The first objective of *The Federalist* was to persuade the people of New York to ratify the Constitution; each paper was addressed "To the People of the State of New York" and published first in a New York newspaper. A second objective was to influence Americans in all 13 states to approve the Constitution.

The authors submerged their political differences in the overall pursuit of a common goal—ratification of the Constitution. Madison and Jay agreed with Hamilton that the Constitution was "a compromise of…many dissimilar interests and inclinations." It did not exactly reflect the ideas on government of any one of the coauthors, but they agreed that it was the best frame of government achievable under the circumstances and far superior to the Articles of Confederation under which the country had functioned since 1781.

After ratification of the Constitution and formation of the federal government, Madison joined Thomas Jefferson in political clashes with Hamilton that led to the establishment of rival political parties: Federalist (Hamilton) versus Democratic-Republican (Jefferson/Madison). These conflicts, however, lay ahead. In 1787–88, Madison and Hamilton were a formidable team in defense of the Constitution.

Hamilton, Madison, and Jay readily agreed on the name of their projected series of essays, *The Federalist*. With this name, they scored a public relations victory against their opponents, who accepted by default the name of Anti-Federalists. This negative label connoted only opposition, with no constructive ideas to improve the government.

The authors of *The Federalist* agreed on certain fundamental principles of constitutional government: republicanism, federalism, separation of powers, and free government.

A republican government is one "in which the scheme of representation takes place" (*The Federalist* No. 10). It is based on the consent of the governed because power is delegated to a small number of citizens who are elected by the rest of the citizens.

In a federal republic, power is divided between a general (federal) government and several state governments. Two levels of government, each supreme in its own sphere, can exercise powers separately and directly on the people. But state governments can neither ignore nor contradict federal statutes that conform to the supreme law, the Constitution. This conception of federalism departed from traditional forms of government, known today as confederations, in which states retained full sovereignty over their internal affairs.

Publius proclaims in *The Federalist* No. 47: "The accumulation of all powers, legislative, executive, and judiciary, in the same hands…may justly be pronounced the very definition of tyranny." So the Constitution provides for a separation of governmental powers among three branches, according to function. But this separation of powers is not complete. Each branch has various constitutional means to participate in the affairs of the other branches, to check and balance their powers, and to prevent one branch of the government from dominating the others.

Republicanism, federalism, and separation of powers are all characteristics of free government. According to *The Federalist*, free government is popular government, limited by the supreme law of the Constitution, established to protect the security, liberty, and property of individuals. A free government is powerful enough to provide protection against external and internal threats and limited enough to prevent tyranny in any form. In particular, free government is designed to guard against the most insidious danger of government by the people—the tyranny of the majority over minorities. This principle applies equally to constitutional protection of religious, ethnic, racial, or other minority groups.

Since its publication in 1788, *The Federalist* has been viewed as an extraordinary work about the principles and practice of constitutional government. *The Federalist* is "the best commentary on the principles of government which ever was written," wrote Thomas Jefferson to James Madison (Nov. 18, 1788). Chief Justice John Marshall agreed in this instance with Jefferson, his longtime political opponent. In *McCulloch* v. *Maryland* (1819), John Marshall wrote that *The Federalist* was "entitled to great respect [by courts] expounding the Constitution." Moreover, he wrote in *Cohens* v. *Virginia* (1821): "[*The Federalist*] is a complete commentary on our Constitution, and it is appealed to by all parties in the questions to which that instrument gave birth." Ever since the founding period, lawyers, judges, politicians, and scholars have used *The Federalist* to guide their decisions about issues of constitutional government.

SEE ALSO

Constitutional democracy; Constitutionalism; Federalism; Republicanism; Separation of powers

FURTHER READING

Carey, George. *The Federalist: Design for a Constitutional Republic.* Urbana: University of Illinois Press, 1989.

Hamilton, Alexander, James Madison, and John Jay. *The Federalist.* Edited by Jacob E. Cooke. Middletown, Conn.: Wesleyan University Press, 1961.

Federal Judicial Center

SEE Administration of federal courts

Federal judicial system

THE JUDICIAL SYSTEM of the United States has three levels: the Supreme Court at the top, the 13 Courts of Appeals in the middle, and the 94 district courts and several specialized courts at the bottom.

The district courts are the courts of original jurisdiction, or trial courts. There are from one to four districts in each state, one in the District of Columbia, and one in each of the four U.S. territories.

The lowest level of the federal judicial system also includes specialized courts. For example, the Court of Claims hears cases involving monetary claims against the United States. The Court of Military Appeals hears appeals of courts-martial, or military trials, of people in the U.S. armed forces. The Tax Court hears cases regarding federal taxes. The Court of Customs and Patent Appeals hears cases involving international trade and claims about the legality of patents (legal assurances of ownership rights granted by the government to inventors).

The 13 Courts of Appeals have appellate jurisdiction; that is, they hear cases on appeal from the federal district courts and other lower courts. There is one U.S. Court of Appeals for each of 11 geographical regions (circuits) of the United States. They are numbered 1 through 11. In addition, there is a U.S. Court of Appeals for the District of Columbia and a U.S. Court of Appeals for the Federal Circuit, which hears cases on appeal from specialized lower courts.

The U.S. Supreme Court is primarily

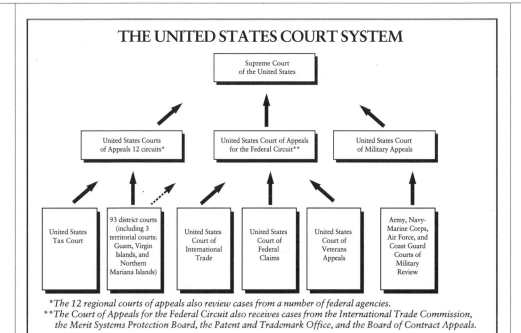

THE UNITED STATES COURT SYSTEM

The 12 regional courts of appeals also review cases from a number of federal agencies.
**The Court of Appeals for the Federal Circuit also receives cases from the International Trade Commission, the Merit Systems Protection Board, the Patent and Trademark Office, and the Board of Contract Appeals.*

an appellate court of last resort. It hears appeals from the federal courts of appeals and the highest state courts in cases involving federal issues or questions, such as claims that a state government action conflicts with the U.S. Constitution or federal law.

SEE ALSO

Circuit Courts of Appeals; Courts of Appeals; Federal district courts

FURTHER READING

Carp, Robert A., and Ronald Stidham. *The Federal Courts.* Washington, D.C.: Congressional Quarterly Press, 1991.

Field, Stephen Johnson

ASSOCIATE JUSTICE, 1863–97

☆ Born: Nov. 4, 1816, Haddam, Conn.
☆ Education: Williams College, B.A., 1837; studied law privately
☆ Previous government service: California House of Representatives, 1850–51; justice, California Supreme Court, 1857–63
☆ Appointed by President Abraham Lincoln Mar. 6, 1863, to a newly created position on the Court
☆ Supreme Court term: confirmed by the Senate Mar. 10, 1863, by a voice vote; retired Dec. 1, 1897
☆ Died: Apr. 9, 1899, Washington, D.C.

STEPHEN FIELD served more than 34 years on the Supreme Court, longer than any other justice except William O. Douglas. During Field's long term, he was a strong supporter of the property rights of individuals.

Justice Field was the Court's leader in using the due process clause of the 14th Amendment to prohibit state governments from regulating or interfering with the property rights of corporations and other businesses or industries. Justice Field viewed a corporation as an individual that could not be deprived of its rights by state governments because of the protection of individual rights guaranteed by Section 1 of the 14th Amendment.

Justice Field and his followers on the Court did not, however, show an equal concern for the rights of people, especially black people, for whose protection the 14th Amendment was drafted and ratified in 1868. They consistently voted as a majority to deny these individual rights to African Americans. Field, for example, voted with the Court's majority in *Plessy v. Ferguson* to establish the "separate but equal" doctrine. That doctrine remained the legal basis for racial segregation in the United States until it was overturned in 1954 by the Court's decision in *Brown* v. *Board of Education.* Justice Field argued that the "equal protection of the laws" required by the 14th Amendment required only equal treatment of people, not their freedom of choice.

In the 1890s, Field's ability to work declined as he became disabled by illness and the infirmities of advanced age. His colleagues repeatedly asked him to retire, but Field refused because he wanted to surpass John Marshall's record for length of service on the Court. He finally retired in 1897, but only after barely exceeding Chief Justice Marshall's record of service of 34 years and five months.

FURTHER READING

Swisher, Carl B. *Stephen J. Field: Craftsman of the Law.* Washington, D.C.: Brookings Institution, 1930.

First Monday in October

S E E Opening Day

Fletcher v. Peck

☆ *6 Cranch 87 (1810)*
☆ *Vote: 4–1*
☆ *For the Court: Marshall*
☆ *Dissenting: Johnson in part*

IN 1795 the state of Georgia sold 35 million acres in the Yazoo area to four land companies. However, the authorization of the land sales was tainted by fraud and bribery involving important mem-

bers of the state legislature who were voted out of office in 1796. New members of the Georgia legislature promptly acted to repeal the statute that had authorized the Yazoo land sales. The 1796 legislation invalidated all property rights gained from the Yazoo Land Act of 1795. People who had purchased Yazoo land under the 1795 statute, however, continued to sell this land to third parties. In 1803 John Peck sold 15,000 acres of Yazoo land to Robert Fletcher. Then Fletcher sued Peck for selling him land that was not his to sell.

The Issue Chief Justice John Marshall avoided any discussion of the reasons for the Georgia legislature's action in repealing the 1795 land act. He said that charges of political corruption associated with land titles and sales were a matter for the state government to decide. According to Marshall, the only question before the U.S. Supreme Court was whether the state legislature could deprive investors of land they had acquired under the corrupt grant authorized by the 1795 law. Was depriving investors of this land, by repealing the land grant that had authorized their purchase of it, a violation of the contract clause of Article 1, Section 10, of the U.S. Constitution?

Opinion of the Court Writing for the Court, Chief Justice John Marshall held that the Georgia legislature's act repealing the Yazoo land grant law was unconstitutional because it violated the contract clause of Article 1, Section 10, of the Constitution. That clause says, "No State shall…pass any…Law impairing the Obligation of Contracts." Thus, concluded Marshall, a state government could not make laws that impaired contracts or interfered with land titles acquired in good faith.

Significance This decision was a legal blow against advocates of stronger state powers and rights within the federal system. Chief Justice Marshall emphatically asserted the right of the U.S. Supreme Court to review and strike down a state law as unconstitutional. Further, Marshall established that contracts and property rights would be protected by the federal courts against state government interference. This constitutional protection of an individual's property rights and contracts encouraged large-scale economic development of the nation.

SEE ALSO

Contract clause; Federalism

Fortas, Abe

ASSOCIATE JUSTICE, 1965–69

☆ *Born: June 19, 1910, Memphis, Tenn.*
☆ *Education: Southwestern College, B.A., 1930; Yale Law School, LL.B., 1933*
☆ *Previous government service: assistant director, corporate reorganization study, Securities and Exchange Commission, 1934–37; assistant director, public utilities commission, Securities and Exchange Commission, 1938–39; counsel to the bituminous coal division, Department of the Interior, 1939–41; director, Division of Power, Department of the Interior, 1941–42; undersecretary of the interior, 1942–46*
☆ *Appointed by President Lyndon B. Johnson July 28, 1965; replaced Arthur J. Goldberg, who resigned*
☆ *Supreme Court term: confirmed by the Senate Aug. 11, 1965, by a voice vote; resigned May 14, 1969*
☆ *Died: Apr. 5, 1982, Washington, D.C.*

ABE FORTAS was the son of Jewish immigrants from England who settled in Tennessee. Through his hard work and intelligence, Fortas won scholarships to Southwestern College and Yale Law School and eventually established a very successful legal practice.

In 1948, Fortas successfully de-fended Lyndon B. Johnson, a member of Congress from Texas. Johnson's election victory had been challenged in court by his opponent, who charged that Johnson won through illegal procedures. Lyndon Johnson never forgot Fortas's help during a critical moment in his political career. After becoming President, Johnson appointed Abe Fortas to the Supreme Court to replace Arthur Goldberg, whom he had encouraged to resign by offering Goldberg the position of U.S. ambassador to the United Nations.

Abe Fortas had won national recognition two years before his appointment to the Supreme Court because he was the winning attorney in the landmark Supreme Court case of *Gideon v. Wainwright* (1963). This case established the right of a poor person to be provided with a lawyer by a state government in all criminal cases involving alleged violations of state law. This case reversed the Court's decision in *Betts* v. *Brady* (1942) and was a significant step forward in the gradual "incorporation" of individual rights in the Bill of Rights under the due process clause of the 14th Amendment.

Fortas showed a strong commitment to the rights of individuals during his brief term on the Court. His two most important opinions involved the rights of children: *In re Gault* (1967) and *Tinker* v. *Des Moines Independent Community School District* (1969).

The *Gault* decision extended to juvenile offenders due process rights of the 5th and 14th Amendments that were previously limited to adults. The *Tinker* decision expanded the 1st Amendment freedom of speech right to include "symbolic speech" expressed through the wearing of black arm bands by students in school to protest U.S. participation in the Vietnam War. Fortas argued that a public school's ban on this form of protest was a violation of a student's right to free speech, as long as this form of protest did not disrupt the functioning of the school or violate the rights of other individuals. Fortas wrote, "It can hardly be argued that either students or teachers shed their constitutional rights to freedom of speech or expression at the schoolhouse gate."

In 1968, Fortas's Supreme Court term came to an abrupt and unhappy end. President Johnson nominated Fortas to be chief justice, replacing Earl Warren, who was retiring. But many senators opposed this appointment, and Johnson was pressured to withdraw the nomination. During this controversy, critics of Fortas charged that he had acted improperly in accepting a large fee, raised by donations from friends and former clients, to teach a course at American University. Several months later, a *Life* magazine article claimed that Justice Fortas behaved wrongly in accepting a large fee from a former client in return for serving on a charitable foundation. The *Life* article also reported that Fortas had returned the money.

These charges influenced some members of Congress to discuss the possibility of starting impeachment proceedings against Fortas in order to remove him from the Court. Fortas strongly denied any improper or illegal activity, but he decided to resign from the Court and returned to private law practice. Thus, he was the first justice to leave the Court because of the threat of impeachment.

SEE ALSO

Gideon v. Wainwright; In re Gault; Tinker v. Des Moines Independent Community School District

FURTHER READING

Kalman, Laura. *Abe Fortas: A Biography.* New Haven: Yale University Press, 1990.
Shogan, James F. *A Question of Judgment: The Fortas Case and the Struggle for the Supreme Court.* Indianapolis: Bobbs-Merrill, 1972.

Frankfurter, Felix

ASSOCIATE JUSTICE, 1939–62

☆ Born: Nov. 15, 1882, Vienna, Austria
☆ Education: City College of New York, B.A., 1902; Harvard Law School, LL.B., 1906
☆ Previous government service: assistant U.S. attorney, Southern District of New York, 1906–9; law officer, Bureau of Insular Affairs, War Department, 1910–14; assistant to the secretary of war, secretary and counsel, President's Mediation Commission, assistant to the U.S. secretary of labor, 1917–18; chairman, War Labor Policies Board, 1918
☆ Appointed by President Franklin D. Roosevelt Jan. 5, 1939; replaced Benjamin Cardozo, who died
☆ Supreme Court term: confirmed by the Senate Jan. 17, 1939, by a voice vote; retired Aug. 28, 1962
☆ Died: Feb. 21, 1965, Washington, D.C.

FELIX FRANKFURTER was the only naturalized citizen of the United States to serve on the Supreme Court. He was born into a Jewish family in Vienna, Austria, and came to New York City in 1894, at the age of 12. He was unable to speak English upon his arrival, but he learned the language quickly and thoroughly. He graduated with honors from the City College of New York and Harvard Law School.

Frankfurter served as the U.S. attorney for the southern district of New York (1906–9), as a federal government official from 1910 to 1918, and then as a law professor at Harvard until 1939, when President Franklin D. Roosevelt appointed him to the Supreme Court. During his 23 years on the Court, Justice Frankfurter was an advocate of judicial restraint, the belief that justices should carefully recognize constitutional limitations and defer to legislative decisions, whenever reasonable, as the legitimate expression of the majority of the people.

In line with his views on judicial restraint, Justice Frankfurter strongly opposed "total incorporation" of the Bill of Rights under the due process clause of the 14th Amendment, which was promoted by his colleague Justice Hugo Black. He argued, for example, that the framers of the 14th Amendment had not intended state governments to follow exactly the requirements of the federal Bill of Rights in dealing with people accused of violating state laws. In *Adamson* v. *California* (1947), he held that the 14th Amendment was "not the basis of a uniform code of criminal procedure federally imposed.... In a federal system it would be a function debilitating to the responsibility of state and local agencies."

Frankfurter was concerned with maintaining the vigor of state and local governments within the federal system. He deplored the trend toward an overwhelming federal government that tended to diminish the functions of state and local governments. He viewed this as a violation of the fundamental constitutional principle of federalism, which originally involved a substantial role for state governments within the Union.

Frankfurter retired from the Court in 1962 after suffering a stroke that greatly weakened him. He died three years later.

SEE ALSO

Federalism; Incorporation doctrine; Judicial activism and judicial restraint

FURTHER READING

Baker, Liva. *Felix Frankfurter.* New York: Coward-McCann, 1969.
Freedman, Max. *Roosevelt and Frankfurter: Their Correspondence.* Boston: Little, Brown, 1967.
Hirsch, Harry N. *The Enigma of Felix Frankfurter.* New York: Basic Books, 1981.
Kurland, Philip B. *Mr. Justice Frankfurter and the Constitution.* Chicago: University of Chicago Press, 1971.
Parrish, Michael E. *Felix Frankfurter and His Times.* New York: Macmillan, 1982.
Simon, James F. "The Antagonists: Hugo Black and Felix Frankfurter." *Constitution* 3, no. 1 (Winter 1991): 26-34.

Freedom of speech and press

THE 1ST AMENDMENT to the Constitution protects free expression through speech or press against suppression by the government: "Congress shall make no law...abridging the freedom of speech, or of the press." All 50 state constitutions contain guarantees of free expression similar to those in the U.S. Constitution. An additional protection for the individual's right to free expression comes from Section 1 of the 14th Amendment: "No State shall make or enforce any law which shall abridge the privileges or immunities of citizens of the United States; nor shall any State deprive any person of life, liberty, or property, without due process of law." The Supreme Court has used this section of the 14th Amendment to apply the 1st Amendment guarantee of freedom of speech and press to cases involving state and local governments.

The right to free speech and press means that individuals may publicly express ideas and information—including expressions generally considered to be unwise, untrue, or unpopular—without fear of punishment by the government. In this way, government officials may be criticized and new ways of thinking and behaving may be advanced. Forms of free speech include the use of symbols, orderly public demonstrations, and radio and television broadcasts. Freedom of speech is an essential characteristic of a constitutional democracy because by exercising this right, individuals can communicate opinions both to other citizens and to their representatives in the government. Through this free exchange of ideas, government officials may become responsive to the people they are supposed to represent.

The first issue of John Peter Zenger's New-York Weekly Journal *in 1733. The New York Provincial Council later ordered that the* Journal *be burned because Zenger had printed criticisms of the New York governor.*

The right to free speech stems from the right to freedom of the press established in England during the 17th century. At that time, however, the right to free speech was specifically extended only to members of Parliament. All presses had to be licensed until 1694, when the law requiring licenses lapsed and was not renewed. But controls on the press continued through prosecution for seditious libel, which is speech and writing critical of the government or public officials. In the British colonies of North America, several colonial charters and constitutions explicitly protected freedom of the press, but the right to free speech, as in England, was guaranteed only to members of the legislative branch of government.

The constitutions of most of the original 13 American states protected freedom of the press, but the right of free speech was again extended only to members of the state legislature. An exception was the Pennsylvania Declaration of Rights (1776), which guaranteed freedom of the press and speech to the people.

Proposals for a bill of rights in the U.S. Constitution, advanced in the first session of Congress by James Madison (June 8, 1789), included freedom of speech and press. These rights to freedom of expression became part of the Constitution's 1st Amendment, ratified by the states in 1791.

From 1791 until the early 1900s, the U.S. Supreme Court heard no cases regarding free speech and free press issues. Then, after World War I, the Court decided several cases arising from enforcement of wartime laws to limit freedom of expression that threatened national security. In *Schenck* v. *United States* and *Abrams* v. *United States* (both 1919), the Court upheld such federal laws, basing its decisions on its "clear and present danger" and "bad tendency" tests.

Not until 1925, in *Gitlow* v. *New York,* did the U.S. Supreme Court assert its authority to deal with free speech and press issues originating at the state level of government. Prior to *Gitlow,* the 1st Amendment rights of free speech and press were held to apply only to the federal government (*Barron* v. *Baltimore,* 1833). In *Gitlow,* the Court acknowledged for the first time that the 1st Amendment freedoms of speech and press were tied fundamentally to the ideas of liberty and due process in the 14th Amendment. Thus, the rights of free speech and press were viewed as part of an individual's liberty that, according to the 14th Amendment, could not be taken from any person without due process of law.

Since *Gitlow,* the U.S. Supreme Court has made several landmark decisions that have expanded free speech and press rights through limitations on state government power to restrain or interfere with these rights. Examples of key Court cases on free speech and press issues, originating in the state courts, are listed below:

• *Stromberg* v. *California* (1931): The Court struck down a California statute outlawing the display of a red flag because it symbolized opposition to the government. This state law was held to be a violation of constitutional rights to freedom of expression.

• *Near* v. *Minnesota* (1931): The Court overturned a state law that barred continued publication of a newspaper because it printed articles that insulted racial and religious minorities and said nasty things about certain people. This law was held to be an example of "prior restraint" of the press in violation of the 1st Amendment.

• *New York Times Co.* v. *Sullivan* (1964): The Court ruled that the 1st Amendment protects the press from libel suits that result from the printing of ar-

Protesters speak out against the Vietnam War in 1967. The 1st Amendment guarantees citizens the right to express their opinions and to criticize government.

ticles that harm the reputation of a public official.

• *Brandenburg* v. *Ohio* (1969): The Court ruled that a state may not forbid or limit speech merely because it advocates the use of force against the government or the violation of the law. Rather, government may limit speech only when it is directly and immediately connected to lawless behavior. The Court departed from the "clear and present danger" doctrine used in *Schenck* v. *United States* and *Abrams* v. *United States*, which permitted government prohibition of speech that had a tendency to encourage or cause lawless behavior.

• *Texas* v. *Johnson* (1989): The Court decided that the state of Texas could not convict and punish a person for burning an American flag during a peaceful political protest demonstration. The state's action in this case, said the Court, violated the 1st Amendment's guarantee of freedom of expression.

Since the 1960s, the Supreme Court has also broadened free speech and press rights in cases originating at the federal level of government. Examples of key cases are *Yates* v. *United States* (1957) and *New York Times Co.* v. *United States* (1971). In *Yates* the court ruled that to prosecute people for violating the Smith Act, which prohibited the advocacy of violent overthrow of the government, there must be proof of overt lawless

actions, not just expression of ideas about illegal behavior. In the *New York Times* case, the Court prevented the federal government from exercising "prior restraint" to stop a newspaper from printing information about the Vietnam War that it wanted to withhold from the public.

Supreme Court decisions in cases originating at the state and federal levels of government have protected speech and press from prior restraint by government, from charges of seditious libel by public officials, and from acts by government to ban or restrict unpopular ideas in speech and print—such as antiwar protests, antigovernment protests, and burning of the country's flag.

Americans have great freedom to say and write what they please without fear of government restrictions. But this freedom has limits pertaining to the time, place, and manner of speech. For example, individuals certainly have the right to speak out for or against candidates competing to win government offices. But they may not use amplifiers to broadcast campaign messages so loudly that residents of a community are disturbed late at night, when most people are in bed. This kind of speech is restricted by law because it unreasonably "disturbs the peace" of a community (*Kovacs* v. *Cooper,* 1949). But the government may not make a law restricting freedom of expression because of the content of the speech. In the *Kovacs* case Justice Felix Frankfurter wrote, "So long as a legislature does not prescribe what ideas may be…expressed and what may not be, nor discriminates among those who would make inroads upon the public peace, it is not for us to supervise the limits the legislature may impose."

Further, individuals do not have freedom under the Constitution to provoke a riot or other violent behavior. In times of national crisis, such as war or rebellion, the government could be justified in limiting freedom of expression that would critically threaten national security. The individual's right to freedom of expression must always be weighed against the community's need for stability and security. At issue is the point at which freedom of expression is sufficiently dangerous to the public welfare to justify constitutionally its limitation in speech, the press, television, or radio.

Issues about constitutional limits on freedom of expression have challenged every generation of Americans and will continue to do so. When and how much should the government limit a person's right to freedom of expression?

The answer of some authorities to this question has been an emphatic affirmation of practically unlimited free speech. Justice Hugo Black was an advocate of unfettered free speech. For example, consider this excerpt from his dissent in *Dennis* v. *United States* (1951):

> [A] governmental policy of unfettered communication of ideas does entail dangers. To the Founders of this Nation, however, the benefits derived from free expression were worth the risk. They embodied this philosophy in the First Amendment's command that "Congress shall make no law…abridging the freedom of speech, or of the press.…" I have always believed that the First Amendment is the keystone of our government, that the freedoms it guarantees provide the best insurance against destruction of all freedom.… [I] cannot agree that the First Amendment permits us to sustain laws suppressing freedom of speech and press on the basis of Congress' or our own notions of mere "reasonableness." Such a doctrine waters down the First Amendment so that it amounts to little more than an admonition to Congress. The Amendment as so construed is not likely to protect any but those "safe" or orthodox views which rarely need its protection.

In contrast to Justice Black's view, Chief Justice Fred M. Vinson, in his majority opinion in *Dennis,* stated a more narrow view of free speech and press, which provides more room for restrictions by government in behalf of the public security:

> Overthrow of the Government by force and violence is certainly a substantial enough interest for the Government to limit speech. Indeed, this is the ultimate value of any society, for if a society cannot protect its very structure from armed internal attack, it must follow that no subordinate value can be protected.

An alternative viewpoint, which strongly supports freedom of speech, while recognizing the need for limits, was written by Justice Louis Brandeis in *Whitney* v. *California* (1927):

> [A]lthough the rights of free speech and assembly are fundamental, they are not in their nature absolute. Their exercise is subject to restriction, if the particular restriction proposed is required to protect the State from destruction or from serious injury, political, economic or moral.…
>
> To justify suppression of free speech there must be reasonable ground to fear that serious evil will result if free speech is practiced.…
>
> [N]o danger flowing from speech can be deemed clear and present, unless the incidence of the evil apprehended is so imminent that it may befall before there is opportunity for full discussion. If there be time to expose through discussion the falsehoods and fallacies, to avert the evil by the processes of education, the remedy to be applied is more speech, not enforced silence. Only an emergency can justify repression.

Brandeis's position—great latitude for free speech, with particular limits associated with the time, manner, and place of that speech—has been the prevalent viewpoint in the United States during most of the 20th century. This viewpoint, however, poses the continuing and complex challenge of making case-by-case judgments about the delicate balance of liberty and order, about the limits on authority and the limits on freedom that in concert sustain a constitutional democracy.

SEE ALSO

Abrams v. United States; Barron v. Baltimore, Brandenburg v. Ohio; Dennis v. United States; Gitlow v. New York; Miami Herald Publishing Co. v. Tornillo; Near v. Minnesota; New York Times Co. v. Sullivan; New York Times Co. v. United States; Prior restraint; Schenck v. United States; Stromberg v. California; Texas v. Johnson; Tinker v. Des Moines Independent Community School District; Whitney v. California; Yates v. United States

FURTHER READING

Blanchard, Margaret A. *Revolutionary Sparks: Freedom of Expression in Modern America*. New York: Oxford, 1992.
Hentoff, Nat. *Free Speech For Me—But Not for Thee: How the American Left and Right Relentlessly Censor Each Other*. New York: HarperCollins, 1992.
Neuborne, Bert. "Cycles of Censorship." *Constitution* 4, no. 1 (Winter 1992): 22–29.
Powe, Lucas A., Jr. *The Fourth Estate and the Constitution: Freedom of the Press in America*. Berkeley: University of California Press, 1991.
Rosenberg, Norman. "Freedom of Speech" and "Freedom of the Press." In *By and for the People: Constitutional Rights in American History*, edited by Kermit L. Hall. Arlington Heights, Ill.: Harlan Davidson, 1991.
Smolla, Rodney A. *Free Speech in an Open Society*. New York: Knopf, 1992.

Free exercise clause

THE 1ST AMENDMENT to the Constitution states, "Congress shall make no law respecting an establishment of religion, or prohibiting the free exercise thereof." Through its free exercise clause, the 1st Amendment protects the individual's right to freedom of conscience and free expression of religious beliefs.

SEE ALSO

Religious issues under the Constitution

Fuller, Melville W.

CHIEF JUSTICE, 1888–1910

☆ *Born: Feb. 11, 1833, Augusta, Maine*
☆ *Education: Bowdoin College, B.A., 1853; Harvard Law School, 1853–55*
☆ *Previous government service: Illinois Constitutional Convention, 1861; Illinois House of Representatives, 1863–64*
☆ *Appointed by President Grover Cleveland Apr. 30, 1888; replaced Morrison R. Waite, who died*
☆ *Supreme Court term: confirmed by the Senate July 20, 1888, by a 41–20 vote; served until July 4, 1910*
☆ *Died: July 4, 1910, Sorrento, Maine*

MELVILLE W. FULLER was an active and loyal member of the Democratic party. He was also a successful lawyer who regularly represented clients in cases before the U.S. Supreme Court. When Chief Justice Morrison Waite died in 1888, President Grover Cleveland, a Democrat, chose to replace him with Fuller, who seemed to share the President's views about politics and constitutional issues.

During his 22 years as chief justice, Fuller guided Supreme Court decisions that supported racial segregation based on the "separate but equal" doctrine. He opposed government regulation of private businesses and of the uses of private property by individuals. In particular, Fuller believed that government had no right to regulate an employer's dealings with workers, such as setting rules about working conditions, payment of wages, or hours of work. These matters, according to Fuller, should be left to free bargaining between employers and workers. In *Adair* v. *United States* (1908), Fuller wrote, "The employer and the employee have equality of right, and any legislation that disturbs that equality is an arbitrary interference with liberty of contract, which no government can legally justify in a free land."

During his term on the Court, Fuller also served on the Venezuela–British Guiana Border Commission and the Permanent Court of Arbitration in The Hague, Netherlands. In these roles, Fuller worked for the peaceful resolution of international conflicts.

FURTHER READING

King, Willard L. *Melville Westin Fuller: Chief Justice of the United States.* Chicago: University of Chicago Press, 1950.

Gibbons v. Ogden

☆ *9 Wheat. 1 (1824)*
☆ *Vote: 6–0*
☆ *For the Court: Marshall*
☆ *Concurring: Johnson*

IN 1807 Robert Fulton made the first successful steamboat run from New York City to Albany. The New York legislature soon granted Fulton and a partner the exclusive right to navigate the waters of New York State. In turn, Fulton and his partner sold Aaron Ogden the right to operate between New York City and the New Jersey shore of the Hudson River.

Meanwhile, Thomas Gibbons secured a license from the U.S. Congress to run two steamships between New York and New Jersey. Competition between Gibbons and Ogden became fierce. Finally, Ogden petitioned a New York state court to order Gibbons to discontinue his business. The state court decided in Ogden's favor, and Gibbons appealed the New York court's decision to the Supreme Court.

The Issue Gibbons argued that under the Constitution, Congress had complete power to regulate interstate commerce. Therefore, his federal license to operate steamboats remained valid despite the ruling of the New York State court. Ogden countered that the congressional commerce power applied only to the transportation and sale of goods, not to navigation. Therefore, he argued, his New York license should prevail and invalidate Gibbons's license. The case raised two issues. First, what did "commerce" include? Did Congress have the power under the commerce clause (Article 1, Section 8) to regulate navigation? Second, did Congress hold an exclusive power or did the states also possess the power to regulate interstate commerce within their boundaries?

Opinion of the Court Chief Justice John Marshall wrote for the Court, which ruled in favor of Gibbons. In doing so, it defined the term *commerce* broadly. Commerce is more than traffic, the Court said. It includes all kinds of business and trade "between nations and parts of nations [the states]," including navigation.

The Court also ruled that should a state law regulating commerce interfere with a federal law, the federal law was always supreme. Consequently, the New York law giving Ogden his monopoly was invalid because it interfered with the federal law under which Gibbons had acquired his license.

The Court did not, however, resolve the second issue in the case—whether states could regulate areas of commerce Congress had not regulated. Nor did the Court decide whether the states could simultaneously regulate commerce that the Congress was regulating. These issues would have to wait several decades to be settled by additional Court rulings.

Significance The *Gibbons* case established a basic precedent because it paved the way for later federal regulation of transportation, communication, buying and selling, and manufacturing. In the 20th century, for example, the Court has ruled that the commerce clause permits Congress to fine a farmer for producing a small amount of wheat for his own use in violation of the quota set by the Department of Agriculture. Little economic activity remains outside the regulatory power of Congress today.

SEE ALSO

Commerce power

FURTHER READING

Baxter, Maurice G. *The Steamboat Monopoly, Gibbons v. Ogden, 1824.* Philadelphia: Philadelphia Book Co., 1972.
Dangerfield, George. "The Steamboat Case." In *Quarrels That Have Shaped the Constitution,* edited by John A. Garraty. New York: Harper & Row, 1987.

Gideon v. Wainwright

☆ *372 U.S. 335 (1963)*
☆ *Vote: 9–0*
☆ *For the Court: Black*
☆ *Concurring: Clark, Douglas, and Harlan*

CLARENCE EARL GIDEON, a penniless Florida drifter, was arrested for the burglary of a Florida pool hall. At his trial Gideon asked for a court-appointed attorney because he could not afford a lawyer. The court denied Gideon's request, and he conducted his own defense.

The Florida court convicted Gideon and sentenced him to five years in prison. In his jail cell, using a pencil and pad of paper, Gideon composed a petition asking the Supreme Court to review his case.

"The question is very simple," wrote Gideon. "I requested the [Florida] court to appoint me an attorney and the court refused." He maintained that the state court's refusal to appoint counsel for him denied him rights "guaranteed by the Constitution and the Bill of Rights" in the 6th and 14th Amendments. The Supreme Court decided to review Gideon's case. Unlike the Florida court, however, the Supreme Court did not expect Gideon to argue his own case. Instead, the Court appointed Abe Fortas, a prominent Washington lawyer and a future Supreme Court justice, to argue Gideon's case. Fortas defended Gideon *pro bono publico* (for the good of the public), donating his time and money for the cause of justice.

The Issue The 6th Amendment states that "in all criminal prosecutions the accused shall enjoy the right ...to have the assistance of counsel for his defense."

Despite the unmistakably clear meaning of this wording, the Supreme Court had ruled in earlier cases that in state courts, needy defendants had a constitutional right to court-appointed lawyers in only two situations: in cases involving the death penalty (*Powell* v. *Alabama,* 1932) and in cases where special circumstances, such as youth or mental incompetence, required furnishing an attorney to assure a fair trial (*Betts* v. *Brady,* 1942).

Does the 6th Amendment right to counsel apply to all criminal cases? Does the due process clause of the 14th Amendment require states to provide lawyers for defendants too poor to hire their own attorneys? Or should the Court continue to follow the precedent set in *Betts* v. *Brady*? The Supreme Court asked the attorneys arguing the

In this petition to the Supreme Court written from his jail cell, Clarence Gideon claimed that he had been denied his constitutional right to an attorney. The Supreme Court ruled unanimously in his favor.

Gideon case specifically to consider whether it should overrule *Betts* v. *Brady*.

Opinion of the Court The Court ruled unanimously in Gideon's favor and did overrule *Betts* v. *Brady*. The Court held that the right to counsel was so fundamental that the 14th Amendment due process clause extended the 6th Amendment guarantee of counsel to *all* defendants in criminal cases.

Justice Hugo Black, who had written a dissenting opinion in *Betts* v. *Brady* 21 years before, now had the pleasure of writing the Court's opinion to overturn the *Betts* decision.

Significance As a result of the ruling, the state of Florida granted Clarence Earl Gideon a new state trial in August 1963. Represented by a court-appointed lawyer, Gideon was found not guilty. The Supreme Court's decision also caused states throughout the nation to review numerous cases. Defendants too poor to afford attorneys' fees, who had been tried without the benefit of counsel, received retrials. The courts acquitted many and released them from prison.

The *Gideon* case reflected the emergence of a nationwide concern with equal justice for the poor. It recognized that, left without the aid of counsel, even intelligent and educated people have very little chance of successfully defending themselves in criminal trials. Most large cities and some states have public defender offices that provide free legal help to poor people in criminal cases. In other areas, trial court judges appoint private lawyers to represent poor defendants.

SEE ALSO

Betts v. Brady; Powell v. Alabama; Rights of the accused; Counsel, right to

FURTHER READING

Lewis, Anthony. *Gideon's Trumpet.* New York: Random House, 1964.

Ginsburg, Ruth Bader

ASSOCIATE JUSTICE, 1993–

☆ *Born: Mar. 15, 1933, Brooklyn, N.Y.*
☆ *Education: Cornell University, B.A., 1954; Harvard Law School, 1956–58; Columbia University Law School, LL.B., 1959*
☆ *Previous government service: law secretary, U.S. District Court, 1959–61; judge, U.S. Court of Appeals for the District of Columbia Circuit, 1980–93*
☆ *Appointed by President Bill Clinton June 14, 1993, to replace Byron White, who resigned*
☆ *Supreme Court term: confirmed by the Senate Aug. 3, 1993, by a 96–3 vote*

ON JUNE 14, 1993, President Bill Clinton nominated Ruth Bader Ginsburg to replace Justice Byron White on the U.S. Supreme Court. She was the second woman, after Justice Sandra Day O'Connor (appointed in 1981), to be named to the Court. She was the first Jew appointed to the Court since Abe Fortas was nominated by President Lyndon B. Johnson in 1965.

In 1960 Justice Felix Frankfurter rejected Ginsburg's application to serve as his law clerk. She had been an honor student at the law schools of two universities, Harvard and Columbia, and had strong recommendations from her professors. While recognizing her great talent, Justice Frankfurter explained that he did not want a woman as his law clerk. This rebuff inspired Ruth Bader Ginsburg to make her mark on constitutional law.

From 1960 to 1980 Ginsburg moved from a job as a federal district court law clerk to an appointment by President Jimmy Carter as a federal appellate court judge. Judge Ginsburg served for 13 years on the U.S. Court of Appeals for the District of Columbia Circuit.

Before serving as a federal appellate

court judge, Ginsburg was a professor of law at Rutgers University (1963–72) and Columbia University (1972–73). From 1973 to 1980 she was an attorney for the American Civil Liberties Union (ACLU), where she started the Women's Rights Project. As an ACLU lawyer, Ginsburg argued six cases before the U.S. Supreme Court and won five of them, including *Reed* v. *Reed*, in which the Court struck down an Idaho law that discriminated against women in the appointment of estate executors. These legal victories greatly advanced the cause of constitutional rights for women.

In nominating Judge Ginsburg for the Supreme Court, President Clinton recognized her outstanding contributions to the development of constitutional law and the rights of women. "Over the course of a lifetime in her pioneering work in behalf of the women of this country," he said, "she has compiled a truly historic record of achievement in the finest traditions of American law and citizenship."

Gitlow v. New York

☆ 268 U.S. 652 (1925)
☆ Vote: 7–2
☆ For the Court: Sanford
☆ Dissenting: Holmes and Brandeis

BENJAMIN GITLOW was a member of the Communist Labor Party of the United States, organized in 1919. He participated in the writing and distribution of a pamphlet published by his party called the *Left Wing Manifesto*. This pamphlet urged the people of the United States to rise up and overthrow their government and bring about a communist revolution. Gitlow was arrested and convicted for violating New York's Criminal Anarchy Law, which made it a crime to advocate violent revolution against the government.

The Issue Gitlow claimed the Criminal Anarchy Law was unconstitutional because it violated his constitutional rights to free speech and press. The 14th Amendment says that a state government cannot deprive a person of liberty without due process of law. Furthermore, Gitlow's lawyers argued that the due process clause of the 14th Amendment could be used to extend 1st Amendment rights of free speech and press to the states. Did New York's Criminal Anarchy Law deprive Gitlow of his constitutional rights to freedom of expression? Could the 14th Amendment's due process clause be used to hold state governments to the free speech and press standards of the 1st Amendment?

Opinion of the Court The Court upheld Gitlow's conviction and concluded that the Criminal Anarchy Law was constitutional. Justice Edward T. Sanford wrote, "[A] state may punish utterances endangering the foundations of organized government and threatening its overthrow by unlawful means." He concluded that Gitlow's pamphlet was not a mere discussion of ideas. Rather, it was "the language of direct incitement" to violent revolution.

The Court, agreed, however, that 1st Amendment free speech and press rights could be applied to the states through the 14th Amendment. Justice Sanford wrote that "for present purposes we may and do assume that freedom of speech and of the press—which are protected by the First Amendment from abridgement by Congress—are among the fundamental personal rights and liberties protected by the due process clause of the Fourteenth Amendment from impairment by the states."

Dissent Justice Oliver Wendell Holmes, with Justice Louis Brandeis

Benjamin Gitlow, a communist who advocated revolution, claimed that he had a right to free speech. The Court, however, upheld a New York law that made it illegal to call for violent overthrow of the government.

concurring, disagreed with the Court's decision to uphold the conviction of Gitlow. Holmes argued that the mere expression of ideas, separated from action, could not be punished under the "clear and present danger" doctrine that he had defined in *Schenck* v. *United States* and modified in his dissent in *Abrams* v. *United States* (both 1919). In his *Gitlow* dissent, Holmes followed his line of reasoning in *Abrams,* in which he stated that unless speech could be linked clearly with immediate violent and unlawful action, it should be permitted. Holmes said, "Every idea is an incitement. It offers itself for belief and, if believed it is acted on unless some other belief outweighs it." Further, Holmes said that there was no evidence that Gitlow's pamphlet was likely to incite violent revolution and that it posed only a remote threat to social order. Holmes and Brandeis agreed strongly with the Court's conclusion that the 1st Amendment should apply to the states.

Significance This case was the foundation for the incorporation of the 1st Amendment under the due process clause of the 14th Amendment in order to limit the states' power to restrict the free speech and press rights of individuals. The incorporation doctrine has been used gradually to apply most of the federal Bill of Rights to the states. Furthermore, beginning in the 1960s the Court rejected the narrow interpretation of free speech expressed by Justice Sanford in this case. The broader interpretation of free speech, expressed by Justice Holmes in dissent, has become the prevailing position of the Court. Thus the *Gitlow* case is important because it provided a foundation for the future expansion of free speech and press rights of individuals.

SEE ALSO
Abrams v. United States; Freedom of speech and press; Incorporation doctrine; Schenck v. United States

Goldberg, Arthur J.

ASSOCIATE JUSTICE, 1962–65

☆ Born: Aug. 8, 1908, Chicago, Ill.
☆ Education: Northwestern University, B.S.L., 1929; J.D., 1929
☆ Previous government service: U.S. secretary of labor, 1961–62
☆ Appointed by President John F. Kennedy Aug. 29, 1962; replaced Felix Frankfurter, who retired
☆ Supreme Court term: confirmed by the Senate Sept. 25, 1962, by a voice vote; resigned July 25, 1965
☆ Subsequent government service: U.S. ambassador to the United Nations, 1965–68
☆ Died: Jan. 19, 1990, Washington, D.C.

ARTHUR J. GOLDBERG was the youngest child of Russian Jewish parents who settled in Chicago. He served less than three years on the Supreme Court, resigning to become the U.S. ambassador to the United Nations.

After graduating from law school, Goldberg became an expert on the legal concerns of labor unions. He often represented unions in legal disputes with employers. In 1961 President John Kennedy appointed Goldberg to be secretary of labor. One year later, the President named Goldberg to the Supreme Court.

During his brief term on the Court, Justice Goldberg supported the expansion of 1st Amendment freedoms of expression and association. He also backed the rights of individuals accused of crimes. In *Escobedo* v. *Illinois* (1964), for example, Justice Goldberg wrote the Court's opinion that overturned the murder conviction of a man who had been denied the 6th Amendment right to counsel during questioning by the police. Justice Goldberg also argued that the police had not advised Escobedo of his right to remain silent and had therefore violated Escobedo's 5th Amendment protection against self-incrimination.

After leaving the Court, Goldberg served for three years as U.S. ambassador to the United Nations. He then returned to the private practice of law in Washington, D.C.

Good faith exception

S E E Exclusionary rule; United States v. Leon

Grand jury

THE 5TH AMENDMENT to the U.S. Constitution provides that "no person shall be held to answer for a capital, or otherwise infamous crime, unless on a presentment or indictment of a Grand Jury, except in cases arising in the land or naval forces, or in the Militia, when in actual service in time of War or public danger." A grand jury is a group of 12 to 20 people convened to hear, in private, evidence presented by the prosecutor against a person accused of a crime. If a majority of the jurors agree that the accused person has committed a crime, an indictment, or formal charge, is issued. In this way, the government is empowered to proceed with its legal action against the accused person.

The grand jury is a means of protecting an accused person against hasty and oppressive action by a prosecutor for the government. In *Wood* v. *Georgia* (1962) the U.S. Supreme Court clearly described the value of the grand jury in protecting the rights of an accused person: "[I]t serves the invaluable function of stand-

This 1973 subpoena commands President Richard Nixon to turn over tapes of his private conversations to the grand jury involved in the Watergate investigation.

ing between the accuser and the accused…to determine whether a charge is founded upon reason or was dictated by an intimidating power or by malice and personal ill will."

S E E A L S O
Due process of law; Rights of the accused

Gray, Horace
ASSOCIATE JUSTICE, 1882–1902

☆ Born: Mar. 24, 1828, Boston, Mass.
☆ Education: Harvard College, A.B., 1845; Harvard Law School, LL.B., 1849
☆ Previous government service: reporter, Massachusetts Supreme Court, 1853–61; associate justice, 1864–73, Massachusetts Supreme Court; chief justice, Massachusetts Supreme Court, 1873–81
☆ Appointed by Chester A. Arthur Dec. 19, 1881; replaced Nathan Clifford, who died
☆ Supreme Court term: confirmed by the Senate Dec. 20, 1881, by a 51–5 vote; served until Sept. 15, 1902
☆ Died: Sept. 15, 1902, Nahant, Mass.

HORACE GRAY was a notable legal scholar with a reputation for basing decisions on careful research. He believed in the separation of legal decisions from politics.

Justice Gray's most important opinion for the Court was in the case of *United States* v. *Wong Kim Ark* (1898). He interpreted the 14th Amendment to mean that anyone born in the United States, regardless of race or national origin, had a right to U.S. citizenship. Therefore, Wong Kim Ark, who was born in the United States to immigrant parents from China, had a natural right to citizenship that could not be denied by the government.

S E E A L S O
United States v. Wong Kim Ark

Grier, Robert C.

ASSOCIATE JUSTICE,
1846–70

☆ Born: Mar. 5, 1794, Cumberland
   County, Pa.
☆ Education: Dickinson College, B.A.,
   1812; studied law privately
☆ Previous government service: judge,
   Allegheny County District Court, Pa.,
   1833–46
☆ Appointed by President James K. Polk
   Aug. 3, 1846; replaced Henry Baldwin,
   who died
☆ Supreme Court term: confirmed by the
   Senate Aug. 4, 1846, by a voice vote;
   retired Jan. 31, 1870
☆ Died: Sept. 25, 1870, Philadelphia, Pa.

ROBERT C. GRIER was a school-
teacher and principal before becoming a
lawyer. He was an active supporter of
the Jacksonian Democratic party. President James K. Polk appointed Grier to
the Supreme Court because of his loyalty
to Democratic party ideas on government and law.

Justice Grier's most important opinion for the Court was the *Prize Cases*
(1863), which supported President
Abraham Lincoln's coastal blockade of
Southern ports during the Civil War.
Owners of ships and cargoes taken by
the federal government as prizes of the
war argued that Lincoln's blockade was
illegal. Writing for the Court, Justice
Grier emphasized the President's duty to
preserve the federal union in a time of
crisis as justification for the blockade
and for the seizure of ships that violated
the blockade.

Griswold v. Connecticut

☆ 381 U.S. 479 (1965)
☆ Vote: 7–2
☆ For the Court: Douglas
☆ Concurring: Goldberg, Harlan, and White
☆ Dissenting: Black and Stewart

ESTELLE GRISWOLD, executive director of the Planned Parenthood League of
Connecticut, provided information to
married people about how to use birth
control devices to prevent pregnancy.
This behavior violated an 1879 Connecticut law, which banned the use of drugs,
materials, or instruments to prevent conception. Griswold was convicted of the
crime of giving married couples advice on
birth control and contraceptive devices.

The Issue The defendant argued
that she had a constitutional right to privacy that was violated by enforcement of
the 1879 state law. Is there a constitutional right to privacy that prevents the
government from intruding into certain
areas of a person's life, such as his or her
choices and actions involving birth control? Could this constitutional right to
privacy be applied to the states through
the due process clause of the 14th
Amendment?

Opinion of the Court The Court
struck down the 1879 Connecticut law
as an unconstitutional invasion of the
individual's right to privacy in personal
relationships between consenting adults.
However, the Court offered differing interpretations of the constitutional right
to privacy.

Writing for the majority, Justice
William O. Douglas said that the 1st,
4th, 5th, and 9th Amendments imply
"zones of privacy that are the foundation
for a general right to privacy." And, he
wrote, the 14th Amendment allows these
implications from the federal Bill of
Rights to be used to limit state governments.
That amendment states, "No State shall
make or enforce any law which shall
abridge the privileges or immunities of
citizens of the United States; nor shall
any State deprive any person of life, liberty, or property without due process of
law."

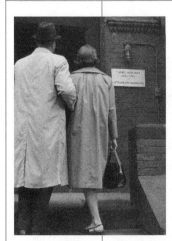

A couple enters a Planned Parenthood clinic in 1965. That year, the Griswold *case determined that the government cannot ban access to birth control information because that would violate an individual's right to privacy.*

Justice Arthur Goldberg argued for a broader view of the right to privacy by using the 9th Amendment: "The enumeration in the Constitution of certain rights shall not be construed to deny or disparage others retained by the people." According to Goldberg, the idea of liberty stated in the 14th Amendment protects personal rights that are not listed in the federal Bill of Rights. These additional rights, protected by the 9th Amendment, are "so rooted in the traditions and conscience of our people as to be ranked fundamental."

Justices Harlan and White presented concurring opinions based solely on the due process clause of the 14th Amendment. Justice Harlan argued that privacy is a fundamental right at the core of due process. There are two conceptions of due process: Procedural due process refers to the necessity of following the rules of the legal process. Substantive due process refers to unspecified rights that are included in the more general definition of due process as legal fairness. Justice Harlan used the idea of substantive due process to justify the protection of an individual's right to privacy from intrusion by the state government.

Dissent The dissenting opinions by Justices Hugo Black and Potter Stewart judged the 1879 Connecticut law to be flawed; Justice Stewart called it "an uncommonly silly law." However, both Black and Stewart argued that the 1879 law did not violate any constitutional right. Stewart wrote, "I can find no such general right of privacy in the Bill of Rights, in any other part of the Constitution, or in any case ever before decided before this Court."

Both Black and Stewart criticized the Court's majority for going beyond

the Constitution to use their judicial power willfully to achieve a desired social outcome. Justice Black concluded, "Use of any such broad, unbounded judicial authority would make of this Court's members a day-to-day constitutional convention." According to Stewart, this unrestrained use of judicial power would lead to a "great unconstitutional shift of power to the courts" and away from the legislative and executive branches, the branches directly accountable to the people through regular elections.

Significance The constitutional right to privacy, affirmed in the *Griswold* case, has been used to support the right to an abortion against restrictive state laws, as in the Court's decision in *Roe* v. *Wade* (1973). This right-to-privacy position has, however, remained controversial.

SEE ALSO
Privacy, right to; Roe v. Wade

Gun control and the right to bear arms

THE 2ND AMENDMENT to the U.S. Constitution says, "A well regulated Militia, being necessary to the security of a free State, the right of the people to keep and bear Arms, shall not be infringed." This provision of the federal Bill of Rights was derived from the contents of the original 13 state constitutions. For example, the Virginia Declaration of Rights (1776) stated that "a well-regulated Militia, composed of the body of the people, trained to arms, is the proper, natural, and safe defense of a free State." The Pennsylvania Constitution of 1776 said, "The people have a right to bear arms for the defense of themselves and the state."

The provisions of the 2nd Amendment have raised many issues and arguments about gun control laws and the constitutional limits on the right of individuals to bear arms. Does the 2nd Amendment primarily protect an individual's right to bear arms and prohibit the government from making and enforcing gun control laws? Or does it primarily guarantee to individuals only the right to bear arms in connection with service in a state's militia forces? Does the 2nd Amendment apply only to the federal government, or does it also limit state governments? What has been the Supreme Court's interpretation?

In *Presser* v. *Illinois* (1886) the Court held that the 2nd Amendment applied only to the federal government and did not prohibit state governments from regulating an individual's ownership or use of guns. In 1982 the Court reaffirmed the *Presser* ruling by refusing to hear a case about an ordinance in Morton Grove, Illinois, that banned handgun possession within the city. The Court let stand a decision by the Seventh Circuit Court of Appeals, *Quilici* v. *Village of Morton Grove* (1983), which exempts state and local laws from 2nd Amendment restrictions. Thus, the 2nd Amendment remains one of the few provisions of the Bill of Rights that is not "incorporated" under the due process clause of

An ad from the National Rifle Association uses the 2nd Amendment to claim that government should not limit a person's right to bear arms.

the 14th Amendment and thereby applied to state governments.

The Court has upheld a federal gun control law, the National Firearms Act of 1934. This law required taxation and registration of sawed-off shotguns and automatic weapons. In *United States* v. *Miller* (1939), the Court ruled that the weapons controlled by the National Firearms Act had no "reasonable relationship to the preservation or efficiency of a well-regulated militia."

Since *Miller*, lower-level courts have upheld various gun control laws. Further, the government may regulate the type of weapon individuals keep. For example, individuals do not have the right to own or keep artillery or rockets for their private use. In *United States* v. *Hale* (1992), the U.S. Court of Appeals for the Eighth Circuit held that "it is not sufficient to prove that the weapon in question was susceptible to military use.... Rather, the claimant of Second Amendment protection must prove that his or her possession of the weapon was reasonably related to a well-regulated militia."

At present, state governments are not prohibited by the 2nd Amendment from enacting gun control laws. Legal issues about these laws have been left to the state legislatures and state courts to decide. State courts have tended to uphold local ordinances and state laws to regulate or control ownership of guns. In 1968, for example, the New Jersey Supreme Court (*Burton* v. *Sills*) upheld a state law that required individuals to obtain permits and licenses for their guns. The New Jersey Supreme Court argued that the 2nd Amendment was "framed in contemplation not of individual rights but of the maintenance of the states' active, organized militia." Further, the federal Seventh Circuit Court of Appeals ruled in the *Quilici* case that the 2nd

This ad, sponsored by Handgun Control Inc., calls for laws banning the sale and use of handguns.

Amendment "had no other effect than to restrict the power of the National Government" in matters pertaining to "those arms which are necessary to maintain well-regulated militia."

SEE ALSO
Incorporation doctrine

FURTHER READING

Alderman, Ellen, and Caroline Kennedy. "The Right to Keep and Bear Arms." *Constitution* 3, no. 1 (Winter 1991): 66–73.
Cress, Lawrence Delbert. "The Right to Bear Arms." In *By and for the People: Constitutional Rights in American History*, edited by Kermit L. Hall. Arlington Heights, Ill.: Harlan Davidson, 1991.
Halbrook, Stephen P. *That Every Man Be Armed: The Evolution of a Constitutional Right*. Albuquerque: University of New Mexico Press, 1985.

Habeas corpus, writ of

ARTICLE 1, SECTION 9, of the U.S. Constitution states: "The privilege of the Writ of Habeas Corpus shall not be suspended, unless when in Cases of Rebellion or Invasion the public Safety may require it." The Latin term *habeas corpus* means "You shall have the body." A writ is a written order from a court of law that requires the performance of a specific act. A writ of habeas corpus requires officials to bring a person whom they have arrested and held in custody before a judge in a court of law, where they must convince the judge that there are lawful reasons for holding the prisoner. If the judge finds their reasons unlawful, then the court frees the suspect. The writ of habeas corpus is a strong protection for individuals from government officials who might want to jail them merely because they belong to unpopular groups or express criticisms of the government.

The privilege of the writ of habeas corpus is rooted in English common law and was specified in Section 39 of the Magna Carta (1215), through which English aristocrats imposed limits on the power of the king. Parliament enacted a habeas corpus statute in 1641, but because it was not entirely effectual, an amendment act was passed in 1679. The Crown was thus prevented from unjustly holding individuals in prison for personal or political reasons. By the end of the 17th century this individual right was solidly established as the appropriate process for curbing illegal imprisonment.

The English habeas corpus acts were not extended to the Anglo-American colonies. However, the writ was one of the widely recognized common law rights of individuals in the American colonies and was frequently invoked before the Revolution. After the Declaration of Independence, the privilege of the writ of habeas corpus was included in several state constitutions enacted prior to the U.S. Constitution of 1787. The Second Article of Compact of the Northwest Ordinance of 1787 also protected this right. The federal Judiciary Act of 1789 provided power to all federal courts "to grant writs of habeas corpus for the purpose of an inquiry into the cause of commitment." Every state of the United States of America has a similar law providing for writs of habeas corpus.

The U.S. Supreme Court has consistently upheld the individual's habeas corpus right, even when this right has been suspended by the federal government to

The Constitution requires that every prisoner be brought before a judge to determine if there are lawful reasons for holding him.

guard public safety and security. In 1861, after the outbreak of the Civil War, President Abraham Lincoln suspended habeas corpus in parts of Maryland. This action was challenged in *Ex parte Merryman* (1861). Chief Justice Roger Taney, sitting as a circuit judge, ruled that only Congress had the right to suspend the writ, but Lincoln ignored the ruling. In *Ex parte Milligan* (1866) the Supreme Court decided that the writ could not be suspended in states (Indiana, in this case) where public order and safety were not endangered by the Civil War. In 1869 Chief Justice Salmon Chase wrote in *Ex parte Yerger* that the privilege of the writ of habeas corpus is "the best and only sufficient defense of personal freedom." Ever since the founding of the United States, Americans have believed the writ of habeas corpus to be a primary protection of their personal liberties.

SEE ALSO
Ex parte Milligan

FURTHER READING
Yackle, Larry W. "Habeas Corpus."
  Constitution 5, no. 1(Winter 1993): 61–66.

Hammer v. Dagenhart

☆ *247 U.S. 251 (1918)*
☆ *Vote: 5–4*
☆ *For the Court: Day*
☆ *Dissenting: Holmes, McKenna, Brandeis, and Clarke*

IN 1916 Congress passed the Keating-Owen Child Labor Act, which banned the interstate shipment of products made by child labor. This federal law applied to businesses that employed children younger than 14 years of age or employed children of ages 14 through 16 for more than eight hours a day or more than six days per week.

Roland H. Dagenhart's two sons,

Reuben (under 14 years old) and John (between 14 and 16 years old), worked at a cotton mill in Charlotte, North Carolina. He did not want his sons to lose their jobs because of the federal law regulating child labor. So Dagenhart brought suit to prevent the federal government from enforcing the Child Labor Act.

The Issue The Child Labor Act was based on Article 1, Section 8, of the Constitution, which gives Congress power to "regulate commerce among the several states." Dagenhart claimed that the Child Labor Act was not a constitutional regulation of commerce. Rather, it regulated conditions of production at the workplace, a power reserved to the states under the 10th Amendment of the Constitution. Dagenhart also argued that the federal law violated the due process clause of the 5th Amendment by taking away his sons' liberty to work. Did Congress, in passing the Child Labor Act, exceed its power to regulate interstate commerce? Did the Child Labor Act violate the 5th Amendment rights of children desiring employment?

Opinion of the Court Justice William Day agreed with the federal government that child laborers need protection but said the state governments, not the federal government, were the proper source of legal regulation. In his opinion, Justice Day wrote that powers "not expressly delegated to the national government are reserved to the people and the

Louisiana children, hired in violation of a state child labor law, shuck oysters for a few cents a day. The Court ruled in the Hammer *case that it was the responsibility of state governments, not the federal government, to regulate child labor.*

states." This is an incorrect statement of the 10th Amendment, which does not include the word *expressly* but says, "The powers not delegated to the United States by the Constitution, nor prohibited by it to the States, are reserved to the States respectively, or to the people." Inclusion of *expressly* in a restatement of the 10th Amendment implies a narrow interpretation of Congress's commerce power and a broad view of powers reserved to the states, which is the position of the Court in this case. Day concluded that it was North Carolina's right to decide the appropriate age of child laborers or their conditions of work. Congress has no power under the Constitution to force child labor laws on the states. To permit it to do so, wrote Justice Day, would be to destroy the system of federalism established by the Constitution.

Dissent Justice Oliver Wendell Holmes argued for a broad interpretation of the federal government's power to regulate interstate commerce, which, he said, is "given…in unqualified terms, [and] the power to regulate [includes] the power to prohibit." Holmes also argued that the Constitution was designed to be adapted to "the felt necessities" and problems of different eras. The Court should interpret the Constitution, said Holmes, to respond to changing times unless the Constitution specifically prevents it from doing so. Holmes concluded: "The public policy of the United States is shaped with a view to the benefit of the nation as a whole.…The national welfare understood by Congress may require a different attitude within its sphere from that of some self-seeking state."

Significance The dissent of Justice Holmes eventually prevailed. In *United States* v. *Darby Lumber Company* (1941), the Court overturned the decision in *Hammer* v. *Dagenhart*. Justice Holmes's dissent in this case became the basis for the Court's decision in the *Darby* case.

SEE ALSO
Commerce power; Federalism; United States v. Darby Lumber Co.

Harlan, John Marshall

ASSOCIATE JUSTICE, 1877–1911

☆ *Born: June 1, 1833, Boyle County, Ky.*
☆ *Education: Centre College, B.A., 1850; studied law at Transylvania University, 1851–53*
☆ *Previous government service: adjutant general of Kentucky, 1851; county judge, Franklin County, Ky., 1858; attorney general of Kentucky, 1863–67*
☆ *Appointed by President Rutherford B. Hayes Oct. 17, 1877; replaced David Davis, who resigned*
☆ *Supreme Court term: confirmed by the Senate Nov. 29, 1877, by a voice vote; served until Oct. 14, 1911*
☆ *Died: Oct. 14, 1911, Washington, D.C.*

JOHN MARSHALL HARLAN belonged to a wealthy and prominent Kentucky family. They were slaveholders and participants in public affairs.

Harlan joined the Republican party and backed the nomination of Rutherford B. Hayes for President in 1876. President Hayes rewarded Harlan with an appointment to the Supreme Court in 1877. Harlan served on the Court for almost 34 years, one of the longest terms in the Court's history. He was known as the Great Dissenter because of his opposition to several important decisions.

Justice Harlan's most famous dissent was in response to the Court's decision in *Plessy* v. *Ferguson* (1896). The Court upheld a Louisiana law requiring black railroad passengers to sit in separate cars, apart from white passengers. The Court argued that this state law was

in line with the 14th Amendment requirement of "equal protection of the laws" because black passengers were treated equally, though separately. Justice Harlan disagreed: "Our Constitution is color-blind, and neither knows nor tolerates classes among citizens." Harlan's dissenting opinion was vindicated in *Brown* v. *Board of Education* (1954), which struck down state laws requiring racial segregation in public schools. But at the time of *Plessy*, Harlan was the only member of the Court who had the vision of justice that would prevail later on, in the decisions of the Warren Court in the 1950s and 1960s.

SEE ALSO
Plessy v. Ferguson

Harlan, John Marshall, II

ASSOCIATE JUSTICE, 1955–71

☆ *Born: May 20, 1899, Chicago, Ill.*
☆ *Education: Princeton University, B.A., 1920; Oxford University, Rhodes Scholar, B.A., 1923; New York Law School, LL.B., 1925*
☆ *Previous government service: assistant U.S. attorney, Southern District of New York, 1925–27; special assistant attorney general of New York State, 1928–30; chief counsel, New York State Crime Commission, 1951–53; judge, U.S. Court of Appeals for the Second Circuit, 1954–55*
☆ *Appointed by President Dwight D. Eisenhower Nov. 8, 1954; replaced Robert Jackson, who died*
☆ *Supreme Court term: confirmed by the Senate Mar. 16, 1855, by a 71–11 vote; retired Sept. 23, 1971*
☆ *Died: Dec. 29, 1971, Washington, D.C.*

JOHN MARSHALL HARLAN II was the grandson of Justice John Marshall Harlan, who served on the Supreme Court from 1877 to 1911. His family was wealthy and prominent and provided Harlan with the best educational opportunities. He studied hard and made the most of his opportunities, winning a prestigious Rhodes Scholarship to study at Oxford University in England.

A lifelong member of the Republican party, Harlan was appointed to the Supreme Court by Republican President Dwight D. Eisenhower. Two of Justice Harlan's most important opinions were written for *National Association for the Advancement of Colored People* v. *Alabama ex rel. Patterson* (1958) and *Poe* v. *Ullman* (1961).

Justice Harlan's opinion in *NAACP* v. *Alabama* was the first Court decision to include freedom of association within the 1st and 14th Amendment provisions for protection of individual liberties. His dissent in *Poe* v. *Ullman* argued for a right to privacy in marital relationships. Four years later, in *Griswold* v. *Connecticut* (1965), a majority of the Court generally agreed with Justice Harlan's ground-breaking views in the *Poe* case, affirming a constitutional right to privacy.

SEE ALSO
Griswold v. Connecticut; Privacy, right to

FURTHER READING
Yarbrough, Tinsley E. *John Marshall Harlan: Great Dissenter of the Warren Court.* New York: Oxford University Press, 1992.

Hazelwood School District v. Kuhlmeier

☆ *484 U.S. 260 (1988)*
☆ *Vote: 6–3*
☆ *For the Court: White*
☆ *Dissenting: Brennan, Marshall, and Stevens*

STUDENTS IN a high school journalism class were involved in the publication of a school-sponsored newspaper. Because the newspaper was produced in the journalism class, it was part of the school curriculum. The journalism students became upset when the school principal deleted two pages from an issue of their newspaper.

The deleted pages contained sensitive information about a student pregnancy and the use of birth control devices and about the divorce of another student's parents. The principal decided that the deleted articles were inappropriate for the intended readers of the school newspaper. But the student journalists claimed that their constitutional rights to freedom of expression were violated by the principal.

The Issue Did the school principal violate the student journalists' 1st Amendment right to freedom of the press when he deleted their articles from the school newspaper?

Opinion of the Court The Court held that the students' constitutional rights were *not* violated in this case. Justice Byron White wrote the majority opinion. He argued that "the First Amendment rights of students in the public schools are not automatically co-extensive with the rights of adults in other settings." The application of these rights to students in schools, therefore, must be tempered by concern for the special conditions and purposes of the school setting.

White held that a "school need not tolerate student speech that is inconsistent with its basic educational mission, even though the government could not censor similar speech outside the school." The school officials have the authority to regulate the contents of a school newspaper because the student journalists are producing this publication as part of the regular program of studies in the school. Thus, the school officials acted in their capacity as educators of these journalism students when

they deleted material from the school newspaper.

Justice White concluded, "It is only when the decision to censor a school-sponsored publication…has no valid educational purpose that the First Amendment is so [involved] as to require judicial intervention to protect students' constitutional rights." In this case, the Court felt that there was a valid educational purpose for limiting the students' freedom of expression.

Dissent Justice William Brennan dissented in this case:

In my view the principal…violated the First Amendment's prohibitions against censorship of any student expression that neither disrupts classwork nor invades the rights of others. . . .

[E]ducators must accommodate some student expression even if it offends them or offers views or values that contradict those the school wishes to inculcate. . . .

The mere fact of school sponsorship does not, as the court suggests, license such thought control in the high school, whether through school suppression of disfavored viewpoints or through official assessment of topic sensitivity. The former would constitute unabashed and unconstitutional viewpoint discrimination, as well as an impermissible infringement of the students' "right to receive information and ideas."

The Supreme Court decided in the Hazelwood *case that school officials have the right to censor the school newspaper if there is a valid educational reason for doing so.*

Significance This decision reinforced the opinion in *Bethel School District No. 403* v. *Fraser* (1986), which held that the 1st Amendment rights of public school students are not exactly the same as the rights of adults in other places. This narrow view of student rights in public schools also prevailed in *New Jersey* v. *T.L.O.* (1985), a case about 4th Amendment rights of protection against unwarranted searches and seizures of an individual's possessions.

S E E A L S O

Bethel School District No. 403 v. Fraser; Student rights under the Constitution; New Jersey v. T.L.O.

Headnotes

S E E Reporter of decisions

Heart of Atlanta Motel v. United States

☆ *379 U.S. 241 (1964)*
☆ *Vote: 9–0*
☆ *For the Court: Clark*
☆ *Concurring: Black, Douglas, Goldberg*

THE CIVIL RIGHTS ACT of 1964 was the most comprehensive civil rights legislation passed by Congress since 1875. Title II of this law prohibited discrimination on the grounds of race, color, religion, or national origin in public accommodations involved in any way in interstate commerce. Its goal was to end discrimination in facilities such as hotels, motels, restaurants, concert halls, theaters, and sports arenas.

Congress based its power to regulate such businesses on the commerce clause in Article 1, Section 8, of the Constitution, which gives Congress the power to regulate commerce among the states. A case challenging the use of the commerce power by Congress to prevent racial discrimination reached the Supreme Court only a few months after the passage of the 1964 Civil Rights Act.

The Heart of Atlanta Motel in downtown Atlanta, Georgia, defied the new law by refusing to rent rooms to blacks. The motel owner claimed that Congress had exceeded its authority under the commerce clause by enacting Title II to regulate local businesses, such as hotels, that were open to the public.

The owner also argued that Title II violated his 5th Amendment rights. The 5th Amendment says that no person shall be "deprived of life, liberty, or property, without due process of law." The motel owner claimed the new Civil Rights Act regulated his private property "without due process of law."

The Issue The case represented a major test of a key part of the new Civil Rights Act. The Constitution gave Congress the clear right to regulate interstate commerce. But did this commerce power permit Congress to prohibit discrimination in privately owned accommodations open to the public within a single state?

Opinion of the Court The Supreme Court unanimously upheld Title II of the Civil Rights Act as a legitimate exercise of the commerce power. Justice Tom Clark, a former district attorney from Texas, wrote that the motel did engage in interstate commerce because it sought out-of-state customers by advertising in national publications and 75 percent of its guests were interstate travelers. Citing testimony from the congressional hearing on the act, Justice Clark pointed out that the difficulty blacks encountered in obtaining accommodations frequently discouraged them from traveling. The motel's discrimination therefore obstructed interstate commerce.

Next, Clark defined the meaning of the commerce power of Congress. He declared that Congress's power to regulate interstate commerce also gave it the authority to regulate local business that "might have a substantial and harmful effect" on interstate commerce.

Clark added that the fact that Congress had used its powers under the commerce clause to achieve a moral goal—stopping discrimination—had no bearing on the decision. "Congress was not restricted by the fact that the particular obstruction to interstate commerce with which it was dealing was also deemed a moral and social wrong," he wrote.

Finally, the Court rejected the charge that Title II violated the motel owner's 5th Amendment rights to private property. "In a long line of cases this Court has rejected the claim that the prohibition of racial discrimination in public accommodations interferes with personal liberty," declared the opinion.

Significance The Supreme Court's decision affirmed that Congress has the constitutional power to promote equality of opportunity and to prevent discrimination. The case greatly aided the cause of the civil rights movement of the 1960s, putting a solid constitutional foundation under legislative and political efforts to promote equal rights for African Americans.

SEE ALSO

Civil rights; Commerce power; Equality under the Constitution

---

Hirabayashi v. United States

☆ *320 U.S. 81 (1943)*
☆ *Vote: 9–0*
☆ *For the Court: Stone*
☆ *Concurring: Douglas, Murphy, and Rutledge*

ON DECEMBER 7, 1941, Japanese air-

Japanese-Americans on the West Coast read a notice about evacuation to internment camps.

craft attacked the U.S. naval base at Pearl Harbor, Hawaii, and won a smashing victory against the surprised American defenders. On December 8, the United States declared war on Japan. A few days later, Germany and Italy declared war on the United States. Thus, the United States was drawn into World War II.

The U.S. government feared that the 112,000 people of Japanese ancestry (most of them citizens of the United States) who lived on the West Coast might be a threat to national security in wartime. On February 19, 1942, President Franklin D. Roosevelt issued Executive Order 9066, giving authority to military commanders to establish special zones in U.S. territory threatened by enemy attack. The order invested the military commanders with power to decide who could come, go, or remain in the special military areas. The President issued this executive order on his own authority, under the Constitution, as commander in chief of the nation's armed forces. On March 21, Congress passed a law in support of the President's executive order. On March 24 General John L. DeWitt proclaimed a curfew between the hours of 8:00 P.M. and 6:00 A.M. for all people of Japanese ancestry living on the Pacific Coast.

Gordon Hirabayashi was an American citizen of Japanese ancestry. Born in the United States, he had never seen Japan. He had done nothing to suggest disloyalty to the United States. Hirabayashi was arrested and convicted for violating General DeWitt's curfew order and for failing to register at a control station in preparation for transportation to a relocation camp, which had been established by federal law.

At the time, Hirabayashi was studying at the University of Washington. He was a model citizen and well-liked student, active in the local YMCA and church organizations. Hirabayashi refused to report to a control center or obey the curfew order because he believed both orders were discriminatory edicts contrary to the very spirit of the United States. He later said: "I must maintain the democratic standards for which this nation lives. . . . I am objecting to the principle of this order which denies the rights of human beings, including citizens."

The Issue Did the U.S. government deprive certain individuals—Americans of Japanese ancestry—of their constitutional rights under the 5th Amendment? The amendment says, "No person shall be...deprived of life, liberty, or property, without due process of law." Did the national emergency of World War II permit the U.S. government to suspend the constitutional rights of Japanese Americans?

Opinion of the Court The Court unanimously upheld the curfew law for Japanese Americans living in Military Area No. 1, the Pacific coastal region of the United States. The Court ruled that the President and Congress had used the war powers provided in the Constitution appropriately. The Court also held that the curfew order did not violate the 5th Amendment.

Writing for the Court, Chief Justice Harlan Fiske Stone said that discrimination based only upon race was "odious to a free people whose institutions are founded upon the doctrine of equality." However, in this case, Stone said, the need to protect national security in time of war necessitated consideration of race and ancestry as reasons for confinement of a group of people.

Significance Gordon Hirabayashi spent more than three years in county jails and federal prisons for his refusal to comply with a law that discriminated against people because of their ancestry. However, he never accepted the judgment against him, and he resolved someday to overturn it. His new day in court came in 1983, when he filed a petition in a federal district court to reopen his case. He eventually won his case, when the Ninth Circuit Court of Appeals ruled in his favor in September 1987. His conviction was overturned on the grounds of misconduct by the law enforcement officials who arrested and detained him.

Throughout his long ordeal, Hirabayashi, like most other Japanese Americans who suffered injustice during World War II, remained a loyal American. After his 1987 legal victory he said: "When my case was before the Supreme Court in 1943, I fully expected that as a citizen the Constitution would protect me. . . . I did not abandon my beliefs and values."

SEE ALSO

Korematsu v. United States

FURTHER READING

Irons, Peter. *The Courage of Their Convictions.* New York: Free Press, 1988.
Irons, Peter. *Justice at War.* New York: Oxford, 1983.
Mydans, Carl. "Internment Remembered." *Constitution* 4, no. 1 (Winter 1992): 43.
Rauch, Rudolph S. "Internment." *Constitution* 4, no. 1 (Winter 1992): 30–42.

Historical Society, Supreme Court

THE SUPREME COURT Historical Society, founded in 1974, is a private, non-profit membership organization with the goal of promoting public knowledge about the history and current operations of the Supreme Court. One of its primary functions is obtaining grants to support research projects on the history of the Court.

The society has more than 2,600 members who support the organization through dues and additional contributions. The society's publication program also yields income through the sale of books and pamphlets. The society manages a gift shop on the ground floor of the Supreme Court Building.

Holmes, Oliver Wendell, Jr.

ASSOCIATE JUSTICE, 1902–32

☆ *Born: Mar. 8, 1841, Boston, Mass.*
☆ *Education: Harvard College, A.B., 1861; Harvard Law School, LL.B., 1866*
☆ *Previous government service: associate justice, Supreme Judicial Court of Massachusetts, 1882–99; chief justice, Massachusetts Supreme Court, 1899–1902*
☆ *Appointed by President Theodore Roosevelt as a recess appointment Aug. 11, 1902; nominated by Roosevelt Dec. 2, 1902; replaced Horace Gray, who died*
☆ *Supreme Court term: confirmed by the Senate Dec. 2, 1902, by a voice vote; retired Jan. 12, 1932*
☆ *Died: Mar. 6, 1932, Washington, D.C.*

OLIVER WENDELL HOLMES, JR., was the son and namesake of a famous Boston physician and writer. He, too, won lasting fame. As a young man, Holmes was honored for uncommon courage as a Union soldier in the Civil War. He was seriously wounded in battle three times. As an older man, Holmes became the most important legal thinker and writer of his time.

In 1881 Holmes published *The Common Law*, which has been recognized as one of the greatest works of American legal scholarship. In this book he developed a "realist" view of law and judging that emphasized "the felt necessities of the time." He argued that law is dynamic and adaptable to the changing conditions of people and their society. He wrote, "The life of law has not been logic; it has been experience."

In 1902 President Theodore Roosevelt named Holmes to the Supreme Court, where he served with distinction. During nearly 30 years on the Court, he wrote 873 opinions, more than any other justice. Holmes wrote so gracefully, forcefully, and cogently that many of his opinions continued to influence the Court long after his death, and several of his memorable phrases have often been quoted by judges, legal scholars, and historians from Holmes's time until today.

Justice Holmes's most notable opinions were written in cases about the limits and latitude of free speech. In *Schenck v. United States* (1919), Holmes, writing for the Court, said that Congress could restrict speech and writing that threatened the safety and security of the United States. He argued that freedom of speech was not unlimited: a person could be punished for "falsely shouting fire in a theater" and causing a panic. Thus, Congress could make laws to punish speech that posed a "clear and present danger" to the security and safety of people .

In *Abrams* v. *United States* (1919), Holmes wrote in dissent to support honest expression of ideas, including highly unpopular views, that posed "no clear and present danger." He expressed his famous "free market of ideas" viewpoint: "The best test of truth is the power of the thought to get itself accepted in the competition of the market." Thus, political protest and criticism are permissible and even valuable because these dissenting views challenge and test the worth of our most cherished beliefs and practices. Through free and open exchange of ideas, including unusual and unpopular opinions, we seek the truth and find ways to improve our lives.

Throughout his long life, which ended in 1932 at the age of 94, Holmes had faith in law as the best means to settle peacefully and fairly the unavoidable conflicts of human life. And he persistently argued, with considerable influence on judges, lawyers, and scholars, for a dynamic and realistic view of the law. Thus, law would always be molded to fit the changing needs of people and their communities.

SEE ALSO

Abrams v. United States; Schenck v. United States

FURTHER READING

Burton, David. *Oliver Wendell Holmes, Jr.* Boston: Twayne, 1980.

Horowitz, Morton J. "The Place of Justice Holmes in American Legal Thought." In *The Transformation of American Law, 1870–1960.* New York: Oxford, 1992.

Novick, Sheldon M. *Honorable Justice: The Life of Oliver Wendell Holmes.* New York: Dell, 1990.

Pohlman, H. L. *Justice Oliver Wendell Holmes: Free Speech and the Living Constitution.* New York: New York University Press, 1991.

Posner, Richard A., ed. *The Essential Holmes: Selections from the Letters, Speeches, Judicial Opinions, and Other Writings of Oliver Wendell Holmes, Jr.* Chicago: University of Chicago Press, 1992.

White, G. Edward. *Justice Oliver Wendell Holmes: Law and the Inner Self.* New York: Oxford, 1993.

Hughes, Charles Evans

ASSOCIATE JUSTICE, 1910–16

CHIEF JUSTICE, 1930–41

☆ *Born: Apr. 11, 1862, Glens Falls, N.Y.*

☆ *Education: Colgate University, 1876–78; Brown University, B.A., 1881; M.A., 1884; Columbia Law School, LL.B., 1884*

☆ *Other government service: special counsel, New York State Investigating Commissions, 1905–6; governor of New York, 1907–11; U.S. secretary of state, 1921–25; U.S. delegate, Washington Armament Conference, 1921; U.S. member, Permanent Court of Arbitration, 1926–30; judge, Permanent Court of International Justice, 1928–30*

☆ *Appointed by President William Howard Taft to be associate justice Apr. 25, 1910; replaced David Brewer, who died; appointed by President Herbert Hoover to be chief justice Feb. 3, 1930; replaced Chief Justice William Howard Taft, who retired*

☆ *Supreme Court term: confirmed as associate justice by the Senate May 2, 1910, by a voice vote; resigned June 10, 1916, to become Republican party candidate for President; confirmed by the Senate as chief justice Feb. 13, 1930, by a 52–26 vote; retired July 1, 1941*

☆ *Died: Aug. 27, 1948, Cape Cod, Mass.*

CHARLES EVANS HUGHES served two terms on the Supreme Court, first as an associate justice (1910–16) and then as the chief justice (1930–41). He resigned from his first Court term to become the Republican party candidate for President. He lost to his Democratic party opponent, President Woodrow Wilson, by only 23 electoral votes.

Hughes served two Republican Presidents, Harding and Coolidge, as secretary of state. In this role, he negotiated several important treaties to limit international weapons buildups and promote world peace. He was a judge on the

Permanent Court of International Justice when President Herbert Hoover appointed him to succeed William Howard Taft as chief justice of the United States.

Under Hughes's leadership, the Supreme Court actively protected the constitutional rights of individuals. In *Stromberg* v. *California* (1931), *Near* v. *Minnesota* (1931), and *DeJonge* v. *Oregon* (1937), Hughes used the due process clause of the 14th Amendment to deny state governments the power to abridge 1st Amendment freedoms of speech, press, and assembly. He also weakened the "separate but equal" doctrine on racial segregation. In his opinion for the Court in *Missouri ex rel. Gaines* v. *Canada* (1938), Hughes wrote that a state university had violated the 14th Amendment's equal protection clause by its refusal to admit a qualified African-American student to its law school.

During President Franklin D. Roosevelt's first term (1933–37), Hughes influenced the Court to reject key parts of the President's New Deal program that, according to the Court's majority, gave the federal government too much power to regulate or direct private businesses in their relationships with workers and consumers. Hughes also successfully resisted Roosevelt's court-packing plan, by which the President had hoped to add justices to the Court who would support his New Deal.

After 1937, however, Hughes began to support important New Deal legislation, to the delight of President Roosevelt and his supporters. It seems that Hughes recognized that the vast majority of the American people supported Roosevelt's programs. They had voted overwhelmingly for his reelection in 1936. So Hughes bowed to the election returns and ceased to be a major obstacle to the President's program.

Upon his retirement in 1941, Hughes was hailed as a great chief justice. In 1942 the American Bar Association honored Hughes with its medal for distinguished contributions to the law.

SEE ALSO

Court-packing plan; Near v. Minnesota; Stromberg v. California

FURTHER READING

Pusey, Merlo. *Charles Evans Hughes.* 2 vols. New York: Macmillan, 1951.

Hunt, Ward

ASSOCIATE JUSTICE, 1873–82

☆ *Born: June 14, 1810, Utica, N.Y.*
☆ *Education: Union College, B.A., 1828; Litchfield Law School, 1829*
☆ *Previous government service: New York Assembly, 1839; mayor, Utica, N.Y., 1844; judge, New York State Court of Appeals, 1866–69; New York State commissioner of appeals, 1869–73*
☆ *Appointed by President Ulysses S. Grant Dec. 3, 1872; replaced Samuel Nelson, who retired ·*
☆ *Supreme Court term: confirmed by the Senate Dec. 11, 1872, by a voice vote; retired Jan. 27, 1882*
☆ *Died: Mar. 24, 1886, Washington, D.C.*

WARD HUNT served only seven years on the Supreme Court. He regularly sided with the Court's majority, led by Chief Justice Morrison R. Waite. Hunt tended to oppose claims by African Americans for equal protection of the laws under the 14th Amendment. He also opposed extension of voting rights for women.

Justice Hunt departed from his usual position to be the lone dissenter in *United States* v. *Reese* (1876), arguing that the federal government had the power to coerce state governments to recognize the voting rights of African Americans guaranteed by the 15th Amendment. However, he returned to his usual position in *United States* v. *Cruikshank* (1876) and went along with the Court's position of indifference to the voting rights of African Americans.

Hylton v. United States

☆ *3 Dall. 171 (1796)*
☆ *Vote: 3–0*
☆ *For the Court: Seriatim opinions by Iredell, Paterson, and Chase*
☆ *Not participating: Cushing, Wilson, and Ellsworth*

IN 1794 Congress passed a law to tax carriages used as passenger vehicles. Daniel Hylton of Virginia refused to pay the tax, and the U.S. government sued Hylton for nonpayment of taxes.

The Issue Daniel Hylton said that the federal carriage tax was a direct tax of the kind prohibited by Article 1, Section 9, of the Constitution. Did Congress have the power to levy a carriage tax on passenger vehicles?

Opinion of the Court The Court upheld Congress's power to tax carriages used as passenger vehicles. The carriage tax law was an *indirect* tax, said the Court, and was not prohibited by Article 1, Section 9, of the Constitution. Justice Paterson wrote, "All taxes on expenses or consumptions are indirect taxes."

Significance This was the first time that the Supreme Court made a judgment about whether an act of Congress was constitutional. By upholding the federal carriage tax, the Court implied that it had the power to overturn it. The justices did not directly discuss the power of judicial review—the power of the Court to declare an act of Congress unconstitutional, or in violation of the Constitution, and therefore void. However, they seemed to believe that they had the power to nullify acts of Congress that

conflicted with the higher law of the Constitution. Justice Samuel Chase wrote that he would use this power of judicial review only "in a very clear case."

In 1803 Chief Justice John Marshall used the case of *Marbury* v. *Madison* to explain and justify the Court's power of judicial review of acts of Congress.

SEE ALSO
Judicial power; Judicial review; Marbury v. Madison

Impeachment

IMPEACHMENT IS the procedure, specified in the U.S. Constitution, by which members of the federal executive or judicial branches can be formally accused of wrongful behavior. The investigation of such accusations may result in their removal from office. According to Article 1, Section 2, of the Constitution, "The House of Representatives…shall have the sole Power of Impeachment"; that is, only the House can bring charges of wrongful behavior against a federal judicial or executive officer, such as the President of the United States or a justice of the U.S. Supreme Court.

According to Article 1, Section 3, "The Senate shall have the sole Power to try all Impeachments. . . . And no Person shall be convicted without the Concurrence of two thirds of the Members present." Only the Senate has the power to try the case of any person who has been impeached, or formally accused, by the House of Representatives. Conviction of the impeached person can be achieved only by a two-thirds vote of the senators present at the impeachment trial.

Article 1, Section 3, of the Constitution states, "Judgment in Cases of Impeachment shall not extend further than

There were three unsuccessful attempts to impeach Justice William O. Douglas. This 1969 cartoon suggests that some members of Congress were upset with the judicial behavior of Justice Douglas.

to removal from Office, and disqualification to hold and enjoy any Office of honor, Trust or Profit under the United States; but the Party convicted shall nevertheless be liable and subject to Indictment, Trial, Judgment and Punishment, according to Law." So, if a person is impeached by the House of Representatives and convicted by the Senate, that person will be removed from federal office and prevented from holding another federal office at any time in the future.

Only one Supreme Court justice has been impeached: Samuel Chase, in 1805, for behaving in a partisan manner. Justice Chase was an outspoken promoter of the Federalist party and an acid critic of the Jeffersonian Republican party. In 1801 Thomas Jefferson became President and the majority in Congress was made up of Jeffersonian Republicans. Justice Chase's flagrant anti-Republican behavior vexed many of the Jeffersonian Republicans, who were determined to strike back at him. The proper moment came in 1805, they believed, after the reelection of Jefferson and a Republican party majority in Congress. The House of Representatives voted to impeach Justice Chase. But the Senate voted not to convict him, and he remained a justice of the Supreme Court until his death in 1811.

The impeachment proceedings against Justice Chase set a precedent that a person should not be impeached and removed from office because of his political opinions. Article 3, Section 1, of the U.S. Constitution says, "The Judges, both of the supreme and inferior Courts, shall hold their Offices during good Behaviour." The key issue in Justice Chase's impeachment trial was whether expression of political opinions was a violation of the constitutional provision for holding office "during good Behaviour."

Was free expression of unpopular political opinions a legitimate reason for removing a justice from office? From Justice Chase's time until today, the answer has been a strong "no." Thus, the independence of Supreme Court justices has been protected against the changing tides of majority political opinion.

SEE ALSO

Chase, Samuel; Independent judiciary; Separation of powers

Implied powers

THE CONSTITUTION of the United States delegates various powers to the three branches of government. For example, Article 1, Section 8, is a list, or enumeration, of powers that Congress may exercise. The final item in this list gives Congress the power "To make all Laws which shall be necessary and proper for carrying into Execution the foregoing powers, and all other Powers vested by this Constitution in the Government of the United States, or in any Department or Officer thereof."

This necessary and proper clause permits Congress to exercise *implied powers;* that is, to identify and use pow-

Regulating the airline industry is a government activity that the Founding Fathers could not have envisioned. Congress assumes this responsibility, however, as an implied power.

ers that are logical extensions or implications of the other powers delegated in the Constitution. For example, the doctrine of implied powers gave Congress justification for making a law to charter a national bank in 1791, even though this power is not specifically listed in the Constitution as one delegated to Congress. This power was implied as "necessary and proper" for the federal government to carry out its enumerated powers, such as borrowing money, regulating currency, and providing for the general welfare of the country.

The issue of the scope of implied powers under the Constitution was first confronted by the Supreme Court in *McCulloch* v. *Maryland* (1819). This case raised the issue of whether Congress had the power to charter a bank under authority of the necessary and proper clause. Writing for a unanimous Court, Chief Justice John Marshall favored a broad construction of Congress's implied powers that clearly included the power to charter a national bank. Marshall wrote, "Let the end be legitimate, let it be within the scope of the Constitution, and all means which are appropriate, which are plainly adapted to that end, which are not prohibited, but consistent with the letter and spirit of the Constitution, are constitutional."

Chief Justice Marshall's viewpoint agreed with ideas expressed earlier by Alexander Hamilton in *The Federalist* No. 23. Hamilton wrote: "[I]t is both unwise and dangerous to deny the federal government an unconfirmed author-

ity in respect to all those objects which are entrusted to its management [grants of power enumerated in the Constitution]." In *The Federalist* No. 44, James Madison wrote that the necessary and proper clause was essential to the effective operation of the federal government. He said, "Without the substance of this power, the whole Constitution would be a dead letter."

Ever since the founding of the United States, scholars, lawyers, judges, and political leaders have argued about the scope of implied powers under the Constitution. Since the decisive opinions of Chief Justice John Marshall, however, the doctrine of implied powers has been solidly established as an important source of federal government power under the Constitution.

SEE ALSO

Constitutional construction; McCulloch v. Maryland

Incorporation doctrine

THE PASSAGE of the 14th Amendment in 1868 established new restrictions on the power of state governments to deprive individuals of civil rights and liberties. Over the course of the 20th century, the Supreme Court has decided that the 14th Amendment incorporates or absorbs most provisions of the federal Bill of Rights, thereby applying these rights to the states.

Prior to the passage of the 14th Amendment, the federal Bill of Rights (Amendments 1 through 10 to the Constitution) was understood to restrict only the actions of the federal government. This common understanding was confirmed by the Supreme Court's decision in *Barron* v. *Baltimore* (1833), which held that the 5th Amendment could not be used to restrict a state or local government from taking private property for public use without providing "just compensation." Thus, following *Barron,* the 1st Amendment freedoms of religion, speech, press, assembly, and petition, for example, checked only the federal government, not the state governments, which retained power to deal with these matters according to their own constitutions and statutes.

In 1868 the 14th Amendment was passed, primarily to protect the civil rights and liberties of former slaves, who had been freed by the Civil War and the 13th Amendment, against state governments that might try to discriminate unfairly against them. Section 1 of the 14th Amendment says, "No State shall make or enforce any law which shall abridge the privileges or immunities of citizens of the United States; nor shall any State deprive any person of life, liberty, or property, without due process of law; nor deny to any person within its jurisdiction the equal protection of the laws." However, during the remainder of the 19th century and the first quarter of the 20th century, the Supreme Court tended to interpret the 14th Amendment narrowly and thus did not use it to enhance significantly the constitutional rights of former slaves or anyone else.

The first departure from this narrow view of the 14th Amendment came in 1897 with the decision in *Chicago, Burlington & Quincy Railroad Co.* v. *Chicago.* The Supreme Court decided that the due process clause of the 14th Amendment required the states, when taking private property for public use, to give the property owners fair compensation. This right is also provided by the just compensation clause of the 5th Amendment to the Constitution. Thus, for the first time, a provision of the Bill of Rights (Amendment 5 in this instance) had been used to limit the power of a state government via the due process clause of the 14th Amendment.

The next opening for the application of the Bill of Rights to the states came in 1908 with the decision in *Twining* v. *New Jersey.* The court decided against application of the self-incrimination clause of the 5th Amendment to the states via the due process clause of the 14th Amendment. The Court stipulated, however, that the due process clause could in principle *incorporate* some rights similar to those in the federal Bill of Rights because they were essential to the idea of due process of law. The Court provided this guideline for future decisions about which rights were due each individual: "Is it [the right in question] a fundamental principle of liberty and justice which inheres in the very idea of free government and is the inalienable right of a citizen of such a government?" With this guideline, *Twining* v. *New Jersey* opened the way to future applications to the states of rights in the federal Bill of Rights via the incorporation doctrine.

In 1925 the door to application of the federal Bill of Rights to the states was opened wider in the case of *Gitlow* v. *New York.* Benjamin Gitlow had been convicted for violating New York's Criminal Anarchy Law, which made it a crime to advocate violent revolution against the government. He claimed that the state of New York had unlawfully denied his 1st Amendment right to free expression under the due process clause of the 14th Amendment. The Court upheld Gitlow's conviction but acknowledged the doctrine of incorporation of 1st Amendment freedoms in the due process clause of the 14th Amendment and their application to the states. The Court asserted that for "present purposes we may and do assume that freedom of speech and of the press—which are protected by the First Amendment from abridgement by Congress—are among the fundamental personal rights and 'liberties' protected by the due process clause of the Fourteenth Amendment from impairment by the states." This idea was reinforced in *Fiske* v. *Kansas* (1927), in which the Court used the 14th Amendment to protect the free speech rights of individuals against a state law.

In 1931, the Court ruled again (in *Near* v. *Minnesota* and *Stromberg* v. *California*) that the 14th Amendment due process clause guaranteed the 1st Amendment rights of freedom of speech (*Stromberg*) and freedom of the press (*Near*) against the power of state governments. Chief Justice Charles Evans Hughes wrote (*Near*), "It is no longer open to doubt that the liberty of the press and of speech is within the liberty safeguarded by the due process clause of the Fourteenth Amendment. It was found impossible to conclude that this essential liberty of the citizen was left unprotected by the general guaranty of fundamental rights of person and property."

Thus the Supreme Court, through its power of judicial review, had extended to all the states beyond doubt the 1st Amendment freedoms of speech and press. What about the other rights in the Bill of Rights? Were they also applicable to the states through the due process clause of the 14th Amendment?

These questions were answered slowly, on a case-by-case basis, from the 1930s through the 1980s. At present, most provisions in the Bill of Rights have been extended nationwide through decisions of the Supreme Court and are generally accepted as legitimate limitations on the powers of state governments. The exceptions are Amendment 2 (the right to bear arms), Amendment 3 (restrictions on the quartering of soldiers), the grand jury indictment clause of Amendment 5, Amendment 7 (requirement of jury trials in civil cases), and the excessive fines and bail clause of Amendment 8.

James Madison, primary author of the Bill of Rights, had wanted to restrict the powers of state governments to interfere with the individual's rights to freedom of speech, press, and religion and to trial by jury in criminal cases. He had proposed to the first federal Congress, in the summer of 1789, that "No state shall infringe the equal rights of conscience, nor the freedom of speech, or of the press, nor of the right to trial by jury in criminal cases." However, this proposal was voted down in Congress, and the principle inherent in it was not revived until ratification of the 14th Amendment in 1868. According to the records of the first Congress, "Mr. Madison conceived this to be the most valuable amendment on the whole list [of amendments that constituted the Bill of Rights]; if there was any reason to restrain the government of the United States from infringing upon these essential rights, it was equally necessary that they should be secured against the state governments."

The Supreme Court, in developing the incorporation doctrine to extend rights in the Bill of Rights to the states, has gradually and securely fulfilled Madison's great hope that the law would be used to limit the power of both federal and state governments in order to protect the inherent rights and liberties of individuals.

SEE ALSO

Barron v. Baltimore; Benton v. Maryland; Bill of Rights; Constitutional law; Due process of law; Duncan v. Louisiana; Everson v. Board of Education of Ewing Township; Gideon v. Wainwright; Gitlow v. New York; Mapp v. Ohio; Near v. Minnesota; Stromberg v. California; Wolf v. Colorado

FURTHER READING

Cortner, Richard. *The Supreme Court and the Second Bill of Rights: The Fourteenth Amendment and the Nationalization of the Bill of Rights.* Madison: University of Wisconsin Press, 1981.

THE DEVELOPMENT OF THE INCORPORATION DOCTRINE

The cases listed below established the incorporation of particular
rights in the Bill of Rights into the due process clause of the 14th Amendment.
Thus these rights were extended to the states.

YEAR	CASE	AMENDMENT	RIGHT
1897	*Chicago, Burlington & Quincy Railroad* v. *Chicago*	5	just compensation
1925	*Gitlow* v. *New York*	1	freedom of speech
1927	*Fiske* v. *Kansas*	1	freedom of speech
1931	*Stromberg* v. *California*	1	freedom of speech
1931	*Near* v. *Minnesota*	1	freedom of press
1937	*DeJonge* v. *Oregon*	1	right to assembly
1939	*Hague* v. *Congress of Industrial Organizations*	1	right to petition
1940	*Cantwell* v. *Connecticut*	1	free exercise of religion
1947	*Everson* v. *Board of Education of Ewing Township*	1	no establishment of religion
1947	*Cole* v. *Arkansas*	6	notice of accusation
1948	*In re Oliver*	6	right to public trial
1949	*Wolf* v. *Colorado*	4	no unreasonable searches and seizures
1961	*Mapp* v. *Ohio*	4	exclusion from trials of illegally seized evidence
1962	*Robinson* v. *California*	8	no cruel and unusual punishment
1963	*Gideon* v. *Wainwright*	6	right to counsel
1964	*Malloy* v. *Hogan*	5	no self-incrimination
1965	*Pointer* v. *Texas*	6	right to confront witnesses
1965	*Griswold* v. *Connecticut*	9	additional and unspecified rights
1966	*Parker* v. *Gladden*	6	right to impartial jury
1967	*Klopfer* v. *North Carolina*	6	right to speedy trial
1967	*Washington* v. *Texas*	6	right to compulsory process for obtaining witnesses
1968	*Duncan* v. *Louisiana*	6	right to jury trial in criminal prosecutions
1969	*Benton* v. *Maryland*	5	no double jeopardy

Independent judiciary

THE INDEPENDENCE of the federal judicial branch is based on the insulation of its members, once appointed and confirmed in their positions, from punitive actions by the legislative and executive branches. According to Article 3 of the Constitution, federal judges may hold their positions "during good Behaviour"; in effect, they have lifetime appointments as long as they satisfy the ethical and legal standards of their judicial offices. Furthermore, Article 3 provides that the legislative and executive branches may not combine to punish federal judges by decreasing payments for their services. The intention of these constitutional provisions is to guard the federal judges against undue influence from the legislative and executive branches in the exercise of their judicial power.

When President Lyndon Johnson (right) nominated Abe Fortas to be chief justice, critics accused Fortas of unethical behavior, and his nomination was withdrawn.

Alexander Hamilton argued for an independent judiciary in *The Federalist* No. 78. He wrote, "The complete independence of the courts of justice is peculiarly essential in a limited Constitution." Hamilton claimed that only an independent judicial branch of government would be able to impartially check excessive exercise of power by the other branches of government.

SEE ALSO
Separation of powers

Individual rights

SEE Bill of Rights; Civil rights; Liberty under the Constitution

In forma pauperis

THE LATIN phrase *in forma pauperis* means "in the manner of a pauper." Appeals for a hearing before the U.S. Supreme Court that are brought by individuals unable to pay court costs are known as *in forma pauperis* petitions. Appellants in such cases are not required to pay the filing fee.

Injunction

AN INJUNCTION is a court order requiring a person to do, or not to do, something in order to protect another's personal or property rights. A person who violates an injunction is in contempt of court and the court may fine or imprison him. An injunction usually is issued to prohibit an action. When it is used to command a positive action, it is called a mandatory injunction.

During the 20th century, courts have used injunctions to protect and promote the civil rights of minorities, especially African Americans. For example, federal courts used injunctions to stop school district officials from continuing racial segregation in schools after the decision in *Brown* v. *Board of Education* (1954). Courts also used injunctions to take positive actions, such as redrawing school district boundaries and ordering the busing of students between districts to achieve racially mixed schools. Thus, federal injunctions have become an important way of protecting the constitutional rights of individuals against infringement by state governments.

SEE ALSO
Brown v. Board of Education

In re

IN RE is a Latin phrase meaning "in the matter of." When *in re* appears in the title of a case, it means that the case does *not* have formal opposing parties. The use of *in re* refers to the object or person that is the primary subject of the case. For example, *In re Winship* (1970) was a case without adversaries. The state did not oppose the person to whom the title refers, Samuel Winship. Thus, Winship was not required in this case to defend himself in any way. Rather, this case dealt only with the standard of proof necessary to incarcerate a 12-year-old boy who had been sentenced and committed to a training school for juvenile offenders. The phrase *in re* is often used in cases involving preadult offenders, which are handled by the juvenile justice system.

SEE ALSO
In re Winship; Juvenile justice

In re Gault

☆ *387 U.S. 1 (1967)*
☆ *Vote: 8–1*
☆ *For the Court: Fortas*
☆ *Concurring: Black, White, and Harlan*
☆ *Dissenting: Stewart*

GERALD GAULT, a 15-year-old boy, made obscene telephone calls to a neighbor. At the time, he was on court-ordered probation for a different act of juvenile delinquency.

As a juvenile, Gault did not have the standard constitutional guarantees of due process, such as the right to counsel, the right to confront or cross-examine one's accuser, the privilege of protection

from self-incrimination, and the right to notice of a legal hearing. The juvenile justice system was separated from the usual criminal processes applied to adults. The intention had been to protect juvenile offenders from the harshness of adult criminal law. But these good intentions could in some cases lead to injustice, which is what Gault's advocates claimed.

If Gault had been tried as an adult, his punishment would have been a $50 fine or two months in jail. As a juvenile offender, he was sentenced to the Arizona State Industrial School until the age of 21, a six-year sentence. Further, Arizona law provided juvenile offenders virtually no due process rights, such as those set out in the 5th and 6th Amendments to the U.S. Constitution.

A state juvenile court judge convicted and sentenced Gerald Gault after two hearings. Gault's father sought his son's release from state-imposed detention on the grounds that he had been denied due process rights guaranteed by the U.S. Constitution.

The Issue Do the due process rights of individuals, specified in the 5th, 6th, and 14th Amendments, apply to juveniles, just as they do to adults accused of crimes?

Opinion of the Court The Court decided that Gerald Gault had been denied his constitutional rights of due process. Justice Abe Fortas declared that "neither the Fourteenth Amendment nor the Bill of Rights is for adults alone. . . . Under our Constitution, the condition of being a boy does not justify a kangaroo court. . . . The essential difference between Gerald's case and a normal criminal case is that safeguards available to adults were discarded in Gerald's case."

Justice Fortas held that due process of law for juveniles required at least four procedural protections of individual

In 1967 the Supreme Court decided in In re Gault *that juveniles deserve some of the same due process rights as adults.*

rights: written notification of specific charges to the juvenile and his parents, assistance of a lawyer, confrontation and cross-examination of witnesses, and protection against self-incrimination.

Justice Fortas argued that the guarantee of these four due process rights for juveniles would not require the state to treat a juvenile accused of delinquency exactly like an adult accused of crime. Rather, these safeguards would protect a juvenile against injustices that otherwise might occur.

Significance This is the Court's most important decision about the rights of juveniles accused of illegal actions. It established that juveniles have certain constitutional rights that cannot be taken away solely because of age. However, the *Gault* decision did not abolish distinctive qualities of a separate juvenile court system. In particular, the due process requirements of *Gault* apply only to the adjudication (hearing and deciding) phase of legal proceedings and not to the conviction phase. Thus, *Gault* does not interfere with the emphasis that juvenile courts have traditionally placed on personalized treatment for rehabilitation of the individual.

SEE ALSO

Due process of law; Juvenile justice

FURTHER READING

Bernard, Thomas J. *The Cycle of Juvenile Justice.* New York: Oxford, 1992.

In re Winship

☆ *397 U.S. 358 (1970)*
☆ *Vote: 6–3*
☆ *For the Court: Brennan*
☆ *Concurring: Harlan*
☆ *Dissenting: Burger, Stewart, and Black*

A 12-YEAR-OLD boy, Samuel Winship, was charged with an act of juvenile delinquency that, if committed by an adult, would be considered larceny. The boy was convicted by a family court judge according to the prevailing New York statute, which required only a "preponderance of the evidence" to justify juvenile detention. Advocates for the convicted juvenile claimed that a higher standard of proof—guilt "beyond a reasonable doubt"—should have been used in this case. That higher standard of proof had historically been the one accepted by the Court in adult criminal proceedings.

The Issue What standard of proof should be necessary to convict a juvenile for an act that would be considered a serious crime if committed by an adult? Should the due process clauses of the 5th and 14th Amendments be interpreted to require proof beyond a reasonable doubt as the standard for conviction of an accused juvenile?

Opinion of the Court Justice William J. Brennan decided that defendants in juvenile proceedings have the constitutional right to the higher standard of proof—"beyond a reasonable doubt." Brennan wrote, "We explicitly hold that the Due Process Clause protects the accused against conviction except upon proof beyond a reasonable doubt of every fact necessary to constitute the crime with which he is charged." Brennan based his opinion on common law and precedent because the "beyond a reasonable doubt" standard is not specifically stated in the U.S. Constitution.

Dissent Justice Hugo Black criticized the Court's majority in this case for stepping beyond the boundaries of its power in order to amend the Bill of Rights. He wrote, "Nowhere in that document is there any statement that conviction of crime requires proof of guilt beyond a reasonable doubt."

Significance The *Winship* decision provided juveniles accused of unlawful behavior with new constitutional protection. As stated by the Court, this higher standard of proof was also legally established for adults accused of criminal behavior.

SEE ALSO

Juvenile justice

FURTHER READING

Bernard, Thomas J. *The Cycle of Juvenile Justice.* New York: Oxford, 1992.

Iredell, James

ASSOCIATE JUSTICE, 1790–99

☆ *Born: Oct. 5, 1751, Lewes, England*
☆ *Education: read law under Samuel Johnston of North Carolina*
☆ *Previous government service: comptroller of customs, Edenton, N.C., 1768–74; collector of customs, Port of North Carolina, 1774–76; judge, Superior Court of North Carolina, 1778; attorney general of North Carolina, 1779–81; North Carolina Council of State, 1787; North Carolina Ratifying Convention, 1788*
☆ *Appointed by President George Washington Feb. 8, 1790*
☆ *Supreme Court term: confirmed by the Senate Feb. 10, 1790, by a voice vote; served until Oct. 20, 1799*
☆ *Died: Oct. 20, 1799, Edenton, N.C.*

JAMES IREDELL was an original member of the Supreme Court. President Washington decided to appoint Iredell because of his good reputation as a legal expert and his skill as a political leader in North Carolina, where he had argued decisively against opponents of the 1787 Constitution.

Iredell had attracted Washington's attention during the debates about ratification of the Constitution. Iredell published a pamphlet opposing the "Objections to the New Constitution" by George Mason, a delegate from Virginia. Iredell also stood firm against the majority of citizens in North Carolina who at first opposed the Constitution of 1787. He eventually helped to persuade North Carolinians to ratify the federal Constitution in 1789.

In dissent from the Court's decision in *Chisholm* v. *Georgia* (1793), Justice Iredell held that a state government could not be sued in a federal court by a person from another state. This position became part of the Constitution in 1795 with ratification of the 11th Amendment.

In *Calder* v. *Bull* (1798), Iredell argued that the Court had authority to declare laws null and void if they violated the Constitution of the United States, the supreme law. This position on the power of judicial review was also implied by the Court, including Iredell, in *Hylton* v. *United States* (1796). In the *Hylton* case, the Court upheld the constitutionality of a federal tax law, and the decision implied that the Court could have ruled this federal law unconstitutional. However, the Court did not discuss the power of judicial review in this case. A few years later, in *Marbury* v. *Madison* (1803), Chief Justice John Marshall argued compellingly for the Court's power of judicial review to strike down acts of Congress that were in violation of the U.S. Constitution.

SEE ALSO

Hylton v. United States; Judicial review

Jackson, Howell E.

ASSOCIATE JUSTICE, 1893–95

☆ Born: Apr. 8, 1832, Paris, Tenn.
☆ Education: West Tennessee College, B.A., 1849; University of Virginia, 1851–52; Cumberland University, 1856
☆ Previous government service: judge, Court of Arbitration for Western Tennessee, 1875–79; Tennessee House of Representatives, 1880; U.S. senator from Tennessee, 1881–86; judge, Sixth Federal Circuit Court, 1886–91; judge, Circuit Court of Appeals, 1891–93
☆ Appointed by President Benjamin Harrison Feb. 2, 1893; replaced Lucius Q. C. Lamar, who died
☆ Supreme Court term: confirmed by the Senate Feb. 18, 1893, by a voice vote; served until Aug. 8, 1895
☆ Died: Aug. 8, 1895, Nashville, Tenn.

HOWELL E. JACKSON achieved an outstanding record of public service in his home state, Tennessee. He was rewarded in 1881 by election to the U.S. Senate, where he developed a close friendship with a senator from Indiana, Benjamin Harrison, and with President Grover Cleveland. In 1886, Jackson left the Senate to accept President Cleveland's appointment to the U.S. Court of Appeals for the Sixth Circuit. In 1893, Jackson was appointed to the Supreme Court by his old friend from the Senate, President Benjamin Harrison.

Jackson served less than two years on the Court because of poor health. In fact, during this time his illness prevented him from participating in several important decisions of the Court.

Jackson's most notable opinion was his dissent in *Pollock* v. *Farmers' Loan and Trust Co.* (1895). The Court decided that the 1894 federal income tax law was unconstitutional. Jackson strongly disagreed, and his position was confirmed in 1913 with passage of the 16th Amendment to the Constitution, which grants power to the federal government to tax incomes "from whatever source derived."

Jackson, Robert H.

ASSOCIATE JUSTICE, 1941–54

☆ Born: Feb. 13, 1842, Spring Creek, Pa.
☆ Education: Albany Law School, 1912
☆ Previous government service: general counsel, Internal Revenue Bureau, 1934–36; special counsel, Securities and Exchange Commission, 1935; assistant U.S. attorney general, 1936–38; U.S. solicitor general, 1938–39; U.S. attorney general, 1940–41
☆ Appointed by President Franklin D. Roosevelt June 12, 1941; replaced Harlan F. Stone, who became chief justice
☆ Supreme Court term: confirmed by the Senate July 7, 1941, by a voice vote; served until Oct. 9, 1954
☆ Died: Oct. 9, 1954, Washington, D.C.

ROBERT H. JACKSON was a Democratic party activist before he became a lawyer. After completing law school, he continued his involvement in the Democratic party of New York and became an ally and close friend of Franklin D. Roosevelt. In 1934 Jackson went to Washington, D.C., to work in the federal government led by President Roosevelt. He eventually became solicitor general in 1938 and attorney general in 1940, and he was also an important adviser to the President. In 1941 President Roosevelt named Jackson to fill a vacancy on the Supreme Court.

Justice Jackson tended to defend the individual against threats of oppression by government officials or by an intolerant majority of the people. In *West Virginia State Board of Education* v. *Barnette* (1943), Jackson upheld the rights of a religious minority, Jehovah's Witnesses, to refrain from participating in a public exercise, saluting the flag and reciting the pledge of allegiance. He wrote: "If there is any fixed star in our constitutional constellation, it is that no official, high or petty, can prescribe what shall be orthodox in politics, nationalism, religion, or other matters of opinion or force citizens to confess by word or act their faith therein."

Jackson, however, also recognized the need for public safety and social order, which could be threatened by unlimited or extreme expressions of individual liberty. He therefore voted with the Court's majority in *Dennis* v. *United States* (1951) to uphold the convictions of American Communist party leaders who promoted the violent overthrow of the U.S. government.

In May 1945, at the end of World War II, President Harry Truman asked Jackson to serve as chief counsel for the United States in the prosecution of Nazi war criminals at the Nuremberg (Germany) war crimes trials. In this role, Jackson developed the legal principles and procedures by which leading Nazis were tried and convicted of war crimes against humanity.

SEE ALSO

West Virginia State Board of Education v. Barnette

FURTHER READING

Gerhart, Eugene C. *America's Advocate: Robert H. Jackson.* Indianapolis: Bobbs-Merrill, 1958.

Jay, John

CHIEF JUSTICE, 1789–95

☆ Born: Dec. 12, 1745, New York, N.Y.
☆ Education: King's College (Columbia University), B.A., 1764; read law with Benjamin Kissam in New York, N.Y.
☆ Previous government service: secretary, Royal Boundary Commission, 1773; Continental Congress, 1774, 1775, 1777, president, 1778–79; New York Provincial Congress, 1776–77;

chief justice, New York State, 1777–78; U.S. minister to Spain, 1779; U.S. secretary of foreign affairs, 1784–89
☆ Appointed by President George Washington Sept. 24, 1789, to be the first chief justice of the United States
☆ Supreme Court term: confirmed by the Senate Sept. 26, 1789, by a voice vote; resigned June 29, 1795
☆ Subsequent government service: governor of New York, 1795–1801
☆ Died: May 17, 1829, Bedford, N.Y.

JOHN JAY was one of the great founders of the United States. Jay was elected to the First Continental Congress in 1774 and at first resisted independence from Great Britain, but he became a fervent patriot in 1776, after the Declaration of Independence.

Jay was the main author of the New York state constitution of 1777. In 1778, he was elected president of the Continental Congress. During the 1780s he was involved in making and conducting foreign policy for the United States.

Although Jay did not attend the Constitutional Convention of 1787, he worked effectively for ratification of the federal Constitution. Toward this end, he wrote five of *The Federalist Papers* (Nos. 2, 3, 4, 5, and 64), which were originally printed in New York newspapers to support the ratification of the U.S. Constitution. Other authors were James Madison and Alexander Hamilton, who were leaders in the movement to write and ratify the Constitution. Later, Hamilton became U.S. secretary of the Treasury under President George Washington, and Madison served as a Virginia member of the House of Representatives in the first federal Congress. Madison became the fourth President of the United States in 1809.

President George Washington appointed Jay as the first chief justice of the United States. The most important decision over which Jay presided was

Chisholm v. *Georgia* (1793), in which the Court ruled that citizens of one state could bring suit in a federal court against another state.

Overall, however, Jay was disappointed at the apparent weaknesses and insignificance of the Court in comparison to the executive and legislative branches of the federal government. Political leaders seemed to pay slight attention to the Court, and few cases were taken to it. For this reason, Jay resigned as chief justice in 1795 to become governor of New York, a position for which he was elected while serving as chief justice.

President John Adams wanted to reappoint Jay as chief justice in 1800, but Jay refused because he believed the Court lacked "the energy, weight and dignity which are essential to its affording due support to the national government." In 1801, he retired from public life.

SEE ALSO

Chisholm v. Georgia

FURTHER READING

Morris, Richard B. *John Jay, the Nation and the Court.* Boston: Boston University Press, 1967.

Johnson, Thomas

A S S O C I A T E   J U S T I C E ,
1 7 9 1 – 9 3

☆ *Born: Nov. 4, 1732, Calvert County, Md.*
☆ *Education: Studied law under Stephen Bordley, Annapolis, Md.*
☆ *Previous government service: Maryland Provincial Assembly, 1762; Annapolis Convention, 1774; Continental Congress, 1774–77; governor of Maryland, 1777–80; Maryland House of Delegates, 1780, 1786–88; Maryland Ratifying Convention, 1788; chief judge, General Court of Maryland, 1790–91*
☆ *Appointed by President George Washington as a recess appointment Aug. 5, 1791; replaced John Rutledge, who resigned; nominated by Washington Oct. 31, 1791*

☆ *Supreme Court term: confirmed by the Senate Nov. 7, 1791, by a voice vote; resigned Jan. 16, 1793*
☆ *Died: Oct. 26, 1819, Frederick, Md.*

THOMAS JOHNSON was an American patriot who fought for the United States in the War of Independence. He became a friend of George Washington, who appointed him to the Supreme Court in 1791.

Johnson served on the Court for only 14 months and wrote only one opinion for the Court. President Washington later appointed Johnson to the committee that planned the new federal city. In 1795, Johnson refused Washington's offer to become secretary of state, and he retired from public life.

Johnson, William

A S S O C I A T E   J U S T I C E ,
1 8 0 4 – 3 4

☆ *Born: Dec. 27, 1771, Charleston, S.C.*
☆ *Education: College of New Jersey (Princeton), B.A., 1790; studied law with Charles Cotesworth Pinckney in Charleston*
☆ *Previous government service: South Carolina House of Representatives, 1794–98, Speaker, 1798; judge, South Carolina Constitutional Court, 1799–1804*
☆ *Appointed by President Thomas Jefferson Mar. 22, 1804; replaced Alfred Moore, who resigned*
☆ *Supreme Court term: confirmed by the Senate Mar. 24, 1804, by a voice vote; served until Aug. 4, 1834*
☆ *Died: Aug. 4, 1834, Brooklyn, N.Y.*

WILLIAM JOHNSON was President Thomas Jefferson's first appointee to the Supreme Court. Of all the justices of the Court under John Marshall, Johnson was the one most likely to disagree with the dominating chief justice. He has been remembered as the first great dissenter of the Supreme Court.

Justice Johnson was a hardworking member of the Court who wrote 112 majority opinions, 21 concurrences, and 34 dissents during 29 years on the Court. Only John Marshall and Joseph Story produced more opinions during Johnson's tenure on the Court.

FURTHER READING

Morgan, Donald G. *Justice William Johnson: The First Dissenter.* Columbia: University of South Carolina Press, 1954.

Johnson v. Transportation Agency of Santa Clara County

☆ *480 U.S. 616 (1987)*
☆ *Vote: 6–3*
☆ *For the Court: Brennan*
☆ *Concurring: O'Connor and Stevens*
☆ *Dissenting: White, Scalia, and Rehnquist*

IN 1978 the Transportation Agency of Santa Clara County, California, created an affirmative action plan to bring about fair representation in its work force of women, minorities, and disabled people. Affirmative action refers to programs or policies to provide opportunities to individuals on the basis of membership in certain groups, such as racial, ethnic, or gender categories that have been discriminated against in the past. The Santa Clara plan did not set aside a certain number of jobs for minorities, women, or the disabled. Rather, it set annual goals as guidelines for decisions about hiring and promoting workers so that eventually there would be "a work force whose composition reflected the proportion of minorities and women in the labor force."

In 1979 the Santa Clara County

Transportation Agency gave notice of a vacancy for the job of road dispatcher. This was a craftworker position, a high-level, skilled job category. None of the 238 jobs in the agency's craftworker category was held by a woman. Paul Johnson and Diana Joyce were the leading candidates, among 12 applicants, for the vacant position.

The interviewers rated both Johnson and Joyce as well qualified. Johnson, however, had a slightly higher job interview score than Joyce did, and the selection panel recommended that he get the position. Nevertheless, Diana Joyce got the job. So Johnson filed a complaint under the federal Civil Rights Act of 1964. He claimed that he was denied the job because of his sex.

The Issue This was the first case to test the legality of sex-based affirmative action plans under Title VII of the Civil Rights Act of 1964. Did the Santa Clara affirmative action plan violate Title VII of the 1964 Civil Rights Act, which prohibits an employer from depriving "any individual of employment opportunities…because of such individual's race, color, religion, sex, or national origin"? Did Santa Clara's voluntary sex-based affirmative action plan deprive Johnson of his 14th Amendment right to "equal protection of the laws"?

In 1987 the Supreme Court upheld an affirmative action plan used by the Transportation Agency of Santa Clara County, California, designed to give more opportunities for skilled jobs to women and minorities.

Opinion of the Court The Court upheld the Santa Clara Transportation Agency's affirmative action plan. Justice William Brennan wrote that it could be legal under Title VII of the 1964 Civil Rights Act to remedy imbalances of female and male workers in a skilled job category. This affirmative action plan was legal, Brennan wrote, because it merely set goals but did not establish quotas for hiring female employees. Further, this plan recognized gender as only one of several factors in decisions about hiring and promotion. Finally, the plan was acceptable because it was only a temporary means to overcome past discrimination against workers based on sex.

Dissent Justice Antonin Scalia argued that this sex-based affirmative action plan was in conflict with the specific words of Title VII of the 1964 Civil Rights Act. He wrote, "The court today completes the process of converting this [Civil Rights Act of 1964] from a guarantee that race or sex will *not* be the basis for employment discrimination, to a guarantee that it often *will*. [W]e effectively replace the goal of a discrimination-free society with the quite incompatible goal of proportionate representation by race and by sex in the workplace."

Significance For the first time, the Court decided that a voluntary sex-based affirmative action plan can be used to overcome the effects of past job discrimination based on gender. Further, the *Johnson* decision clearly endorsed affirmative action as a remedy for past discrimination, as long as it is temporary.

SEE ALSO

Affirmative action; Equality under the Constitution

FURTHER READING

Urofsky, Melvin I. *A Conflict of Rights: The Supreme Court and Affirmative Action.* New York: Scribners, 1991.

Judicial activism and judicial restraint

ARTICLE 3, SECTION 1, of the U.S. Constitution says, "The judicial Power of the United States, shall be vested in one supreme Court, and in such inferior Courts as the Congress may from time to time ordain and establish." Article 3, Section 2, provides that the "judicial Power shall extend to all Cases in Law and Equity, arising under this Constitution, the Laws of the United States, and Treaties made, or which shall be made, under their Authority." Thus, the justices of the U.S. Supreme Court have the power to interpret the Constitution, and laws and treaties of the United States, in response to cases that come before the Court.

In 1796, in *Ware* v. *Hylton,* the Supreme Court held a Virginia statute void because it violated a 1783 peace treaty with Great Britain. In *Marbury* v. *Madison* (1803) the Supreme Court declared a federal law unconstitutional. These cases established the power of judicial review in the Supreme Court—the power to declare acts of the state governments and of the legislative and executive branches of the federal government null and void if they violate provisions of the Constitution. Since the early 19th century, debate has continued over how federal judges should use their powers. Should they practice restraint, or should they actively expand the scope of the Constitution in their interpretations of law, treaties, and constitutional provisions?

Judicial restraint

Those who advocate judicial restraint believe the courts should uphold all acts of Congress and state legislatures unless they clearly violate a specific sec-

The racial integration of college campuses in some parts of the country was largely the result of judicial activism, the principle that the Supreme Court should use its power to correct social injustices such as racial segregation.

tion of the Constitution. In practicing judicial restraint, the courts should defer to the constitutional interpretations of Congress, the President, and others whenever possible. The courts should hesitate to use judicial review to promote new ideas or policy preferences. In short, the courts should interpret the law and not intervene in policy-making.

Over the years eminent Supreme Court Justices such as Felix Frankfurter have called for judicial self-restraint. In *West Virginia State Board of Education* v. *Barnette* (1943), Frankfurter said, "As a member of this Court I am not justified in writing my opinions into the Constitution, no matter how deeply I may cherish them. . . . It can never be emphasized too much that one's own opinion about the wisdom or evil of a law should be excluded altogether when one is doing one's duty on the bench."

Judicial activism

Sometimes judges appear to exceed their power in deciding cases before the Court. They are supposed to exercise judgment in interpreting the law, according to the Constitution. Judicial activists, however, seem to exercise their will to *make* law in response to legal issues before the Court.

According to the idea of judicial activism, judges should use their powers to correct injustices, especially when the other branches of government do not act to do so. In short, the courts should play an active role in shaping social policy on such issues as civil rights, protection of individual rights, political unfairness, and public morality.

Chief Justice Earl Warren (who served from 1954 to 1969) and many members of the Warren Court, such as William O. Douglas, practiced judicial activism when they boldly used the Constitution to make sweeping social changes promoting such policies as school desegregation and to insure that all Americans had the opportunity to vote and to participate in U.S. society. In 1956 Justice Douglas wrote, "[T]he judiciary must do more than dispense justice in cases and controversies. It must also keep the charter of government current with the times and not allow it to become archaic or out of tune with the needs of the day."

Arguments against judicial activism

Opponents of judicial activism argue that activist judges make laws, not just interpret them, which is an abuse of their constitutional power. The issue, they claim, is not whether social problems need to be solved but whether the courts should involve themselves in such problem solving. By making decisions about how to run prisons or schools, argue the critics of judicial activism, the courts assume responsibilities that belong exclusively to the legislative and executive branches of government.

Critics of judicial activism worry that court decisions that so freely "interpret" the meaning of the Constitution will undermine public confidence in and respect for the courts. Justice Byron R. White wrote in *Bowers* v. *Hardwick* (1986), "The Court is most vulnerable and comes nearest to illegitimacy when it deals with judge-made constitutional law having little or no cognizable [knowable] roots in the language or design of the Constitution."

In addition, critics point out that federal judges are not elected; they are appointed for life terms. As a result, when judges begin making policy decisions about social or political changes society should make, they become unelected legislators. Consequently, the people lose control of the right to govern themselves. Further, unlike legislatures, courts are not supposed to be open to influence from interest groups. As a result, the courts may not hear different points of view on complex social issues. In legislatures, by contrast, elected officials are responsive to such interests.

Finally, opponents of judicial activism argue that judges lack special expertise in handling such complex tasks as running prisons, administering schools, or determining hiring policies for businesses. Judges are experts in the law, not in managing social institutions.

Opponents of judicial activism point to the constitutional principle of separation of powers (the division of power among the executive, legislative, and judicial branches of the federal government) and federalism (the division of power between the states and the federal government) to justify judicial restraint. They claim that judicial activism leads to unconstitutional intrusions of federal judicial power into the duties and powers of the executive and legislative branches of government and into the state governments. In *Griswold* v. *Connecticut* (1965), Justice John M. Harlan wrote, "Judicial self-restraint…will be achieved…only by continual insistence upon…the great roles that the doctrines of federalism and separation of powers have played in establishing and preserving American freedoms."

Arguments for judicial activism

Supporters of judicial activism argue that it is necessary to correct injustices and promote needed social changes. They view the courts as institutions of last resort for those in society who lack the political power to influence the other branches of government.

Supporters of judicial activism point out that the courts often step in only after governors and state legislatures have refused to do anything about a problem. For example, neither state legislatures nor Congress acted to ban racially segregated schools, trains, city buses, parks, and other public facilities for decades. Segregation might still exist legally if the Supreme Court had not declared it unconstitutional in 1954.

Supporters of judicial activism also mention that local courts and judges are uniquely qualified to ensure that local officials uphold the guarantees of the Constitution. In fact, with a few exceptions, district court judges have written most of the decisions affecting local institutions. For example, an Alabama judge took over the administration of the prison system in that state because he decided that the conditions in the prisons violated the Constitution's prohibition of "cruel and unusual punishments." Similarly, a Texas judge, a man born and raised in the Lone Star State, ordered sweeping changes in the Texas prison system. And a Massachusetts judge, himself a Boston resident, ordered massive school desegregation in that northern city. In each case, the district judge adopted an activist solution to a problem. But each pursued an activist course because he felt that only such measures would enforce the dictates of the Constitution.

Judicial activists argue that the courts do not create policy as legislatures do. Judges inevitably shape policy, however, as they interpret the law. And, they argue, interpreting the law is the job of the courts. Chief Justice Earl Warren put it this way: "When two [people] come into Court, one may say: 'an act of Congress means this.' The other says it means the opposite. We [the Court] then say it means one of the two or something else in between. In that way we *are* making the law, aren't we?"

Finally, judicial activists argue that the framers of the Constitution expected the courts to interpret the Constitution actively in order to react to new conditions. As Justice Frank Murphy wrote in *Schneiderman* v. *United States* (1943), "The constitutional fathers, fresh from a revolution, did not forge a political strait jacket for the generations to come."

SEE ALSO

Constitutional construction; Judicial power; Judicial review; Separation of powers

FURTHER READING

Wellington, Harry H. *Interpreting the Constitution: The Supreme Court and the Process of Adjudication.* New Haven: Yale University Press, 1991.

Judicial Conference of the United States

SEE Administration of federal courts

Judicial power

ARTICLE 3, Section 1, of the U.S. Constitution says, "The judicial Power of the United States shall be vested in one supreme Court, and in such inferior Courts as the Congress may from time to time order and establish." Section 2 says, "The judicial Power shall extend to all Cases, in Law and Equity, arising under this Constitution, the laws of the United States, and Treaties made, or which shall

be made, under their Authority."

The judicial power specified in the Constitution is the capacity and authority of the U.S. Supreme Court and lower federal courts to hear and decide cases brought before them on the basis of the supreme law—the Constitution—and federal statutes and treaties that conform to the Constitution. The judicial power of the Supreme Court therefore involves interpretation of the law to make decisions in actual controversies that adversaries bring to the Court. Hypothetical cases are not subjects for Supreme Court decisions.

Article 3, Section 2, of the Constitution says that the judicial power of the federal courts can be exercised in two categories of cases: cases defined by the parties to the controversy and cases defined by their substance. The first category includes legal disputes in which the United States is a party, in which the opposing parties are different states of the federal system, or in which the parties are citizens of different states. The second category includes cases about the meaning or application of provisions of the Constitution, federal statutes, or treaties. It also includes cases pertaining to admiralty and maritime law and to ambassadors and officials from other countries.

Judicial review, although not mentioned in the Constitution, has become an important power of the federal judiciary. Judicial review is the power of a court to declare an act of the federal or state government unconstitutional, or unlawful and void. According to this concept, judges in courts of law appraise acts of the legislative and executive branches of federal and state governments to decide whether they are in conflict with the Constitution. All courts,

Chief Justice John Marshall wrote that judicial power involved the review of laws passed by Congress in cases before the Court.

federal and state, may practice judicial review. The Supreme Court of the United States, however, has final say within the judicial system on whether laws or actions violate or are in accord with the U.S. Constitution.

Judicial review is based on three ideas: that the Constitution is the supreme law, that acts contrary to the Constitution are null and void, and that judges in courts of law are responsible for determining if acts violate or agree with the Constitution.

The judicial power, including the power of judicial review, is one of three coordinate and separate powers of government in the United States: legislative, executive, and judicial. Chief Justice John Marshall, in *Osborn* v. *Bank of the United States* (1824), summarized the relationships of the three branches of government: "[T]he legislative, executive, and judicial powers, of every well constructed government, are co-extensive with each other. . . . The executive department may constitutionally execute every law which the Legislative may constitutionally make, and the judicial department [has]…the power of construing every such law." As Marshall wrote in *Marbury* v. *Madison* (1803), "It is emphatically, the province and duty of the judicial department, to say what the law is." The federal judicial power, then, has the authority and capacity to interpret the Constitution and laws and treaties made under it; to apply the law to decisions about cases brought before the courts; and to declare laws unconstitutional if they do not conform to the supreme law, the U.S. Constitution.

SEE ALSO

Judicial review; Jurisdiction; Marbury v. Madison; Separation of powers

FURTHER READING

Abraham, Henry J. *The Judicial Process.* New York: Oxford, 1993.

Judicial review

JUDICIAL REVIEW is the power of the judiciary, or the courts, to determine whether the acts of other branches of government are in accordance with the Constitution. All courts, federal and state, may exercise the power of judicial review, but the Supreme Court of the United States has the final judicial decision on whether laws or actions of local, state, or federal governments violate or conform to the U.S. Constitution, the highest law of the land.

Judges use their power of judicial review only in cases brought before the courts. They consider only actual controversies, not hypothetical questions about the Constitution. Congress cannot, for example, ask the Supreme Court for its advice about whether a bill is constitutional. The Court would make this kind of decision only if the bill became a law and someone challenged it.

Judicial review is not mentioned in the Constitution. However, before 1787 this power was used by courts in several of the American states to overturn laws that conflicted with the state constitution.

Judicial review of state laws

The federal judiciary's power to review state laws is implied in Articles 3 and 6 of the U.S. Constitution. Article 3 says that the federal courts have power to make judgments in all cases pertaining to the Constitution, statutes, and treaties of the United States.

Article 6 implies that the judicial power must be used to protect and defend the authority of the U.S. Constitution with respect to the laws and constitutions of the states: "This Constitution, and the Laws of the United States which shall be made in Pursuance thereof; and all Treaties made, or which shall be

The Supreme Court threw out the Agricultural Adjustment Act in 1936 on the grounds that agriculture is not an interstate activity and cannot be regulated by the federal government.

made under the authority of the United States, shall be the supreme Law of the Land; and the Judges in every State shall be bound thereby, any Thing in the Constitution or Laws of any State to the Contrary notwithstanding." Furthermore, Article 6 declares that all officials of the federal and state governments, including all "judicial Officers, both of the United States and of the several States, shall be bound by Oath or Affirmation, to support this Constitution."

To establish a judicial system for the United States, Congress enacted the Judiciary Act of 1789. Section 25 of this statute provided for review by the U.S. Supreme Court of decisions by state courts that involved issues of federal law.

On the basis of Articles 3 and 6 of the U.S. Constitution and Section 25 of the Judiciary Act of 1789, the Supreme Court in 1796 (*Ware* v. *Hylton*) exercised the power of judicial review to strike down a law of the state government of Virginia. According to the Supreme Court, the Virginia law, which protected Virginia citizens with debts to British creditors from having to pay, was unconstitutional because it violated the 1783 Treaty of Paris, which guaranteed that prewar debts owed to the British would be paid. This judicial decision was generally viewed as consistent with the words of the U.S. Constitution and the intentions of its framers.

Judicial review of federal laws and actions

An open-ended and troublesome question of the founding period was whether the power of judicial review could be used to nullify acts of the legislative or executive branches of the federal government.

In 1788 Alexander Hamilton argued in *The Federalist* No. 78 for judicial review as a means to void all governmental actions contrary to the Constitution. He maintained that limitations on the power of the federal legislative and executive branches in order to protect the rights of individuals "can be preserved in practice no other way than through…courts of justice, whose duty it must be to declare all acts contrary to…the Constitution void. Without this [power of judicial review], all the reservations of particular rights or privileges would amount to nothing."

Hamilton concluded, "No legislative act, therefore, contrary to the Constitution, can be valid. . . . [T]he interpretation of the laws is the proper and peculiar province of the courts. A constitution is…a fundamental law. It therefore belongs to [judges] to ascertain its meaning as well as the meaning of any particular act proceeding from the legislative body."

Marbury v. Madison

The ideas on judicial review in *The Federalist* No. 78 were applied by John Marshall, chief justice of the United States, in *Marbury* v. *Madison* (1803). The specific issue and decision in this case are of little interest or consequence today. However, Chief Justice Marshall's argument for judicial review, which firmly established this power in the federal government's system of checks and balances, has become a strong instrument of the federal courts in securing the constitutional rights of individuals.

In *Marbury* v. *Madison,* the Supreme Court was confronted with an act of Congress that conflicted with a provision of the United States Constitution. The question, in Marshall's words, was "whether an act, repugnant to the constitution, can become the law of the land." He answered that the Constitution is "the fundamental and paramount law of the nation, and consequently, . . . an act of the legislature repugnant to the constitution is void." Marshall argued, from the supremacy clause of Article 6, that *no* act of Congress that violates any part of the Constitution can be valid. Rather, he wrote, it must be declared unconstitutional and repealed.

Marshall concluded with his justification for the Supreme Court's power of judicial review:

> It is, emphatically, the province and duty of the judicial department, to say what the law is. . . . So, if a law be in opposition to the constitution; if both the law and the constitution apply to a particular case, so that the court must either decide that case, conformable to the law, disregarding the constitution; or conformable to the constitution, disregarding the law; the court must determine which of these conflicting rules governs the case; this is of the very essence of judicial duty. If then, the courts are to regard the constitution, and the constitution is superior to any ordinary act of the legislature, the constitution, and not such ordinary act, must govern the case to which both apply.

Marshall used three provisions of the Constitution to justify his arguments for judicial review. The first was Article 3, Section 2, which extends the judicial power to "all Cases, in Law and Equity, arising under this Constitution." Marshall argued, "Could it be the intention of those who gave this power, to say, that in using it, the constitution should not be looked into? That a case arising under the constitution should be decided, without examining the instrument under which it arises? This is too extravagant to be maintained."

Second, Article 6 requires judges to pledge "to support this Constitution." Marshall wrote, "How immoral to impose [this oath] on them, if they were to be used as the instruments . . . for violating what they swear to support!"

Third, Marshall pointed out "that in declaring what shall be the supreme law of the land [Article 6], the constitution itself is first mentioned; and not the laws of the United States, generally, but those only which shall be made in pursuance of the constitution, have that rank."

Finally, Chief Justice Marshall stated "the principle, supposed to be essential to all written constitutions, that a law repugnant to the constitution is void; and that courts, as well as other departments [of the government], are bound by that instrument."

Significance of judicial review

James Madison spoke with foresight during the first federal Congress when, on June 8, 1789, he predicted that the "independent tribunals of justice [federal courts] will consider themselves in a peculiar manner the guardians of those [constitutional] rights . . . [and] resist every encroachment upon rights expressly stipulated . . . by the declaration [bill] of rights."

During the more than 200 years of its existence, the Supreme Court has used its power of judicial review to overturn more than 120 acts of Congress and more than 1,000 state laws. The great majority of these invalidations of federal and state acts have occurred during the 20th century. The Supreme Court declared only 3 federal acts and 53 state laws unconstitutional from 1789 until 1868. Most of the laws declared unconstitutional since 1925 have involved civil liberties guaranteed by the Bill of Rights and subsequent amendments concerned with the rights of individuals. Thus, the Supreme Court has become the guardian of the people's liberties that James Madison said it would be at the inception of the republic.

SEE ALSO

Constitutional democracy; Constitutionalism; Judicial power; Marbury v. Madison; Separation of powers; Ware v. Hylton

FURTHER READING

Clinton, Robert Lowry. *Marbury* v. *Madison and Judicial Review.* Lawrence: University Press of Kansas, 1989.
Ely, John H. *Democracy and Distrust: A Theory of Judicial Review.* Cambridge: Harvard University Press, 1980.
Hall, Kermit L. *The Supreme Court and Judicial Review in American History.* Washington, D.C.: American Historical Association, 1985.
Wolfe, Christopher. *The Rise of Modern Judicial Review.* New York: Basic Books, 1986.

Judiciary Act of 1789

ARTICLE 3 of the U.S. Constitution provides for a Supreme Court to exercise the "judicial Power of the United States." It also empowers Congress to provide through legislation "such inferior Courts as [it] may from time to time ordain and establish." The first federal Congress passed the Judiciary Act of 1789 to establish the structure of the federal court system under the Supreme Court of the United States.

This 1789 law created two lower levels of federal courts. At the lowest level, it created 13 federal district courts, one for each of the 13 states. At the next level, it established three circuit courts to hear appeals from the district courts. At the top of the three-level federal judiciary was the Supreme Court, consisting of the chief justice of the United States and five associate justices.

The Judiciary Act of 1789 stipulated that the Supreme Court, as the court of last resort, would hear questions of law on appeal from lower federal courts. Section 25 of this law gave the Supreme Court the power to exercise judicial review over the highest state courts when they made decisions that involved issues of federal law or the U.S. Constitution.

SEE ALSO

Federal judicial system

FURTHER READING

Marcus, Maeva, ed. *Origins of the Federal Judiciary: Essays on the Judiciary Act of 1789.* New York: Oxford, 1992.

An 1890 banquet celebrated the centennial of the federal judiciary, which was established by the Judiciary Act of 1789. The invitation bore the portraits of the first chief justice, John Jay, and the current one, Melville Fuller.

Judiciary Act of 1869

THIS FEDERAL law set the number of Supreme Court justices at nine, the number that sits on the Court today. It also reformed the circuit courts by establishing a separate circuit court judiciary of nine members, one for each of nine new circuits or regions of the United States. Justices of the Supreme Court still had circuit-riding duties, but they were greatly decreased by the law; now they had to attend circuit court proceedings only once every two years.

SEE ALSO

Circuit Courts of Appeals

Judiciary Act of 1891

THIS FEDERAL law created a new intermediate level for the federal judiciary—nine U.S. Circuit Courts of Appeals (renamed Courts of Appeals in 1948). It eliminated the need for Supreme Court justices to participate in deciding circuit court cases. However, it retained the old circuit courts, which were not eliminated until 1911, when their work was assigned to the federal district courts, the lowest level of the federal judicial system.

The nine Courts of Appeals were staffed with three judges each. Since 1891 the number of the Courts of Appeals has increased to 13, one for each of 11 circuits or regions of the United States. In addition, there is the Court of Appeals for the District of Columbia Circuit and the Court of Appeals for the Federal Circuit. The basic structure of the federal judiciary today, however, was put in place by the Judiciary Act of 1891.

SEE ALSO

Courts of Appeals; Federal judicial system

An 1885 cartoon depicts an overworked Supreme Court. In 1891 the Judiciary Act relieved the Court's burden of deciding circuit court cases by establishing a new level of federal courts.

Judiciary Act of 1925

THIS JUDICIARY Act gave the U.S. Supreme Court expanded power to decide which cases it would accept or reject from lower courts. By limiting the number of cases the Court was required to accept, the Judiciary Act left the Court free to concentrate on cases of great national and constitutional significance.

By sharply limiting the number of cases that would go to the Supreme Court, the 1925 act enhanced the authority and prestige of the Courts of Appeals. These appellate courts became the final review courts for the great majority of appellate cases.

Jurisdiction

THE EXTENT or scope of a court's authority to hear and decide a case properly brought to it is its jurisdiction. There are two types of jurisdiction: original and appellate.

Original jurisdiction is the authority of a court to hear and decide a case for the first time. In general, courts of original jurisdiction are minor courts or trial courts. Federal district courts, for example, are courts of original jurisdiction. Article 3, Section 2, of the U.S. Constitution states that the U.S. Supreme Court has original jurisdiction only in suits involving ambassadors from other countries and in suits to which a state of the United States is a party. For instance, the Court had original jurisdiction in *Georgia* v. *South Carolina* (1990), a case involving the correct location of a boundary between the two states. In all cases except the types listed above, the U.S. Supreme Court has appellate jurisdiction, which is the authority of a court to hear and decide cases brought on appeal from a lower court.

Indeed, the U.S. Supreme Court is primarily an appellate court. Throughout its history, the Court has exercised original jurisdiction in fewer than 160 cases. Article 3, Section 2, of the Constitution provides that "the Supreme Court shall have appellate Jurisdiction, both as to law and fact" with only a few exceptions. However, Article 3 also says that Congress has the power to regulate the nature and scope of the Supreme Court's power of appellate jurisdiction. Using this power, Congress passed the Judiciary Act of 1925 to give greater authority to the Court to decide which cases it would accept or reject on appeal from lower courts. The result was to greatly reduce the number of cases in the Court's caseload.

SEE ALSO
Judicial power

Just compensation

THE 5TH AMENDMENT to the U.S. Constitution states, "No person shall be…deprived of life, liberty, or property, without due process of law; nor shall private property be taken for public use without just compensation." The 5th Amendment recognizes the property rights of individuals and guarantees that the government must provide fair payment to a person whose property is taken for public use. Just compensation is determined by the market value of the property—the amount of money a willing buyer would pay a willing seller for the property in an open and free marketplace. In *Chicago, Burlington & Quincy Railroad Co.* v. *Chicago* (1897) the Su-

preme Court ruled that state and local governments are required to pay "just compensation" when taking private property for public use. In this case a public street in Chicago was opened across a privately owned railroad track.

SEE ALSO
Eminent domain

Justices of the Supreme Court

THERE ARE nine seats on the U.S. Supreme Court: one chief justice and eight associate justices. The number of justices is set by Congress. The Judiciary Act of 1789 created a Supreme Court of six members: five associate justices and a chief justice.

The size of the Court remained at six members until the Judiciary Act of 1801 reduced the number to five. A year later, however, the Judiciary Act of 1802 restored the six-member Court. Congress added a seventh justice in 1807, eighth and ninth justices in 1837, and a tenth justice in 1863.

In 1866, however, Congress reduced the Court to seven members. Through this measure, the Republican party majority in Congress deprived President Andrew Johnson, whom it opposed, of an opportunity to appoint new justices to the Court. After the election of the popular Ulysses S. Grant to the Presidency, Congress passed the Judiciary Act of 1869, which set the Court's membership at nine. This number has remained the same ever since. In 1937, President Franklin Roosevelt attempted unsuccessfully to expand the membership of the court to gain support on the Court for his New Deal programs. He proposed adding one justice to the Supreme Court

The Court headed by Chief Justice Earl Warren. Seated: Tom Clark, Hugo Black, Earl Warren, William Douglas, John Marshall Harlan. Standing: Byron White, William Brennan, Potter Stewart, Abe Fortas.

for every member over 70 years of age, up to a total of six additional justices.

Duties and powers

The chief justice of the United States is the presiding officer of the Supreme Court and the head of the federal judiciary. The eight associate justices work with the chief justice to decide cases that come before the Court. They are expected to make and justify these decisions within the framework of the Constitution and the system of law based on it. The associate justices also collaborate with each other and the chief justice to review all petitions for certiorari (appeals from lower courts for a hearing before the Supreme Court) and decide which of these appeals will be accepted for Supreme Court review.

All associate justices are equal in their formal power. Each associate justice has one vote, and each vote has the same weight. Some justices, however, tend to have more influence than others on Court decisions because they have more skill in reasoning and arguing about legal issues. Some are better at managing human relationships and leading their peers. The justices with more ability to persuade through the force of

intellect or personal style are likely to have a greater impact on the deliberations and decisions of the Court. For example, Justice William Brennan, who served on the Court from 1956 to 1990, had great ability to influence other justices. His colleague Thurgood Marshall said, "There's nobody here that can persuade the way Brennan can persuade."

The chief justice has more authority and power than the associate justices, even though he, too, has only one vote. The chief justice, in presiding over the Court in conference, is able to direct and structure the discussion of cases and thereby to influence the outcome. Further, the chief justice has authority to make up the first version of the discuss list, which is the list of petitions for Supreme Court review that will be considered. By carrying out this task, the chief justice has great power in determining which cases are to be denied a hearing by the Court. Another example of the special role of the chief justice is his power to assign the task of writing the Court's opinion on a case, whenever he is part of the majority in the initial vote in conference. When the chief justice is not part of the majority, the senior justice in the majority makes the assignment. The chief justice tends to make most of the assignments and is thereby able to influence the contents and style of the Court's opinion. For example, the chief may decide to write the opinion of the Court in very important cases, or he may choose an associate justice who tends to agree with him.

Appointment and terms

Both the chief justice and associate justices are appointed by the President of the United States "with the Advice and Consent of the Senate," as provided by Article 2, Section 2, of the U.S. Constitution. They "hold their Offices during good Behaviour," as prescribed by Article 3, Section 1, of the Constitution. This clause practically guarantees appointment for life for those who desire it. Fifty justices have died in office. The justice who served the longest on the Court was William O. Douglas, whose tenure was 36 years and 7 months (1939–75). Justice Oliver Wendell Holmes was the oldest person to serve on the Court. He retired in 1932 at age 90, after 30 years on the Court. By contrast, two associate justices served less than two years. Thomas Johnson had served less than 14 months when he died in 1793, the shortest tenure in the history of the Court. Justice James F. Byrnes served only 16 months before resigning in 1942 to take another job in the federal government.

Salaries of the justices

Article 3, Section 1, of the Constitution says, "The Judges, both of the supreme and inferior Courts, shall…at stated Times, receive for their Services, a Compensation, which shall not be diminished during their Continuance in Office." This provision was designed to keep the judiciary independent by protecting federal judges from threats of pay cuts that might influence their decisions.

The Judiciary Act of 1789 set the chief justice's annual salary at $4,000 and an associate justice's salary at $3,500. Since then, Congress has appropriated larger amounts for judicial salaries. The 1989 Ethics Reform Act provided an annual salary of $124,000 for the chief justice and $118,600 for the associate justices. In 1993 the associate justices received an annual salary of $164,100, and the chief justice was paid $171,500.

Membership of the Court

Since 1789, 96 people have served as associate justices of the U.S. Supreme Court. Five of the 16 chief justices served as associate justices before becoming chief justice: John Rutledge, Edward D. White, Charles Evans Hughes, Harlan F. Stone, and William H. Rehnquist. The overwhelming majority of the justices, including 14 of 16 chief justices, have been white men affiliated with Protestant religions.

The first woman associate justice is Sandra Day O'Connor, who was appointed in 1981 by President Ronald Reagan. Ruth Bader Ginsburg, appointed by President Bill Clinton in 1993, is the second woman to become an associate justice. Two associate justices have been African Americans: Thurgood Marshall, who served from 1967 to 1991, and Clarence Thomas, who was appointed in 1991 to replace Justice Marshall.

Six associate justices have been Jewish: Louis D. Brandeis, Benjamin Cardozo, Felix Frankfurter, Arthur Goldberg, Abe Fortas, and Ruth Bader Ginsburg.

Seven associate justices have been Roman Catholics: Edward D. White, Joseph McKenna, Pierce Butler, Frank Murphy, William Brennan, Antonin Scalia, and Anthony Kennedy. White also served as chief justice. Another Roman Catholic, Roger B. Taney, served only as chief justice.

SEE ALSO

Chief justice; Court-packing plan; Judiciary Act of 1789; Judiciary Act of 1869; Opinions; Seniority

Justiciable questions

THE U.S. SUPREME COURT has held that federal courts may deal only with cases or questions that are justiciable, that is, questions "appropriate for judicial determination" (*Aetna Life Insurance Co.* v. *Haworth,* 1937). In the *Aetna* case Chief Justice Charles Evans Hughes discussed the differences between justiciable questions or issues and those not justiciable. He emphasized that justiciable questions involve a "real and substantial controversy" that can be resolved by a conclusive decision of a court of law.

The U.S. Supreme Court does not provide advisory opinions because they do not pertain to justiciable questions: real cases that are appropriate for a judicial decision. The Court also does not accept cases that require decisions on political questions because they cannot, in the Court's opinion, be resolved on legal or constitutional grounds. Rather, political questions are those appropriate for resolution by the legislative and executive branches of government. For instance, the President, not the Court, decides whether the United States should recognize and maintain diplomatic relations with foreign governments. The Congress, not the Court, decides political questions such as how much federal money should be appropriated to maintain the U.S. armed forces.

SEE ALSO

Advisory opinions; Jurisdiction; Political questions

Juvenile justice

PEOPLE WHO have not reached the legal age of adulthood (usually 18 years old) are considered juveniles under the law. There are special courts of law throughout the United States designed to meet the presumed needs of preadult lawbreakers. These juvenile courts are the core of a system of juvenile justice, with legal procedures that specify what can and cannot be done with, to, and for juveniles by various public officials, including police, prosecutors, judges, and probation officers. The juvenile justice system is separate from the adult criminal justice system.

Juveniles are required to obey the same federal, state, and local laws that adults must obey. Both juveniles and adults, for example, are required to obey laws forbidding such criminal offenses as burglary, arson, rape, and murder. Juveniles also are required to obey laws that adults do not have to obey, such as laws against running away from home, disobeying parents, refusing to attend school (truancy), drinking alcoholic beverages, or participating in consensual sexual activity. Such laws pertain to *status offenses,* so called because they apply only to those with the status of a juvenile.

In most states, people under 18 years old are sent to a juvenile court when they break the law. In a few states, such as New York, those older than 15 who commit criminal offenses are sent to an adult criminal court. In general, juveniles may be tried in an adult court when they commit serious or frequent crimes.

In a few states, such as Pennsylvania, all juveniles accused of homicide (no matter what their age) are sent directly to an adult criminal court. There, the juvenile's lawyer can try to persuade the judge that the accused youth should be

The Juvenile Rights Division of the Legal Aid Society recruits students at New York University law school. The juvenile justice system is separate from the adult system so that rehabilitation may be offered to preadult offenders where possible.

transferred to a juvenile court. If the judge agrees, the case can be sent to a juvenile court.

The original purpose of juvenile courts was to provide special care and treatment for preadult offenders, with the intention of rehabilitating the offender in order to prevent repeated illegal behavior. A symbol of the special concern for preadult offenders in juvenile courts is the manner of naming the cases. The typical title of a juvenile court case is *In re Joe Dokes,* which means "in the matter of . . . ." By contrast, the usual title of a criminal court case is *State* v. *Joe Dokes,* which implies that the defendant is involved in a legal contest with the state. There usually is no suggestion in the name of a juvenile court case that the preadult (Joe Dokes) must defend himself against the state. In return for the special care provided to offenders in the juvenile justice system, juveniles did not have the constitutional rights to due process of law guaranteed to adults in criminal courts, such as the right to counsel, the right to confront and cross-examine witnesses, and the protection against self-incrimination.

During the 1950s critics pointed out that juvenile courts often did not provide special concern for preadult offenders or act in their best interests. Rather, the ju-

venile justice system often appeared only to punish juveniles for their offenses and not to remedy their problems or address their particular needs. So the critics recommended that juveniles accused of criminal offenses should have the constitutional rights of due process, just like adults in criminal courts.

In the case of *In re Gault* (1967), the Supreme Court for the first time confronted the issue of due process rights for juvenile offenders. The Court rejected the traditional claim that a juvenile's rights are sufficiently protected by judges in juvenile courts, who act as substitute parents. Rather, the Court held that juvenile courts must provide the same basic due process rights that the U.S. Constitution guarantees to adults. Writing for the Court, Justice Abe Fortas specified four due process rights that must be provided: written notification of specific charges to the juvenile and his or her parents, assistance of a lawyer, confrontational cross-examination of witnesses, and protection against self-incrimination (the right to remain silent when questioned by prosecutors).

The constitutional rights of preadults in juvenile courts were expanded by the Court in the case of *In re Winship* (1970). The offender, Samuel Winship, was convicted of theft by a juvenile court judge. However, the evidence used to convict Winship was slight. It would not have met the standard of proof typically used in an adult criminal case, which is referred to as proof "beyond a reasonable doubt." This means that the evidence against the accused person is so great that there can be little or no doubt that the person committed the crime. The Court decided that preadults in a juvenile court should have the right to the higher standard of proof available in criminal court proceedings.

In *McKeiver* v. *Pennsylvania* (1971), a juvenile was charged with robbery, larceny, and receiving stolen goods. The defendant's lawyer requested a trial by jury because punishment for these serious offenses could be as much as five years of detention. The state refused the lawyer's request and the defendant was convicted and sentenced without a jury trial. He appealed on the grounds that the right to trial by jury, granted to adults accused of criminal offenses, was unconstitutionally denied to him.

The Supreme Court decided that due process of law for juveniles does not require a trial by jury. Writing for the Court, Justice Harry Blackmun argued that a jury trial would subject juveniles to unnecessary and disruptive adversarial proceedings without the compensating benefits of greater accuracy in fact-finding or determination of guilt or innocence. The *McKeiver* decision indicated that the Court was unwilling to extend all the rights of the criminally accused to juveniles charged with criminal offenses.

In *Schall* v. *Martin* (1984) the Court made another decision that limits the due process rights of juveniles. The Court upheld a New York law that permits a judge to order pretrial confinement for up to 17 days of a juvenile accused of a criminal offense, when there is a significant risk that the juvenile may commit a serious crime before the trial. Justice William Rehnquist emphasized that it is the state's duty to protect the community against criminal acts. The *Schall* decision has influenced other states to enact preventive detention laws similar to the New York law upheld by the Court. Justice Thurgood Marshall dissented from the Court's opinion in *Schall* v. *Martin*. He argued that preventive detention laws give power to judges to treat different juveniles unequally and unfairly.

The *McKeiver* and *Schall* decisions put certain limitations on due process

rights in the juvenile justice system. The due process protections provided by the *Gault* and *Winship* decisions, however, have been firmly established. They have profoundly changed the juvenile justice system in the United States.

Before the *Gault* decision, juveniles had no due process rights. But in exchange for the lack of legal protection from the state, juveniles were supposed to receive benevolent treatment from officials. This pre-*Gault* juvenile justice system permitted competent, caring officials to readily help children. There were no complex due process procedures to get in the way of direct, discreet, and benign behavior on the part of good officials to assist troubled youths. The problem with the pre-*Gault* system was that bad or stupid officials could hurt juveniles, who had no recourse to due process procedures to protect them from abuses of the system.

The post-*Gault* juvenile justice system is concerned more with punishment and prevention of crime than with treatment and reform of troubled youth. Thus, it has become more like the adult criminal justice system, with its adversarial proceedings and guarantees of constitutional due process rights to protect the accused person against the power of the state. Older juveniles accused of serious criminal offenses are likely to be transferred to the criminal courts. Status offenses, such as truancy or disobedience, are still handled by juvenile courts in the traditional paternal and caring manner, with an emphasis on diagnosis and treatment of the psychological and social problems of the offenders.

SEE ALSO
Due process of law; In re Gault; In re Winship; McKeiver v. Pennsylvania

FURTHER READING
Bernard, Thomas J. *The Cycle of Juvenile Justice*. New York: Oxford, 1992.

Katz v. United States

☆ *389 U.S. 347 (1967)*
☆ *Vote: 7–1*
☆ *For the Court: Stewart*
☆ *Concurring: Harlan and White*
☆ *Dissenting: Black*
☆ *Not Participating: Marshall*

CHARLES KATZ was known to be a gambler, and the Federal Bureau of Investigation (FBI) suspected him of engaging in illegal activities in making bets. In particular, the FBI believed he was using a public telephone booth to transmit information about wagers from Los Angeles to Miami and Boston. So FBI agents placed electronic devices outside a telephone booth regularly used by Katz to make his calls. The agents recorded Katz's telephone conversations in order to gather evidence of his illegal gambling activity.

At Katz's trial, the federal government used evidence of his telephone conversations to win a conviction. Katz appealed his conviction on grounds that the evidence introduced against him had been obtained illegally.

The Issue Charles Katz argued that the government had violated his 4th Amendment rights—"The right of the people to be secure in their persons, houses, papers, and effects, against unreasonable searches and seizures." Katz said that the illegally gathered evidence against him should have been excluded from his trial.

Lawyers for the federal government argued that placing a tap on the outside of a public telephone booth was not a violation of the 4th Amendment. They based their argument on the case of *Olmstead* v. *United States* (1928), which had permitted federal government use of electronic surveillance and wiretapping on the grounds that those actions outside

a person's home fell outside the scope of the 4th Amendment.

Opinion of the Court In *Katz*, the Court overturned the decision in *Olmstead* v. *United States*. Justice Potter Stewart argued that the 4th Amendment protects people, not places. It protects an individual's right even in a place accessible to the public, such as a telephone booth on a street corner. Justice Stewart wrote, "[T]he Government's activities in electronically listening to and recording [Katz's] words violated the privacy upon which he justifiably relied while using the telephone booth and thus constituted a 'search and seizure' within the meaning of the Fourth Amendment."

Significance The *Katz* case expanded the scope of 4th Amendment rights to include protection against certain kinds of electronic invasions of an individual's privacy. Since the *Katz* decision, the 4th Amendment has been a means to protect individual privacy in places open to the public.

SEE ALSO

Olmstead v. United States; Searches and seizures

FURTHER READING

Westin, Alvin F. "Civil Liberties in the Technology Age." *Constitution* 3, no. 1 (Winter 1991): 56–64.

In the Katz *case, the Court decided an FBI wiretap of a public phone is illegal. The 4th Amendment, according to the Court, protects people from invasions of their privacy, even in public places.*

Kennedy, Anthony M.

ASSOCIATE JUSTICE, 1988–

☆ Born: July 23, 1936, Sacramento, Calif.
☆ Education: Stanford University, B.A., 1958; London School of Economics, 1957–58; Harvard Law School, LL.B., 1961
☆ Previous government service: judge, Ninth Circuit Court of Appeals, 1975–88
☆ Appointed by President Ronald Reagan Nov. 30, 1987; replaced Louis F. Powell, Jr., who retired
☆ Supreme Court term: confirmed by the Senate Feb. 3, 1988, by a 97–0 vote

ANTHONY M. KENNEDY was, for most of his career, a partner in a law firm and a teacher at the McGeorge School of Law of the University of the Pacific in Stockton, California. President Gerald Ford appointed Kennedy to be a federal appellate court judge, and between 1975 and 1988, Kennedy wrote more than 400 opinions as a federal judge on the Ninth Circuit Court of Appeals.

After his appointment to the Supreme Court in 1988, Justice Kennedy, as a moderate conservative, tended to vote in agreement with Chief Justice William Rehnquist during the 1988–89 term. In 90 percent of the cases, he voted in agreement with the chief justice. Since then, he has shown more independence.

In *Church of the Lukumi Babalu Aye* v. *City of Hialeah* (1993), Kennedy wrote the decision for the Court to strike down a city's ban on ritual animal sacrifice, practiced by the followers of the Santería religion. Kennedy held that the city government of Hialeah, Florida, had violated the 1st Amendment right to free exercise of religion.

Korematsu v. United States

☆ 323 U.S. 214 (1944)
☆ Vote: 6–3
☆ For the Court: Black
☆ Concurring: Frankfurter
☆ Dissenting: Roberts, Murphy, and Jackson

AFTER JAPAN'S attack on Pearl Harbor, Hawaii, on December 7, 1941, more than 100,000 Americans of Japanese ancestry were removed from their homes on the Pacific Coast of the United States and sent to internment camps in the interior of the country. Most of them spent the duration of the war, until August 1945, confined in one of these camps, even though they were loyal U.S. citizens who had done nothing to harm their homeland, the United States.

One such U.S. citizen was Fred Korematsu, born and raised in Alameda County, California. He had never visited Japan and knew little or nothing about the Japanese way of life.

In June 1941, before the official U.S. declaration of war, Fred Korematsu had tried to enlist in the navy. Although the navy was actively recruiting men in anticipation of the U.S. entry into the war, the service did not allow Korematsu to enlist because of poor health. He then went to work in a shipyard as a welder. When the war began, he lost his job because of his Japanese heritage.

On May 9, 1942, General John L. DeWitt ordered all people of Japanese background or ancestry excluded from Military Area No. 1, the Pacific coastal region of the United States. This military order was authorized by an executive order of President Franklin D. Roosevelt (issued on February 19) and an act of Congress (passed on March 21).

Hoping to move to Nevada with his fiancée, who was not of Japanese ancestry, Korematsu ignored the evacuation orders when they came. As a U.S. citizen, he felt the orders should not apply to him in any event. The FBI arrested Korematsu, and he was convicted of violating the orders of the commander of Military Area No. 1.

The Issue The U.S. government justified the internment in two ways. The government claimed that American citizens of Japanese ancestry were more loyal to Japan than to their own country and would spy for Japan. Second, the government claimed that because Japan had attacked the U.S. territory of Hawaii, those Americans of Japanese ancestry might have helped Japan.

Korematsu claimed that military commanders, acting under authority granted by the President and Congress, had denied more than 75,000 U.S. citizens their constitutional rights of due process. The 5th Amendment says, "No person shall be…deprived of life, liberty, or property, without due process of law." Had the government wrongly taken away the constitutional rights of Japanese Americans?

Opinion of the Court The Court upheld the exclusion of Japanese Americans from the Pacific coastal region. The needs of national security in a time of crisis, it said, justified the exclusion orders. The war powers of the President and Congress, specified by the Constitution, provided the legal basis for the majority decision.

Justice Hugo Black admitted that the exclusion orders forced citizens of Japanese ancestry to endure severe hardships. "But hardships are a part of war," said Black, "and war is an aggregation of hardships."

Justice Black maintained that the orders had not excluded Korematsu primarily for reasons of race but for reasons of

U.S. citizens of Japanese ancestry arrive at a relocation center in Santa Anita before being moved to camps further inland.

military security. The majority ruling really did not say whether the relocation of Japanese Americans was constitutional. Rather, the Court sidestepped that touchy issue, emphasizing instead the national crisis caused by the war.

Dissent Three justices—Frank Murphy, Robert Jackson, and Owen Roberts—disagreed with the majority. Justice Roberts thought it a plain "case of convicting a citizen as punishment for not submitting to imprisonment in a concentration camp solely because of his ancestry," without evidence concerning his loyalty to the United States.

Justice Murphy said that the exclusion orders violated the right of citizens to due process of law. Furthermore, Murphy protested that the decision of the Court's majority amounted to the "legalization of racism. Racial discrimination in any form and in any degree has no justifiable part whatever in our democratic way of life."

Murphy admitted that the argument citing military necessity carried weight, but he insisted that such a claim must "subject itself to the judicial process" to determine "whether the deprivation is reasonably related to a public danger that is so 'immediate, imminent, and impending.'"

Finally, Murphy concluded that "individuals must not be left impoverished in their constitutional rights on a plea of military necessity that has neither substance nor support."

Justice Jackson expressed grave concern about the future uses of the precedent set in this case. He wrote:

> A military order, however unconstitutional, is not apt to last longer than the military emergency.... But once a judicial opinion rationalizes such an order to show that it conforms to the Constitution...the Court for all time has validated the principle of racial discrimination in criminal procedures and of transplanting American citizens. The principle then lies about like a loaded weapon ready for the hand of any authority that can bring forward a plausible claim of an urgent need.

Significance The *Korematsu* ruling has never been revoked by law or Supreme Court ruling. In 1980, however, Congress reopened investigations into the treatment of Japanese Americans during World War II and created the Commission on Wartime Relocation and Internment of Civilians. After nearly three years of careful examination of the evidence, which included testimony from 750 witnesses, the commission issued a report on February 25, 1983. The report concluded: "A grave injustice was done to American citizens and resident aliens of Japanese ancestry who, without individual review or any probative evidence against them, were excluded, removed, and detained by the United States during World War II."

In 1988, on the basis of the 1983 report, Congress officially recognized the "grave injustice" of the relocation and internment experience and offered payments of $20,000 as compensation to each person still living who had been detained in a relocation center.

SEE ALSO

Hirabayashi v. United States

FURTHER READING

Irons, Peter. *Justice at War*. New York: Oxford, 1983.

Mydans, Carl. "Internment Remembered." *Constitution* 4, no. 1 (Winter 1992): 43.

Rauch, Rudolph S. "Internment." *Constitution* 4, no. 1 (Winter 1992): 30–42.

Kunz v. New York

☆ *340 U.S. 290 (1951)*
☆ *Vote: 8–1*
☆ *For the Court: Vinson*
☆ *Concurring: Black and Frankfurter*
☆ *Dissenting: Jackson*

A BAPTIST MINISTER, Carl J. Kunz, was denied a permit to preach on the streets of New York City by the city police commissioner. A city ordinance prohibited religious services on public streets without a permit from the city government. The ordinance did not spell out the reasons for denying someone a permit. The Reverend Mr. Kunz was denied a permit because he had a reputation for using obscene words in his speeches to denounce Catholics and Jews. Kunz defied the city ordinance and preached on a street corner without a permit. He was arrested and convicted for violating the city ordinance.

The Issue Were Carl Kunz's rights to freedom of speech and free exercise of religion, guaranteed by the 1st and 14th Amendments, violated by the New York City ordinance that was used to deny him a permit to preach in public?

Opinion of the Court The Court struck down as unconstitutional the New York City ordinance that barred worship services on public streets without a permit. Chief Justice Fred Vinson said that enforcement of the ordinance was an unconstitutional "prior restraint" (advance censorship) on an individual's rights to free speech and free exercise of religion. Vinson ruled that New York could not legally give an administrative official control over the right to speak on religious subjects without "appropriate standards to guide his action."

Dissent Justice Robert Jackson defended the restrictions on Kunz's freedom of expression because the reverend had used "fighting words." Justice Jackson based his dissenting opinion on the "fighting words" doctrine used by the Court in *Chaplinski* v. *New Hampshire* (1942), which held that "the lewd and obscene, the profane, the libelous" and insulting or "fighting words" did not have any "social value" in the search for truth, public order, and safety. Therefore, the Court had ruled that "fighting words" are outside the protection of 1st Amendment guarantees of free speech.

Significance The *Kunz* case established that any broadly worded law restricting freedom of expression in public places is an unconstitutional exercise of prior restraint. The "fighting words" doctrine, employed in the dissenting opinion, has subsequently declined as an argument for restrictions on speech. The only prevailing justification for restricting speech is to prevent direct, immediate, and substantial harm to a vital social interest, such as national security, public order, and the safety of individuals.

SEE ALSO

Freedom of speech and press

Lamar, Joseph R.

ASSOCIATE JUSTICE, 1911–16

☆ *Born: Oct. 14, 1857, Ruckersville, Ga.*
☆ *Education: University of Georgia, 1874–75; Bethany College, B.A., 1877; Washington and Lee University, 1877*
☆ *Previous government service: Georgia House of Representatives, 1886–89; commissioner to codify Georgia laws, 1893; associate justice, Georgia Supreme Court, 1903–5*
☆ *Appointed by President William Howard Taft Dec. 12, 1910; replaced William Henry Moody, who retired*

☆ *Supreme Court term: confirmed by the Senate Dec. 15, 1910, by a voice vote; served until Jan. 2, 1916*
☆ *Died: Jan. 2, 1916, Washington, D.C.*

JOSEPH R. LAMAR belonged to a socially prominent family in Georgia. His ardent studies of law and legal history led to his appointment to a state commission to codify the laws of Georgia. He alone wrote the resulting volume on civil law in Georgia. He later wrote several books on the history of law in Georgia.

During his brief term on the Court, Justice Lamar tended to vote with the majority. He wrote only eight dissents. His only notable opinion for the Court was in a 1911 case, *United States* v. *Grimaud*, which upheld a federal law, the Forest Reserve Act of 1911. This decision gave leeway to federal administrations to "fill in details" when carrying out laws.

Lamar, Lucius Q. C.

ASSOCIATE JUSTICE, 1888–93

☆ *Born: Sept. 17, 1825, Eatonton, Ga.*
☆ *Education: Emory College, B.A., 1845*
☆ *Previous government service: Georgia House of Representatives, 1853; U.S. representative from Mississippi, 1857–60, 1873–77; U.S. senator from Mississippi, 1877–85; U.S. secretary of the interior, 1885–88*
☆ *Appointed by President Grover Cleveland Dec. 6, 1887; replaced William Woods, who died*
☆ *Supreme Court term: confirmed by the Senate Jan. 16, 1888, by a 42–38 vote; served until Jan. 23, 1893*
☆ *Died: Jan. 23, 1893, Macon, Ga.*

LUCIUS LAMAR was a prominent leader of the Confederate States of America and wrote the state of

Mississippi's ordinance of secession from the United States. In 1861 he resigned from the U.S. Congress to become a colonel in the Confederate army and fight against the Union in the Civil War. Years later, Lucius Lamar was called the "Great Pacificator" because of his efforts to reconcile the differences between Americans who had fought on opposing sides in the Civil War.

During the latter half of the 1800s, Lamar served in all three branches of the federal government: as a member of Congress, as the secretary of the interior, and as an associate justice of the Supreme Court. His nomination to the Court by President Grover Cleveland was bitterly opposed by die-hard foes of anyone associated with the Confederate cause. As a result, Lamar was narrowly confirmed by a Senate vote of 42 to 38. He was the first Southerner to take a seat on the Court since his own cousin, John A. Campbell, in 1853. During his brief term on the Court, Lamar tended to vote with the Court majority in opposition to strong state regulation of economic activity.

FURTHER READING

Murphy, James B. *L. Q. C. Lamar, Pragmatic Patriot.* Baton Rouge: Louisiana State University Press, 1973.

Lawyers' Edition

ONE OF the unofficial publications of U.S. Supreme Court decisions is produced by the Lawyers Cooperative Publishing Company. This publication, *United States Supreme Court Reports,* Lawyers' Edition, began in 1882. It is commonly referred to as the *Lawyers' Edition.* Special features of this publication are summaries of briefs in selected cases and annotations of key ideas and arguments in some very significant cases.

The single official version of all U.S. Supreme Court decisions is *United States Reports,* which is published by the U.S. Government Printing Office.

SEE ALSO

Supreme Court Reporter; United States Reports

Legal Counsel, Office of the

SEE Staff of the Court, nonjudicial

Lemon Test

IN LEMON V. KURTZMAN (1971), the Supreme Court stated three standards, or criteria, by which to decide cases involving disputes about the meaning of the 1st Amendment's establishment clause, which concerns government involvement with religion. These three standards are known as the Lemon Test. In order for a statute *not* to violate the establishment clause, it must meet these three conditions: First, it must have a secular or nonreligious purpose. Second, it must neither promote nor restrict religion in its primary effects. Third, it must not bring about an excessive entanglement with religion.

SEE ALSO

Establishment clause; Lemon v. Kurtzman; Religious issues under the Constitution

Lemon v. Kurtzman

☆ *403 U.S. 602 (1971)*
☆ *Vote: 8–0*
☆ *For the Court: Burger*
☆ *Concurring: Brennan and White*
☆ *Not participating: Marshall*

ACCORDING TO Pennsylvania's Non-Public Elementary and Secondary Education Act of 1968, the state could directly support salaries of teachers of secular (nonreligious) subjects in parochial (church-run) and other private schools. The state could also reimburse the nonpublic schools for the purchase of textbooks and other instructional materials used to teach secular subjects. Alton Lemon, a taxpayer and resident of Pennsylvania, believed these state government payments of expenses for parochial schools, which had the primary mission of promoting particular religious beliefs, were unconstitutional. So Lemon brought suit against David Kurtzman, the state superintendent of schools, to stop state payments to parochial schools.

The Issue Did the Pennsylvania law, which authorized state payments to Roman Catholic schools and other private schools with a religious mission, violate the 1st Amendment's religious freedom clause, which said, "Congress shall make no law respecting an establishment of religion, or prohibiting the free exercise thereof"?

Opinion of the Court The Court struck down the Pennsylvania law at issue in this case because it provided for an "excessive entanglement" of the state with institutions (parochial schools) set up for the purpose of promoting religious doctrine. Chief Justice Warren Burger wrote, "The Constitution decrees that religion must be a private matter for the individual, the family, and the institutions of private choice, and that while some involvement and entanglements are inevitable, lines must be drawn."

The Court drew three lines, known ever since as the Lemon Test, to guide decisions in similar cases. For a statute to be constitutional under the establishment clause of the 1st Amendment, it

had to meet these three standards of the Lemon Test: it must have a secular or nonreligious purpose; it must neither promote nor interfere with religion; and it cannot cause an excessive entanglement of government with religion.

Although the Court had maintained a barrier between church and state, Chief Justice Burger said it was "far from being a wall." He was referring to Thomas Jefferson's famous phrase—"a wall of separation between church and state"—which the Court had used previously to interpret the establishment clause of the 1st Amendment. Burger claimed that separation of church and state is "a blurred, indistinct, and a variable barrier depending on all the circumstances of a particular relationship."

Significance The Court maintained a separation of church and state, as it had in several other cases since the 1940s, such as *Everson* v. *Board of Education of Ewing Township* (1947), *Engel* v. *Vitale* (1962), and *Abington School District* v. *Schempp* (1963). Further, the Court attempted to clarify the meaning of the separation of church and state through its three-part Lemon Test. However, the Court, through the opinion of Chief Justice Burger, exhibited uncertainty about when or how this "variable barrier" of separation between church and state might be lowered.

In Lemon *v.* Kurtzman, *the Court ruled that a state cannot pay the salaries of teachers of secular subjects in religious schools. The Court also established a series of guidelines known as the Lemon Test to determine if government involvement with religious schools is constitutional.*

In 1993 the Court upheld student-led prayers at graduation ceremonies when it let stand the Fifth Circuit Court of Appeals decision in *Jones* v. *Clear Creek Independent School District*. But in *Lee* v. *Weisman* (1992), the Court struck down a Rhode Island policy that permitted school officials to include prayers in public high school graduation ceremonies. Further, in *Zobrest* v. *Catalina School District* (1993), the court ruled that government funds can be used to pay for a sign-language interpreter to assist a deaf student in a Catholic school.

SEE ALSO

Abington School District v. Schempp; Engel v. Vitale; Everson v. Board of Education of Ewing Township; Lemon Test; Religious issues under the Constitution

LEXIS

LEXIS IS a computerized legal research service operated by a private corporation, Mead Data Central, Inc. It contains the full text of all Supreme Court decisions from 1790 to the present. The Court electronically transmits its decisions to the LEXIS database on the same day they are made. LEXIS users can access either the citations or the full text of particular Supreme Court decisions and print them out. *United States Law Week,* a weekly publication providing current news about Supreme Court personnel and proceedings, is part of the LEXIS database.

The LEXIS database allows lawyers instant electronic access to Supreme Court opinions.

SEE ALSO

WESTLAW

Liberty under the Constitution

LIBERTY MEANS that a person is free to make choices about, for example, what to say or to do. A primary purpose of constitutional government in the United States is to make the liberty of individuals secure. The preamble to the Constitution proclaims that a principal reason for establishing the federal government is to "secure the Blessings of Liberty to ourselves and our Posterity."

The Bill of Rights, Amendments 1 to 10 of the Constitution, protects the individual's rights to liberty from the power of government. The 1st Amendment, for example, says that Congress shall not take away a person's freedoms of religion, speech, press, assembly, and petition. The 4th Amendment protects personal liberty; it guarantees the right of the people to be secure against unwarranted intrusions into their private lives by forbidding "unreasonable searches and seizures" by government officials. The 5th Amendment prohibits the federal government from taking away a person's "life, liberty, or property, without due process of law." And the 14th Amendment applies the same prohibition against abuses of a person's liberty by state governments.

The freedoms spelled out in the U.S. Constitution are called civil liberties. However, these civil liberties are not granted by government to individuals. Rather, the Constitution assumes that all people automatically have these civil liberties and therefore restrains the government from using its power to abuse individuals. Thus, there is a private realm of life, which government officials cannot invade without violating the Constitution. Within this domain of privacy, indi-

"Justice the Guardian of Liberty" is the inscription on the rear of the Supreme Court Building.

viduals have certain liberties of thought, belief, and action.

The Constitution also guarantees liberty for the people to participate publicly in the political life of their society. The 1st Amendment freedoms, for example, protect a person's right to participate freely in activities to elect representatives in government and to influence public decisions of elected and appointed government officials.

Liberty under the Constitution, then, is secured by limiting the power of government in order to protect the people's rights to freedom. But if the government has too little power, so that law and order break down, then the people's liberties may be lost. Neither freedom of thought nor action is secure in a lawless and disorderly society, where there are no law enforcement officers to protect people against criminals who would abuse them.

So an overriding purpose of constitutional government in the United States has been to provide for the use of sufficient power to maintain order, stability, and security for the liberties of the people. The American Declaration of Independence (1776), for example, clearly and emphatically states, "That to secure these Rights [to Life, Liberty, and the Pursuit of Happiness] Governments are instituted among Men."

Ordered liberty is the desirable condition whereby both public order and personal liberty are secured for the individuals in a society. How can liberty and authority, freedom and power, be combined and balanced? This was the basic political problem of the founding period in the United States, and it continues to challenge Americans today. During the debate on ratification of the Constitution, for example, James Madison wrote to Thomas Jefferson in 1788, "It is a melancholy reflection that liberty should be equally exposed to danger whether the Government have too much or too little power; and that the line which divides these extremes should be so inaccurately defined by experience."

Madison noted the standing threat to liberty posed by insufficient constitutional limits on government. He also recognized that liberty carried to the extreme of license, as in a riot, is equally dangerous to the freedom and rights of individuals. A good constitution is a source of liberty and order, but the right mix of these two factors is sometimes difficult to find and maintain. The challenging questions, of course, are these two: At what point, and under what conditions, should the power of government be limited to protect the rights to liberty of individuals? At what point, and under what conditions, should limits be placed on the freedoms and rights of individuals to protect public order, upon which the security for liberty depends?

In the United States, the Supreme Court has the power and the constitutional responsibility to address authoritatively these broad questions and to resolve disputes about them on a case-by-case basis. Through its power of judicial review, the Court can uphold or overturn, as violations of the Constitution, acts of federal and state governments pertaining to questions of liberty and order. But the questions are never answered for all time. They remain as challenges of a constitutional democracy.

In many of its landmark decisions, the Supreme Court has decided to protect the individual's rights to liberty under the Constitution from an unconstitutional exercise of power by government officials. In *Katz* v. *United States* (1967), for example, the Court prohibited federal law enforcement officials from using evidence against a defendant gained by electronic surveillance (listening in) of his telephone conversations. According to the Court, the federal agents had violated the 4th Amendment guarantee of security "against unreasonable searches and seizures." And in *Texas* v. *Johnson* (1989) the Court struck down, as an unconstitutional violation of 1st Amendment rights to freedom of expression, a state law that banned public protest involving the burning of the American flag.

In other significant decisions, the Court has upheld the constitutional exercise of government power and thereby restricted the rights to liberty of individuals. In *United States* v. *Ross* (1982) the Court upheld the authority of police officers to search an entire automobile they have stopped, without obtaining a warrant (required by the 4th Amendment), if they have "probable cause" to suspect that drugs or other illegally possessed objects are in the vehicle. And in *Kovacs* v. *Cooper* (1949) the Court upheld as constitutional a local law that banned the use of sound-amplifying equipment on city streets to transmit information. In this case, the Court favored the community's desire to avoid noisy disturbances over the individual's presumed constitutional right to freedom of expression.

SEE ALSO

Bill of Rights; Civil rights; Constitutional democracy; Constitutionalism; Judicial review; Katz v. United States; Texas v. Johnson; United States v. Ross

FURTHER READING

Hand, Learned. *The Spirit of Liberty*. New York: Knopf, 1960.
Kammen, Michael. *Spheres of Liberty: Changing Perceptions of Liberty in American Culture*. Ithaca, N.Y.: Cornell University Press, 1986.
Muller, Herbert J. *Freedom in the Western World*. New York: Harper & Row, 1963.
Patterson, Orlando. *Freedom in the Making of Western Culture*. New York: Basic Books, 1991.
Sandoz, Ellis, ed. *The Roots of Liberty*. Columbia: University of Missouri Press, 1993.

Librarian, Supreme Court

SEE Staff of the Court, nonjudicial

Limited government

SEE Constitutional democracy; Constitutionalism; Separation of powers

Livingston, Henry Brockholst

ASSOCIATE JUSTICE, 1807–23

☆ *Born: Nov. 25, 1757, New York, N.Y.*
☆ *Education: College of New Jersey (Princeton), B.A., 1774; studied law with Peter Yates in New York, N.Y.*
☆ *Previous government service: New York Assembly, 1786, 1798–99; judge, New York State Supreme Court, 1802–7*
☆ *Appointed by President Thomas Jefferson as a recess appointment Nov. 10, 1806; replaced William Paterson, who died; nominated by Jefferson Dec. 13, 1806*
☆ *Supreme Court term: confirmed by the Senate Dec. 17, 1806, by a voice vote; served until Mar. 18, 1823*
☆ *Died: Mar. 18, 1823, Washington, D.C.*

HENRY BROCKHOLST LIVING-STON was a patriot who served in the Continental Army during the American War of Independence. After the war, he practiced law in New York and became a leading judge of the New York State Supreme Court.

Justice Livingston was a minor figure on the U.S. Supreme Court, which was dominated at that time by Chief Justice John Marshall. However, he was considered an expert on commercial law.

Lochner v. New York

☆ *198 U.S. 45 (1905)*
☆ *Vote: 5–4*
☆ *For the Court: Peckham*
☆ *Dissenting: Harlan, White, Day, and Holmes*

JOSEPH LOCHNER owned a small bakery shop in Utica, New York. In 1901 the state charged him with violating the Bakeshop Act, a New York law that banned bakers from working more than 10 hours a day or 60 hours a week. Lochner had required an employee, Aman Schmitter, to work more than the 60 hours per week permitted by the state law. The Oneida County Court convicted Lochner, and he appealed his case. After losing in the New York State appellate courts, Lochner appealed to the U.S. Supreme Court.

The Issue Lochner said that the Bakeshop Act violated the 14th Amendment because it deprived him of "life, liberty, or property, without due process of law." Lochner claimed that the Bakeshop Act unconstitutionally interfered with his freedom to make a contract with his workers about pay and hours of work. State officials countered that the Bakeshop Act was intended to

The bakery owned by Joseph Lochner in Utica, New York. In Lochner v. New York, *the Court struck down a state law limiting the number of hours an employee could work.*

protect the health and well-being of workers against employers who might otherwise exploit them.

Opinion of the Court Justice Rufus Peckham, writing for the Court, said the Bakeshop Act was unconstitutional because it took away "the right of the individual to liberty of person and freedom of contract." Under the 14th Amendment, Peckham argued, individuals were free to purchase and sell labor. Therefore, any state law interfering with this "liberty of contract" would be unconstitutional "unless there are circumstances which exclude that right."

This right was not stated in the Constitution. Rather, the Court "found" this right through its interpretation of the due process clause of the 14th Amendment, which says that no state government shall "deprive any person of life, liberty, or property without due process of law." Thus, the Court developed the doctrine of substantive due process, by which it claimed the power to examine the content of laws to determine their fairness. In this way, the Court decides whether laws violate any fundamental rights of individuals, such as rights the Court believes to be associated with "life, liberty, or property." This doctrine of substantive due process was a departure from the traditional understanding of due process solely as government procedures that follow rules of fairness.

Dissent Justice Oliver Wendell Holmes sharply disagreed with the *Lochner* decision and the doctrine of substantive due process upon which it was based. He argued that the Bakeshop Act was a "reasonable" regulation of private business in behalf of a compelling public interest, as determined by a majority of the people's representatives in the state government.

According to Holmes, the Court had no authority to strike down laws made by legislative majorities on the basis of the personal opinions of the justices, which they read into the Constitution through the specious doctrine of substantive due process. Holmes believed that "liberty in the Fourteenth Amendment" was "perverted" when "held to prevent the natural outcome of a dominant opinion" (the legislative majority) unless a "rational and fair man" would conclude that the law violated "fundamental principles" of law and tradition. Holmes charged that the Court overstepped the boundaries of its judicial powers by using substantive due process to substitute its opinion of wise social policy for that of the popularly elected state legislature.

Significance The *Lochner* decision did not stop the movement for legal regulation of the workplace to protect employees. In *Muller* v. *Oregon* (1908), for example, the Court upheld a state law limiting the number of hours per day that women could work. And in *Bunting* v. *Oregon* (1917), the Court sustained a 10-hour workday limit for male workers. However, the Court continued to use the *Lochner* decision as the basis for overseeing legislative regulations of businesses. In 1937, however, the Court overruled *Lochner* v. *New York* with its decision in *West Coast Hotel Co.* v. *Parrish* (1937). In this case, the Court upheld a state law regulating minimum wages for children and women workers.

SEE ALSO

Due process of law; Muller v. Oregon; West Coast Hotel Co. v. Parrish

Lurton, Horace H.

ASSOCIATE JUSTICE, 1910–14

☆ *Born: Feb. 26, 1844, Newport, Ky.*
☆ *Education: Douglas University, 1860; Cumberland Law School, LL.B., 1867*
☆ *Previous government service: judge, Tennessee Supreme Court, 1886–93; judge, U.S. Court of Appeals for the Sixth Circuit, 1893–1909*
☆ *Appointed by President William Howard Taft Dec. 13, 1909; replaced Rufus W. Peckham, who died*
☆ *Supreme Court term: confirmed by the Senate Dec. 20, 1909, by a voice vote; served until July 12, 1914*
☆ *Died: July 12, 1914, Atlantic City, N.J.*

HORACE H. LURTON served in the Confederate Army during the Civil War. He was captured by Union forces and kept in a camp for prisoners of war. After the war, Lurton studied law and set up a private law practice in Clarksville, Tennessee.

During his brief term on the Court, Justice Lurton wrote few opinions. Instead, he usually went along with the Court's majority in deciding cases. He tended to support a strict construction of the Constitution and judicial restraint. Justice Lurton strongly opposed the use of judicial power to overcome social problems. In 1911 he wrote in *North American Review,* "The contention that…the Constitution is to be disregarded if it stands in the way of that which is deemed of public advantage… is destructive of the whole theory upon which our American Commonwealths have been founded."

Majority opinion

THE OPINION of the U.S. Supreme Court in cases that it decides is usually a majority opinion. A majority is one more than half of the justices participating in a decision. When five of the nine justices agree with the opinion of the Court, there is a majority opinion of the Court. When four of seven justices agree (with two justices not participating), there is a majority opinion. All decisions of the Court are by majority vote. In some cases, however, there is not a majority opinion because too many justices write their own concurring opinions. These justices vote with the majority to reach a decision on a case, but they write separate concurring opinions. For example, in 1989 the Court decided *Webster* v. *Reproductive Health Services* by a 5 to 4 vote. However, two justices voting with the majority wrote separate concurring opinions. Only three justices joined the opinion announced by the Court. As a result, there was a plurality opinion in the case, not a majority opinion.

SEE ALSO
Concurring opinion; Dissenting opinion; Opinions; Plurality opinion

Mapp v. Ohio

☆ *367 U.S. 643 (1961)*
☆ *Vote: 6–3*
☆ *For the Court: Clark*
☆ *Concurring: Black, Douglas, and Stewart*
☆ *Dissenting: Harlan, Frankfurter, and Whittaker*

ON MAY 23, 1957, police officers forced their way into the home of Dollree Mapp, whom they suspected of criminal activities. The police claimed they had a search warrant, which is required under the 4th Amendment to the Constitution, but they never proved it. During their unwarranted search of Mapp's house, the police seized obscene pictures, which under an Ohio law were illegal objects for someone to have. Mapp was convicted of possessing obscene pictures and sentenced to prison. Her lawyer appealed to the U.S. Supreme Court.

The Issue The police obtained evidence of Dollree Mapp's illegal behavior through actions that violated the 4th Amendment guarantee against unreasonable searches and seizures. Can evidence obtained through an illegally conducted search be used to convict a person of violating a state law?

Opinion of the Court The Court overturned Dollree Mapp's conviction. Justice Tom Clark wrote that evidence obtained in violation of the 4th Amendment of the U.S. Constitution must be excluded from use in state as well as federal criminal trials. The Court thus applied the exclusionary rule for the first time in ruling against a state government.

Dissent The dissenting opinions were based on opposition to the incorporation doctrine, by which the exclusionary rule associated with the 4th Amendment was applied to a state government through the due process clause of the 14th Amendment. The dissenting justices believed that the 4th Amendment

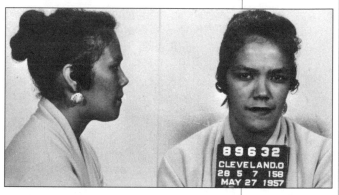

Dollree Mapp's mug shot, taken after she was arrested for possession of obscene pictures. The Supreme Court reversed her conviction because police officers had found these pictures during an illegal search of her house.

guarantees of individual rights were applicable only to the federal government.

Significance The exclusionary rule was created by the Court in *Weeks* v. *United States* (1914). Before the *Mapp* case, however, this rule had never been used against a state government. During the 1980s the Court recognized certain exceptions to the exclusionary rule as used in the *Mapp* case. For example, in *United States* v. *Leon* (1984), the Court ruled that evidence seized on the basis of a mistakenly issued search warrant can be used in a trial, if the warrant was issued in good faith—that is, on presumption that there were valid reasons for issuing the warrant. As a result, the exclusionary rule has been narrowed by this "good faith" exception.

SEE ALSO

Exclusionary rule; Incorporation doctrine; Searches and seizures; United States v. Leon; Weeks v. United States

FURTHER READING

Friendly, Fred W., and Martha J. H. Elliott. "A Knock at the Door: How the Supreme Court Created a Rule to Enforce the Fourth Amendment." In *The Constitution: That Delicate Balance.* New York: Random House, 1984.

Marbury v. Madison

☆ *1 Cranch 137 (1803)*
☆ *Vote: 5–0*
☆ *For the Court: Marshall*

IN THE PRESIDENTIAL election of 1800, Thomas Jefferson, the candidate of the Democratic-Republican party, defeated the Federalist candidate, John Adams. Not only had Adams lost the Presidency but the Federalists had lost control of Congress. Adams and his party feared that Jefferson would ruin the country by undoing everything the Federalists had accomplished in the pre-

vious 12 years. Between the November election and the March inauguration, the Federalists tried to ensure that they would continue to play a role in the U.S. government.

On January 20, 1801, Adams appointed Secretary of State John Marshall to be chief justice of the United States. Although the Senate confirmed this nomination in less than two weeks, Marshall remained secretary of state until Jefferson took office.

Throughout February the Federalists, who controlled Congress, created offices for Adams to fill with loyal supporters. During his last month as President, Adams nominated more than 200 men to new offices. These nominations included 42 justices of the peace for the new national capital at Washington, D.C. Adams appointed William Marbury as one of these justices of the peace.

The Senate received the nominations of the new justices of the peace on March 2 and confirmed them on March 3, Adams's last day in office. In order for the confirmed appointees to assume office, the executive had to complete one more procedure: the President had to sign commissions empowering each man to hold office, and the secretary of state had to place the official seal of the U.S. government on those commissions and supervise their delivery. In those days, officials prepared the commissions by hand. Thus, Adams spent his last evening as President signing commissions. The secretary of state, John Marshall, worked well into the night, affixing the Great Seal of the United States to the commissions and sending them off for delivery. However, in the chaos of Adams's last day in office, a number of commissions, including William Marbury's, though signed and sealed, remained undelivered.

On March 4, 1801, Jefferson became President. Soon after, Marbury asked the new secretary of state, James

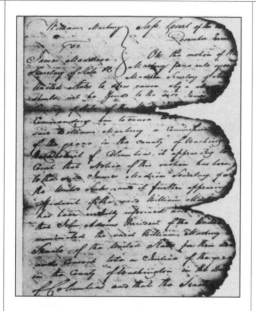

A fragment of the order given to Secretary of State James Madison requiring him to deliver William Marbury's commission to serve as justice of the peace in Washington, D.C.

Madison, for his commission. Madison, after consulting with Jefferson, refused to give Marbury the commission. Marbury then appealed to the Supreme Court for help.

Marbury asked the Court to issue a writ of mandamus directed to Secretary of State James Madison. A writ of mandamus orders a public official to carry out his duties. Marbury argued that he was legally entitled to his commission and that Madison should give it to him. Madison ignored these legal proceedings. Neither he nor Jefferson believed that the Supreme Court could give orders to the other two branches of government. Thus, the Court had to rule on Marbury's case with the knowledge that Madison might ignore the ruling. The man responsible for making the ruling was John Marshall, who as secretary of state had failed to send Marbury his commission in the first place.

The Issue Marbury argued that Section 13 of the Judiciary Act of 1789 gave the Supreme Court authority to issue a writ of mandamus under its original jurisdiction, its power to hear and decide such a case for the first time. The writ would require Secretary of State Madison to deliver Marbury's commis-

sion. Marbury pointed out that an act of Congress had created the office and the Senate had confirmed his Presidential appointment. With the commission legally signed and sealed, delivery of the commission was not, in Marbury's view, a discretionary act on the part of the secretary of state. Madison did not, Marbury claimed, have the authority to choose whether to deliver the commission. Rather, his job required him to deliver it.

Did Marbury have a right to the commission, and did the law provide him a means to obtain it? These were the apparent issues of the case. Chief Justice Marshall, however, asserted another issue: Could the Supreme Court, under the U.S. Constitution, have original jurisdiction in this case? Or, to put it another way, did Section 13 of the Judiciary Act of 1789 contradict or violate the U.S. Constitution?

Opinion of the Court The Court ruled that Marbury was due his commission. Chief Justice John Marshall said, "To withhold his commission is an act" that violates the law.

Marshall held that the writ of mandamus was the proper legal procedure to require a public official to do his duty. Marshall also acknowledged that the Judiciary Act of 1789 authorized the Supreme Court to issue such a writ.

Marshall knew, however, that if he ruled in favor of Marbury, Madison would probably ignore the Court's order to deliver the commission and cause a constitutional crisis. Above all else, Marshall hoped to avoid such a controversy. So one more question remained for Marshall to answer. Could the Supreme Court actually issue the writ of mandamus? If it could, then Marshall had backed himself into a corner. Having admitted that Marbury deserved the writ, he would then have to issue one. But Marshall had an out.

Marbury had directed his request

for a writ of mandamus to the Supreme Court. By asking the Supreme Court to issue the writ, Marbury had asked the Court to take original jurisdiction in the case, to be the first court to consider the request. In complying with such a request, the Supreme Court would act as a trial court. However, the founders of the Supreme Court had designed the Supreme Court as an appellate court—a court to hear appeals from other federal courts and from the state courts. The Constitution, in Article 3, Section 2, Clause 2, spelled out the few types of cases over which the Supreme Court would exercise original jurisdiction. Marshall examined that clause of the Constitution and concluded it did not authorize the Supreme Court to issue a writ of mandamus. Such a writ, he decided, could come only from a lower court.

Thus, Marshall concluded that Section 13 of the Judiciary Act of 1789, which authorized the Court to issue a writ of mandamus, violated the Constitution. Because the Supreme Court could not enforce an unconstitutional law, Marbury did not get his writ.

Marshall's opinion avoided generating a confrontation with Madison and Jefferson. He did not order Madison to give Marbury his commission. Marshall also succeeded in lecturing Madison and Jefferson on their respective responsibilities as secretary of state and President. In addition, by his opinion Marshall successfully asserted the Supreme Court's power to declare acts of Congress unconstitutional. This power is known as judicial review.

Marshall used three provisions of the Constitution to justify his arguments for judicial review. The first was Article 3, Section 2, which extends the judicial power to "all Cases, in Law and Equity, arising under this Constitution." Marshall argued: "Could it be the intention of those who gave this power, to say, that in using it, the constitution should not be looked into? That a case arising under the constitution should be decided, without examining the instrument under which it arises? This is too extravagant to be maintained."

Second, Article 6 requires judges to pledge "to support this Constitution." Marshall wrote, "How immoral to impose [this oath] on them, if they were to be used as the instruments...for violating what they swear to support!"

Third, Marshall pointed out that "in declaring what shall be the supreme law of the land [Article 6], the constitution itself is first mentioned; and not the laws of the United States, generally, but those only which shall be made in pursuance of the constitution, have that rank." Marshall argued from the supremacy clause of Article 6 that no act of Congress that violates any part of the Constitution, the highest law, can be valid. Rather, it must be declared unconstitutional and repealed.

Marshall memorably defined the Supreme Court's duty under the U.S. Constitution:

> It is, emphatically, the province and duty of the judicial department, to say what the law is. . . . So, if a law be in opposition to the constitution; if both the law and the constitution apply to a particular case, so that the court must either decide that case, conformable to the law, disregarding the constitution; or conformable to the constitution, disregarding the law; the court must determine which of these conflicting rules governs the case; this is of the very essence of judicial duty. If then, the courts are to regard the constitution, and the constitution is superior to any ordinary act of the legislature, the constitution, and not such ordinary act, must govern the case to which both apply.

Significance   The *Marbury* decision

provided the constitutional basis for the Supreme Court's power of judicial review of the actions and laws of the federal government. This decision asserted the Court's power to declare invalid those federal laws it finds in conflict with the Constitution. The Court's decision laid the foundation on which the Supreme Court eventually developed into an important branch of the federal government.

Full acceptance of judicial review would not happen until after the Civil War. Regardless, this case established the principle that the courts and government should not enforce unconstitutional federal laws.

SEE ALSO

Judicial power; Judicial review; Judiciary Act of 1789

FURTHER READING

Clinton, Robert Lowry. *Marbury v. Madison and Judicial Review.* Lawrence: University Press of Kansas, 1989.

Garraty, John A. "The Case of the Missing Commissions." In *Quarrels That Have Shaped the Constitution,* edited by John A. Garraty. New York: Harper & Row, 1987.

Marshal, Supreme Court

SEE Staff of the Court, nonjudicial

Marshall, John

CHIEF JUSTICE, 1801–35

☆ Born: Sept. 24, 1755, Germantown, Va.
☆ Education: taught at home by his father and two clergymen; self-educated in law; attended one course on law, College of William and Mary, 1780
☆ Previous government service: Virginia House of Delegates, 1782–85, 1787–90, 1795–96; Executive Council of State, Virginia, 1782–84; recorder, Richmond City Hustings Court, Virginia, 1785–88; U.S. minister to France, 1797–98; Virginia Ratifying Convention, 1788; U.S. representative from Virginia, 1799–1800; U.S. secretary of state, 1800–1801
☆ Appointed by President John Adams Jan. 20, 1801; replaced Oliver Ellsworth, who resigned
☆ Supreme Court term: confirmed by the Senate Jan. 27, 1801, by a voice vote; served until July 6, 1835
☆ Died: July 6, 1835, Philadelphia, Pa.

JOHN MARSHALL was the fourth chief justice of the United States. From his time to ours, he has been called the Great Chief Justice.

Born and raised in the backcountry of Virginia, Marshall was educated mostly at home, with his father as the main teacher. His formal education in the law consisted of one course of lectures by George Wythe, a leading Virginia political leader and legal authority at the College of William and Mary. Marshall, however, had a keen mind that he filled with knowledge through a lifetime of reading, thinking, and interacting with political leaders in the public affairs of Virginia and the United States.

Participation in the American Revolution shaped John Marshall's lifetime loyalty to the United States. He later expressed this loyalty decisively during his tenure on the Supreme Court through opinions that reinforced the power and authority of the federal government over the states. He served in the Continental Army for nearly six years, fought in the battles of Great Bridge, Brandywine, Germantown, and Monmouth and spent the grueling winter with George Washington's forces at Valley Forge. He left the Continental Army in 1781 with the rank of captain. Marshall exhibited intense patriotism and had great admiration for George Washington, which he expressed later in his five-volume biography *Life of George Washington,* published in 1804–7.

President John Adams appointed Marshall to be chief justice in 1801 as one of his final actions before leaving office. Adams's first choice for the job was John Jay, who had been the first chief justice. Jay, however, declined because in his view, widely shared at the time, the Supreme Court was too weak and unimportant; he said that he would not be head of "a system so defective." So John Marshall took the job that Jay refused and transformed it into the most powerful and prominent judicial position in the world.

Marshall brought unity and order to the Court by practically ending *seriatim* opinions (the writing of opinions by various justices). Before Chief Justice Marshall, the Court did not issue a single majority opinion. He, however, influenced the Court's majority to speak with one voice, through an opinion for the Court on each case before it. Of course, members of the Court occasionally wrote concurring or dissenting opinions, as they do today.

Often the Court's voice was John Marshall's. During his 34 years on the Court, the longest tenure of any chief justice, Marshall wrote 519 of the 1,100 opinions issued during that period, and he dissented only eight times.

Chief Justice Marshall's greatest opinions were masterworks of legal reasoning and graceful writing. They stand today as an authoritative commentary on the core principles of the U.S. Constitution.

Marshall's first great decision came in *Marbury* v. *Madison* (1803), in which he ruled that Section 13 of the Judiciary Act of 1789 was void because it violated Article 3 of the Constitution. In this opinion, Marshall made a compelling argument for judicial review, the Court's power to decide whether an act of Congress violates the Constitution. If it does, Marshall wrote, then the legislative act contrary to the Constitution is unconstitutional, or illegal, and could not be enforced. Marshall wrote, "It is emphatically the province and duty of the judicial department to say what the law is.... So if a law be in opposition to the constitution...the constitution and not such ordinary Act, must govern the case to which they both apply."

In a series of great decisions, Marshall also established, beyond legal challenge, the Court's power of judicial review over acts of state government. In *Fletcher* v. *Peck* (1810), *Dartmouth College* v. *Woodward* (1819), *McCulloch* v. *Maryland* (1819), and *Cohens* v. *Virginia* (1821), Marshall wrote for the Court that acts of state government in violation of federal statutes or the federal Constitution were unconstitutional or void.

The Marshall Court's decisions also defended the sanctity of contracts and private property rights against would-be violators in the cases of *Fletcher* v. *Peck* and *Dartmouth College* v. *Woodward*. In *Gibbons* v. *Ogden* (1824), Marshall broadly interpreted Congress's power to regulate commerce (Article 1, Section 8, of the Constitution) and prohibited states from passing laws to interfere with the flow of goods and transportation across state lines.

Chief Justice Marshall's greatest opinions protected private property rights as a foundation of individual liberty. They also rejected claims of state sovereignty in favor of a federal Constitution based on the sovereignty of the people of the United States. Finally, Marshall clearly and convincingly argued for the Constitution as a permanent supreme law that the Supreme Court was established to interpret and defend. "Ours is a Constitution," Marshall wrote in 1819 (*McCulloch* v. *Maryland*), "intended to endure for ages to come, and consequently, to be adapted to the various crises of human affairs."

Only through broad construction of the federal government's powers could the Constitution of 1787 be "adapted" to meet changing times. And only through strict limits on excessive use of the government's powers could the Constitution endure as a guardian of individual rights. The special duty of the Supreme Court, according to Marshall, was to make the difficult judgments, based on the Constitution, about when to impose limits or to permit broad exercise of the federal government's powers.

In 1833, near the end of John Marshall's career, his associate on the Supreme Court, Justice Joseph Story, wrote a "Dedication to John Marshall" that included these words of high praise: "Your expositions of constitutional law…constitute a monument of fame far beyond the ordinary memorials of political or military glory. They are destined to enlighten, instruct and convince future generations; and can scarcely perish but with the memory of the Constitution itself." And so it has been, from Marshall's time until our own, that his judgments and commentaries on the Constitution have instructed and inspired Americans.

SEE ALSO

Cohens v. Virginia; Dartmouth College v. Woodward; Fletcher v. Peck; Judicial review; Marbury v. Madison; McCulloch v. Maryland

FURTHER READING

Baker, Leonard. *John Marshall: A Life in Law*. New York: Macmillan, 1974.
Rudko, Frances H. *John Marshall, Statesman and Chief Justice*. Westport, Conn.: Greenwood Press, 1991.
Stites, Francis N. *John Marshall: Defender of the Constitution*. Boston: Little, Brown, 1981.
White, G. Edward. *The Marshall Court and Cultural Change*. New York: Oxford University Press, 1991.

Marshall, Thurgood

ASSOCIATE JUSTICE, 1967–91

☆ Born: July 2, 1908, Baltimore, Md.
☆ Education: Lincoln University, B.A., 1930; Howard University Law School, LL.B., 1933
☆ Previous government service: judge, Second Circuit Court of Appeals, 1961–65; U.S. solicitor general, 1965–67
☆ Appointed by President Lyndon B. Johnson June 13, 1967; replaced Tom C. Clark, who retired
☆ Supreme Court term: confirmed by the Senate Aug. 30, 1967, by a 69–11 vote; retired Oct. 1, 1991
☆ Died: Jan. 24, 1993, Bethesda, Md.

THURGOOD MARSHALL, the great-grandson of a slave, was the first African-American justice of the Supreme Court. He began his historic career in 1933, as a civil rights lawyer for the National Association for the Advancement of Colored People (NAACP). In 1940 Marshall became head of the NAACP Legal Defense Fund. In this position, he led the NAACP's legal fight against racial segregation and denial of individual rights of black people. Marshall successfully argued 29 out of 32 cases before the U.S. Supreme Court.

In 1954 Thurgood Marshall achieved his biggest victory for the NAACP in *Brown* v. *Board of Education*. In this landmark case, Marshall convinced the Supreme Court to decide that racial segregation in public schools was unconstitutional. This was the beginning of the eventual ending of state government laws that denied equal rights to black people.

In 1961 President John F. Kennedy appointed Marshall to the U.S. Court of Appeals for the Second Circuit. In 1965 President Lyndon B. Johnson selected Marshall to be solicitor general of the United States, the top lawyer for the U.S.

government in federal court cases. Marshall was the first African American to serve as the solicitor general and to argue cases for the government at the Supreme Court.

During his 24 years on the Court, Justice Marshall wrote many opinions on various issues pertaining to federal jurisdiction, antitrust laws, and civil rights. He wrote numerous dissenting opinions about equal protection of the laws, the rights of minorities, and capital punishment. He strongly opposed the death penalty, which in his opinion was a violation of the 8th Amendment prohibition of "cruel and unusual punishment." Throughout his long career in law, Thurgood Marshall was an outspoken advocate for the rights and opportunities of minorities, especially for African Americans and poor people.

During his final years on the Court, Justice Marshall often wrote strong dissents to call attention to his views about unmet needs for social justice. He opposed the conservative tendencies of the Court during the 1980s and was a staunch ally of Justice William Brennan in arguing for liberal positions. He remained on the Court only one term after Brennan retired, citing declining health as a major reason for his retirement. Marshall's death in 1993 brought an outpouring of praise for his remarkable career.

SEE ALSO

Brown v. Board of Education; Civil rights; National Association for the Advancement of Colored People (NAACP)

FURTHER READING

Aldred, Lisa. *Thurgood Marshall.* New York: Chelsea House, 1990.
Rowan, Carl T. *Dream Makers, Dream Breakers: The World of Thurgood Marshall.* Boston: Little, Brown, 1993.
Tushnet, Mark V. *Making Civil Rights Law: Thurgood Marshall and the Supreme Court, 1936–1961.* New York: Oxford, 1993.

Martin v. Hunter's Lessee

☆ *1 Wheat. 304 (1816)*
☆ *Vote: 6–0*
☆ *For the Court: Story*
☆ *Not participating: Marshall*

THOMAS, SIXTH LORD FAIRFAX, owned more than 5 million acres of valuable land in the northern area of western Virginia. In 1781 Lord Fairfax died and left his property to a nephew, Denny Martin, a British subject. However, during the War of Independence, Virginia had passed laws confiscating the property of Loyalists, such as Lord Fairfax, who supported Great Britain. The state sold the land to private owners, including David Hunter, who denied Denny Martin's claim to his uncle's property. Martin challenged Hunter's right to this property and filed a lawsuit against him.

The state courts of Virginia decided in favor of Hunter, so Martin took his case to the U.S. Supreme Court. In *Fairfax's Devisee* v. *Hunter's Lessee*

Lord Fairfax owned land in the northern neck of Virginia. When his nephew inherited the land, the state of Virginia tried to deny the claim but the Supreme Court decided that the inheritance was protected by a U.S. treaty with Great Britain.

(1813), the Court decided in favor of Martin. (Chief Justice John Marshall did not participate in this decision because of financial interests in the land at issue.)

Writing for the Court, Justice Joseph Story overturned the Virginia laws used to take the Fairfax lands, reasoning that Martin's inheritance was protected by the Treaty of Paris (1783) and Jay's Treaty (1794). Both of these treaties between the United States and Great Britain pledged that the property of Loyalists in the United States would be protected by the federal government. Justice Story pointed to Article 6 of the Constitution, which included treaties of the United States as part of the "supreme Law of the Land." Further, Article 6 said that "the Judges in every State shall be bound thereby, any thing in the Constitution or Laws of any State to the Contrary notwithstanding." Finally, Justice Story referred to Section 25 of the Judiciary Act of 1789, which provided for review by the U.S. Supreme Court of decisions by state courts that involved the U.S. Constitution, federal laws, and treaties.

Justice Story ordered the Virginia Court of Appeals to carry out the decision of the U.S. Supreme Court. The Virginia judges refused to obey the order, however. They claimed that Section 25 of the Judiciary Act of 1789 was not valid because it violated the powers and rights of state governments in the federal Union.

The Issue Virginia's refusal to comply with Justice Story's ruling brought the case back to the U.S. Supreme Court. The issue cut to the heart of the federal Union. Did the Supreme Court have authority over all state laws and state judicial decisions that involved the U.S. Constitution, federal laws, and treaties? Or did each state have authority under the U.S. Constitution to defy certain kinds of federal treaties or decisions if it did not approve of them?

Opinion of the Court Once again, Joseph Story wrote for the Court. (Chief Justice Marshall again declined to participate because of a possible conflict of interest.) Justice Story decided that the U.S. Supreme Court had jurisdiction in this case, and he rebuked the Virginia judges who had refused to comply with the Court's orders. Contrary to the views of the Virginia judges, Story argued that the U.S. Supreme Court's appellate jurisdiction extended to all cases involving federal issues, not merely to cases coming to it from lower federal courts.

Story asserted that Article 25 of the Judiciary Act of 1789 was constitutional and was necessary to the enforcement of federal laws and treaties as part of the supreme law of the land, as defined by Article 6 of the Constitution. He rejected Virginia's claim to equal sovereignty with the United States and argued that the American people, not the states, had created the federal Union.

Finally, Justice Story insisted that to enforce the supremacy clause of Article 6, the U.S. Supreme Court had the final power to interpret the U.S. Constitution. Without this power over state governments, Story insisted, there could be no enduring federal Union.

Significance The Court's judgment, expressed by Justice Story, has been called the greatest argument ever made for judicial review of state laws and court decisions by the U.S. Supreme Court. Story's opinion also gave great strength to the nationalists' side of the ongoing argument about state powers and rights in the federal system of the United States. The claims of extreme states' rights advocates, however, were not subdued until after the Civil War.

S E E A L S O

Federalism; Judicial power; Judicial review; Jurisdiction

Matthews, Stanley

ASSOCIATE JUSTICE, 1881–89

☆ *Born: July 21, 1824, Cincinnati, Ohio*
☆ *Education: Kenyon College, B.A., 1840*
☆ *Previous government service: assistant prosecuting attorney, Hamilton County, Ohio, 1845; clerk, Ohio House of Representatives, 1848–49; judge, Hamilton County Court of Common Pleas, 1851–53; Ohio Senate, 1855–58; U.S. attorney for the Southern District of Ohio, 1858–61; judge, Superior Court of Cincinnati, 1863–65; counsel, Hayes-Tilden electoral commission, 1877; U.S. senator from Ohio, 1877–79*
☆ *Appointed by President James A. Garfield Mar. 14, 1881; replaced Noah Swayne, who retired*
☆ *Supreme Court term: confirmed by the Senate May 12, 1881, by a 24–23 vote; served until Mar. 22, 1889*
☆ *Died: Mar. 22, 1889, Washington, D.C.*

STANLEY MATTHEWS's political connections led to his appointment to the Supreme Court. He campaigned for Presidential candidate Rutherford B. Hayes in 1876. Then he served as a lawyer for Hayes at the 1877 electoral commission that decided the contested Presidential election in favor of Hayes. Consequently, Hayes appointed Matthews to fill a vacancy on the Court, but the Senate blocked the nomination. They recalled his involvement in a controversial federal case in 1859, when Matthews served as the U.S. attorney for southern Ohio. Although Matthews had sided publicly with the cause of abolishing slavery, he vigorously prosecuted an abolitionist for helping two fugitive slaves to escape to freedom. Many senators objected to Matthews because of his role as prosecuting attorney in this case. Matthews was renominated by President Hayes's successor, James A. Garfield, but he was still opposed by many sena-tors and was barely confirmed, by a vote of 24–23.

The controversy about Matthews's appointment to the Court eventually died down and he served satisfactorily as an associate justice. He wrote 232 opinions for the Court and 5 dissents in a Supreme Court career of less than eight years.

McCulloch v. Maryland

☆ *4 Wheat. 316 (1819)*
☆ *Vote: 7–0*
☆ *For the Court: Marshall*

CONGRESS CHARTERED the Second Bank of the United States in 1816 to provide a sound national currency. But the bank soon proved very unpopular in many states. Maryland passed a law that levied an extremely high tax on any bank in the state without a state charter. At the time, the Second Bank of the United States was the only bank operating in Maryland that was not chartered by the state. McCulloch, the cashier of the Baltimore branch of the Bank of the United States, refused to pay the tax. Maryland sued McCulloch and won in the Maryland courts.

Officials of the bank appealed to the U.S. Supreme Court. They claimed the state tax interfered unconstitutionally with the federally chartered bank. Maryland argued that Congress had no power to charter the bank and that the state had the power to tax the bank.

The Issue The Constitution did not expressly give Congress the power to charter a national bank. However, Article 1, Section 8, Clause 18, did grant Congress the power to "make all laws which shall be necessary and proper for carrying into Execution the foregoing Powers." Did this "necessary and proper" clause give Congress adequate power only to do those few things indispensable for carrying out its listed, or delegated, powers? Or did it ensure that Congress could do nearly anything it wanted, such as chartering a national bank, to exercise its delegated powers?

In addition, did states have the power to tax a national bank? Was national law or state law supreme in this case?

Opinion of the Court The Court upheld the power of Congress to create a national bank. Chief Justice John Marshall wrote that the Constitution did not need to expressly authorize Congress to establish a bank. Such expressly listed congressional powers as the power to tax, to spend money, to borrow money, and to support the army and navy implied that Congress had the power to establish a bank.

At the same time, the Court ruled that the states could not tax the bank. Marshall declared that allowing states to tax part of the national government would interfere with national supremacy. "The power to tax involves the power to destroy."

Thus, the Court established two important constitutional principles. The first, the implied powers doctrine, stated that the legal system should interpret broadly the necessary and proper clause of the Constitution to let Congress choose the means it wished to employ to carry out the powers the Constitution

expressly gave it. Marshall wrote, "Let the end be legitimate, let it be within the scope of the Constitution, and all means which are appropriate, which are plainly adapted to that end, which are not prohibited, but consist with the letter and spirit of the Constitution, are constitutional."

The second principle, national supremacy, forbids the states to intrude into the constitutional operations of the federal government. It reinforced the supremacy of the Constitution and federal laws over state laws that conflict with them.

Significance The *McCulloch* decision has been used to support a broad construction of the Constitution that enables the federal government to apply the supreme law flexibly to meet the new problems of changing times. In the *McCulloch* case Chief Justice Marshall made a memorable statement, which is often quoted to support a broad interpretation of the federal government's constitutional powers: "This…is…a constitution we are expounding, intended to endure for ages to come, and consequently, to be adapted to the various crises of human affairs."

Today, many bills Congress passes to some extent draw their legitimacy from the necessary and proper clause and the broad construction of the Constitution exemplified in Marshall's *McCulloch* opinion. For example, federal laws pertaining to the regulation of airlines or broadcasting are based on the necessary and proper clause, not on express powers of Congress specified in the Constitution.

The *McCulloch* decision also strengthened the Court's powers of judicial review over acts of state governments. Thus, it pleased advocates of federal supremacy and infuriated supporters of state powers and rights. The vision of national supremacy under the Constitution, expressed in Chief Justice Mar-

The Bank of the United States in Philadelphia. The Supreme Court decided that the necessary and proper clause of the Constitution gave Congress the power to establish a national bank.

shall's *McCulloch* opinion, has prevailed in the 20th century.

SEE ALSO

Constitutional construction; Federalism; Implied powers

FURTHER READING

Gunther, Gerald. *John Marshall's Defense of McCulloch v. Maryland.* Stanford, Calif.: Stanford University Press, 1969.

Hammond, Bray. "The Bank Cases." In *Quarrels That Have Shaped the Constitution,* edited by John A. Garraty. New York: Harper & Row, 1987.

McKeiver v. Pennsylvania

☆ *403 U.S. 528 (1971)*
☆ *Vote: 6–3*
☆ *For the Court: Blackmun*
☆ *Concurring: White, Harlan, and Brennan*
☆ *Dissenting: Douglas, Black, and Marshall*

JOSEPH McKEIVER, 16 years old, was a juvenile defendant who had been accused of serious acts of delinquency—robbery and receiving stolen goods. He faced the possible punishment of detention for five years. McKeiver asked for a trial by jury, but the state of Pennsylvania denied his request. McKeiver was convicted and sentenced without a jury trial. He appealed his conviction on the grounds that his constitutional right to a trial by jury had been violated.

The Issue Adults accused of crimes have a constitutional right to trial by jury. This right is included in the 6th Amendment, and it is applicable to the states through the due process clause of the 14th Amendment. Is this right to trial by jury required in state proceedings against a juvenile accused of unlawful behavior?

Opinion of the Court The Court decided that due process of law for juveniles does not require a trial by jury. Justice Harry Blackmun stated a standard of "fundamental fairness" for due process in juvenile cases. Thus, a right to trial by jury in juvenile cases had to be balanced against the special requirements of juvenile justice. Justice Blackmun feared that a jury trial would subject juveniles to unnecessary and disruptive adversarial proceedings without providing compensating benefits of greater accuracy in fact-finding or determination of guilt.

Significance The Court decided in another case about a juvenile offender, *In re Gault* (1967), to extend constitutional rights of due process to juvenile court proceedings. The *McKeiver* decision, however, indicated that the Court was unwilling to extend all the rights of the criminally accused to juveniles accused of serious crimes. According to this decision, states are not required to provide a jury trial for a juvenile, but they may choose to do so. To date, none has done so.

SEE ALSO

In re Gault; Juvenile justice; Trial by jury

FURTHER READING

Bernard, Thomas J. *The Cycle of Juvenile Justice.* New York: Oxford, 1992.

McKenna, Joseph

ASSOCIATE JUSTICE, 1898–1925

☆ *Born: Aug. 10, 1843, Philadelphia, Pa.*
☆ *Education: Benicia Collegiate Institute, 1865*
☆ *Previous government service: district attorney, Solano County, Calif., 1866–70; California Assembly, 1875–76; U.S. representative from California, 1885–92; judge, U.S. Court of Appeals for the Ninth Circuit, 1892–97; U.S. attorney general, 1897*
☆ *Appointed by President William McKinley Dec. 16, 1897; replaced Stephen J. Field, who retired*

☆ Supreme Court term: confirmed by
the Senate Jan. 21, 1898, by a voice
vote; retired Jan. 5, 1925
☆ Died: Nov. 21, 1926, Washington, D.C.

JOSEPH McKENNA was the son of immigrants from Ireland. He was a successful politician who served seven years in
the U.S. House of Representatives,
where he became a friend of William
McKinley. When McKinley became
President, he appointed his old friend to
fill a vacancy on the Supreme Court.

Justice McKenna served on the
Court for 27 years. He joined in the
Court's opinions to regulate various
kinds of economic activity under the
"commerce clause" of Article 1, Section
8, of the Constitution. He also supported
regulation of businesses under the Pure
Food and Drug Act.

During his later years on the Court,
McKenna's reasoning powers seemed to
decline. His associates urged him to resign, which he did in 1925, at age 83.

FURTHER READING

McDevitt, Matthew. *Joseph McKenna.*
1946. Reprint. New York: Da Capo, 1974.

McKinley, John

*A S S O C I A T E J U S T I C E,
1 8 3 7 – 5 2*

☆ Born: May 1, 1780, Culpeper County, Va.
☆ Education: self-educated in the law
☆ Previous government service: Alabama
House of Representatives, 1820, 1831,
1836; U.S. senator from Alabama,
1826–31; U.S. representative from
Alabama, 1833–35
☆ Appointed by President Martin Van
Buren as a recess appointment Apr. 22,
1837, to a newly created position on
the Supreme Court; nominated by Van
Buren Sept. 18, 1837
☆ Supreme Court term: confirmed by the
Senate Sept. 25, 1837, by a voice vote;
served until July 19, 1852
☆ Died: July 19, 1852, Lexington, Ky.

JOHN McKINLEY was a loyal supporter of the Jacksonian Democrats,
who backed the Presidential candidacies
of Andrew Jackson and Martin Van
Buren. After Van Buren became President, he rewarded McKinley with an appointment to the Supreme Court.

Justice McKinley was a strong supporter of states' rights and slavery. However, he was an unproductive and medio-
cre associate justice who wrote only 20
opinions for the Court during his 15
years of service. He usually voted with
the Court's majority and dissented only
when joined by at least one other justice.
He wrote no opinions that contributed
significantly to the development of constitutional law.

McLean, John

*A S S O C I A T E J U S T I C E,
1 8 3 0 – 6 1*

☆ Born: Mar. 11, 1785, Morris County, N.J.
☆ Education: studied at home with
private tutors; read law in the office of
Arthur St. Clair, Jr., in Cincinnati
☆ Previous government service: exam-
iner, U.S. Land Office, Cincinnati,
Ohio, 1811–12; U.S. representative
from Ohio, 1813–16; judge, Ohio
Supreme Court, 1816–22; commis-
sioner, General Land Office, 1822–23;
U.S. postmaster general, 1823–29
☆ Appointed by President Andrew
Jackson Mar. 6, 1829; replaced Robert
Trimble, who died
☆ Supreme Court term: confirmed by the
Senate Mar. 7, 1829, by a voice vote;
served until Apr. 4, 1861
☆ Died: Apr. 4, 1861, Cincinnati, Ohio

JOHN McLEAN was President Andrew
Jackson's first appointment to the Supreme Court. During his 32 years on the
Court, however, Justice McLean moved
away from Jacksonian views, which fa-

vored states' rights, to support nationalism and the federal government's power to regulate foreign and interstate commerce.

Justice McLean's dislike of slavery and states' rights was expressed in his famous dissent in the Dred Scott case (*Scott* v. *Sandford*, 1857). In opposition to the Court's majority, he argued that Congress could ban slavery in the territories of the United States, that blacks could be citizens, and that Dred Scott was a free man because he had lived in a free state and a free territory. This dissent was vindicated by ratification of the 13th and 14th Amendments, which overturned the *Dred Scott* decision.

SEE ALSO
Scott v. Sandford

FURTHER READING
Weisenburger, Francis P. *The Life of John McLean*. 1937. Reprint. New York: Da Capo, 1971.

McReynolds, James Clark

ASSOCIATE JUSTICE, 1914–41

☆ Born: Feb. 3, 1862, Elkton, Ky.
☆ Education: Vanderbilt University, B.S., 1882; University of Virginia, LL.B., 1884
☆ Previous government service: assistant U.S. attorney, 1903–7; U.S. attorney general, 1913–14
☆ Appointed by President Woodrow Wilson Aug. 19, 1914; replaced Horace H. Lurton, who died
☆ Supreme Court term: confirmed by the Senate Aug. 29, 1914, by a 44–6 vote; retired Jan. 31, 1941
☆ Died: Aug. 24, 1946, Washington, D.C.

JAMES MCREYNOLDS was an outspoken man with strong views and a disagreeable personality. He was intolerant of colleagues with opposing views and expressed his feelings through rude behavior. He disliked Associate Justices Louis Brandeis and Benjamin Cardozo so much that he would not speak to them. Brandeis and Cardozo were Jews and critics accused McReynolds of anti-Semitism. He also seemed to favor racial segregation and to be prejudiced against female attorneys.

Justice McReynolds was a harsh critic of President Franklin D. Roosevelt's New Deal programs and joined several majority opinions to strike down New Deal legislation between 1934 and 1936. During President Roosevelt's second term, however, the Court shifted to majority support of New Deal enactments. Justice McReynolds therefore became a bitter dissenter during his last years on the Court.

Miami Herald Publishing Co. v. Tornillo

☆ *418 U.S. 241 (1974)*
☆ *Vote: 9–0*
☆ *For the Court: Burger*
☆ *Concurring: Brennan, Rehnquist, and White*

IN SEPTEMBER 1972, the *Miami Herald* printed editorials that were highly critical of Pat Tornillo, a candidate for the Florida House of Representatives. The editorials faulted Tornillo's judgment and character and advised voters not to support him.

Tornillo demanded that the *Miami Herald* print his response to its critical editorials. When the newspaper's publisher refused, Tornillo pointed to a 1913 Florida law that provided that "if a candidate for nomination in election is as-

The second draft of the Supreme Court's decision in Miami Herald Publishing Co. v. Tornillo. *This copy belonged to Justice Thurgood Marshall.*

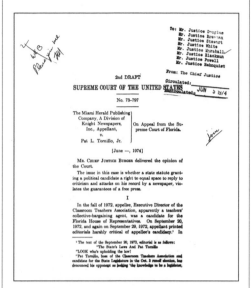

sailed regarding his personal character or official record by any newspaper, the candidate has a right to demand that the newspaper print…any reply the candidate may make to the newspaper's charges."

The *Miami Herald*'s publisher continued to ignore Tornillo's request, so Tornillo filed suit, asking that the Florida "right to reply" law be enforced in his behalf.

The Florida Supreme Court upheld the "right to reply" law as furthering the "broad societal interest in the free flow of information to the public." The *Miami Herald* appealed to the U.S. Supreme Court.

The Issue The 1st Amendment to the U.S. Constitution says, "Congress shall make no law…abridging the freedom of speech, or of the press." The 1st Amendment freedoms of speech and press have been applied by the Court to the states through the due process clause of the 14th Amendment. Did the Florida "right to reply" law violate the *Miami Herald*'s constitutional right to freedom of the press?

Opinion of the Court The Court reversed the Florida Supreme Court judgment and declared the "right to reply" law unconstitutional. Chief Justice War-

ren Burger concluded that the 1913 Florida statute was a clear violation of the 1st Amendment guarantee of a free press. Burger wrote, "The choice of material to go into a newspaper, and the decisions made as to…treatment of public issues and public officials—whether fair or unfair—constitute the exercise of editorial control and judgment."

Significance This case established that the government cannot force a newspaper publisher to print and distribute particular information. However, the Court has upheld government "right to reply" regulations with regard to news broadcasting, as in *Red Lion Broadcasting Co., Inc.* v. *Federal Communications Commission* (1969). That is because the broadcast media, unlike print media, have a limited number of frequencies or channels available, so the only way to provide for access to different points of view is a "right to reply" regulation that can be imposed by the Federal Communications Commission.

SEE ALSO

Freedom of speech and press; Incorporation doctrine

FURTHER READING

Powe, Lucas A., Jr. *American Broadcasting and the First Amendment.* Berkeley: University of California Press, 1987.

Miller, Samuel Freeman

ASSOCIATE JUSTICE, 1862–90

☆ *Born: Apr. 5, 1816, Richmond, Ky.*

☆ *Education: Transylvania University, M.D., 1838; studied law privately*

☆ *Previous government service: justice of the peace and member of the Knox County Court, Ky., 1840s*

☆ *Appointed by President Abraham Lincoln July 6, 1862; replaced Peter V. Daniel, who died*

☆ *Supreme Court term: confirmed by the Senate July 16, 1862, by voice vote; served until Oct. 13, 1890*

☆ *Died: Oct. 13, 1890, Washington, D.C.*

SAMUEL MILLER participated in more than 5,000 decisions of the Supreme Court during his 28 years of service. Before Justice Miller, no other member of the Court had written as many opinions.

During and after the Civil War, Miller voted to sustain President Abraham Lincoln's actions to suspend habeas corpus and to try civilians in military courts in cases involving charges of disloyalty to the Union. A writ of habeas corpus requires officials to bring a person whom they have arrested and held in custody before a judge in a court of law. If a judge finds their reasons for holding the person unlawful, then the court frees the suspect.

However, Justice Miller's greatest influence on constitutional law was in his decision to support state government rights and powers. Thus, he opposed a broad interpretation of the 14th Amendment that would involve the Court as "a perpetual censor upon all legislation of the states." He asserted this opinion for the Court in the *Slaughterhouse Cases* (1873). In this decision, Justice Miller advanced a narrow interpretation of the 14th Amendment that supported state government authority over the privileges and immunities of citizenship instead of emphasizing the federal government's power in these matters. Justice Miller concluded that it would be a violation of the Constitution to bring protection of all civil rights under the authority of the federal government. This would, he wrote, "fetter and degrade the state governments by subjecting them to the control of Congress."

Justice Miller and his supporters on the Court effectively blocked the use of the 14th Amendment to protect black Americans from state government acts that would restrict their civil rights, especially their right to "equal protection of the laws." This narrow interpretation of the 14th Amendment persisted until the middle of the 20th century.

SEE ALSO
Slaughterhouse Cases

FURTHER READING
Fairman, Charles. *Mr. Justice Miller and the Supreme Court.* Cambridge: Harvard University Press, 1938.

Minersville School District v. Gobitis

☆ *310 U.S. 586 (1940)*
☆ *Vote: 8–1*
☆ *For the Court: Frankfurter*
☆ *Dissenting: Stone*

ONE DAY in 1936, Lillian Gobitis, age 12, and her brother William, age 10, came home from school with news that distressed their parents. They had been expelled from their Minersville, Pennsylvania, school for refusing to salute the American flag during the morning patriotic exercises.

The Gobitis family belonged to the Jehovah's Witnesses faith. This religion taught that saluting the flag was like worshiping a graven image (an idol), an offense against God's law.

Lillian and William's parents asked the Minersville school board to excuse their children from the flag salute requirement. The board refused, and the Gobitises placed their children in a private school. Mr. Gobitis then sued the school board to stop it from requiring children attending the public schools to salute the flag. Federal district and appellate judges upheld Gobitis's suit. The Minersville school board then appealed to the Supreme Court.

The Issue Could public school officials force Jehovah's Witnesses to salute

Walter Gobitis and his children, William and Lillian, after they were expelled from school for refusing to salute the American flag. As Jehovah's Witnesses, they claimed that saluting the flag violated their religious beliefs.

the American flag even though doing so contradicted their religious beliefs? The Witnesses claimed the Minersville school board's regulation violated their 1st Amendment right to the "free exercise" of religion.

Opinion of the Court The Court voted to sustain the lower courts' rulings and uphold the flag salute requirement. Justice Felix Frankfurter wrote the majority opinion. He argued that religious liberty had to give way to state authority as long as the state did not directly promote or restrict religion. Because it met this requirement, the school board's flag salute requirement was constitutional.

Frankfurter called the controversy a "tragic issue" that defied the Court to find a clear-cut solution. However, he argued that national unity is the basis for national security. If a local school board believed that a compulsory flag salute promoted national unity, then the Court should not prevent it from requiring students to salute the flag.

Dissent Justice Harlan Fiske Stone was the lone dissenter in the *Gobitis* case. He considered religious freedom to be outside the jurisdiction of political authority. Stone argued that when the state attempts to force children to express a belief they do not really hold, it violates their 1st Amendment rights to freedom of speech and free exercise of religion. Furthermore, he suggested that there were other ways to instill patriotism in students.

Significance Within three years, the majority of the Court would come to

agree with Stone's opposition to the *Gobitis* decision. *Gobitis* established a precedent, but that precedent did not last. Two factors influenced the Court's determination to overrule it: the reaction of the public and the legal community and changes in the Court's membership.

To Justice Frankfurter's surprise, a substantial public outburst greeted the *Gobitis* decision. More than 170 newspapers opposed the decision. The stance of the *St. Louis Post-Dispatch* typified the nationwide criticism. "We think this decision of the United States Supreme Court is dead wrong," declared its editorial. Members of the legal profession, exerting influence on the justices, strongly condemned the decision. Articles in legal journals opposed the decision nearly unanimously and agreed with the dissent of Justice Stone.

Over a three-year period the membership of the Court changed. This change proved a second factor leading to the overruling of *Gobitis*. The first new member was Robert H. Jackson, an advocate of civil liberties for minorities. Then Wiley B. Rutledge, known for strong views in favor of freedom of religion, joined the Court. In addition, Justice Stone, who had stood alone against the *Gobitis* decision, became chief justice. A new point of view prevailed on the Court after these changes in membership.

The Court reversed the *Gobitis* decision in 1943 in the case of *West Virginia State Board of Education* v. *Barnette,* which said that Jehovah's Witnesses in public schools had the right to refuse to participate in required flag salute ceremonies.

SEE ALSO

Religious issues under the Constitution; West Virginia State Board of Education v. Barnette

FURTHER READING

Irons, Peter. *The Courage of Their Convictions.* New York: Free Press, 1988.

Minority rights

S E E Affirmative action; Constitutional democracy; Civil rights; Equality under the Constitution; Liberty under the Constitution

Minton, Sherman

ASSOCIATE JUSTICE, 1949–56

☆ Born: Oct. 20, 1890, Georgetown, Ind.
☆ Education: Indiana University, LL.B., 1925; Yale University, LL.M., 1927
☆ Previous government service: Indiana public counselor, 1933–34; U.S. senator from Indiana, 1935–41; administrative assistant to the President, 1941; federal judge, Seventh Circuit Court of Appeals, 1941–49
☆ Appointed by President Harry S. Truman Sept. 15, 1949; replaced Wiley B. Rutledge, who died
☆ Supreme Court term: confirmed by the Senate Oct. 4, 1949, by a 48–16 vote; retired Oct. 15, 1956
☆ Died: Apr. 9, 1965, New Albany, Ind.

SHERMAN MINTON graduated from Indiana University, where he excelled as a scholar and a varsity athlete in football and basketball. After holding a minor position in the state government, he entered national politics in 1934, winning a seat in the U.S. Senate. A Democrat, he strongly supported the New Deal programs of President Franklin D. Roosevelt.

Justice Minton supported the authority of the executive and legislative branches to make policies without interference from the judiciary. So he tended to favor a broad interpretation of the constitutional powers of the federal government.

Minton's term on the Court was cut short by a severe case of anemia that caused physical weakness and exhaustion. This condition forced him to retire after only seven years of service. As a result, his impact on constitutional law was minimal. He tended to favor government regulations over the civil liberties and rights of individuals. Justice Minton was an avid supporter of national security objectives, which he expressed as the writer of the Court's opinion in *Adler* v. *Board of Education.* This ruling upheld a New York law that banned members of subversive organizations, such as the Communist party, from teaching in public schools.

Miranda v. Arizona

☆ 384 U.S. 436 (1966)
☆ Vote: 5–4
☆ For the Court: Warren
☆ Dissenting: Clark, Harlan, White, and Stewart

IN 1963 Ernesto Miranda was arrested for kidnapping and attacking a young woman near Phoenix. The woman identified him at the police station and the police questioned him for two hours. No one told him that he had the right to refuse to answer questions or to see a lawyer. Miranda confessed. He was tried and convicted on the basis of his confession.

Miranda appealed his conviction to the U.S. Supreme Court. His lawyer claimed the police violated Miranda's 5th Amendment protection against self-incrimination. The 5th Amendment says, "No person…shall be compelled in any criminal case to be a witness against himself."

Arizona's lawyers argued that Miranda could have asked for a lawyer at any time during questioning. He had not done so. They also said no one had forced him to confess. Because he had given his confession voluntarily, the prosecution could use it in court.

The Issue Does the 5th Amendment require the police to inform suspects of their right to remain silent and that anything they say can be held against them? Could the police use evidence obtained without such warnings in court?

Opinion of the Court The Court struck down Miranda's conviction, ruling that the 5th Amendment requires police to inform suspects in their custody that they have the right to remain silent, that anything they say can be held against them, and that they have a right to consult a lawyer. The police must give these warnings, the Court said, before any questioning of a suspect can take place. A defendant can then voluntarily waive these rights.

The Court added that if a suspect wants to remain silent or to contact a lawyer, police interrogation must stop until the suspect is ready to talk again or a lawyer is present. The prosecution cannot use any confessions obtained in violation of this rule in court.

Chief Justice Earl Warren argued that the U.S. system of justice is based on the idea that an individual is innocent until proved guilty. The government, he claimed, must produce evidence against an accused person. It cannot resort to forcing suspects to prove themselves guilty.

Dissent In a strong dissent, Justice John Harlan argued: "It's obviously going to mean the disappearance of confessions as a legitimate tool of law enforcement." He concluded, "[T]he thrust of the new rule is to negate all pressures, to reinforce the nervous or ignorant suspect, and ultimately to discourage any confession at all."

Significance The *Miranda* decision was controversial. Many law enforcement officials complained the decision

WARNING AS TO YOUR RIGHTS

You are under arrest. Before we ask you any questions, you must understand what your rights are.

You have the right to remain silent. You are not required to say anything to us at any time or to answer any questions. Anything you say can be used against you in court.

You have the right to talk to a lawyer for advice before we question you and to have him with you during questioning.

If you cannot afford a lawyer and want one, a lawyer will be provided for you.

If you want to answer questions now without a lawyer present you will still have the right to stop answering at any time. You also have the right to stop answering at any time until you talk to a lawyer.   P-4475

Police officers must read the Miranda warning to all suspects to notify them of their constitutional rights.

"handcuffed the police." However, in 1986, in *Moran* v. *Burbine*, the Court referred to the *Miranda* case as a decision that "embodies a carefully crafted balance designed to fully protect both the defendant's and society's interests."

Ever since the *Miranda* decision, police have carried cards that they use to read suspects their rights. This message has become known as the Miranda warnings, which consist of four points: the right to remain silent, the reminder that anything said by the suspect can be used against him, the right to a lawyer, and the reminder that a lawyer will be provided free if the suspect cannot afford to hire one.

SEE ALSO
Counsel, right to; Rights of the accused

FURTHER READING
Baker, Liva. *Miranda: Crime, Law and Politics*. New York: Atheneum, 1983.

Moody, William Henry
ASSOCIATE JUSTICE, 1906–10

☆ Born: Dec. 23, 1853, Newbury, Mass.
☆ Education: Harvard College, A.B., 1876; Harvard Law School, 1876–77
☆ Previous government service: city solicitor, Haverhill, Mass., 1888–90; district attorney, Eastern District of Massachusetts, 1890–95; U.S. representative from Massachusetts, 1895–1902; U.S. secretary of the navy, 1902–4; U.S. attorney general, 1904–6
☆ Appointed by President Theodore Roosevelt Dec. 3, 1906; replaced Henry B. Brown, who retired
☆ Supreme Court term: confirmed by the Senate Dec. 12, 1906, by a voice vote; retired Nov. 20, 1910
☆ Died: July 2, 1917, Haverhill, Mass.

WILLIAM MOODY became a friend of Theodore Roosevelt in 1895. The two men shared similar interests and ideas;

when Roosevelt became President, he appointed Moody as secretary of the navy. In 1904, President Roosevelt chose Moody to be the U.S. attorney general. In 1906, he named Moody an associate justice of the Supreme Court.

Justice Moody's most important opinion for the Court came in *Twining* v. *New Jersey* (1908). Moody, writing for the Court, refused to apply to a state government the 5th Amendment right of an accused person to refuse to testify against himself, to avoid self-incrimination. He argued that this right of the individual, as granted in the federal Bill of Rights, could not be used to restrict state governments because the Bill of Rights applies only to the federal government. This decision was later overturned, but it had force and influence for many years.

Justice Moody's impact on constitutional law was limited by his very short term of service on the Court. He was forced to retire because of the crippling disease of rheumatism.

SEE ALSO
Twining v. New Jersey

Moore, Alfred

ASSOCIATE JUSTICE, 1800–1804

☆ Born: May 21, 1755, New Hanover County, N.C.
☆ Education: studied law under his father
☆ Previous government service: North Carolina General Assembly, 1782, 1792; attorney general of North Carolina, 1782–91; judge, North Carolina Superior Court, 1799
☆ Appointed by President John Adams Dec. 6, 1799; replaced James Iredell, who died
☆ Supreme Court term: confirmed by the Senate Dec. 10, 1799, by a voice vote; resigned Jan. 26, 1804
☆ Died: Oct. 15, 1810, Bladen County, N.C.

ALFRED MOORE was a strong supporter of an independent United States of America during the 1770s conflict with the British. He served in the First North Carolina Regiment in the War of Independence and was recognized for his courage and ability as a military leader.

During the 1780s, Moore backed the movement for a strong federal government, which resulted in the framing of the Constitution of 1787. He helped to achieve ratification of the Constitution in North Carolina.

Moore served briefly on the Supreme Court because of ill health. In 1800, he wrote his only opinion for the Court in a case involving the capture of a French vessel by the U.S. navy during the undeclared naval war with France in 1798. The vessel had been owned by an American before its capture by the French. The court ruled that the former owner had to pay one-half the value of the ship in order to reclaim it from the U.S. government.

Muller v. Oregon

☆ 208 U.S. 412 (1908)
☆ Vote: 9–0
☆ For the Court: Brewer

IN THE EARLY 1900s state legislatures began passing laws aimed at reforming working conditions. Employers soon challenged the new laws. As a result, the Supreme Court began to face questions regarding the constitutionality of these reform laws.

A case arose in 1907 that dramatically changed how the Supreme Court made decisions about such social reform legislation. That year, Curt Muller, a Portland, Oregon, laundry owner, was

Workers at the laundry of Curt Muller, who challenged an Oregon law that limited the workday for women to 10 hours. The Supreme Court upheld the Oregon law.

charged with violating an Oregon law that set a maximum 10-hour workday for women working in laundries. Muller challenged the law as a violation of his "liberty to contract," which he claimed was guaranteed by the 14th Amendment.

Muller argued that the due process clause of the 14th Amendment prevented the state from interfering with his liberty to enter into any contracts, including those setting wages and hours for workers, necessary for running his business. (The amendment states, in part, "nor shall any State deprive any person of life, liberty, or property, without due process of law.") The Supreme Court had supported this interpretation of the 14th Amendment in several earlier cases.

Louis D. Brandeis, a brilliant lawyer who later became a distinguished Supreme Court justice, argued the case for Oregon. Brandeis took a startling new approach. He presented sociological, medical, and statistical information to show that long hours of hard labor had a harmful effect upon women's health. He claimed the Court must consider whether the Oregon law was a reasonable attempt to protect public health and safety. A state law might be allowed to interfere with the 14th Amendment's presumed guarantee of liberty of contract if it could be justified as protecting public health against real dangers.

How could the Court decide when a state law met such a standard? Brandeis argued that the Court could not rely merely on legal precedents and the vague words of the Constitution in judging such cases. It also had to consider relevant facts about the social conditions that led to the law in the first place.

The Issue Brandeis defined the question before the Court: Did the consideration of social conditions justify the Oregon law's interference with the 14th Amendment supposed guarantee of liberty of contract?

Would the Court accept Brandeis's novel thesis that it should consider relevant social facts in deciding the case? Or would the Court, as it had in the past, decide the case strictly through reference to legal arguments?

Opinion of the Court The Court accepted Brandeis's argument, ruling unanimously to uphold Oregon's law. The factual evidence Brandeis supplied proved convincing. The Court ruled that longer working hours might harm women's ability to bear children. Thus, the state's limitation of those hours was a justified interference with liberty of contract and property and within the state's regulatory power.

Significance The *Muller* case established that lawyers could use social facts and statistics as well as strictly legal arguments in the briefs they presented to the Supreme Court. A brief is a document summarizing the facts and legal arguments that a lawyer gives to a court when appealing a case. Today we call a brief that contains substantial nonlegal data a *Brandeis brief*. Ever since the *Muller* case, lawyers have used relevant social data in their arguments before the Court. When deciding subsequent cases—*Brown* v. *Board of Education* (1954), for example—the Supreme Court has recognized that information about social conditions could appropriately supplement legal principles.

SEE ALSO

Brandeis brief

FURTHER READING

Mason, Alpheus Thomas. "The Case of the Overworked Laundress." In *Quarrels That Have Shaped the Constitution,* edited by John A. Garraty. New York: Harper & Row, 1987.

Munn v. Illinois

☆ *94 U.S. 113 (1877)*
☆ *Vote: 7–2*
☆ *For the Court: Waite*
☆ *Dissenting: Field and Strong*

MUNN V. ILLINOIS was the first of a famous series of cases known as the *Granger Cases.* These cases dealt with issues resulting from the rapid growth of manufacturing and transportation companies that began after the Civil War ended in 1865.

Many of these companies, particularly those formed by railroad concerns and operators of huge grain warehouses, began to abuse the nearly complete control they had over hauling and storing farm products, especially grain. The railroads and grain warehouses charged farmers very high prices and often tried to cheat them. By the 1870s, the situation had deteriorated so much that even the *Chicago Tribune,* a newspaper known for its pro-business sympathies, called the grain warehouses "bloodsucking insects."

In response to such conditions, a large, politically powerful farm group, the Grange, developed. Farmers in the Granger movement influenced state legislatures in the Midwest to pass laws regulating the prices railroads, ware-

houses, and public utilities charged for hauling freight and storing grain.

The Issue The railroads and grain warehouses fought against state regulation of their businesses in the courts. They claimed the states' Granger laws violated the Constitution in three ways: they infringed on Congress's right to regulate interstate commerce, they violated the Constitution's prohibition against interfering with contracts, and they violated the 14th Amendment by depriving businesses of their liberty and property without due process of law.

The *Munn* case posed a clear and important question for a nation with rapidly developing industries. Did the Constitution permit a state to regulate privately owned businesses?

Opinion of the Court The Court ruled in favor of the states. It said the Illinois state legislature could fix maximum rates for grain storage in Chicago and other places in the state. Chief Justice Morrison R. Waite set forth a doctrine that both Congress and state legislatures still use to regulate many private business activities—the doctrine of "business affected with a public interest."

Waite said that when the activity of a company "has public consequences and affect(s) the community at large," it is a "business affected with a public interest." Under the Constitution the states

Ira Munn's grain warehouse was on the right side of the Chicago River. When Munn ignored state laws regulating the rates he could charge for storage, the case went to the Supreme Court. The Court ruled that states could regulate privately owned businesses.

can regulate such a business, and the owner of such a business "must submit to be controlled by the public for the common good."

Dissent Justice Stephen J. Field argued against the *Munn* opinion as an invasion of private property rights, which he said were protected against state power by the due process clause of the 14th Amendment. Justice Field wanted to limit the use of state "police power" to regulate businesses.

Significance The Court's decision established the power of state government to regulate businesses other than public utilities. Today, state legislatures exercise tremendous regulatory powers over such matters as working conditions, transportation of goods and people, and manufacturing of products for sale to the public. The constitutional basis for much of this activity rests directly on the Court's decision in *Munn* v. *Illinois*.

Murphy, Frank

*A S S O C I A T E   J U S T I C E ,
1 9 4 0 – 4 9*

☆ *Born: Apr. 13, 1890, Harbor Beach, Mich.*

☆ *Education: University of Michigan, B.A., 1912; LL.B., 1914*

☆ *Previous government service: chief assistant attorney general, Eastern District of Michigan, 1919–20; judge, Recorder's Court, Detroit, Mich., 1923–30; mayor of Detroit, 1930–33; governor general of the Philippines, 1933–35; U.S. high commissioner to the Philippines, 1935–36; governor of Michigan, 1937–39; U.S. attorney general, 1939–40*

☆ *Appointed by President Franklin D. Roosevelt Jan. 4, 1940; replaced Pierce Butler, who died*

☆ *Supreme Court term: confirmed by the Senate Jan. 15, 1940, by a voice vote; served until July 19, 1949*

☆ *Died: July 19, 1949, Detroit, Mich.*

FRANK MURPHY was a strong supporter of Franklin D. Roosevelt's 1932 campaign for the Presidency. After serving as an administrator of the U.S. territory of the Philippines and as U.S. attorney general, Murphy was appointed by President Roosevelt to the Supreme Court.

As an associate justice, Murphy was a strong defender of minority rights. His most notable opinions were written in dissent of the Court's decisions to favor federal or state government interests above the rights of individuals.

Justice Murphy's dissent in *Korematsu* v. *United States* (1944) has been regarded as an example of the best opinions to be found in the Supreme Court literature. In this wartime case, the Court upheld the right of the government to relocate and confine all persons of Japanese ancestry living on the Pacific coast of the United States. The Court's majority argued that this action was necessary to protect national security during the war against Japan. Justice Murphy disagreed and said the relocation was "utterly revolting among a free people who have embraced the principles set forth in the Constitution of the United States."

Murphy's dissent in the *Korematsu* case is honored today as a courageous and correct view of the case. And the majority opinion in that case tends to be criticized, in Murphy's terms, as "legalization of racism."

S E E   A L S O
Korematsu v. United States

F U R T H E R   R E A D I N G
Fine, Sidney. *Frank Murphy: The Washington Years.* Ann Arbor: University of Michigan Press, 1984.
Howard, J. Woodford. *Mr. Justice Murphy: A Political Biography.* Princeton, N.J.: Princeton University Press, 1968.

National Association for the Advancement of Colored People (NAACP)

THE NATIONAL ASSOCIATION for the Advancement of Colored People (NAACP) is a private, not-for-profit organization founded in 1909 to protect and expand the civil rights of African Americans. The NAACP has used both political and legal strategies to carry out its mission. In 1939 the NAACP Legal Defense Fund (LDF) was created to support legal strategies on behalf of civil rights for African Americans. From 1940 to 1961 Thurgood Marshall was the director of the LDF. He was primarily responsible for winning 29 victories for the LDF in cases before the Supreme Court. Marshall and the LDF helped the NAACP to win its greatest legal victory, the Supreme Court decision in *Brown* v. *Board of Education* (1954), which outlawed racial segregation in public schools. Marshall went on to become an associate justice of the Supreme Court.

The NAACP carefully monitors the President's nominations of Supreme Court justices and other federal judges. The purpose is to encourage the appointment of people who are likely to agree with the organization's views on civil rights.

SEE ALSO
Brown v. Board of Education; Civil rights

National Labor Relations Board v. Jones & Laughlin Steel Corp.

☆ *301 U.S. 1 (1937)*
☆ *Vote: 5–4*
☆ *For the Court: Hughes*
☆ *Dissenting: Sutherland, Van Devanter, McReynolds, and Butler*

IN JULY 1935 the Jones & Laughlin Steel Corporation fired 10 workers at its Aliquippa, Pennsylvania, plant. They were leaders of a local unit of the American Federation of Labor (AFL), a national labor union. The managers of the

Thurgood Marshall (sitting on the table) with his staff at the NAACP. Under Marshall's leadership, the Legal Defense Fund successfully argued cases before the Supreme Court to secure civil rights for African Americans.

steel company wanted to stop their workers from joining the labor union.

On July 5, 1935, four days before Jones & Laughlin dismissed the 10 labor union leaders, President Franklin D. Roosevelt signed into law the National Labor Relations Act, often called the Wagner Act after New York senator Robert Wagner, the law's major sponsor in Congress. This new federal law made it illegal for an employer to fire or otherwise harass a worker because he belonged to a labor union. The law also protected the right of workers at a company to designate, by majority vote, a labor union to represent them as their sole bargaining agent with their employer. The Wagner Act applied to all businesses either engaged directly in interstate commerce or whose operations affected interstate commerce. Thus, the law could be applied to a business such as Jones & Laughlin Steel Corporation, which shipped steel across state lines.

The government set up the National Labor Relations Board (NLRB) to enforce the Wagner Act. On April 9, 1936, the NLRB charged Jones & Laughlin with violating the Wagner Act by discharging the 10 workers because they were labor union leaders. The company was ordered to reinstate the men and to give them back pay for the period they were not permitted to work. Jones & Laughlin's response was to challenge the NLRB and the Wagner Act as unconstitutional.

The Issue Lawyers for Jones & Laughlin argued that the Wagner Act was based on an excessively broad interpretation of the commerce powers of Congress specified in Article 1, Section 8, of the U.S. Constitution. According to Jones & Laughlin, Congress did not have power under the commerce clause to regulate the relationships of managers and workers of a private corporation. Furthermore, the company claimed, the Wagner Act violated the due process clause of the 5th Amendment, which had been held in previous decisions of the Court to protect the "liberty of contract" between employers and employees. The federal government had no power, said the Jones & Laughlin lawyers, to interfere with the rights of private property owners and workers to bargain about wages, hours of work, and working conditions.

Opinion of the Court The Court sustained the Wagner Act as a constitutional exercise of Congress's commerce power and ruled that it did not violate the 5th Amendment's due process clause. Chief Justice Charles Evans Hughes wrote that the Wagner Act's purpose was to reduce the possibility of strikes, which could disrupt the production and distribution of products and thereby increase the bargaining power to achieve satisfactory working conditions. Strikes could be prevented, Hughes said, by protecting the right of workers to organize labor unions. Hughes also rejected the "liberty of contract" argument based on the due process clause of the 5th Amendment. He emphasized that the Wagner Act in fact *enhanced* workers' power to bargain through a democratically elected representative of a labor union.

Significance In this decision, the Court affirmed President Roosevelt's position that the federal government has the power under the Constitution to regulate the economic system. The *Jones & Laughlin* decision was a departure from several decisions between 1933 and 1937 in which the Court had firmly rejected President Roosevelt's New Deal programs.

The Court's opposition had so angered the President that, following his landslide victory in the 1936 election, he threatened to change the membership of the Court in his favor. On February 5, 1937, Roosevelt announced that he would ask Congress to enact legislation to enable the President to add up to six additional justices to the Court. With such a law, he could immediately add new justices to the Court who would be likely to vote for his economic regulation policies. This Court-packing plan was abandoned by President Roosevelt after the Court made decisions he agreed with in *Jones & Laughlin* and other 1937 cases.

The upholding of the Wagner Act by the Court greatly changed labor-management relations throughout the United States. It led to an enormous growth in the membership and power of labor unions, which were influential in improving wages, hours of work, and working conditions.

SEE ALSO

Commerce power; Court-packing plan

FURTHER READING

Cortner, Richard C. *The Jones & Laughlin Case.* New York: Knopf, 1970.

Natural law

THE THEORY of natural law holds that there is a certain order in nature from which humans, by use of their reason, can derive standards for human conduct. For example, Saint Thomas Aquinas (a 13th-century European scholar and Roman Catholic priest), in his *Summa Theologica,* attempted to derive natural law from his understanding of the divine law revealed by God.

By contrast, philosophers of the European Age of Enlightenment (from the 1680s through the 1700s) such as John Locke in his *Two Treatises of Government* (1690) ignored the idea of divine law and based their concept of natural law on the fundamental human desire

for self-preservation and fulfillment. Accordingly, Locke and other Enlightenment thinkers held that the laws of nature imply government based on consent of the governed as the way to secure natural rights of individuals to life, liberty, and property. The natural law standard for judging the worth of government was the effectiveness of the government in securing the natural rights of individuals. These rights were thought to exist prior to the people's establishment of their government, and all people were entitled to these rights by virtue of their humanity. All were bound to respect and abide by these natural rights because of their capacity to know and justify them through human reason.

The Enlightenment conception of natural law and natural rights influenced the founders of constitutional government in the United States. This influence is evident in the text of the Declaration of Independence and the preambles to the first state constitutions of the original 13 states. However, there were other important influences on the constitutional thought of the founders, such as the political and legal ideas brought to America from England and the experiences in establishing and developing their colonial governments.

The idea of natural law was used from time to time in debates about constitutional issues. For example, both sides in the slavery controversy, from the 1780s to the 1860s, appealed to natural law as justification for their views. Nineteenth-century opponents of strong government regulation of private business also appealed to natural law to support their constitutional arguments. However, during the 20th century, natural law theories have had little influence on the decisions of Supreme Court justices or the thoughts of most legal scholars.

British philosopher John Locke based his concept of natural law on the universal human desires for life, liberty, and property.

Legal protection of individual rights has not been based on natural law doctrines but on the principles and precedents stemming from interpretation of the U.S. Constitution and federal statutes.

SEE ALSO

Constitutional democracy; Constitutionalism; Constitutional law

FURTHER READING

Arkes, Hadley. "Natural Law." *Constitution* 4, no. 1 (Winter 1992): 13–20.

Near v. Minnesota

☆ *283 U.S. 697 (1931)*
☆ *Vote: 5–4*
☆ *For the Court: Hughes*
☆ *Dissenting: Butler, Van Devanter, Sutherland, and McReynolds*

IN 1927 Jay Near and Howard Guilford established the *Saturday Press* in Minneapolis. Near, an experienced journalist, was known for his bigotry against Catholics, blacks, Jews, and organized labor. He specialized in reporting scandals in a sensational manner.

From its first issue, the *Saturday Press* hammered away at alleged ties between gangsters and police in a series of sensational stories. The paper proved especially tough on city and county government officials.

The *Saturday Press* attacked, among others, county prosecutor Floyd Olson, who later became a three-term Minnesota governor. The *Saturday Press* called him "Jew lover" Olson and accused him of dragging his feet in the investigation of organized crime. Olson was enraged. On November 21, 1927, he filed a complaint under Minnesota's Public Nuisance Abatement Law with the county district judge. Olson charged that the *Saturday Press* had defamed various politicians, the county grand jury, and the entire Jewish community.

The county judge issued a temporary restraining order against the *Saturday Press* prohibiting publication of the paper under the Public Nuisance Abatement Law. That law was known as a "gag law" because it authorized a form of censorship called prior restraint. Prior restraint allows government officials to restrict a newspaper or magazine *in advance* from publishing materials of which they disapprove.

Near and Guilford obeyed the restraining order issued against them. They claimed, however, that it was unconstitutional. As the Minnesota courts dealt with this case, Howard Guilford withdrew from the legal battle. More important, Near recruited a rich and powerful ally. Robert McCormick, the publisher of the *Chicago Tribune,* sympathized with Near for a number of reasons. Like Near, the bigoted McCormick disliked blacks, Jews, and other minorities. McCormick had also fought numerous legal battles over articles published in his paper. These struggles had taught McCormick the importance of defending the 1st Amendment. He did not want the Illinois legislature to copy the Minnesota gag law. And so the interests of the rich publisher in Chicago and those of the poor scandalmonger in Minnesota coincided. Near wanted his little paper back in business; McCormick wanted a free press. McCormick committed the *Tribune*'s full resources to the case. His lawyers represented Near in future legal proceedings.

The Minnesota Supreme Court decided against Near and upheld the Public Nuisance Abatement Law. Near, with McCormick's support, appealed to the U.S. Supreme Court.

The Issue Near's attorney claimed that the Minnesota Public Nuisance Abatement Law allowed prior restraint and thus violated the 1st Amendment, which guarantees freedom of speech and press, and the 14th Amendment, which forbids the states to "deprive any person of life, liberty, or property, without due process of law." He argued that the Constitution guaranteed freedom of the press as a fundamental right. No state could take the right away through prior restraint.

Near's attorney admitted that the *Saturday Press* article was "defamatory" of government officials. But, he added, "So long as men do evil, so long will newspapers publish defamation." The attorney argued, "Every person does have a constitutional right to publish malicious, scandalous and defamatory matter, though untrue and with bad motives, and for unjustifiable ends." Such a person could be punished afterward. The remedy, then, was not censorship of an offending newspaper by prior restraint. Rather, the state should bring specific criminal charges against such a newspaper after it published the material.

Minnesota argued that the Public Nuisance Abatement Law was constitutional and that the injunction against the *Saturday Press* was not prior restraint. The injunction was issued only after the *Saturday Press* had attacked the reputations of public officials. Thus, the law punished an offense already committed. The Constitution was designed to protect individual freedoms, not serve the purposes of wrongdoers, such as Near and his scandalous *Saturday Press*.

Opinion of the Court The Court ruled in favor of Jay Near and held that the Minnesota Public Nuisance Abatement Law was a prior restraint on the press that violated both the 1st Amendment and the due process clause of the 14th Amendment.

Chief Justice Charles Evans Hughes, in the majority opinion, declared the Minnesota law "the essence of censor-

The state of Minnesota issued an injunction banning publication of the Saturday Press, *but the Supreme Court ruled in* Near v. Minnesota *that such prior restraint of the newspaper was illegal.*

ship." He stated that libel laws, not newspaper closures, should counter false charges and character assassinations. He emphasized that the right to criticize government officials was one of the foundations of the American nation.

Hughes stressed that "this statute [the Public Nuisance Abatement Law] raises questions of grave importance transcending the local interests involved in the particular action. It is no longer open to doubt that the liberty of the press…is within the liberty safeguarded by the due process clause of the Fourteenth Amendment from invasion by state action."

Dissent Justice Pierce Butler argued that the Minnesota law was not an example of prior restraint. Rather, it allowed public officials to control unacceptable publications after reading the published material. Butler also argued that the U.S. Supreme Court had imposed on a state government "a federal restriction that is without precedent." He was referring to the fact that this decision was the first time that the Court used the due process clause of the 14th Amendment to apply the 1st Amendment right to freedom of the press to a state. Butler and his colleagues in dissent said this should not be done.

Significance Jay Near was triumphant when he learned of the Court's verdict. In October 1932 Near again began to publish the *Saturday Press*. The paper did not survive, however, and in April 1936 Near died in obscurity.

The Court's ruling also pleased Colonel McCormick. He wrote Chief Justice Hughes: "I think your decision in the Gag Law case will forever remain one of the buttresses of free government."

As a result of *Near* v. *Minnesota*, the United States has built a tradition against prior restraints unlike any other in the world. This tradition has helped keep the free press from censorship by government officials merely because it is critical of them.

In 1971 the Supreme Court relied on the *Near* precedent in the Pentagon Papers case (*New York Times Co.* v. *United States*). In that case the federal government attempted to stop the *New York Times* from publishing secret documents describing the history of U.S. involvement in the Vietnam War. The Court ruled against the government and permitted publication of the documents.

SEE ALSO

Freedom of press and speech; Incorporation doctrine; New York Times Co. v. United States; Prior restraint

FURTHER READING

Friendly, Fred W. *Minnesota Rag: The Dramatic Story of the Landmark Court Case That Gave New Meaning to Freedom of the Press.* New York: Random House, 1981.
Murphy, Paul L. "The Case of the Miscreant Purveyor of Scandal." In *Quarrels That Have Shaped the Constitution,* edited by John A. Garraty. New York: Harper & Row, 1987.

Necessary and proper clause

SEE Constitutional construction; Implied powers

Nelson, Samuel

ASSOCIATE JUSTICE, 1845–72

☆ Born: Nov. 10, 1792, Hebron, N.Y.
☆ Education: Middlebury College, B.A., 1813
☆ Previous government service: postmaster, Cortland, N.Y., 1820–23; New York State Constitutional Convention, 1821; Presidential elector, 1820; judge, Sixth Circuit Court of New York, 1823–31; associate justice, New York Supreme Court, 1831–37; chief justice, New York Supreme Court, 1837–45

☆ Appointed by President John Tyler Feb. 4, 1845; replaced Smith Thompson, who died
☆ Supreme Court term: confirmed by the Senate Feb. 14, 1845, by a voice vote; retired Nov. 28, 1872
☆ Died: Dec. 13, 1873, Cooperstown, N.Y.

SAMUEL NELSON was the son of Scotch-Irish parents who came to North America in the 1760s. After admission to the New York bar in 1817, he began a career in law and politics. In 1823 he was appointed to the position of judge on the Sixth Circuit Court of New York. For nearly the rest of his life, Nelson occupied judicial positions in the state of New York and on the U.S. Supreme Court.

During his 27 years on the Supreme Court, Nelson performed satisfactorily but without distinction. His decisions tended to favor states' rights and judicial self-restraint. In his opinion for the Court in *Georgia* v. *Stanton* (1868), Justice Nelson showed his strong belief in judicial restraint to the point of deciding against states' rights. He decided against the attempts of two Southern states to obstruct Reconstruction policies of the federal government. He held that the case presented by the Southern states should be dismissed because it involved "political questions" that the Supreme Court could not decide.

New Jersey v. T.L.O.

☆ 469 U.S. 325 (1985)
☆ Vote: 6–3
☆ For the Court: White
☆ Dissenting: Stevens, Brennan, and Marshall

A TEACHER at a New Jersey high school discovered a student smoking cigarettes in a school bathroom, which was a violation of school rules. The

teacher took the student to the principal's office. The assistant principal questioned the student, who denied she had been smoking in the bathroom. The school official then demanded to see her purse. After opening it, he found cigarettes, cigarette rolling papers that are commonly associated with the use of marijuana, a pipe, plastic bags, money, a list of students who owed her money, and two letters that contained evidence that she had been involved in marijuana dealings.

As a result of this search of the student's purse and the seizure of items in it, the state brought delinquency charges against the student in New Jersey Juvenile Court. The student (identified in the case only by her initials, T.L.O.) countered with a motion to suppress evidence found in her purse as a violation of her constitutional rights against unreasonable and unwarranted searches and seizures.

The Issue Is the 4th Amendment prohibition of unreasonable and unwarranted searches and seizures applicable to officials in a public school with regard to its students?

Opinion of the Court The Supreme Court decided that the 4th Amendment prohibition of *unreasonable* searches and seizures is applicable to searches conducted by public school officials, but that in this case a warrantless search of the student's purse *was* reasonable and permissible.

Justice Byron White wrote the opinion of the Court. He said that school officials may search a student in school as long as "there are reasonable grounds for suspecting that the search will turn up evidence that the student has violated or is violating either the law or the rules of the school."

Dissent Justice John Paul Stevens wrote in dissent:

> The search of a young woman's purse by a school administrator is a serious

invasion of her legitimate expectations of privacy…. Because [the student's] conduct was neither unlawful nor significantly disruptive of school order or the educational process, the invasion of privacy associated with the forcible opening of T.L.O.'s purse was entirely unjustified at its inception….

> The rule the Court adopts today is so open-ended that it may make the Fourth Amendment virtually meaningless in the school context. Although I agree that school administrators must have broad latitude to maintain order and discipline in our classrooms, that authority is not unlimited.

Significance This decision indicated that the Court did not view the rights of students in a public school as equivalent to the rights of adults in a nonschool setting. Police need to demonstrate "probable cause" that individuals they search have violated or are violating a law. School officials, by contrast, need to have only "reasonable suspicion" of unlawful conduct to justify a search of students in school. School authorities, in this view, may restrict the rights of students in behalf of the school's compelling educational purpose.

SEE ALSO

Searches and seizures; Student rights under the Constitution

New York Times Co. v. Sullivan

☆ *376 U.S. 254 (1964)*
☆ *Vote: 9–0*
☆ *For the Court: Brennan*

ON MARCH 29, 1960, the *New York Times* printed a full-page advertisement paid for by two black civil rights organizations. L. B. Sullivan, an elected city

Police Commissioner L. B. Sullivan (right) in court during his libel suit against the New York Times.

commissioner of Montgomery, Alabama, read the advertisement and decided to bring a libel suit against the *New York Times* and the sponsors of the advertisement. Libel is the act of slandering, or hurting a person's reputation by saying negative things about him that are untrue or misleading.

Sullivan was upset about the advertisement because it described civil rights activities in southern states, including Alabama, and appealed for donations of money to support the programs of the ad's two sponsors. The ad also included an eight-line description of events in Montgomery, Alabama, that criticized the city police for abuses against black demonstrators. Sullivan's name was not mentioned, but he was offended because he was in charge of the Montgomery police department. So he claimed that false and exaggerated charges against the city police were slanders against him in his role as police commissioner.

State courts in Alabama decided in favor of Sullivan. Sullivan proved that there were several errors about details, but not main points, in the advertisement. The state courts concluded that he had been libeled and awarded him $500,000 in damages. The *New York Times* appealed this decision to the U.S. Supreme Court.

The Issue L. B. Sullivan argued that the advertisement in this case was libelous because it contained untrue statements. He claimed that the Constitution does not protect speech that is false or misleading about the actions of a person. The *New York Times* argued that the libel law of Alabama, which permitted restrictions on untrue speech, was an infringement on 1st Amendment freedoms to express criticisms of public officials. To what extent do constitutional protections of free speech limit a state government's power to award damages in a libel action brought by a government official against his critics?

Opinion of the Court The U.S. Supreme Court reversed the decision of the Alabama Supreme Court. Justice William Brennan argued that the Alabama libel law threatened 1st Amendment freedoms of speech and press by "raising... the possibility that a good-faith critic of government will be penalized for his criticism." Brennan said that "debate on public issues should be uninhibited, robust, and wide-open, and that it may well include vehement, caustic, and sometimes unpleasantly sharp attacks on government and public officials."

Brennan maintained that "erroneous statement is inevitable in free debate." Therefore, even false statements about public officials must be protected if citizens and the media are to act effectively as critics of their government. Therefore, the Court concluded, public officials may not be awarded damages for defamatory statements about their official conduct merely because the statements are false. Rather, the offended public official must prove actual malice. That is, he must demonstrate that "the statement was made with...knowledge that it was false or with reckless disregard of whether it was false or not."

Significance This decision has made it very difficult for public officials to bring libel actions against the media. As a result, freedom of expression about the actions of government has been greatly expanded. The media have been encouraged to play the role of watchdog and exposer of questionable or improper actions by public officials, such as corrupt or foolish behavior.

SEE ALSO

Freedom of speech and press

FURTHER READING

Lewis, Anthony. *Make No Law: The Sullivan Case and the First Amendment.* New York: Random House, 1991.

New York Times Co. v. United States

☆ *403 U.S. 713 (1971)*
☆ *Vote: 6–3*
☆ *For the Court: per curiam opinion; Douglas, Stewart, White, Marshall, Black, and Brennan writing separately*
☆ *Dissenting: Burger, Blackmun, and Harlan*

IN JUNE 1971, the *New York Times* and the *Washington Post* started to publish a series of articles based on U.S. government documents that became known as the Pentagon Papers. The Pentagon is the headquarters of the U.S. Department of Defense, the compiler of these documents, which included information about U.S. military involvement in Vietnam and federal government policies on the Vietnam War that was classified as top secret. Federal officials did not want the Pentagon Papers released to the public and printed only 15 copies. Daniel Ellsberg, a researcher involved in compiling and editing the Pentagon Papers, made a photocopy of these documents and gave most of them to Neil Sheehan of the *New York Times.*

A team of *Times* reporters wrote a series of articles on U.S. involvement in the Vietnam War based on the top secret information in the Pentagon Papers. A short time later, Daniel Ellsberg also provided materials from the Pentagon Papers to the *Washington Post,* and articles based on these documents began to appear in that paper, too.

The federal government objected to the publication in daily newspapers of information it classified as top secret. Government officials claimed that wide distribution of information in the Pentagon Papers would be damaging to national security. So the government brought legal action against the *New York Times* and the *Washington Post* to stop them, and other newspapers, from publishing articles about the Pentagon Papers.

The Issue Representatives of the *New York Times* said the federal government's attempt to stop publication of articles about the Pentagon Papers was an example of prior restraint—when the government restricts a publication in advance from publishing certain information—and a violation of freedom of the press guaranteed in the 1st Amendment. The federal government argued that publication of this top secret information would put the lives of soldiers in danger and give assistance during wartime to enemies of the United States. Do the needs of national security during wartime outweigh the value of free and open communication of information? Does the President's constitutional duty as commander in chief of the armed forces require that he have power to restrict publication of military secrets?

Federal judge Gerhard Gesell hears arguments in the Pentagon Papers case. The Supreme Court ruled that publication of the Pentagon Papers was not a sufficient threat to national security to justify prior restraint.

What are the constitutional limits on a free press during wartime?

Opinion of the Court The Court rejected the federal government's arguments for prior restraint on the publication of information from the Pentagon Papers. The Court concluded that the government failed to show that publication of this information about the Vietnam War would cause such serious harm as to outweigh the value of free expression of information.

Dissent Chief Justice Warren Burger emphasized the complexity of this kind of case. He agreed in principle with constitutional limits on prior restraint. But he also argued that there are limits on 1st Amendment freedoms. He said, "[T]he imperative of a free and unfettered press comes into collision with another imperative, the effective functioning of a complex modern government and specifically the effective exercise of certain constitutional powers of the Executive." He referred to the constitutional powers of the President pertaining to conduct of foreign policy and command of military forces.

Significance The Supreme Court decision in this case was a clear defeat for advocates of prior restraint under conditions of wartime or other national crises. The decision also encouraged the media in their efforts to check federal government officials or hold them accountable by obtaining and publishing information that the government wants to keep from public view.

SEE ALSO
Freedom of speech and press; Prior restraint

FURTHER READING
The Pentagon Papers as Published by the New York Times. New York: Bantam, 1971.
Unger, S. J. *The Papers and the Papers: An Account of the Legal and Political Battles over the Pentagon Papers*. New York: Dutton, 1972.

Nomination of justices

SEE Appointment of justices; Rejection of Supreme Court nominees

Northern Securities Co. v. United States

☆ *193 U.S. 197 (1904)*
☆ *Vote: 5–4*
☆ *For the Court: Harlan*
☆ *Concurring: Brewer*
☆ *Dissenting: White, Holmes, Fuller, and Peckham*

J. P. MORGAN, James J. Hill, and Edward H. Harriman were powerful stock market speculators and investors who were interested mainly in railroads. Each desperately desired to control the three leading railroads linking the Great Lakes and the Pacific Northwest. In 1901 they battled fiercely on the stock exchange to gain control of the railroads. None of the three succeeded, so they settled their differences and joined together to form the Northern Securities Company to control the three railroads. They chartered their company under New Jersey laws.

In 1890, however, Congress had passed the Sherman Antitrust Act in an effort to prevent the growth of business monopolies. (A monopoly is the exclusive control of an industry by a single owner or company.) This law prohibited trusts, or business combinations "in restraint of trade or commerce among the several States." Congress had the power to pass that law under the commerce clause of the Constitution (Article 1, Section 8), which had been defined broadly in the Supreme Court case *Gibbons* v. *Ogden* (1824). But the Sherman Antitrust Act was vague. What did "restraint of trade and commerce" mean?

The government argued that the Northern Securities Company was guilty of the very thing the law forbade. The Sherman Act aimed to prevent monopolies from taking over an industry or an aspect of an industry. The Northern Securities Company controlled *all* of the major railroads throughout a huge section of the country. If the Court allowed the three competing railroads to merge into one giant company, competition in the area would disappear. Because people had no alternative method of transportation, the Northern Securities Company would have been able to charge them exorbitant fees. Serving only the narrow interests of Morgan, Hill, and Harriman, this monopoly would harm the public and nation.

The Northern Securities Company argued that the federal government could not interfere with its affairs because it was merely a holding company created by a stock transaction. (A holding company is created solely to hold the ownership rights to two or more companies. But the holding company, as an administrative convenience, does not by itself deal in commerce.) Legally, under New Jersey laws, the corporation therefore did not deal in commerce. Federal government interference would violate state powers as protected by the 10th Amendment.

The Issue Did the combination of railroads under the Northern Securities Company represent a "restraint of trade or commerce" covered by the Sherman Antitrust Act? Or was the combination just a stock transaction, not commerce? If it was the latter, it merited legal recognition under New Jersey law and 10th Amendment protection.

As often happens in Supreme Court cases, however, this specific question reflected a larger, more general issue. Could the national government regulate the activities of the huge, powerful businesses that were developing in the nation? A decision in favor of the Northern Securities Company would greatly limit the effectiveness of the Sherman Antitrust Act and the ability of the government to gain some control over business.

Opinion of the Court The Court ruled in favor of the government. It found that the Northern Securities Company intended to eliminate competition among the railroads involved. Hence, the company was "a combination in restraint of interstate commerce" and was illegal under the Sherman Antitrust Act.

The Court interpreted the act broadly. Justice John Harlan wrote that a combination of businesses, a trust, did not need to engage directly in commerce to violate the act. If it restrained commerce in any way, a trust was illegal.

Dismissing the argument that the Sherman Act violated state powers under the Constitution, Harlan said a state law could not confer immunity from federal law. In regulating interstate commerce, Congress superseded the states' power to create corporations. Acting within its legitimate sphere, such as regulating commerce, the national government was supreme.

Dissent Chief Justice Edward D. White argued that Congress could not regulate the ownership of stock through laws such as the Sherman Antitrust Act because this was a violation of powers reserved to the states by the 10th Amendment. He also claimed that a broad interpretation of the Sherman Act would have a negative effect on business.

Significance The Court's decision helped establish increased government control of trusts and monopolies. The *Northern Securities* case symbolized the federal government's right and duty to regulate the national economy for the public good. The Court's ruling gave the federal government the authority to begin to exercise stricter supervision of the growing number of large American corporations. For example, the Federal Trade Commission Act of 1914 provided for regulation of businesses to prevent activities that would reduce competition in the marketplace or cheat consumers.

SEE ALSO

Commerce power

FURTHER READING

Apple, R. W., Jr. "The Case of the Monopolistic Railroadmen." In *Quarrels That Have Shaped the Constitution,* edited by John A. Garraty. New York: Harper & Row, 1987.

Nullification

IN THE YEARS preceding the Civil War, some supporters of state powers and rights developed the doctrine of nullification. Advocates of nullification claimed that state governments had the power, under the U.S. Constitution, to declare a federal law unconstitutional, or unlawful and void.

John C. Calhoun of South Carolina, then Vice President of the United States, was the leading proponent of nullification. In the essay *South Carolina Exposition and Protest* (1828), Calhoun argued that the Constitution and federal Union were established by sovereign states, not by the people of the United States. Thus, the state governments have authority to decide whether acts of the federal government are constitutional or not. If a state government decided that the federal government had exceeded constitutional limits on its powers, then the state could call a special convention to nullify the law, thereby declaring that the law would *not* be enforced in the state. The nullification doctrine was linked to the claim that a state had a right to secede from, or leave, the federal Union.

John Calhoun believed each state had the power to nullify federal laws.

In 1832, during a controversy about a federal tariff law, South Carolina attempted to use Calhoun's nullification doctrine to declare the federal statute unconstitutional. There was talk of secession. President Andrew Jackson responded with the threat of military force to suppress actions that he viewed as rebellious violations of the U.S. Constitution. The crisis ended with a compromise about the terms of the disputed federal tariff law.

Arguments about the nullification doctrine and the right of secession were settled, once and for all, by the Civil War (1861–65). After the Union victory over the Confederate states, there was no more serious advocacy of a state's right to nullify a federal law or to secede from the federal Union. The Supreme Court, in *Texas v. White* (1869), concluded that the Constitution created "an indestructible Union, composed of indestructible states."

SEE ALSO

Constitutionalism; Federalism; Implied powers; Texas v. White

FURTHER READING

Lence, Ross M., ed. *Union and Liberty: The Political Philosophy of John C. Calhoun.* Indianapolis: Liberty Fund, 1992.

Obiter dictum

IN WRITING an opinion, justices of the Supreme Court or judges of a lower court sometimes make statements that are not necessary to the legal reasoning of the decision in the case. Such a statement is called *obiter dictum,* which is Latin for "said in passing." Occasionally, obiter dicta (the plural of the term) have become important in the development of constitutional law. Justice Edward T. Sanford, for example, made a statement in passing (obiter dictum) in

Gitlow v. *New York* (1925) that greatly influenced the incorporation of 1st Amendment free speech and press rights under the due process clause of the 14th Amendment. Justice Sanford wrote, "[W]e may act to assume that freedom of speech and of the press…are among the fundamental personal rights and liberties protected by the due process clause of the Fourteenth Amendment from impairment by the States."

Justice Sanford's statement was not part of his reasoning in the decision of this case. Nevertheless, it soon influenced decisions of the Court in two important cases: *Near* v. *Minnesota* and *Stromberg* v. *California* (both 1931), which applied the 1st Amendment freedoms of speech (*Stromberg*) and the press (*Near*) to the states through the due process clause of the 14th Amendment.

SEE ALSO

Gitlow v. New York; Near v. Minnesota; Stromberg v. California

O'Connor, Sandra Day

ASSOCIATE JUSTICE, 1981–

☆ *Born: Mar. 26, 1930, El Paso, Tex.*
☆ *Education: Stanford College, B.A., 1950; Stanford University Law School, LL.B., 1952*
☆ *Previous government service: assistant attorney general, Arizona, 1965–69; Arizona Senate, 1969–75, majority leader of the Arizona Senate, 1973–74; judge, Maricopa County Superior Court, Arizona, 1975–79; judge, Arizona Court of Appeals, 1979–81*
☆ *Appointed by President Ronald Reagan Aug. 19, 1981; replaced Potter Stewart, who retired*
☆ *Supreme Court term: confirmed by the Senate Sept. 21, 1981, by a 99–0 vote*

SANDRA DAY O'CONNOR was the first woman to be appointed and con-firmed to the U.S. Supreme Court . She was a brilliant student, and her record at Stanford University Law School was outstanding. However, she had difficulty, at first, in pursuing a career in the law because of her gender. She was an outstanding woman in a profession traditionally dominated by men. Many male lawyers did not want to work with women, and O'Connor had a hard time getting a job she wanted. One prominent law firm offered her a job as a secretary.

Through persistence and competence, O'Connor earned recognition as a lawyer, as a state senator in Arizona, and as a judge in the Arizona state court system. She also found time to raise three sons with her husband, John O'Connor.

In 1981, President Ronald Reagan appointed Sandra Day O'Connor to the U.S. Supreme Court. Justice O'Connor has appeared to resist overturning *Roe* v. *Wade* (1973), which granted women the right to have an abortion, although she has tended to narrow the scope of that decision by upholding state-level regulations "not unduly burdensome" to the woman. She has also shaped Supreme Court rulings on affirmative action and separation of church and state with regard to state government actions. She appears to favor strict neutrality over strict separation in the state's treatment of religion. And in response to state-level affirmative action cases, she has tended to favor a strict scrutiny test that would permit programs to rectify prior discrimination by the state government.

FURTHER READING

Cook, Beverly B. "Justice Sandra Day O'Connor: Transition to a Republican Court Agenda." In *The Burger Court: Political and Judicial Profiles*, edited by Charles M. Lamb and Stephen C. Halpern, 238–75. Urbana: University of Illinois Press, 1991.

Gherman, Beverly. S*andra Day O'Connor: Justice for All.* New York: Viking, 1991.

Huber, Peter. *Sandra Day O'Connor*. New York: Chelsea House, 1990.

Olmstead v. United States

☆ *277 U.S. 438 (1928)*
☆ *Vote: 5–4*
☆ *For the Court: Taft*
☆ *Dissenting: Holmes, Brandeis, Butler, and Stone*

IN 1919, the 18th Amendment to the U.S. Constitution was ratified. It banned the sale, transportation, and importation of alcoholic beverages. Congress passed the National Prohibition Act to implement the 18th Amendment. Roy Olmstead, however, defied the National Prohibition Act by conducting a large-scale business to transport liquor throughout the state of Washington and British Columbia in Canada.

Federal agents gained evidence of Olmstead's illegal business by tapping the telephone line in one of his company's offices and the telephone lines into the homes of four of his workers. The agents listened to his telephone conversations and took notes about illegal activities.

Roy Olmstead and several others were convicted of conspiracy to violate the National Prohibition Act. Olmstead appealed his conviction to the Supreme Court. He claimed that the wiretap violated his rights under the 4th Amendment, which says, "The right of the people to be secure in their persons, houses, papers, and effects, against unreasonable searches and seizures, shall not be violated." Further, he argued that searches and seizures are unreasonable unless officials conducting them have obtained warrants only for "probable cause" that the person to be searched has violated or is violating the law. He also pointed to the 5th Amendment right that "no person…shall be compelled in any criminal case to be a witness against himself."

The Issue Was the use of evidence obtained through a telephone wiretap a violation of an individual's 4th and 5th Amendment rights? Should evidence obtained through a telephone wiretap be excluded from the trial of a person accused of a crime?

Opinion of the Court The Court upheld Olmstead's conviction. Chief Justice William Howard Taft wrote that conversations were not protected by the 4th Amendment and that the wiretaps on the telephone lines were not an invasion of the defendant's house or office. Taft agreed with the decision in *Weeks* v. *United States* (1914) that evidence obtained illegally must be excluded from a defendant's trial. However, he concluded that the evidence against Roy Olmstead was gathered legally.

Dissent Justice Louis D. Brandeis wrote an eloquent dissent that took account of the new technologies involved in this case; the electronic devices involved in the case did not exist when the 4th Amendment was written and ratified.

The wiretaps by federal agents, said Brandeis, were an invasion of privacy, which violated the intention of those who wrote and ratified the Constitution. According to Brandeis, they "sought to protect Americans in their beliefs, their thoughts, their emotions and their sensations. They conferred, as against the government, the right to be let alone—the most comprehensive of rights and the right most valued by civilized men." He asserted that to protect the person's right to privacy, every "unjustifiable intrusion by the government…whatever the means employed" must be viewed as a violation of the 4th Amendment. In addition, he said, use of evidence gathered illegally, such as through telephone wiretaps, violates the 5th Amendment.

Significance The *Olmstead* case was the first one in which the Court considered the impact of new electronic

Louis Brandeis dissented in the Olmstead *case, claiming that a federal wiretap of a person's phone is an illegal invasion of privacy. Later, using Brandeis's dissent, the Court overturned the* Olmstead *decision.*

technology on the constitutional rights of individuals accused of criminal activity. It was also the first case in which a general right to privacy was asserted as a fundamental right—the basis of the dissenting opinion by Justice Brandeis.

The Court's decision in *Olmstead* was overturned in *Katz* v. *United States* (1967), which concluded that wiretaps and other forms of electronic surveillance are violations of the 4th Amendment. In Title III of the Crime Control and Safe Streets Act of 1968, Congress banned wiretapping to gain evidence against individuals in the United States except when it was approved in advance by a federal judge according to guidelines in the 1968 act. In the long run the dissenting views of Justice Brandeis prevailed concerning the use of wiretapping to gather evidence of criminal behavior. Brandeis's views about privacy as a general constitutional right are still controversial, although this idea has influenced opinions in several key cases. These include *Griswold* v. *Connecticut* (1965) and *Roe* v. *Wade* (1973), which dealt with the issues of birth control and abortion.

SEE ALSO

Griswold v. Connecticut; Katz v. United States; Privacy, right to; Roe v. Wade; Searches and seizures

FURTHER READING

Murphy, Walter F. *Wiretapping on Trial: A Case Study in the Judicial Process.* New York: Random House, 1965.

One person, one vote

S E E Baker v. Carr; Reynolds v. Sims

Opening day

SINCE 1917 the first Monday in October has been the official opening day of the annual term of the Supreme Court. The chief justice ceremoniously opens the session at 10:00 A.M. New justices, if any, take their oath of office, and attorneys are admitted to the bar of the Supreme Court. The Court shows its respect to retired and deceased colleagues and Supreme Court officers through brief statements of tribute. Since 1975 the opening day has also included oral arguments.

Opinions

THE SUPREME COURT presents its decisions on cases to the public through written opinions. The opinions announce the outcomes of cases decided by the Court and provide the legal reasoning in support of the decisions.

When the chief justice is part of the majority opinion on a case, he may either write the Court's opinion himself or assign it to another justice in the majority group. When the chief justice is not part of the Court's majority, the most senior associate justice in the majority group assigns the task of writing the opinion. The writing of minority or dissenting opinions is not assigned. The justices who wish to write them merely assume this responsibility voluntarily.

When the justice assigned to write the Court's opinion completes a first draft, the opinion is distributed to the other eight justices, who may join the opinion. Sometimes, the opinion is modified to satisfy one or more justices,

This 1978 play, which accurately foreshadowed the appointment of the first woman to the Court, took its title from the Court's traditional opening day. Fifteen years later, the first woman justice, Sandra Day O'Connor, swore in actress Jane Alexander as head of the National Endowment for the Arts.

The first page of a Supreme Court opinion.

NOTICE: This opinion is subject to formal revision before publication in the preliminary print of the United States Reports. Readers are requested to notify the Reporter of Decisions, Supreme Court of the United States, Washington, D.C. 20543, of any typographical or other formal errors, in order that corrections may be made before the preliminary print goes to press.

SUPREME COURT OF THE UNITED STATES

No. 91–2024

LAMB'S CHAPEL AND JOHN STEIGERWALD, PETITIONERS *v.* CENTER MORICHES UNION FREE SCHOOL DISTRICT ET AL.

ON WRIT OF CERTIORARI TO THE UNITED STATES COURT OF APPEALS FOR THE SECOND CIRCUIT

[June 7, 1993]

JUSTICE WHITE delivered the opinion of the Court.

Section 414 of the New York Education Law (McKinney 1988 and Supp. 1993), authorizes local school boards to adopt reasonable regulations for the use of school property for 10 specified purposes when the property is not in use for school purposes. Among the permitted uses is the holding of "social, civic and recreational meetings and entertainments, and other uses pertaining to the welfare of the community; but such meetings, entertainment and uses shall be non-exclusive and open to the general public." §414(c).[1] The list of permitted uses does not include meetings for religious purposes, and a New York appellate court in *Trietley* v. *Board of Ed. of Buffalo,* 409 N. Y. S. 2d 912, 915 (App. Div. 1978), ruled that local boards could not allow student bible clubs to meet on school property because "[r]eligious purposes are not included in the enumerated purposes for which a school

[1] Section 414(e) authorizes the use of school property "[f]or polling places for holding primaries and elections and for the registration of voters and for holding political meetings. But no meetings sponsored by political organizations shall be permitted unless authorized by a vote of a district meeting, held as provided by law, or, in cities by the board of education thereof."

who otherwise will not sign it. These differences and compromises are discussed among the justices in meetings and in written messages in response to drafts of opinions that have been circulated.

If a justice agrees with the Court's decision but disagrees somewhat with the written opinion of the Court, he or she may write a concurring opinion, one that reaches the same conclusion but using different legal reasoning. Justices who disagree with the Court's decision on a case may write a dissenting opinion.

SEE ALSO
Concurring opinion; Dissenting opinion; Majority opinion; Per curiam; Plurality opinion; Seriatim opinions

Oral argument

AFTER THE COURT decides to hear a case, the clerk of the Court schedules the oral argument on the case. At this time, attorneys for both sides of the case speak before the justices in the Supreme Court chamber, or courtroom. Each side is limited to a 30-minute oral presentation. The attorneys may not read a set speech. They usually interact with the justices, who ask them questions. The justices may interrupt an advocate with questions or comments whenever they wish. About one-third of the counsel's 30-minute presentation is taken up with questions or remarks by justices. The effective advocate makes skillful responses to the questions of the justices. Those who stumble in responding or try to evade the question are likely to make a bad impression on the Court. During oral arguments, passionate exchanges at times occur between advocate and justices or between different justices who take exception to the reasoning or style of the commentary.

The justices read briefs, which are the lawyers' summaries of their arguments, and other documents regarding each case, such as memoranda about the case prepared by their law clerks and records from the trial court, before the day of the oral argument. As a result, they are likely to bring questions and concerns about the issues to the oral argument. This hearing gives the justices an opportunity to test the worth of the arguments on both sides of the case. Moreover, through this open hearing the justices demonstrate to the public that arguments on both sides of the case will be considered and challenged before a decision is made.

In presenting their oral arguments before the Supreme Court, 19th-century lawyers delivered eloquent speeches that sometimes lasted for days. Today, lawyers still must present a compelling speech even though they are not allowed to read their remarks and are limited to 30 minutes.

Orders list

THE CLERK of the Supreme Court prepares orders lists that appear near the end of volumes of the *United States Reports,* the official record of the Court's opinions. Each orders list is made up of brief summaries of the Court's actions on a particular day regarding certain cases under review but does not include opinions. For example, the Court may decide to refuse or accept a writ of appeal; it may deny or accept petitions for a writ of certiorari (an order for a lower court to send the official record of a case to the Supreme Court). Orders may treat such matters as stays of execution for a person scheduled for capital punishment, permissions to file amicus curiae briefs (which are filed by individuals or organizations not involved in a particular case but who have a special interest in the issue under review), or actions on disbarment of attorneys (expulsion from the legal profession).

SEE ALSO
United States Reports

Original intent

THE METHOD of interpreting the U.S. Constitution according to the literal intentions of its authors is known as original intent. Advocates of this method of constitutional interpretation claim that judges are obligated to find out what the framers intended by the words they used in writing the Constitution. Robert H. Bork, a legal scholar who favors original intent, stated in 1984, "It is necessary to establish the proposition that the framers' intentions…are the sole premise from which constitutional analysis may proceed."

Critics of the original intent method say that most of the framers did not expect those who came after them to be bound strictly by their work. Rather, they claim, the framers expected that the basic principles of the Constitution would be retained but details would be adapted to meet the changing and unforeseen circumstances of the future.

Justice William J. Brennan, for example, opposed the doctrine of original intent. He said in a 1985 speech, "We current Justices read the Constitution in the only way we can: as Twentieth Century Americans. We look to the history of the time of framing and to the intervening history of interpretation. But the ultimate question must be, what do the words of the text mean in our time. For the genius of the Constitution rests not in any static meaning it might have had in a world that is dead and gone, but in the adaptability of its great principles to cope with current problems and current needs."

Defenders of original intent, however, argue that the rule of law cannot be maintained unless judges apply the Constitution to current controversies as the framers intended it to be applied. If original intent is ignored, they claim, then judges become lawmakers, not law interpreters, as they are supposed to be. Robert H. Bork, for example, told the Senate Judiciary Committee in 1987, "How should a judge go about finding the law? The only legitimate way, in my opinion, is by attempting to discern what those who made the law intended…. If a judge abandons intention as his guide, there is no law available to him and he begins to legislate a social agenda for the American people. That goes way beyond his legitimate power."

The 1787 Constitutional Convention in Philadelphia. Some legal scholars today believe that courts should try to determine the original intent of the founders when applying the law.

Is it the duty of the judges to keep the Constitution in tune with the times? No, say the advocates of original intent. Rather, they argue, it is the duty of judges to maintain an unbroken continuity of constitutional meaning from the founding era to their own times.

SEE ALSO
Constitutional construction; Judicial activism and judicial restraint

Original jurisdiction

SEE Jurisdiction

Palko v. Connecticut

☆ 302 U.S. 319 (1937)
☆ Vote: 8–1
☆ For the Court: Cardozo
☆ Dissenting: Butler

FRANK PALKO robbed a store in Connecticut and shot and killed two police officers. He was tried for first-degree murder. The jury, however, found Palko guilty of the lesser crime of second-degree murder. He was sentenced to life in prison. The state prosecutors appealed this conviction and won a second trial, at which new evidence against Palko was introduced.

The judge at the first trial had refused to allow Palko's confession to be used as evidence against him. The absence of this evidence led to a lesser sentence for the defendant. At the second trial, however, all available evidence was used. As a result, Palko was convicted of the more serious charge of first-degree murder and sentenced to death.

Frank Palko appealed to the U.S. Supreme Court. His appeal was based on the 5th Amendment, which guarantees that no one should endure double jeopardy—that is, be put on trial twice for the same crime. The 5th Amendment, however, applies only to actions of the federal government. So Palko also pointed to the 14th Amendment provision that no state can "deprive any person of life, liberty, or property, without due process of law." Palko claimed that the 5th Amendment protection against double jeopardy could be applied to a state government through the due process clause of the 14th Amendment.

The Issue There was no question about Palko's guilt or innocence. The issue was whether he had been unconstitutionally subjected to double jeopardy. Does the 14th Amendment's due process clause encompass the 5th Amendment's prohibition of double jeopardy? Or does the 5th Amendment apply only to actions of the federal government?

Opinion of the Court Palko's appeal was denied. His basic argument— "[W]hatever is forbidden by the Fifth Amendment is forbidden by the Fourteenth also"—was rejected. In reaching this conclusion, the Court proposed a new test to determine which rights of an accused person, as stated in the federal Bill of Rights, are so fundamental that they apply equally to the state and federal governments. Justice Benjamin Cardozo wrote that fundamental rights are "the very essence of a scheme of ordered liberty," without which justice is not possible. To deprive an individual of these rights is "a hardship so acute and shocking that our polity will not endure it."

According to Cardozo, the 5th Amendment rights claimed by Palko in this case were important but were not "principles of justice so rooted in the traditions and conscience of our people as

Writing in the Palko case, Benjamin Cardozo outlined the process by which certain "fundamental rights" in the Bill of Rights should be applied to state governments.

to be ranked fundamental." Thus, the Court would not apply to the states in this case the 5th Amendment right of protection against double jeopardy.

Significance The *Palko* case was an important contribution in creating an acceptable test to guide the Court's use of the 14th Amendment's due process clause in limiting the actions of state governments. Justice Cardozo created the "fundamental rights" test in the *Palko* opinion. According to this test, the 14th Amendment's due process clause does not necessarily incorporate the federal Bill of Rights. However, it does open the way for a case-by-case consideration of what and how to select parts of the federal Bill of Rights to apply them to the states. In 1969 the Court overruled *Palko* in *Benton* v. *Maryland*. Double jeopardy became one of the provisions of the federal Bill of Rights to be selectively incorporated into the 14th Amendment and applied to the states.

SEE ALSO

Benton v. Maryland; Double jeopardy; Incorporation doctrine

Pardon power

ARTICLE 2, SECTION 2, of the U.S. Constitution states, "The President... shall have Power to grant Reprieves and Pardons for Offenses against the United States, except in cases of Impeachment." President Jimmy Carter, for example, used this pardon power to officially forgive all individuals who had illegally evaded the military draft during the Vietnam War. The men who were pardoned were forever exempt from criminal prosecutions or other penalties for breaking this federal law.

Paterson, William

ASSOCIATE JUSTICE, 1793–1806

☆ Born: Dec. 24, 1745, County Antrim, Ireland
☆ Education: College of New Jersey (Princeton), B.A., 1763, M.A., 1766; studied law under Richard Stockton
☆ Previous government service: New Jersey Provincial Congress, 1775–76; New Jersey State Constitutional Convention, 1776; attorney general of New Jersey, 1776–83; Constitutional Convention, 1787; U.S. senator from New Jersey, 1789–90; governor of New Jersey, 1790–93
☆ Appointed by President George Washington Mar. 4, 1793; replaced Thomas Johnson, who resigned
☆ Supreme Court term: confirmed by the Senate Mar. 4, 1793, by a voice vote; served until Sept. 9, 1806
☆ Died: Sept. 9, 1806, Albany, N.Y.

WILLIAM PATERSON, born in Ireland, was one of the founders of the United States of America. He helped to draft the first constitution of New Jersey in 1776 and the U.S. Constitution in 1787. At the Constitutional Convention, Paterson was the main author of the New Jersey Plan, an outline of how the government should be set up that he introduced as an alternative to the Virginia Plan of James Madison and Edmund Randolph. Several parts of the New Jersey Plan were combined with the Vir-

The specter of those who died in the Vietnam War hovers over President Jimmy Carter as he contemplates pardoning draft dodgers. Carter did issue the pardon.

ginia Plan to create the foundation of the U.S. Constitution.

Paterson participated in the 1st Congress of the United States as a senator from New Jersey. He worked with Oliver Ellsworth of Connecticut to draft the Judiciary Act of 1789, which created the federal judicial system.

President George Washington appointed Paterson to the Supreme Court in 1793. Justice Paterson consistently argued for the supremacy of the federal government in cases about state powers and rights. For example, in *Ware* v. *Hylton* (1796), he decided that an act of the Virginia state government was unconstitutional because it violated the U.S. government's treaty of peace with Great Britain. According to Article 6 of the U.S. Constitution, valid treaties of the United States are part of the supreme law of the land, which all state governments are bound to obey.

William Paterson was injured critically in 1804 while riding circuit for the Court. In those days, justices of the Supreme Court were responsible also for duties on the federal Circuit Courts of Appeals. Each circuit court encompassed a certain region of the United States. Riding circuit involved traveling from place to place to hear cases on appeal from lower courts. During one of those trips in 1804, the horses pulling Justice Paterson's carriage bolted, overturning the vehicle and severely injuring Paterson. He never recovered and died in 1806. The city of Paterson, New Jersey, which he helped to plan, is named after him.

SEE ALSO

Ware v. Hylton

FURTHER READING

O'Connor, John E. *William Paterson: Lawyer and Statesman.* New Brunswick, N.J.: Rutgers University Press, 1979.

Peckham, Rufus W.

ASSOCIATE JUSTICE, 1896–1909

☆ *Born: Nov. 8, 1838, Albany, N.Y.*
☆ *Education: studied law in his father's law firm*
☆ *Previous government service: district attorney, Albany County, N.Y., 1869–72; judge, New York Supreme Court, 1883–86; judge, New York Court of Appeals, 1886–95*
☆ *Appointed by President Grover Cleveland Dec. 3, 1895; replaced Howell Jackson, who died*
☆ *Supreme Court term: confirmed by the Senate Dec. 9, 1895, by a voice vote; served until Oct. 24, 1909*
☆ *Died: Oct. 24, 1909, Altamont, N.Y.*

RUFUS W. PECKHAM was named to the Supreme Court in 1895. In the previous year, his brother, Wheeler H. Peckham, had been nominated by President Grover Cleveland and rejected by the Senate. The Senate, however, readily confirmed Rufus Peckham's nomination.

During his 13 years on the Court, Justice Peckham favored property rights and contract rights of individuals. He usually opposed state government regulation of businesses and working conditions in favor of economic liberty. His most notable opinion for the Court was in *Lochner* v. *New York* (1905). He ruled that a New York law limiting the length of the workday for bakers was unconstitutional because it violated the rights of workers and employers to freely make contracts.

SEE ALSO

Lochner v. New York

Per curiam

PER CURIAM is Latin for "by the court." An opinion designated "by the

Court," as a body, instead of by one member, is called a per curiam decision. In *Brandenburg* v. *Ohio* (1969), for example, the opinion of the court was not attributed to a particular justice. Instead, it was announced as a per curiam decision. This kind of opinion is used to summarily deal with an issue in a concise and unsigned opinion that signifies the general authority of the Court.

Pitney, Mahlon

ASSOCIATE JUSTICE, 1912–22

☆ Born: Feb. 5, 1858, Morristown, N.J.
☆ Education: College of New Jersey (Princeton), B.A., 1879, M.A., 1882
☆ Previous government service: U.S. representative from New Jersey, 1895–99; New Jersey Senate, 1899–1901; president, New Jersey Senate, 1901; associate justice, New Jersey Supreme Court, 1901–8; chancellor of New Jersey, 1908–12
☆ Appointed by President William Howard Taft Feb. 19, 1912; replaced John Marshall Harlan, who died
☆ Supreme Court term: confirmed by the Senate Mar. 13, 1912, by a 50–26 vote; retired Dec. 31, 1922
☆ Died: Dec. 9, 1924, Washington, D.C.

MAHLON PITNEY was a strong supporter of individual rights, especially economic liberty and property rights. He tended to oppose strong government regulation of economic activities.

Pitney, however, tended to support limits on freedom of expression when it appeared to threaten national security. In *Pierce* v. *United States* (1920), for example, Justice Pitney upheld the prosecution of individuals under the Espionage Act of 1917 because their freedom of expression, he argued, threatened the security of the U.S. government.

Justice Pitney believed that the individual's right to contract was the most important constitutional right. He, therefore, tended to oppose the interests of labor unions as a threat to the economic liberty of individuals. However, he showed great concern for compensation of workers injured at the workplace. In *New York Railroad Company* v. *White* (1917) and several subsequent cases, Justice Pitney upheld state government laws that required employers to compensate workers for injuries suffered during their employment.

Plea bargaining

PLEA BARGAINING is the process by which a person accused of a crime may bargain with the prosecutor to receive a lesser punishment. Typically, the accused person will plead guilty, sometimes to a lesser charge than the original one (to manslaughter rather than murder, for example). This process saves the government the time and cost of a jury trial in exchange for a reduced sentence.

Defendants who plead guilty as part of a plea bargain give up three constitutional rights: the right of trial by jury, the right to confront and question one's accusers, and the right to refuse to incriminate oneself. In *Boykin* v. *Alabama* (1969) the Court ruled that plea bargaining is constitutional as long as the defendant gives up his constitutional rights

When a defendant consents to a plea bargain, he gives up his right to trial by jury and deals directly with the prosecutor and judge.

voluntarily and with full comprehension of the trade-offs of the deal.

Plessy v. Ferguson

☆ *163 U.S. 537 (1896)*
☆ *Vote: 7–1*
☆ *For the Court: Brown*
☆ *Dissenting: Harlan*
☆ *Not participating: Brewer*

THE RATIFICATION of the 13th Amendment in 1865, shortly after the end of the Civil War, abolished slavery in the United States. However, prejudices against blacks remained strong. Southern states began to pass laws to keep blacks separated from whites. A group of black leaders in Louisiana formed a Citizens' Committee to deliberately test the constitutionality of one such law, the Separate Car Law.

Acting for the Citizens' Committee, Homer Plessy, a Louisiana resident who was one-eighth black, bought a first-class ticket for a train in Louisiana. Plessy took a seat in the railroad car reserved for whites only, ignoring the coach marked "colored only." When Plessy refused to move to the coach reserved for "colored," he was arrested. He had violated the Louisiana law requiring separate railroad accommodations for blacks and whites.

The Citizens' Committee and Plessy claimed the Louisiana law denied him the "equal protection of the laws" guaranteed by the 14th Amendment. Plessy's lawyers also claimed the law violated the 13th Amendment ban on slavery by destroying the legal equality of the races and, in effect, reintroducing slavery.

The Issue Did a state law requiring segregation of the races violate the 13th Amendment ban on slavery or the 14th Amendment guarantee of equal protection of the laws for all citizens?

Opinion of the Court The Supreme Court ruled against Plessy. The Court held that the "equal protection of the laws" clause of the 14th Amendment allowed a state to provide "separate but equal" facilities for blacks. Justice Henry Brown wrote that the 14th Amendment aimed "to enforce the absolute equality of the two races before the law, but in the nature of things it could not have been intended to abolish distinctions based upon color, or to enforce social…equality."

The Court also ruled that the Louisiana law did not violate the 13th Amendment ban on slavery. Brown said a law "which implies merely a legal distinction between the white and colored races… has no tendency to…reestablish a state of involuntary servitude [slavery]."

Dissent Justice John M. Harlan dissented in the *Plessy* decision. Harlan, a native of Kentucky and a former slaveholder, argued strongly against dividing people by race. He declared, "[I]n the eye of the law there is in this country no superior, dominant, ruling class of citizens. There is no caste here. Our Constitution is color-blind and neither knows nor tolerates classes among citizens." Justice Harlan's view finally pre-

Even into the mid-20th century, public facilities such as railroad waiting rooms were usually segregated in southern states. The Court ruled in Plessy v. Ferguson *that segregation was legal as long as the separate facilities were equal.*

vailed in 1954, when the Supreme Court overruled the *Plessy* decision in the case of *Brown* v. *Board of Education.*

Significance The "separate but equal" doctrine established by the Court served to justify segregation in many states for the next half century. The *Plessy* decision reinforced state-ordered segregation, which had become a fact of life in the southern states. State laws required blacks to use separate toilets, water fountains, streetcars, and waiting rooms. Blacks had to attend different schools and remained separated from whites in prisons, hospitals, parks, theaters, and other public facilities. By 1920 segregation regulated every facet of life in the South. Blacks and whites could not eat at the same restaurants, stay in the same hotels, use the same elevators, or visit the same beaches, swimming pools, or amusement parks. Blacks and whites attended separate public schools, and in some states at the end of each school year the school board had to store the books from black schools separately from the books from white schools. One state required the segregation of public telephones, while another prohibited blacks and whites from playing checkers together.

Born in segregated hospitals, educated in segregated schools, employed at workplaces that kept blacks and whites separated, and buried in the segregated cemeteries of segregated churches, the people of the South endured the all-pervasive influence of segregation. The separation of the races was one of the most important aspects of southern life. *Plessy* v. *Ferguson* gave this entire system legitimacy. Although that decision established the well-known doctrine of "separate but equal," in actual practice separate but *unequal* was the rule throughout the South.

The "separate but equal" doctrine was upheld by Supreme Court rulings for the next 50 years. For decades, however, the Court refused to examine the actual conditions in the South to determine if equality existed along with separateness. Not until the 1930s and 1940s did the Supreme Court begin to enforce the "equal" part of the doctrine. And not until 1954 did the Court directly face the more basic question of whether separating whites and blacks was an inherently discriminating act that by nature ensured unequal treatment. In *Brown* v. *Board of Education* (1954), the Court overturned the *Plessy* decision, declaring, in a now-famous phrase, "Separate educational facilities are inherently unequal."

SEE ALSO

Brown v. Board of Education; Civil rights; Equality under the Constitution; Segregation, de facto and de jure

FURTHER READING

Kull, Andrew. "The 14th Amendment That Wasn't." *Constitution* 5, no. 1 (Winter 1993): 68–75.
Woodward, C. Vann. "The Case of the Louisiana Traveler." In *Quarrels That Have Shaped the Constitution,* edited by John A. Garraty. New York: Harper & Row, 1987.

Plurality opinion

The U.S. Supreme Court decides cases by majority vote; more than half of the justices participating must vote in favor of the decision. If the justices in the majority agree to sign a single opinion, they produce a majority opinion for the Court. Now and then, however, there are so many individual concurring opinions that the opinion that garners the most votes is called not a majority opinion but a plurality opinion.

For example, in *Dennis* v. *United States* (1951), the Court decided the case by a vote of 6 to 2 (one justice did not participate). Two justices wrote separate concurring opinions and thereby made it impossible for there to be a single majority opinion for the Court. Instead, there was a plurality opinion (signed by four justices), supported in many respects by two justices' concurring opinions, and opposed by the other two justices' dissenting opinions. Thus, Chief Justice Vinson announced the decision of the Court based on a plurality opinion.

SEE ALSO

Concurring opinion; Dissenting opinion; Majority opinion; Opinions

Political questions

THE SUPREME COURT may decide not to accept a case because it involves what it considers to be political questions, which are outside the scope of the Court's authority. Political questions may include problems clearly in the domain of Congress or the President. These are questions that, in the Court's opinion, defy resolution on legal or constitutional grounds. For example, the Court has ruled that the President, not the Court, should determine whether the United States should recognize a certain foreign government.

The political questions doctrine is a limitation that the Court has imposed upon its own powers of judicial review. Only the Supreme Court itself decides which cases involve political questions, thereby disqualifying them for review and judgment by the Court. Such political questions are referred to as nonjusticiable. Justiciable questions, by contrast, are those the Supreme Court accepts as appropriate for its review and judgment.

In *Pacific States Telephone & Telegraph* v. *Oregon* (1912), the Court faced an issue that it decided was outside the scope of judicial review. The issue pertained to Article 4, Section 4, of the Constitution, which says, "The United States shall guarantee to every State in the Union a Republican Form of Government...." The Pacific States Telephone & Telegraph Company argued that the state of Oregon was enacting laws in a non-republican manner, which violated Article 4, Section 4. The state had passed a tax of 2 percent on the income of all telephone and telegraph companies in the state. This tax law was passed through a popular initiative and referendum, not strictly and exclusively by the state legislature. The people of the state used an initiative to petition the government to pass the tax law; in response to this initiative, the voters of Oregon were permitted to decide in a public election (a referendum, which was also called for by the voters) whether to pass the law.

SEE ALSO

Judicial power; Judicial review; Justiciable questions

In 1912 Oregon passed a law taxing telephone companies. One company claimed that the state was violating the Constitution because the law had been passed by popular election, not by the legislature. The Supreme Court claimed that this was a political question, not subject to its review.

Popular sovereignty

POPULAR SOVEREIGNTY is government based on the consent of the people. Government, established by free choice of the people, is expected to serve the people, who have sovereignty, or supreme power.

Popular sovereignty is the basis of constitutional government in the United States. The U.S. Constitution clearly establishes government in the name of the people. The preamble says: "We the people of the United States…do ordain and establish this Constitution for the United States of America."

Popular sovereignty was exercised according to Article 7 of the Constitution, which required that nine states approve the proposed frame of government before it could become the supreme law of the United States. The people chose representatives to ratification conventions who freely decided to approve the Constitution in the name of those who elected them. Popular sovereignty was also recognized in Article 5 of the Constitution, which provides for amendments to the Constitution through decisions by

POGHKEEPSIE,
July 2d, 1788.

JUST ARRIVED

BY EXPRESS,

The Ratification of the New Conſtitution by the Convention of the State of Virginia, on Wedneſday the 25th June, by a majority of 10 ; 88 agreeing, and 78 diſſenting to its adoption.

"WE the Delegates of the People of Virginia, duly elected in Purſuance of a Recommendation of the General Aſſembly, and now met in Convention, having fully and fairly inveſtigated and diſcuſſed the Proceedings of the Federal Convention, and being With theſe Impreſſions, with a ſolemn Appeal to the Searcher of Hearts for the Purity of our Intentions, and under the Conviction, that whatſoever Imperfections may exiſt in the Conſtitution, ought rather to be examined in the Mode preſcribed therein, than to bring the Uni-

The ratification of the U.S. Constitution by individual states was an example of popular sovereignty, or government based on the consent of the people.

elected representatives of the people. Finally, popular sovereignty is reflected in Article 1, which requires that representatives to Congress be elected by the people.

Popular sovereignty, or government by the people, implies majority rule. People elect representatives in government by majority vote, and these representatives of the people make laws by majority vote.

SEE ALSO

Constitutional democracy; Constitutionalism; Republicanism

FURTHER READING

Morgan, Edmund S. *Inventing the People: The Rise of Popular Sovereignty in England and America.* New York: Norton, 1988.

Powell, Lewis F., Jr.

ASSOCIATE JUSTICE, 1972–87

☆ *Born: Sept. 19, 1907, Suffolk, Va.*
☆ *Education: Washington and Lee University, B.S., 1929; Washington and Lee University Law School, LL.B., 1931; Harvard Law School, LL.M., 1932*
☆ *Previous government service: chairman, Richmond School Board, Va., 1952–61; Virginia State Board of Education, 1961–69; president, Virginia State Board of Education, 1968–69*
☆ *Appointed by President Richard Nixon Oct. 21, 1971; replaced Hugo L. Black, who retired*
☆ *Supreme Court term: confirmed by the Senate Dec. 6, 1971, by an 89–1 vote; retired June 26, 1987*

LEWIS F. POWELL, JR., belonged to a respected family with deep roots in Virginia. The first American Powell was one of the original settlers of Jamestown in 1607.

Though a member of the Virginia establishment, Powell opposed the long-established practice of racial segregation in the public schools. As chairman of the Richmond School Board, he presided over the peaceful integration of the city's schools in the wake of the *Brown* v. *Board of Education* (1954) decision. He also stood up to leading Virginians who resisted statewide integration of schools. As a member of the Virginia State Board of Education, he led the successful racial integration of the state's public schools.

As a justice of the Supreme Court, Powell tried to balance the needs of society against the rights of individuals. His most famous opinion for the Court was *Regents of the University of California* v. *Bakke* (1978), a case about the legality of a plan that provided special opportunities for minority group applicants (such as African Americans) to gain admission to the university. Powell characteristically sought the middle ground between competing claims for preferences based on race and equality of individual rights in decisions about whom to admit to the state university. Powell decided against the establishment of rigid racial quotas for minorities seeking admission to the university. However, he also upheld the principle of "affirmative action" as one factor, among others, that could be considered in making decisions about admitting students to the university. Affirmative action means making a special effort to provide opportunities for members of groups that had been discriminated against in the past. Considering the racial identity of an applicant as a positive factor in making a decision about student admissions could be done to compensate for the negative effects of past discrimination.

SEE ALSO
Regents of the University of California v. Bakke

FURTHER READING
Haupt, Donna. "A Justice Reflects." *Constitution* 2, no. 3 (Fall 1990): 16–25.

Landynski, Jacob W. "Justice Lewis F. Powell, Jr.: Balance Wheel of the Court." In *The Burger Court: Political and Judicial Profiles,* edited by Charles M. Lamb and Stephen C. Halpern. Urbana: University of Illinois Press, 1991: 276–314.

Powell v. Alabama

☆ *287 U.S. 45 (1932)*
☆ *Vote: 7–2*
☆ *For the Court: Sutherland*
☆ *Dissenting: Butler and McReynolds*

ON MARCH 25, 1931, nine African-American youths, ranging in age from 12 to 20, were arrested near Scottsboro, Alabama. They were accused of having raped two white women. A hostile crowd gathered outside the jail in Scottsboro and shouted insults at the young men.

The nine youths were quickly indicted and a trial date was set for six days later. The nine defendants were too poor to hire an attorney to represent them. According to Alabama law, the judge was required to appoint counsel to assist them because they were accused of a capital offense (a crime punishable by death). The judge responded to this legal requirement by declaring that every licensed lawyer in Scottsboro was assigned to represent the nine men. No one attorney, however, took personal responsibility for their defense.

On the day of the trial, two attorneys did show up to defend the accused youths. They asked the judge to postpone the trial so they could have time to prepare their defense. But the judge refused, and the lawyers had only 30 minutes before the trial started to consult with the defendants.

The trial was conducted quickly. Eight of the nine defendants were found guilty and sentenced to death. The jury was unable to reach a decision about one of the defendants.

The nine "Scotts-boro boys" are guarded by the Alabama militia on their way to the courthouse. When eight of the defendants were found guilty of rape and sentenced to death, the case was appealed to the Supreme Court because they had been denied adequate counsel.

The decision was appealed to the Alabama Supreme Court, which upheld the conviction of seven of the defendants. The conviction of one defendant was reversed because he was a juvenile (only 12 years old). The Alabama Supreme Court ruling with regard to the other seven was appealed to the U.S. Supreme Court.

The Issue The defendants, too poor to hire a lawyer, were tried, convicted, and sentenced to death without effective assistance of an attorney. However, the 14th Amendment to the U.S. Constitution says, "No state shall…deprive any person of life, liberty, or property, without due process of law."

Were due process rights denied to the defendants in this case? Do people without means to obtain a lawyer have the right to counsel at the government's expense?

Opinion of the Court Writing for the Court, Justice George Sutherland overturned the convictions of the defendants. This decision was based on the due process clause of the 14th Amendment. Justice Sutherland argued that the right to counsel is an essential element of due process. Further, he rejected claims by the prosecutors that the defendants were given effective legal assistance. He pointed to the last-minute assignment of counsel for the defense as inadequate.

Justice Sutherland wrote about the critical importance of effective legal counsel, without which a fair trial is impossible. A defendant, he said, "lacks both the skill and knowledge adequately to prepare his defense, even though he has a perfect one. He requires the guiding hand of counsel at every step in the proceedings against him. Without it, though he be not guilty, he faces the danger of conviction because he does not know how to establish his innocence."

Dissent Justice Pierce Butler, joined in dissent by Justice James McReynolds, argued that the defendants had received adequate legal assistance. Further, they said that the Court's reversal of the convictions was unjustified interference with the operations of a state court system.

Significance In the *Powell* case the Court decided for the first time that the 14th Amendment required states to provide legal help for poor defendants in order to guarantee a fair trial. After *Powell,* state governments were required to provide counsel for poor defendants in all capital cases.

By contrast, the assistance of counsel clause of the 6th Amendment to the Constitution required the federal government to provide counsel for indigent defendants in both capital and noncapital cases. Federal and state government requirements regarding the assistance of counsel were not brought into conformity until 1963 with the decision in *Gideon* v. *Wainwright.* In this landmark case, the Court ruled for the first time that the 6th Amendment assistance of counsel clause applied to state governments. The Court incorporated the 6th Amendment right to an attorney under the due process clause of the 14th Amendment. The states have to provide legal assistance to indigent defendants, in both capital and noncapital cases, in order to guarantee that the defendant receives the constitutional right to due process in criminal justice proceedings.

Following the Court's decision in *Powell,* the case was returned to Alabama for retrial of the seven youths on rape charges. This time, the defendants were represented by counsel, as required by the Supreme Court decision. However, they were again convicted and sentenced to death. Once again, they appealed their conviction and the case returned to the U.S. Supreme Court as *Norris* v. *Alabama* (1935). This appeal was based on the exclusion of blacks from the jury pool for the trial. The Court again overturned the convictions on the grounds that the 14th Amendment due process rights of the defendants were violated by systematic exclusion of jurors because of race.

The case was returned once more to Alabama for a jury trial. In subsequent state trials, the defendants were convicted again. However, none of them was sentenced to the death penalty. After several years of very complicated proceedings, all of the defendants were released from prison on parole, the last one in 1950.

SEE ALSO

Counsel, right to; Due process of law; Gideon v. Wainwright; Incorporation doctrine

FURTHER READING

Carter, Dan T. *Scottsboro—A Tragedy of the American South.* Rev. ed. Baton Rouge: Louisiana State University Press, 1979.

Precedent

APPEALS COURTS in the United States, including the Supreme Court, follow precedent, or past decisions, in making new ones. Once a case has been decided, similar cases are supposed to be decided in the same way. This practice is based on the doctrine of *stare decisis,* a Latin phrase meaning "Let the decision stand." The principle of *stare decisis* gives stability and predictability to the law. Decisions of the Supreme Court are binding on all lower courts in the United States, and they also serve as guidelines for subsequent Supreme Court decisions.

Occasionally, however, the Court departs from precedent to decide a case in a new way. Its decision in *Brown* v. *Board of Education* (1954), for example, rejected the precedent of "separate but equal" that had been established in *Plessy* v. *Ferguson* (1896) to support racial segregation.

SEE ALSO

Constitutional law; Dissenting opinion; Judicial review

Prior restraint

PRIOR RESTRAINT is a form of censorship in which government officials restrict a newspaper or magazine in advance from publishing materials of which they disapprove. The 1st Amendment guarantee of a free press precludes the government's use of prior restraint to control the content of a publication. This 1st Amendment ban on prior restraint was applied to state governments through the due process clause of the 14th Amendment in *Near* v. *Minnesota*

(1931). In this landmark decision, the Court ruled that an injunction to stop publication of a newspaper with objectionable content was an example of prior restraint and therefore unconstitutional. The Court did not rule, however, that a publisher was protected from legal action *after* publishing questionable material.

SEE ALSO

Freedom of speech and press; Near v. Minnesota; New York Times Co. v. United States

Privacy, right to

THE WORD *privacy* cannot be found in the Constitution of the United States. Yet Americans have tended to believe in a constitutional right to privacy—the right to be secure against unlawful intrusions by government into certain protected areas of life. Ever since the founding era, most Americans have recognized public and private domains of society. The public domain is open to regulation by government. For example, the people expect their police officers to keep order on the streets of a community, a function that involves certain limits on the free movement of people. The private domain, by contrast, is generally closed to invasion and control by government and can be entered and regulated by police officers only for a compelling public purpose and according to due process of law.

There are continuing legal issues about the boundaries between the public and private domains of society because these two realms of life are inextricably bound together. Thus, for example, the government can constitutionally justify certain regulations of private property owners to protect the public against abuses, such as pollution of the environment. Further, the government may con-

stitutionally enter a person's home to prevent individuals from conducting activities that violate the public interest, such as molesting children. When, and under what circumstances, does a person's right to privacy end and the public's authority to regulate behavior in the public interest begin? This is an ongoing problem in the courts.

Justice Louis D. Brandeis argued for a general constitutional right to privacy in a famous dissent in O*lmstead* v. *United States* (1928): "The makers of our Constitution undertook to secure conditions favorable to the pursuit of happiness…. They conferred, as against the Government, the right to be let alone—the most comprehensive of rights and the right most valued by civilized men." Justice Brandeis pointed to the 4th Amendment protections against "unreasonable searches and seizures" and the 5th Amendment guarantees against self-incrimination as examples of constitutional protection against "unjustifiable intrusion by the Government upon the privacy of the individual."

For more than 30 years after the *Olmstead* case, the Court avoided serious discussions of a constitutional right to privacy. Then, in *Poe* v. *Ullman* (1961), Justices John Marshall Harlan and William O. Douglas argued in dissent for the individual's right to privacy against a Connecticut law banning the use of birth control devices, even by married couples. Harlan pointed to the 14th Amendment's provision that "no State shall make or enforce any law which shall…deprive any person of life, liberty, or property, without due process of law." According to Harlan, the state law at issue unconstitutionally deprived individuals of their liberty, without due process of law, to use birth control devices, which was "an intolerable and unjustifiable invasion of privacy." Thus, Harlan linked the 14th Amendment's guarantee

THE DECISION TO HAVE A BABY COULD SOON BE BETWEEN YOU, YOUR HUSBAND AND YOUR SENATOR.

A pro-choice advertisement from Planned Parenthood. A woman's right to have an abortion, established in the Roe v. Wade decision in 1973, is based on an implied constitutional right to privacy.

of liberty to the right to privacy.

In *Griswold* v. *Connecticut* (1965), the Court overturned the decision in *Poe* v. *Ullman* (1961). The Court decided that the Connecticut law against contraception was unconstitutional and based its decision on a constitutional right to privacy. However, the justices disagreed about where in the Constitution this right to privacy could be found.

Justice William O. Douglas found a general right to privacy which, he believed, can be interpreted from the words of parts of the Bill of Rights (the 1st, 3rd, 4th, and 5th Amendments). He argued that the state of Connecticut had specifically violated the right to marital privacy, which fits within the "zone of privacy" one can infer from the text of the Bill of Rights.

Justice Arthur Goldberg's concurring opinion in *Griswold* emphasized the 9th Amendment: "The enumeration in the Constitution of certain rights shall not be construed to deny or disparage others retained by the people." Justice Goldberg held that the right to privacy in marital relationships was one of those rights not written in the Constitution that was nonetheless "retained by the people." Justice Goldberg wrote, "To

hold that a right so basic and fundamental and so deep-rooted in our society as the right to privacy in marriage may be infringed because the right is not guaranteed in so many words by the first eight amendments to the Constitution is to ignore the Ninth Amendment and to give it no effect whatsoever."

Justice John Marshall Harlan also concurred with the Court's opinion in the *Griswold* case. However, Harlan based his decision on the due process clause of the 14th Amendment, as he had done in his dissent in the *Poe* case four years earlier.

Justices Hugo L. Black and Potter Stewart dissented from the Court's opinion in *Griswold*. They argued that a general right to privacy cannot be inferred from any part of the Constitution. Further, they criticized the Court's majority for deciding this case according to personal opinion instead of following the text of the Constitution. Justice Black wrote, "I like my privacy as well as the next one, but I am nevertheless compelled to admit that government has a right to invade it unless prohibited by some specific constitutional provision." In *Griswold,* Black found no "specific constitutional provision" that prohibited the state government's regulation of the private behavior at issue in this case.

Support for a right to privacy has continued since the *Griswold* decision. In *Katz* v. *United States* (1967), the Court overturned the decision in *Olmstead* v. *United States* (1928). The Court held that the 4th and 5th Amendments protect an individual's right to privacy against electronic surveillance and wiretapping by government agents, even in a place open to the public, such as a telephone booth on a city street. In *Roe* v. *Wade* (1973), the Court ruled that the right to privacy included a woman's choice to have an abortion during the first three months of pregnancy.

While continuing to recognize a constitutional right to privacy, the Court has acted recently to set limits on it. In *Skinner* v. *Railway Labor Executives Association* (1989) and *National Treasury Employees Union* v. *Von Raab* (1989), the Court has upheld federal regulations that provide for drug testing of railroad and customs workers, even without warrants or reasonable suspicion of drug use. In these cases, the Court decided that the need for public safety was a compelling reason for limiting the individual's right to privacy against government regulation.

Since the 1960s the often-contested right to privacy has been established in a line of Supreme Court decisions. As Justice Harry A. Blackmun wrote in *Thornburgh* v. *American College of Obstetricians and Gynecologists* (1986), "Our cases long have recognized that the Constitution embodies a promise that a certain private sphere of individual liberty will be kept largely beyond the reach of government."

The exact meaning and limits of this widely recognized right to privacy, however, will continue to be controversial. Every extension of the right to privacy limits the power of government to regulate behavior for the public good, which citizens of a constitutional democracy expect. By contrast, every expansion of government's power to regulate the behavior of individuals diminishes the "private sphere of individual liberty" cherished by citizens of a constitutional democracy. How to justly balance and blend these contending factors, so that both are addressed but neither one is sacrificed to the other, is an ongoing issue of the Supreme Court and the citizenry of the United States.

SEE ALSO

Griswold v. Connecticut; Katz v. United States; Olmstead v. United States; Roe v. Wade

FURTHER READING

Barnett, Randy, ed. *The Rights Retained by the People: The History and Meaning of the Ninth Amendment.* Fairfax, Va.: George Mason University Press, 1989.

Van Burkleo, Sandra F. "The Right to Privacy." In *By and for the People: Constitutional Rights in American History,* edited by Kermit L. Hall. Arlington Heights, Ill.: Harlan Davidson, 1991.

Westin, Alan F. *Privacy and Freedom.* New York: Atheneum, 1968.

Probable cause

THE 4TH AMENDMENT to the U.S. Constitution requires that "no [search or arrest] warrants shall issue, but upon probable cause." Thus, government officials may not obtain a warrant to search or arrest someone unless they have probable cause, or good reasons, to believe that the person may be involved in criminal behavior of some kind. Judges, not law enforcement officers, have the authority to decide if there is probable cause for issuing a warrant to search or arrest someone. In *Terry* v. *Ohio* (1968), however, the Court adjusted this standard to allow police officers to stop and frisk suspects if they consider it necessary to protect themselves, even without probable cause for arrest.

SEE ALSO

Searches and seizures; Terry v. Ohio

Property rights

THE FOUNDERS of the United States believed that the right to acquire, own, and use private property was an essential element of a free society. John Adams expressed a prevailing opinion of his times when he wrote in 1790, "Property must

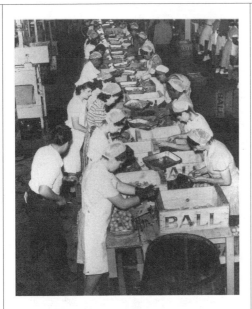

be secured or liberty cannot exist."

Land ownership was one kind of property right the founders wanted to protect. They were also concerned about rights to other kinds of property, such as personal goods (clothing, tools, houses, and animals, for instance), ideas, inventions, and money. Property takes many forms that represent both wealth and the means of creating or producing wealth.

A main purpose of the U.S. Constitution of 1787 was to limit the power of government in order to protect individual rights, including property rights. The framers used separation of powers, with checks and balances, to constitutionally limit the government for the purpose of guarding individual property rights and other fundamental rights. The framers of the Constitution and of the Bill of Rights also provided protections for property rights in specific clauses.

For example, Article 1, Section 10, states, "No State shall…pass any Bill of Attainder…or Law impairing the Obligation of Contracts." By prohibiting bills of attainder, or the punishment of a person by a legislative act (rather than by a court of law), the Constitution protects individuals from legislative actions to arbitrarily deprive them of property or

punish them in some other way. By prohibiting legislative actions interfering with the terms of a contract, the Constitution protects property rights involved in the contract. Further, in Article 1, Section 8, Congress is granted the power to protect the property rights of inventors and writers to their ideas and creations "by securing for limited Times to Authors and Inventors the exclusive Right to their respective Writings and Discoveries." Finally, Article 1, Section 9, prohibits Congress from levying direct taxes on individuals unless they are apportioned according to population. This constitutional provision limited the Congress's power to impose land taxes, thereby protecting a person's private property from acquisition by the federal government. (The 16th Amendment, passed in 1913, permits the federal government to levy taxes on the income of individuals, whatever the source.)

The 5th Amendment to the U.S. Constitution (ratified in 1791 as part of the Bill of Rights) says, "No person shall be…deprived of life, liberty, or property, without due process of law; nor shall private property be taken for public use without just compensation." The 14th Amendment (ratified in 1868) provides protection for private property rights by prohibiting any state government from taking a person's property "without due process of law." The 5th and 14th Amendments limit the power of the federal and state governments to abuse the property rights of individuals.

Chief Justice John Marshall strongly supported private property rights of individuals as a bulwark of personal liberty and as a stimulus to productive use of resources. Marshall believed, as did most other leaders of his time, that security in the ownership of property helped a person to resist domination by others, especially government officials. Chief Justice Marshall's opinions in *Fletcher* v. *Peck*

(1810) and *Dartmouth College* v. *Woodward* (1819) bolstered the "Obligation of Contracts" cited in Article 1, Section 10, of the Constitution as a guarantee of private property rights.

If the Constitution set limits on the power of government to violate property rights, it also implied that there are limits on the rights of individuals in behalf of the public good. For example, Chief Justice Roger Taney was a strong supporter of private property rights. In *Charles River Bridge* v. *Warren Bridge* (1837), however, Taney held that property rights in a contract could sometimes be overridden to permit development of innovations or improvements to benefit the public. In *West River Bridge Co.* v. *Dix* (1848), the Taney Court held that the contract clause of the Constitution did not protect a corporation from the state's right of eminent domain—its power to take private property, with fair compensation, to use for the public good.

There has been persistent tension between the private property rights of individuals and the public's need for limitations or regulations on private property rights. Justice John M. Harlan stressed in *Chicago, Burlington & Quincy Railroad Company* v. *Chicago* (1897), "Due protection of the rights of property has been regarded as a vital principle of republican institutions." Justice Harlan also wrote (*Mugler* v. *Kansas,* 1887), "All property in this country is held under the implied obligation that the owner's use of it shall not be injurious to the community." However, he qualified this recognition of the government's authority to regulate property rights by insisting that there were "limits beyond which legislation cannot rightfully go."

At times the Court has tilted to the government-regulation side of the debate on property rights. In *Munn* v. *Illinois* (1877), for instance, the Court upheld an Illinois law regulating the price for storing grain in privately owned storage elevators. Chief Justice Morrison R. Waite wrote, "When private property is devoted to a public use, it is subject to public regulation."

More often, however, from the 1870s until the 1930s the Court seemed to oppose any government laws that interfered with the free market, such as state laws regulating wages or working conditions of employees. In *Lochner* v. *New York* (1905), for example, the Court overturned a New York law that restricted hours of work in bakeries. Writing for the Court, Justice Rufus W. Peckham argued that the New York law violated the "liberty of contract" protected by the 14th Amendment.

The *Lochner* decision set the trend for Court rulings on state regulation of private property rights for the next 30 years. Not until 1937, when the Court upheld federal laws regulating the economy for the public good (in *National Labor Relations Board* v. *Jones & Laughlin Steel Corp.* and *West Coast Hotel Co.* v. *Parrish*), did the trend shift away from the resistance to many kinds of public regulations of private property rights. In the *Parrish* case, Chief Justice Charles Evans Hughes rejected the "liberty of contract" idea that had prevailed in the *Lochner* decision and other subsequent decisions. He wrote for the Court, "Liberty under the Constitution is… necessarily subject to the restraints of due process, and regulation [of a private business by a state government to protect the health, welfare, and personal rights of workers] which is adopted in the interests of the community is due process."

During the middle years of the 20th century, from 1937 until the 1960s, the Court tilted strongly toward public regulation of private property for the public good and away from 19th-century views on the connection of private property rights to personal liberty. For example,

Justice Hugo Black wrote in *Marsh* v. *Alabama* (1946), "Ownership does not always mean absolute domination. The more an owner, for his advantage, opens up his property for use by the public in general, the more do his rights become circumscribed by the statutory and constitutional rights of those who use it.... Thus, the owners of privately held bridges, ferries, turnpikes, and railroads may not operate them as freely as a farmer does his farm. Since these facilities are built and operated primarily to benefit the public and since their operation is essentially a public function, it is subject to state regulation."

Since the 1970s, however, the Court has tended to reemphasize private property rights in a continuing quest for a just balance between private property rights and the public good. Justice Potter Stewart expressed in *Lynch* v. *Household Finance Corporation* (1972) the Court's renewed emphasis on property rights as a key to liberty and a free society: "In fact, a fundamental interdependence exists between the personal right to liberty and the personal right in property. Neither could have meaning without the other."

SEE ALSO

Charles River Bridge v. Warren Bridge; Contract clause; Dartmouth College v. Woodward; Fletcher v. Peck; Lochner v. New York; Munn v. Illinois; National Labor Relations Board v. Jones & Laughlin Steel Corp.; West Coast Hotel Co. v. Parrish

FURTHER READING

Bakken, Gordon Morris. "Property Rights." In *By and for the People: Constitutional Rights in American History*, edited by Kermit L. Hall. Arlington Heights, Ill.: Harlan Davidson, 1991.
Ely, James W., Jr. *The Guardian of Every Other Right: A Constitutional History of Property Rights*. New York: Oxford, 1992.
Epstein, Richard. *Takings: Private Property and the Power of Eminent Domain*. Cambridge: Harvard University Press, 1985.

Public Information Office

SEE Staff of the Court, nonjudicial

Recusal

A JUDGE may recuse himself or herself, or refuse to participate in deciding a case, because of a special interest in the outcome that could influence his or her decision. The term *recuse* is derived from the Latin word *recusare*, which means "to refuse." Chief Justice John Marshall, for example, recused himself in the case of *Martin* v. *Hunter's Lessee* (1816) because he had served as attorney to one of the parties (Martin) in an earlier phase of the case. In addition, he had a financial stake in the outcome of the case.

Reed, Stanley F.

ASSOCIATE JUSTICE, 1938–57

☆ *Born: Dec. 31, 1884, Minerva, Ky.*

☆ *Education: Kentucky Wesleyan College, B.A., 1902; Yale College, B.A., 1906; legal studies at University of Virginia and Columbia University*

☆ *Previous government service: Kentucky General Assembly, 1912–16; general counsel, Federal Farm Board, 1929–32; general counsel, Reconstruction Finance Corporation, 1932–35; special assistant to the U.S. attorney general, 1935; U.S. solicitor general, 1935–38*

☆ *Appointed by President Franklin D. Roosevelt Jan. 15, 1938; replaced George Sutherland, who retired*

☆ *Supreme Court term: confirmed by the Senate Jan. 25, 1938, by a voice vote; retired Feb. 25, 1957*

☆ *Died: Apr. 2, 1980, Huntington, N.Y.*

STANLEY REED was a prominent defender of the New Deal policies of President Franklin D. Roosevelt. As a lawyer for the federal government, he defended New Deal programs in several important Supreme Court cases. His reward was appointment in 1938 by President Roosevelt to a vacancy on the Supreme Court.

Justice Reed continued to support the economic programs of President Roosevelt's New Deal. He tended to favor broad exercise of the federal government's power to regulate commerce or trade among the states (Article 1, Section 8, of the Constitution). However, Justice Reed tended to have a narrow view of freedom of expression when he thought it threatened national security or public order.

Reed retired from the Court in 1957, but he continued to assist the Court of Claims and the Court of Appeals for the District of Columbia. In 1980, he died at the age of 95, having lived longer than any other justice of the Supreme Court.

Reed v. Reed

☆ *404 U.S. 71 (1971)*
☆ *Vote: 7–0*
☆ *For the Court: Burger*

SALLY AND CECIL REED were the separated parents of a deceased son, Richard Reed. Both parents petitioned an Idaho court for appointment as the administrator of their son's estate. The Court denied Sally Reed's petition in favor of Cecil Reed. This decision was based on an Idaho statute that preferred males to females in choosing administrators of estates.

Sally Reed sued Cecil for the right to administer Richard's estate, which was valued at less than $1,000. She claimed that the Idaho law giving preference to a male over a female violated the 14th Amendment guarantee of "equal protection of the laws." Ruth Bader Ginsburg, as a lawyer for the American Civil Liberties Union, argued Sally Reed's case before the Supreme Court.

The Issue The 14th Amendment says, "No State shall…deny to any person within its jurisdiction the equal protection of the laws." However, in past cases the Court had not used the "equal protection" clause of the 14th Amendment to overturn laws that discriminated against individuals on the basis of gender. The Court had used what it called a rational basis test to uphold sex-based laws. According to this test, such laws were constitutional unless one could prove they were not reasonably connected to a compelling public interest. Did the Idaho law in this case violate the equal protection clause of the 14th Amendment? Was there any compelling public reason for sustaining this law?

Opinion of the Court The Court decided this case in favor of Sally Reed, ruling that the Idaho statute did not meet the rational basis test. Chief Justice Warren E. Burger wrote, "To give a mandatory preference to members of either sex…merely to accomplish the elimination of hearings on the merits, is to make the very kind of arbitrary legislative choice forbidden by the Equal Protection Clause of the Fourteenth Amendment."

Significance This case was the first to rule that laws mandating gender discrimination are violations of the 14th Amendment. The Court has used the precedent established in the *Reed* case to strike down many laws that unfairly discriminated against women. For instance, in *Kahn* v. *Shevin* (1974) it ruled that a Florida law that gave a property tax exemption to widowers (males), but not to widows (females) was unconstitutional.

SEE ALSO
Equality under the Constitution

Regents of the University of California v. Bakke

☆ *438 U.S. 265 (1978)*
☆ *Vote: 5–4*
☆ *For the Court: Powell*
☆ *Concurring: Burger, Rehnquist, Stevens, and Stewart*
☆ *Dissenting: Blackmun, Brennan, Marshall, and White*

IN 1972 there were 2,664 applicants for admission to the medical school of the University of California at Davis. From this large pool of applicants, the medical school intended to select 100 students. Eighty-four of the 100 openings were to be filled according to usual procedures of the standard admissions program. Sixteen of the 100 places were to be filled through a special affirmative action program designed to increase the number of disadvantaged students from certain minority groups, such as African Americans, Latinos, and Native Americans.

Students applying for admission through the affirmative action program did not have to meet the same standards as students applying through the regular admissions program. For example, requirements for grade point averages and scores on standardized tests of scholastic aptitude and achievement were lower for those seeking admission through the special program.

Allan Bakke, a white male, wanted to become a doctor. In 1972 he applied through the regular program for admission to the Davis medical school. He was

White protesters call for an end to racial discrimination—against whites. Allan Bakke, rejected by a University of California medical school, had charged that black applicants did not have to meet the same requirements that he did.

rejected even though his grade point average and standardized test scores were higher than those of several students admitted to the medical school through the affirmative action program.

In 1973 Bakke again tried to gain admission to the Davis medical school. This time he was one of 3,737 applicants for 100 vacancies. Once again, 16 places were set aside for applicants through the special affirmative action program. Bakke was rejected a second time, even though he appeared to be more qualified, based on certain statistical indicators, than several applicants admitted through both the affirmative action program and the regular process.

Bakke claimed he was a victim of unequal and unfair treatment. He sued for admission to the state medical school.

The Issue Bakke argued that the medical school's admissions program violated the "equal protection of the laws" guarantee of the 14th Amendment. Bakke also claimed that the university's affirmative action admissions program conflicted with Title VI of the Civil Rights Act of 1964, which forbids discrimination based on race or ethnicity in programs supported by federal funds.

The University of California defended its special admissions program as necessary to compensate for past injustices suffered by members of certain disadvantaged groups. The special admissions program, university officials said, was one way to open new opportunities for individual members of groups that in the past had not enjoyed these opportunities to the same degree as other members of society.

Allan Bakke, however, questioned whether the affirmative action admissions program went too far in trying to provide new opportunities for members of certain disadvantaged groups. To Bakke, the medical school's affirmative action admissions program seemed to be "reverse discrimination" based on race or ethnicity. Therefore, he asserted, it violated federal statutes and the U.S. Constitution.

Opinion of the Court The Court was so sharply divided in its response to this case that the majority could not agree on a common opinion for the Court. Lewis F. Powell was designated to announce the decision, but the four concurring justices wrote separate opinions, which were mixed in their reasons for supporting or opposing different aspects of the Court's decision.

A majority decided that Allan Bakke must be admitted to the University of California Medical School at Davis. Justice Powell noted that Bakke had been excluded from competition for one of the 16 positions reserved for individuals seeking admission through the special affirmative action program. Therefore, Powell concluded, Bakke had been denied "equal protection of the laws" as required by the 14th Amendment.

Justice Powell wrote, "The guarantees of the Fourteenth Amendment extend to all persons.... The guarantee of equal protection cannot mean one thing when applied to one individual and something else when applied to a person of another color. If both are not accorded the same protection, then it is not equal."

The Court held that a university may use admissions standards involving race or ethnicity as one part of a complex admissions process. But "fixed quotas"—guaranteeing a certain number of positions for students of a particular race or ethnicity—cannot be used. Race and ethnic background may be viewed favorably in making decisions about when to admit a person to a university program. But they cannot be the sole factor in determining whether to admit or reject someone.

Dissent Justices William Brennan, Byron White, Thurgood Marshall, and Harry Blackmun voted against admission of Bakke to the medical school. And they would have upheld the quota-based admissions system of the medical school. However, they joined with Justice Powell to permit "race conscious programs in the future," as long as they are only one factor considered in a multifactor admissions process. Thus, the four dissenters from the decision to admit Bakke to the medical school blocked the other four justices (Warren Burger, William Rehnquist, John Paul Stevens, and Potter Stewart), who would have prohibited any use of a person's race as a factor in deciding whom to admit to a university program.

The four dissenters defended the affirmative action admissions program of the medical school:

> The Davis program does not simply advance less qualified applicants; rather it compensates applicants, who it is uncontested are fully qualified to study medicine, for educational disadvantages that it was reasonable to conclude were a product of state-fostered discrimination. Once admitted, these students must satisfy the same degree requirements as regularly admitted students.

Significance This case was the Court's first major statement on whether affirmative action programs are constitutional. And the results were mixed. The rejection of Allan Bakke as a result of the medical school's special admissions program was declared in violation of the U.S. Constitution. However, race could be an important factor in admissions programs, as long as it was not the sole or dominating factor in making an admissions decision.

Allan Bakke certainly benefited from the Court's decision. He graduated in 1982 from the University of California Medical School at Davis and later served as a resident at the prestigious Mayo Clinic in Rochester, Minnesota. However, the *Bakke* decision has had only slight impact on university admissions programs, which shun explicitly stated quotas but tend to consider race and ethnicity as important factors in admissions decisions. This matter remains complex and controversial.

SEE ALSO
Affirmative action

FURTHER READING
Friendly, Fred W., and Martha J. H. Elliott. "Bakke and the Equal Protection Clause." In *The Constitution: That Delicate Balance.* New York: Random House, 1984.
Wilkinson, J. Harvie. *From Brown to Bakke: The Supreme Court and School Integration, 1954–1978.* New York: Oxford, 1979.

Rehnquist, William H.

ASSOCIATE JUSTICE, 1972–86

CHIEF JUSTICE, 1986–

☆ Born: Oct. 1, 1924, Milwaukee, Wis.
☆ Education: Stanford University, B.A., 1948, M.A., 1949; Harvard University, M.A., 1950; Stanford University Law School, LL.B., 1951
☆ Previous government service: law clerk to Justice Robert H. Jackson of the Supreme Court, 1952–53; assistant U.S. attorney general, 1969–71

☆ Appointed by President Richard Nixon to the position of associate justice Oct. 21, 1971; replaced John Marshall Harlan II, who retired; appointed chief justice by President Ronald Reagan June 20, 1986; replaced Chief Justice Warren E. Burger, who retired
☆ Supreme Court term: confirmed by the Senate as associate justice Dec. 10, 1971, by a 68–26 vote; confirmed by the Senate as chief justice Sept. 17, 1986, by a 65–33 vote

WILLIAM H. REHNQUIST ranked first in his class at Stanford Law School, which also included Justice Sandra Day O'Connor. And he was a distinctive member of the Supreme Court under Chief Justice Warren Burger. Justice Rehnquist dissented more than any other member of that Court. In 1986, President Reagan named Rehnquist the Chief Justice of the United States.

Rehnquist has tended to support the rights and powers of state governments within the federal system. He strongly believes that the Constitution limits the federal government so that the state governments have substantial powers in many areas. He has favored state law enforcement powers over the rights of accused persons, as in *New York* v. *Quarles* (1984) and *United States* v. *Leon* (1984). He also has upheld state rules that restrict abortion rights but has stopped short of total opposition to *Roe* v. *Wade* (1973), the landmark case restricting states from taking away the abortion rights of women.

Rehnquist emphasizes limitations of judicial power and tries to avoid judicial infringement of the legitimate powers of the legislative and executive branches of government. The judicial branch, according to Rehnquist, should scrupulously avoid political questions and restrict itself to exercising judgment according to the words of the Constitution and the intentions of the framers.

FURTHER READING

Davis, Sue. "Justice William H. Rehnquist: Right-Wing Ideologue or Majoritarian Democrat?" In *The Burger Court: Political and Judicial Profiles,* edited by Charles M. Lamb and Stephen C. Halpern, Urbana: University of Illinois Press, 1991: 315–42.

Davis, Sue. *Justice Rehnquist and the Constitution.* Princeton, N.J.: Princeton University Press, 1989.

Rehnquist, William H. *The Supreme Court—How It Was—How It Is.* New York: Morrow, 1987.

Savage, David G. *Turning Right: The Making of the Rehnquist Supreme Court.* New York: Wiley, 1992.

Judge Robert Bork testifies before the Senate Judiciary Committee in 1987. The committee rejected his nomination because of his conservative philosophy.

Rejection of Supreme Court nominees

ACCORDING TO Article 2, Section 2, of the Constitution, the President "shall nominate, and by and with the Advice and Consent of the Senate, shall appoint . . . Judges of the Supreme Court." The President's nominees for seats on the Supreme Court must be approved by a majority vote of the Senate. Thus, one part of the legislative branch has the power to check the power of appointment of the executive branch.

From 1789 to 1993 the Senate either rejected by formal vote, or informally turned away, 28 Presidential nominees to the Supreme Court. The Senate officially rejected 11 nominees by majority vote. Seventeen nominations were either withdrawn by the President before a formal vote, or no action was taken by the Senate on the nomination, thereby defeating it.

The Senate first formally voted to reject a nominee in 1811, when the senators refused to confirm President James Madison's nomination of Alexander Wolcott. The vote was 9 senators for Wolcott and 24 against him. The main reason for rejection was doubt about his competence.

Four nominees have been voted down by the Senate during the period from 1900 to 1993: John Parker, nominated by President Herbert Hoover in 1930 (by a vote of 39 to 41); Clement Haynsworth, nominated by President Richard Nixon in 1969 (by a vote of 45 to 55); G. Harrold Carswell in 1970, nominated by Nixon (by a vote of 45 to 51); and Robert H. Bork, nominated by President Ronald Reagan in 1987 (by a vote of 42 to 58).

Both John Parker and Robert Bork were defeated because important interest groups opposed them. Parker, for example, was defeated by two votes in the Senate because of pressure exerted by labor unions, whose leaders believed him to be opposed to more federal regulation of businesses to improve wages and working conditions. Bork's defeat in the Senate was influenced by civil rights and feminist groups, who disliked his conservative ideas about a woman's right to an abortion and government programs to advance opportunities of minorities and women. Furthermore, some senators opposed Bork because they disagreed with his conservative legal philosophy, which emphasized judicial restraint and a strict construction of the Constitution. For example, Bork could find no justification in the Constitution for the Court's decision in *Roe* v. *Wade* (1973), which affirmed a woman's right to an abortion during a certain period of pregnancy. He believed that the issue of abortion rights should be decided by state legislatures, not by the federal judiciary. Despite disagreements with his legal and political ideas, most of Robert Bork's opponents respected the high quality of his intellect, legal work, and personal integrity.

By contrast, President Nixon's nomination of Clement Haynsworth in 1969 failed largely because most senators had doubts about his competence and character. The Senate also rejected Nixon's nomination of G. Harrold Carswell the following year because of doubts about Judge Carswell's ability to do the job.

In general, reasons for the Senate's rejection of the President's nominees to the Court have included political opposition to the President making the nomination, rather than strong dislike of the nominee; disagreement with the nominee's views on controversial public issues; lack of confidence in the nominee's

REJECTION OR WITHDRAWAL OF SUPREME COURT NOMINATIONS

NOMINEE	YEAR	NOMINATED BY	ACTION
John Rutledge	1795	George Washington	Withdrawn
Alexander Wolcott	1811	James Madison	Rejected
John Crittenden	1828	John Quincy Adams	None
Roger B. Taney*	1835	Andrew Jackson	None
John Spencer	1844	John Tyler	Rejected
Reuben Walworth	1844	John Tyler	Withdrawn
Edward King	1844	John Tyler	None
Edward King	1845	John Tyler	Withdrawn
John Read	1845	John Tyler	None
George Woodward	1845	James K. Polk	Rejected
Edward Bradford	1852	Millard Fillmore	None
George Badger	1853	Millard Fillmore	None
William Micou	1853	Millard Fillmore	None
Jeremiah Black	1861	James Buchanan	Rejected
Henry Stanbery	1866	Andrew Johnson	None
Ebenezer Hoar	1869	Ulysses S. Grant	Rejected
George Williams	1873	Ulysses S. Grant	Withdrawn
Caleb Cushing	1874	Ulysses S. Grant	Withdrawn
Stanley Matthews*	1881	Rutherford B. Hayes	None
William Hornblower	1893	Grover Cleveland	Rejected
Wheeler Peckham	1894	Grover Cleveland	Rejected
John Parker	1930	Herbert C. Hoover	Rejected
Abe Fortas*	1968	Lyndon B. Johnson	Withdrawn
Homer Thornberry	1968	Lyndon B. Johnson	None
Clement Haynsworth	1969	Richard M. Nixon	Rejected
G. Harrold Carswell	1970	Richard M. Nixon	Rejected
Robert Bork	1987	Ronald Reagan	Rejected
Douglas Ginsburg	1987	Ronald Reagan	Withdrawn

*Roger Taney was nominated twice, the second time for the office of chief justice, and was confirmed. Stanley Matthews was nominated a second time and confirmed. Abe Fortas was a sitting justice when President Johnson nominated him for the office of chief justice; a controversy ensued, leading to withdrawal of the nomination and the resignation of Fortas from the Supreme Court.

qualifications; doubts about the judicial ethics or the personal morality of the nominee; and strong opposition to the nominee by large or influential special interest groups.

SEE ALSO

Appointment of justices; Senate Judiciary Committee

FURTHER READING

Abraham, Henry J. *Justices and Presidents: A Political History of Appointments to the Supreme Court*. New York: Oxford, 1992.

Religious issues under the Constitution

THE 1ST AMENDMENT to the U.S. Constitution requires that "Congress shall make no law respecting an establishment of religion, or prohibiting the free exercise thereof." There are two parts to this constitutional provision about religion: the establishment clause and the free exercise clause.

Establishment clause

Americans have always agreed that the establishment clause bans government actions establishing or promoting an official religion. Americans have argued vehemently, however, about whether the establishment clause strictly prohibits all government involvement in support of religion.

Thomas Jefferson wrote in 1802 that the intent of the 1st Amendment was to build "a wall of separation between church and state." Justice Hugo Black agreed with Jefferson in writing for the Court in *Everson* v. *Board of Education of Ewing Township* (1947), the case that began the ongoing contemporary debate about the meaning of the establishment clause. Justice Black wrote that neither federal nor state governments can act to "aid one religion, aid all religions, or prefer one religion over another." The *Everson* decision was the first time the Court applied the 1st Amendment's establishment clause to the states through the due process clause of the 14th Amendment.

Justice Black, like Thomas Jefferson, held an *absolutist* position on the meaning of the establishment clause. Absolutists argue for complete separation of government from religious activity. According to the absolutists, religious activity should be carried out solely in the private sphere of society, free of both government interference and government support.

Since the earliest years of the republic, many Americans have disagreed with the absolutist position on church-state relations. For example, Justice William O. Douglas, writing for the Court in *Zorach* v. *Clauson* (1952), argued that the 1st Amendment "does not say that in every and all respect there shall be a separation of church and state." In *Zorach,* the Court approved a program whereby public school students could be released during school hours to receive religious instruction, but not within the public school facilities. The *Zorach* decision was the first in which the Court accommodated a relationship between church and state in a nonpreferential and voluntary program of religious education. However, *Zorach* was a very small breach in the "wall of separation" supported by the *Everson* case and later Court rulings.

Since the *Everson* decision in 1947, the Court has for the most part rejected the nonpreferentialist interpretation of the establishment clause, in which minimal government support of religion is permitted as long as it does not give preference to a particular religious denomination. Other key cases supporting strict

In this cartoon, the Supreme Court tries to balance the scales of justice with a Bible on one side and the Constitution on the other. The separation between church and state is an essential part of the Constitution.

separation of church and state are *Engel* v. *Vitale* (1962), *Abington School District* v. *Schempp* (1963), and *Wallace* v. *Jaffree* (1985). With these decisions, the Court has overturned state laws that require or sanction prayer and Bible-reading activities in public schools. These prohibitions apply even when the prayers or religious activities at issue are nondenominational, nonpreferential, and voluntary.

In *Lee* v. *Weisman* (1992) the Court prohibited prayers as part of a public school's formal graduation ceremony. A major factor in the case was the direction of the ceremony by school officials. The Court stressed that under the establishment clause, public authorities are forbidden to sanction even nondenominational or supposedly voluntary prayers. Finally, in this case, as in others of its type, the Court emphasized the importance of protecting the rights of individuals in the minority against the control or coercion of majority rule and peer pressure. However, students remain free to organize, on their own and without school support, voluntary religious programs associated with graduation from school. In 1993 the Supreme Court let stand, without comment, a decision of the U.S. Court of Appeals for the Fifth Circuit that upheld a Texas public school district's policy of permitting stu-

dents to lead voluntary prayers at graduation ceremonies.

In 1985 Justice William Rehnquist expressed strong opposition to the absolutist position developed by the Court since the *Everson* decision. In his dissent in *Wallace* v. *Jaffree*, Rehnquist wrote, "The establishment clause did not require government neutrality between religion and irreligion nor did it prohibit the federal government from providing non-discriminatory aid to religions."

Justice Rehnquist and others support a position referred to as *nonpreferentialist*. The position rejects Jefferson's "wall of separation" viewpoint. Non-preferentialists assert that government should be able to aid religious activity, as long as the support would be provided equally to all religions. That is, no religious denomination would be favored or preferred over others.

The Lemon Test, developed by the Court in *Lemon* v. *Kurtzman* (1971), was an attempt to accommodate some modest relationships between church and state. The test involves three standards for deciding whether federal or state aid to religious schools or programs is constitutional. The Lemon Test says that a statute does not violate the establishment clause if its purpose is secular or nonreligious, if it neither promotes nor restricts religion in its primary effects, and if it does not bring about excessive government entanglement with religion.

During the 1980s the Supreme Court moved slightly in the direction of accommodation between church and state. In *Marsh* v. *Chambers* (1983), the Court held that the Nebraska legislature could begin its sessions with prayers led by a paid chaplain. In *Lynch* v. *Donnelly* (1984) the Court upheld the placing of a crèche, a Christian nativity scene, at public expense on public property in front of a city hall at Christmastime. The display, the Court held, was permissible because it was within the context of a larger exhibit that emphasized secular or nonreligious objects, such as a Santa Claus, reindeers, and talking wishing wells. However, in *Allegheny County* v. *American Civil Liberties Union, Greater Pittsburgh Chapter* (1989), the Court ruled that an exclusively religious exhibit, a Jewish menorah and a crèche, could not be displayed in a government building because this kind of religious exhibit violated the establishment clause.

Another move toward accommodation of church and state was made by the Court in *Zobrest* v. *Catalina School District* (1993). The Court ruled that a deaf student at a private parochial school (run by the Catholic church) could be assisted by a publicly funded sign-language interpreter. This kind of aid helps the student, not the Church, said the Court. It therefore does not violate the 1st Amendment's establishment clause.

Free exercise clause

The free exercise clause of the 1st Amendment has not provoked as much controversy as the establishment clause. This clause clearly indicates that government must neither interfere with religious practices of individuals nor prescribe their religious beliefs. From the founding era of the United States until today, most Americans have heartily agreed that individuals have the right to freely express their religious beliefs in the private sphere of society.

The Court has protected the free-exercise rights of religious minorities since the 1940s. In *Cantwell* v. *Connecticut* (1940) the free exercise clause was for the first time "incorporated" by the Court under the due process clause of the 14th Amendment and applied to state governments. The outcome was the protection of the right of Jehovah's Witnesses, a minority religion, to peacefully distribute religious information to people

in their neighborhoods with the aim of winning converts.

In *West Virginia State Board of Education* v. *Barnette* (1943) the Court struck down a state flag-salute law because it forced some students, who were Jehovah's Witnesses, to violate their religious beliefs. Writing for the Court, Justice Robert Jackson emphasized that the individual's right to free exercise of religion was placed by the 1st Amendment "beyond the reach of majorities and officials." He emphasized that it was the Court's responsibility to protect this constitutional right of individuals against the power of majority rule, whenever the majority, acting through representatives in government, might try to deny that right to unpopular minority groups.

Like freedom of speech, the individual's free exercise of religion is not absolute. The Court has ruled that in some instances religious expression may be limited on behalf of the public good.

In *Reynolds* v. *United States* (1879), for example, the Supreme Court upheld a federal law against the practice of polygamy—having multiple spouses—in federal territories. The Court ruled that the anti-polygamy law did not violate the right to free exercise of religion of a member of the Church of Jesus Christ of Latter-Day Saints (Mormons), who claimed it was his religious obligation to

Jehovah's Witnesses gather for a convention in 1950 in New York City. The 1st Amendment guarantees that citizens will not be prohibited from practicing the religion of their choice.

have more than one wife. Writing for the Court, Chief Justice Morrison Waite argued that the federal law prohibiting polygamy, even when practiced for religious reasons, was necessary for the good of the community. He wrote, "Suppose one believed that human sacrifices were a necessary part of religious worship, would it be seriously contended that the civil government [could] not interfere to prevent a sacrifice?"

In order to restrict an individual's free exercise of religion, the government must demonstrate a compelling public interest as its reason. Thus, in *Sherbert* v. *Verner* (1963), the Court ruled that a state could not refuse unemployment compensation benefits to a worker who would not make herself available for employment on Saturday because this was the special day of worship of her religion (she was a Seventh-Day Adventist). An entitlement such as state unemployment benefits cannot be denied to someone because of her religious practices.

By contrast, in *Employment Division, Department of Human Resources of Oregon* v. *Smith* (1990), the Court ruled against state employees who were denied unemployment benefits after being dismissed from their jobs for religion-related reasons. The employees, who were Native Americans, practiced a religion with rituals involving the smoking of peyote, an illegal substance under state law. Because they were dismissed for violating a state law, the Court upheld the state's denial of unemployment compensation. Writing for the Court, Justice Antonin Scalia argued that "the right of free exercise does not relieve an individual of the obligation to comply with a valid and neutral law of general applicability."

In 1993, however, the Court struck down a city ordinance that banned ritual animal sacrifice by a religious group. The Court held in *Church of the Lukumi Babalu Aye* v. *City of Hialeah* (1993) that the ordinance violated the 1st Amendment's free exercise clause because it suppressed, without a compelling argument on behalf of the public good, a religious ceremony fundamental to members of a church.

Continuing controversy

The fiercest arguments today about religion-related constitutional rights pertain to the establishment clause, not the free exercise clause. The absolutists and the nonpreferentialists strongly disagree about such issues as state-sponsored prayer in schools and neutral or nonpreferential support for religious practices in public places or with public funds. Public opinion polls have revealed more than 70 percent of Americans to be against the absolutist, or strict separation, position. However, a slim majority of the Court has continued to favor an interpretation of the establishment clause that maintains strict separation of church and state.

The primary author of the 1st Amendment, James Madison, expressed clear and strong views on the subject of religious establishment and liberty in his "Memorial and Remonstrance Against Religious Assessments" (1785). Madison wrote, "We maintain therefore that in matters of Religion, no man's right is abridged by the institution of Civil Society, and that Religion is wholly exempt from its cognizance.… [And] if religion be exempt from the authority of the Society at large, still less can it be subject to that of the Legislative Body." Madison used this essay to defeat a bill in the Virginia legislature to provide financial support for religion on a nonpreferential basis. The argument between separationists and nonpreferentialists, however, had just begun. This burning issue about religious liberty and church-state connections, raised in 1785, is still with us today.

SEE ALSO

Abington School District v. Schempp; Engel v. Vitale; Establishment clause; Everson v. Board of Education of Ewing Township; Free exercise clause; Lemon Test; Lemon v. Kurtzman; Wallace v. Jaffree; West Virginia State Board of Education v. Barnette; Zorach v. Clauson

FURTHER READING

Alley, Robert S., ed. *James Madison on Religious Liberty*. Buffalo, N.Y.: Prometheus Books, 1985.

Alley, Robert S., ed. *The Supreme Court on Church and State*. New York: Oxford, 1988.

Curry, Thomas J. *The First Freedoms: Church and State in America to the Passage of the First Amendment*. New York: Oxford, 1986.

Levy, Leonard W. *The Establishment Clause: Religion and the First Amendment*. New York: Macmillan, 1986.

Miller, William Lee. *The First Liberty: Religion and the American Republic*. New York: Paragon House, 1985.

Urofsky, Melvin I. "The Religion Clauses." In *By and for the People: Constitutional Rights in American History*, edited by Kermit L. Hall. Arlington Heights, Ill.: Harlan Davidson, 1991.

Reporter of decisions

IN 1816 Congress officially created the office of reporter of decisions of the Supreme Court. The reporter, with a staff of nine, records and edits all the Court's case decisions. Since 1955 audio tapes have been made of oral arguments before the Court. These recordings are stored at the National Archives. The reporter oversees the process of printing and publishing the record of the Court's decisions in *United States Reports*, the official publication of the Court's decisions.

The reporter also supervises the printing of a headnote for each decision of the Court. The headnote is a summary of the case that includes background facts, the legal reasoning used in the decision, and the voting record of the justices on the case. The headnote also tells whether the lower court's ruling has been affirmed or overturned by the Supreme Court's decision. Each headnote contains this statement: "The syllabus [headnote] constitutes no part of the opinion of the Court but has been prepared by the Reporter of Decisions for the convenience of the reader."

The first reporter of decisions was Alexander Dallas, who served unofficially on the job from 1790 to 1800. He was self-appointed, but the Court gave its approval to his work. He was not paid by the federal government, but he tried to make a profit through sales of his published reports. William Cranch, the second reporter, also worked unofficially at this job from 1801 to 1815. Henry Wheaton, who served from 1816 to 1827, was the first official reporter of the Supreme Court. The early reporters of decisions did their work laboriously by hand. Today, the reporter and his staff use audiotape and recorders, photocopy machines, and high-speed computers and printers to process information and produce the formal record of the Court's work.

SEE ALSO

Staff of the Court, nonjudicial; United States Reports

Republicanism

REPUBLICANISM IS the belief in the worth of a republic, a type of government that is based on the consent of the governed and is conducted by elected representatives of the people. In a republican government, the people are sovereign, or supreme, because their representatives serve at their pleasure for the common good. Today, people tend to use the terms *republic* and *representative democracy* interchangeably. In contrast to a republic, a *pure* or *direct democracy* is a form of government in which the people govern directly—in a town meeting, for example—instead of through representatives whom they elect.

In *The Federalist* No. 39, James Madison presented the idea of republicanism that is embodied in the U.S. Constitution:

> What, then, are the distinctive characters of the republican form?…
>
> If we resort for a criterion…we may define a republic to be…a government which derives all its powers directly or indirectly from the great body of the people, and is administered by persons holding their offices during pleasure for a limited period, or during good behavior. It is essential to such a government that it be derived from the great body of the society, not from an inconsiderable proportion or a favored class of it.… It is *sufficient* for such a government that the persons administering it be appointed, either directly or indirectly, by the people; and that they hold their appointments by either of the tenures just specified.

In the world of the 1780s, the republican form of government was rare; monarchies and aristocracies prevailed. These non-republican forms of government function without representation of or participation by the common people. In an absolute monarchy, the monarch (the king or queen or both) rules; and in an aristocracy, a small elite group of aristocrats or nobles exercises power in government. Power usually is based on heredity in a monarchy or aristocracy; titles are passed from father to children (usually sons).

Americans in the 1780s were committed to republicanism, rather than a monarchy, aristocracy, or other non-republican form of government. They agreed that the rights and liberty of individuals could best be secured through a republican form of government. As a result, they built republicanism into the U.S. Constitution. Article 4, Section 4, says, "The United States [federal government] shall guarantee to every State in this Union a Republican Form of Government."

SEE ALSO

Constitutional democracy; Constitutionalism; Liberty under the Constitution

FURTHER READING

Rahe, Paul. *Republics Ancient and Modern.* Chapel Hill: University of North Carolina Press, 1992.

Reversals of Supreme Court decisions

THE SUPREME COURT has the last word, within the American judicial system, on questions of constitutional interpretation. However, a Supreme Court decision regarding interpretation of the Constitution can be overturned by a constitutional amendment. A Court decision on interpretation of federal laws can be overturned by Congressional enactment of a new law.

Reversals by Constitutional amendment

The people, through their representatives in government, can use Article 5 of the Constitution to overturn the Court's decisions. Article 5 provides that constitutional amendments can be proposed by a two-thirds vote of the members of each house of Congress or by a special convention that Congress calls after two-thirds of the state legislatures have voted to request it. For a proposed amendment to be ratified, three-fourths of the states

A black school in 1904. Although the Court decided in Plessy v. Ferguson *that racially segregated public facilities were legal,* Brown v. Board of Education *reversed that decision and demanded full integration of public schools.*

must approve it, either by their legislatures or by conventions especially convened for this purpose. To date, all amendments have been proposed by Congress, and all but one (the 21st) have been ratified by state legislatures. The 21st Amendment was ratified by state conventions.

Of the 27 amendments to the Constitution, 4 clearly were enacted to overturn unpopular Supreme Court decisions. The 11th Amendment overturned *Chisholm* v. *Georgia* (1793) by guaranteeing the immunity of states from lawsuits by citizens of another state or a foreign country. The 14th Amendment nullified *Scott* v. *Sandford* (1857) by guaranteeing the civil rights and citizenship of African Americans. The 16th Amendment overrode *Pollock* v. *Farmers' Loan and Trust Co.* (1895) by giving Congress the power to levy an income tax. The 26th Amendment negated *Oregon* v. *Mitchell* (1970) by permitting 18-year-olds to vote in state elections. Many other attempts to enact constitutional amendments to override Supreme Court decisions have failed.

Reversals of Court decisions by Congress

Congress has a rather simple and direct way to negate unpopular decisions of the Court that have nullified federal statutes: It can pass a new law. For example, Congress passed the Civil Rights Act of 1991 to overturn the Court's decision in *Ward's Cove Packing Company* v. *Atonio* (1989). In *Ward's Cove*, the Court decided that an individual proving discrimination by an employer could still be dismissed or demoted from a desired job as long as the employer could prove that the discriminating practice was necessary to maintain his business. The Civil Rights Act of 1991 makes it illegal for an employer to claim "business necessity" as a reason for intentional job discrimi-

nation against an individual based on race, color, ethnic origin, and gender.

Although most bills that have been introduced to overturn Supreme Court decisions have *not* been passed, the power of Congress to negate certain kinds of Court decisions is an important part of the American constitutional system of separation of powers and checks and balances.

S E E A L S O
Amendments to the Constitution; Precedent; Separation of powers

---

Reynolds v. Sims

☆ 377 U.S. 533 (1964)
☆ *Vote: 8–1*
☆ *For the Court: Warren*
☆ *Concurring: Stewart and Clark*
☆ *Dissenting: Harlan*

BY THE EARLY 1920s the distribution of the U.S. population had clearly changed since the 19th century. For the first time, more Americans were living in cities than in rural areas. This change created inequities between the populations of urban and rural state legislative districts.

By 1960 nearly every state had some urban legislative districts populated by at least twice as many people as rural districts in the state. In Alabama, for example, the smallest congressional district had a population of 6,700 and the largest had a population of 104,000. In a representative democracy people's votes possess equal value only when each member of a legislative body represents the same number of people. Clearly, the people in more populous urban districts and the people in less populous rural districts were not represented equally. As a result, city and suburban problems did not receive appropriate attention in state

Birmingham, Alabama, in 1963. In Reynolds v. Sims, *the Supreme Court ruled that Alabama had to reapportion its legislative districts so that people living in urban areas had the same representation as rural voters.*

legislatures dominated by representatives from farming and rural districts.

The domination by rural interests also meant that state legislatures refused to redistrict to ensure that each member of the legislature would represent roughly the same number of people. Some simply ignored sections in their state constitutions requiring redistricting every 10 years. Others merely redistricted in ways that continued to favor rural interests. There was little voters could do to change things through the ballot box.

During the 1960s the Supreme Court heard a series of cases challenging the apportionment (distribution) of state legislative districts. In *Reynolds* v. *Sims,* voters in Jefferson County, Alabama, claimed that the unequal representation of citizens in Alabama districts violated the equal protection clause of the 14th Amendment.

The Issue The 14th Amendment declares: "No state…shall deny to any person within its jurisdiction the equal protection of the laws." Did Alabama and other states violate the equal protection rights of voters by setting up legislative districts that contained unequal numbers of people?

Opinion of the Court The Supreme Court ruled that the 14th Amendment required states to establish equally populated electoral districts for both houses of state legislatures. Chief Justice Earl Warren declared that plans for setting up legislative districts could not discriminate

against people on the basis of where they live (city versus country, in this case) any more than they could on the basis of race or economic status.

The Court rejected the idea that state legislatures, like Congress, could create senate districts on the basis of area rather than population. The Constitution, which allotted equal representation to states in the U.S. Senate no matter what their size, recognized the states as "sovereign entities." Political subdivisions within a state (such as counties or regions), however, did not possess the status of sovereign entities. Thus, Warren argued, the people of a state must benefit from equal representation in *both* houses of a state legislature. "Legislators represent people, not trees or acres," Warren declared.

The Court ruled that state legislatures did not have to draw legislative districts with "mathematical exactness or precision." However, such districts did have to be based "substantially" on equal population. The Court thus established the key principle of "one person, one vote."

Dissent Justice John Marshall Harlan argued that this case did not pertain to violation of constitutional rights. Rather, he said, it involved a political question that should be decided by elected representatives of the people, not by the Court.

Significance The *Reynolds* decision had a major impact on state legislatures. After the decision, 49 state legislatures reapportioned their legislative districts on the basis of equal population. Oregon had already done so in 1961. The decision caused a fundamental shift in American politics by declaring unconstitutional the practices that enabled rural minorities to control state legislatures. The decision also affected national politics because state legislatures draw the lines for U.S. congressional districts.

FURTHER READING
Cortner, Richard C. *The Apportionment Cases.* Knoxville: University of Tennessee Press, 1970.

Rights of the accused

A PRIMARY PURPOSE of government is to enforce law and order. The federal and state constitutions of the United States, for example, grant certain powers to government officials so they can maintain an orderly society and protect the lives, property, and rights of the people. Federal and state government officials have the duty of preventing some individuals from harming others through criminal acts such as theft, assault, rape, and murder. Nevertheless, criminal behavior has become a serious threat to many American communities where violence, theft, and illegal drug use are rampant. Most Americans, therefore, want law enforcement officials to be tough on criminals, to apprehend and punish them.

There are, however, constitutional limits on the power of government officials in order to prevent them from abusing the rights of individuals, including those accused of criminal behavior. From colonial times until the present, Americans have believed in an old English saying: "It is better for 99 guilty persons to go free than for one innocent person to be punished." In the United States, a person accused of a crime is presumed innocent until proved guilty. The burden of proving the suspect guilty is upon the government prosecutors.

Americans want their federal and state governments to be both powerful and limited, so that freedom and order are balanced. On the one side, government officials should have enough power to keep order so that people are safe and secure. On the other side, the power of government officials to enforce law and order should be sufficiently limited so that they cannot oppress anyone.

Constitutional rights of the accused

The U.S. Constitution, especially the Bill of Rights (Amendments 1 to 10), protects individuals from wrong or unjust accusations and punishments by law enforcement officials.

Amendment 4 protects individuals against unreasonable and unwarranted searches and seizures of their property. It establishes conditions for the lawful issuing and use of search warrants by government officials in order to protect the right of individuals to security "in their persons, houses, papers and effects." There must be a "probable cause" for issuing a warrant to authorize a search or arrest, and the place to be searched, the objects sought, and the person to be arrested must be precisely described.

Amendment 5 states certain legal and procedural rights of individuals. For example, the government may not act against an individual in the following ways:

• Hold an individual to answer for a serious crime unless the prosecution presents appropriate evidence to a grand jury that indicates the likely guilt of the individual.

• Try an individual more than once for the same offense.

• Force an individual to act as a witness against himself in a criminal case.

• Deprive an individual of life, liberty or property without due process of law (fair and proper legal proceedings).

Amendment 6 guarantees people suspected or accused of a crime certain protections against the power of government. It provides these rights to individuals:

• A speedy public trial before an unbiased jury picked from the state and community in which the crime was committed.

• Information about what the individual has been accused of and why the accusation has been made.

• A meeting with witnesses offering testimony against the individual.

• Means of obtaining favorable witnesses, including the right to subpoena, or legally compel, witnesses to testify in court.

• Help from a lawyer.

Amendment 8 protects individuals from overly harsh punishments and excessive fines and bail (the amount of money required to secure a person's release from custody while awaiting trial).

Amendment 14 provides general protection for the rights of the accused against the powers of state governments. This amendment forbids state governments from making and enforcing laws that will deprive any individual of life, liberty, or property "without due process of law"; it also says that a state government may not deny to any person under its authority "the equal protection of the laws."

The U.S. Constitution includes other protections of individual rights that are not in the Bill of Rights or subsequent amendments. For example, Article 1, Section 9, prohibits government from suspending the privilege of the writ of habeas corpus. A writ of habeas corpus requires officials to bring a person whom they have arrested and held in custody before a judge in a court of law. The officials must convince the judge that there are lawful reasons for holding the person. If the judge finds their reasons unlawful, then the court frees the suspect. Thus, the writ of habeas corpus protects individuals from government officials who might want to jail them arbitrarily—because they belong to unpopular groups or express criticisms of the government, for instance.

Article 1, Section 9, also prohibits enactment by the federal government of bills of attainder and ex post facto laws.

A bill of attainder is a law that punishes an individual solely by means of legislation, without a trial or fair hearing in a court of law. An ex post facto (literally, "after the fact") law makes an action a crime after it was committed.

Article 1, Section 10, prohibits state governments from enacting bills of attainder and ex post facto laws.

Article 3, Section 2, provides individuals accused of a crime the right to trial by jury.

Article 3, Section 3, protects individuals against arbitrary accusations of treason—an attempt to overthrow the government or to give aid and support to enemies of the United States, such as countries waging war against it. This article also establishes rigorous standards for convicting a person of treason.

The Constitution guarantees specific rights, such as the right to a speedy trial, to those accused of crimes in order to prevent the abuse of power by officials.

Sources of rights of the accused

American ideas about the rights of the accused—criminal defendants—can be traced to the great English documents of liberty, such as the Magna Carta (1215), the Petition of Right (1628), and the English Bill of Rights (1689). These documents embodied the principles of limited government and the rule of law, which all were bound to obey, even the king. For example, Section 39 of the Magna Carta said that no "freeman" could be put in prison except "by the lawful judgment of peers or the law of the land." This was the beginning of due process of law and rights for individuals accused of crimes. These ideas were developed in England and brought to the North American colonies in the 1600s.

American colonists expanded their English legal heritage to provide new and higher levels of protection for the rights of the accused. The Massachusetts Body of Liberties (1641), for example, established many provisions that appeared later in the federal Bill of Rights, such as the rights to trial by jury, to challenge jurors, to have assistance of counsel, to know the charges of criminal behavior, to reasonable bail, and to protection against cruel or unusual punishment.

By the time of the American Revolution, legal protections for those accused of crimes were a generally accepted part of government. The Declaration of Independence (1776) accused the British king of, among other charges, violating the due process rights of Americans, such as "depriving us, in many cases, of the Benefits of Trial by Jury."

The new constitutions of the first 13 states of the United States, written between 1776 and 1783, included ample provisions for the rights of the accused. These state constitutions reflected an American consensus about the general importance of due process of law in criminal proceedings and about specific protections for the rights of accused persons. The rights of the accused expressed in the U.S. Constitution (1787) and Bill of Rights (1791) were drawn from the provisions in the original 13 state constitutions.

Rights of the accused under Constitutional law

Throughout most of U.S. history, the federal Bill of Rights had little impact on individuals accused of crimes. Most criminal cases in the American federal system were (and will be) within the jurisdiction of state governments. And the U.S. Supreme Court ruled in *Barron* v. *Baltimore* (1833) that the federal Bill of Rights restrained only the federal government. As a result, the rights of the accused guaranteed by Amendments 4, 5, 6, and 8 of the U.S. Constitution were not applicable to law enforcement activities of state governments. Most defen-

dants, therefore, could look only to their state constitutions and bills of rights for legal protection against police power.

The 14th Amendment, ratified in 1868, appeared to impose certain legal restrictions on the states in criminal proceedings. This amendment stated, "No state shall…deprive any person of life, liberty, or property, without due process of law, nor deny to any person within its jurisdiction the equal protection of the laws."

In *Hurtado* v. *California* (1884), the U.S. Supreme Court faced the question of whether the due process clause of the 14th Amendment required a state government to provide the 5th amendment guarantee of a grand jury indictment in criminal proceedings. The Court ruled that the 14th Amendment did not incorporate, or include, any part of the 5th Amendment and thereby make it binding on state governments. *Hurtado,* like *Barron* v. *Baltimore,* implied that the federal Bill of Rights could be used only to limit the federal government.

Justice John Marshall Harlan dissented from the Court's opinion in *Hurtado* v. *California.* He argued that the intent of the 14th Amendment was "to impose upon the States the same restrictions, in respect of proceedings involving life, liberty, and property, which had been imposed upon the general government." Harlan concluded that the rights of the accused in the federal Bill of Rights could be applied to the states through the 14th Amendment's due process clause.

Justice Harlan's dissent in *Hurtado* prevailed in the long run. In *Powell* v. *Alabama* (1932) the U.S. Supreme Court ruled that the due process clause of the 14th Amendment required assistance of a lawyer for defendants charged in a state court with a crime punishable by death. In *Cole* v. *Arkansas* (1947) the Court used the 14th Amendment's due process clause to apply to a state the 6th Amendment's requirement of notice of accusation to a defendant. And in *In re Oliver* (1948), the 6th Amendment requirement of a public trial was imposed upon the states through the 14th Amendment. Further, in *Wolf* v. *Colorado* (1949), the Court incorporated the 4th Amendment's protections against unreasonable searches and seizures into the 14th Amendment.

The Supreme Court's case-by-case application of the rights of the accused listed in the federal Bill of Rights to the states moved ahead dramatically during the 1960s. This rapid change, often called a "due process revolution," took place under the leadership of Chief Justice Earl Warren. The following cases applied virtually all of the 4th, 5th, 6th, and 8th Amendment rights of the accused to the states through the due process clause of the 14th Amendment:

• *Mapp* v. *Ohio* (1961): Evidence obtained in violation of 4th Amendment rights must be excluded from the state's prosecution of criminal defendants.

• *Robinson* v. *California* (1962): State governments cannot use cruel and unusual punishments in violation of the 8th Amendment.

• *Gideon* v. *Wainwright* (1963): The 6th Amendment right to counsel must be provided to all defendants.

• *Malloy* v. *Hogan* (1964): Defendants in state courts have the 5th Amendment right of protection against self-incrimination.

• *Pointer* v. *Texas* (1965): States must observe the 6th Amendment right of defendants to confront witnesses against them.

• *Parker* v. *Gladden* (1966): Defendants in state courts have the 6th Amendment right to an impartial jury.

• *Miranda* v. *Arizona* (1966): Police are required to advise suspects of their 5th Amendment right of protection against self-incrimination and 6th Amendment right to an attorney.

• *Klopfer* v. *North Carolina* (1967): Defendants in state courts have the 6th Amendment right to a speedy trial.

• *Washington* v. *Texas* (1967): Defendants in state courts have the 6th Amendment right to subpoena witnesses to testify in their favor.

• *Duncan* v. *Louisiana* (1968): States must guarantee the defendant's 6th Amendment right to a jury trial in criminal cases.

• *Benton* v. *Maryland* (1969): State law enforcers cannot subject a person to double jeopardy; that is, they cannot deprive individuals of their 5th Amendment right not to be tried twice for the same crime.

Controversies about rights of the accused

The Warren Court's due process revolution nationalized the rights of the accused in the federal Bill of Rights; that is, people accused of crimes anywhere in the United States could expect the same legal protections.

Many Americans hailed the due process revolution. Others, however, criticized it for caring too much for the rights of accused criminals and too little for the victims of crime and the law-abiding majority of the people. The critics claimed that such decisions as *Mapp, Malloy,* and *Miranda* restricted police too much and made it too easy for criminals to evade punishment.

During his 1968 Presidential campaign, Richard Nixon sided with the critics when he said, "Let us always respect, as I do, our courts and those who serve on them, but let us also recognize that some of our courts have gone too far in weakening the peace forces as against the criminal forces in this country." After winning the Presidency, Nixon appointed a new chief justice, Warren

Burger, who agreed with him about issues of law, order, and the rights of the accused. From 1970 to 1971 President Nixon appointed three more justices: Harry Blackmun, Lewis Powell, and William Rehnquist. Later, Presidents Ronald Reagan and George Bush also expressed strong concern for the rights of crime victims and criticized the overemphasis on the rights of criminal suspects.

Despite high-level objections to some aspects of the due process revolution of the Warren Court, none of the Court's rulings on the rights of the accused has been overruled. Only minor modifications have been made in the *Mapp* and *Miranda* decisions about certain 4th and 5th Amendment rights. In *New York* v. *Quarles* (1984), the Court decided that police officers could, in order to protect themselves against harm, question a suspect about possession of weapons before advising the suspect of his Miranda rights to remain silent and obtain counsel. In *United States* v. *Leon* (1984) the Court adopted a "good faith exception" to the exclusionary rule established by the *Mapp* decision. This means that evidence obtained illegally may be used to prosecute a defendant if the police who obtained it thought they were acting legally at the time.

In a free society, there will always be arguments about the proper balance between liberty and order, between the rights of criminal suspects and the public's need for safety and security against crime. The exact meaning and practical applications of due process of law will continue to be debated in public forums and courts of law. Such constructive controversies are signs of a healthy constitutional democracy.

SEE ALSO

Benton v. Maryland; Bill of Rights; Counsel, right to; Double jeopardy; Due process of law; Duncan v. Louisiana; Exclusionary rule; Gideon v. Wainwright; Grand jury; Habeas corpus, writ of; Incorporation doctrine; Juvenile justice; Mapp v. Ohio; Miranda v. Arizona; Powell v. Alabama; Searches and seizures; Trial by jury; United States v. Leon; Wolf v. Colorado

FURTHER READING

Bodenhamer, David J. *Fair Trial: Rights of the Accused in American History*. New York: Oxford, 1992.
Bodenhamer, David J. "Trial Rights of the Accused." In *By and for the People: Constitutional Rights in American History*, edited by Kermit L. Hall. Arlington Heights, Ill.: Harlan Davidson, 1991.
Bodenhamer, David J., and James W. Ely, Jr. *The Bill of Rights in Modern America after Two Hundred Years*. Bloomington: Indiana University Press, 1993.
Graham, Fred. *The Due Process Revolution: The Warren Court's Impact on Criminal Law*. New York: Hayden, 1970.
Walker, Samuel. *Popular Justice: A History of American Criminal Law*. New York: Oxford, 1980.
Walker, Samuel. "Rights Before Trial." In *By and for the People: Constitutional Rights in American History*, edited by Kermit L. Hall. Arlington Heights, Ill.: Harlan Davidson, 1991.

Roberts, Owen J.

ASSOCIATE JUSTICE, 1930–1945

☆ *Born: May 2, 1875, Germantown, Pa.*
☆ *Education: University of Pennsylvania, A.B., 1895, LL.B., 1898*
☆ *Previous government service: special deputy attorney general, Eastern District of Pennsylvania, 1918; special U.S. attorney, 1924–30*
☆ *Appointed by President Herbert Hoover May 9, 1930; replaced Justice Edward Terry Sanford, who died*
☆ *Supreme Court term: confirmed by the Senate May 20, 1930, by a voice vote; resigned July 31, 1945*
☆ *Died: May 17, 1955, West Vincent Township, Pa.*

OWEN J. ROBERTS served on the Supreme Court during an era of crisis and controversy, which included the Great Depression and World War II. He initially participated with the Court's majority in opposing President Franklin Roosevelt's New Deal programs. Later, he switched his position to join the Court's majority in favor of New Deal programs and laws. His change in position seemed to reflect a great change in popular opinion signaled by President Roosevelt's landslide victory in the 1936 election.

Justice Roberts's most notable Supreme Court opinion came in dissent in *Korematsu* v. *United States* (1944). The Court upheld the compulsory movement of Japanese Americans during World War II to internment centers because they were viewed as a threat to national security following Japan's attack on Pearl Harbor in Hawaii. Roberts, however, disagreed and wrote: "[This] is the case of convicting a citizen as a punishment for not submitting to imprisonment in a concentration camp, based on his ancestry . . . without evidence or inquiry concerning his loyalty and good disposition towards the United States. . . . I need hardly labor the conclusion that constitutional rights have been violated." Justice Roberts's dissent in the *Korematsu* case is viewed by most Americans today as the correct opinion.

SEE ALSO
Korematsu v. United States

Robing room

BEFORE EACH session of the Court, the justices go to the robing room on the main floor of the Supreme Court Building, next to the Conference Room. The robing room contains nine closets, one for each justice, which hold the judicial robes. In this room, the justices put on their robes before appearing in public for a session of the Court.

Roe v. Wade

☆ *410 U.S. 113 (1973)*
☆ *Vote: 7–2*
☆ *For the Court: Blackmun*
☆ *Concurring: Douglas, Stewart, and Burger*
☆ *Dissenting: White and Rehnquist*

IN AUGUST 1969 an unmarried pregnant woman living in Texas wanted to terminate her pregnancy by having an abortion. Her doctor refused this request because Texas law made it a crime to have an abortion unless the operation was necessary to save the mother's life. So the woman sought legal help and filed suit against Henry Wade, district attorney for Dallas County, Texas. Throughout the legal proceedings, the woman was identified as Jane Roe to protect her anonymity. The plaintiff later was identified by the media as Norma McCorvey.

Jane Roe argued that the Texas abortion laws were unconstitutional. So she requested an injunction to restrain Henry Wade from enforcing them.

The Issue Roe's lawyers claimed that the Texas abortion laws violated her rights under the due process clause of the 14th Amendment, which prohibited states from depriving their citizens of life, liberty, or property without due process of law. Does the 14th Amendment protect the right of a woman to have an abortion? Are state laws prohibiting abortion unconstitutional?

Opinion of the Court The Court ruled that the Texas statutes on abortion were unconstitutional and that a woman did have the right to terminate her pregnancy. Justice Harry Blackmun wrote, "The right of privacy . . . whether it is to be found in the Fourteenth Amendment's concept of personal liberty . . . or . . . in the Ninth Amendment's reservation of rights to the people, is broad enough to

Sarah Weddington argued Jane Roe's case before the Supreme Court and claimed that a Texas law banning abortion was unconstitutional.

In 1989, 16 years after the Roe *decision, the debate between pro-abortion and anti-abortion forces is still strong. At a demonstration in Texas, Planned Parenthood banners assert women's right to abortion.*

encompass a woman's decision whether or not to terminate her pregnancy."

Justice Blackmun recognized that a woman's right to an abortion could be limited by "a compelling state interest" to protect her health and life. Based on medical evidence, Justice Blackmun concluded that during the "second trimester" of a woman's pregnancy (months 4 to 6), the state might intervene to regulate abortion to protect the mother's well-being. And the state could regulate or prohibit abortion during the third trimester (months 7 to 9). However, during the first trimester (months 1 to 3) of a pregnancy, it seemed unlikely that there would be "a compelling state interest" to restrict abortion rights to protect the health and life of the mother.

Dissent Justice Byron White could not find in the Constitution the right to privacy upon which the *Roe* decision was based. He wrote, "I find nothing in the language or history of the Constitution to support the Court's judgment.... This issue, for the most part, should be left with the people and the political processes the people have devised to govern their affairs." Justices White and William Rehnquist both objected to the Court's involvement in a question they believed should be left to state governments to decide, without interference from the federal courts. They also believed that the *Roe* decision unjustly disregarded the protection due to the life of the fetus.

Significance The *Roe* decision has generated continuing controversy. Women's rights advocates have hailed *Roe* as a landmark victory. Its critics can be roughly divided into two groups: those who oppose the decision because they believe abortion is murder and those who believe that the Court improperly substituted its policy preference for the will of the people as expressed through their elected representatives in state governments.

Justice Byron White accurately remarked in his dissent that the right to an abortion is an issue about which "reasonable men may easily and heatedly differ." And so it has been since 1973, when the *Roe* case was decided.

Efforts to modify or overturn the *Roe* decision have continued. In *Webster* v. *Reproductive Health Services* (1989), for example, the court upheld provisions of a Missouri law that restricted the right to an abortion, a retreat from the *Roe* decision that stopped short of overturning it. *Rust* v. *Sullivan* (1991) limited the access of poor women to abortions by forbidding federally funded clinics, such as those run by Planned Parenthood, to advise patients about abortion.

SEE ALSO

Abortion rights; Privacy, right to; Webster v. Reproductive Health Services

FURTHER READING

Faux, Marian. *Roe v. Wade.* New York: Macmillan, 1988.
Garrow, David J. *Liberty and Sexuality: The Right to Privacy and the Making of Roe v. Wade, 1923–1973.* New York: Macmillan, 1993.
Rosenberg, Rosalind. "The Abortion Case." In *Quarrels That Have Shaped the Constitution,* edited by John A. Garraty. New York: Harper & Row, 1987.
Tribe, Laurence H. *Abortion: The Clash of Absolutes.* New York: Norton, 1990.
Weddington, Sarah. *A Question of Choice.* New York: Putnam, 1992.

Rule of Four

PETITIONERS SEEKING review of a case by the Supreme Court will petition the Court for a writ of certiorari, an order from the Supreme Court to a lower court requiring that a record of a case be sent to the Court for review. If at least four of the nine justices vote in favor of this action, the Court will grant a petition for certiorari. This procedure is known as the Rule of Four.

SEE ALSO
Certiorari, writ of

Rule of law

SEE Constitutionalism

Rules of the Court

DURING ITS first term, in 1790, the Supreme Court established rules for its activities. Since then, the Court has occasionally revised the rules. The rules and revisions are published in the *United States Reports*.

Changes in the rules may be proposed by one or more of the justices, by members of the bar, or by committees of lawyers and members of the federal judiciary that the Court creates to review the rules. By tradition, the justices agree upon revisions of the rules by consensus, not by a formal majority vote.

The rules cover various aspects of the Court's work. For example, there are rules to be followed by attorneys in Court proceedings. Rule 38 regulates an advocate's behavior during the oral argument, when a case is heard by the Court. The attorney presenting an oral argument may speak no longer than 30 minutes and may not read the oral argument. The rule says, "The Court looks with disfavor on any oral argument that is read from a prepared text." There are rules on the format, content, and length of certain documents involved in Court proceedings. For example, Rule 33 says that a lawyer's brief, submitted to the Court in advance of the oral argument in a case, must not be more than 50 typeset pages in length. Rule 34 specifies the contents and format of a brief and states, "Briefs must be compact, logically arranged with proper headings, concise, and free from burdensome, irrelevant, immaterial, or scandalous matter." One group of rules specifies the duties of the Court's officers, such as the clerk, librarian, and reporter of decisions. Another category of rules pertains to the Court's jurisdiction, or the types of cases it has the authority to review and hear. As of 1993, there were 48 rules of the Court.

Rutledge, John

ASSOCIATE JUSTICE, 1790–91

CHIEF JUSTICE (UN-CONFIRMED), 1795

☆ Born: Sept. 1739, Charleston, S.C.
☆ Education: privately tutored at home; studied law at the Middle Temple, London
☆ Other government service: South Carolina Commons House of Assembly, 1761–76; attorney general of South Carolina, 1764–65; Stamp Act Congress, 1765; Continental Congress, 1774–76, 1776–78; governor of South Carolina, 1779–82; judge of the Court of Chancery of South Carolina, 1784–91; chief, South Carolina delegation to the Constitutional Convention, 1787; South Carolina Ratifying Convention, 1788; chief justice, South Carolina Court of Common Pleas, 1791

☆ *Appointed by President George Washington to be an associate justice Sept. 24, 1789, as one of the original members of the U.S. Supreme Court; appointed by Washington as a recess appointment July 1, 1795, to be chief justice; replaced Chief Justice John Jay, who resigned*

☆ *Supreme Court term: confirmed by the Senate as an associate justice Sept. 26, 1789, by a voice vote; resigned Mar. 5, 1791; sworn in as recess appointment to position of chief justice Aug. 12, 1795; the Senate rejected his appointment as chief justice by a vote of 14 to 10 and his service was terminated on Dec. 15, 1795*

☆ *Died: June 21, 1800, Charleston, S.C.*

JOHN RUTLEDGE was one of the founders of the United States. He was a member of the Continental Congress and the Constitutional Convention of 1787. He was also a member of the committee that wrote the first constitution of South Carolina in 1776.

In 1789 President George Washington appointed Rutledge to be one of the original associate justices of the U.S. Supreme Court. Rutledge resigned in 1791, having written no opinions for the Supreme Court. He left the Supreme Court to become chief justice of South Carolina, which at that time was considered a more important position.

In 1795 President Washington appointed Rutledge to replace John Jay as chief justice of the United States. Jay had resigned to become governor of New York. Rutledge presided over the Court (without Senate confirmation) from August 12 to December 15, 1795, while the Congress was in recess. However, the Senate refused to confirm his nomination because of political disagreements with Rutledge, who had spoken publicly against a treaty negotiated by John Jay with the British government. The Senate had ratified the Jay Treaty in 1794 and many members were angered by Rutledge's promotion of public criticism of the Senate about the matter. So President Washington named Oliver Ellsworth to be the chief justice, and the Senate confirmed this appointment.

Rutledge was so shaken by the Senate's rejection of his nomination that he tried to drown himself. He recovered from this suicide attempt but spent the rest of his life in seclusion. He died at the age of 60 in Charleston, South Carolina.

SEE ALSO

Rejection of Supreme Court nominees

Rutledge, Wiley B.

ASSOCIATE JUSTICE, 1943–49

☆ *Born: July 20, 1894, Cloverport, Ky.*

☆ *Education: University of Wisconsin, B.A., 1914; University of Colorado, LL.B., 1922*

☆ *Previous government service: judge, U.S. Court of Appeals for the District of Columbia, 1939–43*

☆ *Appointed by President Franklin D. Roosevelt Jan. 11, 1943; replaced James F. Byrnes, who resigned*

☆ *Supreme Court term: confirmed by the Senate Feb. 8, 1943, by a voice vote; served until Sept. 10, 1949*

☆ *Died: Sept. 10, 1949, York, Maine*

WILEY B. RUTLEDGE was a strong supporter of President Franklin Roosevelt's New Deal. As dean of the University of Iowa Law School, Rutledge spoke against the Supreme Court majority that opposed President Roosevelt's policies in key Court cases. The President rewarded Rutledge with an appointment to the U.S. Court of Appeals for the District of Columbia. As an appellate court judge, Rutledge consistently supported the President's New Deal. When James F. Byrnes retired from the Court in 1942, President Roosevelt picked Rutledge to replace him.

During his six years on the Court, Justice Rutledge was a strong defender of 1st Amendment freedoms. His only lapses from this position were his votes with the majority in the Japanese-American internment cases of World War II (e.g., *Korematsu* v. *United States* and *Hirabayashi* v. *United States*), in which he supported the government's right to detain Japanese Americans on the basis that they might be a threat to national security.

FURTHER READING

Harper, Fowler. *Justice Rutledge and the Bright Constellation.* Indianapolis: Bobbs-Merrill, 1965.

San Antonio Independent School District v. Rodriguez

☆ *411 U.S. 1 (1973)*
☆ *Vote: 5–4*
☆ *For the Court: Powell*
☆ *Concurring: Stewart*
☆ *Dissenting: Douglas, Brennan, White, and Marshall*

DEMETRIO RODRIGUEZ was a Mexican American living in San Antonio, Texas. His children, along with many other Mexican-American students, attended the Edgewood Independent Schools. Rodriguez and other Mexican-American parents were upset about the poor educational facilities and programs provided in their school district. They believed that public funds for schools were administered unfairly in Texas. It seemed to them that school districts with mostly higher-income families received more resources than those with mostly Mexican-American students or students of lower economic status.

Demetrio Rodriguez complained to leaders of the Mexican American Legal Defense and Education Fund (MALDEF) about unequal funding of Texas schools that deprived the Mexican-American students and other students from low-income families of fair educational opportunities. MALDEF filed suit against Texas on behalf of Rodriguez and several other San Antonio parents. The suit charged that the Texas system for financing schools was unconstitutional because it violated the "equal protection of the laws" provision of the 14th Amendment.

The Issue MALDEF argued that a high-quality education is a fundamental constitutional right of individuals. This right, acording to MALDEF, was denied to Mexican-American children and others from low-income families who were required to attend public schools with few resources and poor facilities. At fault was the Texas school finance system, which distributed funds unequally—providing much more for some public schools than others. Was this system, as MALDEF claimed, a violation of the 14th Amendment?

Opinion of the Court The right to an education, the Court decided, is not a fundamental right guaranteed by the Constitution. Justice Lewis Powell wrote, "[A]t least where wealth is concerned the Equal Protection Clause does not require absolute equality or precisely equal advantages. So, the Texas system for financing public schools does not violate the Fourteenth Amendment."

Dissent Justice Thurgood Marshall disagreed with the Supreme Court's opinion. He wrote, "[T]he majority's holding can only be seen as a retreat from our historic commitment to equality of educational opportunity and as unsupportable acquiescence in a system which deprives children in their earliest years of the chance to reach their full potential as citizens."

Significance The *Rodriguez* decision seemed to impede attempts to fundamentally reform distribution of funds to public schools within a state. The Court appeared to validate state funding systems designed to maintain grossly unequal and unfair distributions of resources to public schools. Since the *Rodriguez* decision, however, several states have decided, without the coercion of a U.S. Supreme Court decision, to reform and equalize their school funding systems.

Sanford, Edward Terry

ASSOCIATE JUSTICE, 1923–30

☆ Born: July 23, 1865, Knoxville, Tenn.
☆ Education: University of Tennessee, B.A., 1883; Harvard, A.B., 1884, M.A., 1889; Harvard Law School, LL.B., 1889
☆ Previous government service: special assistant to the U.S. attorney general, 1906–7; assistant U.S. attorney general, 1907–8; federal judge, U.S. District Court for the Middle and Eastern Districts of Tennessee, 1908–23
☆ Appointed by President Warren G. Harding Jan. 24, 1923; replaced Mahlon Pitney, who retired
☆ Supreme Court term: confirmed by the Senate Jan. 29, 1923, by a voice vote; served until Mar. 8, 1930
☆ Died: Mar. 8, 1930, Washington, D.C.

EDWARD TERRY SANFORD served only seven years on the Supreme Court, after 15 years of service as a federal district judge in Tennessee. His one notable achievement came in the area of constitutional rights. Writing for the Court in *Gitlow* v. *New York* (1925), Justice Sanford denied free speech and press rights to a publisher who advocated violent overthrow of the government. However, he also wrote that the 1st Amendment freedoms of speech and press "are among the fundamental personal rights and liberties protected by the due process clause of the Fourteenth Amendment from impairment by the states."

Two years later, in *Fiske* v. *Kansas* (1927), Justice Sanford wrote the opinion for the Court when it overturned, for the first time, a state law on grounds that it violated the 1st and 14th Amendments to the Constitution in denying an individual his freedom of speech. Thus, Justice Sanford laid the foundation for the later Court decisions to "incorporate" most of the Bill of Rights into the due process clause of the 14th Amendment, thereby prohibiting state governments from violating the Bill of Rights.

SEE ALSO

Gitlow v. New York; Incorporation doctrine

Santa Clara County v. Southern Pacific Railroad Co.

☆ 118 U.S. 394 (1886)
☆ Vote: 9–0
☆ For the Court: Harlan

THE STATE of California tried to collect taxes owed by the Southern Pacific and Central Pacific railroads. Advocates for the railroad companies claimed that the due process clause of the 14th Amendment made the state tax levy against them unconstitutional. The 14th Amendment says that no state shall "deprive any person of life, liberty, or property without due process of law." The railroad company advocates argued that the state tax levy was an unconstitutional denial of their rights to property.

The Issue Was a corporation protected against state interference with its rights in the same way that a person was protected? If not, the California taxes on the railroads should be enforced. If so, the taxes could be declared invalid.

When the Southern Pacific Railroad Company objected to taxes imposed by the state of California, the Court sided with the railroad. It ruled that the company had the same rights to liberty and property as a person.

Opinion of the Court The Court did not directly address the 14th Amendment issue in its opinion. Indeed, Chief Justice Morrison Waite announced, even before the Court heard oral arguments, that the Court would not deal with the question of "whether the provision in the Fourteenth Amendment to the Constitution which forbade a state to deny to any person within its jurisdiction the equal protection of the Constitution, applied to these corporations. We are all of the opinion that it does."

Having established that the Court would apply the 14th Amendment protection of constitutional rights to corporations in the same way as it did to individuals, the Court focused on the narrow issue of whether the state of California could tax fences on the railroad companies' property. The Court decided against the state of California, ruling that the state tax law was a violation of the 14th Amendment due process rights of the corporation, defined by the Court as a person.

Significance Corporations were established in constitutional law as "persons" within the meaning of the 14th Amendment. By using the due process guarantees of the 14th Amendment, corporation lawyers were able to protect businesses from many kinds of state government regulations put forward in behalf of the public good. This view of corporations as persons protected by the

14th Amendment was not fully overturned until the 1930s. In *West Coast Hotel Co.* v. *Parrish* (1937), for example, the Court upheld a state law regulating wages of women workers of a private business. The Court refused to protect the rights of the business as a person under the 14th Amendment.

SEE ALSO
West Coast Hotel Co. v. Parrish

Scalia, Antonin

ASSOCIATE JUSTICE, 1986–

☆ *Born: Mar. 11, 1936, Trenton, N.J.*
☆ *Education: Georgetown University, B.A., 1957; Harvard Law School, LL.B., 1960*
☆ *Previous government service: general counsel, White House Office of Telecommunications Policy, 1971–72; chairman, Administrative Conference of the United States, 1972–74; assistant U.S. attorney general, Office of Legal Counsel, 1974–77; judge, U.S. Court of Appeals for the District of Columbia Circuit, 1982–86*
☆ *Appointed by President Ronald Reagan June 24, 1986; replaced William H. Rehnquist, who became chief justice*
☆ *Supreme Court term: confirmed by the Senate Sept. 17, 1986, by a 98–0 vote*

ANTONIN SCALIA is the first American of Italian ancestry to become a Supreme Court Justice. He is one of seven children of Eugene and Catherine Scalia, who came to the United States from Italy. Scalia is the first Roman Catholic to be appointed to the Court since William Brennan in 1957.

Justice Scalia has been a strong force on the Court in decisions protecting the constitutional rights of individuals and demanding equal protection of the laws. He has also favored government regulations that protect the safety and security

of the community, even if this would mean limitations on the rights of certain individuals.

Schechter Poultry Corp. v. United States

☆ 295 U.S. 495 (1935)
☆ Vote: 9–0
☆ For the Court: Hughes

DURING THE early 1930s President Franklin D. Roosevelt fought the Great Depression by proposing many economic recovery programs. The centerpiece of his efforts was the National Industrial Recovery Act (NIRA) of 1933, managed by the National Recovery Administration (NRA).

Under that law, Congress granted the President authority to approve codes of fair competition for different industries. Drawn up by trade and industry groups themselves, each of these codes included standards of minimum wages and maximum hours of work. Presidential approval of the code for an industry gave that code the force of law.

By 1935 many industries had started to ignore the NIRA. The government decided to bring a test case before the Supreme Court in the hope that a ruling in favor of NIRA codes would encourage industries to accept the codes.

A case involving four brothers who ran a poultry business became a key test of Roosevelt's program. The Schechters bought live poultry outside New York State and sold it in New York City. The government convicted the brothers of violating several provisions of the NIRA live poultry code in order to keep their prices below those of competitors. Prosecutors also charged them with selling thousands of pounds of diseased chickens to a local butcher. The Schechters ap-

pealed to the Supreme Court. The press called the suit the "sick chicken case."

The Issue The case involved three questions: Did the economic crisis facing the nation justify resorting to the NIRA? Did the Constitution allow Congress to delegate so much power to the President? And did the law come under Congress's power to regulate interstate commerce?

Opinion of the Court The NIRA lost on all counts. The Supreme Court ruled that the economic problems of the nation did not justify the NIRA. Chief Justice Charles Evans Hughes wrote that "extraordinary conditions do not create or enlarge constitutional power."

Second, the Court said that under the Constitution only Congress has the power to make laws. If Congress wanted to delegate any of this power to the President, it had to set clear standards to guide the executive branch in making detailed applications of the general law. The NIRA was unconstitutional because, in effect, it gave trade and industry groups unregulated power to create any laws they wanted.

Finally, the Court recognized that although the Schechters bought their poultry in many states, they processed and sold it only in New York. Thus, the Schechters' operation was a local concern not directly affecting interstate commerce, and so it was beyond federal control.

This cartoon supported the National Industrial Recovery Act, which was designed to spur the economy by granting the President the power to approve codes of fair competition. However, in the Schecter case the Supreme Court ruled the NIRA unconstitutional.

Significance The decision at first appeared to devastate President Roosevelt's New Deal economic recovery program. But by 1937 the Supreme Court began upholding new laws passed to fulfill New Deal objectives. The National Labor Relations Act of 1935, for example, was upheld by the Court in *National Labor Relations Board* v. *Jones & Laughlin Steel Corp.* (1937).

The *Schechter* case established the principle that in domestic affairs Congress may not delegate broad legislative powers to the President without also outlining clear standards to guide the President in employing these powers. This principle stands today.

FURTHER READING

Freidel, Frank. "The Sick Chicken Case." In *Quarrels That Have Shaped the Constitution*, edited by John A. Garraty. New York: Harper & Row, 1987.

Schenck v. United States

☆ *249 U.S. 47 (1919)*
☆ *Vote: 9–0*
☆ *For the Court: Holmes*

DURING WORLD WAR I, Congress passed the Espionage Act of 1917. This law made it illegal to encourage insubordination in the armed forces or to use the mails to distribute materials urging resistance to the government.

Charles Schenck, general secretary of the Socialist party in the United States, was an outspoken critic of America's role in the war. Schenck printed and mailed about 15,000 leaflets to men eligible for the draft. The leaflets denounced the draft as involuntary servitude (slavery) and therefore a violation of the 13th Amendment. The pamphlets also argued that participation in World War I did not serve the best interests of the American people.

Schenck was arrested and convicted of violating the Espionage Act of 1917. At his trial, Schenck claimed his 1st Amendment right to free speech had been violated. The 1st Amendment states: "Congress shall make no law…abridging the freedom of speech, or of the press."

The Issue Did the Espionage Act of 1917, under which Schenck was arrested, violate the 1st Amendment protection of free speech? The *Schenck* case also posed a larger question about potential limitations on free speech. For the first time in its history, the Supreme Court faced directly the question of whether the government might limit speech under special circumstances.

Opinion of the Court The Court decided against Schenck, ruling that the Espionage Act of 1917 did not violate the 1st Amendment rights of free speech and free press.

Justice Oliver Wendell Holmes wrote the Court's opinion. He set forth a test to determine when government might limit free speech. Holmes said, "The most stringent protection of free speech would not protect a man in falsely shouting fire in a theatre and causing a panic." When spoken or written words "create a clear and present danger" of bringing about evils that Congress has the authority to prevent, the government may limit speech.

Holmes reasoned that during peacetime the 1st Amendment would have protected Schenck's ideas. During a wartime emergency, however, urging men to resist the draft presented a "clear and present danger" to the nation. Holmes declared: "When a nation is at war, many things that might be said in time of peace are such a hindrance to its efforts that their utterance will not be… protected by any constitutional right."

Police in Cambridge, Massachusetts, load communist propaganda into a wagon in 1919. That year the Supreme Court upheld the conviction of Charles Schenck, who had been arrested for distributing Socialist party leaflets that criticized the U.S. role in World War I.

Significance The *Schenck* decision established important precedents. First, it set up the "clear and present danger" test. This formula was applied to many subsequent free speech cases. In addition, the decision announced that certain speech may be permissible in peacetime but not in wartime. Thus, the *Schenck* case established that the 1st Amendment protection of free speech is not an absolute guarantee. Under conditions such as those Holmes described, the government may constrain speech.

Later, in another free speech case, (*Abrams* v. *United States,* 1919), Holmes wrote a dissenting opinion that modified the "clear and present danger" test set forth in *Schenck*. In his *Abrams* dissent, Holmes emphasized that a "clear and present danger" must be directly connected to specific actions that would bring about evil consequences. If the imminent danger could not be demonstrated, then speech could not be lawfully limited. In the 1950s and 1960s, the modified version of Holmes's "clear and present danger" test prevailed in the Court's opinions. In *Yates* v. *United States* (1957), for example, the Court protected the freedom of expression of Communist party members. And in *Brandenburg* v. *Ohio* (1969), the Court protected free speech by a racist Ku Klux Klan leader.

SEE ALSO
Abrams v. United States; Brandenburg v. Ohio; Freedom of speech and press; Seditious libel; Yates v. United Staes

Scott v. Sandford

☆ *19 How. 393 (1857)*
☆ *Vote: 7–2*
☆ *For the Court: Taney*
☆ *Dissenting: Curtis and McLean*

WHEN THE Constitution was written in 1787, it permitted slavery. Many of the framers owned slaves; others opposed slavery. During the Constitutional Convention they hotly debated the issue of how to deal with slavery, and the problem continued to plague the new nation. By the 1850s some states had forbidden slavery, while others still protected it.

In 1854 Dred Scott, a slave, was taken by his master to Rock Island, Illinois, a town in a free state. His master later took him to the Wisconsin Territory (an area that is now part of Minnesota), where the Missouri Compromise of 1820, a federal law, had forbidden slavery. His master then brought Scott back to Missouri, a slave state. Scott brought suit against his master, claiming that he was a free man because he had resided in areas that had banned slavery.

The Issue The case involved three issues: (1) Scott had lived in the free state of Illinois. Had he become free while living there? Should Missouri have to recognize that freedom? (2) Scott had traveled to a federal territory that Congress had declared a free territory in the Missouri Compromise of 1820. Had he become free while living there, and should Missouri have to recognize that freedom? (3) Did the Supreme Court have the jurisdiction, or power, to hear this case?

Scott claimed that his master had freed him by taking him to Illinois, where slavery was not allowed. Therefore, any slave taken there became free. Once Scott became free in Illinois, no Missouri law could turn him into a slave again. Scott's lawyers further argued that Missouri must recognize the laws of any other state in the Union.

Scott also claimed that he was free under the Missouri Compromise. Passed by Congress and recognized as the law of the land since 1820, the Missouri Compromise prohibited slavery in all the federal territories north of Missouri. When Scott's master took him to Fort Snelling in the Wisconsin Territory, Scott had also become free there. Even if Missouri chose not to recognize the laws of Illinois, the Constitution required all states to recognize the laws of Congress, as the supremacy clause of the Constitution (Article 6, Clause 2) clearly stated.

Finally, Scott's lawyers argued that the Supreme Court did have the power to hear this case. Article 3, Section 2, of the Constitution established the jurisdiction, the authority to hear cases, of the federal courts. This jurisdiction extended to cases "between citizens of different states." Scott's master was now dead, leaving Scott technically under the control of his dead master's brother-in-law, John F. A. Sanford, who lived in New York. (The case is called *Scott* v. *Sandford* because a court clerk misspelled the name of the defendant.) Scott claimed that if he was free, then he had to be a citizen of Missouri. As such, he could sue a citizen of New York in federal court.

Opinion of the Court The Supreme Court ruled against Scott on all three issues. In an extraordinary decision, all nine judges wrote opinions that totaled 248 pages. Chief Justice Roger B. Taney's 55-page opinion of the court expressed the collective view of the majority.

Taney first argued that Scott could not sue in a federal court because he was

When Dred Scott, a slave, sued for his freedom because he had traveled with his owner to a state that banned slavery, the Supreme Court denied his claim and stated that black people, whether enslaved or free, had no rights as citizens.

not a citizen of the United States. Taney said that no black person, slave or free, could be a citizen. Taney wrote, "The question is simply this: Can a negro, whose ancestors were imported into this country and sold as slaves, become a member of the political community formed and brought into existence by the Constitution of the United States?" Taney answered his own question: "We think they are not…included, and were not intended to be included, under the word 'citizens' in the Constitution." Rather, Taney asserted that at the time the Constitution was written, blacks were "considered as a subordinate and inferior class of beings, who had been subjugated by the dominant race, and whether emancipated or not…had no rights or privileges but such as those who held the power and the Government might choose to grant them."

Having concluded that Scott had no right to sue in a federal court, Taney might have stopped. However, the issue of slavery in the federal territories was an important political question, and Taney wanted to let the nation know where the Court stood on it. So he examined Scott's other claims.

The Court easily disposed of the claim to freedom based on Illinois law. Taney held that Scott lost whatever claim to freedom he had while in Illinois when he left the state, and no law or precedent obligated Missouri to enforce the Illinois law.

Scott's claim based on the Missouri Compromise presented more complications. Considering the Missouri Compromise, passed by Congress in 1820, as the law of the land would obligate the state of Missouri to recognize it. Taney, however, decided that the ban on slavery in the Missouri Compromise was unconstitutional. He reasoned that the territories belonged to all the citizens of the United States. Under the Constitution's

5th Amendment, no one could deprive a person of his property without "due process of law" and "just compensation." But the Missouri Compromise would deprive men like Scott's owner of their property simply for entering federal territories. Thus, the Court held that the Missouri Compromise was unconstitutional. For only the second time, the Supreme Court declared an act of Congress unconstitutional. This power of judicial review of acts of Congress had first been used by the Court in *Marbury* v. *Madison* (1803).

Dissent In a 69-page dissent, Justice Benjamin R. Curtis took Taney to task at every point. Curtis pointed out that at the time of the ratification of the Constitution blacks voted in a number of states, including Massachusetts, Pennsylvania, and North Carolina. Thus, Curtis argued, free blacks had always been citizens of the nation, and if Scott was free the Court had jurisdiction to hear his case. Curtis also argued in favor of the constitutionality of the Missouri Compromise, which he pointed out had existed as accepted law for more than three decades and served as the basis of the sectional understanding that had kept the North and South together in one Union.

Significance Taney had hoped to settle the issue of slavery in the territories through the *Scott* verdict. Instead, Taney's decision itself became a political issue. Abraham Lincoln and Stephen A. Douglas argued over its merits in their famous debates of 1858. Instead of lessening sectional tensions, Taney's decision exacerbated them and helped bring on the Civil War.

When the Civil War was finally over, the 13th Amendment (1865) ended slavery. The 14th Amendment (1868) gave blacks citizenship. Thus, by amending the Constitution, the people overturned the *Scott* decision.

SEE ALSO
Jurisdiction

FURTHER READING
Fehrenbacher, Don E. *The Dred Scott Case: Its Significance in American Law and Politics.* New York: Oxford, 1978.
Fehrenbacher, Don E. "The Dred Scott Case." In *Quarrels That Have Shaped the Constitution,* edited by John A. Garraty. New York: Harper & Row, 1987.

Searches and seizures

THE 4TH AMENDMENT to the U.S. Constitution says, "The right of the people to be secure in their persons, houses, papers, and effects, against unreasonable searches and seizures, shall not be violated, and no Warrants shall issue, but upon probable cause, supported by Oath or affirmation, and particularly describing the place to be searched, and the persons or things to be seized."

The principle in the 4th Amendment is clear: the privacy of the individual is protected against arbitrary intrusion by agents of the government. In 1949 Justice Felix Frankfurter wrote (*Wolf* v. *Colorado*): "The security of one's privacy against arbitrary intrusion by the police is basic to a free society. The knock at the door, whether by day or by night, as a prelude to a search, without authority of law but solely on the authority of the police, did not need the commentary of recent history to be condemned as inconsistent with the conception of human rights enshrined in the history and the basic constitutional documents of English-speaking peoples."

The 4th Amendment protection against unreasonable searches and seizures is reinforced by the clause that requires a warrant, or court authorization, for such searches and seizures. A warrant should not be issued, of course, unless

An agent of the Drug Enforcement Agency aims at a suspect in a car. The Supreme Court has ruled that police can search a car without a warrant.

there is a finding of "probable cause" by a neutral magistrate or judge.

The 4th Amendment principle of personal security against unlawful intrusion is clear enough. But the exact meaning of the key phrases and their precise application in specific cases requires interpretation and judgment—the duties of the federal courts. What constitutes "unreasonable searches and seizures"? What exactly is the meaning of "probable cause"? Are there any situations that justify a warrantless search by government officials? If so, what are they, and what are the justifications?

In making judgments about 4th Amendment rights, the federal courts attempt to balance liberty and order—the rights of the individual to freedom from tyranny and the needs of the community for stability, security, and safety. Judges must decide when to provide more or less latitude for the rights of individuals suspected of criminal behavior.

The Supreme Court ruled on what is "unreasonable" in *Weeks* v. *United States* (1914). Evidence seized illegally by federal government agents—without probable cause or a search warrant—must be excluded from a defendant's trial, according to the Court. This exclusionary rule applied, however, only to federal government officials. The Court did not establish the exclusionary rule as a limitation on state governments until 1961, in *Mapp* v. *Ohio*.

The Supreme Court established a "good faith" exception to the exclu-

sionary rule in *United States* v. *Leon* (1984). The Court ruled that evidence seized as the result of a mistakenly issued search warrant can be used in a trial as long as the warrant was issued on good faith that there was probable cause for issuing it.

Judges, not law enforcement officers, are supposed to determine whether or not there is probable cause for issuing a search warrant. Evidence seized by police with a valid search warrant can, of course, be used against the defendant in a trial. There are, however, exceptions to the requirement of a warrant to justify a search and seizure of evidence. The Supreme Court ruled, for example, in *Terry* v. *Ohio* (1968) that police may stop and search a suspect's outer clothing for a gun or other weapons without a warrant if they suspect a crime is about to be committed. Further, police may stop and search automobiles without first obtaining a warrant if they have a reasonable suspicion that illegal goods are inside or that illegal actions are about to take place.

The accompanying table of cases on 4th Amendment rights demonstrates the evolution of constitutional rights in the 20th century. As it shows, the incorporation of the 4th Amendment into the due process clause of the 14th Amendment did not occur until 1949, in the case of *Wolf* v. *Colorado*. Since that time, however, most of the 4th Amendment cases have involved actions at the state level of government. On balance, decisions in these cases have gradually enhanced the rights of individuals against the power of government.

SEE ALSO

Bill of Rights; Exclusionary rule; Incorporation doctrine; Katz v. United States; Mapp v. Ohio; New Jersey v. T.L.O.; Olmstead v. United States; Probable cause; Terry v. Ohio; United States v. Leon; United States v. Ross; Weeks v. United States; Wolf v. Colorado

THE EVOLUTION OF 4TH AMENDMENT RIGHTS

Weeks v. United States (1914) A person may require that evidence obtained in a search shall be excluded from use against him in a federal court if the evidence was seized illegally—without probable cause or a search warrant.

Carroll v. United States (1925) Federal agents can conduct searches of automobiles without a warrant whenever they have a reasonable suspicion of illegal actions.

Olmstead v. United States (1928) Wiretaps by federal agents are permissible where no entry of private premises has occurred.

Wolf v. Colorado (1949) The 4th Amendment protections apply to searches by state officials as well as federal agents. However, state judges are not required to exclude evidence obtained by searches in violation of 4th Amendment rights.

Mapp v. Ohio (1961) Evidence obtained in violation of 4th Amendment rights must be excluded from use in state and federal trials.

Katz v. United States (1967) Electronic surveillance and wiretapping are within the scope of the 4th Amendment because it protects whatever an individual wants to preserve as private, including conversations and behavior, even in a place open to the public.

Terry v. Ohio (1968) The police may stop and frisk, or search, a suspect's outer clothing for dangerous weapons without first obtaining a warrant if they suspect that a crime is about to be committed.

Chimel v. California (1969) Police may search without a warrant only the immediate area around the suspect from which he could obtain a weapon or destroy evidence. But a person's entire dwelling cannot be searched merely because he is arrested there.

Marshall v. Barlow's, Inc. (1978) Federal laws cannot provide for warrantless inspections of businesses that are otherwise legally regulated by a federal agency. A federal inspector must obtain a search warrant when the owner of the business to be inspected objects to a warrantless search.

United States v. Ross (1982) Police officers may search an entire vehicle they have stopped without obtaining a warrant if they have probable cause to suspect that drugs or other contraband is in the vehicle.

United States v. Leon (1984) Evidence seized on the basis of a mistakenly issued search warrant can be introduced in a trial if the warrant was issued in good faith—that is, on presumption that there were valid grounds for issuing the warrant.

New Jersey v. T.L.O. (1985) School officials do not need a search warrant or probable cause to conduct a reasonable search of a student. The school officials may search a student if there are reasonable grounds for suspecting that the search will uncover evidence that the student has violated or is violating either the law or the rules of the school.

California v. Greenwood (1988) The police may search through garbage bags and other trash containers that people leave outside their houses in order to obtain evidence of criminal activity. This evidence may subsequently be used as the basis for obtaining a warrant to search a person's house.

Michigan v. Sitz (1990) The police may stop automobiles at roadside checkpoints and examine the drivers for signs of intoxication. Evidence obtained in this manner may be used to bring criminal charges against the driver.

Minnesota v. Dickerson (1993) Police do not need a warrant to seize narcotics that were found when frisking or quickly searching a suspect for concealed weapons. Evidence seized in this way can be used to bring criminal charges against a suspect.

Seditious libel

SEDITIOUS LIBEL is the crime of making public statements that threaten to undermine respect for the government, laws, or public officials. The Sedition Act of 1798 made it a crime to criticize, ridicule, or erode the authority of the federal government, the President, or other federal officials. This law was used by government officials to prosecute members of the Republican party, headed by Thomas Jefferson, who were rivals to the ruling Federalist party, headed by President John Adams. After Jefferson's victory in the Presidential election of 1800, the Sedition Act of 1798 was allowed to expire.

Controversy about seditious libel emerged during World War I, with passage of the Sedition Act of 1918. In *Abrams* v. *United States* (1919) the court upheld the federal government's use of this law to convict Jacob Abrams of distributing leaflets that severely criticized President Woodrow Wilson and the U.S. government. The Court's decision in *Abrams* was based on the "clear and present danger" test stated by Justice Oliver Wendell Holmes in *Schenck* v. *United States* (1919). Justice Holmes, however, wrote a stinging dissent against the Court's use of the "clear and present danger" test in *Abrams* to limit freedom of speech and press. Holmes stressed that a "clear and present danger" exists only when speech can be connected immediately and directly to specific acts of lawless behavior threatening the security of the United States. If the imminent danger could not be demonstrated, said Holmes, then speech could not be lawfully limited.

Arguments about the constitutionality of seditious libel laws under the 1st Amendment, however, continued until the 1960s, when the U.S. Supreme Court made landmark decisions about this traditional limitation on freedom of speech and press.

In *New York Times Co.* v. *Sullivan* (1964) the Court ruled against a civil libel suit by a public official who tried to collect damages from critics who had denounced him in a newspaper advertisement. In rejecting the suit, the Court compared it to seditious libel prosecutions undertaken to prevent negative speech about the government. The Court concluded that such efforts to limit freedom of speech and press were not permitted by the U.S. Constitution.

In *Garrison* v. *Louisiana* (1964) the Supreme Court overturned a criminal libel conviction. And in *Brandenburg* v. *Ohio* (1969) the court used ideas from Justice Holmes's dissent in *Abrams* to strike down a state law on seditious libel. Thus, the Court acted against seditious libel prosecutions, civil or criminal, and thereby protected the freedom to criticize or otherwise speak out against government actions or officials.

SEE ALSO

Abrams v. United States; Brandenburg v. Ohio; Freedom of speech and press; New York Times Co. v. Sullivan; Schenck v. United States

Segregation, de facto and de jure

DE JURE (Latin for "from the law") segregation is the separation of people on the basis of race as required by law. For example, after the Civil War and the ending of slavery by the 13th Amendment to the Constitution (1865), the governments of the former slave states found new ways to discriminate against

The sign in this Atlanta park indicates that by city regulation blacks were allowed to enter only as servants. The Court has ruled that such de jure segregation is unconstitutional.

black Americans. They enacted laws to require separate public facilities for blacks and whites. Blacks were required, for example, to attend separate schools, to use separate public rest rooms, and to use separate public drinking fountains. The separate facilities for blacks were supposed to be equal to the facilities provided for whites. This "separate but equal" doctrine was endorsed by the Supreme Court decision in *Plessy* v. *Ferguson* (1896). In reality, however, the facilities for black people were rarely, if ever, equal in quality to those provided for whites.

Racial separation that exists as a matter of custom rather than as a legal requirement is known as *de facto* (Latin for "in fact") segregation. For example, one neighborhood may include only white families, and another nearby neighborhood may include only black families. However, this racial segregation may have developed informally in response to social and economic factors, not as a requirement of the law.

De jure segregation has been declared unconstitutional by the U.S. Supreme Court. In *Brown* v. *Board of Education* (1954) the Court ruled against de jure racial segregation in public schools. In subsequent cases the Court outlawed racial discrimination in other areas of public life. In 1964 Congress passed the Civil Rights Act, which outlawed de jure segregation.

The Court has ruled in *Milliken* v. *Bradley* (1974) that courts of law can remedy de facto segregation only if it was caused by specific acts of government. In *Washington* v. *Seattle School District No. 1* (1982) the Court upheld voluntary acts by state agencies to overcome de facto segregation.

SEE ALSO

Brown v. Board of Education; Civil rights; Equality under the Constitution; Plessy v. Ferguson

---

Selection of justices

SEE Appointment of justices; Rejection of Supreme Court nominees

---

Self-incrimination, privilege against

THE 5TH AMENDMENT to the U.S. Constitution guarantees that "no person...shall be compelled in any criminal case to be a witness against himself." Thus, a criminal defendant has the right to refuse to answer questions that could result in a conviction for a crime.

The 5th Amendment right to avoid self-incrimination was extended to the states when the U.S. Supreme Court incorporated this right into the due process clause of the 14th Amendment in *Malloy* v. *Hogan* (1964). In *Miranda* v. *Arizona* (1966) the Court required law enforcement officers to inform suspects of their 5th Amendment right to remain silent.

Critics have complained that the Court's decision in the *Miranda* case helps criminals resist prosecution. Justice Arthur Goldberg, however, saw the 5th Amendment as a great guarantee of individual rights. In *Murphy* v. *Waterfront*

Commission of New York (1964) Goldberg wrote, "[T]he privilege [of avoiding self-incrimination] while sometimes a shelter to the guilty, is often a protection to the innocent."

SEE ALSO

Incorporation doctrine; Miranda v. Arizona; Rights of the accused

Senate Judiciary Committee

ESTABLISHED IN 1816, the Judiciary Committee is one of the standing, or permanent, committees of the U.S. Senate. In 1868 the Senate directed the Judiciary Committee to examine and screen, for the full Senate, all Presidential nominations to the Supreme Court. Since then, one of the highly visible and very important duties of the committee is its investigations and recommendations about Presidential nominations to the Supreme Court.

The full Senate sends the President's judicial nominations to the Judiciary Committee for review. The committee holds public hearings to consider the merits of each person nominated to fill a vacancy on the Supreme Court. The nominee is invited to appear before the committee to answer questions about his or her background, qualifications, and ideas about law and the U.S. Constitution.

In 1925 Harlan F. Stone became the first nominee to appear before the committee for a hearing. He was subsequently confirmed by the Senate. Since 1955, when John Marshall Harlan II appeared before the Senate Judiciary Committee, all nominees have participated in formal committee hearings.

The committee concludes its hearings on Supreme Court nominations with a vote and a recommendation to the full Senate. The committee's recommendation tends to be decisive. A likely negative committee vote sometimes influences the nominee to withdraw from the process. In 1968 President Lyndon Johnson withdrew his nomination of Abe Fortas for the office of chief justice, when it became clear during the confirmation hearings that the Senate Judiciary Committee would vote against Fortas. A negative recommendation sent by the committee to the full Senate for discussion and vote usually ends in the defeat of the nominee.

SEE ALSO

Appointment of justices; Rejection of Supreme Court nominees

Seniority

SENIORITY REFERS to the length of time each justice has served on the Court. Certain rules and procedures of the Court are based on seniority. Only the chief justice is exempt from considerations of seniority.

The senior associate justices, those with the longest periods of service, may choose to occupy the larger chambers, or offices, in the Supreme Court Building. The four senior justices also get the better (more spacious) places around the Court's conference table. The most

The seating of the justices is arranged by seniority, with the newest justices sitting on the ends.

junior justice serves as the doorkeeper during the Court's private conferences. He or she is also the designated receiver and sender of messages during the conferences.

In the Courtroom, the chief justice is seated at the center. The senior associate justice sits to the right of the chief, and the second most senior to his left. The other justices take their places in alternating order of seniority, with the most junior associate justice at the far left of the bench.

During the conferences, the justices speak in order of seniority, from the most senior to the most junior. By speaking first, the senior justices are able to shape the terms of arguments on issues. And, in any case in which the chief justice is not part of the Court's majority, the senior associate justice in the majority has the duty of assigning the writing of the Court's opinion. (If the chief justice is part of the majority, he assigns the writing of the opinion.)

Separate but equal doctrine

IN 1896 in *Plessy* v. *Ferguson,* the Supreme Court ruled that a state law requiring racial segregation in public transportation was constitutional as long as the separate facilities were equal. This "separate but equal" doctrine was used to justify racial segregation in public schools and a wide variety of other public facilities. In 1954 the Court overturned the "separate but equal" doctrine in *Brown* v. *Board of Education.*

SEE ALSO

Brown v. Board of Education; Civil rights; Equality under the Constitution; Plessy v. Ferguson; Segregation, de facto and de jure

Separation of powers

SEPARATION OF powers, a major principle of the U.S. Constitution, is the distribution of power among three branches of government: the legislative, the executive, and the judicial. The legislative branch (Congress) has the power, according to Article 1 of the Constitution, to make certain kinds of laws. In Article 2, the Constitution says that the executive branch (headed by the President) has the power to enforce or carry out laws. The judicial branch (headed by the Supreme Court) is established in Article 3 of the Constitution to interpret and apply the law in federal court cases.

Further, legislative power is divided between the two houses of Congress: the Senate and the House of Representatives. Both houses must pass a bill for it to become law.

Separation of powers among the three branches of the federal government is the fundamental constitutional means for achieving limited government and protecting the people against abuses of power. Limited government means that officials cannot act arbitrarily. Rather, they are bound by the higher law of the Constitution, which guides and limits their use of power in order to protect the liberties of the people and prevent tyranny. James Madison summarized this view of the need for separation of powers in *The Federalist* No. 47: "The accumulation of all powers, legislative, executive, and judiciary, in the same hands, whether of one, a few, or many, and whether hereditary, self-appointed, or elected, may justly be pronounced the very definition of tyranny."

In *The Federalist* No. 48, Madison emphasized that the separation of powers in the U.S. Constitution is complemented by a system of checks and bal-

In this cartoon, the legislative branch marches with President Franklin Roosevelt, representing the executive branch. However, the Supreme Court, headed by Chief Justice Charles Evans Hughes, maintained the separation of powers as it over-ruled much of Roosevelt's New Deal legislation.

ances, whereby one branch can block or check an action of another branch in order to maintain a balance of power in the government. Madison said that unless the separate branches of government "be so far connected and blended [balanced] as to give each a constitutional control [check] over the others the degree of separation… essential to a free government can never in practice be duly maintained."

There are many examples of ways that one branch of the government checks the actions of another branch to maintain a balance of powers so that no branch can continually dominate the others. The President, for example, can check Congress by vetoing bills it has passed. But the President's veto can be overturned by a subsequent two-thirds vote of Congress. The President can appoint executive branch officials and federal judges, including justices of the Supreme Court. The Senate, however, must approve these appointments by majority vote. The President is commander in chief of the armed forces. But only Congress can enact legislation to provide funds needed by the armed forces and their commander to carry out missions. The President makes treaties with foreign governments, but the Senate has the power to confirm or reject them. Additional examples of the checks and balances system are listed in Articles 1, 2, and 3 of the Constitution.

The Supreme Court uses the power of judicial review to check the executive and legislative branches of government and to maintain the separation of powers. This power enables the Court to declare acts of the executive or legislative branches unconstitutional (in violation of some part of the Constitution). Thus, the Court can declare null and void actions of the other branches that exceed or contradict their powers as expressed in the Constitution.

The Court established its power of judicial review of the federal legislative and executive branches in *Marbury* v. *Madison* (1803). Since that time, the Court has exercised the power of judicial review to declare more than 120 acts of Congress and the President unconstitutional. In *Youngstown Sheet & Tube* Co. v. *Sawyer* (1952), for example, the Court ruled that President Harry Truman's use of an executive order to temporarily take control of privately owned steel mills was unconstitutional. Writing for the Court, Justice Hugo Black explained: "In the framework of our Constitution, the President's power to see that the laws are faithfully executed refutes the idea that he is to be a lawmaker. The Constitution limits his functions in the lawmaking process to the recommending of laws he thinks wise and the vetoing of laws he thinks bad."

As the preceding examples indicate, each branch of the government has some influence over the actions of the others, but no branch can exercise its powers without cooperation from the others. Each branch has some say in the work of the others as a way to check and limit the power of the others.

In this system of separation of powers, with its checks and balances, no branch of the government can accumulate too much power. But each branch, and the government generally, is supposed to have enough power to do what the people expect of it. So the government is supposed to be both limited and strong; neither too strong for the liberty of the people nor too limited to be effective in maintaining order, stability, and security for the people. This is the theory of separation of powers as a means to a limited but effective government.

Justice Louis D. Brandeis nicely summed up the founders' purposes and reasons for separation of powers in a dissenting opinion in *Myers* v. *United States* (1926): "The doctrine of the separation of powers was adopted by the Convention of 1787, not to promote efficiency but to preclude the exercise of arbitrary power. The purpose was not to avoid friction but, by means of the inevitable friction incident to the distribution of the governmental powers among three departments, to save the people from autocracy."

SEE ALSO

Constitutional democracy; Constitutionalism; Federalist, The; Impeachment; Independent judiciary; Judicial activism and judicial restraint; Judicial power; Judicial review; Marbury v. Madison; Reversals of Supreme Court decisions; Youngstown Sheet & Tube Co. v. Sawyer

FURTHER READING

Carey, George. *The Federalist: Design for a Constitutional Republic*. Urbana: University of Illinois Press, 1991.

Diamond, Martin. *The Founding of the Democratic Republic*. Itasca, Ill.: F. E. Peacock, 1981.

Fisher, Louis. *Constitutional Conflicts between Congress and the President*. Princeton, N.J.: Princeton University Press, 1985.

Fisher, Louis. *Constitutional Dialogues*. Princeton, N.J.: Princeton University Press, 1988.

Pious, Richard M. "A Prime Minister for America." *Constitution* 4, no. 3 (Fall 1992): 4–14.

Vile, M. J. C. *Constitutionalism and the Separation of Powers*. New York: Oxford, 1967.

Seriatim opinions

SERIATIM is the Latin word for "severally," or "in a series." When appellate court judges render seriatim opinions, each one presents a separate judgment on a case; no one writes an opinion for the court as a whole. From its origin until 1803, the U.S. Supreme Court followed the practice of writing seriatim opinions. But under Chief Justice John Marshall this practice stopped and the Court began the practice, which is nearly always employed today, of having one justice write a majority opinion for each case decided by the Court.

SEE ALSO

Concurring opinion; Dissenting opinion; Majority opinion; Opinions; Plurality opinion

Shiras, George, Jr.

ASSOCIATE JUSTICE, 1892–1903

☆ *Born: Jan. 26, 1832, Pittsburgh, Pa.*

☆ *Education: Ohio University, 1849–51; Yale College, B.A., 1853; studied law at Yale and privately*

☆ *Previous government service: none*

☆ *Appointed by President Benjamin Harrison July 19, 1892; replaced Joseph P. Bradley, who died*

☆ *Supreme Court term: confirmed by the Senate July 26, 1892, by a voice vote; retired Feb. 23, 1903*

☆ *Died: Aug. 2, 1924, Pittsburgh, Pa.*

GEORGE SHIRAS, JR., was a successful lawyer before his appointment to the Supreme Court. However, he had no prior experience in government service, unlike all other Supreme Court justices.

Justice Shiras strongly supported property rights and economic liberty. Thus, he voted to strike down or limit federal and state regulations of businesses in the cases of *United States* v. *E. C. Knight* (1895) and *Allegeyer* v. *Louisiana* (1897). In *Wong Wing* v. *United States* (1896), however, Justice Shiras wrote for the Court in protecting the rights of illegal aliens against unduly harsh punishments that disregarded 5th and 6th Amendment rights of due process and trial by jury.

FURTHER READING

Shiras, Winfield. *Justice George Shiras, Jr. of Pittsburgh*. Pittsburgh: University of Pittsburgh Press, 1953.

Slaughterhouse Cases

☆ *16 Wall. 36 (1873)*
☆ *Vote: 5–4*
☆ *For the Court: Miller*
☆ *Dissenting: Field, Bradley, Chase, and Swayne*

IN 1869 the Louisiana legislature passed a law incorporating the Crescent City Live-Stock Landing and Slaughter House Company. This law required that all butchering of animals in New Orleans had to be done at the facilities of the new Crescent City Company. According to state officials, the reason for passing this law was to protect the health and safety of the community. They claimed that local butchers were causing pollution and spreading diseases by using unsanitary procedures when they slaughtered animals to be processed into food products. By combining all butchering work in one place, the state officials claimed they could regulate this work in order to reduce health risks.

The local butchers were outraged. The new law forced them to take their business to one location and pay high fees for slaughtering their animals there. They argued that the new law was passed primarily to benefit the owners of the Crescent City Company, not the public good.

The local butchers formed their own organization, the Butchers' Benevolent Association, and hired a lawyer, John A. Campbell, who had been a U.S. Supreme Court justice. Campbell sued the Cres-

cent City Company for depriving the local butchers of their right to property. He argued that this is a basic right of individuals, protected by the privileges and immunities clause of the 14th Amendment, which says, "No state shall make or enforce any law which shall abridge the privileges or immunities of citizens of the United States." Further, Campbell argued that the state law at issue deprived the local butchers of their property rights primarily for the private profit of the Crescent City Company and not for the good of the community, as had been claimed.

In 1870 the issue went to the Louisiana Supreme Court, which upheld the state law and rejected the suit of the Butchers' Benevolent Association. The butchers appealed to the U.S. Supreme Court.

The Issue Did the Louisiana law creating the Crescent City Live-Stock Landing and Slaughter House Company violate the property rights of local butchers under the privileges and immunities clause of the 14th Amendment?

Opinion of the Court In a close vote (5 to 4), the Court upheld the Louisiana law at issue and decided against the suit brought by the Butchers' Benevolent Association. Writing for the Court, Justice Samuel F. Miller held that the Louisiana state government had not violated the 14th Amendment by creating the

New Orleans slaughterhouses in the 1860s. In the Slaughterhouse Cases, the Court decided that a company's right to property was subject to state regulation.

Crescent City Company and giving it control of the slaughterhouse business in New Orleans.

Justice Miller argued that the 14th Amendment's privileges and immunities clause did not protect the butchers' property rights or their right to work. Further, he narrowly interpreted the privileges and immunities clause to pertain only to very few rights of national citizenship that states could not abridge or take away. According to Justice Miller, rights of property and labor were not among these few fundamental rights protected by the 14th Amendment from abridgment by state governments. Rather, these rights were subject to state regulation for the good of the community, said Justice Miller. He also argued that the primary purpose of the 14th Amendment (which was enacted after the Civil War) was to protect the rights of African Americans and not to expand or add to the rights of white people.

Dissent Justice Stephen J. Field argued that property rights and the right to labor *were* among the privileges and immunities protected from state interference by the 14th Amendment. Justices Joseph Bradley and Noah Swayne also contended that the Louisiana law violated the 14th Amendment by depriving the butchers of property without due process of law. Finally, all of the dissenting justices rejected the Court's argument that the 14th Amendment was designed to protect the rights only of black Americans.

Significance Justice Miller's opinion for the Court strictly limited future applications of the privileges and immunities clause of the 14th Amendment. This clause might have been used to allow federal government protection for a wide range of fundamental rights, including the federal Bill of Rights, against infringement by state governments. The *Slaughterhouse* decision, by rejecting a broad interpretation of the privileges and immunities clause, made this constitutional provision virtually useless as a guarantee of the most important individual rights. Individuals therefore had to depend upon their state constitutions and governments for protection of their basic rights. This put black people, newly freed from slavery, at a disadvantage in seeking such protection from southern state governments dominated by former slaveholders. One positive outcome of the *Slaughterhouse* decision, however, was the encouragement given to states in the 1870s and 1880s to regulate economic activities for the good of the community; that is, to protect public health, safety, or morals.

SEE ALSO
Property rights

Smith v. Allwright

☆ *321 U.S. 649 (1944)*
☆ *Vote: 8–1*
☆ *For the Court: Reed*
☆ *Dissenting: Roberts*

LONNIE SMITH, an African American, lived in Harris County, Texas. On July 27, 1940, Smith was stopped from voting in the Democratic party's primary election for selecting the party's nominees for U.S. senator, representative to Congress, and several state offices. Smith met all the Texas qualifications for eligibility to vote. He was denied the ballot by Democratic party election officials only because of his race.

Smith sought help from the National Association for the Advancement of Colored People (NAACP). One of the NAACP lawyers who helped him was Thurgood Marshall, a future justice of the U.S. Supreme Court. Lonnie Smith

In 1942, Maryland election officials show a black man how to vote. Not until 1944, however, did the Supreme Court rule that blacks must be allowed to vote in primary elections as well as general elections.

sued Allwright, a Democratic party election judge, for illegally denying him the right to vote.

The Issue The 15th Amendment to the Constitution clearly protected Lonnie Smith's right to vote: "The right of citizens of the United States to vote shall not be denied or abridged by the United States or any State on account of race, color, or previous condition of servitude." In addition, Section 1 of the 14th Amendment protected Smith's rights against state government interference.

However, the Democratic party was a private organization, not part of the Texas state government. So party officials claimed they could deny Smith the right to participate in a Democratic party primary election without violating the 14th and 15th Amendments, which limited only the federal and state governments, not private associations. They argued that as long as Smith was allowed to vote in the final general election, where he could choose between the Democratic and Republican candidates, his constitutional right to vote was protected.

Smith and his lawyers disagreed. They pointed out that the Democratic party dominated politics and government in Texas. The candidates who won the Democratic party primary election almost always won the subsequent general election. So, by denying Smith and

other black citizens the right to vote in the primary election, the Democratic party was preventing them from effectively participating in electing their representatives in government.

Did the 14th and 15th Amendment protections of the right to vote apply to the primary elections of a political party?

Opinion of the Court Lonnie Smith and the NAACP won this case. The Court held that political party primary elections are operated in association with state government machinery set up to choose state and federal officials. Thus, the 14th and 15th Amendments to the U.S. Constitution could be used to protect Smith's right to vote in the Democratic party primary election.

Justice Stanley Reed wrote:

> The United States is a constitutional democracy. Its organic law grants to all citizens a right to participate in the choice of elected officials without restriction by any State because of race. This grant to the people of the opportunity for choice is not to be nullified by a state through casting its electoral process in a form which permits a private organization to practice racial discrimination in the election. Constitutional rights would be of little value if they could be thus indirectly denied.

Significance This decision overturned *Grovey* v. *Townsend* (1935), which had permitted racial discrimination in the conduct of a party primary election. *Smith* v. *Allwright* was the beginning of legal developments that culminated in the 1960s in full voting rights for African Americans through the passage of the Voting Rights Act of 1965. This federal law was affirmed by the Court in *South Carolina* v. *Katzenbach* (1966) as constitutional under the 15th Amendment.

SEE ALSO

Civil rights; Equality under the Constitution

FURTHER READING

Rogers, Donald W., ed. *Voting and the Spirit of Democracy: Essays in the History of Voting and Voting Rights in America.* Urbana: University of Illinois Press, 1992.

Solicitor general

THE PRESIDENT of the United States appoints the solicitor general to represent the federal executive department before the Supreme Court. Congress created the position of solicitor general in 1870 as part of the Department of Justice. The solicitor general assists the attorney general of the United States, who heads the Department of Justice.

The main duty of the solicitor general is to argue the executive branch's position in cases being heard by the Supreme Court. The solicitor general maintains offices at both the Justice Department headquarters and the Supreme Court building. As a result, a close working relationship has developed between the solicitor general and the justices of the Court.

Thurgood Marshall, an associate justice from 1967 to 1991, served as solicitor general from 1965 to 1967. In this role, he won the Supreme Court's affirmation of the Voting Rights Act of 1965 in *South Carolina* v. *Katzenbach* (1966).

Thurgood Marshall is sworn in as solicitor general in 1965. President Lyndon Johnson stands to the left of Marshall.

FURTHER READING

Sachs, Andrea. "The Government's Advocate." *Constitution* 3, no. 3 (Fall 1991): 4–14.
Salokar, Rebecca Mae. *The Solicitor General: The Politics of Law.* Philadelphia: Temple University Press, 1992.

Souter, David H.

ASSOCIATE JUSTICE, 1990–

☆ Born: Sept. 17, 1939, Melrose, Mass.
☆ Education: Harvard College, A.B., 1961; Harvard Law School, LL.B., 1965
☆ Previous government service: attorney general of New Hampshire, 1976–78; superior judge, New Hampshire, 1978–83; justice, New Hampshire Supreme Court, 1983–90; judge, Federal Court of Appeals of the First Circuit, 1990
☆ Appointed by President George Bush July 25, 1990; replaced Justice William Brennan, who retired
☆ Supreme Court term: confirmed by the Senate Oct. 2, 1990, by a vote of 90–9

DAVID H. SOUTER was President George Bush's first appointment to the Supreme Court. President Bush was determined to nominate a noncontroversial person who would be readily confirmed by the Senate, without conflict and acrimony. The President also wanted a justice who favored judicial restraint and policy-making only by the legislative and the executive branches of government. Souter clearly was the President's man. He had neither written nor publicly said anything controversial enough that could be used to deny his confirmation. Further, he seemed to agree with the President about judicial self-restraint in interpreting the Constitution.

During his confirmation hearings before the Senate Judiciary Committee, Souter performed cautiously and competently. He was confirmed by the Senate and took his seat as the 105th justice of the U.S. Supreme Court.

During his first few years on the Court, Justice Souter has been a capable justice. He has tended to side with the Court's conservative majority, but he clearly has demonstrated intellectual flexibility and independence. For example, he joined the Court's 1993 decision in *Church of the Lukumi Babalu Aye* v. *City of Hialeah,* which struck down a local law banning animal sacrifice as part of a religious ritual. Souter wrote a concurring opinion that protected the 1st Amendment right of free exercise of religion. Souter's concurring opinion, however, was more strongly and broadly stated than the opinion of the Court, written by Justice Anthony Kennedy. Justice Souter has also been a frequent dissenter from the Court majority.

Staff of the Court, nonjudicial

MORE THAN 319 permanent staff members assist the justices in carrying out the business of the U.S. Supreme Court. Most of these employees of the Court work for one of the five officers, whose jobs were established by law: administrative assistant to the chief justice, clerk of the Court, reporter of decisions, marshal, and librarian.

Administrative assistant to the chief justice

The administrative assistant, with a staff of three, assists the chief justice in management of nonjudicial business, such as the administration of the Judicial Conference of the United States, the Federal Judicial Center, and the Administrative Office of the United States Courts.

The administrative assistant also supervises personnel matters and budgets of the Court.

Clerk of the Court

The clerk of the court oversees a staff of 25 people. Among other duties, they manage dockets (agendas) and calendars of the Court, keep track of petitions and briefs that are submitted to the Court, notify lower courts of Supreme Court actions and decisions, and advise lawyers, upon request, about rules and procedures of the Court.

Reporter of decisions

The reporter supervises a staff of nine people who are responsible for recording, editing, and printing the opinions of the Court. The reporter of decisions oversees the official publication of the Supreme Court case decisions in *United States Reports,* which is printed by the U.S. Government Printing Office.

Marshal

With a staff of more than 200 people, the marshal of the Supreme Court manages the security, physical facilities, and payroll of the Court. The marshal receives all important visitors to the Supreme Court Building. He also takes charge of the safety of justices when they carry out formal duties outside the Supreme Court Building.

The marshal declares the beginning of each public session of the Court. He stands at one side of the bench and announces, "The Honorable, the chief justice and the associate justices of the Supreme Court of the United States." As the justices file into the courtroom, the marshal declares, "Oyez, oyez, oyez [Hear ye]: All persons having business before the Honorable, the Supreme Court of the United States, are admonished to draw near and give their attention, for the Court is now sitting. God save the United States and this honorable Court."

Librarian

A staff of 25 helps the librarian of the Supreme Court manage more than 250,000 books and several computerized databases. The librarian supervises the library in the Supreme Court Building and arranges for interlibrary loans.

In addition to the five court officers described above, other employees work for the Office of the Legal Counsel, Office of the Curator, Public Information Office, and the Data Systems Office.

Office of the Curator

The curator of the Supreme Court has the duty of recording and preserving the history of the Court. Chief Justice Warren Burger established the Office of the Curator in 1973. The office collects and preserves memorabilia, such as photographs, prints, manuscripts, and videotapes, that are related to the lives and work of the justices.

Items from the collections of the curator are used in the two exhibits the curator's staff prepares each year. These exhibits are presented in the lower Great Hall of the Supreme Court Building.

The curator's staff responds regularly to requests for information about the Supreme Court from scholars, the justices, other federal judges, and the general public. The staff also conducts hourly lectures and tours for the thousands of visitors who annually visit the Supreme Court Building.

Office of the Legal Counsel

Two attorneys assist the Court with legal research. The attorneys prepare for the justices summaries and analyses of the cases in which the Court has original jurisdiction (cases not on appeal from lower courts, but heard for the first time by the Supreme Court). This office serves as a general counsel for the Court; that is, it provides legal information for the justices upon request. Unlike the justices' law clerks, who serve short terms, the Office of the Legal Counsel provides the continuous legal research services of experienced attorneys.

Public Information Office

A staff of four people works for the Public Information Office. This office distributes 4,000 slip opinions on Supreme Court cases—preliminary, unedited full-text reports on opinions that are circulated within three days of decisions. The slip opinions help newspaper reporters and broadcasters to publicize news of Supreme Court opinions quickly; without the slip opinions, they would have to wait for the fully edited and official publication of the Court opinions. The Public Information Office maintains a press room and broadcast booths for the use of journalists. One hundred seventy-five bench copies of the Court's opinions, preliminary full-text reports, are provided to reporters on the day the opinion is announced by the Court. The Public Information Office also transmits the bench copies of opinions electronically to legal database services, such as LEXIS and WESTLAW.

SEE ALSO
Clerk of the Court; Clerks of the justices; Reporter of decisions

Standing to sue

A PERSON who has the right to bring legal action against another party has standing to sue that party. A party who is injured by another party has standing to sue that party, if the injured one can show that his rights were violated. A party has standing to sue the government only if that party has been injured by the government. For example, if local police conduct an illegal search of a person's home, the person has standing to sue the government under the 4th and 14th Amendments to the Constitution.

By contrast, if a person has no justifiable connection to an alleged wrongful action by the government, then the person has no standing to sue in that regard. For example, a citizen of the United States does not have standing to sue the federal government for recognizing a foreign government that has been charged with violations of international law.

Stare decisis

SEE Precedent

State courts

SOME CASES that go to the Supreme Court originated in the courts of the 50 states. The direct line of appeal, however, is only from the highest appellate court of a state. For example, a case originating in a trial court in Indiana must be appealed first to the Indiana Supreme Court before it can be heard by the U.S. Supreme Court.

In addition, state-level cases may be appealed to the U.S. Supreme Court only if they involve federal questions—issues pertaining to the U.S. Constitution, federal treaties, or federal laws. State courts are required to act in accordance with the Constitution, as well as federal statutes and treaties made under the Constitution. They must recognize the supremacy of federal law—acts of Congress as well as the Constitution—over state law. And they must interpret fed-

eral law in accordance with prevailing decisions of the U.S. Supreme Court.

SEE ALSO
Federalism; Judicial review

Statute

A STATUTE is a written law enacted by a legislature. A federal statute is a law enacted by Congress. State statutes are enacted by state legislatures; those that violate the U.S. Constitution may be struck down by the Supreme Court if the issue is appealed to the Court.

Stevens, John Paul

ASSOCIATE JUSTICE, 1975–

☆ *Born: Apr. 20, 1920, Chicago, Ill.*
☆ *Education: University of Chicago, B.A., 1941; Northwestern University School of Law, J.D., 1947*
☆ *Previous government service: law clerk to Justice Wiley B. Rutledge, 1947–48; associate counsel, Subcommittee on the Study of Monopoly Power, House Judiciary Committee, 1951; U.S. Attorney General's National Committee to Study the Antitrust Laws, 1953–55; judge, Seventh Circuit Court of Appeals, 1970–75*
☆ *Appointed by President Gerald R. Ford Nov. 28, 1975; replaced William O. Douglas, who retired*
☆ *Supreme Court term: confirmed by the Senate Dec. 17, 1975, by a 98–0 vote*

JOHN PAUL STEVENS has been an independent thinker on the Court. He has often written separate concurring opinions and dissenting opinions.

Justice Stevens has tended to support national government authority in cases on federalism, which has restricted the powers and independent activities of state governments. In particular, he has favored broad interpretations of the Constitution's "commerce clause" (Article 1, Section 8), which grants power to Congress to regulate trade among the states.

Justice Stevens has tended to support protection of individual rights, especially 1st Amendment freedoms of religion, speech, and assembly. He wrote notably for the Court, for example, in *Wallace* v. *Jaffree* (1985) to defend strict separation of church and state.

SEE ALSO
Wallace v. Jaffree

FURTHER READING
Canon, Bradley C. "Justice John Paul Stevens: The Lone Ranger in a Black Robe." In *The Burger Court: Political and Judicial Profiles,* edited by Charles M. Lamb and Stephen C. Halpern, 343–74. Urbana: University of Illinois Press, 1991.

Stewart, Potter

ASSOCIATE JUSTICE, 1958–81

☆ *Born: Jan. 23, 1915, Jackson, Mich.*
☆ *Education: Yale College, B.A., 1937; fellow, Cambridge University, 1937–38; Yale Law School, LL.B., 1941*
☆ *Previous government service: Cincinnati City Council, Ohio, 1950–53; vice mayor of Cincinnati, 1952–53; judge, Sixth Circuit Court of Appeals, 1954–58*
☆ *Appointed by President Dwight D. Eisenhower as a recess appointment Oct. 14, 1958; replaced Harold H. Burton, who retired; nominated by Eisenhower Jan. 17, 1959*
☆ *Supreme Court term: confirmed by the Senate May 5, 1959, by a 70–17 vote; retired July 3, 1981*
☆ *Died: Dec. 7, 1985, Hanover, N.H.*

POTTER STEWART was an especially strong defender of individual rights pro-

tected by the 1st, 4th, and 14th Amendments. For example, in *Katz* v. *United States* (1967), Stewart strengthened the protection of the 4th Amendment against government's invasion of an individual's privacy. He argued that private conversations must be protected against police interception no matter where the conversation takes place. Stewart wrote: "The Fourth Amendment protects people not places." Thus, a microphone placed against the wall of a telephone booth by federal investigators was held to be a violation of the 4th Amendment's ban on "unwarranted searches and seizures" and a violation of the right of privacy.

Justice Stewart had a way with words and many of his statements in Supreme Court opinions have become famous quotations. For example, he admitted his difficulty in stating an exact definition of pornography in *Jacobellis* v. *Ohio* (1964); Stewart wrote this often-quoted statement about pornography: "I know it when I see it."

SEE ALSO
Katz v. United States

FURTHER READING
Yarbrough, Tinsley E. "Justice Potter Stewart: Decisional Patterns in Search of Doctrinal Moorings." In *The Burger Court: Political and Judicial Profiles,* edited by Charles M. Lamb and Stephen C. Halpern, 375–406. Urbana: University of Illinois Press, 1991.

Stone, Harlan Fiske

ASSOCIATE JUSTICE, 1925–41

CHIEF JUSTICE, 1941–46

☆ *Born: Oct. 11, 1872, Chesterfield, N.H.*
☆ *Education: Amherst College, B.A., 1894, M.A., 1897, LL.D., 1913; Columbia University Law School, LL.B., 1898*

☆ *Previous government service: U.S. attorney general, 1924–25*

☆ *Appointed by President Calvin Coolidge to be an associate justice Jan. 5, 1925; replaced Joseph McKenna, who retired; appointed chief justice by President Franklin D. Roosevelt June 12, 1941; replaced Chief Justice Charles Evans Hughes, who retired*

☆ *Supreme Court term: confirmed as an associate justice by the Senate Feb. 5, 1925, by a 71–6 vote; confirmed by the Senate as chief justice June 27, 1941, by a voice vote; served until Apr. 22, 1946*

☆ *Died: Apr. 22, 1946, Washington, D.C.*

HARLAN FISKE STONE was the only university professor ever to become chief justice of the United States. As a Republican appointed by Democratic President Franklin Roosevelt, Stone is one of only two chief justices nominated by a President from a different political party. (Chief Justice Edward White was the other one.)

Before entering federal government service, Stone was a professor and dean of the Columbia University School of Law (1910–23). He served under President Calvin Coolidge as attorney general of the United States before Coolidge named Stone as associate justice of the Supreme Court. The great respect among the other justices for Stone led President Roosevelt to appoint him to the office of chief justice in 1941.

Throughout his term on the Supreme Court, Harlan Fiske Stone followed the principle of judicial self-restraint, which he stated in a dissenting opinion in *United States* v. *Butler* (1936). In this case, the Court struck down as unconstitutional the Agricultural Adjustment Act, which was part of the New Deal. Justice Stone could find no constitutional basis for this decision and claimed it was based on the anti–New Deal policy preferences of the Court's majority, which were used to override the policy-making majority in

Congress. Justice Stone wrote that the President and Congress are restrained by the "ballot box and the processes of democratic government. . . . The only check on our own exercise of power is our own sense of [judicial] self-restraint."

According to Justice Stone, the Court should leave the making of policies and laws to the executive and legislative branches. The Court should not substitute its policy preferences for those of the democratically elected Congress and President because this would be an unconstitutional overextension of the Court's power.

Justice Stone opposed the judicial activism of the justices who opposed, for conservative political reasons, the New Deal programs of President Roosevelt. Later, as chief justice, Stone opposed the judicial activism of liberal justices who wanted to expand the power and benefits of organized labor.

Chief Justice Stone acted strongly to support 1st Amendment freedoms in the "flag salute cases" of 1940 and 1943; he dissented against the Court's majority in *Minersville School District* v. *Gobitis* (1940), which upheld a state law requiring students in public schools to salute the U.S. flag and pledge allegiance to the United States. Three years later, Chief Justice Stone was instrumental in organizing the Court's majority in *West Virginia State Board of Education* v. *Barnette* (1943), which overturned the *Gobitis* decision. Thus, a state law requiring students in public schools to salute the flag was struck down as a violation of the free exercise of religion by Jehovah's Witnesses.

Chief Justice Stone, however, led the majority in the Japanese-American internment cases, which restricted individual rights of Japanese Americans in favor of national security concerns during World War II. For example, in the cases of *Korematsu* v. *United States* (1944) and *Hirabayashi* v. *United States* (1943), Chief Justice Stone voted to uphold federal laws restricting the freedom of Japanese Americans on the presumption, without evidence, that they might aid Japan, a World War II enemy of the United States. Most Americans today believe these cases were decided unjustly.

SEE ALSO

Hirabayashi v. United States; Judicial activism and judicial restraint; Korematsu v. United States; Minersville School District v. Gobitis; West Virginia State Board of Education v. Barnette

FURTHER READING

Konefsky, S. J. *Chief Justice Stone and the Supreme Court.* New York: Macmillan, 1946.
Mason, Alpheus Thomas. *Harlan Fiske Stone: Pillar of the Law.* New York: Viking Press, 1956.

Story, Joseph

ASSOCIATE JUSTICE, 1812–45

☆ *Born: Sept. 18, 1779, Marblehead, Mass.*
☆ *Education: Harvard College, A.B., 1798; read law with Samuel Sewall and Samuel Putnam in Boston, 1799–1801*
☆ *Previous government service: Massachusetts House of Representatives, 1805–8, Speaker, 1811; U.S. representative from Massachusetts, 1808–9*
☆ *Appointed by President James Madison Nov. 15, 1811; replaced William Cushing, who died*
☆ *Supreme Court term: confirmed by the Senate Nov. 18, 1811, by a voice vote; served until Sept. 10, 1845*
☆ *Died: Sept. 10, 1845, Cambridge, Mass.*

JOSEPH STORY was one of the greatest justices of the Supreme Court. He worked in close partnership with Chief Justice John Marshall to establish the supremacy of the U.S. Constitution and the federal government over state constitutions and governments. He also acted with Marshall to uphold private property rights and economic liberty as fundamental principles of the Constitution. Finally, his peers generally agreed that Story was the greatest legal scholar and educator of his times.

Justice Story's greatest opinion for the Court was *Martin* v. *Hunter's Lessee* (1816), in which he upheld the constitutionality of Section 25 of the Judiciary Act of 1789. The constitutional question was whether or not the U.S. Supreme Court should have the power of judicial review over decisions of state courts, as specified in Section 25 of the Judiciary Act of 1789. Justice Story successfully argued for the constitutionality of Section 25, which bolstered the supremacy of the federal government in its relationships with the states. This decision was vindicated, once and for all, by Chief Justice John Marshall (with Story's support) in *Cohens* v. *Virginia* (1821).

Most of Chief Justice Marshall's great decisions were products of close collaboration with Justice Story. He endorsed and helped to develop John Marshall's broad construction of the Constitution. Likewise, Justice Story provided substance and technical precision for Chief Justice Marshall's great opinions about commercial law, contracts, and private property. Like Marshall, Story believed that protection of private property rights was necessary for the preservation of free government.

Throughout his long tenure on the Court, Justice Story found time to be a scholar and educator. He reorganized legal education at the Harvard Law School and served there as a distinguished professor of law. He also wrote several volumes that have become classics of legal scholarship. For example, his *Commentaries on the Constitution* (originally published in 1833) influenced constitutional thought throughout the 19th century. Story's achievements as a teacher and scholar made the Harvard Law School the biggest and best in the United States.

Justice Story's influence on the Court declined after the death of John Marshall in 1835, who was replaced as chief justice by Roger B. Taney. Under Taney's leadership, the Court reflected the ideas of Jacksonian democracy, not Marshall's federalism. The Jacksonians, unlike Marshall, tended to resist strong emphasis on federal government power. States' rights and powers were favored more than before, causing Justice Story to become a dissenter on the Court. Despite Story's declining status on the Taney Court, his influence outside the Court remained strong. His published commentaries on various aspects of the law shaped legal thinking long after his death.

SEE ALSO

Cohens v. Virginia; Martin v. Hunter's Lessee

FURTHER READING

Dunne, Gerald T. *Justice Joseph Story and the Rise of the Supreme Court.* New York: Simon & Schuster, 1970.
McClellan, James. *Joseph Story and the American Constitution: A Study in Political and Legal Thought.* Norman: University of Oklahoma Press, 1990.
Newmyer, R. Kent. "The Lost Legal World of Joseph Story." *Constitution* 4, no. 1 (Winter 1992): 58–65.
Newmyer, R. Kent. *Supreme Court Justice Joseph Story: Statesman of the Old Republic.* Chapel Hill: University of North Carolina Press, 1985.

Strict scrutiny

SEE Equality under the Constitution; Suspect classifications; Time, place, and manner rule

Stromberg v. California

☆ *283 U.S. 359 (1931)*
☆ *Vote: 7–2*
☆ *For the Court: Hughes*
☆ *Dissenting: Butler and McReynolds*

YETTA STROMBERG was a 19-year-old counselor at a summer camp for children in California. She was also an active member of the Young Communist League. Stromberg taught the children about communist ideas and praised the communist government of the Soviet Union. In teaching one of her lessons, Stromberg had the children make a replica of the red flag of the U.S.S.R. She and the children raised the banner and recited a pledge of allegiance to it.

The sheriff of San Bernardino County arrested Yetta Stromberg for teaching activities that violated a 1919 state law prohibiting the display of a red flag "as an emblem of opposition to organized government." After her conviction under the California law, Stromberg appealed to the U.S. Supreme Court.

The Issue Stromberg argued that the state of California had denied her right to freedom of speech guaranteed by the 1st and 14th Amendments to the U.S. Constitution. California attorneys claimed that the state law used to convict Stromberg was within the state's power to maintain order and safety.

Opinion of the Court Chief Justice Charles Evans Hughes, writing for the Court, overturned the conviction of Yetta Stromberg. The California "red flag law" was declared unconstitutional because it violated "the conception of liberty under the due process clause of the Fourteenth Amendment [which] embraces the right of free speech [in the First Amendment]."

Significance The *Stromberg* case was one of the Court's early uses of the

14th Amendment to incorporate the 1st Amendment's right to free speech—that is, to protect this right from infringement by a state government. The 14th Amendment states, "No State shall . . . deprive any person of life, liberty, or property, without due process of law."

In addition, in *Stromberg* the Court for the first time protected the substance of symbolic speech (a flag display) against state government restriction.

SEE ALSO

Freedom of speech and press; Gitlow v. New York; Incorporation doctrine; Near v. Minnesota

FURTHER READING

Murphy, Paul L. *The Meaning of Freedom of Speech*. Westport, Conn.: Greenwood, 1972.
Smolla, Rodney. *Free Speech in an Open Society*. New York: Knopf, 1992.

Strong, William

ASSOCIATE JUSTICE, 1870–80

☆ Born: May 6, 1808, Somers, Conn.
☆ Education: Yale University, B.A., 1828, M.A., 1831
☆ Previous government service: U.S. representative from Pennsylvania, 1847–51; justice, Pennsylvania Supreme Court, 1857–68
☆ Appointed by President Ulysses Grant Feb. 7, 1870; replaced Robert C. Grier, who retired
☆ Supreme Court term: confirmed by the Senate Feb. 18, 1870, by a voice vote; retired Dec. 14, 1880
☆ Died: Aug. 19, 1895, Lake Minnewaska, N.Y.

WILLIAM STRONG rarely wrote opinions for the Court during his 10-year term as an associate justice. He tended to side with the majority in decisions supporting property and contractual rights.

Justice Strong had a mixed record in civil rights cases. He joined the Court's majority in the *Slaughterhouse Cases* (1873) to restrict the rights of individuals under the 14th Amendment. However, he wrote for the Court in *Strauder* v. *West Virginia* (1880) the decision to strike down a state law excluding black people from juries. In a related case, *Ex parte Virginia* (1880), Justice Strong upheld a section of the Civil Rights Act of 1875 that banned racial discrimination in jury selection.

Justice Strong retired from the Court in robust health at the age of 72. He wanted to set an example for three colleagues on the Court who continued to serve despite age-related health problems that interfered with their performance. Within two years, the three resigned.

Student rights under the Constitution

JUSTICE ABE FORTAS, writing for the U.S. Supreme Court in *Tinker* v. *Des Moines Independent Community School District* (1969), stated, "It can hardly be argued that either students or teachers shed their constitutional rights to freedom of speech or expression at the schoolhouse gate." The Supreme Court has ruled that some constitutional rights of students in public schools are the same as those of other people in the United States. Other constitutional rights, however, are not the same for children and adults. For example, people younger than 18 years old are not eligible to vote in public elections. Further, state governments may constitutionally deny to children certain privileges available to adults, such as licenses to drive automobiles or to marry.

The Supreme Court has also held that certain constitutional rights of adults or students outside of school are not necessarily the same for students in a public school. During the 20th century, the U.S. Supreme Court has decided cases about such constitutional rights of students as freedom of speech and press, religious freedom, freedom of assembly and association, protection against unreasonable searches and seizures, and due process of law.

Free speech and press

In 1969, the Supreme Court upheld student rights to free speech in a landmark decision, *Tinker* v. *Des Moines Independent Community School District*. The Court ruled that students who wore black armbands to school to protest U.S. involvement in the Vietnam War had a constitutional right to such freedom of expression. In this case and others, however, the Court has affirmed the authority of school officials to regulate freedom of expression with regard to the time, place, and manner of the spoken or written messages. School officials may therefore limit student speech in order to prevent serious disruption of the teaching and learning processes of the school.

For example, in *Bethel School District No. 403* v. *Fraser* (1986), the Court upheld the restriction of a student's speech by school officials because the speech was obscene and therefore disrupted the educational process. Chief Justice Warren Burger, writing for the Court, declared, "The undoubted freedom to advocate unpopular and controversial views in schools and classrooms must be balanced against the society's countervailing interest in teaching students the boundaries of socially appropriate behavior."

In *Hazelwood School District* v. *Kuhlmeier* (1988) the Court upheld restrictions by school officials on the content of articles printed in a school newspaper. The students' writing for this publication was viewed by the Court as part of the school curriculum and therefore subject to regulation by school authorities. Justice Byron White, writing for the Court, argued, "A school need not tolerate student speech that is inconsistent with its basic educational mission, even though the government could not censor similar speech outside the school." The Court in this case emphasized that the constitutional rights of students in public schools are not necessarily and always the same as the rights of individuals in other places. The Court also stressed that the rights of students in extracurricular activities of the school are broader than their rights in activities of the school's formal program of studies. Thus, Justice White concluded, "It is only when the decision to censor a school sponsored publication…has no valid educational purpose [or is not part of the school curriculum] that the First Amendment [can be used] to protect students' constitutional rights."

Protection against unreasonable searches and seizures

The Court has ruled (*New Jersey* v. *T.L.O.*, 1985) that the 4th Amendment rights of public school students are not exactly the same as the rights of adults in nonschool settings. In the *T.L.O.* case, the Court permitted school officials to conduct a search of a student's purse without a warrant, on the grounds that this action was reasonable under the circumstances. There was reason to suspect that the search would turn up evidence of violation of either the law or school rules, so the warrantless search was upheld even though a similar search outside of school would have been ruled unconstitutional.

In line with the *T.L.O.* decision, federal courts have upheld warrantless searches of student lockers when there is a reasonable suspicion of uncovering evidence of actions violating laws or school rules. School authorities may suspend or expel students from school for possession of illegal drugs, alcohol, or weapons uncovered by warrantless searches of lockers or purses.

Due process rights

The 5th and 14th Amendments to the Constitution guarantee due process of law—certain legal procedural rights—to individuals charged with breaking the law and to those facing deprivation of life, liberty, or property by the government. In *Goss* v. *Lopez* (1975) the Supreme Court considered the due process rights of students suspended from school for violating school rules. The Court held that public school officials must follow minimal due process procedures when suspending a student from school for 10 days or less. Students facing such suspension, ruled the Court, must at least receive oral or written notice of charges against them and an opportunity for a hearing to present their side regarding the charges. However, the Court said that due process rights for short-term suspensions do not require that the students charged with wrongdoing have the rights to assistance of legal counsel, to question witnesses against them, and to call their own witnesses to refute the charges against them, which are due process rights specified in the 6th Amendment to the Constitution. Further, the Court said that notice of charges and a hearing should be provided before suspension, unless a student's presence in school threatens the safety, property, or educational opportunities of others.

In its *Goss* ruling, the Court emphasized that it was responding only to an issue about suspensions of 10 days or less. It advised school officials that "longer suspensions or expulsion for the remainder of the school term, or permanently, may require more formal procedures."

In *Honig* v. *Doe* (1988) the Supreme

Court ruled on the due process rights of disabled students. Before school officials expel a disabled student from school, they must determine whether the offending behavior was caused by the student's disability. If so, the student cannot be expelled from school. However, the disabled student may be suspended from school, for no more than 10 days, even if the offending behavior stemmed from the disability. If the offending behavior was not caused by the student's disability, the student may be expelled, following careful observance of due process rights, just like a student without a disability. However, a disabled student expelled from school may not be totally deprived of educational services by the public school system.

The Supreme Court in *Ingraham* v. *Wright* (1977) decided that school officials may carry out corporal (physical) punishment as a means of disciplining students without providing due process rights to the student. Lower federal courts have, however, spelled out minimal due process procedures for corporal punishment, which involve prior notice to students about the kinds of misbehavior that could result in corporal punishment and administration of such punishment by one school official in the presence of another school official. Even

In a school setting, students do not have all the constitutional rights that they have outside of school. Free speech, for example, may be limited if it disrupts the educational process.

though the Supreme Court has neither banned nor strictly limited corporal punishment in schools, many school districts and some state legislatures have regulated or eliminated this kind of punishment.

Student rights to religious liberty

The Supreme Court has upheld the right of students in public schools to free exercise of religious belief. In *West Virginia State Board of Education* v. *Barnette* (1943), the Court overturned a state flag-salute law. The Court held that the state law forced some students (Jehovah's Witnesses) to salute the flag even though this action violated their religious beliefs.

The Supreme Court has consistently opposed state and local laws that require public school students to pray or otherwise engage in religious activities during the school day or during school-sponsored extracurricular activities. This restriction has been maintained even when the religious content of the prayers or other activities has been nondenominational, nonpreferential, and voluntary, as long as the government has sanctioned the activity. The Court has held (in *Engel* v. *Vitale*, 1962; *Abington School District* v. *Schempp*, 1963; and *Wallace* v. *Jaffree*, 1985) that these kinds of public school–sanctioned religious activities violate the establishment clause of the 1st Amendment to the Constitution.

Further, in *Stone* v. *Graham* (1980) the Court ruled unconstitutional a state law that required copies of the Ten Commandments to be displayed in public school classrooms because it violated the 1st Amendment's establishment clause. And in 1992 (*Lee* v. *Weisman*) the Court prohibited prayers as part of an official public school graduation ceremony. However, students are free to organize, on their own and without school sup-

port, voluntary religious programs associated with graduation. In 1993, the Court let stand a decision of the Court of Appeals for the Fifth Circuit (*Jones* v. *Clear Creek Independent School District*) that ruled that a Texas school district's policy allowing students to voluntarily lead prayers at public school graduation ceremonies does not violate the 1st Amendment's establishment clause.

The Supreme Court rulings on prayer and religious programs in public schools do not prohibit individuals from quietly praying, on their own, during the school day or during school-sponsored extracurricular activities. Further, the Court's rulings do not prohibit teaching and learning about religious beliefs in history or literature courses, as long as teachers refrain from the indoctrination of particular religions.

The Court has supported student rights to free speech and free exercise of religion by upholding the federal Equal Access Act in *Board of Education of the Westside Community Schools* v. *Mergens* (1990). This federal law states that it is unlawful for "any public secondary school which receives Federal financial assistance and which has a limited open forum to deny equal access or a fair opportunity to, or discriminate against, any students who wish to conduct a meeting within the limited open forum on the basis of the religious, political, philosophical, or other content of the speech at such meetings." The Court has ruled that the federal Equal Access Act does not violate the establishment clause and does provide opportunity for students to voluntarily form a religious club and hold meetings of their organization on school premises after school hours.

In *Lamb's Chapel* v. *Center Moriches Union Free School District* (1993) the Supreme Court held that a New York public school district violated the freedom of expression and free exercise of religion rights of a church-supported group by not letting it use school facilities to hold a meeting after completion of the formal school day. The public school officials opened school buildings to other community groups for meetings. Thus, it was unlawful, said the Court, for them to deny access to a church group because the group wanted to exhibit and discuss films about their religious beliefs.

SEE ALSO

Abington School District v. Schempp; Bethel School District No. 403 v. Fraser; Engel v. Vitale; Hazelwood School District v. Kuhlmeier; New Jersey v. T.L.O.; Tinker v. Des Moines Independent Community School District; West Virginia State Board of Education v. Barnette; Wallace v. Jaffree

FURTHER READING

Weeks, J. Devereux. *Student Rights under the Constitution.* Athens: Carl Vinson Institute of Government, University of Georgia, 1992.

Supreme Court Reporter

SINCE 1883 the West Publishing Company has regularly issued the *Supreme Court Reporter,* an unofficial record of U.S. Supreme Court decisions. The contents of the decisions in the *Supreme Court Reporter* are the same as in the official edition, *United States Reports,* which is issued by the U.S. Government Printing Office. Summaries of all cases are prepared by West. In addition, tables of key words, phrases, and statutes are developed to help readers interpret information in the full-text reports of the Court's opinions.

SEE ALSO
United States Reports

Suspect classifications

THE EQUAL protection clause of the 14th Amendment and the due process clause of the 5th Amendment restrict state and federal governments from discriminating against individuals. Not all discrimination by the government, however, is unconstitutional. The law may treat classes of individuals differently if it is reasonable to do so and there is a compelling government interest. A state government may, for example, discriminate on the basis of age in determining who is eligible to obtain a driver's license because such discrimination is reasonable and serves the compelling government interest of promoting public safety.

Suspect classifications, by contrast, are assumed to be unreasonable and cannot be justified as necessary to achieve a compelling government interest. Government discrimination against suspect classifications of individuals has been judged by the Supreme Court to be unconstitutional. It considers both race and religion to be suspect classifications; therefore, any government discrimination against racial or religious groups is unlikely to be upheld. When discrimination involving suspect classifications is challenged in court, the government has the very difficult, if not impossible, task of demonstrating that the discrimination is necessary to achieve a compelling state interest. This heavy burden of proof is known as the test of strict scrutiny.

In contrast to the ordinary scrutiny of the Court, strict scrutiny is undertaken on the assumption that the challenged government act is unconstitutional. Only in very few cases has a challenged government act passed the test of strict scrutiny.

Sutherland, George

ASSOCIATE JUSTICE,
1922–38

☆ *Born: Mar. 25, 1862,*
 Buckinghamshire, England
☆ *Education: University of Michigan*
 Law School, 1883
☆ *Previous government service: Utah*
 Senate, 1896–1900; U.S. representa-
 tive from Utah, 1901–3; U.S. senator
 from Utah, 1905–17; chairman,
 advisory committee to the Washington
 Conference for the Limitation of
 Naval Armaments, 1921; U.S. counsel,
 Norway–United States arbitrations,
 The Hague, Netherlands, 1921–22
☆ *Appointed by President Warren G.*
 Harding Sept. 5, 1922; replaced Justice
 John H. Clarke, who resigned
☆ *Supreme Court term: confirmed by the*
 Senate Sept. 5, 1922, by a voice vote;
 retired Jan. 17, 1938
☆ *Died: July 18, 1942, Stockbridge,*
 Mass.

GEORGE SUTHERLAND was a strong
advocate of private rights and limited
government. He opposed extensive government regulation of businesses as an
invasion of property rights and contractual rights. For example, he wrote for the
Court in *Adkins* v. *Children's Hospital*
(1923), the decision that struck down a
minimum wage law for female workers.
Justice Sutherland argued that this law
interfered unconstitutionally with a
woman's right to negotiate a contract.

Justice Sutherland was capable of
defending the civil rights of accused
people as vigorously as property rights.
In *Powell* v. *Alabama* (1932), he overturned the conviction of black youths
sentenced to death for an assault on a
white girl because they had been denied
their constitutional right to legal counsel
(provided by Amendment 6).

Justice Sutherland's views in support of
economic liberty and against heavy-handed
government regulation of businesses put

him at odds with President Franklin
Roosevelt's New Deal programs. He was
known as one of the Court's "Four Horse-
men"—the hard-line opponents of the New
Deal. The Court's movement in 1937
toward acceptance of the New Deal influenced Sutherland to retire from the Court
in 1938.

SEE ALSO
Powell v. Alabama

Swayne, Noah H.

ASSOCIATE JUSTICE,
1862–81

☆ *Born: Dec. 7, 1804, Frederick County,*
 Va.
☆ *Education: studied law privately*
☆ *Previous government service:*
 Coshocton County, Va., prosecuting
 attorney, 1826–29; Ohio House of
 Representatives, 1830, 1836; U.S.
 attorney for Ohio, 1830–41; Colum-
 bus City councilman, Ohio, 1834
☆ *Appointed by President Abraham*
 Lincoln Jan. 22, 1862; replaced John
 McLean, who died
☆ *Supreme Court term: confirmed by the*
 Senate Jan. 24, 1862, by a 38–1 vote;
 retired Jan. 24, 1881
☆ *Died: June 8, 1884, New York, N.Y.*

NOAH H. SWAYNE was a zealous foe
of slavery, which led him to join the Republican party and support Abraham
Lincoln for the presidency. He became
President Lincoln's first Supreme Court
appointment.

Justice Swayne readily supported
Lincoln's Civil War policies. For example, he backed the President's blockade of southern ports in the *Prize Cases*
(1863), and he sustained the use of military trials for civilian defendants in *Ex
parte Vallandigham* (1864). After the
war, Justice Swayne continued to back
Republican party programs.

Sweatt v. Painter

☆ *339 U.S. 629 (1950)*
☆ *Vote: 9–0*
☆ *For the Court: Vinson*

HERMAN MARION SWEATT was a post office worker in Houston, Texas, who wanted to become a lawyer. He applied for admission to the law school of the University of Texas. Sweatt's application to this racially segregated law school was turned down solely because he was black.

Sweatt turned for help to the National Association for the Advancement of Colored People (NAACP) and its chief legal counsel, Thurgood Marshall, who would later become an associate justice of the U.S. Supreme Court.

The NAACP and Sweatt filed suit to demand his admission to the University of Texas. The trial court judge continued, or postponed, the case for six months to give the state government time to set up a law school for black people that could admit Herman Sweatt. At the end of the six-month period, the judge dismissed Sweatt's suit because the state was setting up a law school to which he could be admitted.

Sweatt, however, was not satisfied. He claimed that the new law school for blacks would be greatly inferior to the University of Texas law school. But the Texas courts decided that the two law schools—one for whites and the other for blacks—were "substantially equivalent." Sweatt and the NAACP appealed to the U.S. Supreme Court.

The Issue This case was a test of the "separate but equal" doctrine established by the Court in *Plessy* v. *Ferguson* (1896). Did the separate Texas law schools—one for white students and the other for blacks—satisfy the 14th Amendment requirement that "No state shall...deny to

any person within its jurisdiction the equal protection of the laws"?

Opinion of the Court The Court decided in favor of Sweatt. Chief Justice Fred M. Vinson concluded that the new law school for black students could not be equal to the University of Texas law school, which had a long tradition, a highly regarded faculty, and ample resources. The racially segregated law schools of Texas violated the equal protection clause of the 14th Amendment.

Significance This decision was a clear rejection of the long-standing "separate but equal" doctrine set forth in *Plessy* v. *Ferguson* (1896), and it pointed the way to a more sweeping decision against that doctrine that occurred four years later in *Brown* v. *Board of Education* (1954).

SEE ALSO

Brown v. Board of Education; Civil rights; Equality under the Constitution; National Association for the Advancement of Colored People (NAACP), Plessy v. Ferguson; Segregation, de facto and de jure

Taft, William Howard

*CHIEF JUSTICE,
1 9 2 1 – 3 0*

☆ *Born: Sept. 15, 1857, Cincinnati, Ohio*
☆ *Education: Yale College, B.A., 1878; University of Cincinnati Law School, LL.B., 1880*
☆ *Previous government service: assistant prosecuting attorney, Hamilton County, Ohio, 1881–83; assistant county solicitor, Hamilton County, 1885–87; judge, Ohio Superior Court, 1887–90; U.S. solicitor general, 1890–91; federal judge, Sixth Circuit, 1892–1900; chairman, Philippine Commission, 1900–1901; civil governor of the Philippines, 1901–4; U.S. secretary of war, 1904–8; President of the United States, 1909–13; joint chairman, National War Labor Board, 1918–19*
☆ *Appointed by President Warren G. Harding June 30, 1921; replaced Chief Justice Edward D. White, who died*

☆ Supreme Court term: confirmed by the Senate June 30, 1921, by a voice vote; retired Feb. 3, 1930
☆ Died: Mar. 8, 1930, Washington, D.C.

WILLIAM HOWARD TAFT is the only President of the United States to also serve as chief justice of the United States. Of the two positions, chief justice was the one to which he most strongly aspired. From his youth to old age, Taft ardently desired to sit on the Supreme Court. When he was 63 years old, his ambition was fulfilled when President Warren G. Harding appointed him to the Court.

Taft's opportunity to achieve his ambition was affected by one of his decisions as President. When Chief Justice Melville Fuller died in 1910, President Taft had considered two men as his replacement: Charles Evans Hughes and Edward D. White. Hughes was 17 years younger than White, whom Taft appointed to be the new chief justice. If President Taft had picked Hughes instead of White, his lifelong dream might not have been attained.

Chief Justice Taft was a great judicial administrator. He influenced Congress to pass the Judiciary Act of 1925, which gave the Court almost total authority to choose what cases it would decide. And Taft influenced Congress to appropriate money for construction of the magnificent Supreme Court Building in which the Court conducts its work today. (Since 1860, the Court had been conducting its business on the first floor of the Capitol, in the old Senate chamber.) Chief Justice Taft was also known as a skillful manager of the Court's work load and an adept mediator among his colleagues.

Chief Justice Taft was a great administrator, but he was not as accomplished at formulating doctrine or writing opinions. Though he wrote 249 opinions for the Court, he left no landmark decisions or enduring interpretations of the Constitution. His most significant opinion was in *Myers* v. *United States* (1926). The Court ruled that the President had the power to remove an executive appointee, a postmaster, without the consent of the Senate. Taft said: "I never wrote an opinion I felt to be so important in its effect."

SEE ALSO

Buildings, Supreme Court

FURTHER READING

Mason, Alpheus Thomas. W*illiam Howard Taft: Chief Justice.* New York: Simon & Schuster, 1964.

Taney, Roger Brooke

CHIEF JUSTICE, 1836–64

☆ Born: Mar. 17, 1777, Calvert County, Md.
☆ Education: Dickinson College, B.A., 1795; read law in the office of Judge Jeremiah Chase in Annapolis, Md.
☆ Previous government service: Maryland House of Delegates, 1799–1800; Maryland Senate, 1816–21; attorney general of Maryland, 1827–31; U.S. attorney general, 1831–33; acting U.S. secretary of war, 1831; U.S. secretary of the Treasury, 1833–34 (appointment rejected by the Senate)
☆ Appointed by President Andrew Jackson Dec. 28, 1835; replaced John Marshall, who died
☆ Supreme Court term: confirmed by the Senate Mar. 15, 1836, by a 29–15 vote; served until Oct. 12, 1864
☆ Died: Oct. 12, 1864, Washington, D.C.

CHIEF JUSTICE Roger Brooke Taney is linked inseparably with his infamous opinion in *Scott* v. *Sandford* (1857), which sanctioned slavery and denied the rights of black Americans. Yet Taney freed his own slaves, which he inherited. He also has been ranked by legal schol-

ars as one of the great justices in Supreme Court history.

Roger Taney began his career in the federal government as a staunch Jacksonian Democrat. He served President Andrew Jackson's interests ably as U.S. attorney general, acting secretary of war, and secretary of the Treasury.

In 1835, President Jackson appointed Taney to fill a vacancy on the Supreme Court. The Senate, however, rejected the appointment because of disagreements with Taney's performance as secretary of the Treasury. A few months later, Chief Justice John Marshall died, and President Jackson turned again to Taney. This time the Senate confirmed the President's appointment, after a bitter debate, and Roger Taney succeeded John Marshall as chief justice of the United States.

Chief Justice Taney's greatest opinion was *Charles River Bridge* v. *Warren Bridge* (1837). Writing for the Court, Taney rejected the claim of owners of the Charles River Bridge that their charter, granted by the state of Massachusetts, implicitly gave them a monopoly and thereby prevented the state from granting rights to another company to build a second bridge over the same river. The Charles River Bridge Company, which charged passengers a toll for crossing its bridge, did not want any competition from a second company. In deciding against the monopoly claims of the Charles River Bridge Company, Taney sought to balance private property rights with the public good. He wrote: "The object and end of government is to promote the happiness and prosperity of the community. . . . While the rights of private property are sacredly guarded, we must not forget that the community also has rights, and that the happiness and well-being of every citizen depends on their faithful preservation."

With this decision, Chief Justice Taney defined a major, continuing issue of American constitutional law. From Taney's time until today, jurists have tried, as he did, to balance the sometimes competing claims of private property rights and the community's rights.

Taney's tenure on the Court was marked by growing concerns to protect state government powers and rights within the federal system. This trend was in sharp contrast to the Marshall Court's persistent concern with establishing federal government supremacy over the states. The Taney Court emphasized the sovereignty of the states over matters within their jurisdiction, as provided by the U.S. Constitution, such as maintaining public order, building public facilities, and regulating local businesses.

Taney's conception of states' rights shaped his decisions about slavery. He held that the power to maintain slavery or to free slaves belonged solely to the state governments. His views were expressed memorably and disastrously in *Scott* v. *Sandford* (1857). In this decision, Taney asserted that black Americans could not be citizens of the United States; that the U.S. Constitution protected private property rights, including the right to own slaves; that each state had exclusive power to make decisions about slavery or emancipation of slaves; and that the federal government had no power to ban slavery in the territories of the United States. The *Dred Scott* decision fanned the flames of conflict between the so-called slave states and free states and was one important cause of the Civil War.

SEE ALSO
Charles River Bridge v. Warren Bridge; Federalism; Scott v. Sandford

FURTHER READING
Lewis, Walker. *Without Fear or Favor: A Biography of Chief Justice Roger Brooke Taney.* Boston: Houghton Mifflin, 1965.
Newmyer, R. Kent. *The Supreme Court Under Marshall and Taney.* Arlington Heights, Ill.: Harlan Davidson, 1986.
Swisher, Carl B. *Roger B. Taney.* New York: Macmillan, 1974.

Terms of the Supreme Court

A TERM of the U.S. Supreme Court is the period of time when the Court is in session. The Judiciary Act of 1789 required that the Court terms begin on the first Monday in February and August. The terms of the Court have been changed, from time to time, by Congress. In 1979 the Court began its current practice of holding sessions throughout the year with periodic recesses. According to law, the Supreme Court begins each annual term on the first Monday in October. This practice was started in 1917.

The Court is in session to hear oral arguments on Monday, Tuesday, and Wednesday for two weeks of each month from October until the end of April. A session may also be held on Monday of the third week of the month. During May and June, the Court is in session to deliver opinions on cases heard during the term. However, some opinions are announced earlier in the term. The justices spend time away from the Court during the summer. But they also continue their work on petitions for hearing cases on appeal from lower courts. The justices meet in late September to take care of unfinished business and to prepare for the new term beginning in October.

SEE ALSO
Decision days; Opening day

```
              SUPREME COURT OF THE UNITED STATES
                SCHEDULE FOR OCTOBER TERM 1993
1993          M    T    W
October       4    5    6              (Argument)
              H    12   13             (Argument)
              18                       (No Argument)
         RECESS - October 19 through October 31    (2 weeks)
November      1    2    3              (Argument)
              8    9                   (Argument)
              15                       (No Argument)
         RECESS - November 16 through November 28  (2 weeks)
November      29   30                  (Argument)
December                 1             (Argument)
              6    7    8              (Argument)
              13                       (No Argument)
         RECESS - December 14 through January 9    (4 weeks)
1994
January       10   11   12             (Argument)
              H    18   19             (Argument)
              24                       (No Argument)
         RECESS - January 25 through February 20   (4 weeks)
February      H    22   23             (Argument)
              28                       (Argument)
March              1    2              (Argument)
              7                        (No Argument)
         RECESS - March 8 through March 20         (2 weeks)
March         21   22   23             (Argument)
April         28   29   30             (Argument)
              4                        (No Argument)
         RECESS - April 5 through April 17         (2 weeks)
April         18   19   20             (Argument)
              25   26   27             (Argument)
              2                        (No Argument)
         RECESS - May 3 through May 15             (2 weeks)
May           16, 23, 31               (No Argument)
June          6, 13, 20, 27            (No Argument)
```

This schedule shows which days the Supreme Court will be in session and when it will hear arguments during the 1993 term.

Terry v. Ohio

☆ *392 U.S. 1 (1968)*
☆ *Vote: 8–1*
☆ *For the Court: Warren*
☆ *Concurring: Harlan, Black, and White*
☆ *Dissenting: Douglas*

A POLICE OFFICER in plain clothes, Martin McFadden, was patrolling downtown Cleveland when he observed two men acting suspiciously. They were walking back and forth in front of a store, pausing to look into the window. They soon were joined by a third man, who talked with them.

Officer McFadden thought the three men were preparing to rob the store. He confronted the three men, identified himself as a police officer, and frisked them to see if they were armed. He found that one of the men, John Terry, was carrying a pistol. A second man also had a concealed weapon. So McFadden arrested them on concealed weapons charges.

Terry and his companions were convicted. Terry, however, appealed to the U.S. Supreme Court. He claimed that his 4th Amendment and 14th Amendment rights had been violated because Officer McFadden had searched him without a warrant.

The Issue Was the warrantless search of Terry a violation of the 4th Amendment protection against unreasonable searches and seizures and the 14th Amendment guarantee of due process of law in state proceedings?

Opinion of the Court The Court decided against Terry. The policeman's "stop and frisk" action in this case was constitutional because it was reasonable under the circumstances. The Court made its decision "by balancing the need to search against the invasion which the search entails."

Chief Justice Earl Warren concluded, "[W]here a police officer observes unusual conduct which leads him reasonably to conclude…that criminal activity may be afoot and that the person…may be armed and presently dangerous…he is entitled for the protection of himself and others in the area to conduct a carefully limited search of the outer clothing of such persons in an attempt to discover weapons which might be used to assault him."

Significance *Terry* was the first case to recognize "stop and frisk" as a legal practice by police officers under certain conditions. It has become an established exception to the standard requirement of a search warrant. However, police can stop and frisk a person only when they have reason to believe their lives are in danger. The search must be limited to the area of the body in which the police suspect the presence of weapons.

SEE ALSO
Searches and seizures

Test cases

A TEST CASE is one in which an individual or a group intentionally violates a law in order to bring a case to court. The purpose is to test the constitutionality of the law. For example, in 1989 Congress passed a law against flag burning. Soon afterward, protesters broke this law because they wanted to bring a test case to the courts. Thus, the case of *United States* v. *Eichman* (1990) was tried and eventually taken to the U.S. Supreme Court. The Court decided that the federal flag-burning law was unconstitutional and overturned it—exactly the outcome desired by those who initiated the test case.

Texas v. Johnson

☆ *491 U.S. 397 (1989)*
☆ *Vote: 5–4*
☆ *For the Court: Brennan*
☆ *Concurring: Kennedy*
☆ *Dissenting: Rehnquist, White, O'Connor, and Stevens*

THE REPUBLICAN PARTY held its 1984 convention in Dallas, Texas. During one of the convention sessions, a group of demonstrators marched through the streets nearby to protest the policies of President Ronald Reagan, a Republican, who was overwhelmingly supported by delegates at the convention.

When the protest march ended, one of the demonstrators, Gregory Johnson, displayed the American flag, soaked it with kerosene, and set it on fire. As the flag burned, the demonstrators cheered. Some of them chanted, "America, the red, white, and blue, we spit on you."

Police officers arrested Johnson and charged him with violating the flag desecration law of the state of Texas. He was convicted and sentenced to one year in jail and a fine of $2,000. The Texas Court of Criminal Appeals reversed the decision, on the grounds that the decision was a violation of his free speech rights and the Texas and U.S. Constitutions, and the state appealed to the U.S. Supreme Court.

The Issue Advocates for Texas argued that its flag desecration law was a constitutional means to preserve the flag as a symbol of national unity. Further, this state law could be used to stop behavior that threatened to disrupt public order. Johnson argued that his conviction under Texas state law was a violation of 1st Amendment guarantees of freedom of expression as extended to the state through the due process clause of the 14th Amendment. Is flag burning, in the circumstances of this case, protected by the U.S. Constitution? Was the Texas statute on flag desecration constitutional?

Opinion of the Court The Court ruled in favor of Johnson. Justice William Brennan based his opinion on the prevailing free speech doctrine that justifies limitations only when the speech in question incites others directly and imminently to violence or other unlawful behavior. But there was no evidence that Johnson's "symbolic speech" (expression of an idea through an action, such as burning a flag) was an immediate threat to public order and safety. Brennan concluded, "If there is a bedrock principle underlying the First Amendment, it is that Government may not prohibit the expression of an idea simply because society finds the idea itself offensive or disagreeable."

MONUMENT TO THE FIRST AMENDMENT

The Supreme Court ruled in Texas v. Johnson *that flag burning, as an example of symbolic speech, is protected by the 1st Amendment right to freedom of speech.*

Dissent Chief Justice William Rehnquist emphasized that freedom of expression may be limited in behalf of a legitimate government interest, such as preventing incitement of a riot or the desecration of a revered national symbol. Rehnquist wrote that the American flag is a "visible symbol embodying our Nation." It is not just "another symbol" and therefore deserves special protection against desecration.

Justice John Paul Stevens wrote that the American flag represents values, such as liberty and equality, that "are worth fighting for." Thus, it cannot be "true that the flag…is not itself worthy of protection from unnecessary desecration."

Significance This decision was very controversial. Public opinion polls showed that more than 80 percent of Americans opposed it and wanted a constitutional amendment or a federal law to reverse the *Johnson* decision. President George Bush also condemned the Court's decision.

Congress subsequently passed the Flag Protection Act of 1989, which provided penalties of one year in jail and a $1,000 fine for desecration of the American flag. This federal law had a very short life. The Court declared it unconstitutional in *United States* v. *Eichman* (1990). Thus, the Court's position in the *Johnson* case has prevailed.

SEE ALSO
Freedom of speech and press

Texas v. White

☆ *7 Wall. 700 (1869)*
☆ *Vote: 6–3*
☆ *For the Court: Chase*
☆ *Dissenting: Grier, Miller, and Wayne*

IN 1861, early in the Civil War, Texas seceded from the Union to join the Confederate States of America. After the war, Texas was temporarily governed under the Reconstruction policies of the federal government. This Reconstruction government of Texas brought suit to recover state-owned bonds (certificates of debt) that the state's Confederate government had sold.

Buyers of these bonds, such as George White, argued that Texas was at that time not a state and therefore could not sue anyone in a federal court. White based his claim on the fact that Texas had not yet been fully restored to the Union.

The Issue Was Texas able to file a suit in the U.S. Supreme Court, given the facts of its secession, its status as a Confederate state during the Civil War, and its current status under Reconstruction policies? Did the U.S. Supreme Court have jurisdiction in this case?

Opinion of the Court The Court ruled against White, and Texas was able to get back its bonds. In his opinion, Chief Justice Salmon Chase set forth enduring ideas about the nature of the federal Union. He stated that the Constitution created "an indestructible Union, composed of indestructible States." Thus, secession was illegal, and in a legal sense Texas had never left the Union. Therefore, as a full-fledged state of the federal Union, Texas could file suit in the federal courts.

Significance Chief Justice Chase's decision established that secession was not valid under the U.S. Constitution. A constitutional argument that had persisted from the founding of the United States through the Civil War was finally settled.

Thomas, Clarence

ASSOCIATE JUSTICE, 1991–

☆ *Born: June 23, 1948, Savannah, Ga.*

☆ *Education: Holy Cross College, B.A., 1970; Yale Law School, LL.B., 1973*

☆ *Previous government service: assistant to the Missouri attorney general, 1973–77; legislative assistant to U.S. Senator John Danforth, 1979–81; assistant secretary of education, Civil Rights Division, 1981–82; chairman, Equal Employment Opportunity Commission, 1982–90; judge, U.S. Court of Appeals for the District of Columbia Circuit, 1990–91*

☆ *Appointed by President George Bush July 1, 1991; replaced Thurgood Marshall, who retired*

☆ *Supreme Court term: confirmed by the Senate Oct. 15, 1991, by a vote of 52–48*

CLARENCE THOMAS became, at the age of 43, the second black associate justice of the Supreme Court of the United States. He replaced Thurgood Marshall, the first African American on the Court. Thomas's road to the pinnacle of judicial power, however, was filled with obstacles.

Clarence Thomas rose to prominence from humble origins. He was raised by his grandfather, Myers Anderson, after his father abandoned him. Although poor, Anderson was a proud man with high hopes for his grandson. He pushed Thomas to excel in school and provided discipline and stability for his grandson. Thomas responded with high achievement in school that led him eventually to graduate from Yale Law School in 1973.

Thomas's first job as a lawyer was in Missouri, where he worked for the attorney general, John Danforth. Later, Danforth was elected to the U.S. Senate as a Republican, and Thomas went to Washington as the Senator's legislative assistant. During the 1980s, Thomas, with support from Senator Danforth, achieved top-level jobs in the U.S. Department of Education and the Equal Employment Opportunity Commission.

In 1990, President George Bush appointed Thomas to the U.S. Court of Appeals for the District of Columbia Circuit. Eighteen months later, Thurgood Marshall resigned from the Supreme Court at the age of 82. On July 1, 1991, President Bush nominated Thomas to replace Justice Marshall. The President said: "If credit accrues to him for coming up through a tough life as a minority in this country, so much the better. It proves he can do it, get the job done. And so that does nothing but enhance the Court, in my view."

Standing next to the President, Clarence Thomas replied: "In my view, only in America could this have been possible. . . . As a child I could not dare dream that I would ever see the Supreme Court, not to mention be nominated to it."

The move from nomination to Senate confirmation was difficult for Thomas and the President. After several days of hearings, the Senate Judiciary Committee was sharply divided along partisan lines in its evaluation of Thomas. The Democrats, with one exception, clearly opposed his nomination, and the Republican members of the committee favored it. The committee vote was deadlocked, seven members for Thomas and seven against him.

Suddenly, the confirmation process became embroiled in controversy. Anita Hill, a former employee of Thomas at the U.S. Department of Education and the Equal Employment Opportunity Commission, charged him with sexual harassment. The Senate Judiciary Committee conducted special sessions to examine these charges by Hill. After three days of intense and acrimonious discussion of this issue, the Senate Judiciary Committee concluded its work and sent Thomas's nomination to the Senate for a final decision. The Senate committee vote remained at seven for Thomas and seven against him.

The Senate voted to confirm Justice Thomas by a vote of 52 to 48. This was the closest vote of approval for a Supreme Court appointment in more than 100 years. Eleven Democrats joined 41 Republicans to vote for Justice Thomas.

During his short time on the Court, Justice Thomas has performed carefully and competently. He usually joins with Justice Antonin Scalia when presenting concurring or dissenting opinions. Thomas appears determined to demonstrate his qualifications to serve on the Supreme Court.

Thompson, Smith

ASSOCIATE JUSTICE, 1823–43

☆ *Born: Jan. 17, 1768, Amenia, N.Y.*
☆ *Education: College of New Jersey (Princeton), B.A., 1788; read law with James Kent in Poughkeepsie, N.Y.*
☆ *Previous government service: New York Assembly, 1800; New York Constitutional Convention, 1801; associate justice, New York Supreme Court, 1802–14; New York State Board of Regents, 1813; chief justice, New York Supreme Court, 1814–18; U.S. secretary of the navy, 1819–23*
☆ *Appointed by President James Monroe as a recess appointment Sept. 1, 1823; replaced Henry Brockholst Livingston, who died; nominated by Monroe Dec. 8, 1823*
☆ *Supreme Court term: confirmed by the Senate Dec. 19, 1823, by a voice vote; served until Dec. 18, 1843*
☆ *Died: Dec. 18, 1843, Poughkeepsie, N.Y.*

SMITH THOMPSON served on the Supreme Court for 20 years. During this lengthy period of service, however, he had only a slight impact on constitutional law. He developed a position on regulation of commerce at odds with the prevailing view of the Court, which gave broad powers of commercial regulation to the federal government. By contrast, Justice Thompson held that states could regulate commerce in all cases except those that conflicted with a federal law. This position was known as the doctrine of concurrent commerce powers; that is, the federal government and the state government could act jointly in most cases to regulate commerce. Thompson's position influenced the judicial thought of Roger B. Taney, John Marshall's successor as chief justice.

Justice Thompson's most significant opinion was his dissent in *Cherokee Nation* v. *Georgia* (1831). The state of Georgia asserted control over Cherokee lands within the state that had been granted to the Native Americans by a treaty with the federal government. Thompson argued that the Cherokee were an independent and sovereign nation, despite their status as a conquered people, and must be treated like other sovereign nations in legal dealings with the U.S. government. This dissenting opinion became the majority position, expressed by John Marshall, in *Worcester* v. *Georgia* (1832).

Time, place, and manner rule

THE U.S. SUPREME COURT has developed the time, place, and manner rule to determine whether government regulations or limitations of free speech are legal. According to this guideline, regulations about free speech may be constitutional if they are neutral concerning the content of the speech and deal only with the time, place, and manner of speech.

For example, people may talk freely to each other in public, but they may not talk at a time or place that would block traffic. Individuals may freely criticize government officials, but they may not express themselves in a manner that would interfere with the necessary work of the government. Individuals have the right to speak in favor of candidates for election to government offices. But they may not use a loudspeaker in a residential neighborhood at three o'clock in the morning to broadcast their messages because this would unfairly disturb sleeping residents of the community. In *Kovacs* v. *Cooper* (1949), for example, the Court upheld a local law restricting the use of sound-amplifying equipment on public streets.

When a free-speech regulation is challenged in court, the judges always inquire whether the regulation is neutral with regard to the content of the speech. If not, the Court will apply the test of strict scrutiny; that is, a compelling public interest must be demonstrated as justification for regulating the content of speech. Otherwise, the regulation will be overturned as unconstitutional. An example of a compelling public interest that could pass the strict scrutiny test is protecting the safety of individuals who might be endangered by the unregulated speech.

SEE ALSO

Freedom of speech and press

Tinker v. Des Moines Independent Community School District

☆ *393 U.S. 503 (1969)*
☆ *Vote: 7–2*
☆ *For the Court: Fortas*
☆ *Concurring: Stewart and White*
☆ *Dissenting: Black and Harlan*

IN DECEMBER 1965 some students in Des Moines, Iowa, decided to publicly express their opposition to the war in Vietnam by wearing black armbands. Des Moines school administrators, however, decided upon a policy that forbade the wearing of a black armband in school. Students who violated the policy would be suspended from school until they agreed to comply with the policy.

On December 16, Mary Beth Tinker and Christopher Eckhardt wore armbands to school. John Tinker did the same thing the next day. As a consequence, the three students were sus-

Mary Beth and John Tinker wore black armbands to protest the Vietnam War. Their school suspended them for wearing the armbands, but the Supreme Court ruled that the school's action violated the students' right to free speech.

pended from school and told not to return unless they removed their armbands. They stayed away from school until the early part of January 1966.

The three students filed a complaint, through their parents, against the school officials. They sought an injunction to prevent the officials from punishing them for wearing black armbands to school.

The Issue Did the school district's policy of prohibiting the wearing of black armbands in school violate the students' 1st Amendment right to free speech, as extended to the states through the due process clause of the 14th Amendment?

Opinion of the Court The Court decided by a vote of 7 to 2 that the school district had violated the students' right to free speech under the 1st and 14th Amendments to the Constitution. In previous cases, such as *Stromberg* v. *California,* the Court had ruled that 1st Amendment free speech rights were incorporated by the due process clause of the 14th Amendment, which provides that no state shall "deprive any person of life, liberty [such as free speech], or property, without due process of law."

Justice Abe Fortas wrote the majority opinion, in which he stated that the wearing of black armbands to protest the Vietnam War was a form of "symbolic speech" protected by the 1st Amendment. Therefore, a public school ban on this form of protest was a violation of the students' right to free speech, as long as the protest did not disrupt the functioning of the school or violate the

rights of other individuals. Justice Fortas wrote, "First Amendment rights applied in light of the special characteristics of the school environment, are available to teachers and students. It can hardly be argued that either students or teachers shed their constitutional rights to freedom of speech or expression at the schoolhouse gate."

Dissent Justice Hugo Black was one of the two dissenters in this case. He wrote:

> While I have always believed that under the First and Fourteenth Amendments neither the State nor the Federal Government has any authority to regulate or censor the content of speech, I have never believed that any person has a right to give speeches or engage in demonstrations where he pleases and when he pleases. This Court has already rejected such a notion....
>
> One does not need to be a prophet or the son of a prophet to know that after the Court's holding today some students in Iowa schools and indeed in all schools will be ready, able, and willing to defy their teachers on practically all orders....
>
> This case, therefore, wholly without constitutional reasons in my judgment, subjects all the public schools in the country to the whims and caprices of their loudest-mouthed, but maybe not their brightest students.

Significance *Tinker* is one of the most important cases on the constitutional rights of students in public schools. It supports the protection of free expression that does not disrupt the educational purposes of the school or violate the rights of other students.

In subsequent cases involving students in public schools, such as *Bethel School District No. 403* v. *Fraser* (1986) and *Hazelwood School District* v. *Kuhlmeier* (1988), the Court supported the power of public school officials to limit freedom of expression by students if such expression—in these cases, a vulgar speech and the publication of sensitive material in the student newspaper—disrupted the schools' educational mission.

SEE ALSO

Bethel School District No. 403 v. Fraser; Freedom of speech and press; Hazelwood School District v. Kuhlmeier; Student rights under the Constitution

FURTHER READING

Irons, Peter. *The Courage of their Convictions.* New York: Free Press, 1988.

Todd, Thomas

ASSOCIATE JUSTICE, 1807–26

☆ Born: Jan. 23, 1765, King and Queen County, Va.
☆ Education: Liberty Hall (Washington and Lee University), B.A., 1783; read law under Harry Innes, Bedford County, Va.
☆ Previous government service: clerk, federal district for Kentucky, 1789–92; clerk, Kentucky House of Representatives, 1792–1801; clerk, Kentucky Court of Appeals, 1799–1801; judge, Kentucky Court of Appeals, 1801–6; chief justice of Kentucky, 1806–7
☆ Appointed by President Thomas Jefferson Feb. 28, 1807, to occupy a new seat on the Court
☆ Supreme Court term: confirmed by the Senate Mar. 3, 1807, by a voice vote; served until Feb. 7, 1826
☆ Died: Feb. 7, 1826, Frankfort, Ky.

THOMAS TODD was a veteran of the American War of Independence. At the age of 16, he served in the Continental Army. Before the war was over, Todd went to college and prepared to become a lawyer. In 1783, Todd moved to the western frontier in Kentucky, where he practiced law and served as a clerk in the government.

During his nearly 19 years on the Su-preme Court, Justice Todd wrote only 14 opinions. He mostly followed the leadership of Chief Justice John Marshall, even though he was appointed by President Thomas Jefferson, a political foe of Marshall.

Tort

A TORT is a civil wrong, other than a contract violation, done by one party to another party. By contrast, a crime is a violation of a government's laws; these are the statutes that pertain to wrongs against society, which the government has authority to punish through its law enforcement powers.

Torts involve violations of civil law, not criminal law. They usually are the responsibility of state courts, but the U.S. Supreme Court sometimes becomes involved when the tort law of a state conflicts with the Constitution or federal laws.

Trial by jury

A TRIAL involves public examination of a legal issue in a court of law. A jury is a group of supposedly impartial citizens selected to determine the facts and sit in judgment of a defendant in a trial. The jury, at the end of the trial, reaches a verdict of guilty or innocent, which determines whether the defendant is freed or punished.

The right of an individual to a trial by jury is provided in three parts of the U.S. Constitution. Article 3, Section 2, says, "The Trial of all Crime, except in Cases of Impeachment, shall be by Jury." Amendment 6 says, "In all criminal prosecutions, the accused shall enjoy the right to a speedy and public trial." Amendment 7 says, "In Suits at common law, where the value in controversy shall exceed twenty dollars, the right to trial by jury shall be preserved."

The Supreme Court ruled in *Baldwin* v. *New York* (1970) that the right to a trial by jury is provided to any adult accused of a crime if the potential punishment is incarceration for more than six months. And, according to the 7th Amendment, a trial by jury is available to those involved in a common lawsuit (federal civil, or noncriminal, case) if the controversy involves more than $20.

In a trial by jury of a criminal case, the jury has the power to decide whether the accused person is guilty or innocent. The jury also may make decisions, within legally prescribed limits, about degrees of criminal behavior (for example, whether a person is guilty of murder or merely manslaughter) and the severity of punishment for a guilty person.

The traditional size of a jury, 12 people, is based on English legal traditions that were brought to America during the colonial era. However, some states have experimented with smaller juries, especially in trials of less serious crimes. The U.S. Supreme Court ruled in *Williams* v. *Florida* (1970) that a six-person jury is not necessarily a violation of the constitutional guarantee of due process of law. Further, Section 48 of the Federal Rules of Civil Procedure permits the parties in a dispute to agree to a jury of less than 12 members.

Another tradition has been the requirement of a unanimous decision by a jury in reaching a verdict. Some states, however, have experimented with rules that permit verdicts by juries that are less than unanimous. Usually, these rules have required large majorities, such as 9 or 10 jurors, in reaching a verdict.

The Supreme Court decided in *Min-neapolis and St. Louis Railway Company* v. *Bombolis* (1916) that jury verdicts in state court proceedings based on less than a unanimous vote were not denials of the fair legal procedures required by the due process clause in the Constitution. Later, however, in *Burch* v. *Louisiana* (1979), the Court overturned a Louisiana law that permitted verdicts to be reached by a 5-to-1 vote of a six-person jury. In contrast to some state court practices, the unanimous verdict rule remains the standard in federal cases involving a jury trial.

SEE ALSO

Bill of Rights; Rights of the accused

FURTHER READING

Bodenhamer, David J. *Fair Trial: Rights of the Accused in American History.* New York: Oxford, 1992.

Trimble, Robert

ASSOCIATE JUSTICE, 1826–28

☆ Born: Nov. 17, 1776, Berkeley County, Va.
☆ Education: read law under George Nicholas and James Brown, Lexington, Ky.
☆ Previous government service: Kentucky House of Representatives, 1802; judge, Kentucky Court of Appeals, 1807–9, 1810; U.S. district attorney for Kentucky, 1813–17; U.S. district judge for Kentucky, 1817–26
☆ Appointed by President John Quincy Adams Apr. 11, 1826; replaced Thomas Todd, who died
☆ Supreme Court term: confirmed by the Senate May 9, 1826, by a voice vote; served until Aug. 25, 1828
☆ Died: Aug. 25, 1828, Paris, Ky.

ROBERT TRIMBLE was the son of pioneers who arrived in the territory of Kentucky in 1780. Trimble took advantage of an opportunity to go to school and attended the Bourbon Academy. Later, he prepared for a career in law by studying with two local attorneys. Trimble became a successful lawyer and judge in Kentucky.

Trimble was the only Supreme Court appointment of President John Quincy Adams. He was the first federal district judge to become a justice of the Supreme Court. Like President Adams, he favored a strong federal government. Justice Trimble served briefly on the Court and wrote only 16 opinions before his sudden death from an undiagnosed illness.

Twining v. New Jersey

☆ *211 U.S. 78 (1908)*
☆ *Vote: 8–1*
☆ *For the Court: Moody*
☆ *Dissenting: Harlan*

NEW JERSEY charged Albert Twining with the crime of reporting false information to a state government bank examiner. Twining refused to testify at his state court trial, an action that the judge interpreted, in his charge to the jury, as an admission of guilt. Under New Jersey law, the judge could make such an interpretation.

Twining was convicted and the New Jersey Supreme Court upheld the conviction. Twining, however, argued that he had a constitutional right to protection against giving evidence against himself. He pointed to the 5th Amendment to the U.S. Constitution, which says, "No person shall be…compelled in any criminal case to be a witness against himself." Twining appealed to the U.S. Supreme Court.

The Issue Did the New Jersey trial court judge's instructions to the jury violate the 5th Amendment guarantee of protection against self-incrimination? If

so, could this part of the federal Bill of Rights be applied to a state government through the due process clause of the 14th Amendment, which says, "No state shall…deprive any person of life, liberty, or property, without due process of law"?

Opinion of the Court Justice William H. Moody recognized that the trial judge violated the self-incrimination clause of the 5th Amendment. However, he upheld the conviction of Twining because, in the Court's view, the self-incrimination clause in the federal Bill of Rights could not be applied to a state government via the due process clause of the 14th Amendment. However, the Court stated that this due process clause could in principle incorporate some fundamental rights in the federal Bill of Rights, if these rights were judged essential to the idea of fairness in due process of law. Justice Moody provided this guideline for future decisions about which rights could be incorporated and applied to state governments: "Is it [the right in question] a fundamental principle of liberty and justice which inheres in the very idea of free government and is the inalienable right of a citizen of such a government?"

The Court decided that the 5th Amendment's self-incrimination clause was not one of the "fundamental principles" of the federal Bill of Rights that could be applied to state governments through the 14th Amendment. But Justice Moody's guidelines did open the way for future applications to the states of selected rights in the federal Bill of Rights.

Dissent Justice John Marshall Harlan concluded that the 5th Amendment's self-incrimination clause did apply to the states through the 14th Amendment. In his opinion, this right to remain silent was a fundamental part of the principle of liberty embedded in the Constitution.

Significance The Court rejected *total incorporation*—the idea that Amendments 1 to 8 of the federal Bill of Rights could be completely applied to the states through the due process clause of the 14th Amendment. However, the Court did provide an opening for *selective incorporation*—the idea that certain parts of the federal Bill of Rights could be applied to the states on a case-by-case basis. During the 20th century, the Court has selectively incorporated most provisions of the federal Bill of Rights through the due process clause of the 14th Amendment, thereby applying these fundamental rights to the states.

S E E   A L S O
Incorporation doctrine; Rights of the accused; Self-incrimination, privilege against

United States Reports

ALL DECISIONS of the Supreme Court of the United States are recorded in an authorized publication, the *United States Reports*. This series of volumes was initially compiled by Alexander J. Dallas, the Court's first reporter (1790–1800). Dallas's work was approved by the Court, although he held no official position and sold the publication of his work for profit. The position of reporter of the Supreme Court was not established by Congress until 1816.

Private publishers issued the *United States Reports* until 1922. Since then, the U.S. Government Printing Office has been the publisher.

The Court's decisions are not reported exclusively in the *United States Reports*. They also appear, for example, in *Supreme Court Reporter; United States Law Week,* a weekly publication that covers Supreme Court news and proceedings, including the full text of all Court decisions on cases; and the legal databases LEXIS and WESTLAW. However, the only official report of the Court's decisions is in *United States Reports.* This is the version that must be cited in all briefs and memoranda to the Court, and it should be listed first in any multiple listing of sources of a citation.

S E E   A L S O
Reporter of decisions

United States v. Curtiss-Wright Export Corp.

☆ *299 U.S. 304 (1936)*
☆ *Vote: 7–1*
☆ *For the Court: Sutherland*
☆ *Dissenting: McReynolds*
☆ *Not participating: Stone*

IN 1934, Bolivia and Paraguay were at war with each other. Both countries needed military weapons from abroad, and American weapons makers were eager to sell to them. At the same time, the American public and Great Britain wanted the United States to help end the war by stopping all arms sales to the two nations.

On May 28, 1934, Congress passed a joint resolution giving President Franklin Delano Roosevelt authority to place an embargo, or ban, on selling weapons to Bolivia and Paraguay. Four days later, Roosevelt declared the embargo in effect because he believed it would help restore peace. The federal government later indicted the Curtiss-Wright Corporation for violating the embargo by selling armed aircraft to Bolivia. Curtiss-Wright claimed that the Constitution did not allow Congress to give the President power to declare an embargo.

The Issue Did Congress's joint resolution unconstitutionally delegate legislative power to the executive branch? Or did Congress have the authority to delegate broad discretionary powers in foreign affairs to the President?

Opinion of the Court The Supreme Court ruled to uphold the President's embargo. The Court distinguished between the powers exercised by Congress and the President in "external" (foreign) affairs and "internal" (domestic) affairs. The Court said that the national government could take action in conducting foreign affairs that might exceed its authority to direct domestic policy.

Writing for the majority, Justice George Sutherland reasoned that since the United States had existed as a sovereign nation before the adoption of the Constitution, it retained powers to influence international affairs that were neither implied nor listed in the Constitution. These powers stemmed from the simple unspoken reality that the United States existed in a world of nations and must have powers to meet its international responsibilities just as other sovereign nations did. This idea established a new precedent, the doctrine of inherent powers.

Further, the Court ruled that Congress could delegate broad discretionary powers to the President to cope with foreign affairs issues. This verdict contrasted with the Court's ruling on domestic affairs, which limited Congress to delegating legislative powers to the President only if it also set clear guidelines for using those delegated powers.

Dissent Although Justice James McReynolds dissented in this case, he filed no opinion.

Significance The *Curtiss-Wright* decision recognized the broad responsibility of the executive branch of the national government for foreign affairs, giving the President great freedom in directing the nation's foreign policy. Justice Sutherland wrote: "[T]he President alone has the power to speak as a representative of the nation." He described the President's power in foreign affairs as "plenary [full] and exclusive." The President is "the sole organ of the federal government in…international relations." This decision thereby provided the foundations for strong and decisive Presidential leadership in world affairs.

FURTHER READING

Divine, Robert A. "The Case of the Smuggled Bombers." In *Quarrels That Have Shaped the Constitution,* edited by John A. Garraty. New York: Harper & Row, 1987.

United States v. Darby Lumber Co.

☆ *312 U.S. 100 (1941)*
☆ *Vote: 9–0*
☆ *For the Court: Stone*

IN 1938, the U.S. Congress passed the Fair Labor Standards Act, which set minimum wages, maximum hours, and overtime pay regulations for workers in businesses involved in interstate commerce—that is, in shipping their products across state lines. Enactment of this federal law was based on Congress's power "to regulate Commerce…among the several States" (Article 1, Section 8, of the Constitution).

The Darby Lumber Company claimed that the Fair Labor Standards Act was unconstitutional, so it filed suit to prevent enforcement of this federal law.

The Issue The Darby Lumber Company argued that Congress exceeded its powers under the commerce clause of the Constitution when it passed the Fair Labor Standards Act. It claimed that, according to the 10th Amendment to the Constitution, the power to regulate

Women can peaches in California for shipment around the country. In 1941 the Supreme Court upheld the Fair Labor Standards Act, which set minimum wages and maximum hours for workers in industries involved in interstate commerce.

wages, hours of work, working conditions, and so forth belongs to the states. (The amendment states, "The powers not delegated to the United States by the Constitution, nor prohibited by it to the States, are reserved to the States respectively, or to the people.") This claim was based on the Supreme Court's decision in *Hammer* v. *Dagenhart* (1918). Was enactment of the Fair Labor Standards Act a constitutional exercise of the commerce power, or did this federal law violate the 10th Amendment of the Constitution? Further, did the Fair Labor Standards Act violate the due process clause of the 5th Amendment by taking away the right of employers and workers to bargain freely about wages and working conditions?

Opinion of the Court The Court upheld the Fair Labor Standards Act. Writing for the Court, Justice Harlan F. Stone based his opinion on the dissent of Justice Oliver Wendell Holmes in *Hammer* v. *Dagenhart* (1918). Agreeing with Holmes, Stone argued that the federal government's power to regulate commerce among the states should be interpreted broadly. Thus, the power to regulate wages and working conditions can, said Justice Stone, be tied to the power to regulate interstate commerce. Stone wrote, "The conclusion is inescapable that *Hammer* v. *Dagenhart*...should be and now is overruled."

Significance This decision expanded the federal government's power to regulate national economic affairs. Further, this opinion rejected the argument, advanced in *Hammer* v. *Dagenhart,* that the 10th Amendment strictly limits the enumerated, or specifically listed, powers of Congress. Instead, it established a broad interpretation of the Congress's commerce power.

SEE ALSO

Commerce power; Federalism; Hammer v. Dagenhart

United States v. E. C. Knight Co.

☆ *156 U.S. 1 (1895)*
☆ *Vote: 8–1*
☆ *For the Court: Fuller*
☆ *Dissenting: Harlan*

IN 1890 Congress passed the Sherman Antitrust Act, which seemed to outlaw business monopolies. A monopoly has control over the means of producing and selling a product or service. The Sherman Antitrust Act provided that "every contract, combination in the form of trust or otherwise, or conspiracy, in restraint of trade or commerce among the several states, or with foreign nations, is hereby declared to be illegal." So, according to this federal law, any business that acted to restrain trade by controlling most or all of a particular business activity would seem to be illegal.

In the late 19th century the American Sugar Refining Company was the

The Sugar Trust (second from right) marches with other major trusts in a triumphant parade. When the federal government filed suit against the Sugar Trust for violating the Sherman Antitrust Act, the Supreme Court ruled in favor of the trust, even though it controlled 90 percent of the sugar refining business in the country.

dominant maker of sugar in the United States. It was known as the Sugar Trust. In 1892 the Sugar Trust acquired four Philadelphia sugar refineries, including the E. C. Knight Company. As a result, the American Sugar Refining Company controlled 98 percent of sugar manufacturing in the United States. The federal government filed suit under the Sherman Antitrust Act to prevent the "restraint of trade or commerce among the several states" by the American Sugar Refining Company's takeover of nearly all the sugar refining businesses in the United States.

The Issue Was the Sugar Trust in violation of the Sherman Antitrust Act? Did its control of 98 percent of the sugar refining business in the United States constitute an illegal restraint of trade or commerce?

Opinion of the Court In its first interpretation of the Sherman Antitrust Act, the Court decided against the federal government. It upheld the lower court's dismissal of the government's suit. The Sherman Antitrust Act, according to the Court, did not apply to a trust that refined 98 percent of the sugar sold throughout the United States.

Writing for the Court, Chief Justice Melville Fuller argued that a monopoly of the production of refined sugar did not necessarily lead to an illegal restraint of trade, which was what the Sherman Antitrust Act prohibited. Fuller said that production and commerce were two very different kinds of business activity. He wrote that only the distribution or sale of a product (such as refined sugar) was subject to federal regulation under the commerce clause of the Constitution (Article 1, Section 8). By contrast, Congress did not have the power under the Constitution to regulate the manufacturing of a product that occurred within the boundaries of a state. This power, according to Fuller, belonged to the government of the state in which a manufacturing company was located. So the federal government suit against the Sugar Trust exceeded the scope of the Sherman Antitrust Act, and it could not be applied to E. C. Knight.

Dissent Justice John Marshall Harlan argued that the Sugar Trust's near monopoly of the production of refined sugar gave it power to dominate the distribution and sale of this product. For example, the Sugar Trust could control the market price of refined sugar.

Therefore, the Sugar Trust was in violation of the Sherman Antitrust Act.

Justice Harlan argued for a broad interpretation of the federal government's commerce power. He believed that Congress had the authority to regulate business to prevent any interference with free trade among the states. He wrote, "The general [federal] government is not placed by the Constitution in such a condition of helplessness that it must fold its arms and remain inactive while capital combines…to destroy competition."

Significance The *E. C. Knight* decision opened the way to large-scale combinations of manufacturing businesses whose production activities had been ruled beyond the scope of the Sherman Antitrust Act. Further, this decision diminished the power of the federal government to regulate economic activity.

The *E. C. Knight* ruling prevailed until the end of the 1930s, when the Court took a different position on the federal government's power, under the commerce clause, to regulate the economy. For example, in *National Labor Relations Board* v. *Jones & Laughlin Steel Corp.* (1937) and *West Coast Hotel Co.* v. *Parrish* (1937), the Court upheld federal and state laws regulating wages and working conditions of private businesses. These decisions emphasized a broad interpretation of the federal government's commerce power, which could include the interrelated issues of production and distribution of goods and services. After the erosion of the *Knight* decision in 1937, the federal government exercised broad authority to regulate economic activity for the public good.

SEE ALSO

Commerce power; National Labor Relations Board v. Jones & Laughlin Steel Corp.; West Coast Hotel Co. v. Parrish

United States v. Leon

☆ *468 U.S. 897 (1984)*
☆ *Vote: 6–3*
☆ *For the Court: White*
☆ *Concurring: Blackmun*
☆ *Dissenting: Brennan, Marshall, and Stevens*

IN 1981 the police in Burbank, California, received information about drug dealing by two residents of their city. So the police began to regularly watch the Burbank home of the two suspects, where they spotted an automobile owned by Alberto Leon, another suspected drug dealer.

The Burbank police obtained a search warrant from a local judge, searched the residence, and found illegal drugs belonging to Alberto Leon. This evidence led to Leon's arrest and conviction.

The Issue Leon's lawyer argued that the search warrant used by the Burbank police was not valid because there was no "probable cause" for the police to request it or for the judge to issue it. As a result, the evidence against Leon gathered by the police should have been thrown out under the exclusionary rule established in *Mapp* v. *Ohio* (1961), according to which evidence obtained in violation of a person's constitutional rights cannot be used to prosecute the person. Should the evidence against Leon be excluded because it was obtained through procedures that violated the 4th Amendment guarantee to "the right of the people to be secure in their persons, houses, papers, and effects, against unreasonable searches and seizures"? Or should the Court permit an exception to the exclusionary rule when the police make a "good faith" mistake in obtaining and using a search warrant?

In the Leon *case, the Court ruled that even if police or federal agents search a house with an invalid warrant, any evidence found can be used in a trial if the officers were acting in "good faith" when they sought the warrant.*

Opinion of the Court The Court acknowledged that the police used an invalid search warrant to obtain evidence against Leon. Nonetheless, the Court ruled against Leon and permitted a "good faith" exception to the exclusionary rule. The exclusionary rule is not a constitutional right, said Justice Byron White, but merely serves to limit oppressive police actions. However, when police act on "good faith" to obtain valid evidence of criminal behavior, the exclusionary rule does not apply to the case.

Dissent Justice William Brennan, who had established the exclusionary rule in *Mapp* v. *Ohio*, opposed any "good faith" exception to this rule. He feared that this exception would lead to an increase in illegal police behavior in gathering evidence against people suspected of criminal behavior.

Significance The *Leon* decision narrowed the exclusionary rule protections under the 4th Amendment of the Constitution. This outcome was hailed by many law enforcement officials, who often felt frustrated by judicial decisions that permitted a criminal to avoid conviction because of a technical error by the police. However, defenders of the exclusionary rule argued against any exceptions to it because of their strong commitment to 4th Amendment rights.

SEE ALSO
Exclusionary rule; Mapp v. Ohio; Searches and seizures

United States v. Nixon

☆ *418 U.S. 683 (1974)*
☆ *Vote: 8–0*
☆ *For the Court: Burger*
☆ *Not participating: Rehnquist*

BEGINNING WITH George Washington, several Presidents have asserted the right to withhold information from Congress or from a court. The right of the President to do this has come to be called *executive privilege.* Presidents have often made such claims in the area of foreign affairs. In 1974, however, President Richard Nixon claimed executive privilege for another reason.

In the spring of 1972, employees of President Nixon's reelection committee burglarized the Democratic party headquarters in the Watergate office complex in Washington and planted illegal electronic bugging equipment. Eventually, seven of President Nixon's top aides, including former attorney general John Mitchell, were indicted for their role in planning the Watergate break-in, as it came to be known, and for obstructing justice by trying to cover up their actions. During Senate hearings on the break-in and the cover-up, a Nixon aide admitted that there were secretly recorded tapes of Nixon's conversations with his aides. A special prosecutor investigating the Watergate break-in subpoenaed the tapes for use as evidence in the criminal investigations.

President Nixon refused to surrender the tapes. He claimed that the principle of executive privilege protected the record of his private conversations from such a subpoena. He argued that the actions of many past Presidents clearly established the tradition of executive privilege. He also claimed that to allow another branch of government, the courts, to obtain the tapes would destroy the separation of powers established by the Constitution and would weaken the Presidency.

The Issue Did the constitutional principle of separation of powers and the tradition of executive privilege prevent the courts from requiring the President to turn over material needed as evidence in a criminal trial?

Opinion of the Court The Court ordered President Nixon to turn over the tapes and other documents to the trial court for use as evidence. The Supreme Court rejected the claim that either separation of powers or executive privilege could make the President immune from the judicial process. The Court's ruling established the precedent that unless important military or diplomatic secrets affecting national security were involved, the need to ensure a fair trial outweighed the principle of executive privilege. The decision limited the concept of executive privilege by determining that a President could not use it to prohibit disclosure of criminal conduct.

At the same time, the Court's decision acknowledged the constitutionality of executive privilege in certain other situations. The Constitution does not mention executive privilege, and until the Court reached this decision, legal scholars had frequently debated whether any real constitutional basis supported the doctrine.

In *United States* v. *Nixon,* Chief Justice Warren Burger, a Nixon appointee, said that Presidents and their aides must be free to consider alternatives as they make decisions. In order to do so, they must possess the confidence to express themselves freely without fear that the public will gain access to their ideas. Thus, Burger wrote, "[Executive] privilege is fundamental to the operation of government and inextricably rooted in the separation of powers under the Constitution."

Significance President Nixon obeyed the Court's decision and turned over the tapes to the special prosecutor. Nixon claimed the demand for the tapes was a political maneuver by his enemies. However, this claim could not stand up in the face of a unanimous Court decision written by a Nixon appointee and supported by two other Nixon appointees. The tapes revealed that Nixon had participated in the cover-up. When the contents of these tapes became public knowledge, even Nixon's strongest supporters in Congress believed that he could no longer remain in office. Some Republican congressmen said they would have to vote for his impeachment, and leading Republican senators publicly announced that they saw no way he could avoid conviction. Nixon became the first U.S. President to resign from office.

SEE ALSO
Executive privilege; Separation of powers

United States v. O'Brien

☆ *391 U.S. 367 (1968)*
☆ *Vote: 7–1*
☆ *For the Court: Warren*
☆ *Concurring: Harlan*
☆ *Dissenting: Douglas*
☆ *Not participating: Marshall*

IN THE 1960s, the United States was fighting a war in Vietnam. The war was controversial, and many Americans protested against the selective service system, which drafted young men into the armed forces of the United States. Some of the antiwar protests involved the destruction of draft registration cards, which were issued to all men eligible for induction into the U.S. military. Congress in 1965 amended the Selective Service Act to make it a crime for anyone to "destroy or mutilate" a draft registration card.

On March 31, 1966, David O'Brien burned his draft card during an antiwar demonstration at an entrance to a South Boston courthouse. Agents of the Federal Bureau of Investigation (FBI) saw O'Brien burn his draft card and arrested him for violating the Selective Service Act, as amended in 1965.

The Issue David O'Brien claimed that he had publicly burned his draft card to express his opposition to the Vietnam War. This "symbolic speech" was, in his opinion, permissible because of his 1st Amendment right to free speech. His attorney pointed to the Court's opinion in *Stromberg* v. *California* (1931), which ruled that symbolic speech was protected from government prohibition by the 1st Amendment.

The federal government's attorney argued that O'Brien's actions seriously interfered with its legitimate business because he wanted "to influence others to adopt his anti-war beliefs" and thwart the government's ability to conduct the war. The government argued that the requirements of national security justified limitations on symbolic speech.

Was the 1965 amendment to the Selective Service Act, which banned destruction of draft cards, a valid limitation on free speech? Or was this federal statute an unconstitutional violation of the 1st Amendment?

Opinion of the Court The Court upheld the 1965 law and rejected David O'Brien's claims that it violated his right to free speech. Chief Justice Earl Warren wrote:

A protester holds aloft his draft card in a demonstration against the Vietnam War. In the O'Brien *case, the Supreme Court upheld the law that prohibited the burning of draft cards, ruling that it was not "symbolic speech" protected by the 1st Amendment.*

We cannot accept the view that an apparently limitless variety of conduct can be labeled "speech" whenever the person engaging in the conduct intends thereby to express an idea. However, even on the assumption that the alleged communicative element in O'Brien's conduct is sufficient to bring into play the First Amendment, it does not necessarily follow that the destruction of a registration certificate is a constitutionally protected activity. This Court has held that when "speech" and "nonspeech" elements are combined in the same course of conduct, a sufficiently important governmental interest in regulating the nonspeech element can justify incidental limitations on First Amendment freedoms.... [W]e think it clear that a government regulation is sufficiently justified if it is within the constitutional power of the Government; if it furthers an important or substantial governmental interest; if the governmental interest is unrelated to the suppression of free expression; and if the incidental restriction on alleged First Amendment freedoms is no greater than is essential to the furtherance of that interest.

Significance The Court provided guidelines for subsequent decisions about when the government could regulate symbolic speech. These guidelines required the government to have a valid, compelling interest, such as the necessity for a military draft, unrelated to the purpose of suppressing free speech. Moreover, any restrictions on free speech could be no broader than was necessary to carry out that valid interest. The *O'Brien* guidelines, or tests, for deciding permissible limits on free speech are now an established part of constitutional law.

SEE ALSO

Freedom of speech and press; Stromberg v. California

United States v. Ross

☆ *456 U.S. 798 (1982)*
☆ *Vote: 6–3*
☆ *For the Court: Stevens*
☆ *Concurring: Blackmun and Powell*
☆ *Dissenting: White, Marshall, and Brennan*

DETECTIVE MARCUM of the Washington, D.C., Metropolitan Police received a telephone call about criminal activity in a local neighborhood. The caller reported that a man was selling drugs in the vicinity of 439 Ridge Street. The informer described the drug seller and his automobile in detail.

Marcum and two other police officers, Detective Cassidy and Sergeant Gonzales, quickly went to check out the reported drug dealing on the city streets. They found the car of the alleged drug dealer and used the license plate number to obtain information about the owner, Albert Ross.

The police officers stopped Albert Ross's car, asked him to step outside, and searched him. Sergeant Gonzales, looking through the automobile window, noticed a bullet on the front seat. He entered the car, searched it for weapons, and found a pistol in the glove compartment. The officers arrested Ross for violating the local firearms code.

The officers unlocked the trunk of the car and found a bag and a small pouch. Plastic envelopes in the bag contained white powder, which later proved to be heroin. The pouch contained $3,200 in cash.

Ross was charged with possession of an illegal substance, heroin, with intent to sell it. He, in turn, accused the police of violating his constitutional rights by searching his car and containers in the car without first obtaining a search warrant. His attorney filed a motion asking that the evidence obtained without a warrant be excluded from Ross's trial. Ross's motion was denied, and he was convicted. His attorney appealed and the case eventually went to the U.S. Supreme Court.

The Issue The 4th Amendment to the Constitution guarantees the "right of the people to be secure in their persons, houses, papers, and effects against unreasonable searches and seizures…and no warrants shall issue, but upon probable cause." However, cars have been treated differently from houses ever since *Carroll* v. *United States* (1925), when the Court held that police could search an automobile without a warrant when they had a reasonable suspicion of criminal activity. The justification for this exception to the usual 4th Amendment requirements was that a car can be quickly driven away while police take time to obtain a search warrant. The opportunity to obtain evidence of illegal activity would then be lost.

If cars could be stopped by police and searched without a warrant, legal questions still remained about how far such a search could extend. Was it legal for police to search a car's glove compartment or trunk without a warrant? Can police examine containers spotted

In 1982 the Supreme Court ruled that police officers could search compartments of a car and containers inside a car without first obtaining a search warrant. The general right to search a car without a warrant had been established in 1925.

in a car, such as boxes or pouches, without obtaining a warrant from a magistrate?

Opinion of the Court Justice John Paul Stevens held that police officers do not need to obtain a warrant before they search compartments of a car or containers found in the vehicle. They can conduct such searches as long as they can demonstrate "probable cause" to believe that they will find evidence of illegal activity. This is the same standard needed to obtain a search warrant prior to conducting a search and seizing evidence.

Justice Stevens wrote, "If probable cause justifies the search of a lawfully stopped vehicle, it justifies the search of every part of the vehicle and its contents that may conceal the object of the search."

Dissent Justices Thurgood Marshall, William Brennan, and Byron White argued that the Court's decision gave a police officer the same authority as a judge to determine probable cause. They said that this was a wrongful blurring of the constitutional separation of judicial powers and executive or law enforcement powers. Justice Marshall feared that the Court's opinion was "a first step toward an unprecedented 'probable cause' exception to the warrant requirement." If this exception were to occur, Marshall said, the constitutional rights of individuals would be unjustly limited.

Significance The Court's decision in *Ross* extended the automobile exception to 4th Amendment requirements established in *Carroll* v. *United States* (1925). In effect, the *Ross* decision gave the power to determine "probable cause" to police officers rather than to a court.

Since the *Ross* case, the Court has continued to support the automobile exception to usual search and seizure standards. As a result, the 4th Amendment protections against automobile searches are minimal.

SEE ALSO

Carroll v. United States; Probable cause; Searches and seizures; Terry v. Ohio

United States v. United States District Court

☆ *407 U.S. 297 (1972)*
☆ *Vote: 8–0*
☆ *For the Court: Powell*
☆ *Concurring: Burger, Douglas, and White*
☆ *Not participating: Rehnquist*

IN 1968 Congress passed the Omnibus Crime Control and Safe Streets Act, which provided for court-approved electronic surveillance to fight certain kinds of crimes. This law also provided that "nothing contained [in the section about electronic surveillance] shall limit the constitutional power of the President to take such measures as he deems necessary to protect the United States against the overthrow of the Government."

President Richard Nixon used this section of the act to use electronic surveillance (telephone wiretaps, for example) to monitor American citizens suspected of activities dangerous to the security of the United States. The Nixon administration did so without first showing "probable cause" and obtaining a warrant, or permission, from a court, as required by the 4th Amendment.

Electronic surveillance had been used by the Nixon administration against defendants accused of bombing a Central Intelligence Agency office in Ann Arbor, Michigan. Before their trial, the defendants petitioned the U.S. District Court for the Eastern District of Michigan to require the federal government to

President Richard Nixon and Attorney General John Mitchell argued that they should not have to turn over to the courts information gained through electronic surveillance of defendants accused of bombing a CIA office.

produce any information about them obtained from electronic surveillance. The U.S. attorney general, John Mitchell, said that such information existed, but he refused to release it. The district court, however, ruled that the Nixon administration's use of electronic surveillance violated the 4th Amendment and ordered the federal government to turn over the requested information. The federal government appealed this ruling to the U.S. Supreme Court.

The Issue The Nixon administration argued that disclosure of the requested information "would prejudice the national interest." Further, the Nixon administration held that Article 2 of the Constitution implied that the President had power to use electronic surveillance or any other means necessary to gather information to protect the federal government from destruction. Did the needs of national security, for which the President is responsible under the U.S. Constitution, outweigh the protection of individual rights guaranteed by the U.S. Constitution, such as the 4th Amendment right to protection against unwarranted governmental searches and seizures of one's private possessions? Was the federal government required to obey the district court's order to disclose certain information obtained through electronic surveillance conducted without a warrant?

Opinion of the Court The Supreme court upheld the federal district court's order. The Court stressed that this case involved protection of 1st and 4th Amendment rights. It viewed the electronic surveillance project of the Nixon administration as a discouragement to free and open exchange of information by individuals critical of the government.

Significance The decision in this case was a strong statement about the primary importance of constitutional rights. Not even pervasive social upheavals and threats to national security could justify denial of fundamental rights of liberty and justice for all individuals.

FURTHER READING

Westin, Alvin F. "Civil Liberties in the Technology Age." *Constitution* 3, no. 1 (Winter 1991): 56–64.

United States v. Wong Kim Ark

☆ *169 U.S. 649 (1898)*
☆ *Vote: 6–2*
☆ *For the Court: Gray*
☆ *Dissenting: Fuller and Harlan*
☆ *Not participating: McKenna*

WONG KIM ARK was born in San Francisco, California, in 1873. His parents had gone to California from China. They were not citizens of the United States but retained their status as subjects of the emperor of China.

Wong Kim Ark traveled to China in 1894. When he returned to California one year later, federal agents refused him admission to the United States because, they said, he was Chinese and not a citizen of the United States. Wong Kim Ark claimed U.S. citizenship because he was born in the United States.

The Issue The 14th Amendment says, "All persons born or naturalized in the United States, and subject to the jurisdiction thereof, are citizens of the United States and of the State wherein

A scene from San Francisco's Chinatown at the turn of the century. In 1898 the Supreme Court ruled that anyone born in the United States, regardless of ancestry, has the rights of a U.S. citizen.

they reside." The federal government argued that Wong Kim Ark was not a citizen of the United States because his parents were Chinese. Thus, neither Wong Kim Ark nor his parents were "subject to the jurisdiction" of the United States. Rather, claimed the federal government, they were subject to the jurisdiction of China. Did a person of Chinese descent, born in the United States, have the right of U.S. citizenship?

Opinion of the Court The decision favored Wong Kim Ark. Justice Horace Gray held that the common law tradition and the 14th Amendment clearly guaranteed U.S. citizenship to all people born in the country. The ethnic identity or place of birth of the person's parents could not be used to deny citizenship to a person born in the United States.

Significance This case immediately established the citizenship rights of people of Asian descent born in the United States. It also established the general rule of *jus soli* (a Latin term meaning the "right based on soil")— the determination of citizenship by place of birth. The *Wong Kim Ark* case rejected the general rule of *jus sanguinis* (a Latin term meaning the "right based on blood")—the determination of citizenship by the ethnicity of the parents. Given the rule of *jus soli*— embodied in the 14th Amendment— Wong Kim Ark was entitled to all privileges and rights of U.S. citizenship on equal terms with any other citizen, whether naturalized (by legal procedure) or natural-born, as he was.

SEE ALSO

Citizenship

United Steelworkers of America v. Weber

☆ *443 U.S. 193 (1979)*
☆ *Vote: 5–2*
☆ *For the Court: Brennan*
☆ *Dissenting: Burger and Rehnquist*
☆ *Not participating: Powell and Stevens*

THE UNITED Steelworkers of America, a labor union, made an agreement with the Kaiser Aluminum and Chemical Company to set up a training program to develop the skills of workers at a Kaiser plant in Gramercy, Louisiana. Half of the places in the program were reserved for black workers. In the past, black workers in this region had been denied opportunities to become highly skilled craftworkers, and most of them worked at low-paying, menial jobs. The company's voluntary and temporary plan was designed to overcome past job discrimination and to create new opportunities for black workers.

Brian Weber, a white unskilled worker and a member of the union, applied for a position in the new job training program. He was rejected. However, black workers with less seniority than Weber were selected in order to fill the 50 percent quota reserved for black workers in the new training program.

Seniority refers to the amount of time a worker has been employed in a job. Labor unions often use seniority as a standard for distributing benefits of one kind or another; those with more years of service get preference in promotions to better jobs or positions in job training programs.

Weber charged that his rejection for admission to the job training program was unfair because it was based on

An apprentice steelworker on the job. The Supreme Court ruled in 1979 that companies can establish affirmative action plans to choose workers for their training programs.

race, not the usual standard of seniority. He claimed this was a violation of Title VII of the Civil Rights Act of 1964, which forbids an employer to discriminate against an employee "because of such individual's race, color, religion, sex, or national origin." Weber sued the union and his employer.

The Issue Was the plan for selecting applicants to the job training program, set up by the United Steelworkers of America in agreement with the Kaiser plant, a violation of Title VII of the Civil Rights Act of 1964? Was Brian Weber illegally denied admission to the new job training program at the Kaiser plant in Gramercy, Louisiana?

Opinion of the Court The Court held that the plan for selecting applicants to the job training program did not violate the Civil Rights Act of 1964. Justice William Brennan wrote that the plan for selecting applicants was in line with the intent of the Civil Rights Act to "break down old patterns of racial segregation and hierarchy."

Brennan emphasized that the race-based quota in the plan was temporary and resulted from a voluntary agreement between a labor union and an employer. Further, he said, the purpose was not to maintain a racial balance but to overcome a long-standing racial imbalance in employment opportunity.

Dissent Chief Justice Warren Burger and Justice William Rehnquist argued that the plan for admission to the job training program conflicted with the words and the intent of the 1964 Civil Rights Act. According to the dissenters, the federal law clearly prohibits discrimination on the basis of race in selecting participants for a job training program.

Significance This was the first case in which the Court decided an issue about an employer's affirmative action plan—a program that gives favored treatment to members of certain groups

supposed to have suffered from past discrimination in employment opportunities. The decision encouraged private employers to experiment with temporary and voluntary affirmative action plans.

SEE ALSO

Affirmative action

Van Devanter, Willis

ASSOCIATE JUSTICE, 1911–37

☆ *Born: Apr. 17, 1859, Marion, Ind.*
☆ *Education: Indiana Asbury University (DePauw University), B.A., 1878; University of Cincinnati Law School, LL.B., 1881*
☆ *Previous government service: city attorney, Cheyenne, Wyo., 1887–88; Wyoming Territorial Legislature, 1888; chief justice, Wyoming Territory Supreme Court, 1889–90; assistant U.S. attorney general, 1897–1903; judge, U.S. Court of Appeals for the Eighth Circuit, 1903–1910*
☆ *Appointed by President William Howard Taft Dec. 12, 1910; replaced William Moody, who retired*
☆ *Supreme Court term: confirmed by the Senate Dec. 15, 1910, by a voice vote; retired June 2, 1937*
☆ *Died: Feb. 8, 1941, Washington, D.C.*

WILLIS VAN DEVANTER moved, as a young man, from his settled community in Indiana to Cheyenne in the Wyoming Territory. On the last western frontier, he built a successful career in law and politics that led him back east to federal government service in Washington, D.C.

Van Devanter served 26 years on the Supreme Court, where he exercised great influence on his colleagues during most of his long term. He rarely wrote opinions; his average number of opinions per year was only 14. (Most justices wrote more than 50 per year.) Justice Van Devanter influenced the other justices through face-to-face discussions about the cases before the Court. He often influenced the direction and substance of opinions written by others.

Justice Van Devanter argued persistently for limited government and against the expansion of the federal government's power to regulate businesses and the relationships between employers and workers. Accordingly, he reacted strongly against the New Deal programs of President Franklin D. Roosevelt. He succeeded in influencing the Court to strike down several New Deal laws during President Roosevelt's first term of office. However, by 1936 the tide had turned against him. Public opinion was strongly on the side of Roosevelt's New Deal. The President's new appointments to the Court reflected this public mood and Roosevelt's views. As a result, Van Devanter decided to retire from the Court in 1937.

Vinson, Fred M.

CHIEF JUSTICE, 1946–53

☆ *Born: Jan. 22, 1890, Louisa, Ky.*
☆ *Education: Centre College, B.A., 1909, LL.B., 1911*
☆ *Previous government service: commonwealth's attorney, 32nd District of Kentucky, 1921–24; U.S. Representative from Kentucky, 1924–29, 1931–38; judge, U.S. Court of Appeals for the District of Columbia Circuit, 1938–43; director, U.S. Office of Economic Stabilization, 1943–45; administrator, Federal Loan Agency, 1945; director, U.S. Office of War Mobilization and Reconversion, 1945; U.S. secretary of the Treasury, 1945–46*
☆ *Appointed by President Harry S. Truman June 6, 1946; replaced Harlan Fiske Stone, who died*
☆ *Supreme Court term: confirmed by the Senate June 20, 1946, by a voice vote; served until Sept. 8, 1953*
☆ *Died: Sept. 8, 1953, Washington, D.C.*

FRED M. VINSON became the 13th chief justice of the United States in 1946. This was the capstone of a long and meritorious career in all three branches of the federal government. Chief Justice Vinson served only seven years, until his death in 1953, as chief justice. These were years of tumult and controversy involving the Court in issues of patriotism and loyalty to the United States and issues of civil liberties and equal protection against racial discrimination.

Chief Justice Vinson acted strongly against individuals he viewed as a threat to the government of the United States. In *Dennis* v. *United States* (1951), for example, he upheld the Smith Act, which provided for criminal convictions of anyone advocating violent overthrow of the U.S. government. In the *Dennis* case, several leaders of the American Communist party were punished.

Chief Justice Vinson supported equal rights for black Americans in several opinions. For example, he led the Court in overturning state laws that unfairly discriminated against black people in *Sweatt* v. *Painter* (1950) and *McLaurin* v. *Board of Regents* (1950). These rulings helped to set the stage for the Court's landmark decision in *Brown* v. *Board of Education* (1954), which marked the beginning of the end of racial segregation in public schools and other institutions.

SEE ALSO

Dennis v. United States; Sweatt v. Painter

FURTHER READING

Palmer, Jan S. *The Vinson Court Era*. New York: AMS Press, 1990.
Pritchett, C. Herman. *Civil Liberties and the Vinson Court*. Chicago: University of Chicago Press, 1954.

Waite, Morrison R.

*CHIEF JUSTICE,
1874–88*

☆ *Born: Nov. 29, 1816, Lyme, Conn.*
☆ *Education: Yale College, B.A.,
1837*
☆ *Previous government service: Ohio
House of Representatives, 1850–52;
president, Ohio Constitutional
Convention, 1873–74*
☆ *Appointed by President Ulysses S.
Grant Jan. 19, 1874; replaced Salmon
P. Chase, who died*
☆ *Supreme Court term: confirmed by the
Senate Jan. 21, 1874, by a 63–0 vote;
served until Mar. 23, 1888*
☆ *Died: Mar. 23, 1888, Washington, D.C.*

MORRISON R. WAITE had no judicial
experience before his appointment as
chief justice, and he had never presented
a case before the Supreme Court. President Ulysses S. Grant appointed Waite to
head the Supreme Court because of his
effectiveness in representing the United
States in an international arbitration case
in Geneva.

At first, Chief Justice Waite was not
respected by other members of the Supreme Court because of his lack of experience. He eventually won their acceptance and respect for his hard work and
leadership of the Court.

Chief Justice Waite often decided in
favor of the power and rights of state
governments. For example, in his most
notable opinion, *Munn* v. *Illinois*
(1877), Chief Justice Waite upheld an Illinois law that set maximum rates that
could be charged by grain elevator owners. He supported the power of the state
of Illinois to regulate the use of private
property "when such regulation becomes necessary for the public good."

In the *Munn* case, and similar cases
involving state laws, Waite believed that
the political process, not the Courts, was
the correct avenue for opponents of the

laws. In *Munn* v. *Illinois,* Waite wrote:
"For protection against abuse by legislatures, the people must resort to the polls,
not to the courts." Waite believed that
the legislative branch of government, not
the judicial branch, should always take
the lead in making public policy. The judiciary, he argued, should restrain itself
to questions of legal interpretation.

Under Waite's leadership, the Court
tended to narrowly interpret the rights of
black Americans under the 14th and
15th Amendments to the U.S. Constitution. Waite argued that most civil rights
were associated with state citizenship,
which should be guaranteed by the state
governments, not the federal government. This viewpoint, which often prevailed on the Court at this time, meant
that the civil rights of black Americans
varied considerably depending upon the
state in which they lived. In many states,
their rights were not equal to those of
white Americans, and the Supreme
Court, under Waite, was reluctant to intervene into the states' affairs to secure
these rights.

SEE ALSO

Judicial activism and judicial restraint;
Munn v. Illinois

FURTHER READING

Magrath, Peter C. *Morrison R. Waite: The
Triumph of Character.* New York:
Macmillan, 1963.

Wallace v. Jaffree

☆ *472 U.S. 38 (1985)*
☆ *Vote: 6–3*
☆ *For the Court: Stevens*
☆ *Concurring: Powell and O'Connor*
☆ *Dissenting: Burger, White, and
Rehnquist*

FROM 1978 TO 1982 the Alabama legislature passed three laws pertaining to
prayer in public schools. The 1978 law

Ishmael Jaffree on the steps of the Supreme Court. When Jaffree's children reported that their teachers were leading prayers in school, he filed suit against the state for violating the constitutional separation of church and state.

authorized schools to provide a daily minute of silence for meditation. A 1981 law provided for a similar period "for meditation or voluntary prayer." A third law, enacted in 1982, allowed teachers to lead "willing students" in a prescribed prayer.

In 1982 Ishmael Jaffree filed suit against the school board of Mobile County to challenge the 1981 and 1982 Alabama laws permitting a period of silence and prayer in public schools. Jaffree decided to file this suit after his three children reported that their teachers had led prayers in school. Jaffree claimed that the 1981 and 1982 Alabama statutes on prayer in public schools violated the establishment clause of the 1st Amendment to the U.S. Constitution, which prohibited the states from making laws regarding the establishment of religion. He cited Supreme Court decisions such as *Engel* v. *Vitale* (1962) and *Abington School District* v. *Schempp* (1963) to support his argument. In both cases, the Court found that state-mandated religious activities in public schools were unconstitutional.

A federal district court ruled against Jaffree, stating that the *Engel* and *Schempp* cases were decided incorrectly. This district court ruling was overturned by the U.S. Court of Appeals for the 11th Circuit. The Court of Appeals followed the precedents of the *Engel* and *Schempp* cases and held that the 1981 and 1982 Alabama laws violated the establishment clause of the 1st Amendment as applied to the states through the 14th Amendment. The state of Alabama appealed the federal appellate court's decision to the U.S. Supreme Court.

The Issue The Supreme Court summarily upheld the appellate court's decision to strike down the 1982 statute, which clearly authorized teachers and students to set aside time for expression of prayer in public schools. According to the Court, this was a clear violation of the 1st Amendment's establishment clause. Therefore, the Court agreed to hear oral arguments only about the 1981 statute, which authorized the moment of silence for "meditation or voluntary prayer." Does a state law authorizing a moment of silence in a public school, for the express purpose of prayer, violate the 1st Amendment provisions on religion: "Congress shall make no law respecting an establishment of religion, or prohibiting the free exercise thereof"?

Opinion of the Court The Court decided for Jaffree and overturned the Alabama law at issue in this case because of the law's religious purpose and intentions. Justice John Paul Stevens relied upon the Court's previous rulings in *Abington School District* v. *Schempp* (1963) and *Lemon* v. *Kurtzman* (1971) to justify the *Jaffree* decision.

Dissent Justice William Rehnquist argued for a totally new interpretation of the 1st Amendment's establishment clause. He rejected the idea of a "wall of separation" between church and state. And he opposed the precedents of *Schempp* and *Lemon* as bases for making decisions about establishment clause issues. Instead, Rehnquist claimed that the 1st Amendment was designed only to prevent the government from favoring one religion over another. As long as all religions were treated neutrally or equally (non-preferentially), said Rehnquist, the government could provide support for religion in public schools.

Significance This case is notable for what it did not decide. The question of a legislated moment of silence without specific provision for prayer was not addressed. As a result, moments of silence continue to be observed in the public schools of more than 25 states, including Alabama.

SEE ALSO

Abington School District v. Schempp; Engel v. Vitale; Establishment clause; Lemon v. Kurtzman; Religious issues under the Constitution

FURTHER READING

Irons, Peter. *The Courage of Their Convictions.* New York: Free Press, 1988.

Ware v. Hylton

☆ *3 Dall. 199 (1796)*
☆ *Vote: 4–0*
☆ *For the Court: seriatim opinions by Chase, Paterson, Wilson, and Cushing*
☆ *Not participating: Ellsworth and Iredell*

THE TREATY OF PARIS (1783), which ended the American War of Independence, guaranteed that prewar debts owed by Americans to British subjects would be recoverable. The state of Virginia, however, had passed legislation during the war to protect citizens of Virginia who had debts to British creditors against demands for repayment of the debts. Ware, the financial agent of a British subject, sought payment of a debt owed his client by Daniel Hylton, a Virginia citizen, so Ware took his case to a federal court.

The Issue Article 6 of the Constitution says that "all Treaties made, or which shall be made, under the Authority of the United States, shall be the supreme Law of the Land; and the Judges in every State shall be bound thereby, any Thing in the Constitution or Laws of any State to the Contrary notwithstanding." Given the precise wording of the Constitution about treaties as supreme law, was it possible for Virginia to violate a provision of the 1783 Treaty of Paris about payment of debts to British subjects?

Hylton's attorney was John Marshall, a future chief justice of the United States. Marshall argued that a U.S. treaty could not override a state law enacted before the Constitution was written in 1787 and before the Treaty of Paris was ratified. Ware argued that the Virginia law at issue violated the U.S. Constitution and, therefore, should be struck down by the Court.

Opinion of the Court The Supreme Court decided against Hylton and the state of Virginia. It ruled that the Treaty of Paris was part of the supreme law of the United States and its provisions took precedence over any state law that conflicted with it. The Court declared the state law unconstitutional and therefore null and void. Justice Samuel Chase wrote, "A treaty cannot be the supreme law of the land…if any act of a state legislature can stand in its way…. [L]aws of any states, contrary to a treaty shall be disregarded [as]…null and void."

Significance John Marshall lost the only case he argued before the Supreme Court, which he later dominated for 34 years. Ironically, the Court's sweeping defense of federal supremacy over conflicting state laws was in keeping with Marshall's subsequent opinions for the Court.

This case marks the Court's first use of judicial review to strike down a state action because it violated the U.S. Constitution. This power, implied by Article 6 of the U.S. Constitution, is spelled out in Section 25 of the Judiciary Act of 1789.

SEE ALSO

Federalism; Judicial review

Warren, Earl

*CHIEF JUSTICE,
1953–69*

☆ *Born: Mar. 19, 1891, Los Angeles,
Calif.*

☆ *Education: University of California at
Berkeley, B.L., 1912, J.D., 1914*

☆ *Previous government service: deputy
city attorney, Oakland, Calif., 1919–
20; deputy assistant district attorney,
Alameda County, Calif., 1920–23;
chief deputy district attorney, Alameda
County, 1923–25; district attorney,
Alameda County, 1925–39; attorney
general of California, 1939–43;
governor of California, 1943–53*

☆ *Appointed by President Dwight D.
Eisenhower as a recess appointment
Oct. 2, 1953; replaced Chief Justice
Fred M. Vinson, who died; nominated
by Eisenhower Jan. 11, 1954*

☆ *Supreme Court term: confirmed by the
Senate Mar. 1, 1954, by a voice vote;
retired June 23, 1969*

☆ *Died: July 9, 1974, Washington, D.C.*

EARL WARREN, the son of immigrants from Norway, had a profound influence on constitutional law in the United States. As the 14th chief justice of the United States, he presided over a judicial revolution in the 1950s and 1960s.

Warren's public life before becoming chief justice gave little hint of what he would do on the Court. His career was conducted exclusively in California local and state politics from 1919 until 1953, when he joined the Supreme Court. During World War II, as attorney general and governor of California, Warren vigorously supported the federal order removing people of Japanese ancestry from the Pacific Coast of the United States and confining them in grim camps. He believed, without any evidence, that these people could threaten the national security of the United States during its war with Japan. At the end of his life, Warren expressed remorse: "I have since deeply regretted the removal order and my own testimony advocating it, because it was not in keeping with our American concept of freedom and the rights of citizens."

Governor Warren moved to the Supreme Court through his participation in the Presidential election of 1952, when he helped Dwight D. Eisenhower win the Republican party nomination for President. After winning the Presidency, Eisenhower rewarded Earl Warren with the appointment to the office of chief justice.

Eisenhower later said this appointment was "the biggest damn-fool mistake I ever made." Supreme Court scholars, however, have lauded Warren as one of the Court's all-time great justices. What did Warren do to disappoint Eisenhower and win the acclaim of scholars?

Earl Warren presided over the Supreme Court during a period of great controversy and change. Under his leadership, the Court stated new ideas on equal protection of the laws, the rights of persons accused of crime, freedom of expression, and representation in government.

Chief Justice Warren's greatest opinion was written in 1954, at the beginning of his 16-year term. In *Brown* v. *Board of Education*, Chief Justice Warren skillfully influenced the Court's unanimous decision to strike down state laws that required separate schools to be provided for black and white students. This decision overturned the 1896 ruling in *Plessy* v. *Ferguson* that had sanctioned racial segregation in public facilities.

Several decisions of the Warren Court greatly expanded the constitutional rights of those suspected or accused of crime. For example, state law enforcement officials were required to exclude illegally obtained evidence in criminal proceedings (*Mapp* v. *Ohio*, 1961), to guarantee the right to competent legal assistance for an accused person (*Gideon* v. *Wainwright*, 1963), and to inform people of their right against self-incrimination (*Griffin* v. *California*, 1965, and *Miranda* v. *Arizona*, 1966). These decisions overruled earlier Court rulings that had allowed the states to deviate from strict observance of the federal Bill of Rights. The Warren Court moved decisively to apply the rights of an accused person, as outlined in the federal Bill of Rights, to all of the states under the due process clause of the 14th Amendment to the U.S. Constitution.

The Warren Court's most significant ruling on freedom of expression came in *New York Times Co.* v. *Sullivan* (1964). The Court held that a public official may not sue and recover damages for libel against a person who has written untrue statements about him unless there was a complete and reckless disregard for truth. The Court's intention was to remove barriers to the free flow of information about government officials that is a necessary part of the democratic process.

Chief Justice Warren considered the Court's rulings on a series of "reapportionment cases" to be its most important contribution to constitutional law. These decisions, beginning with *Baker* v. *Carr* (1962) and culminating in *Reynolds* v. *Sims* (1964), established the principle of "one person, one vote" in state and federal elections. State governments were required to apportion, or divide, the state, for purposes of political representation, into districts based solely on population, with the districts as nearly equal in population as was possible. This decision ended the practice of creating districts to unfairly inflate representation in government of some groups at the expense of other groups.

Chief Justice Warren believed it was the Court's responsibility to protect the civil liberties and rights of individuals against overbearing majorities acting privately or through their representatives in government. Warren also believed that

the Court should be an active partner with the other branches of government in achieving social justice and protection of the individual against the powers of the state.

SEE ALSO

Brown v. Board of Education; Incorporation doctrine; Judicial activism and judicial restraint; Miranda v. Arizona; Reynolds v. Sims

FURTHER READING

Schwartz, Bernard. *Superchief: Earl Warren and His Supreme Court.* New York: New York University Press, 1983.
White, G. Edward. *Earl Warren: A Public Life.* New York: Oxford University Press, 1982.

Washington, Bushrod

ASSOCIATE JUSTICE, 1798–1829

☆ Born: June 5, 1762, Westmoreland County, Va.
☆ Education: College of William and Mary, B.A., 1778; read law with James Wilson in Philadelphia, Pa.
☆ Previous government service: Virginia House of Delegates, 1787; Virginia Ratifying Convention, 1788
☆ Appointed by President John Adams as a recess appointment Sept. 29, 1798; replaced James Wilson, who died; nominated by Adams Dec. 19, 1798
☆ Supreme Court term: confirmed by the Senate Dec. 20, 1798, by a voice vote; served until Nov. 26, 1829
☆ Died: Nov. 26, 1829, Philadelphia, Pa.

BUSHROD WASHINGTON was George Washington's favorite nephew, who inherited his uncle's property at Mount Vernon. He served in the Continental Army under his Uncle George during the War of Independence. He studied law under James Wilson, whom Bushrod Washington succeeded on the Supreme Court.

Bushrod Washington served on the Supreme Court for 31 years, but he wrote no important decisions. Rather, his contributions came as an ardent supporter of Chief Justice Marshall's opinions. His ties to John Marshall were so close that another associate justice, William Johnson, said that they "are commonly estimated as a single judge."

Justice Washington and Chief Justice Marshall were together on the Supreme Court for 29 years. They disagreed only three times.

Wayne, James M.

ASSOCIATE JUSTICE, 1835–67

☆ Born: 1790, Savannah, Ga.
☆ Education: College of New Jersey (Princeton), B.A., 1808; read law under Charles Chauncey in New Haven, Conn.
☆ Previous government service: Georgia House of Representatives, 1815–16; mayor of Savannah, 1817–19; judge, Savannah Court of Common Pleas, 1820–22; judge, Georgia Superior Court, 1822–28; U.S. Representative from Georgia, 1829–35
☆ Appointed by President Andrew Jackson Jan. 7, 1835; replaced William Johnson, who died
☆ Supreme Court term: confirmed by the Senate Jan. 9, 1835, by a voice vote; served until July 5, 1867
☆ Died: July 5, 1867, Washington, D.C.

JAMES M. WAYNE served 32 years as an associate justice of the U.S. Supreme Court. During this time he was torn by his conflicting loyalties to the South and to the federal Union. He was a slaveholder from Georgia who believed in the power and right of each state to decide, without federal interference, about the institution of slavery. He was also committed to the preservation of the United States of America.

When the Civil War erupted, Justice Wayne remained loyal to the Union and remained on the Supreme Court. His

son, by contrast, resigned from the U.S. Army and became the adjutant general of the Confederate state of Georgia. In 1861, Georgia declared Justice Wayne an "enemy alien" and confiscated his property.

During the Civil War, Justice Wayne supported President Abraham Lincoln's policies in the *Prize Cases* (1863), upholding Lincoln's blockade of Southern ports, and in *Ex parte Vallandigham* (1864), which permitted the conviction of a civilian Confederate sympathizer in a military court.

FURTHER READING

Lawrence, Alexander A. *James Moore Wayne: Southern Unionist.* Chapel Hill: University of North Carolina Press, 1943.

Webster v. Reproductive Health Services

☆ 492 U.S. 490 (1989)
☆ Vote: 5–4
☆ For the Court: Rehnquist
☆ Concurring: Scalia and O'Connor
☆ Dissenting: Blackmun, Brennan, Marshall, and Stevens

IN 1986 the state of Missouri passed a law that placed certain restrictions on the performance of abortions. This law was challenged as an unconstitutional violation of women's rights by Reproductive Health Services, a federal organization providing assistance for women seeking abortions. A district court and circuit court of appeals struck down the Missouri law because it placed restrictions on a woman's right to choose an abortion, which was established in *Roe* v. *Wade* (1973). The state of Missouri appealed to the U.S. Supreme Court.

The Issue At issue was the constitutionality of the Missouri law restricting a woman's right to an abortion, which violated the precedent established by the Court in *Roe* v. *Wade.*

Opinion of the Court Chief Justice William Rehnquist reported the opinion of a divided Court. A bare majority upheld two of several provisions of the Missouri law: "[W]e uphold the Act's restrictions on the use of public employees and facilities for the performance or assistance of non-therapeutic abortions [those not necessary to save a mother's life]." The other provision of the Missouri law upheld by the Court was a requirement that "before a physician performs an abortion on a woman he has reason to believe is carrying an unborn child of twenty or more weeks…the physician shall first determine if the unborn child is viable [capable of life outside the womb]." Thus, the *Webster* decision modified the second-trimester rule in *Roe* v. *Wade,* which held that all regulations on abortion rights during the fourth through sixth months of pregnancy must be related to protecting the health of the mother. The *Webster* decision, however, stopped short of overturning *Roe,* which antiabortion advocates had wanted.

Dissent Justice Harry Blackmun, author of the Court's opinion in *Roe* v. *Wade,* wrote a passionate dissent. He wrote, "Today, *Roe* v. *Wade* (1973) and the fundamental right of women to decide whether to terminate a pregnancy survive but are not secure." According to Justice Blackmun, the Court's decision in the *Webster* case "implicitly invites every state legislature to enact more and more restrictive abortion regulations in order to provoke more and more test cases, in the hope that sometime down the line the Court will return the law of procreative freedom to the severe limitations that generally prevailed in this country before January 22, 1973."

Significance This case fueled the heated public controversy about the abortion rights issue. Pro-choice groups, who favored abortion rights, saw the Court's decision as an assault on their position. Their opponents cheered it as the beginning of the end for *Roe* v. *Wade.* Both sides increased their attempts to influence state government officials to support their views in this ongoing dispute.

SEE ALSO

Abortion rights; Roe v. Wade

Weeks v. United States

☆ *232 U.S. 383 (1914)*
☆ *Vote: 9–0*
☆ *For the Court: Day*

LOCAL POLICE and U.S. marshals suspected Weeks of criminal behavior. His house was searched twice, first by local police and then by a U.S. marshal. Incriminating evidence was found and used to charge Weeks with the crime of sending lottery tickets through the mail.

Neither search of Weeks's home was authorized by a search warrant. So Weeks petitioned a federal court for the return of his property because it had been taken in violation of the 4th and 5th Amendments to the Constitution. The 4th Amendment requires government officials to obtain a warrant before they can search a person's home. The 5th Amendment says that no person can be "deprived of life, liberty, or property, without due process of law." Weeks's petition for return of his property went to the U.S. Supreme Court.

The Issue Did the warrantless search of Weeks's house by a federal officer violate his constitutional rights?

Could Weeks's property, taken in a warrantless search, be kept by the government and used against Weeks in court?

Opinion of the Court Justice William R. Day narrowed the case to the consideration of Weeks's 4th Amendment rights, which clearly were violated by the federal marshal's warrantless search of his home. The judgment against Weeks was reversed because the evidence used against him was obtained illegally. His illegally seized property was returned to him and could not be used in any trial.

Significance This case was the origin of the exclusionary rule, which requires that evidence obtained in violation of a person's constitutional rights must be excluded from any legal proceedings against him. Prior to the *Weeks* case, courts admitted illegally seized evidence because the rights of the individual were considered secondary to society's need for the punishment of criminal behavior.

SEE ALSO
Exclusionary rule; Searches and seizures

West Coast Hotel Co. v. Parrish

☆ *300 U.S. 379 (1937)*
☆ *Vote: 5–4*
☆ *For the Court: Hughes*
☆ *Dissenting: Sutherland, Butler, McReynolds, and Van Devanter*

ELSIE PARRISH worked as a chambermaid at the Cascadian Hotel in Wenatchee, Washington. Her pay was $12 for a 48-hour week. This was less than the amount required by the state of Washington's minimum wage law. So Elsie Parrish brought suit against her employer. The state supreme court decided in favor of Parrish, but the hotel owners appealed to the U.S. Supreme Court.

The Issue One year earlier, in *Morehead* v. *New York ex rel. Tipaldo* (1936), the Court ruled a New York State minimum wage law unconstitutional. The Court argued for liberty of contract between employer and employee to decide without government regulation about wages and hours of work. This liberty of contract was held to be protected from state government regulations by the due process clause of the 14th Amendment. Did the state of Washington's minimum wage law violate the 14th Amendment?

Opinion of the Court The Court upheld the state minimum wage law and reversed the decisions in *Morehead* v. *New York ex rel. Tipaldo* (1936) and *Adkins* v. *Children's Hospital* (1923), upon which the *Morehead* decision was based. In *Adkins,* the Court declared unconstitutional an act of Congress

In 1937 the Supreme Court ruled that a Washington state minimum wage law, which protected workers from exploitation by employers, was constitutional.

that established a minimum wage for children and women workers in the District of Columbia. The dissenting view in *Morehead*—by Chief Justice Charles Evans Hughes and Justices Louis Brandeis, Benjamin Cardozo, and Harlan Fiske Stone—was the foundation for the Court's opinion in this case, written by Hughes. Justice Owen Roberts joined the four *Morehead* dissenters to form the Court majority in this case.

Chief Justice Hughes rejected the idea of liberty of contract set forth in the *Adkins* and *Morehead* cases. He wrote:

> The Constitution does not speak of freedom of contract. It speaks of liberty and prohibits the deprivation of liberty without due process of law. In prohibiting that deprivation the Constitution does not recognize an absolute and uncontrollable liberty.... The liberty safeguarded is liberty in a social organization which requires the protection of law against the evils which menace the health, safety, morals, and welfare of the people. Liberty under the Constitution is thus necessarily subject to the restraints of due process, and regulation which is adopted in the interests of the community is due process.

Significance Justice Roberts's vote in support of the Washington State minimum wage law was a complete change from his vote in the *Morehead* case, and it made the difference in the *Parrish* case. Reporters called it "the switch in time that saved nine." This reference was to the court-packing plan of President Franklin D. Roosevelt. He had been frustrated by several of the Court's decisions against his New Deal programs involving government regulation of businesses on behalf of the public good. So the President had proposed that Congress enact legislation to enable him to appoint six new justices to the Supreme Court. After the *Parrish* decision, however, the President backed away from his plan to alter the membership of the Court.

The *Parrish* decision provided legal support for Congress to pass the Fair Labor Standards Act in 1938, which included a minimum wage provision for businesses involved in interstate commerce. The *Parrish* decision also provided a precedent for federal court decisions against liberty of contract claims that would endanger important community interests and the public good.

SEE ALSO
Court-packing plan

WESTLAW

WEST PUBLISHING COMPANY has a computerized research service— WESTLAW—that contains a database of all Supreme Court decisions since 1790. Data on current decisions are sent electronically to the WESTLAW database from the Court and can be accessed via computer on the same day the decision is made. The database contains the full text of all decisions of the Court, summaries of recent decisions, and reports about changes in Supreme Court rules. The WESTLAW database also contains information about orders, such as the schedule for oral arguments, stays of execution, and invitations or permissions to file amicus curiae (friend of the court) briefs on cases scheduled to be heard by the Court, and cases accepted on appeal or denied review by the Court.

SEE ALSO
LEXIS

West Virginia State Board of Education v. Barnette

☆ *319 U.S. 624 (1943)*
☆ *Vote: 6–3*
☆ *For the Court: Jackson*
☆ *Concurring: Black, Douglas, and Murphy*
☆ *Dissenting: Frankfurter, Roberts, and Reed*

THE GOVERNMENT of West Virginia made a law that required students in public schools to salute the flag and pledge allegiance to it. Refusal to comply with this act would be considered insubordination punishable by expulsion from school. Readmission to school would be granted only on condition that the student comply with the flag-salute law. Furthermore, expelled students would be considered unlawfully absent from school, and their parents or guardians would be liable to prosecution.

Some children and their parents, who were Jehovah's Witnesses, refused to obey the flag-salute law on the grounds that it violated their religious beliefs. They viewed the flag of the United States as a "graven image," and their religion forbade them to "bow down to" or "worship a graven image." They argued that God's law was superior to the laws of the state. In turn, the local school authorities, backed by the West Virginia Board of Education, moved to punish the children and parents who would not obey the law. Thus, several West Virginia Jehovah's Witnesses families, including the family of Walter Barnette, sued for an injunction to stop enforcement of the flag-salute law.

The Issue Did the West Virginia flag-salute law violate the constitutional right to religious freedom of children professing the religion of Jehovah's Witnesses?

Opinion of the Court The Court ruled that the West Virginia flag-salute requirement was unconstitutional. Justice Robert H. Jackson said that public officials could act to promote national unity through patriotic ceremonies. However, they could not use compulsion of the kind employed in this case to enforce compliance. In particular, the 1st Amendment to the Constitution (applied to the state government through the due process clause of the 14th Amendment) prohibited public officials from forcing students to salute the flag against their religious beliefs. Justice Jackson concluded with one of the most quoted statements in the annals of the Supreme Court:

> The very purpose of a Bill of Rights was to withdraw certain subjects from the vicissitudes of political controversy, to place them beyond the reach of majorities and officials and to establish them as legal principles to be applied by the courts. One's right to life, liberty, and property, to free speech, a free press, freedom of worship and assembly, and other fundamental rights may not be submitted to vote; they depend on the outcome of no elections....
>
> If there is any fixed star in our constitutional constellation, it is that no official, high or petty, can prescribe

In 1943 the Supreme Court ruled that a West Virginia law requiring students to salute the American flag was unconstitutional.

what shall be orthodox in politics, nationalism, religion, or other matters of opinion or force citizens to confess by word or act their faith therein. If there are any circumstances which permit an exception, they do not now occur to us.

Dissent Justice Felix Frankfurter concluded that the state school board had the constitutional authority to require public school students to salute the flag. He wrote that by not complying with the law, minorities can disrupt government and civil society, and therefore the Court should support the duly enacted legislation at issue in this case, which clearly reflected the will of the majority in West Virginia. If citizens of West Virginia dislike laws enacted by their representatives in the state legislature, then they should try to influence the legislature to change the laws. According to Justice Frankfurter, the Supreme Court had overstepped its authority in placing its judgment above that of the elected legislature and school boards in West Virginia. "The courts ought to stand aloof from this type of controversy," he concluded.

Frankfurter especially objected to Jackson's argument that questions associated with the Bill of Rights should be beyond the reach of local officials and legislatures. Frankfurter believed judges had a duty to respect and give in to the discretion of legislatures and the laws they passed.

Significance The *Barnette* decision overturned the Court's ruling, only three years earlier, in *Minersville School District* v. *Gobitis,* which had upheld a Pennsylvania law requiring students in public schools to pledge allegiance to the American flag. The two flag-salute cases show how the Supreme Court can change its mind about the meaning of the Constitution. Applications of the doctrine of *stare decisis*—the use of precedent, or previously decided cases, to decide new cases—create stability in the law. However, allowing for exceptions to *stare decisis* and overruling precedents are ways the Court adapts the Constitution to changing conditions.

The *Barnette* case set a new precedent that the legal system has followed to this day. Federal courts applying the *Barnette* precedent have turned back several attempts by officials to establish new flag-salute requirements.

SEE ALSO

Free exercise clause; Minersville School District v. Gobitis; Religious issues under the Constitution; Student rights under the Constitution

FURTHER READING

Dillard, Irving. "The Flag-Salute Cases." In *Quarrels That Have Shaped the Constitution,* edited by John A. Garraty. New York: Harper & Row, 1987.

White, Byron R.
ASSOCIATE JUSTICE, 1962–93

☆ *Born: June 8, 1917, Fort Collins, Colo.*
☆ *Education: University of Colorado, B.A., 1938; Rhodes Scholar, Oxford University, 1939; Yale Law School, LL.B., 1946*
☆ *Previous government service: law clerk to Chief Justice Fred M. Vinson, 1946–47; deputy U.S. attorney general, 1961–62*
☆ *Appointed by President John F. Kennedy Mar. 30, 1962; replaced Charles E. Whittaker, who retired*
☆ *Supreme Court term: confirmed by the Senate Apr. 11, 1962, by a voice vote; retired June 28, 1993*

BYRON R. WHITE was an excellent scholar-athlete at the University of Colorado. He ranked first in his class as a scholar, and he was a star on the varsity teams in football, basketball, and baseball. His prowess as a running back in football brought him national fame as an All American and earned him the nickname of Whizzer.

After graduation from college Whizzer White played one season for the Pittsburgh Steelers and led the National Football League in yards gained as a running back. Then he went to England as a Rhodes Scholar to study at Oxford. There he met John F. Kennedy, a future President of the United States.

During World War II, White joined the navy and served in the Pacific theater of the war, where he again met John Kennedy, an officer in the navy. Later, when Kennedy campaigned for President, Byron White supported him, which led to his appointment to the Supreme Court by Kennedy.

Justice White consistently supported equal protection of the law and civil rights of minorities, especially black Americans. However, he was cautious about expanding the rights of people suspected of criminal activity. For example, he dissented from the Warren Court majority in *Miranda* v. *Arizona* (1966) to argue that the Court's decision would unduly hamper efforts by police to obtain a confession from those suspected of criminal behavior. And he wrote for the Burger Court majority in *United States* v. *Leon* (1984) to establish a "good faith" exception to the exclusionary rule established by the Warren Court in *Mapp* v. *Ohio* (1961). The *Leon* case established that when police act on good faith to obtain evidence of criminal behavior without a valid search warrant, the evidence does not have to be excluded from the trial. Justice White also wrote for the Court in *New Jersey* v. *T.L.O.* (1985), which permitted public school officials to disregard the 4th Amendment protection against "unwarranted searches and seizures" when inspecting the personal belongings of students in school who are presumed to be hiding evidence of unlawful behavior.

SEE ALSO

New Jersey v. T.L.O.; United States v. Leon

FURTHER READING

Kramer, Daniel C. "Justice Byron R. White: Good Friend to Polity and Solon." In *The Burger Court: Political and Judicial Profiles*, edited by Charles M. Lamb and Stephen C. Halpern, 407–32. Urbana: University of Illinois Press, 1991.

White, Edward D.

ASSOCIATE JUSTICE, 1894–1910

CHIEF JUSTICE, 1910–21

☆ *Born: Nov. 3, 1845, Lafourche Parish, La.*
☆ *Education: Mount St. Mary's College, 1856; Georgetown University, B.A., 1861; studied law under Edward Bermudez in New Orleans*
☆ *Previous government service: Louisiana Senate, 1874; associate justice, Louisiana Supreme Court, 1878–1880; U.S. senator from Louisiana, 1891–94*
☆ *Appointed by President Grover Cleveland to be an associate justice Feb. 19, 1894; replaced Samuel Blatchford, who died; appointed by President William Howard Taft to be chief justice Dec. 12, 1910; replaced Melville Fuller, who died*
☆ *Supreme Court term: confirmed by the Senate as associate justice Feb. 19, 1894, by a voice vote; confirmed by the Senate as chief justice Dec. 12, 1910, by a voice vote; served until May 19, 1921*
☆ *Died: May 19, 1921, Washington, D.C.*

EDWARD D. WHITE was the first associate justice to be promoted to chief justice of the U.S. Supreme Court. It seems that President William Howard Taft appointed him, instead of a much younger man, in order to keep open the possibility that Taft himself might become chief justice after retirement from the Presidency.

During his 27 years on the Court, White's single major contribution to legal doctrine was his controversial "rule of reason" used to interpret the Sherman Antitrust Act. This federal law was written to outlaw all combinations of businesses for the purpose of restraining trade. White, however, argued that only "unreasonable" restraints were banned by the Sherman Antitrust Act. Of course, what is "reasonable" or "unreasonable" is a matter of interpretation that may vary from one person to another. Chief Justice White's "rule of reason" doctrine gained a majority in *Standard Oil* v. *United States* (1911), which decided that the Standard Oil monopoly had to be broken up.

White was succeeded as chief justice by William Howard Taft in 1921. The former President's long-standing ambition to be chief justice was fulfilled at last.

FURTHER READING

Highsan, Robert B. *Edward Douglass White: Defender of the Conservative Faith*. Baton Rouge: Louisiana State University Press, 1981.

Whitney v. California

☆ *274 U.S. 357 (1927)*
☆ *Vote: 9–0*
☆ *For the Court: Sanford*
☆ *Concurring: Brandeis and Holmes*

CHARLOTTE ANITA WHITNEY was a socialist who helped to found the Communist Labor Party (CLP), an organization dedicated to bringing about fundamental changes in the political and economic systems of the United States, by violent means if necessary. The ultimate goal of the CLP was public owner-

ship of the means of production of goods and services and a redistribution of wealth to benefit the masses of workers. California police arrested Whitney because of her socialist and CLP activities.

The state charged Whitney with violating the California Criminal Syndicalism Act of 1919. According to this law, criminal syndicalism was defined as "advocating, teaching or aiding…sabotage …or unlawful acts of force and violence…as a means of accomplishing a change in industrial ownership or control, or effecting any political change."

Whitney was tried and convicted solely on the basis of her involvement with the CLP, an organization that advocated the use of violent revolution to bring about social changes.

The Issue At first, the Court refused to hear the *Whitney* case on the grounds that no federal issue was involved. But Whitney's attorneys proved that in the California Court of Appeals, questions had been raised about possible conflicts of the California Criminal Syndicalism Act with the due process and equal protection clauses of the 14th Amendment. So the Supreme Court accepted the case.

Did the California law used to convict Charlotte Anita Whitney violate her 14th Amendment rights? Moreover, did it also violate her 1st Amendment right of free speech as applied to the states through the due process clause of the 14th Amendment?

Opinion of the Court The Court upheld the California Criminal Syndicalism Act. Justice Edward Sanford concluded that the state's power and duty to maintain public safety and order outweighed the claims of the defendant about protection of her individual rights.

In his concurring opinion, Justice Louis D. Brandeis argued that Whitney's attorneys should have used the "clear and present danger" doctrine, developed in preceding cases by Brandeis and

Oliver Wendell Holmes, to distinguish between mere expression of ideas and ideas that would result in actions that would endanger public safety and order. Whitney had claimed that the California law violated the U.S. Constitution, but, said Brandeis, "she did not claim that it was void because there was no clear and present danger of serious evil" that would result from her speech and actions. This version of the "clear and present danger" doctrine had been expressed by Justice Oliver Wendell Holmes in *Abrams* v. *United States* (1919).

Justice Brandeis set forth an often-quoted statement about the latitude and limits of free speech:

> [A]lthough the rights of free speech and assembly are fundamental, they are not in their nature absolute. Their exercise is subject to restriction, if the particular restriction proposed is required to protect the State from destruction or from serious injury, political, economic, or moral....
>
> [T]o justify suppression of free speech there must be reasonable ground to fear that serious evil will result if free speech is practiced....
>
> [N]o danger flowing from speech can be deemed clear and present unless the incidence of the evil apprehended is so imminent that it may befall before there is opportunity for full discussion. If there be time to expose through discussion the falsehoods and fallacies, to avert the evil by the process of education, the remedy to be applied is more speech, not enforced silence. Only an emergency can justify repression. Such must be the rule if authority is to be reconciled with freedom. Such, in my opinion, is the command of the Constitution. It is therefore always open to Americans to challenge a law abridging free speech and assembly by showing that there was no emergency justifying it.

Significance Justice Brandeis's concurring opinion has the tone of a dissent. It immediately influenced the life of Charlotte Anita Whitney. The California governor, C. C. Young, pardoned her only a few months after the Supreme Court decision; he gave reasons similar to the ideas in Justice Brandeis's opinion.

In 1969 the Supreme Court overturned the *Whitney* decision in its ruling in *Brandenburg* v. *Ohio*. The ideas of Justice Brandeis influenced the Court's reasoning in this case; it pointed out a defense of free speech rights that could have prevailed for Whitney, if only she and her attorney had used this line of reasoning to support her case.

SEE ALSO
Abrams v. United States; Brandenburg v. Ohio; Freedom of speech and press

Whittaker, Charles E.

ASSOCIATE JUSTICE, 1957–62

☆ *Born: Feb. 22, 1901, Troy, Kans.*
☆ *Education: University of Kansas City Law School, LL.B., 1924*
☆ *Previous government service: federal judge, U.S. District Court for Western Missouri, 1954–56; judge, U.S. Eighth Circuit Court of Appeals, 1956–57*
☆ *Appointed by President Dwight D. Eisenhower Mar. 2, 1957; replaced Stanley Reed, who retired*
☆ *Supreme Court term: confirmed by the Senate Mar. 19, 1957, by a voice vote; retired Mar. 31, 1962*
☆ *Died: Nov. 26, 1973, Kansas City, Mo.*

CHARLES E. WHITTAKER was appointed to the Supreme Court in 1957, after serving briefly as a federal district court judge in Missouri and as a judge of the U.S. Eighth Circuit Court of Appeals. He had risen to these distinguished positions through hard work and persistence.

Justice Whittaker's brief term on the Court was undistinguished. He wrote few opinions, none of them memorable, and he was generally viewed as the weakest thinker on the Court. He retired due to poor health.

Wilson, James

ASSOCIATE JUSTICE, 1789–98

☆ Born: Sept. 14, 1742, Fifeshire, Scotland
☆ Education: University of St. Andrews, Scotland; read law in the office of John Dickinson, Philadelphia, Pa.
☆ Previous government service: first Provincial Convention at Philadelphia, 1774; Continental Congress, 1775–77, 1783, 1785–87; Constitutional Convention, 1787; Pennsylvania Ratifying Convention, 1787
☆ Appointed by President George Washington Sept. 24, 1789, as one of the original members of the U.S. Supreme Court
☆ Supreme Court term: confirmed by the Senate Sept. 26, 1789, by a voice vote; served until Aug. 21, 1798
☆ Died: Aug. 21, 1798, Edenton, N.C.

JAMES WILSON traveled to the British colony of Pennsylvania from rural Scotland and helped to found a new nation, the United States of America. He served in the Continental Congress during the American War of Independence and participated influentially in the Constitutional Convention of 1787. Historians have rated him as one of the most important framers of the Constitution because many of his ideas were included in the final draft of this document.

In 1789, President George Washington appointed Wilson to the first Supreme Court of the United States. He was generally viewed as the best legal scholar among the original appointments to the Court. However, Justice Wilson's performance did not match his potential, and he contributed little of lasting significance as a Supreme Court justice.

His brief term on the Court was marred by heavy personal problems, including great indebtedness. Wilson's worries led to illness and death, in poverty, at the age of 55.

FURTHER READING

Smith, Page. *James Wilson: Founding Father.* Chapel Hill: University of North Carolina Press, 1956.

Wolf v. Colorado

☆ 338 U.S. 25 (1949)
☆ Vote: 6–3
☆ For the Court: Frankfurter
☆ Dissenting: Douglas, Murphy, and Rutledge

DR. WOLF, a Colorado physician, was suspected of performing abortions secretly, in violation of state laws. But the police were unable to obtain evidence to prove their suspicions. A deputy sheriff assigned to the case took Dr. Wolf's appointment book from his office, without the doctor's knowledge. The police contacted people listed in this appointment book about Dr. Wolf's medical practice. Through these interviews the police gained enough evidence to convict Wolf of conspiracy to commit abortions.

The Issue Wolf said his constitutional rights had been violated. He pointed to the 4th Amendment to the U.S. Constitution: "The right of the people to be secure in their persons, houses, papers, and effects, against unreasonable searches and seizures, shall not be violated." He also pointed to the 14th Amendment: "No state…shall deprive any person of life, liberty, or property, without due process of law."

Wolf's attorney asked the Court to

overturn his client's conviction because it was based on illegally obtained evidence. He cited the Court's decision in *Weeks* v. *United States* (1914). In that case, evidence obtained in violation of the 4th Amendment was excluded from consideration by prosecutors.

Were Wolf's 4th Amendment rights violated? Are the 4th Amendment guarantees against unreasonable searches and seizures incorporated by the due process clause of the 14th Amendment and thus applicable to the states? Should evidence obtained in violation of the 4th Amendment be excluded by judges from consideration at the trial of a defendant?

Opinion of the Court Justice Felix Frankfurter agreed that the 4th Amendment was applicable to the states through the 14th Amendment. He wrote eloquently about the fundamental right of the individual to be secure against arbitrary intrusion by agents of the government. Frankfurter said, "The security of one's privacy against arbitrary intrusion by the police is basic to a free society. The knock on the door, whether by day or by night, as a prelude to a search, without authority of law but solely on the authority of the police [is] inconsistent with the conception of human rights enshrined in the history and basic constitutional documents of English-speaking peoples."

The Court held that 4th Amendment protection applies to searches by state officials as well as by federal agents. However, the exclusionary rule established in the *Weeks* case was not applied to the states. State judges were not re-

Felix Frankfurter ruled in the Wolf case that citizens must be secure in their homes and businesses against unreasonable invasions of their privacy.

quired to exclude evidence obtained by searches in violation of 4th Amendment rights, so Wolf's conviction was upheld.

Dissent Justice William O. Douglas argued that the exclusionary rule must be used to enforce 4th Amendment rights. Without the exclusion of illegally obtained evidence, he noted, the constitutional protections against unreasonable searches and seizures are practically worthless.

Significance This was the first time that 4th Amendment rights were incorporated by the 14th Amendment and applied to the states, a precedent that has been followed ever since the *Wolf* case. In 1961, in *Mapp* v. *Ohio*, the Court accepted the dissenting position of the *Wolf* case and applied the exclusionary rule to the states, thus overturning the *Wolf* decision.

SEE ALSO

Exclusionary rule; Incorporation doctrine; Mapp v. Ohio; Searches and seizures; Weeks v. United States

Woodbury, Levi

ASSOCIATE JUSTICE, 1845–51

☆ Born: Dec. 22, 1789, Francestown, N.H.
☆ Education: Dartmouth College, B.A., 1809; Tapping Reeve Law School, 1810
☆ Previous government service: clerk, New Hampshire Senate, 1816; associate justice, New Hampshire Superior Court, 1817–23; governor of New Hampshire, 1823–24; Speaker, New Hampshire House of Representatives, 1825; U.S. senator from New Hampshire, 1825–31, 1841–45; U.S. secretary of the navy, 1831–34; U.S. secretary of the Treasury, 1834–41
☆ Appointed by President James K. Polk as a recess appointment Sept. 20, 1845; replaced Joseph Story, who died; nominated by Polk Dec. 23, 1845

☆ *Supreme Court term: confirmed by the Senate Jan. 3, 1846, by a voice vote; served until Sept. 4, 1851*
☆ *Died: Sept. 4, 1851, Portsmouth, N.H.*

LEVI WOODBURY was a Jacksonian Democrat who served less than six years on the Supreme Court. During his brief term, he tended to side with the majority on the Taney Court. He especially favored the rights and powers of the states in cases regarding conflicts with the federal government. In general, Woodbury's judicial career lacked distinction.

Woods, William B.

ASSOCIATE JUSTICE, 1881–87

☆ *Born: Aug. 3, 1824, Newark, Ohio*
☆ *Education: Western Reserve College, 1841–44; Yale College, B.A., 1845*
☆ *Previous government service: mayor of Newark, Ohio, 1856; Ohio House of Representatives, 1858–62, Speaker, 1858–60, minority leader, 1860–62; chancellor, Middle Chancery District of Alabama, 1868–69; judge, U.S. Circuit Court for the Fifth Judicial Circuit, 1869–80*
☆ *Appointed by President Rutherford B. Hayes Dec. 15, 1880; replaced William Strong, who retired*
☆ *Supreme Court term: confirmed by the Senate Dec. 21, 1880, by a 39–8 vote; served until May 14, 1887*
☆ *Died: May 14, 1887, Washington, D.C.*

WILLIAM B. WOODS served briefly on the Supreme Court during the 1880s. His main contributions to constitutional law came through his narrow interpretation of the 14th Amendment. For example, he sided with the Court's majority in the *Civil Rights Cases* (1883) to declare unconstitutional the Civil Rights Act of 1875, which was designed to use federal authority to protect black Americans against abuse of their rights by state government.

Writing for the Court in *Presser* v. *Illinois* (1886), Justice Woods argued that the Bill of Rights restricted only the federal government and could not be applied to the states through the 14th Amendment. This position was not overturned until the second quarter of the 20th century. In general, Justice Woods favored limitations on federal power in favor of state powers and rights.

Worcester v. Georgia

☆ *6 Pet. 515 (1832)*
☆ *Vote: 5–1*
☆ *For the Court: Marshall*
☆ *Dissenting: Baldwin*

IN THE EARLY 19th century, the Cherokee people owned a vast area of land in Georgia. They organized a thriving community with a constitution and republican institutions of government. They clearly meant to live as a free and sovereign, or self-governing, people. Georgia state government officials, however, had a different view of Cherokee destiny. They enacted laws that placed Cherokee lands under the control of Georgia county governments.

The Cherokees objected to Georgia's efforts to rule them. They brought suit directly to the U.S. Supreme Court on grounds that they were an independent nation whose rights had been violated by the state of Georgia. Writing for the Court, Chief Justice John Marshall, in *Cherokee Nation* v. *Georgia* (1831), held that the Court had no jurisdiction, under the U.S. Constitution, to deal with this issue because the Cherokees were "a domestic, dependent nation"—not a truly sovereign nation.

The Cherokee newspaper published articles in both the Cherokee language and English. Chief Justice John Marshall ruled in Worcester v. Georgia *that the Cherokees were an independent nation, not subject to the laws of Georgia.*

In March 1831 the Georgia militia arrested Samuel A. Worcester and thereby reopened the legal issue of Cherokee rights in the United States. Worcester was a white Christian missionary who lived among the Cherokee people. He was charged by the Georgia government with violation of a law prohibiting "all white persons [from] residing within the limits of the Cherokee nation…without a license or permit from his excellency the [Georgia] governor." A Georgia state court found Worcester guilty and sentenced him to four years in the state penitentiary. Worcester appealed to the U.S. Supreme Court.

The Issue Worcester's attorneys claimed that the Georgia law he violated was unconstitutional because it conflicted with U.S.–Cherokee treaties, the contract and commerce clauses of the U.S. Constitution, and the sovereign status of the Cherokee nation. Should the national rights of the Cherokees be recognized? Should the Georgia law at issue in this case be declared void?

Opinion of the Court Chief Justice John Marshall decided against Georgia. He wrote that the Cherokee and other "Indian nations" were "distinct, independent political communities, retaining their original natural rights." This was a dramatic change from the Court's decision one year earlier in *Cherokee Nation v. Georgia.* Marshall overturned

Worcester's conviction and ordered his release from prison.

Significance President Andrew Jackson and the executive branch of the federal government refused to abide by the Court's decision. Worcester remained in jail and served his four-year sentence. The Georgia government moved against the Cherokee people, who were eventually forced to move west of the Mississippi River.

Chief Justice Marshall's *Worcester* opinion departed from his *Cherokee Nation* opinion. Nevertheless, the *Cherokee Nation* opinion prevailed in subsequent cases, to the disadvantage of the people classified in the 1831 case as "domestic, dependent nations."

FURTHER READING

Perdue, Theda. *The Cherokee.* New York: Chelsea House, 1988.

Yates v. United States

☆ *354 U.S. 298 (1957)*
☆ *Vote: 6–1*
☆ *For the Court: Harlan*
☆ *Dissenting: Clark*
☆ *Not participating: Brennan and Whittaker*

CONGRESS PASSED the Smith Act in 1940 to limit the political activities of radical opponents of the U.S. government, such as the Communist Party of the United States (CPUSA). The Smith Act made it a crime for anyone knowingly to advocate the forcible overthrow of the U.S. government or to organize or participate in any group committed to the purpose of violent revolution against the U.S. government. Oleta O'Connor Yates was one of 14 members of the CPUSA convicted for violating the Smith Act.

The Issue Could the Smith Act be

used to prohibit advocacy of violent overthrow of the government merely as an idea (but not as a direct incitement to forcible political revolution)? Was the Smith Act a violation of the 1st Amendment to the Constitution, which guarantees the individual's rights to freedom of speech, press, petition, and assembly? Should the convictions of Yates and her associates be upheld or reversed?

Opinion of the Court The convictions of Yates and her associates were reversed, but the Smith Act was not ruled unconstitutional. Rather, the Court's interpretation of the Smith Act was narrowed to the point of making it virtually unenforceable. Justice John Marshall Harlan emphasized the difference between advocating ideas (abstractions) and advocating immediate illegal action directed toward violent overthrow of the government. Harlan ruled that Yates and her associates were doing merely the former. Yates and the others therefore had been wrongly convicted under an incorrect interpretation of the Smith Act, said Justice Harlan.

Significance The *Yates* opinion took the "teeth" out of the Smith Act. Given the Court's restrictive interpretation of the law, it became very difficult to enforce. After the *Yates* case, there were no more prosecutions carried out to enforce the Smith Act.

SEE ALSO
Freedom of speech and press

Youngstown Sheet & Tube Co. v. Sawyer

☆ *343 U.S. 579 (1952)*
☆ *Vote: 6–3*
☆ *For the Court: Black*
☆ *Concurring: Frankfurter, Douglas, Jackson, Burton, and Clark*
☆ *Dissenting: Vinson, Reed, and Minton*

IN THE SPRING of 1952, the United States was in the midst of the Korean War, and the nation's steelworkers were about to go on strike. Harry Truman and his advisers feared a long strike could bring disaster: U.S. troops in Korea might run short of weapons and ammunition.

The President acted forcefully. On April 8, a few hours before the expected start of the strike, Truman issued Executive Order No. 10340. This order directed Secretary of Commerce Charles Sawyer to take control of the nation's steel mills temporarily and to keep them running. The steel companies accepted the order but moved to fight Truman's action in court.

Taking temporary control of the steel mills was not the only alternative open to Truman. The President had another way to deal with the strike. He chose not to use it.

In 1947 Congress had passed the Taft-Hartley Act. Under this law, the President could get a court order delaying the strike for 80 days. During this "cooling off" period, the steelworkers' union and the mill owners would have tried to settle their differences.

Truman disliked the Taft-Hartley Act. He thought it was anti-labor. He had vetoed it in 1947, but Congress had overridden his veto. He had never used the law and would not do so in the steel strike.

Furthermore, Truman believed the blame for the strike did not lie with the steelworkers. The union had already postponed the strike four times in an effort to reach a settlement. Government arbitrators had recommended a compromise, which the union had accepted. The steel companies had rejected those recommendations, even though in 1951 the companies earned their greatest profits in

President Harry Truman announces on radio and TV that he has seized the nation's steel mills. The Supreme Court, however, ordered the President to return the mills to their owners.

more than 30 years. President Truman believed the steel companies were using the emergency of the Korean War to force the steelworkers to accept low wages. Under such circumstances Truman held the companies, and not the workers, responsible for the crisis in the industry, and he decided to seize the steel mills.

The steel companies quickly challenged Truman's action in the federal district court in Washington, D.C. Within a few days the case went to the Supreme Court.

The Issue President Truman's order was a remarkable assertion of Presidential power. The President was not carrying out or acting under a law passed by Congress. No law authorized a President to seize and operate the steel mills. By his order, President Truman was, in effect, making law—a power reserved to Congress by Article 1 of the Constitution.

Had the President overstepped the constitutional boundary that separated the functions of the legislative and executive branches? Or did the Constitution give Truman powers to protect the nation in times of national emergency?

The steel companies argued that the President's order clearly violated the Constitution. They said neither the Constitution nor existing laws gave him authority to seize private property. In addi-

tion, Congress had already set up procedures to handle the strike in the Taft-Hartley Act. Thus, they claimed the President had exceeded his constitutional authority.

The President argued that his authority, as chief executive under Article 2 of the Constitution, gave him power to keep steel production going in times of national emergency. In addition, he argued that his power as commander in chief allowed him to take actions necessary to protect the lives of U.S. troops. This power included ensuring a steady flow of steel to produce weapons.

Opinion of the Court On June 2 the Supreme Court ruled against the President. The Court judged Truman's seizure of the steel mills an unconstitutional exercise of power.

Justice Hugo L. Black, in the majority opinion, said that the President had no power, as either chief executive or commander in chief, to seize private property—even temporarily and during a national emergency. Black said that the power to authorize such an action belonged to Congress, not to the President. Thus, Truman could not seize the steel mills unless Congress passed legislation enabling him to do so. Because Congress had not done so, the seizure was illegal.

Black noted that, in writing the 1947 Taft-Hartley Act, Congress had considered letting Presidents seize factories in the event of strikes but had rejected the idea. Thus, by his executive order Truman had attempted to make his own law. Yet the Constitution, Black said, did not permit him to do so. The Constitution limited the President "to the recommending of laws he thinks wise and the vetoing of laws he thinks bad."

Dissent Three justices, all Truman appointees, issued a strong dissent. They argued that during a grave national crisis, such as the Korean War, the Constitution allowed the President to exercise unusual powers. Chief Justice Fred Vinson wrote, "Those who suggest that this is a case involving extraordinary powers should be mindful that these are extraordinary times." Vinson added that Truman's actions followed the tradition of taking extraordinary actions in times of crisis established by such Presidents as Abraham Lincoln, Grover Cleveland, Woodrow Wilson, and Franklin Roosevelt.

Significance The *Youngstown* decision required the government to return the steel mills to their owners immediately. Truman promptly complied with the Court's ruling even though he strongly disagreed with it. The steel strike began, and it lasted for 53 days. When it ended, the steel companies agreed to a contract within one cent of the settlement recommended by the government arbitrators. Truman never used the Taft-Hartley Act to intervene. The President did claim that in the summer and fall of 1952 the strike caused some shortages of ammunition.

In this decision, the Court clearly established that there are limits on the powers a President can derive from the Constitution, even during a national emergency. For nearly 20 years Presidential power had been growing through a series of crises including the Great Depression and World War II. The *Youngstown* decision had the effect of slowing this steady growth.

This case shows how strong Presidents can try to expand the powers of the office. It also demonstrates how the Supreme Court can act to preserve the separation of powers inherent in the U.S. constitutional system.

SEE ALSO

Constitutionalism; Separation of powers

FURTHER READING

Donovan, Robert J. "Truman Seizes Steel." *Constitution* 2, no. 3 (Fall 1990): 48–57.

Marcus, Maeva. *Truman and the Steel Seizure Case: The Limits of Presidential Power.* New York: Oxford, 1992.

Westin, Alan F. *The Anatomy of a Constitutional Law Case: Youngstown Sheet & Tube v. Sawyer.* New York; Columbia University Press, 1990.

Zorach v. Clauson

☆ *343 U.S. 306 (1952)*
☆ *Vote: 6–3*
☆ *For the Court: Douglas*
☆ *Dissenting: Black, Frankfurter, and Jackson*

IN 1948 the New York City public schools introduced a "released time" program for religious education, under which students could leave the public schools before the end of the regular school day to attend religious classes of their choosing. During the 1940s and 1950s these programs were widespread. Tessim Zorach, a resident of New York City, complained that the city school system's "released time" program violated the establishment clause of the 1st Amendment.

The Issue The 1st Amendment of the Constitution prohibits government from enacting laws "respecting an establishment of religion." Does this mean that there must be complete separation of church and state? Or does this establishment clause permit certain kinds of governmental association with religion, as long as the government does not discriminate in its treatment of different religions?

Opinion of the Court Justice William O. Douglas upheld the New York City "released time" program because the religious instruction was not carried out in public school buildings. Rather, public school students could choose to participate, during the official school day, in religious instruction outside the

The Zorach *case decided that a New York law allowing students to be released early from public school in order to attend religious instruction was not in violation of the Constitution.*

public schools. Douglas emphasized that a "released time" program in Champaign, Illinois, had been declared unconstitutional only because religious instruction was provided in the public school buildings during the school day (*Illinois ex rel. McCollum* v. *Board of Education,* 1948).

Justice Douglas wrote these often-quoted words in support of permissible governmental accommodation of religion:

> We are a religious people whose institutions suppose a Supreme Being.... When the state encourages religious instruction or cooperates with religious authorities by adjusting the schedule of public events to sectarian needs, it follows the best of our traditions. For it then respects the religious nature of our people and accommodates the public service to their spiritual needs. To hold that it may not would be to find in the Constitution a requirement that the government show a callous indifference to religious groups. That would be preferring those who believe in no religion over those who do believe.

Dissent Justice Hugo Black emphasized that the location of religious instruction involved in "released time"

programs was not relevant. It was the connection between government-supported public schools and the content of the religious instruction that, according to Black and the other dissenters, was not permitted by the 1st Amendment as applied to the states through the 14th Amendment. Black wrote that the resources and authority of the public schools had been unconstitutionally put at the service of private religious groups.

Significance "Released time" programs expanded in the wake of the *Zorach* decision. However, they declined in use and importance in the 1970s and 1980s. The enduring importance of the *Zorach* case is the argument for a constitutional accommodation of government and religion provided by Justice Douglas. In line with this opinion, the Court ruled in *Zobrest* v. *Catalina School District* (1993) that local government funds could be used to pay for a sign-language interpreter to assist a deaf student at a private school operated by the Catholic church.

SEE ALSO

Establishment clause; Religious issues under the Constitution

FURTHER READING

Alley, Robert S. *The Supreme Court on Church and State.* New York: Oxford, 1988.

Zurcher v. The Stanford Daily

☆ *436 U.S. 547 (1978)*
☆ *Vote: 5–3*
☆ *For the Court: White*
☆ *Dissenting: Stewart, Marshall, and Stevens*
☆ *Not participating: Brennan*

IN APRIL 1971 a group of demonstrators seized the administrative offices of

Stanford University Hospital. They blocked entrances and would not permit people to move freely through the facility. The Palo Alto city police confronted the demonstrators and a riot resulted. Several police officers were injured. The *Stanford Daily,* a student newspaper, published a report of the riot that included pictures.

The identities of the rioters could not be determined from the pictures published in the newspaper. The police, however, thought the photographer might have other pictures in his office that could be used to identify some of the rioters. They obtained a warrant and searched the offices of the *Stanford Daily,* but they found no additional pictures. However, while they searched for pictures the police saw confidential papers in the newspaper's files. These papers included information about the management of the newspaper and the personal activities of students.

The *Stanford Daily* brought suit against the police. The student publishers claimed that the police's search of their offices violated their constitutional rights under the 1st, 4th, and 14th Amendments.

The Issue The students argued that a reasonable police search of a newspaper office should be based on a subpoena, not a warrant. A subpoena is an order requiring a person to appear before a court of law. A subpoena issued by a local court would have required representatives of the student newspaper to submit to police, for their examination, any pictures in their possession about the riot. This procedure, the students said, would have eliminated the possibility of police seeing confidential documents in their files not related to the purpose of the search. The city government replied that the warrant was legally obtained and the subsequent search properly conducted.

Was there a violation of the student newspaper's 4th Amendment rights to protection against unreasonable searches? And did the case involve a violation of the 1st Amendment guarantee of a free press?

Opinion of the Court Justice Byron White ruled against the *Stanford Daily.* He referred to the intentions of those who proposed and ratified the federal Bill of Rights: they did not, he wrote, "forbid warrants where the press was involved." Justice White emphasized that the press should not have special privileges with regard to the authorization of search warrants. Further, he contended that requiring a subpoena before the issuance of a search warrant would unduly interfere with effective enforcement of the law.

Dissent Justice Potter Stewart argued that the search without a subpoena was a violation of 1st and 4th Amendment rights because police were able to examine sensitive papers having no relationship to the purpose of the search. This kind of invasion of privacy, wrote Stewart, could intimidate newspaper publishers and thereby interfere with freedom of the press.

Significance The *Zurcher* decision prompted Congress to pass the Privacy Protection Act of 1980. This law prohibits federal government agents from carrying out searches and seizures in newspaper offices on "work-product materials unless the reporter or writer is suspected of committing a crime or there is some life-threatening situation." This federal law does not apply to state or local police, however. Thus the *Zurcher* ruling stands as a legal precedent.

SEE ALSO

Freedom of speech and press; Searches and seizures

APPENDIX 1
TERMS OF THE JUSTICES
OF THE U.S. SUPREME COURT

PRESIDENT/JUSTICE	OATH TAKEN	TERM END
George Washington		
John Jay*	19 Oct. 1789	R 29 June 1795
John Rutledge	15 Feb. 1790	R 5 Mar. 1791
William Cushing	2 Feb. 1790	D 13 Sept. 1810
James Wilson	5 Oct. 1789	D 21 Aug. 1798
John Blair, Jr.	2 Feb. 1790	R 25 Oct. 1795
James Iredell	12 May 1790	D 20 Oct. 1799
Thomas Johnson	R 19 Sep. 1791	
	6 Aug. 1792	R 16 Jan. 1793
William Paterson	11 Mar. 1793	D 9 Sept. 1806
John Rutledge*†	R 12 Aug. 1795	15 Dec. 1795
Samuel Chase	4 Feb. 1796	D 19 June 1811
Oliver Ellsworth*	8 Mar. 1796	R 15 Dec. 1800
John Adams		
Bushrod Washington	R 9 Nov. 1798	
	4 Feb. 1799	D 26 Nov. 1829
Alfred Moore	21 Apr. 1800	R 26 Jan. 1804
John Marshall*	4 Feb. 1801	D 6 July 1835
Thomas Jefferson		
William Johnson	8 May 1804	D 4 Aug. 1834
Henry Brockholst Livingston	R 20 Jan. 1807	
	2 Feb. 1807	D 18 Mar. 1823
Thomas Todd	4 May 1807	D 7 Feb. 1826
James Madison		
Joseph Story	3 Feb. 1812	D 10 Sept. 1845
Gabriel Duvall	23 Nov. 1811	R 14 Jan. 1835
James Monroe		
Smith Thompson	10 Feb. 1824	D 18 Dec. 1843
John Quincy Adams		
Robert Trimble	16 June 1826	D 25 Aug. 1828
Andrew Jackson		
John McLean	11 Jan. 1830	D 4 Apr. 1861
Henry Baldwin	18 Jan. 1830	D 21 Apr. 1844
James M. Wayne	14 Jan. 1835	D 5 July 1867
Roger B. Taney*	28 Mar. 1836	D 12 Oct. 1864
Philip P. Barbour	12 May 1836	D 25 Feb. 1841
John Catron	1 May 1837	D 30 May 1865
Martin Van Buren		
John McKinley	9 Jan. 1838	D 19 July 1852
Peter V. Daniel	10 Jan. 1842	D 31 May 1860
John Tyler		
Samuel Nelson	27 Feb. 1845	R 28 Nov. 1872

PRESIDENT/JUSTICE	OATH TAKEN	TERM END
James K. Polk		
Levi Woodbury	R 23 Sept. 1845	
	3 Jan. 1846	D 4 Sept. 1851
Robert C. Grier	10 Aug. 1846	R 31 Jan. 1870
Millard Fillmore		
Benjamin R. Curtis	R 10 Oct. 1851	R 30 Sept. 1857
Franklin Pierce		
John A. Campbell	11 Apr. 1853	R 30 Apr. 1861
James Buchanan		
Nathan Clifford	21 Jan. 1858	D 25 July 1881
Abraham Lincoln		
Noah H. Swayne	27 Jan. 1862	R 24 Jan. 1881
Samuel F. Miller	21 July 1862	D 13 Oct. 1890
David Davis	10 Dec. 1862	R 4 Mar. 1877
Stephen J. Field	20 May 1863	R 1 Dec. 1897
Salmon P. Chase*	15 Dec. 1864	D 7 May 1873
Ulysses S. Grant		
William Strong	14 Mar. 1870	R 14 Dec. 1880
Joseph P. Bradley	23 Mar. 1870	D 22 Jan. 1892
Ward Hunt	9 Jan. 1873	R 27 Jan. 1882
Morrison R. Waite*	4 Mar. 1874	D 23 Mar. 1888
Rutherford B. Hayes		
John Marshall Harlan	10 Dec. 1877	D 14 Oct. 1911
William B. Woods	5 Jan. 1881	D 14 May 1887
James A. Garfield		
Stanley Matthews	17 May 1881	D 22 Mar. 1889
Chester A. Arthur		
Horace Gray	9 Jan. 1882	D 15 Sept. 1902
Samuel Blatchford	3 Apr. 1882	D 7 July 1893
Grover Cleveland		
Lucius Q. C. Lamar	18 Jan. 1888	D 23 Jan. 1893
Melville W. Fuller*	8 Oct. 1888	D 4 July 1910
Benjamin Harrison		
David Brewer	6 Jan. 1890	D 28 Mar. 1910
Henry B. Brown	5 Jan. 1891	R 28 May 1906
George Shiras, Jr.	10 Oct. 1892	R 23 Feb. 1903
Howell E. Jackson	4 Mar. 1893	D 8 Aug. 1895
Grover Cleveland		
Edward D. White	12 Mar. 1894	P 18 Dec. 1910
Rufus W. Peckham	6 Jan. 1896	D 24 Oct. 1909

PRESIDENT/JUSTICE	OATH TAKEN	TERM END
William McKinley		
Joseph McKenna	26 Jan. 1898	R 5 Jan. 1925
Theodore Roosevelt		
Oliver Wendell Holmes, Jr.	8 Dec. 1902	R 12 Jan. 1932
William R. Day	2 Mar. 1903	R 13 Nov. 1922
William H. Moody	17 Dec. 1906	R 20 Nov. 1910
William H. Taft		
Horace H. Lurton	3 Jan. 1910	D 12 July 1914
Charles E. Hughes	10 Oct. 1910	R 10 June 1916
Edward D. White*†	19 Dec. 1910	D 19 May 1921
Willis Van Devanter	3 Jan. 1911	R 2 June 1937
Joseph R. Lamar	3 Jan. 1911	D 2 Jan. 1916
Mahlon Pitney	18 Mar. 1912	R 31 Dec. 1922
Woodrow Wilson		
James C. McReynolds	5 Sept. 1914	R 31 Jan. 1941
Louis D. Brandeis	5 June 1916	R 13 Feb. 1939
John H. Clarke	1 Aug. 1916	R 18 Sept. 1922
Warren G. Harding		
William H. Taft*	11 July 1921	R 3 Feb. 1930
George Sutherland	2 Oct. 1922	R 17 Jan. 1938
Pierce Butler	2 Jan. 1923	D 16 Nov. 1939
Edward T. Sanford	5 Feb. 1923	D 8 Mar. 1930
Calvin Coolidge		
Harlan F. Stone	2 Mar. 1925	P 2 July 1941
Herbert C. Hoover		
Charles E. Hughes*†	24 Feb. 1930	R 1 July 1941
Owen J. Roberts	2 June 1930	R 31 July 1945
Benjamin N. Cardozo	14 Mar. 1932	D 9 July 1938
Franklin D. Roosevelt		
Hugo L. Black	19 Aug. 1937	R 17 Sept. 1971
Stanley F. Reed	31 Jan. 1938	R 25 Feb. 1957
Felix Frankfurter	30 Jan. 1939	R 28 Aug. 1962
William O. Douglas	17 Apr. 1939	R 12 Nov. 1975
Frank Murphy	18 Jan. 1940	D 19 July 1949
Harlan F. Stone*†	3 July 1941	D 22 Apr. 1946
James F. Byrnes	8 July 1941	R 3 Oct. 1942
Robert H. Jackson	11 July 1941	D 9 Oct. 1954
Wiley B. Rutledge	15 Feb. 1943	D 10 Sept. 1949
Harry S. Truman		
Harold H. Burton	1 Oct. 1945	R 13 Oct. 1958
Fred M. Vinson*	24 June 1946	D 8 Sept. 1953
Tom Clark	24 Aug. 1949	R 12 June 1967
Sherman Minton	12 Oct. 1949	R 15 Oct. 1956

PRESIDENT/JUSTICE	OATH TAKEN	TERM END
Dwight D. Eisenhower		
Earl Warren*	R 5 Oct. 1953	
	2 Mar. 1954	R 23 June 1969
John M. Harlan II	28 Mar. 1955	R 23 Sept. 1971
William J. Brennan, Jr.	R 16 Oct. 1956	
	22 Mar. 1957	R 20 July 1990
Charles E. Whittaker	25 Mar. 1957	R 31 Mar. 1962
Potter Stewart	R 14 Oct. 1958	
	15 May 1959	R 3 July 1981
John F. Kennedy		
Byron R. White	16 Apr. 1962	R 28 June 1993
Arthur J. Goldberg	1 Oct. 1962	R 25 July 1965
Lyndon B. Johnson		
Abe Fortas	4 Oct. 1965	R 14 May 1969
Thurgood Marshall	2 Oct. 1967	R 1 Oct. 1991
Richard M. Nixon		
Warren E. Burger*	23 June 1969	R 26 Sept. 1986
Harry A. Blackmun	9 June 1970	
Lewis F. Powell, Jr.	7 Jan. 1972	R 26 June 1987
William H. Rehnquist	7 Jan. 1972	P 26 Sept. 1986
Gerald R. Ford		
John Paul Stevens	19 Dec. 1975	
Ronald Reagan		
Sandra Day O'Connor	25 Sept. 1981	
William H. Rehnquist*†	26 Sept. 1986	
Antonin Scalia	26 Sept. 1986	
Anthony M. Kennedy	18 Feb. 1988	
George Bush		
David H. Souter	9 Oct. 1990	
Clarence Thomas	1 Nov. 1991	
Bill Clinton		
Ruth Bader Ginsberg	10 Aug. 1993	

NOTES

President/Justice column:
Presidents are listed in the shaded lines; the justices whom they appointed are in untinted lines.
* = chief justice
† = nomination for promotion to chief justice only; see prior listing for service as associate justice

Oath Taken column:
R = recess appointment; the justice took office before being confirmed by the Senate; he may have taken a second oath after confirmation

Term End column:
D = died
P = promoted to chief justice (see separate listing for service as chief justice)
R = retirement/resignation

VISITING THE
SUPREME COURT BUILDING

The public may visit the Supreme Court Building at 1 First Street, S.E., Washington, D.C., every week of the year, Monday through Friday, from 9:00 A.M. until 4:30 P.M. except on legal holidays. More than 700,000 people annually visit the Supreme Court Building. Visitors have access only to certain parts of the ground floor and first floor of the Supreme Court Building. The floor plans on this page show the areas open to visitors. Only the rooms with labels in the diagrams are accessible; all others are closed to visitors.

Visitors can see a film about the Court in a room on the ground floor. Staff members of the curator's office also give lectures about the Court and its history. Courtroom lectures are presented daily, every hour on the half hour, from 9:30 A.M. to 3:30 P.M., when the Court is not in session.

The courtroom includes seats for about 300 visitors, which are available on a first come, first seated basis. Demand is usually high. The Court is in session to hear oral arguments in the Court chamber (courtroom) from 10:00 A.M. to noon and from 1:00 to 3:00 P.M. on Monday, Tuesday, and Wednesday, for two-week periods each month, beginning on the first Monday in October until the end of April of each year. A session may also be held on Monday of the third week of the month. From mid-May through June, the courtroom sessions convene at 10:00 A.M. The Court uses these sessions to deliver its opinions on cases heard previously.

The exhibit hall on the ground floor contains portraits and statues of the justices and other displays of documents and memorabilia relating to the work of the Court. The curator prepares two exhibits a year using the Court's collections of photographs, prints, films, manuscripts, and other memorabilia. The curator's office also collects decorative and fine arts.

The kiosk of the Supreme Court Historical Society, on the ground floor next to the exhibit hall, sells books and other materials that provide visitors with additional information about the Supreme Court Building and the operations of the Court.

This floor plan indicates the parts of the Supreme Court Building open to the public.

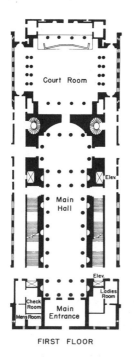

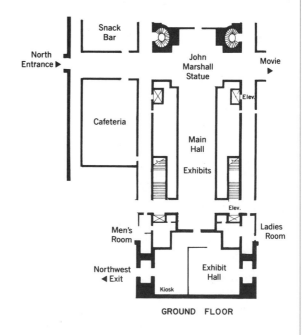

FURTHER READING

Many entries in this volume include references to books dealing with that specific subject. The following volumes are more general in scope. They provide useful ideas and information for your further study of the Supreme Court and its role in the constitutional history of the United States.

Abraham, Henry J. *The Judicial Process.* New York: Oxford University Press, 1993.

Anastaplo, George. *The Constitution of 1787: A Commentary.* Baltimore: Johns Hopkins University Press, 1989.

Arbetman, Lee, and Richard L. Roe. *Great Trials in American History.* St. Paul, Minn.: West, 1985.

Bailyn, Bernard, ed. *The Debate on the Constitution: Federalist and Antifederalist Speeches, Articles, and Letters During the Struggle Over Ratification.* 2 vols. New York: Library of America, 1993.

Baum, Laurence. *The Supreme Court.* Washington, D.C.: Congressional Quarterly, 1992.

Bernstein, Richard B., and Jerome Agel. *Amending America: If We Love the Constitution So Much, Why Do We Keep Trying to Change It?* New York: Random House, 1993.

Bowen, Catherine Drinker. *Miracle at Philadelphia: The Story of the Constitutional Convention.* 1966. Reprint. Boston: Little, Brown, 1987.

Burt, Robert A. *The Constitution in Conflict.* Cambridge: Harvard University Press, 1992.

Collier, Christopher, and James Lincoln Collier. *Decision in Philadelphia: The Constitutional Convention of 1787.* New York: Random House, 1986.

Cox, Archibald. *The Court and the Constitution.* Boston: Houghton Mifflin, 1987.

Currie, David P. *The Constitution in the Supreme Court: The First Hundred Years.* Chicago: University of Chicago Press, 1985.

Currie, David P. *The Constitution in the Supreme Court: The Second Century.* Chicago: University of Chicago Press, 1991.

Currie, David P. *The Constitution of the United States: A Primer for the People.* Chicago: University of Chicago Press, 1988.

Epstein, Lee, and Thomas G. Walker. *Constitutional Law for a Changing America.* Washington, D.C.: Congressional Quarterly, 1992.

Friedman, Lawrence M. *A History of American Law.* 2nd rev ed. New York: Simon & Schuster. 1986.

Friedman, Leon, and Fred L. Israel, eds. *The Justices of the United States Supreme Court, 1789–1991.* 5 vols. Rev. ed. New York: Chelsea House, 1992.

Friendly, Fred W., and Martha J. H. Elliott. *The Constitution: That Delicate Balance.* New York: Random House, 1984.

Garraty, John A., ed. *Quarrels That Have Shaped the Constitution.* New York: Harper & Row, 1987.

Hall, Kermit L. *The Magic Mirror: Law in American History.* New York: Oxford, 1989.

Hall, Kermit L., ed. *By and for the People: Constitutional Rights in American History.* Arlington, Ill.: Harlan Davidson, 1991.

Hall, Kermit L., ed. *The Oxford Companion to the Supreme Court of the United States.* New York: Oxford, 1992.

Hall, Kermit L., William M. Wiecek, and Paul Finkelman. *American Legal History: Cases and Materials.* New York: Oxford, 1991.

Harrell, Mary Ann, and Burnett Anderson. *Equal Justice Under Law.* Washington, D.C.: Supreme Court Historical Society, 1982.

Horowitz, Morton J. *The Transformation of American Law, 1870–1960: The Crisis of Legal Orthodoxy.* New York: Oxford, 1992.

Horowitz, Morton J. *The Transformation of American Law, 1780–1860.* New York; Oxford, 1992.

Irons, Peter. *The Courage of Their Convictions. Sixteen Americans Who Fought Their Way to the Supreme Court.* New York: Free Press, 1988.

Irons, Peter, ed. *May It Please the Court: The Most Significant Oral Arguments Made Before the Supreme Court Since 1955.* New York: New Press, 1993.

Johnson, John W. *Historic U.S. Court Cases, 1690–1990, An Encyclopedia.* New York: Garland, 1992.

Kelly, Alfred H., Winfred A. Harbison, and Herman Belz. *The American Constitution: Its Origins and Development.* New York: Norton, 1990.

Ketchum, Ralph. *Framed for Posterity: The Enduring Philosophy of the Constitution.* Lawrence: University Press of Kansas, 1993.

Levy, Leonard W., Kenneth L. Karst, and Dennis J. Mahoney, editors. *Encyclopedia of the American Constitution.* 4 vols. New York: Macmillan, 1986.

Lutz, Donald S. *The Origins of American Constitutionalism.* Baton Rouge: Louisiana State University Press, 1988.

Marcus, Maeva. *Origins of the Federal Judiciary.* New York: Oxford, 1992.

Meltzer, Milton. *The Bill of Rights: How We Got It and What It Means.* New York: Crowell, 1990.

Peck, Robert S. *We the People: The Constitution in American Life.* New York: Abrams, 1987.

Perry, H. W., Jr. *Deciding to Decide: Agenda Setting in the United States Supreme Court.* Cambridge: Harvard University Press, 1991.

Ritchie, Donald A. *The U.S. Constitution.* New York: Chelsea House, 1989.

Schwartz, Bernard. *The Great Rights of Mankind: A History of the American Bill of Rights.* Madison, Wis.: Madison House, 1992.

Schwartz, Bernard. *A History of the Supreme Court.* New York: Oxford, 1993.

Schwartz, Bernard. *Main Currents in American Legal Thought.* Durham, N.C.: Carolina Academic Press, 1993.

Shapiro, Fred R., ed. *American Legal Quotations.* New York: Oxford, 1993.

Shnayerson, Robert. *The Illustrated History of the Supreme Court of the United States.* New York: Abrams, 1986.

Urofsky, Melvin I. *A March of Liberty: A Constitutional History of the United States.* New York: Knopf, 1988.

Wagman, Robert J. *The Supreme Court: A Citizen's Guide.* New York: Pharos Books, 1993.

Wiecek, William M. *Liberty Under Law: The Supreme Court in American Life.* Baltimore: Johns Hopkins University Press, 1988.

Witt, Elder. *Guide to the U.S. Supreme Court.* Washington, D.C.: Congressional Quarterly, 1989.

Witt, Elder. *The Supreme Court and Individual Rights.* Washington, D.C.: Congressional Quarterly, 1988.

Witt, Elder. *The Supreme Court at Work.* Washington, D.C.: Congressional Quarterly, 1990.

Woodward, Bob, and Scott Armstrong. *The Brethren: Inside the Supreme Court.* New York: Simon & Schuster, 1979.

The Supreme Court library.

INDEX

John J. Patrick is director of the Social Studies Development Center, professor of education, and director of the ERIC Clearinghouse for Social Studies/Social Science Education at Indiana University. He has also taught history, civics, and government at the secondary level. His many publications include *Lessons on the Constitution, Lessons on the Federalist Papers, A Teacher's Guide to the Constitution, Liberty and Order in Constitutional Government, James Madison and The Federalist Papers, Resources for Teachers on the Bill of Rights, Ideas of the Founders on Constitutional Government,* and the textbooks *American Political Behavior* and *History of the American Nation.* Professor Patrick was the chief consultant to the video series *The U.S. Constitution,* produced by the Agency for Instructional Technology, as well as for several other award-winning video series. He has recently served as senior consultant to the civic education program in Poland sponsored by the Mershon Center of The Ohio State University and the Polish Ministry of National Education.